T0213937

Lecture Notes in Computer Science 12014

More information about this series at http://www.springer.com/series/7407

Roberto Moreno-Díaz · Franz Pichler ·
Alexis Quesada-Arencibia (Eds.)

Computer Aided Systems Theory – EUROCAST 2019

17th International Conference
Las Palmas de Gran Canaria, Spain, February 17–22, 2019
Revised Selected Papers, Part II

 Springer

Editors
Roberto Moreno-Díaz
University of Las Palmas de Gran Canaria
Las Palmas de Gran Canaria, Spain

Franz Pichler
Johannes Kepler University Linz
Linz, Austria

Alexis Quesada-Arencibia
University of Las Palmas de Gran Canaria
Las Palmas de Gran Canaria, Spain

ISSN 0302-9743   ISSN 1611-3349 (electronic)
Lecture Notes in Computer Science
ISBN 978-3-030-45095-3   ISBN 978-3-030-45096-0 (eBook)
https://doi.org/10.1007/978-3-030-45096-0

LNCS Sublibrary: SL1 – Theoretical Computer Science and General Issues

This Springer imprint is published by the registered company Springer Nature Switzerland AG
The registered company address is: Gewerbestrasse 11, 6330 Cham, Switzerland

Preface

The concept of CAST as a computer-aided systems theory was introduced by Franz Pichler in the late 1980s to refer to computer theoretical and practical development as tools for solving problems in system science. It was thought of as the third component (the other two being CAD and CAM) required to complete the path from computer and systems sciences to practical developments in science and engineering.

Franz Pichler, of the University of Linz, organized the first CAST workshop in April 1988, which demonstrated the acceptance of the concepts by the scientific and technical community. Next, Roberto Moreno-Díaz, of the University of Las Palmas de Gran Canaria, joined Franz Pichler, motivated and encouraged by Werner Schimanovich, of the University of Vienna (present honorary chair of Eurocast), and they organized the first international meeting on CAST (Las Palmas February 1989), under the name EUROCAST 1989. The event again proved to be a very successful gathering of systems theorists, computer scientists, and engineers from most European countries, North America, and Japan.

It was agreed that the EUROCAST international conference would be organized every two years, alternating between Las Palmas de Gran Canaria and a continental European location. Since 2001 the conference has been held exclusively in Las Palmas. Thus, successive EUROCAST meetings took place in Krems (1991), Las Palmas (1993), Innsbruck (1995), Las Palmas (1997), and Vienna (1999), before being held exclusively in Las Palmas in 2001, 2003, 2005, 2007, 2009, 2011, 2013, 2015, 2017 and 2019, in addition to an extra-European CAST conference in Ottawa in 1994. Selected papers from these meetings were published as Springer *Lecture Notes in Computer Science* volumes 410, 585, 763, 1030, 1333, 1798, 2178, 2809, 3643, 4739, 5717, 6927, 6928, 8111, 8112, 9520, 10671, and 10672, respectively, and in several special issues of *Cybernetics and Systems: An International Journal*. EUROCAST and CAST meetings are definitely consolidated, as shown by the number and quality of the contributions over the years.

With EUROCAST 2019 we celebrated our 30th anniversary. It took place at the Elder Museum of Science and Technology of Las Palmas, during February 17–22, and it continued with the approach tested at previous conferences as an international computer-related conference with a truely interdisciplinary character. As in the previous conferences, the participants profiles were extended to include fields that are in the frontier of science and engineering of computers, information and communication technologies, and the fields of social and human sciences. The best paradigm is the Web, with its associate systems engineering, CAD-CAST tools, and professional application products (Apps) for services in the social, public, and private domains.

There were specialized workshops, which, on this occasion, were devoted to the following topics:

1. Systems Theory and Applications, chaired by Pichler (Linz) and Moreno-Díaz (Las Palmas)
2. Pioneers and Landmarks in the Development of Information and Communication Technologies, chaired by Pichler (Linz) and Seising (Munich)
3. Stochastic Models and Applications to Natural, Social and Technical Systems, chaired by Nobile and Di Crescenzo (Salerno)
4. Theory and Applications of Metaheuristic Algorithms, chaired by Affenzeller, Wagner (Hagenberg), and Raidl (Vienna)
5. Model-Based System Design, Verification and Simulation, chaired by Nikodem (Wroclaw), Ceska (Brno), and Ito (Utsunomiya)
6. Applications of Signal Processing Technology, chaired by Huemer, Zagar, Lunglmayr, and Haselmayr (Linz)
7. Artificial Intelligence and Data Mining for Intelligent Transportation Systems and Smart Mobility, chaired by Sanchez-Medina (Las Palmas), del Ser (Bilbao), Vlahogianni (Athens), García (Madrid), Olaverri-Monreal (Linz), and Acosta (La Laguna)
8. Computer Vision and Machine Learning for Image Analysis and Applications, chaired by Penedo (A Coruña), Rádeva (Barcelona), and Ortega-Hortas (A Coruña)
9. Computer and Systems Based Methods and Electronic Technologies in Medicine, chaired by Rozenblit (Tucson), Maynar (Las Palmas), and Klempous (Wroclaw)
10. Advances in Biomedical Signal and Image Processing, chaired by Fridli (Budapest), Huemer, Kovacs, and Böck (Linz)
11. Systems Concepts and Methods in Touristic Flows, chaired by Palma-Méndez (Murcia), Rodriguez, and Moreno-Díaz Jr. (Las Palmas)
12. Systems in Industrial Robotics, Automation and IoT, chaired by Jacob (Kempten), Stetter (Munich), and Markl (Vienna)

In this conference, as in previous ones, most of the credit for the success is due to the workshop chairs. They and the sessions chairs, with the counseling of the International Advisory Committee, selected from 172 presented papers. After oral presentations and subsequent corrections, 123 revised papers are included in this volume.

The event and this volume were possible thanks to the efforts of the workshop chairs in the diffusion and promotion of the conference, as well as in the selection and organization of all the material. The editors would like to express their thanks to all the contributors, many of whom have already been Eurocast participants for years, and particularly to the considerable interaction of young and senior researchers, as well as to the invited speakers: Prof. Paul Cull, from Oregon State University, USA; Prof. Christoph Stiller, from Karlsruhe Institute of Technology (KIT), Germany; and Prof. Bruno Buchberger, from the Research Institut for Symbolic Computation (RISC), Johannes Kepler University Linz, Austria. We would also like to thank the Director of the Elder Museum of Science and Technology, D. José Gilberto Moreno, and the museum staff. Special thanks are due to the staff of Springer in Heidelberg for their valuable support.

November 2019

Roberto Moreno-Díaz
Franz Pichler
Alexis Quesada-Arencibia

Organization

EUROCAST 2019 was organized by the Universidad de Las Palmas de Gran Canaria, Spain, Johannes Kepler University Linz, Austria, and Museo Elder de la Ciencia y la Tecnología, Spain.

Conference Chair

Roberto Moreno-Díaz   Universidad de Las Palmas de Gran Canaria, Spain

Program Chair

Franz Pichler   Johannes Kepler University Linz, Austria

Honorary Chair

Werner Schimanovich   Austrian Society for Automation and Robotics, Austria

Organizing Committee Chair

Alexis Quesada-Arencibia   Universidad de Las Palmas de Gran Canaria, Spain

Contents – Part II

Artificial Intelligence and Data Mining for Intelligent Transportation Systems and Smart Mobility

Computer Vision, Machine Learning for Image Analysis and Applications

Computer and Systems Based Methods and Electronic Technologies in Medicine

Advances in Biomedical Signal and Image Processing

Systems Concepts and Methods in Touristic Flows

Systems in Industrial Robotics, Automation and IoT

Contents – Part I

Pioneers and Landmarks in the Development of Information and Communication Technologies

Stochastic Models and Applications to Natural, Social and Technical Systems

Theory and Applications of Metaheuristic Algorithms

Model-Based System Design, Verification and Simulation

Applications of Signal Processing Technology

Robust Factor Analysis Parameter Estimation

Rui Zhou$^{(\boxtimes)}$, Junyan Liu, Sandeep Kumar, and Daniel P. Palomar

Department of Electronic and Computer Engineering, The Hong Kong
University of Science and Technology, Kowloon, Hong Kong
{rui.zhou,jliubl}@connect.ust.hk,
{eesandeep,palomar}@ust.hk

Abstract. This paper considers the problem of robustly estimating the
parameters of a heavy-tailed multivariate distribution when the covariance matrix is known to have the structure of a low-rank matrix plus
a diagonal matrix as considered in factor analysis (FA). By assuming
the observed data to follow the multivariate Student's t distribution, we
can robustly estimate the parameters via maximum likelihood estimation (MLE). However, the MLE of parameters becomes an intractable
problem when the multivariate Student's t distribution and the FA structure are both introduced. In this paper, we propose an algorithm based
on the generalized expectation maximization (GEM) method to obtain
estimators. The robustness of our proposed method is further enhanced
to cope with missing values. Finally, we show the performance of our
proposed algorithm using both synthetic data and real financial data.

Keywords: Robust parameter estimation · Factor analysis · Student's
t · Generalized expectation maximization · Missing values

1 Introduction

Factor analysis (FA) is of great significance in various fields like finance, statistics, and cognitive ratio [11,14]. A basic FA model can be written as $\mathbf{x} = \boldsymbol{\mu} + \mathbf{Bf} + \boldsymbol{\varepsilon}$, where $\mathbf{x} \in \mathbb{R}^p$ is the observed vector, $\boldsymbol{\mu} \in \mathbb{R}^p$ is a constant vector, $\mathbf{B} \in \mathbb{R}^{p \times r} \, (r \ll p)$ is the factors loading matrix, $\mathbf{f} \in \mathbb{R}^r$ is a vector of low-dimensional common factors, and $\boldsymbol{\varepsilon} \in \mathbb{R}^p$ is a vector of uncorrelated noise. For example, in a financial market, $\mathbf{x}$ can be the return of stocks, and $\mathbf{f}$ can be some macroeconomic factors like growth rate of the GDP, inflation rate, unemployment rate, etc. [2]. FA model typically assumes that $\mathbf{f}$ and $\boldsymbol{\varepsilon}$ are uncorrelated and both zero-mean, and the covariance matrix of $\mathbf{f}$ is an $r \times r$ identity matrix, denoted by $\mathbf{I}_r$. Following this, the covariance matrix of $\mathbf{x}$ can be expressed as $\boldsymbol{\Sigma} = \mathbf{BB}^T + \boldsymbol{\Psi}$, where $\boldsymbol{\Psi}$ is a $p \times p$ diagonal matrix containing the variance of noise at its diagonal. Note that, with the FA structure, the number of parameters of the covariance matrix has been greatly reduced from $p(p+1)/2$ to $p(r+1)$. Therefore, the estimation of $\boldsymbol{\Sigma}$ could be improved due to the FA structure.

This work was supported by the Hong Kong RGC 16208917 research grant.

R. Moreno-Díaz et al. (Eds.): EUROCAST 2019, LNCS 12014, pp. 3–11, 2020.
https://doi.org/10.1007/978-3-030-45096-0_1

1.1   Related Works

Learn from Σ: A large amount of literature has focused on estimating the covariance matrix with FA structure. One choice is decomposing the estimated Σ into the sum of a low-rank matrix and a diagonal matrix, e.g., constrained minimum trace factor analysis (MTFA) [13]. But a main drawback is imposing the hard equality constraint $\Sigma = \mathbf{B}\mathbf{B}^T + \mathbf{\Psi}$, which does not allow any differences between Σ and $\mathbf{B}\mathbf{B}^T + \mathbf{\Psi}$. Its application is restricted as the exact Σ is usually not observed. Another choice is to approximate the target matrix by a FA structured one. A naive method is to obtain $\hat{\mathbf{B}}$ firstly via principal component analysis (PCA) and then $\hat{\mathbf{\Psi}}$ by taking directly the residual's sample variance. A joint estimation method over $\mathbf{B}$ and $\mathbf{\Psi}$ is usually chosen to minimize $\|\Sigma - (\mathbf{B}\mathbf{B}^T + \mathbf{\Psi})\|_F^2$, where $\|\cdot\|_F$ denotes the Frobenius norm of a matrix. This problem can be solved by applying PCA iteratively [11].

Learn from Data: Different from works mentioned above, the MLE for FA directly learns the parameters from raw data. It assumes that the data are generated from a certain statistical model, typically the multivariate Gaussian distribution, and then the parameters are estimated by maximizing the likelihood function. However, a disadvantage of the estimators under the Gaussian assumption is sensitiveness to outliers [2]. A popular way to obtain a more robust estimation result is to consider some robust heavy-tailed distribution, such as multivariate Student's t or multivariate Skew t [15,16] instead of Gaussian. The two aforementioned methods both assume that $\mathbf{f}$ and ε follow the same heavy tail distribution sharing the same degrees of freedom. As $\mathbf{f}$ and ε are not observed, such an assumption is very restrictive and difficult to verify in practice.

1.2   Contributions

This paper considers more general and practically verifiable assumptions on the FA model: we only assume that the observation $\mathbf{x}$ follows a multivariate Student's t distribution and the FA structure with no additional restrictions on $\mathbf{f}$ and ε. For this more general model, we propose an efficient algorithm to estimate the parameters based on the generalized expectation maximization (GEM) [1] method. In addition, we use the PX-EM [7] method to accelerate the GEM. Our proposed algorithm can be easily extended to other situations, e.g., when observed data contains missing values [6] or when it follows the multivariate Skew t distribution. With synthetic data, our proposed algorithm shows great estimation accuracy and robustness to outliers and missing data, which is very meaningful in practical applications. We also consider real market data in the numerical results, where the global minimum variance portfolio is designed using our estimator and compared with those using other estimators.

2   Gaussian FA Problem

Given the sample covariance matrix of the observed data as $\mathbf{S}$, the MLE problem for FA under the Gaussian distribution assumption (GFA) is given as below:

$$\underset{\Sigma,\mathbf{B},\mathbf{\Psi}}{\text{maximize}} \quad \log|\Sigma^{-1}| - \text{Tr}\left(\Sigma^{-1}\mathbf{S}\right)$$

$$\text{subject to} \quad \Sigma = \mathbf{B}\mathbf{B}^T + \mathbf{\Psi} \tag{1}$$

$$\mathbf{\Psi} = \text{Diag}\left(\psi_1, \ldots, \psi_p\right) \succ \mathbf{0}.$$

The solution to problem (1) would be $\Sigma^\star = \mathbf{S}$ if the structure constraints were ignored, but becomes intractable when the FA structure is imposed. Here we introduce two algorithms for solving problem (1).

Alternating Algorithm: Problem (1) can be solved by an alternating optimization approach, which can be performed by alternately updating $\mathbf{B}$ and $\mathbf{\Psi}$ (note that this actually corresponds to an alternating optimization over a factor model decomposition of Σ^{-1} instead of an alternating optimization over $\mathbf{B}$ and $\mathbf{\Psi}$, cf. [9,10]). For fixed $\mathbf{\Psi}$, the optimal update for $\mathbf{B}$ is given next.

Lemma 1 ([9]). *Given a feasible $\mathbf{\Psi}$, the optimal $\mathbf{B}^\star$ maximizing problem (1) is $\mathbf{B}^\star = \mathbf{\Psi}^{\frac{1}{2}}\mathbf{U}\mathbf{D}^{\frac{1}{2}}$ where $\mathbf{U}\boldsymbol{\Lambda}\mathbf{U}^T$ is the eigenvalue decomposition (EVD) of $\mathbf{\Psi}^{-\frac{1}{2}}\mathbf{S}\mathbf{\Psi}^{-\frac{1}{2}}$ and $\mathbf{D} = Diag\left(d_1, \ldots, d_r, 0, \ldots, 0\right)$ with $d_i = \max\left(\lambda_i - 1, 0\right)$.*

For fixed $\mathbf{B}$, the update for $\mathbf{\Psi}$ is set as $\text{Diag}\left(\mathbf{S} - \mathbf{B}\mathbf{B}^T\right)$.

MM Algorithm: Recently, a majorization-minimization (MM) [12] based method has been proposed in [4] to obtain the optimal Σ. Plugging the optimal $\mathbf{B}^\star$ from Lemma 1 in (1), we can achieve a concentrated version of (1).

Lemma 2 ([4]). *Denoting $\mathbf{\Phi} = \mathbf{\Psi}^{-1}$, the problem (1) is equivalent to minimizing $f\left(\boldsymbol{\phi}\right)$, where $f\left(\boldsymbol{\phi}\right) = f_1\left(\boldsymbol{\phi}\right) - f_2\left(\boldsymbol{\psi}\right)$ with $f_1\left(\boldsymbol{\phi}\right) = \sum_{i=1}^{p}\left(-\log\phi_i + S_{ii}\phi_i\right)$, $f_2\left(\boldsymbol{\phi}\right) = -\sum_{i=1}^{r}\left(\log\left(\max\{1, \lambda_i^*\}\right) - \max\{1, \lambda_i^*\} + 1\right)$ and $\{\lambda_i^*\}_{i=1}^{r}$ are the top r eigenvalues of $\mathbf{S}^* = \mathbf{\Phi}^{\frac{1}{2}}\mathbf{S}\mathbf{\Phi}^{\frac{1}{2}}$. Besides, $f_1\left(\boldsymbol{\phi}\right)$ and $f_2\left(\boldsymbol{\phi}\right)$ are both convex in $\boldsymbol{\phi}$.*

By linearizing the $f_2\left(\boldsymbol{\phi}\right)$ using its sub-gradient, we can majorize $f\left(\boldsymbol{\phi}\right)$ by $\bar{f}\left(\boldsymbol{\phi}\right) - \sum_{i=1}^{p}\left(-\log\phi_i + S_{ii}\phi_i - \nabla_i^{(k)}\phi_i\right)$, where $\nabla^{(k)}$ is a subgradient of $f_2\left(\boldsymbol{\phi}\right)$ at the kth iteration. The $\nabla^{(k)}$ can be calculated as $\nabla_i^{(k)} = \left(\mathbf{\Phi}^{-\frac{1}{2}}\mathbf{U}^*\mathbf{D}_1\mathbf{U}^{*T}\mathbf{\Phi}^{\frac{1}{2}}\mathbf{S}\right)_{ii}$ where $\mathbf{U}^*\boldsymbol{\Lambda}^*\mathbf{U}^{*T}$ is the EVD of $\mathbf{\Phi}^{\frac{1}{2}}\mathbf{S}^{(k)}\mathbf{\Phi}^{\frac{1}{2}}$ and $\mathbf{D}_1 = \text{Diag}\left(d_1, \ldots, d_r, 0, \ldots 0\right)$ with $d_i = \max\{0, 1 - 1/\lambda_i^*\}$ [4,5]. Then the update of $\mathbf{\Phi}$ can be easily obtained as $\phi_i^{(k+1)} = \left(S_{ii}^{(k)} - \nabla_i^{(k)}\right)^{-1}$ for $i = 1, \ldots, p$. By iteratively taking the above procedure, we can get a converged sequence of $\phi^{(k)}$. Finally we can set $\mathbf{\Psi} = \mathbf{\Phi}^{-1}$ and compute $\mathbf{B}$ via Lemma 1.

It should be noted that the two algorithms are the same and can be verified by matrix algebra.

3   Problem Statement

The p-dimensional multivariate Student's t distribution, denoted as $\boldsymbol{t}_p\left(\boldsymbol{\mu}, \boldsymbol{\Sigma}, \nu\right)$, has the probability density function (pdf)

$$f(\mathbf{x}|\boldsymbol{\theta}) = \frac{\Gamma\left(\frac{\nu+p}{2}\right)}{\Gamma\left(\frac{\nu}{2}\right)\nu^{\frac{p}{2}}\pi^{\frac{p}{2}}|\boldsymbol{\Sigma}|^{\frac{1}{2}}} \left[1 + \frac{1}{\nu}(\mathbf{x}-\boldsymbol{\mu})^T \boldsymbol{\Sigma}^{-1}(\mathbf{x}-\boldsymbol{\mu})\right]^{-\frac{\nu+p}{2}} \tag{2}$$

where $\boldsymbol{\theta} = (\boldsymbol{\mu}, \boldsymbol{\Sigma}, \nu)$, ν is the degrees of freedom, $\boldsymbol{\Sigma}$ is the scale $p \times p$ positive definite matrix, $\boldsymbol{\mu}$ is the p-dimensional mean vector, and $\Gamma(a) = \int_0^\infty t^{(a-1)} \exp(-t)\, dt$ is the gamma function. Note that the covariance matrix of $\mathbf{x}$ is $\frac{\nu}{\nu-2}\boldsymbol{\Sigma}$, and it is not defined for $\nu \leq 2$. Interestingly, the above multivariate Student's t distribution can be represented in a hierarchical structure as $\mathbf{x}|\tau \overset{i.i.d}{\sim} \mathcal{N}_p\left(\boldsymbol{\mu}, \frac{1}{\tau}\boldsymbol{\Sigma}\right)$ with $\tau \overset{i.i.d}{\sim} \text{Gamma}\left(\frac{\nu}{2}, \frac{\nu}{2}\right)$, where $\mathcal{N}_p(\boldsymbol{\mu}, \boldsymbol{\Sigma})$ is the multivariate Gaussian distribution with mean vector $\boldsymbol{\mu}$ and covariance matrix $\boldsymbol{\Sigma}$. $\text{Gamma}(a, b)$ means gamma distribution with shape a and rate b, whose pdf is $f(\tau) = b^a \tau^{(a-1)} \exp(-b\tau)/\Gamma(a)$.

We consider that the observed p-dimensional data $\mathbf{x}_t, t = 1, \dots, T$ follows the independent and identical distributed (i.i.d.) multivariate Student's t distribution, i.e., $\mathbf{x}_t \sim t_p(\boldsymbol{\mu}, \boldsymbol{\Sigma}, \nu)$. Besides, we assume that $\mathbf{x}_t$ follows the FA model, which means $\boldsymbol{\Sigma} = \mathbf{B}\mathbf{B}^T + \boldsymbol{\Psi}$. Note that we omit a scaling factor in order to simplify the notation (recall that here $\boldsymbol{\Sigma}$ refers to the scale matrix). A natural approach is to obtain the parameter estimation through MLE method, i.e., maximizing $L(\boldsymbol{\theta}|\mathbf{X}) = \sum_t \log f(\mathbf{x}_t|\boldsymbol{\theta})$ w.r.t. $\boldsymbol{\theta}$, where $\mathbf{X} \in \mathbb{R}^{T \times p}$ with $\mathbf{x}_t$ along the t-th row.

4   Problem Solution

It is very difficult to directly solve the above MLE problem as the objective function and constraints are both non-convex. The expectation maximization (EM) algorithm is a powerful iterative method to handle such problem [8]. By incorporating the latent data $\mathbf{Z}$, EM can be employed to convert the maximization for $L(\mathbf{X}|\boldsymbol{\theta})$ to the maximization for a sequence of simpler and solvable problems. In each iteration, it requires $Q(\boldsymbol{\theta}|\boldsymbol{\theta}^{(k)})$, which is the expected log-likelihood function of $L(\mathbf{X}|\boldsymbol{\theta})$ with respect to the current conditional distribution of $\mathbf{Z}$ given the $\mathbf{X}$ and the current estimate of the parameter $\boldsymbol{\theta}^{(k)}$. Then it finds $\boldsymbol{\theta}^{(k+1)}$ by maximizing $Q(\boldsymbol{\theta}|\boldsymbol{\theta}^{(k)})$. However, the computational cost of solving the subproblem might still be rather heavy and make the whole EM algorithm impractical. That is when the GEM algorithm can help. The GEM is an iterative method based on the EM philosophy but requiring an improvement at each iteration instead of a full maximization as in EM.

4.1   The RFA Algorithm

In this section, we propose a robust factor analysis (RFA) algorithm to solve the above problem. By incorporating the latent variables τ from the multivariate Student's t hierarchical structure, the log-likelihood function of the complete data $(\mathbf{X}, \boldsymbol{\tau})$ is given in (3). Note that $\boldsymbol{\tau}$ corresponds to $\mathbf{Z}$ in our application.

$$L\left(\boldsymbol{\theta}|\mathbf{x},\boldsymbol{\tau}\right) = \frac{T}{2}\log|\boldsymbol{\Sigma}^{-1}| - \frac{1}{2}\mathrm{Tr}\left(\boldsymbol{\Sigma}^{-1}\sum_{t=1}^{T}\tau_t\left(\mathbf{x}_t - \boldsymbol{\mu}\right)\left(\mathbf{x}_t - \boldsymbol{\mu}\right)^{T}\right)$$

$$+ \frac{T\nu}{2}\log\frac{\nu}{2} + \frac{\nu}{2}\sum_{t=1}^{T}\left(\log\tau_t - \tau_t\right) - T\log\Gamma\left(\frac{\nu}{2}\right) + const. \tag{3}$$

Expectation Step: The expectation step of the GEM algorithm is to find the conditional expectation of $L\left(\boldsymbol{\theta}|\mathbf{X},\boldsymbol{\tau}\right)$ over $\boldsymbol{\tau}$ given the observed $\mathbf{X}$ and the current estimation of $\boldsymbol{\theta}$, i.e., $\boldsymbol{\theta}^{(k)}$. Since the conditional expectation of τ_t and $\log\tau_t$ for $t = 1,\ldots,T$ can be directly calculated as

$$e_{1,t}^{(k)} = \mathrm{E}\left(\tau_t|\mathbf{x}_t,\boldsymbol{\theta}^{(k)}\right) = \frac{\nu^{(k)} + p}{\nu^{(k)} + d\left(\mathbf{x}_t,\boldsymbol{\mu}^{(k)},\boldsymbol{\Sigma}^{(k)}\right)}$$

$$e_{2,t}^{(k)} = \mathrm{E}\left(\log\tau_t|\mathbf{x}_t,\boldsymbol{\theta}^{(k)}\right) = \psi\left(\frac{\nu^{(k)} + p}{2}\right) - \log\frac{\nu^{(k)} + d\left(\mathbf{x}_t,\boldsymbol{\mu}^{(k)},\boldsymbol{\Sigma}^{(k)}\right)}{2}$$

where $d\left(\mathbf{x},\boldsymbol{\mu},\boldsymbol{\Sigma}\right) = \left(\mathbf{x} - \boldsymbol{\mu}\right)^{T}\left(\boldsymbol{\Sigma}\right)^{-1}\left(\mathbf{x} - \boldsymbol{\mu}\right)$ is the Mahalanobis distance between $\mathbf{x}_t$ and $\boldsymbol{\mu}$ [6], then the expectation of the complete data log likelihood (3) is

$$Q\left(\boldsymbol{\theta}|\boldsymbol{\theta}^{(k)}\right) = \frac{T}{2}\log|\boldsymbol{\Sigma}^{-1}| - \frac{1}{2}\mathrm{Tr}\left(\boldsymbol{\Sigma}^{-1}\left(\sum_{t=1}^{T}e_{1,t}^{(k)}\left(\mathbf{x}_t - \boldsymbol{\mu}\right)\left(\mathbf{x}_t - \boldsymbol{\mu}\right)^{T}\right)\right)$$

$$+ \frac{T\nu}{2}\log\frac{\nu}{2} + \frac{\nu}{2}\sum_{t=1}^{T}\left(e_{2,t}^{(k)} - e_{1,t}^{(k)}\right) - T\log\Gamma\left(\frac{\nu}{2}\right) + const. \tag{4}$$

Maximization Step: Here we divide the parameters update into two parts. *Update of $\boldsymbol{\mu}$ and ν:* It is easy to see that $\boldsymbol{\mu}$ and ν are actually decoupled in $Q\left(\boldsymbol{\theta}|\boldsymbol{\theta}^{(k)}\right)$ and thus can be easily obtained by setting their derivative to zero. Then the update scheme for $(\boldsymbol{\mu},\nu)$ is

$$\boldsymbol{\mu}^{(k+1)} = \sum_{t=1}^{T}e_{1,t}^{(k)}\mathbf{x}_t \bigg/ \sum_{t=1}^{T}e_{1,t}^{(k)} \tag{5}$$

$$\nu^{(k+1)} = \underset{\nu>0}{\mathrm{argmax}}\left\{\frac{T\nu}{2}\log\frac{\nu}{2} + \frac{\nu}{2}\sum_{t=1}^{T}\left(e_{2,t}^{(k)} - e_{1,t}^{(k)}\right) - T\log\Gamma\left(\frac{\nu}{2}\right)\right\}. \tag{6}$$

According to Proposition 1 in [6], $\nu^{(k+1)}$ always exists and can be found by bisection search. Interestingly, the update for $\boldsymbol{\mu}$ and ν are independent from each other and irrelevant to $\boldsymbol{\Sigma}$.

Update of $\boldsymbol{\Sigma}$: Fixing $\boldsymbol{\mu}$ and ν, maximizing $Q(\boldsymbol{\theta}|\boldsymbol{\theta}^{(k)})$ w.r.t. $\boldsymbol{\Sigma}$ is reduced to a GFA problem with $\mathbf{S}^{(k)} = \frac{1}{T}\sum_{t=1}^{T} e_{1,t}^{(k)} (\mathbf{x}_t - \boldsymbol{\mu}^{(k+1)}) (\mathbf{x}_t - \boldsymbol{\mu}^{(k+1)})^T$, which can be solved by any of the two iterative methods described in Sect. 2, which require several iterations until convergence. Considering that solving $\boldsymbol{\Sigma}$ exactly would require several iterations and could be time-consuming, we can instead only run the algorithms for one round, which would correspond to implementing the GEM instead of EM.

4.2   An Acceleration Scheme: PX-EM

A drawback of the EM algorithm is the slow convergence. The parameter expanded EM (PX-EM) [7] was proposed as an efficient method to accelerate the classical EM method and can be applied here. A well-known application of PX-EM on multivariate Student's t case is to assume that we have $\tau \overset{i.i.d}{\sim} \alpha\text{Gamma}\left(\frac{\nu}{2}, \frac{\nu}{2}\right)$ in the Student's t hierarchical structure, where α is the expanded parameter.

PX-E step: The PX-E step needs only a few modifications on the original expectation step. Specifically, the Mahalanobis distance should be calculated as $d(\mathbf{x}_t, \boldsymbol{\mu}_*, \boldsymbol{\Sigma}_*/\alpha)$, where $(x)_*$ is the corresponding notation of x in the parameter expanded statistical model.

PX-M step: The update schemes for parameters is similar to those in EM with only few changes. The update of $\boldsymbol{\mu}$ and ν keeps unchanged but the update of $\boldsymbol{\Sigma}$ depends on $(\mathbf{S}^{(k)})_* = \alpha^{(k)}\mathbf{S}^{(k)}$. The update of the new parameter α is $\alpha^{(k+1)} = \frac{\alpha^{(k)}}{T}\sum_{t=1}^{T} e_{1,t}^{(k)}$. After the algorithm achieves convergence, the real parameters should be recovered as $\boldsymbol{\mu} = \boldsymbol{\mu}_*$, $\boldsymbol{\Sigma} = \boldsymbol{\Sigma}_*/\alpha$ and $\nu = \nu_*$.

4.3   Robust Enhancement to Missing Data

Due to measurement problems or transmission/storage errors, the observed data $\mathbf{x}_t$ might contain some missing values, which has been well studied, cf. [6]. It turns out that the missing values can be regarded as latent data like $\boldsymbol{\tau}$. The new $Q\left(\boldsymbol{\theta}|\boldsymbol{\theta}^{(k)}\right)$ at expectation step has the same expression w.r.t. $\boldsymbol{\theta}$ as in (4) [6]. Therefore the maximization step can also be achieved by first updating $\boldsymbol{\mu}$ and ν, and then $\boldsymbol{\Sigma}$ with FA structure imposed.

5   Numerical Experiments

5.1   Synthetic Data

We generate synthetic data following the multivariate Student's t distribution. The basic dimension setting is $p = 100$ and $r = 5$. The true distribution parameters are chosen as follows: ν_{true} is set to be 7, the elements of $\boldsymbol{\mu}_{\text{true}}$ are drawn i.i.d. from $\mathcal{N}(0,1)$, $\mathbf{B}_{\text{true}}$ comes from BARRA industry model [3] with each sector has size 20, diagonal elements of $\mathbf{\Psi}_{\text{true}}$ are generated independently from an exponential distribution with mean 10. The initial $\boldsymbol{\mu}^{(0)}$, $\nu^{(0)}$ are set as the sample mean and 10, and $\mathbf{\Psi}^{(0)}$, $\mathbf{B}^{(0)}$ are given by the naive PCA method. The convergence condition is set as $|L^{(k+1)} - L^{(k)}| \leq 10^{-6}|L^{(k)}|$.

Convergence Illustration: In Fig. 1, we compare the convergence of our proposed methods. The log-likelihood function of the observed data increases monotonically with the iterations and can finally converge. The PX-EM can significantly accelerate the convergence in this case. Then, in Fig. 2, we show the parameter estimation convergence. The parameter estimation normalized errors are defined as $\text{NE}(\boldsymbol{\mu}) = \|\hat{\boldsymbol{\mu}} - \boldsymbol{\mu}_{\text{true}}\|_2/\|\boldsymbol{\mu}_{\text{true}}\|_2$, $\text{NE}(\boldsymbol{\Sigma}) = \|\hat{\boldsymbol{\Sigma}} - \boldsymbol{\Sigma}_{\text{true}}\|_F/\|\boldsymbol{\Sigma}_{\text{true}}\|_F$ and $\text{NE}(\nu) = |s(\hat{\nu}) - s(\nu_{\text{true}})|/|s(\nu_{\text{true}})|$ for $\boldsymbol{\mu}$, $\boldsymbol{\Sigma}$ and ν, where $s(\nu) = \frac{\nu}{\nu-2}$. In Fig. 2, we can find all the errors are decreasing and finally converge.

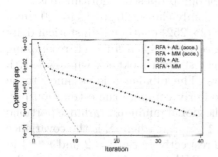

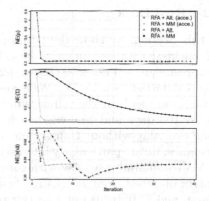

Fig. 1. Optimality gap vs iterations.   **Fig. 2.** Estimation error vs iterations.

Robustness Illustration: We compare our proposed RFA methods in covariance matrix estimation with sample covariance matrix (SCM), Student's t (Stu-t) estimation (without FA structure) [6], GFA, and iterative PCA (Iter-PCA) estimation. The results shown below are averaged over 100 different realizations of $\mathbf{X}$ following Gaussian distribution. In Fig. 3, we change the sample number n but fixing $p = 100$. All methods show better performance when n goes large while our proposed RFA method always gives the best result. In Fig. 4, we randomly pick some rows of $\mathbf{X}$ and element-wisely add outliers drawn from $\mathcal{N}(0,50)$. It is significant that our proposed RFA method can still hold a good estimation while the results from non-robust estimation methods are totally destroyed. The results owe to the robustness of Student's t assumption in resisting the outliers. In Fig. 5, we randomly pick some rows of $\mathbf{X}$ and randomly set 10% values be missing for each row. Our proposed robust FA algorithm will be directly fed with incomplete data while for other methods we need to manually remove the rows containing the missing values. It is impressive that our proposed robust FA method can keep the lowest and almost unchanged performance.

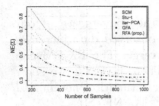 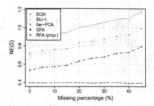

Fig. 3. Average NE (Σ) when n changes.   **Fig. 4.** Average NE (Σ) with outliers.   **Fig. 5.** Average NE (Σ) with missing values.

5.2 Real Data

In this Section, we show the performance of our proposed algorithm based on the backtest with real financial data. We randomly choose 50 stocks for 10 times from Standard & Poor's 500 list and 2 years (2×252) continuous historical daily prices data between 01 Dec 2008 and 01 Dec 2018. Then for each resampling dataset, we perform the rolling window backtest with lookback window length set to 100 days and test window be 5 days. The rebalance is assumed to be done everyday without transaction cost. To fairly compare the estimation performance, we are particularly interested in the global minimum variance portfolio (GMVP): minimize $\mathbf{w}^T \Sigma \mathbf{w}$ with constraint $\mathbf{1}^T \mathbf{w} = 1$, where Σ is the covariance matrix obtained from various methods. We respectively set $r = 2$ and $r = 4$ in Figs. 6 and 7. It turns out that our proposed RFA method can achieve smaller out-of-sample risk with less uncertainty.

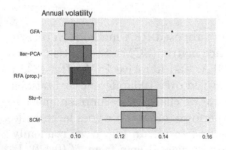 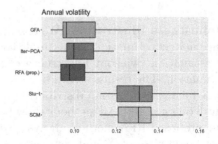

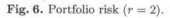

Fig. 6. Portfolio risk ($r = 2$).   **Fig. 7.** Portfolio risk ($r = 4$).

6   Conclusion

In this paper, we have proposed the RFA algorithm to obtain the MLE of the multivariate Student's t distribution with FA structure imposed. The algorithm was based on the EM framework and had great estimation accuracy and robustness to outliers and missing values. The backtest over real financial data has shown advantages and practical usefulness of our proposed RFA algorithm.

References

1. Dempster, A.P., Laird, N.M., Rubin, D.B.: Maximum likelihood from incomplete data via the EM algorithm. J. Roy. Stat. Soc. B **39**(1), 1–38 (1977)
2. Feng, Y., Palomar, D.P.: A signal processing perspective on financial engineering. Found. Trends® Signal Process. **9**(1–2), 1–231 (2016)
3. Heckman, L., Narayanan, S.R., Patel, S.A.: Country and industry importance in European returns. J. Invest. **10**, 27–34 (1999). SSRN 169455
4. Khamaru, K., Mazumder, R.: Computation of the maximum likelihood estimator in low-rank factor analysis. arXiv preprint arXiv:1801.05935 (2018)
5. Lewis, A.S.: Derivatives of spectral functions. Math. Oper. Res. **21**(3), 576–588 (1996)
6. Liu, C., Rubin, D.B.: ML estimation of the t distribution using EM and its extensions ECM and ECME. Statistica Sinica **5**, 19–39 (1995)
7. Liu, C., Rubin, D.B., Wu, Y.N.: Parameter expansion to accelerate EM: the PX-EM algorithm. Biometrika **85**(4), 755–770 (1998)
8. Moon, T.K.: The expectation-maximization algorithm. IEEE Signal Process. Mag. **13**(6), 47–60 (1996)
9. Ramírez, D., Santamaria, I., Van Vaerenbergh, S., Scharf, L.L.: An alternating optimization algorithm for two-channel factor analysis with common and uncommon factors, pp. 1743–1747 (2018)
10. Santamaria, I., Scharf, L.L., Via, J., Wang, H., Wang, Y.: Passive detection of correlated subspace signals in two MIMO channels. IEEE Trans. Signal Process. **65**(20), 5266–5280 (2017)
11. Sardarabadi, A.M., van der Veen, A.J.: Complex factor analysis and extensions. IEEE Trans. Signal Process. **66**(4), 954–967 (2018)
12. Sun, Y., Babu, P., Palomar, D.P.: Majorization-minimization algorithms in signal processing, communications, and machine learning. IEEE Trans. Signal Process. **65**(3), 794–816 (2017)
13. Ten Berge, J.M., Snijders, T.A., Zegers, F.E.: Computational aspects of the greatest lower bound to the reliability and constrained minimum trace factor analysis. Psychometrika **46**(2), 201–213 (1981)
14. Tsay, R.S.: Analysis of Financial Time Series, vol. 543. Wiley, New York (2005)
15. Wang, W.L., Liu, M., Lin, T.I.: Robust skew-t factor analysis models for handling missing data. Stat. Methods Appl. **26**(4), 649–672 (2017)
16. Zhang, J., Li, J., Liu, C.: Robust factor analysis using the multivariate t-distribution. Statistica Sinica **24**(1), 291–312 (2014)

Multiple-Model Estimation Applied to Unequal, Heterogeneous State Space Models

Dirk Weidemann$^{(\boxtimes)}$ and Edmond Skeli

Institute of System Dynamics and Mechatronics,
University of Applied Sciences Bielefeld, Bielefeld, Germany
{dirk.weidemann,edmond.skeli}@fh-bielefeld.de

Abstract. Multiple-model estimation is useful to detect both structural and parametric changes of technical systems and has been used in areas such as target tracking and fault diagnosis. Known approaches to multiple-model estimation, such as Generalized-Pseudo-Bayesian approaches or the Interacting-Multiple-Model approach, apply a stochastic filter for each model and calculate the estimate by appropriately mixing the moments calculated by each filter. However, it has to be taken into account that in the context of fault diagnosis the individual mathematical models often have unequal, heterogeneous state spaces. Thus, multi-model estimation approaches have to be appropriately adapted, otherwise biased estimates will be calculated. In contrast to known multiple-model estimation approaches to unequal, heterogeneous state spaces, where the necessary adaptions are only done for the model conditional means and covariance matrices, we propose an approach, where the model conditional probability density functions are adapted so that non-Gaussian filters can also be used.

Keywords: Multiple-model estimation · Heterogeneous state spaces

1 Introduction

Multiple-model estimation is useful to detect both structural and parametric changes of technical systems and has been successfully used in many areas such as target tracking [4] and fault diagnosis [6]. As indicated by the name, multiple-model estimation approaches do not utilise a single model in order to describe the behaviour of the system, but rather a finite set of models $\mathcal{M} = \{m^{(1)}, m^{(2)}, \ldots, m^{(q)}\}$, where $q \in \mathbb{N}$ is the cardinal number of $\mathcal{M}$. The discrete dynamics, i.e. the switching between these models, which are also denoted as modes, is usually governed by a Markov-chain, while the continuous dynamics of each model of $\mathcal{M}$ is given either by differential or differential-algebraic

This work was funded by the European Union and the federal state of North Rhine-Westphalia, Germany.

© Springer Nature Switzerland AG 2020
R. Moreno-Díaz et al. (Eds.): EUROCAST 2019, LNCS 12014, pp. 12–19, 2020.
https://doi.org/10.1007/978-3-030-45096-0_2

equations. The objective of multiple-model estimation is to estimate both the discrete and the continuous state, i.e. a hybrid state. Consequently, theses estimation approaches belong to the class of hybrid estimation, cf. [3].

In order to estimate the hybrid state multiple-model estimation approaches apply a stochastic filter for each model and aggregate the model conditional estimates in an appropriate way. Note, that the aggregation of model conditional estimates is only possible and meaningful if all models have the same state space. However, in the context of model-based diagnosis this requirement is not met if faults are modelled by augmented states since state augmentation leads to an increasing state dimension. Thus, the individual models $m \in \mathcal{M}$ differ in the dimension of their state space. Moreover, different augmented states usually describe different physical effects (in an electronic system, for example, the augmented state of one model may describe changes of an inductor, while the augmented state of another model describes the change of a capacitor) such that the models have unequal, heterogeneous state spaces, which has to be taken into account when aggregating model conditional estimates to avoid a biased hybrid estimate.

Multiple-model estimation with unequal, heterogeneous state spaces is a rather recent research topic and is addressed in [2,5] in the context of the Interacting-Multiple-Model (IMM) approach, which is a suboptimal multiple-model estimation approach. In contrast to [2,5], where the necessary adaptions are only done for the model conditional means and covariance matrices, we propose an approach, where the model conditional probability density functions (pdfs) are adapted so that non-Gaussian filters can also be used. The proposed approach is applied to both the IMM and the second-order Generalized-Pseudo-Bayesian (GPB2) approach.

2 Modelling of Systems Subject to Faults

In the context of fault diagnosis multiple-model estimation approaches are usually used when fault identification is required in addition to fault detection and fault localisation. Concerning fault identification, it has to be taken into account that faults can affect sensors, actuators and the system itself and that fault magnitudes can posses an arbitrary characteristic with respect to time. In order to use only as many models as necessary, i.e. to keep the cardinal number of $\mathcal{M}$ as small as possible, it is reasonable to model faults by augmented state variables. If the system is modelled by a set of semi-explicit differential algebraic equations, which is denoted as DAE system in the following, the augmented states are additional differential states. Let the nonlinear DAE system of index one

$$\dot{x}_{\mathrm{d}}^{(\mathrm{ff})} = \phi_{\mathrm{d}}^{(\mathrm{ff})}(x_{\mathrm{d}}^{(\mathrm{ff})}, x_{\mathrm{a}}, u, t), \qquad g_{\mathrm{a}}^{(\mathrm{ff})}(x_{\mathrm{d}}^{(\mathrm{ff})}, x_{\mathrm{a}}, u, t) = 0,$$
$$y = h^{(\mathrm{ff})}(x_{\mathrm{d}}^{(\mathrm{ff})}, x_{\mathrm{a}}, u, t) \tag{1}$$

describe the behaviour of the fault-free system, with $\det(\partial g_{\mathrm{a}}^{(\mathrm{ff})}/\partial x_{\mathrm{a}}) \neq 0$ and $x_{\mathrm{d}}^{(\mathrm{ff})} \in \mathbb{R}^{n_{\mathrm{d}}}$ denoting the differential, $x_{\mathrm{a}} \in \mathbb{R}^{n_{\mathrm{a}}}$ the algebraic states, $u \in \mathbb{R}^{m}$ the inputs, and $y \in \mathbb{R}^{p}$ the measured outputs. Thus, $g_{\mathrm{a}}^{(\mathrm{ff})}(\cdot) \in \mathbb{R}^{n_{\mathrm{a}}}$ holds.

Considering the hydraulic cylinder described in Sect. 4, the faults are due to internal and external leakages. In both cases the faults are assumed to occur abruptly with constant magnitude, such that the dynamics of the fault magnitudes can be modelled by $\dot{x}_{\mathrm{d,aug}}^{(i)} = 0$ with $i \in \{\mathrm{in}, \mathrm{ex}\}$. Let $x_{\mathrm{d}}^{(i)} = [(x_{\mathrm{d}}^{(\mathrm{ff})})^{\mathrm{T}}, x_{\mathrm{d,aug}}^{(i)}]^{\mathrm{T}}$ with $x_{\mathrm{d,aug}}^{(i)} \in \mathbb{R}$ be the differential states of the system subject to an internal and external leakage, respectively, such that

$$\dot{x}_{\mathrm{d}}^{(i)} = \phi_{\mathrm{d}}^{(i)}(x_{\mathrm{d}}^{(i)}, x_{\mathrm{a}}, u, t) = \begin{bmatrix} \phi_{\mathrm{d}}^{(\mathrm{ff})}(x_{\mathrm{d}}^{(i)}, x_{\mathrm{a}}, u, t) \\ 0 \end{bmatrix}, \qquad g_{\mathrm{a}}^{(i)}(x_{\mathrm{d}}^{(i)}, x_{\mathrm{a}}, u, t) = 0,$$

$$y = h^{(i)}(x_{\mathrm{d}}^{(i)}, x_{\mathrm{a}}, u, t) \tag{2}$$

with $\det(\partial g_{\mathrm{a}}^{(i)}/\partial x_{\mathrm{a}}) \neq 0$ and $g_{\mathrm{a}}^{(i)}(\cdot) \in \mathbb{R}^{n_{\mathrm{a}}}$ hold.

Thus, the dynamic behaviour of the hydraulic cylinder subject to two faults can be modelled by an hybrid automaton with the hybrid state $\xi = [z, x_{\mathrm{d}}^{\mathrm{T}}, x_{\mathrm{a}}^{\mathrm{T}}]^{\mathrm{T}}$ comprising three discrete-state states, i.e modes $z \in \mathcal{M} = \{m^{(\mathrm{ff})}, m^{(\mathrm{in})}, m^{(\mathrm{ex})}\}$ as well as the continuous differential and algebraic states. The continuous dynamics in each mode is represented by the corresponding nonlinear DAE system, while a Markov-chain is used to describe the discrete dynamics, cf. [6].

3   Multiple-Model Estimation Approaches

Considering that the optimal multiple-model estimation approach can not be realized in practice, since the computational effort increases exponentially with $k \in \mathbb{N}$ (cf. [1,3]), where k denotes the sampling instant, suboptimal approaches such as the GPB2 approach or the IMM approach have to be used.

The recursive cycle of both the GPB2 and the IMM algorithms is graphically shown in Figs. 1 and 2, respectively, where, for the sake of simplicity, the set $\mathcal{M}$ contains only two models. At the beginning of each cycle the posteriori density calculated by a stochastic filter related to the model $m^{(i)}$ with $i \in \{1, 2\}$ is given by $p(x_k | m_k^{(i)}, y_{1:k})$, where $m_k^{(i)}$ indicates that the behaviour of the system is modelled by the model $m^{(i)}$ during the time interval $t \in (k - 1, k]$ and $y_{1:k} = (y_1, y_2, \ldots, y_{k-1}, y_k)$ contains all measurements up to the time instant k. As depicted in both figures, mode transitions take place immediately after the time instant k since ϵ is assumed to be a sufficiently small positive constant. Note, that the conditional pdf after a mode transition is not only conditioned on $m_k^{(i)}$ but on the mode sequence $m_k^{(i)}, m_{k+1}^{(j)}$ with $i, j \in \{1, 2\}$. Depending on the algorithm, mode stochastic filtering (GPB2) or merging of mode sequences ending in the same mode (IMM) is performed first. As depicted in Figs. 1 and 2, merging of the mode sequences corresponds to mixing of pdfs which are dependent on those mode sequences, where $\mu_{k+1}^{(ji)} = P(m_k^{(j)} | m_{k+1}^{(i)}, y_{1:k+1})$ and $\mu_k^{(ji)} = P(m_k^{(j)} | m_{k+1}^{(i)}, y_{1:k})$ with $i, j \in \{1, 2\}$ are the mixing probabilities of the GPB2 and IMM approach, respectively. Finally, all mode conditional pdfs are fused to calculate the continuous state pdf $p(x_{k+1} | y_{1:k+1})$ according to (7).

However, the application of the suboptimal multiple-model estimation approaches described above to models with unequal, heterogeneous state spaces requires adapting the conditional pdfs after mode transitions and before fusing the mode conditioned results. Both adaptions are described below.

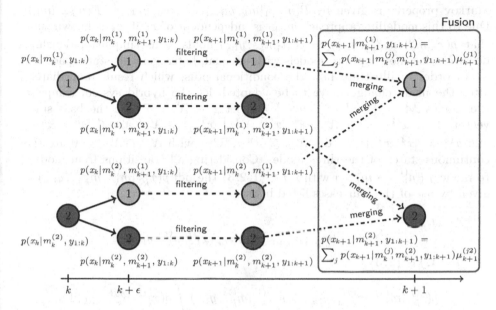

Fig. 1. Recursive cycle of the GBP2 approach

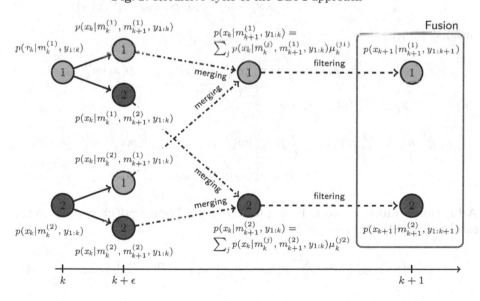

Fig. 2. Recursive cycle of the IMM approach

Adaption After Mode Transitions. Applying multiple-model estimation approaches to models with homogeneous state spaces the discrete dynamics, i.e. the mode transitions are usually modelled by a finite Markov-chain. The characteristic property of a Markov-chain is that m_{k+1} is only dependant on m_k but neither on m_ν with $\nu \in \{0, 1, \ldots, k-1\}$ nor $y_{1:k}$. In mathematical terms, the Markov property is given by $P(m_{k+1}|m_k, m_{k-1}, \ldots, m_0, y_{1:k}) = P(m_{k+1}|m_k)$. Due to this modelling approach m_{k+1} is independent of x_k if m_k is known such that $p(x_k|m_k^{(i)}, m_{k+1}^{(j)}, y_{1:k}) = p(x_k|m_k^{(i)}, y_{1:k})$ holds. This simple relationship, however, does not apply to models with unequal, heterogeneous state spaces.

In order to illustrate how the conditional pdfs, which result immediately after the mode change, have to be adapted, let the hybrid system comprise the modes $\mathcal{M} = \{m^{(1)}, m^{(2)}, m^{(3)}\}$ and let $x \in \mathcal{X} \subseteq \mathbb{R}^n$ be the base state vector. Then $x^{(1)} = x \in \mathcal{X} \subseteq \mathbb{R}^n$, $x^{(2)} = [x^T, x_{e,2}^T]^T \in \mathcal{X} \times \mathcal{X}_{e,2} \subseteq \mathbb{R}^n \times \mathbb{R}^{n_{e,2}}$, and $x^{(3)} = [x^T, x_{e,3}^T]^T \in \mathcal{X} \times \mathcal{X}_{e,3} \subseteq \mathbb{R}^n \times \mathbb{R}^{n_{e,3}}$ with $\mathcal{X}_{e,2} \cap \mathcal{X}_{e,3} = \emptyset$ are the continuous states of the three modes. Considering all transitions from mode i to mode j ($m_k^{(i)} \to m_{k+1}^{(j)}$) with $i, j \in \{1, 2, 3\}$ the pdf $p(x_k^{(j)}|m_k^{(i)}, m_{k+1}^{(j)}, y_{1:k})$ is given by one of the four cases listed below:

(i) $i = j$

$$p(x_k^{(i)}|m_k^{(i)}, m_{k+1}^{(i)}, y_{1:k}) = p(x_k^{(i)}|m_k^{(i)}, y_{1:k}), \tag{3}$$

(ii) $i = 1, j \in \{2, 3\}$

$$p(x_k^{(j)}|m_k^{(1)}, m_{k+1}^{(j)}, y_{1:k}) = p(x_k^{(1)}|m_k^{(1)}, y_{1:k}) \int p(x_k^{(j)}|m_k^{(j)}, y_{1:k}) \mathrm{d}x_k$$

$$= p(x_k^{(1)}|m_k^{(1)}, y_{1:k}) p(x_{e,j,k}|m_k^{(j)}, y_{1:k}), \tag{4}$$

(iii) $i = \{2, 3\}, j = 1$

$$p(x_k^{(1)}|m_k^{(i)}, m_{k+1}^{(1)}, y_{1:k}) = \int p(x_k^{(i)}|m_k^{(i)}, y_{1:k}) \mathrm{d}x_{e,i,k} = p(x_k|m_k^{(i)}, y_{1:k}), \tag{5}$$

(iv) $i = \{2, 3\}, j = \{2, 3\}$ with $i \neq j$

$$p(x_k^{(j)}|m_k^{(i)}, m_{k+1}^{(j)}, y_{1:k}) = \int p(x_k^{(i)}|m_k^{(i)}, y_{1:k}) \mathrm{d}x_{e,i,k} \int p(x_k^{(j)}|m_k^{(j)}, y_{1:k}) \mathrm{d}x_k$$

$$= p(x_k|m_k^{(i)}, y_{1:k}) p(x_{e,j,k}|m_k^{(j)}, y_{1:k}). \tag{6}$$

Adaption Before Fusion. Fusing the mode conditional pdfs according to the total probability theorem yields the pdf

$$p(x_{k+1}|y_{1:k+1}) = \sum_{i=1}^{q} p(x_{k+1}|m_{k+1}^{(i)}, y_{1:k+1}) P(m_{k+1}^{(i)}|y_{1:k+1}) \tag{7}$$

of the continuous states as a mixture of pdfs, each conditioned on a mode, where $P(m_{k+1}^{(i)}|y_{1:k+1})$ denotes the probability of the i-th mode. Obviously, mixing of pdfs succeeds only if the mode conditional pdfs are defined on the same domain. However, this requirement is clearly not met if unequal, heterogeneous state space models are used. Thus, the mode conditional pdfs have to be suitably adapted. In order to explain how to adapt the mode conditional pdfs, assume that $\mathcal{M} = \{m^{(1)}, m^{(2)}, m^{(3)}\}$ contains only three modes. Note, that the states $x^{(1)}$, $x^{(2)}$, and $x^{(3)}$ of each mode are already defined above. A straightforward but unstructured approach to adapt the mode conditional pdfs $p(x_{k+1}^{(i)}|m_{k+1}^{(i)}, y_{1:k+1})$ with $i \in \{1, 2, 3\}$ is to multiply each of them by an arbitrarily chosen but constant pdf $p^*(x, x_{e,2}, x_{e,3})$. Even though this unstructured approach ensures that the domains of the resulting pdfs are identical it generally also alters the statistical quantities of each mode conditional pdf leading to a biased estimate. An approach to adapt the mode conditional pdfs that does not change the mode-conditioned filter results is given by

$$p(x_{k+1}^*|m_{k+1}^{(1)}, \cdot) = p(x_{k+1}^{(1)}|m_{k+1}^{(1)}, \cdot)p(x_{e,2,k+1}|m_{k+1}^{(2)}, \cdot)p(x_{e,3,k+1}|m_{k+1}^{(3)}, \cdot), \quad (8)$$

$$p(x_{k+1}^*|m_{k+1}^{(2)}, \cdot) = p(x_{k+1}^{(2)}|m_{k+1}^{(2)}, \cdot)p(x_{e,3,k+1}|m_{k+1}^{(3)}, \cdot), \quad (9)$$

$$p(x_{k+1}^*|m_{k+1}^{(3)}, \cdot) = p(x_{k+1}^{(3)}|m_{k+1}^{(3)}, \cdot)p(x_{e,2,k+1}|m_{k+1}^{(2)}, \cdot) \quad (10)$$

with $x^* = [x^T, x_{e,2}^T, x_{e,3}^T]^T$, where $y_{1:k+1}$ is not explicitly listed for space reasons.

4   Numerical Results

The system under consideration is a hydraulic cylinder, which is described in detail in [6]. The aim is to distinguish between a fault-free operation of the system $(m^{(ff)})$ and an operation subject to either an internal $(m^{(in)})$ or an external leakage $(m^{(ex)})$. The duty cycle of the cylinder is shown in Fig. 3, where altering backgrounds indicate 4 distinctive phases of the duty cycle. Moreover, u_1, u_2 denote the pressures at the hydraulic ports, $p_{c,1}$, $p_{c,2}$ the pressures in the hydraulic compartments, and s the displacement of piston rod.

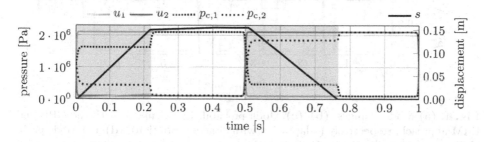

Fig. 3. Duty cycle of the fault-free system.

The results of both the GPB2 and IMM approache, both of which use an UKF for each mode (cf. [6]), are shown in Fig. 4 for eight consecutive duty cycles. Altering operation modes (see Fig. 4 **(a)** are imposed to the simulated system in different working cycle phases by abruptly changing the fault magnitudes. Figure 4 **(b)** and (c) show results, where the pdfs $p(x_\ell^{(i)}|m_\ell^{(i)}, y_{1:\ell})$ with $i \in \{\text{ff}, \text{in}, \text{ex}\}$ and $\ell \in \{k, k+1\}$ have been adapted with $p(x_{\text{d,aug},\ell}^{(j)}|m_\ell^{(j)}, y_{1:\ell}) = \delta(x_{\text{d,aug},\ell}^{(j)} - \hat{x}_{\text{d,aug},\ell}^{(j)})$ with $j \in \{\text{ex}, \text{in}\}$ and $j \neq i$, where $\hat{x}_{\text{d,aug},\ell}^{(j)}$ is the mean calculated by the filter of the j-th mode. This adaption, however, does not lead to a reliable mode estimation since several mode transitions have neither been detected by the GPB2 approach nor the IMM approach.

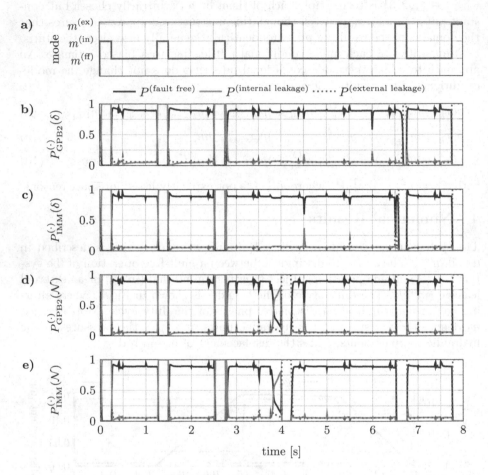

Fig. 4. (a) Mode changes, (b)–(c) Mode probabilities calculated with the GPB and IMM approach, respectively (adaptation with dirac distribution), (d)–(e) Mode probabilities calculated with the GPB and IMM approach, respectively (adaptation with normal distribution).

Better mode estimation results are obtained adapting $p(x_\ell^{(i)}|m_\ell^{(i)}, y_{1:\ell})$ with $p(x_{\text{d,aug},\ell}^{(j)}|m_\ell^{(j)}, y_{1:\ell}) = \mathcal{N}(x_{\text{d,aug},\ell}^{(j)}; \hat{x}_{\text{d,aug},\ell}^{(j)}, (\sigma_{\text{d,aug},\ell}^{(j)})^2)$, where $(\sigma_{\text{d,aug},\ell}^{(j)})^2$ is the variance calculated by the filter of the j-th mode. The corresponding results depicted in Fig. 4 (d) and (e) show, the more moments calculated by the filter of the j-th mode are take into account, the better are the estimated results. The same holds true to the estimated fault magnitudes, however, these estimates are not shown for space reasons.

5 Conclusion

If well known approaches to multiple-model estimation, such as the GPB2 approach or the IMM approach, are used in the context of fault diagnosis, the mode specific models usually have unequal, heterogeneous state spaces. Thus, it is necessary to adapt the mode conditional pdfs calculated by the related filters after mode transitions and before fusion. While adapting mode conditional pdfs with dirac distributions does not lead to a reliable estimation, the mode can be estimated with sufficient accuracy, if mode conditional pdfs are appropriately adapted with normal distributions.

References

1. Bar-Shalom, Y., Li, X., Kirubarajan, T.: Estimation with Applications to Tracking and Navigation. Wiley, New York (2001)
2. Granstroem, K., Willet, P., Bar-Shalom, Y.: Systematic approach to IMM mixing for unequal dimension states. IEEE Trans. Aerosp. Electron. Syst. **51**(5), 2975–2986 (2015)
3. Hofbaur, M.: Hybrid Estimation of Complex Systems. Springer, Heidelberg (2005). https://doi.org/10.1007/b105591
4. Li, X.R., Jilkov, V.P.: Survey of maneuvering target tracking - Part V: multiple-model methods. IEEE Trans. Aerosp. Electron. Syst **41**(4), 1255–1320 (2005)
5. Lopez, R., Danes, P., Royer, F.: Extending the IMM filter to heterogeneous-order state space models. In: Proceedings of the 49th Conference on Decision and Control, Atlanta, USA, pp. 7360–7374 (2010)
6. Weidemann, D., Alkov, I.: Fault diagnosis of nonlinear differential-algebraic systems using hybrid estimation. In: Rauh, A., Senkel, L. (eds.) Variable-Structure Approaches. ME, pp. 283–307. Springer, Cham (2016). https://doi.org/10.1007/978-3-319-31539-3_10

A Gradient Ascent Approach for Multiple Frequency Estimation

Yuneisy E. Garcia Guzman[1,2(✉)], Michael Lunglmayr[1,2], and Mario Huemer[1,2]

[1] Johannes Kepler University Linz, Linz, Austria
{yuneisy.garcia_guzman,michael.lunglmayr,mario.huemer}@jku.at
[2] Institute of Signal Processing, Linz, Austria

Abstract. This work investigates a new approach for frequency estimation of multiple complex sinusoids in the presence of noise. The algorithm is based on the optimization of the least squares (LS) cost function using a gradient ascent algorithm. The paper studies the performance of the proposed method and compares it to other estimation techniques such as root-multiple signal classification (root-MUSIC) and the discrete-time Fourier transform (DTFT). Simulation results show the performance gains provided by the proposed algorithm in different scenarios.

Keywords: Frequency estimation · DTFT · Gradient ascent · root-MUSIC · Cramer-Rao lower bound

1 Introduction

Frequency estimation has been an active research area in the last decades. Several methods have been proposed in the literature for solving this problem [1]; among the classic super-resolution techniques are the multiple signal classification (MUSIC) [2], its variant root-MUSIC [3], and the estimation of signal parameters via rotational invariance techniques (ESPRIT) [4,5], which exploit subspace methods to achieve high-resolution. Some of the limitations of these methods include an inferior performance in scenarios with low signal to noise ratios (SNRs) and a high computational complexity as a consequence of the required computation of the eigenvalue decomposition (EVD) of the measurement signal's covariance matrix. On the other hand, the discrete-time Fourier transform (DTFT) algorithm is a low computational complexity solution, which achieves a suitable performance for small SNRs. However, it introduces an estimation error due to the interactions of different frequency components. Recently a new approach has been introduced in [6], which does not require EVD of the covariance matrix and avoids inversion of data dependent matrices of large dimensions [6].

© Springer Nature Switzerland AG 2020
R. Moreno-Díaz et al. (Eds.): EUROCAST 2019, LNCS 12014, pp. 20–27, 2020.
https://doi.org/10.1007/978-3-030-45096-0_3

The present research proposes an enhanced algorithm for frequency estimation of multiple complex sinusoids in the presence of noise based on [6]. It features lower computational complexity than the super-resolution techniques, and shows a comparable and in some SNR regions even an improved performance. The main idea of this approach is to find the least squares (LS) estimate of the parameters of the multiple complex sinusoids. Two principal steps are needed for accomplishing this task. In the first step, the DTFT performs a coarse search of the frequencies, and in the second step, a gradient ascent (GA) algorithm is applied to obtain the optimal solution of the LS problem. Moreover, a numerical approximation technique (central difference method) is used for computing the gradient at each iteration, and the low complexity recursive method proposed in [6] is employed for the inversion of the occurring data dependent matrices.

2 Signal Model

We consider N samples of a signal $z[n]$ consisting on Q multiple complex sinusoids

$$z[n] = \sum_{q=1}^{Q} a_q e^{j2\pi f_q n} + v[n], \tag{1}$$

where f_q and a_q represent the normalized frequency and complex amplitude of the qth complex exponential, and $v[n]$ represents the additive complex Gaussian noise with variance σ^2 [6]. Equation (1) can be expressed in matrix/vector form as

$$\mathbf{z} = \mathbf{H}(\mathbf{f})\mathbf{a} + \mathbf{v} \tag{2}$$

where $\mathbf{a} = [a_1, a_2, \ldots, a_Q]^T$, $\mathbf{v} = [v[0], v[1], \ldots, v[N-1]]^T$, $\mathbf{f} = [f_1, f_2, \ldots, f_Q]^T$, and

$$\mathbf{H}(\mathbf{f}) = \begin{bmatrix} 1 & 1 & \cdots & 1 \\ e^{j2\pi f_1} & e^{j2\pi f_2} & \cdots & e^{j2\pi f_Q} \\ \vdots & \vdots & \vdots & \vdots \\ e^{j2\pi f_1(N-1)} & e^{j2\pi f_2(N-1)} & \cdots & e^{j2\pi f_Q(N-1)} \end{bmatrix}. \tag{3}$$

In the following we will also use the DTFT of $z[n]$

$$Z(f) = \sum_{n=0}^{N-1} z[n] e^{-j2\pi fn} \tag{4}$$

which can also be written in matrix/vector form

$$\mathbf{Z}(\mathbf{f}) = \mathbf{H}^H(\mathbf{f})\mathbf{z}. \tag{5}$$

The LS cost function can be expressed as

$$J_{LS}(\mathbf{a}, \mathbf{f}) = (\mathbf{z} - \mathbf{H}(\mathbf{f})\mathbf{a})^H (\mathbf{z} - \mathbf{H}(\mathbf{f})\mathbf{a}), \tag{6}$$

and based on this formulation the least squares estimate of the parameter $\mathbf{a}$ can be obtained by

$$\hat{\mathbf{a}} = (\mathbf{H}^H(\mathbf{f})\mathbf{H}(\mathbf{f}))^{-1}\mathbf{H}^H(\mathbf{f})\mathbf{z}. \tag{7}$$

Substituting (7) in (6) we get

$$\begin{aligned} J_{LS}(\hat{\mathbf{a}}, \mathbf{f}) &= \mathbf{z}^H(\mathbf{I} - \mathbf{H}(\mathbf{f})(\mathbf{H}^H(\mathbf{f})\mathbf{H}(\mathbf{f}))^{-1}\mathbf{H}^H(\mathbf{f}))\mathbf{z} \\ &= \mathbf{z}^H\mathbf{z} - \mathbf{z}^H\mathbf{H}(\mathbf{f})(\mathbf{H}^H(\mathbf{f})\mathbf{H}(\mathbf{f}))^{-1}\mathbf{H}^H(\mathbf{f})\mathbf{z}. \end{aligned} \tag{8}$$

The problem translates into maximizing the function

$$J(\mathbf{f}) = \underbrace{\mathbf{z}^H\mathbf{H}(\mathbf{f})}_{\mathbf{Z}^H(\mathbf{f})}\underbrace{(\mathbf{H}^H(\mathbf{f})\mathbf{H}(\mathbf{f}))^{-1}}_{N\mathbf{C}_Q}\underbrace{\mathbf{H}^H(\mathbf{f})\mathbf{z}}_{\mathbf{Z}(\mathbf{f})}. \tag{9}$$

Note that $J(\mathbf{f})$ is finally expressed as a function of the DTFT of the signal and the matrix $\mathbf{C}_Q = \frac{1}{N}\mathbf{H}^H(\mathbf{f})\mathbf{H}(\mathbf{f})$ which depends of the frequency differences [6]. Using the function $W(f) = e^{-j\pi f(N-1)}\sin(\pi fN)/(N\sin(\pi f))$, $\mathbf{C}_Q$ can be written as

$$\mathbf{C}_Q = \begin{bmatrix} 1 & W(f_1 - f_2) & \dots & W(f_1 - f_Q) \\ W(f_2 - f_1) & 1 & \dots & W(f_2 - f_Q) \\ \vdots & \vdots & \vdots & \vdots \\ W(f_Q - f_1) & W(f_Q - f_2) & \vdots & 1 \end{bmatrix}. \tag{10}$$

Figure 1(a) shows the cost function $J(\mathbf{f})$ for $Q = 2$ and for the frequency values $f_1 = 0.2$, $f_2 = 0.25$, and Fig. 1(b) highlights the gradients of the cost function in the interesting regions.

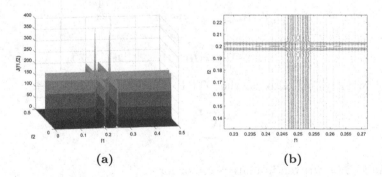

(a)   (b)

Fig. 1. (a) Cost function for $f_1 = 0.2$ and $f_2 = 0.25$. (b) Gradients of the cost function.

3 Gradient Ascent for Frequency Estimation

Considering the cost function (9), the LS estimate of the frequencies is given by

$$\hat{\mathbf{f}} = \max_{\mathbf{f}} \frac{1}{N} \mathbf{Z}^H(\mathbf{f}) \mathbf{C}_Q^{-1} \mathbf{Z}(\mathbf{f}). \tag{11}$$

For solving the above optimization problem we apply a gradient method with the update

$$\hat{\mathbf{f}}^{(k)} = \hat{\mathbf{f}}^{(k-1)} + \mu \nabla J(\hat{\mathbf{f}}^{(k-1)}) \tag{12}$$

where $\nabla J(\hat{\mathbf{f}}^{(k-1)})$ is the gradient of the cost function $J(\mathbf{f})$ evaluated in the current point and μ is the stepsize. In our algorithm, we approximate the partial derivatives using a center finite-difference method as

$$\frac{\partial J}{\partial f_q} = \frac{J(\hat{\mathbf{f}}^{(k-1)} + \epsilon \cdot \mathbf{e}_q) - J(\hat{\mathbf{f}}^{(k-1)} - \epsilon \cdot \mathbf{e}_q)}{2\epsilon}, \qquad q = 1, 2, \ldots Q, \tag{13}$$

where ϵ is a small constant and $\mathbf{e}_q \in \mathbb{R}^Q$ is a unit vector pointing in the qth direction, e.g., $\mathbf{e}_1 = [1, 0, 0, \ldots, 0]^T$.

It is well known that the gradient ascent technique is sensible to initialization, for this reason we choose as a starting point the estimated frequencies provided by the DTFT.

Note that the computation of the expression (13) implies to evaluate the cost function and therefore to calculate a matrix inversion. We have used an iterative procedure proposed in [6], which provides an efficient means to derive $\mathbf{C}_Q^{-1}$. Using the matrix inversion lemma, $\mathbf{C}_Q^{-1}$ can be expressed as [6]

$$
\begin{aligned}
\mathbf{C}_Q^{-1} &= \begin{bmatrix} \mathbf{C}_{Q-1} & \mathbf{x}_Q \\ \mathbf{x}_Q^H & 1 \end{bmatrix}^{-1} \\
&= \begin{bmatrix} (\mathbf{C}_{Q-1} - \mathbf{x}_Q \mathbf{x}_Q^H)^{-1} & -(\mathbf{C}_{Q-1} - \mathbf{x}_Q \mathbf{x}_Q^H)^{-1} \mathbf{x}_Q \\ -\mathbf{x}_Q^H (\mathbf{C}_{Q-1} - \mathbf{x}_Q \mathbf{x}_Q^H)^{-1} & 1 + \mathbf{x}_Q^H (\mathbf{C}_{Q-1} - \mathbf{x}_Q \mathbf{x}_Q^H)^{-1} \mathbf{x}_Q \end{bmatrix} \\
&= \begin{bmatrix} \mathbf{C}_{Q-1}^{-1} & \mathbf{0} \\ \mathbf{0}^T & 0 \end{bmatrix} + \frac{1}{1 - \delta_Q} \begin{bmatrix} \mathbf{y}_Q \mathbf{y}_Q^H & -\mathbf{y}_Q \\ -\mathbf{y}_Q^H & 1 \end{bmatrix}
\end{aligned} \tag{14}
$$

where $\mathbf{0}$ is the zero vector and

$$
\begin{aligned}
\mathbf{x}_Q &= [W(f_1 - f_Q) \ W(f_2 - f_Q) \ldots W(f_{Q-1} - f_Q)]^T \\
\delta_Q &= \mathbf{x}_Q^H \mathbf{C}_{Q-1}^{-1} \mathbf{x}_Q, \quad \mathbf{y}_Q = \mathbf{C}_{Q-1}^{-1} \mathbf{x}_Q.
\end{aligned} \tag{15}
$$

The matrix inversion can be computed iteratively starting from $(\mathbf{C}_1)^{-1} = 1$. Finally, the proposed method is summarized in Algorithm 1.

Algorithm 1: Gradient Ascent for Frequency estimation

---

1 **Input:** $\hat{\mathbf{f}}^{(0)} = \hat{\mathbf{f}}_{\text{DTFT}}$, ϵ, τ, μ, N_{iter}
2 **Initialization:** $\nabla J = 0$
3 **for** $k = 1 : N_{iter}$ **do**
4   **for** $q = 1 : Q$ **do**
5          $\frac{\partial J}{\partial f_q} = \frac{J(\hat{\mathbf{f}}^{(k-1)} + \epsilon \cdot \mathbf{e}_q) - J(\hat{\mathbf{f}}^{(k-1)} - \epsilon \cdot \mathbf{e}_q)}{2\epsilon}$
6          $\nabla J(q) = \frac{\partial J}{\partial f_q}$
7   **end**
8      $\hat{\mathbf{f}}^{(k)} = \hat{\mathbf{f}}^{(k-1)} + \mu \nabla J(\hat{\mathbf{f}}^{(k-1)})$
9      $\tilde{\mu} = \mu$
10   **while** $J(\hat{\mathbf{f}}^{(k)}) < J(\hat{\mathbf{f}}^{(k-1)})$ **do**
11          $\tilde{\mu} = \tilde{\mu}/2$
12          $\hat{\mathbf{f}}^{(k)} = \hat{\mathbf{f}}^{(k-1)} + \tilde{\mu} \nabla J(\hat{\mathbf{f}}^{(k-1)})$
13   **end**
14   **if** $\left\| \nabla J(\hat{\mathbf{f}}^{(k-1)}) \right\| < \tau$ **then**
15   break
16   **end**
17 **end**
18 **Output:** $\hat{\mathbf{f}} = \hat{\mathbf{f}}^{(k)}$

---

4   Simulation Results

The simulation results have been obtained using 100 test cases for averaging. The measurement noise samples are drawn from an i.i.d complex Gaussian random process with zero mean and variance σ^2. The performance is evaluated in terms of the mean square error (MSE) between the estimated and the correct frequency vector; both sorted in ascending order

$$\text{MSE} = E[\|\boldsymbol{\omega} - \hat{\boldsymbol{\omega}}\|^2] = E[\sum_{i=1}^{Q} (\omega_i - \hat{\omega}_i)^2] \tag{16}$$

where $\omega_i = 2\pi f_i$ are the normalized angular frequencies and $\boldsymbol{\omega} = [\omega_1, \omega_2, \ldots \omega_Q]$. The proposed algorithm (DTFT+GA) is compared with state-of-the-art approaches for different scenarios.

Figure 2 depicts a scenario with $N = 200$ and normalized frequencies $\omega_1 = 0.40$ and $\omega_2 = 0.60$. All the amplitudes were considered equal to one. In addition to the MSE of the considered estimation methods, we also show the Cramer-Rao lower bound (CRB) [7]. It can be noticed that DTFT+GA improves the behavior of the DTFT for high SNRs since it does not flatten out, but achieves lower MSE values in that region. Moreover, it outperforms the root-MUSIC algorithm in the low SNR region and shows a comparable performance in the high SNR region.

Figure 3 shows a scenario with normalized frequencies $\omega_1 = 0.30$ and $\omega_2 = 0.35$. The rest of the simulation parameters are the same as before. This simulation demonstrates the effectiveness of DTFT+GA for the case where the

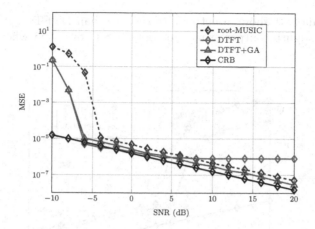

Fig. 2. MSE versus SNR for $\omega_1 = 0.40$ and $\omega_2 = 0.60$. Simulation parameters: $N_{iter} = 30$, $\epsilon = 10^{-4}$, $\tau = 10^{-6}$, $\mu = 0.0004$.

frequencies are closer to each other. Note that the DTFT performance flattens out at a higher MSE compared to the example above. This comes from the fact that the individual peaks in the spectrum around ω_1 and ω_2 influence each other, such that their maxima are slightly displaced. The DTFT+GA and the root-MUSIC still show about the same performance as in the first example.

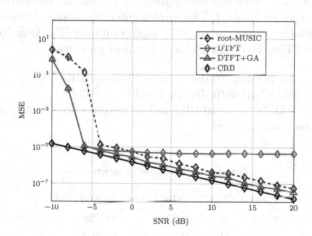

Fig. 3. MSE versus SNR for $\omega_1 = 0.30$ and $\omega_2 = 0.35$.

In order to evaluate how the performance of the algorithms is affected when the number of estimated frequencies increases, we ran a simulation with 10 normalized frequencies selected uniformly at random in the interval $(0, \pi]$. We considered a minimum difference between frequencies of 10^{-2}. The results are illustrated in Fig. 4. It can be noticed that DTFT+GA still shows a comparably good performance. It shows a better performance than DTFT in the high SNR region and it slightly outperforms the root-MUSIC over the whole simulated SNR region.

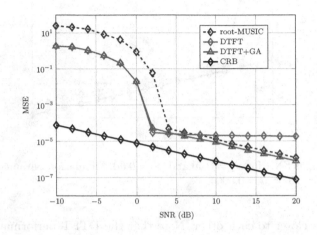

Fig. 4. MSE versus SNR for 10 normalized frequencies.

In order to get a rough idea of the computational times of the algorithms, we selected three cases with different parameter values and compared them. The results are displayed in Table. 1. The implementations were written in MATLAB 2008a, and simulations were run on a HP laptop running Windows 10 64-bit with an Intel(R) Core(TM) i7-7600 CPU and 16GB of memory.

- Case 1: $N = 150$, SNR = 10 dB, $\omega_1 = 0.30$, $\omega_2 = 0.40$.
- Case 2: $N = 200$, SNR = 10 dB, $\omega_1 = 0.30$, $\omega_2 = 0.40$.
- Case 3: $N = 500$, SNR = 10 dB, and 10 frequencies selected uniformly at random in the interval $(0, \pi]$.

Table 1. Runtimes in seconds

Case	DTFT	DTFT+GA	root-MUSIC
Case 1	0.0047	0.0210	0.0388
Case 2	0.0078	0.0260	0.0982
Case 3	0.0174	0.3466	0.6742

Note that the runtime of the DTFT+GA method lies in between the runtimes of the DTFT and the root-MUSIC for all regarded scenarios. The fact that after the computation of the DTFT, a gradient ascent technique is applied increases the computational time of DTFT+GA with respect to the DTFT method, as expected. On the other hand, it is less complex than root-MUSIC. This is due to the fact that it does not require EVD of the covariance matrix and avoids large matrix inversions. Note that we have used the Matlab function for root-MUSIC that is already relying on compiled libraries. We therefore expect to be able to further clearly increase the runtime gap between DTFT+GA and root-MUSIC by using a more efficient programming language, e.g, a C implementation.

5   Conclusions

In this work we investigated an efficient multiple frequency estimation algorithm that uses a combination of DTFT and gradient ascent. The algorithm outperforms the DTFT based frequency estimation in the high SNR region. Moreover, it shows a better performance than the subspace based root-MUSIC algorithm for low SNRs and a comparable performance in the high SNR region. The performance gains over the DTFT increase in scenarios with quite close frequencies. The DTFT+GA approach also offers a good trade-off between complexity and performance. It requires additional effort compared to the DTFT, but avoids EVD and large matrix inversions as required for subspace-based techniques. We therefore consider the DTFT+GA approach more appropriate for digital hardware implementation than the subspace-based techniques.

Acknowledgements. This work is supported by: the COMET-K2 "Center for Symbiotic Mechatronics" of the Linz Center of Mechatronics (LCM), funded by the Austrian federal government and the federal state of Upper Austria.

References

1. Van Trees, H.: Optimum Array Processing. Part IV of Detection, Estimation and. Wiley, New York (2002)
2. Schmidt, R.: Multiple emitter location and signal parameter estimation. IEEE Trans. Antennas Propag. **34**, 276–280 (1986)
3. Rao, B., Hari, K.: Performance analysis of Root-Music. IEEE Trans. Acoust. Speech Signal Process. **37**, 1939–1949 (1989)
4. Kailath, T.: ESPRIT-estimation of signal parameters via rotational invariance techniques. Opt. Eng. **29**, 296 (1989, 1990)
5. Haardt, M., Nossek, J.: Unitary ESPRIT: how to obtain increased estimation accuracy with a reduced computational burden. IEEE Trans. Signal Process. **43**, 1232–1242 (1995)
6. Abeysekera, S.: Least-squares multiple frequency estimation using recursive regression sum of squares. In: 2018 IEEE International Symposium on Circuits and Systems (ISCAS) (2018)
7. Stoica, P., Nehorai, A.: MUSIC, maximum likelihood, and Cramer-Rao bound. IEEE Trans. Acoust. Speech Signal Process. **37**, 720–741 (1989)

Enhanced Transform-Domain LMS Based Self-interference Cancellation in LTE Carrier Aggregation Transceivers

Christian Motz$^{(\boxtimes)}$ (ID), Oliver Ploder (ID), Thomas Paireder (ID), and Mario Huemer (ID)

Christian Doppler Laboratory for Digitally Assisted RF Transceivers for Future Mobile Communications, Institute of Signal Processing, JKU, Linz, Austria
christian.motz@jku.at

Abstract. Modern radio frequency transceivers for wireless communication standards operating in frequency division duplex suffer from an unwanted Tx leakage signal. In combination with carrier aggregation this might harm the receiver in form of a so-called modulated spur interference. Different digital interference cancellation techniques have been proposed but suffer from a slow adaptation rate due to the high correlation of the involved Long Term Evolution (LTE) signals. This work derives and analyzes a new form of the Least-Mean-Squares (LMS) algorithm that incorporates knowledge of the signal statistics. Simulations show that the presented algorithm can effectively improve the cancellation and adaptation performance for real world interference scenarios.

Keywords: Interference cancellation · LTE · Adaptive filter · LMS

1 Introduction

Modern radio frequency (RF) transceivers for wireless communication standards usually support frequency division duplex (FDD) operation and employ carrier aggregation (CA). Then, the transmitter (Tx) and the receiver (Rx) paths are connected via the duplexer to the common antenna and operate simultaneously. The limited Tx-Rx stop-band isolation of the duplexer leads to an unwanted Tx leakage signal into the receiver(s) which can generate interferences like modulated-spurs. This causes a deterioration of the signal-to-noise ratio (SNR) of the wanted signal. In [3,5] a system model has already been derived and a cancellation scheme based on the Least-Mean-Squares (LMS) algorithm has been suggested. Also mixed signal solutions have been presented in the literature [2,6]. In the influence of the Long Term Evolution (LTE) uplink signal statistics on the adaptation speed of the LMS algorithm. We show that a high eigenvalue spread is inherent to the single carrier frequency-division multiple access (SC-FDMA) transmission scheme resulting in slow adaptation. In addition, we present a novel low-complexity algorithm, namely the Model-Based (MB)-LMS, for the cancellation of the modulated-spur interference which

© Springer Nature Switzerland AG 2020
R. Moreno-Díaz et al. (Eds.): EUROCAST 2019, LNCS 12014, pp. 28–35, 2020.
https://doi.org/10.1007/978-3-030-45096-0_4

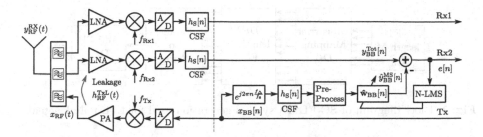

Fig. 1. Block diagram: LTE CA transceiver with proposed modulated spur cancellation.

is based on the Transform-Domain (TD)-LMS. In the MB-LMS approach the statistical model of the SC-FDMA transmit data is incorporated into the algorithm. This improves the adaptation speed, which is important for applications in RF transceivers because several parameters change frequently during operation [1].

2 Modulated Spurs

Figure 1 shows the basic architecture of an FDD RF transceiver employing CA. The duplexer, connecting the Tx and Rx paths to the antenna, has a limited stopband attenuation which allows for parts of the Tx signal to leak into the RX paths. Furthermore, due to the several clock sources and dividers needed for all possible CA scenarios, cross-talk between the LO lines of the receivers, together with device nonlinearities spurs may be created. If the frequency of such a spur falls near the Tx frequency, this can lead to a downconversion of the distorted Tx leakage signal into one or more of the receive bands. This so-called modulated spur possibly interferes with the received signal and ultimately diminishes the receiver's sensitivity. In [5] an equivalent baseband model of the modulated spur problem is derived and the LMS algorithm is applied for cancellation. In [3] several adaptive algorithms are compared for the modulated spur problem and a variable step-size (VSS) normalized LMS is suggested. In this contribution we will build upon the same system model. Baseband equivalent signals have the subscript BB. The received signal for RX1 consists of three components: (1) the wanted RX signal denoted by $y_{\mathrm{BB}}^{\mathrm{RX}}[n]$, (2) a noise term referred to as $n_{\mathrm{BB}}[n]$ and (3) the modulated spur interference $x_{\mathrm{BB}}^{\mathrm{s}}[n]$. Therefore, the total received signal at the output of the analog-to-digital converters can be modelled as

$$y_{\mathrm{BB}}^{\mathrm{Tot}}[n] = A_{\mathrm{LNA}}\left(y_{\mathrm{BB}}^{\mathrm{RX}}[n] + n_{\mathrm{BB}}[n] + x_{\mathrm{BB}}^{\mathrm{s}}[n]\right) * h_{\mathrm{s}}[n]. \qquad (1)$$

Here A_{LNA} denotes the low noise amplifier (LNA) gain, and $h_{\mathrm{s}}[n]$ describes the impulse response of the channel select filter (CSF). The leakage signal based on the baseband (BB) transmit data $x_{\mathrm{BB}}^{\mathrm{TX}}[n]$ can be written as

$$x_{\mathrm{BB}}^{\mathrm{s}}[n] = A_{\mathrm{PA}} A_{\mathrm{sp}}\left(x_{\mathrm{BB}}^{\mathrm{TX}}[n]\, e^{j2\pi n \frac{f_{\Delta}}{f_{\mathrm{s}}}}\right) * h_{\mathrm{BB}}^{\mathrm{TX,L}}[n], \qquad (2)$$

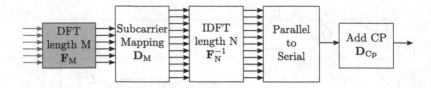

Fig. 2. Block diagram of SC-FDMA symbol generation used for LTE uplink signals.

where the factors A_{PA} and A_{sp} represent the gain of the power amplifier (PA) and the spur, respectively. The frequency shift results from the spur offset $f_\Delta = f_{\mathrm{Tx}} - f_{\mathrm{sp}}$ which is known. The equivalent BB impulse response of the TX-RX leakage channel $h_{\mathrm{BB}}^{\mathrm{TX,L}}[n]$ with respect to f_{sp} is the only unknown. Consequently, adaptive filtering algorithms can be applied to estimate this leakage channel. Then, the right part of Fig. 1 allows to generate an estimate of the modulated spur interference signal which can be used for the cancellation in the receive path.

3   LTE Uplink Signal Generation

As shown before the modulated spur interference is based on the BB trans-mit signal. The RF transceiver in this paper is shown from the user equipment perspective, meaning the transmit path corresponds to the LTE uplink, where SC-FDMA is used as the transmission scheme. The generation of SC-FDMA symbols is shown in Fig. 2, where M input symbols are processed at once to create the time samples needed for the transmission in the BB. The subcarrier mapping allows for dynamic multi user access by assigning different parts of the overall bandwidth to different users. In the following a linear model of the form

$$\mathbf{x}' = \mathbf{A}\,\mathbf{d} \tag{3}$$

is derived for the SC-FDMA symbol generation, where $\mathbf{d}$ denotes the QAM symbols and $\mathbf{x}'$ the samples of the symbol. This allows to study the statistics of the LTE BB signal in more detail. The discrete Fourier transform (DFT) operation of given length M can be formulated as a multiplication with the DFT matrix $\mathbf{F}_{\mathrm{M}}$ where the DC part of the signal is denoted by the first row. As it is more convenient to consider only a spectrum centered around DC, we define the general remapping $\mathbf{S}_{\mathrm{K}}$ as follows

$$\mathbf{S}_{\mathrm{K}} = \begin{bmatrix} \mathbf{0}^{K/2 \times K/2} & \mathbf{I}^{K/2} \\ \mathbf{I}^{K/2} & \mathbf{0}^{K/2 \times K/2} \end{bmatrix}, \tag{4}$$

and apply it after the DFT with $K = M$. Moving on in the chain, the subcarrier mapping can be described by applying the $N \times M$ matrix

$$\mathbf{D}_{\mathrm{Map}} = \begin{bmatrix} \mathbf{0}^{L_0/2 \times M} \\ \mathbf{I}^M \\ \mathbf{0}^{(N-(M+L_0)) \times M} \\ \mathbf{0}^{L_0/2 \times M} \end{bmatrix}. \tag{5}$$

Of course, this is just an example of a possible mapping, the exact matrix depends on the position and bandwidth of granted uplink transmission resources. Further, L_0 denotes the number of guard subcarriers. For LTE with 20 MHz bandwidth, only 1200 out of the available 2048 subcarriers can be used, considering full resource block (RB) allocation. The remaining subcarriers are always set to zero to avoid spectral leakage outside of the designated bandwidth. The inverse discrete Fourier transform (IDFT) is formulated by a multiplication with the remapping matrix $\mathbf{S}_N$ and the inverse DFT matrix. Adding the cyclic prefix (CP) can be modeled via the matrix

$$\mathbf{D}_{\mathrm{Cp}} = \begin{bmatrix} \mathbf{0}^{L_{\mathrm{Cp}} \times (N - L_{\mathrm{Cp}})} & \mathbf{I}^{L_{\mathrm{Cp}}} \\ \mathbf{I}^N \end{bmatrix}, \tag{6}$$

with L_{Cp} denoting the CP length. The desired model (3) already considers the generation of $N + L_{\mathrm{Cp}}$ time samples out of the M input symbols, consequently, the parallel to serial conversion does not need to be modeled as an extra step. Lastly, according to the LTE standard, the signal needs to be frequency shifted by half the subcarrier spacing, to avoid transmission of data at the DC subcarrier. This shift can be achieved by applying the diagonal matrix $\mathbf{H}_S = \mathrm{diag}\,(s_i)$ with $s_i = e^{j\pi\Delta f/f_s\, i}$ where Δf denotes the subcarrier spacing. Combining the whole signal chain finally yields the desired representation of the LTE uplink symbol generation

$$\mathbf{x}' = \mathbf{A}\,\mathbf{d} = \mathbf{H}_S \mathbf{D}_{\mathrm{Cp}} \mathbf{F}_N^{-1} \mathbf{S}_N \mathbf{D}_{\mathrm{Map}} \mathbf{S}_M \mathbf{F}_M\, \mathbf{d}\,. \tag{7}$$

For LMS based algorithms the second order statistics of the input signal influences the adaptation rate. For a linear model the transformed covariance matrix is given by

$$\mathbf{C}_{\mathbf{x}'\mathbf{x}'} = \mathbf{A}\,\mathbf{C}_{\mathbf{dd}}\,\mathbf{A}^H\,. \tag{8}$$

Assuming an independent and identical distribution of the input data $\mathbf{d}$, $\mathbf{C}_{\mathbf{dd}}$ reduces to a scaled identity matrix. Inspecting $\mathbf{C}_{\mathbf{x}'\mathbf{x}'}$ in detail reveals that it is a Toeplitz matrix. This implies that the vector $\mathbf{x}'$ can be interpreted as a section of a wide-sense stationary (WSS) signal. Later in this work, the elements of $\mathbf{x}'$ form the input samples of LMS-based adaptive filters with length L. The covariance matrix of the input data for the adaptive algorithm $\mathbf{C}_{\mathbf{xx}}$ is given by the northwest submatrix of size $L \times L$. Numerical evaluations revealed that $\mathbf{C}_{\mathbf{xx}}$ exhibits a high eigenvalue spread even for fully allocated LTE uplink signals. In real world scenarios mostly partial allocations occur which show an even higher eigenvalue spread. Consequently, LMS based modulated spur cancellation schemes that do not account for this fact, suffer from slow adaption rates.

4 Algorithm

4.1 TD-LMS

One well known method to reduce the negative effects of correlated signals on the performance of the LMS algorithm is the TD-LMS [7] described in Algorithm 1. The idea is to apply a unitary transformation $\mathbf{T}$ to the input data

---

Algorithm 1. Transform Domain Least Mean Squares Algorithm

1: **function** TD-LMS($\mathbf{x}_{1,\ldots,N}, y_{1,\ldots,N}$)
2: Initialization $\mathbf{p}[0] := \mathbf{0}$, $\mathbf{w}[0] := \mathbf{0}$
3:     **for** $n = 1 : N$ **do**
4:         $\mathbf{u}[n] = \mathbf{T}\,\mathbf{x}[n]$
5:         $p_l[n] = (1 - \alpha)\, p_l[n-1] + \alpha\, |u_l[n]|^2$, $l = 1, \ldots, L$
6:         $\mathbf{P}[n] = \mathrm{diag}(1/p_1[n], \ldots, 1/p_N[n])$
7:         $\hat{y}[n] = \mathbf{w}[n-1]^T \mathbf{u}[n]$
8:         $e[n] = y[n] - \hat{y}[n]$
9:         $\mathbf{w}[n] = \mathbf{w}[n-1] + \mu\, e[n]\mathbf{P}[n]\mathbf{u}[n]^*$
10:     **return** $\hat{y}_{1,\ldots,N}$

$\mathbf{x}[n] = [x[n], x[n-1], \ldots, x[n-L+1]]^T$, where L is the LMS filter length. In a second step a power normalization is applied which aims to equalize power differences of the transformed input vector. The idea of the TD-LMS is to bring the covariance matrix of the LMS input close to an identity matrix. This represents the best case for the LMS in terms of the input covariance matrix. The covariance matrix of the input $\mathbf{x}[n]$ and the covariance matrix of the transformed input $\mathbf{u}[n] = \mathbf{T}\,\mathbf{x}[n]$ are related by $\mathbf{C_{uu}} = \mathbf{T}\,\mathbf{C_{xx}}\,\mathbf{T}^H$. The aim of the unitary transformation in the TD-LMS is to bring the covariance matrix close to a diagonal matrix. Common transformations such as the DFT or the Discrete Cosine transform (DCT) have been proven to have this property for many types of signals or at least fulfill it approximately. Furthermore, they are similarity transformations that preserve eigenvalues. Consequently, we end up with a covariance matrix similar to

$$\mathbf{C_{uu}} \approx \mathrm{diag}(\lambda_1, \ldots, \lambda_L), \qquad (9)$$

with λ_l being the eigenvalues of the input covariance matrix $\mathbf{C_{xx}}$. Then, the power estimation for each component of the transformed input vector is applied. Due to the fact that $\mathbf{C_{uu}}$ is diagonal or at least diagonal dominant, for zero-mean input signals the estimated variances are a good approximation of the eigenvalues λ_l. The power equalization within the update equation can again be seen as a linear transformation. If the power estimation is close to the eigenvalues, then using the inverse to normalize the data will indeed bring the covariance matrix seen by the LMS close to the identity matrix.

4.2 MB-LMS

Next, we show how the TD-LMS can be modified if the covariance matrix of the input signal is known, such as for LTE signals. First of all, it is still useful to apply a unitary transformation, because this class of transformations can be computed efficiently in our application by utilizing a sliding window structure. For LTE uplink signals it turns out that the DCT performs better than the DFT. The recursive power estimation and successive equalization can however be modified. Based on the knowledge of $\mathbf{C_{xx}}$ and thus $\mathbf{C_{uu}}$ we can choose $\mathbf{P}$ in a way that brings $\mathbf{C_{vv}}$ close to the identity matrix in advance. One natural choice is

$$\mathbf{P} = \mathrm{diag}(1/[\mathbf{C_{uu}}]_{11}, \ldots, 1/[\mathbf{C_{uu}}]_{LL}) \tag{10}$$

with $[\mathbf{C_{uu}}]_{ll}$ denoting the lth-element of the main diagonal. Finally, the MB-LMS is similar to Algorithm 1. The recursive power estimation $p_l[n]$ is not required, because the normalization matrix $\mathbf{P}[n]$ is precomputed according to (10). This leads to a lower complexity compared to the TD-LMS. The right part of Fig. 1 shows how the algorithm can be used to cancel modulated spur interference. The pre-processing block contains the transformation and normalization of the input data according to the equations above.

4.3 Stability Analysis

To derive the stability bound, we consider the a priori error $e[n]$ according to [4]. There, $e[n + 1]$ is approximated by a first order Taylor series, and only the derivative with respect to $\mathbf{w}$ is considered. In our case this yields

$$e[n + 1] \approx e[n] + \left. \frac{\partial e}{\partial \mathbf{w}} \right|_{\mathbf{w}=\mathbf{w}[n-1]} \cdot (\mathbf{w}[n] - \mathbf{w}[n - 1])$$

$$e[n + 1] \approx e[n] - \mu\, c[n]\mathbf{u}[n]^T \mathbf{P}\, \mathbf{u}[n]^*. \tag{11}$$

For $|e[n]|$ to converge in the mean squared error sense, it must stand that [4]

$$|1 - \mu\, \mathbf{u}[n]^H \mathbf{P}\, \mathbf{u}[n]| < 1 \tag{12}$$

Solving for μ finally yields the wanted lower and upper bound for the step size

$$0 < \mu < \frac{2}{\mathbf{u}[n]^H \mathbf{P}\, \mathbf{u}[n]}. \tag{13}$$

This result is very similar to the Normalized Least-Mean-Squares (N-LMS) algorithm, with the difference that the transformed input vector $\mathbf{u}[n]$ is used and that a weighted vector norm is used instead of the L_2-norm. For simulations a normalized weight update is used utilizing this step size bound.

5   Simulation Results

To evaluate the performance of the algorithm, we conduct a series of simulations for modulated spur interference scenarios. The duplexer stop-band is approximated by an FIR filter. The impulse responses are based on real world duplexers for LTE communication devices, where S-parameter measurements of the stop-band have been acquired in order to fit impulse responses. The measurements have been done under different operating conditions such as varying temperature to yield models covering a large range of real world scenarios. We compare our algorithm with the N-LMS and the traditional TD-LMS. The normalized mean-squared-error (NMSE) given by

$$\text{NMSE}_{\text{dB}} = 10 \log_{10} \left(\frac{\text{E}\left[\left| y_{\text{BB}}^{\text{MS}}[n] - \hat{y}_{\text{BB}}^{\text{MS}}[n] \right|^2 \right]}{\text{E}\left[\left| y_{\text{BB}}^{\text{MS}}[n] \right|^2 \right]} \right) \tag{14}$$

allows us to compare the interference suppression in a normalized manner. Each algorithm is tested with 41 fitted duplexer models. In addition, we use ensemble averaging with 250 runs for each scenario to account for the stochastic nature of the algorithms. We evaluate different levels of the interference. Note that the wanted received signal acts as a noise term for the adaptation, too. Therefore, we define the SNR for the adaptive algorithm as follows:

$$\text{SNR}_{\text{dB}} = 10 \log_{10} \left(\frac{\text{E}\left[\left| y_{\text{BB}}^{\text{MS}}[n] \right|^2 \right]}{\text{E}\left[\left| y_{\text{BB}}^{\text{RX}}[n] + w_{\text{BB}}[n] \right|^2 \right]} \right) \tag{15}$$

In the first scenario we choose an interference level of 30 dB and an LTE uplink signal with 20 MHz bandwidth and 100 RBs allocated. Figure 3a shows the results, where best and worst case performance of each algorithm are plotted. The best case performance of all algorithms is almost the same. Though, the N-LMS exhibits a huge performance spread over the different duplexer models. Only the MB-LMS shows almost no difference between best and worst case and thus outperforms the other algorithms. This is very crucial for an RF transceiver: for the specification of the interference level, one has to consider the worst case. The second scenario uses an interference level of 10 dB and 25 allocated RBs (on the left side of the spectrum). Again the MB-LMS is the only one not

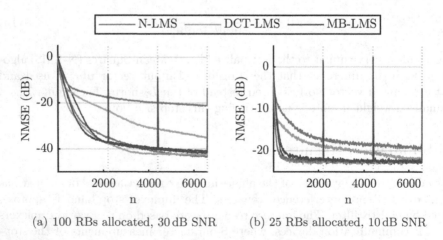

(a) 100 RBs allocated, 30 dB SNR   (b) 25 RBs allocated, 10 dB SNR

Fig. 3. Performance evaluation of the MB-LMS for cancellation of a modulated spur interference scenario for different RB allocations in the uplink signal and different interference levels.

exhibiting a noticeable performance spread. However, the performance gain is lower compared to the first scenario. Another interesting aspect are the error spikes of all algorithms at the symbol transitions (marked by the vertical dotted lines). They result from the non-stationary signal statistics at these transitions.

6 Conclusion

This paper addressed challenges in the cancellation of the modulated spur interference in RF transceivers. A model of the second order statistics for the involved LTE signals is derived to analyze their influence for adaptive algorithms such as the LMS which is commonly used for this type of interference cancellation. Then, a refined form of the TD-LMS is derived that incorporates knowledge based on the signal statistics without increasing computational complexity. Simulations demonstrated that the presented algorithm improves the cancellation performance substantially in real world interference scenarios.

Acknowledgment. The authors wish to acknowledge DMCE GmbH & Co KG as part of Intel for supporting this work carried out at the Christian Doppler Laboratory for Digitally Assisted RF Transceivers for Future Mobile Communications. The financial support by the Austrian Federal Ministry for Digital and Economic Affairs and the National Foundation for Research, Technology and Development is gratefully acknowledged.

References

1. Dahlman, E., Parkvall, S., Sköld, J.: 4G LTE/LTE-Advanced for Mobile Broadband, 2nd edn. Elsevier Academic Press, Amsterdam (2014)
2. Elmaghraby, A., et al.: A mixed-signal technique for TX-induced modulated spur cancellation in LTE-CA receivers. IEEE Trans. Circuits Syst. I: Regul. Pap. **65**(9), 3060–3073 (2018)
3. Gebhard, A., Kanumalli, R.S., Neurauter, B., Huemer, M.: Adaptive self-interference cancelation in LTE-A carrier aggregation FDD direct-conversion transceivers. In: 2016 IEEE Sensor Array and Multichannel Signal Processing Workshop (SAM), pp. 1–5, July 2016
4. Hanna, A.I., Mandic, D.P.: A fully adaptive normalized nonlinear gradient descent algorithm for complex-valued nonlinear adaptive filters. IEEE Trans. Signal Process. **51**(10), 2540–2549 (2003)
5. Kanumalli, R.S., Gebhard, A., Elmaghraby, A., Mayer, A., Schwartz, D., Huemer, M.: Active digital cancellation of transmitter induced modulated spur interference in 4G LTE carrier aggregation transceivers. In: 2016 IEEE 83rd Vehicular Technology Conference (VTC Spring), pp. 1–5, May 2016
6. Sadjina, S., Krzysztof, D., Kanumalli, R.S., Huemer, M., Pretl, H.: A circuit technique for blocker-induced modulated spur cancellation in 4G LTE carrier aggregation transceivers. In: 2017 Austrochip Workshop on Microelectronics (Austrochip), pp. 23–28, October 2017
7. Sayed, A.H.: Fundamentals of Adaptive Filtering. Wiley, Hoboken (2003)

Kernel Adaptive Filters: A Panacea for Self-interference Cancellation in Mobile Communication Transceivers?

Christina Auer[1]([✉]), Andreas Gebhard[1], Christian Motz[1], Thomas Paireder[1], Oliver Ploder[1], Ram Sunil Kanumalli[1], Alexander Melzer[2], Oliver Lang[2], and Mario Huemer[1,2]

[1] Christian Doppler Laboratory for Digitally Assisted RF Transceivers for Future Mobile Communications, Johannes Kepler University Linz, Linz, Austria
christina.auer@jku.at
[2] Institute of Signal Processing, Johannes Kepler University Linz, Linz, Austria

Abstract. In frequency division duplex transceivers, the non-ideal analog duplexer has only a limited stop-band attenuation, and therefore a part of the transmit signal leaks into the receive path. Although operating on a different frequency band, non-ideal effects in the receive path cause different kinds of self-interferences, which can have a higher power level than the actual wanted receive signal. A possible way to tackle this problem are adaptive filters. These approaches are mostly model based, and for each kind of interference a different algorithm is needed. Kernel adaptive filtering offers the possibility to deal with different sorts of interferences with the same algorithm. In this work, we investigate the capabilities of kernel adaptive filtering to cancel especially the second-order intermodulation distortion (IMD2) and the transmitter (Tx)-harmonics interference.

Keywords: Kernel adaptive filter · KLMS · Interference cancellation · LTE · Mobile transceiver

1 Introduction

Today's radio frequency (RF) transceivers in mobile communication devices support the operation in frequency division duplex (FDD) mode, in which they are simultaneously transmitting and receiving at different frequencies. The demand for higher data throughput is ever increasing. One way to fulfill this requirement is carrier aggregation (CA) as it is supported by the 'Long Term Evolution Advanced' (LTE-A)-standard. With this approach the number of transmitters and receivers integrated in a single chip increases. A simplified RF transceiver with one transmit and two receive paths connected via the duplexer to one common antenna is shown in the system model in Fig. 1, for further details see [1].

This duplexer usually provides a limited transmit (Tx) to receive (Rx) stop-band attenuation of around 50 dB in nowadays transceivers [2]. Therefore, part

© Springer Nature Switzerland AG 2020
R. Moreno-Díaz et al. (Eds.): EUROCAST 2019, LNCS 12014, pp. 36–43, 2020.
https://doi.org/10.1007/978-3-030-45096-0_5

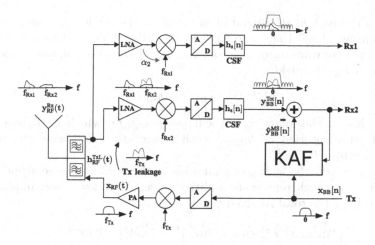

Fig. 1. System model of an LTE FDD transceiver for mobile devices.

of the Tx signal leaks into the Rx paths. In combination with nonlinearities in the transmit and/or in the receive chains [3] and with crosstalk issues this can lead to interferences that overlap the wanted receive signal in FDD mode. With the increasing numbers of Tx- and Rx-paths also the number of possible interference scenarios is increasing steadily. Some interferences only occur when CA is applied. In this paper we address Tx-harmonics and second-order intermodulation distortion (IMD2) interferences [1], which are discussed in detail in the following section.

There are different approaches for the digital cancellation of transmitter induced nonlinear self-interferences discussed in the existing literature. One prominent approach is adaptive filtering, another one are least squares (LS) type methods. For the second-order intermodulation distortion (IMD2) cancellation in [4] a Volterra kernel based LS approach was applied, and in [1] a particular least mean squares (LMS) type algorithm, the IMD2LMS was designed. For the problem of Tx-harmonics, data preprocessing and classical LMS filtering was applied in [5]. To the best of our knowledge we are the first investigating kernel adaptive filtering (KAF) as a potential method for the cancellation of all sources of self-interferences with the same algorithm.

2 Problem Statement

In this section, we derive analytical models for the Tx-harmonics and second-order intermodulation distortion (IMD2) interference [1] with the help of Fig. 1. In the transmitter the digital complex transmit signal $x_{\mathrm{BB}}[n]$ is analog-to-digital converted resulting in the complex analog signal $x_{\mathrm{BB}}(t)$, up-converted to the transmit carrier frequency f_{Tx} by the mixer, and fed into the power amplifier (PA) with gain A_{PA}, which gives

$$x_{\mathrm{RF}}(t) = A_{\mathrm{PA}} \Re\left\{ x_{\mathrm{BB}}(t) e^{j 2\pi f_{Tx} t} \right\}. \tag{1}$$

Due to the limited stop-band attenuation of the duplexer, a small fraction of the transmit signal leaks into the receive paths. This leakage signal can be modeled by a convolution of the transmit signal with the impulse response of the duplexer $h_{\mathrm{RF}}(t)$, yielding

$$y_{\mathrm{RF}}^{\mathrm{TxL}}(t) = x_{\mathrm{RF}}(t) * h_{\mathrm{RF}}(t). \tag{2}$$

We note that in the following we will use $h_{\mathrm{BB}}(t; f)$, which is the equivalent baseband representation of $h_{\mathrm{RF}}(t)$ with respect to f following the relation $h_{\mathrm{RF}}(t) = 2\Re\{h_{\mathrm{BB}}(t; f)e^{j2\pi f t}\}$.

At the receiver, the leakage signal adds to the wanted receive signal $y_{\mathrm{RF}}^{\mathrm{Rx}}(t)$ and to $w_{\mathrm{RF}}(t)$, which represents additive noise. After low noise amplification with gain A_{LNA} the total received signal reads as

$$y_{\mathrm{RF,LNA}}^{\mathrm{Tot}}(t) = A_{\mathrm{LNA}} \left[y_{\mathrm{RF}}^{\mathrm{TxL}}(t) + y_{\mathrm{RF}}^{\mathrm{Rx}}(t) + w_{\mathrm{RF}}(t) \right]. \tag{3}$$

So far we assumed ideal transmit and receive paths. In the following two possible non-ideal effects leading to self-interferences are described.

2.1   Tx-Harmonics

Tx-harmonics appear, e.g., due to a nonlinearity of the PA. When the transceiver is operating in receive CA mode, one of the generated Tx-harmonics can fall in an Rx band and degrade the signal-to-noise ratio (SNR) of the desired Rx signal. This is also explained in detail in [5]. In this work we limit our analysis to the second harmonic which is most likely to fall into an Rx band and additionally has the highest power of all harmonics. In order to investigate the performance of the nonlinear kernel least mean squares (KLMS) algorithm, we include a second order term in our PA model (1)

$$x_{\mathrm{RF}}(t) = A_{\mathrm{PA}}\Re\left\{x_{\mathrm{BB}}(t)e^{j2\pi f_{Tx}t}\right\} + \underbrace{\beta_2 A_{\mathrm{PA}}^2 \Re\left\{x_{\mathrm{BB}}(t)e^{j2\pi f_{Tx}t}\right\}^2}_{\tilde{x}_{\mathrm{RF}}(t)}. \tag{4}$$

Furthermore, we assume that $\tilde{x}_{\mathrm{RF}}$ falls into the band of the second CA receive path Rx2. We can reformulate $\tilde{x}_{\mathrm{RF}}(t)$ as

$$\tilde{x}_{\mathrm{RF}}(t) = \beta_2 \frac{A_{\mathrm{PA}}^2}{2}\Re\{x_{\mathrm{BB}}(t)^2 e^{j4\pi f_{Tx}t}\} + \beta_2 \frac{A_{\mathrm{PA}}^2}{2} |x_{\mathrm{BB}}(t)|^2. \tag{5}$$

This signal is now leaking via the duplexer into the receive chain. Considering the subsequent mixing process in the receiver, the relevant remaining part is the first term in (5). Therefore, (2) becomes

$$\tilde{y}_{\mathrm{RF}}^{\mathrm{TxL}}(t) = \tilde{x}_{\mathrm{RF}}(t) * h_{\mathrm{RF}}(t) = \beta_2 \frac{A_{\mathrm{PA}}^2}{2}\Re\left\{\left(x_{\mathrm{BB}}(t)^2 * h_{\mathrm{BB}}^{\mathrm{H2}}(t)\right) e^{j4\pi f_{Tx}t}\right\} \tag{6}$$

with $h_{\mathrm{BB}}^{\mathrm{H2}}(t) := h_{\mathrm{BB}}(t; 2f_{Tx})$ according to the definition given in the previous subsection. After the low noise amplifier (LNA) and the down conversion with the frequency f_{Rx2} we obtain

$$\tilde{y}_{\text{mixer}}^{\text{TxH2}}(t) = \beta_2 \frac{A_{\text{PA}}^2 A_{\text{LNA}}}{4} \left(\left(x_{\text{BB}}(t)^2 * h_{\text{BB}}^{\text{H2}}(t) \right) e^{j2\pi(2f_{\text{Tx}} - f_{\text{Rx2}})t} \right.$$

$$\left. + \left(x_{\text{BB}}(t)^2 * h_{\text{BB}}^{\text{H2}}(t) \right)^* e^{-j2\pi(2f_{\text{Tx}} + f_{\text{Rx2}})t} \right). \quad (7)$$

Before the analog-to-digital conversion the ideally assumed anti-aliasing filter attenuates the signal components far away from the baseband. The resulting time-discrete received signal at the output of the channel select filter (CSF) $h_s[n]$ is

$$\tilde{y}_{\text{BB}}^{\text{TxH2}}[n] = \beta_2 \frac{A_{\text{PA}}^2 A_{\text{LNA}}}{4} \left(\left(x_{\text{BB}}[n]^2 * h_{\text{BB}}^{\text{H2}}[n] \right) e^{j2\pi \frac{2f_{\text{Tx}} - f_{\text{Rx2}}}{f_s} n} \right) * h_s[n], \quad (8)$$

where f_s is the sampling frequency.

2.2 (2nd Order) Intermodulation Distortion

The IMD2 interference can occur due to a coupling between a mixer's RF- and local oscillator (LO) input in the receive path [1]. The total received signal (3) at the mixer is not only multiplied with the LO signal, but also with a copy of itself. With the mixer RF-to-LO terminal coupling coefficient $\alpha_2 = \alpha_2^{\text{I}} + j\alpha_2^{\text{Q}}$ for the I- and Q-path of the mixer, the output of the mixer can be described as

$$y_{\text{RF,mixer}}^{\text{Tot}}(t) = y_{\text{RF,LNA}}^{\text{Tot}}(t)\alpha_1 e^{-j2\pi f_{\text{Rx1}}t} + \alpha_2 (y_{\text{RF,LNA}}^{\text{Tot}}(t))^2 \quad (9)$$

where α_1 is the down-conversion gain. Inserting (2) and (3) into (9), and using the definition given in the previous subsection $h_{\text{BB}}^{\text{TxL}}(t) := h_{\text{BB}}(t; f_{\text{Tx}})$ yields

$$y_{\text{RF,mixer}}^{\text{Tot}}(t) = \alpha_1 \frac{A_{\text{LNA}}}{2} y_{\text{BB}}^{\text{Rx}}(t) + \alpha_1 \frac{A_{\text{LNA}}}{2} w_{\text{BB}}(t)$$

$$+ \frac{\alpha_2}{2} \left[\left| A_{\text{LNA}} A_{\text{PA}} x_{\text{BB}}(t) * h_{\text{BB}}^{\text{TxL}}(t) \right|^2 + \left| y_{\text{BB}}^{\text{Rx}}(t) \right|^2 \right. \quad (10)$$

$$\left. + 2\Re\{y_{\text{BB}}^{\text{Rx}}(t) w_{\text{BB}}^*(t)\} + |w_{\text{BB}}(t)|^2 \right]$$

where $y_{\text{BB}}^{\text{Rx}}(t)$ denotes the baseband equivalent wanted receive signal and $w_{\text{BB}}(t)$ represents additive noise in the equivalent baseband. Note that the contributions that are attenuated by the anti-aliasing filter of the analog-to-digital converter (ADC) are already omitted here. The term $\left| A_{\text{LNA}} A_{\text{PA}} x_{\text{BB}}(t) * h_{\text{BB}}^{\text{TxL}}(t) \right|^2$ contains the leakage signal and is called the IMD2 interference. For strong IMD2 interference signals, all the remaining terms in the squared brackets in (10) are negligible. Since various components in a receive chain create unwanted DC, receivers usually employ a DC cancellation. This behavior is essential for the IMD2 problem, thus, we include it in our model as follows $\bar{h}_s[n] = h_s[n] * h_{\text{DC}}[n]$, where $h_{\text{DC}}[n]$ describes a DC notch filter. After sampling with the ADC and filtering the total discrete-time received signal in the baseband is approximated by

$$y_{\text{BB}}^{\text{Tot}}[n] = \alpha_1 \frac{A_{\text{LNA}}}{2} y_{\text{BB}}^{\text{Rx}}[n] * \bar{h}_s[n] + \alpha_1 \frac{A_{\text{LNA}}}{2} w_{\text{BB}}[n] * \bar{h}_s[n] \qquad (11)$$

$$+ \underbrace{\frac{\alpha_2}{2} \left| A_{\text{LNA}} A_{\text{PA}} x_{\text{BB}}[n] * h_{\text{BB}}^{\text{TxL}}[n] \right|^2 * \bar{h}_s[n]}_{y_{\text{BB}}^{\text{IMD2}}[n]}. \qquad (12)$$

The baseband equivalent discrete-time duplexer impulse response in (2.2) is a scaled and sampled version of the continuous-time baseband impulse response according to $h_{\text{BB}}^{\text{TxL}}[n] = T_s h_{\text{BB}}^{\text{TxL}}(t)|_{t=nT_s}$. In general the complex-valued IMD2 interference can be expressed as

$$y_{\text{BB}}^{\text{IMD2}}[n] = y_{\text{BB}}^{\text{IMD2,I}}[n] + j y_{\text{BB}}^{\text{IMD2,Q}}[n] = \xi \left| x_{\text{BB}}[n] * h[n] \right|^2 * \bar{h}_s[n] \qquad (13)$$

with $h[n] = \sqrt{\frac{\alpha_2^I}{2}} A_{\text{LNA}} A_{\text{PA}} h_{\text{BB}}^{\text{TxL}}[n]$ and $\xi = 1 + j\frac{\alpha_2^Q}{\alpha_2^I}$, cf. [1].

3   Kernel Adaptive Filtering

In the LMS algorithm a *linear* finite impulse response filter is assumed. In case of a highly nonlinear mapping between the desired output y and the input vector $\mathbf{x}$ containing the data samples, the LMS often performs poorly. In this section we describe an extension of the LMS algorithm that utilizes the kernel trick in order to account for nonlinear mappings between y and $\mathbf{x}$. The final algorithm is denoted as KLMS [6].

The main idea of the kernel method is to transform the vector of the data $\mathbf{x} \in X$ from the input space X into a higher dimensional feature space F via the transformation φ. Formally speaking, we replace $\mathbf{x}$ by $\varphi(\mathbf{x})$, short φ. Since we transform $\mathbf{x}$ into the feature space, also the weights $\mathbf{w}$ from the LMS have to live in this space. Starting with the equations of the LMS, see [7], we replace $\mathbf{w}$ by $\boldsymbol{\omega}$, $\mathbf{x}$ by φ and set $\boldsymbol{\omega}_1 = \mathbf{0}$ such that

$$\hat{y}_n = \boldsymbol{\omega}_n^T \varphi_n$$
$$e_n = y_n - \hat{y}_n \qquad (14)$$
$$\boldsymbol{\omega}_{n+1} = \boldsymbol{\omega}_n + \mu e_n \varphi_n$$

where $\hat{y}_n$ denotes the output of the KLMS, and μ the step size. Unwinding the iteration of $\boldsymbol{\omega}$ we get

$$\boldsymbol{\omega}_{n+1} = \left(\boldsymbol{\omega}_{n-1} + \mu e_{n-1} \varphi_{n-1} \right) + \mu e_n \varphi_n = \cdots = \mu \sum_{j=1}^n e_j \varphi_j. \qquad (15)$$

Inserting $\boldsymbol{\omega}_{n+1}$ into the formula for $\hat{y}_{n+1}$, it follows

$$\hat{y}_{n+1} = \boldsymbol{\omega}_{n+1}^T \varphi_{n+1} = \mu \sum_{j=1}^n e_j \varphi_j^T \varphi_{n+1}. \qquad (16)$$

Algorithm 1. THE KERNEL LEAST MEAN SQUARE ALGORITHM

1: **function** KLMS($\mathbf{x}_{1,...,N}, y_{1,...,N}$)
2: Initialization $e_1 := y_1$
3:    **for** $n = 1 : N - 1$ **do**
4:       $\hat{y}_{n+1} = \mu \sum_{j=1}^{n} e_j \kappa(\mathbf{x}_j, \mathbf{x}_{n+1})$
5:       $e_{n+1} = y_{n+1} - \hat{y}_{n+1}$
6:    **end for**
7:    **return** $\hat{y}_{2,...,N}$
8: **end function**

Since the kernel trick says that the inner product in the feature space can be replaced by the evaluation of the kernel function $\varphi^{\mathrm{T}}(\mathbf{x})\varphi(\mathbf{y}) = \kappa(\mathbf{x}, \mathbf{y})$; $\forall \mathbf{x}, \mathbf{y} \in \mathbb{R}^n$ we can rewrite Eq. (16) as

$$\hat{y}_{n+1} = \mu \sum_{j=1}^{n} e_j \kappa(\mathbf{x}_j, \mathbf{x}_{n+1}). \tag{17}$$

Note that in our case the input space is $X = \mathbb{R}^P$, and therefore, the kernel function is $\kappa : \mathbb{R}^P \times \mathbb{R}^P \to \mathbb{R}$. The kernel can also be understood as a similarity map, saying how similar two vectors are. Therefore, in (17) the current input vector is compared with all the previous input vectors. These kernel evaluations are weighted with the errors between the corresponding approximated signal and the desired signal, then they are summed up. The final algorithm for the KLMS is shown in Algorithm 1. Two very prominent examples of kernels are the Gauss kernel $\kappa(\mathbf{x}, \mathbf{y}) := \exp\left(-\frac{\|\mathbf{x}-\mathbf{y}\|^2}{2h^2}\right)$, where h is the kernel parameter, and the polynomial kernel $\kappa(\mathbf{x}, \mathbf{y}) := \|1 + \mathbf{x}^{\mathrm{T}}\mathbf{y}\|^m$ with $m \in \mathbb{R}$ and $\forall \mathbf{x}, \mathbf{y} \subset \mathbb{R}^n$.

4 Simulation Results

In this section the performance of the KLMS method is assessed based on system simulations for the two different interference problems discussed in Sect. 2. An FDD scenario with LTE 10 signals is used. The highly frequency-selective duplexer is approximated by a 15 tap finite impulse response (FIR) system.

In Figs. 2 and 3 a comparison of the KLMS algorithm [8] with state-of-the-art algorithms is given in terms of the normalized mean squared error (NMSE). First, we investigate the Tx-harmonics problem introduced in Sect. 2.1, and second, the IMD2 problem from Sect. 2.2. In the figures on the left hand side a fully allocated signal is used and in the figures on the right hand side a scenario with a narrow allocation is shown.

Figure 2 compares the KLMS algorithm and the ordinary LMS algorithm [7] for the case that a second order harmonic Tx interference (TxH2) superimposes the receive signal. While the KLMS can work with the plain signal $x_{\mathrm{BB}}[n]$ itself, the linear LMS needs preprocessing. Specifically it requires the squared signal $x_{\mathrm{BB}}[n]^2$ as input, which requires an interpolation beforehand, since the squaring

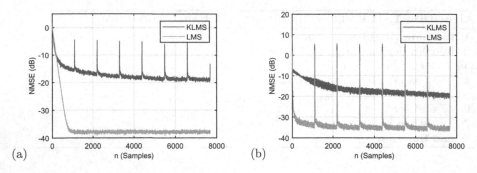

Fig. 2. Performance comparison on TxH2 for (a) full and (b) narrow allocation

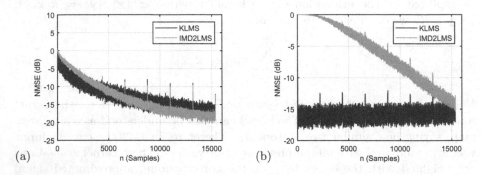

Fig. 3. Performance comparison on IMD2 for (a) full and (b) narrow allocation

doubles the bandwidth. Note that thermal noise and the wanted receive signal act as noise for the adaptive algorithms. For this simulation we set the SNR of the wanted signal, regarding the thermal noise, for the adaptive algorithm to 30 dB. For the KLMS we chose the polynomial kernel and step size $\mu = 0.9$, for the LMS $\mu = 0.25$. These step sizes have been chosen such that a further reduction of them do not significantly increase the steady-state performance of the algorithms. It can be observed that the LMS outperforms the KLMS. Additionally, in the case of full allocation, the spikes are suppressed due to the preprocessing step (interpolation and squaring) of the LMS. Though one has to point out that this preprocessing step requires the knowledge of the order of the harmonic distortion. This kind of model knowledge is not required by the KLMS algorithm.

In Fig. 3 the performances of the KLMS and the IMD2LMS [1] algorithm are compared for an IMD2 interference scenario. For the KLMS we chose the Gauss kernel with the parameter $h = 0.02$ and step size $\mu = 0.9$. Note that the IMD2LMS has particularly been developed and optimized for the IMD2 self-interference problem. Still, its performance is comparable to that of the KLMS for full allocation, see Fig. 3(a), here an SNR of 10 dB is chosen. For the IMD2LMS we chose $\mu = 0.04$. More importantly, in case of a narrow allocation and an SNR of 30 dB in Fig. 3(b) the KLMS adapts way faster than the IMD2LMS. Also the parameter choice for the IMD2LMS algorithm is crucial, since for many choices the algorithm becomes unstable. This and the slow adaptation speed are major drawbacks of the IMD2LMS that can be overcome by employing the KLMS.

5   Discussion and Conclusion

In this paper, the KLMS is applied to self-interference cancellation in RF transceivers for mobile communications. Specifically, we addressed the problems of second order harmonics and IMD2. In the first case the classical LMS outperforms the more general non-model based kernel algorithm. However, in contrast to the KLMS, the LMS algorithm requires a detailed model description of the problem, which is incorporated in a preprocessing step. In the second case the IMD2LMS, which is particularly designed for the IMD2 problem, outperforms the KLMS in case of full allocation. However, for a narrow band allocation the KLMS adapts way faster and is more robust. To conclude, the results do not allow to give a clear answer to the question raised originally.

Acknowledgment. The financial support by the Austrian Federal Ministry of Science, Research and Economy and the National Foundation for Research, Technology and Development is gratefully acknowledged.

References

1. Gebhard, A., Motz, C., Kanumalli, R.S., Pretl, H., Huemer, M.: Nonlinear least-mean-squares type algorithm for second-order interference cancellation in LTE-A RF transceivers. In: Proceedings of the 51st Asilomar Conference on Signals, Systems, and Computers (ACSSC 2017), pp. 802–807. Pacific Grove (2017)
2. Ericsson and ST-Ericsson: "R4-126964, REFSENS with one UL carrier for NC intra-band CA," Ericsson, Technical report, November 2012. https://www.3gpp.org/DynaReport/TDocExMtg-R4-65-29023.htm
3. Razavi, B.: Design considerations for direct-conversion receivers. IEEE Trans. Circ. Syst. II: Analog Digit. Sig. Proc. 44(6), 428–435 (1997)
4. Kiayani, A., Anttila, L., Valkama, M.: Modeling and dynamic cancellation of TX-RX leakage in FDD transceivers. In: 2013 IEEE 56th International Midwest Symposium on Circuits and Systems (MWSCAS 2013), pp. 1089–1094, Columbus (2013)
5. Gebhard, A.: Self-interference cancellation and rejection in FDD RF-transceivers, Ph.D. dissertation, Johannes Kepler University Linz, Linz, Austria (2019)
6. Liu, W., Principe, J., Haykin, S.: Kernel Adaptive Filtering. Wiley, Hoboken (2010)
7. Kay, S.M.: Fundamentals of statistical signal processing. In: Oppenheim, A.V. (ed.) Prentice Hall, Upper Saddle River (1993)
8. Bouboulis, P., Theodoridis, S.: Extension of Wirtinger's calculus to reproducing Kernel Hilbert spaces and the complex Kernel LMS. IEEE Trans. Signal Process. 59(3), 964–978 (2011)

Acoustic Monitoring – A Deep LSTM Approach for a Material Transport Process

Adnan Husaković[1]([✉]), Anna Mayrhofer[1], Eugen Pfann[2], Mario Huemer[2], Andreas Gaich[2], and Thomas Kühas[1]

[1] Primetals Technologies Austria GmbH, Turmstr. 44, 4031 Linz, Austria
{adnan.husakovic,anna.mayrhofer,thomas.kuehas}@primetals.com
[2] Institute of Signal Processing, Johannes Kepler University, 4040 Linz, Austria
{eugen.pfann,mario.huemer,andreas.gaich}@jku.at

Abstract. Robust classification strongly depends on the combination of properly chosen features and the classification algorithm. This paper investigates an autoencoder for feature fusion together with recurrent neural networks such as the Long Short-Term Memory neural networks (LSTMs) in different configurations applied to a dataset of a material transport process. As an important outcome the investigations show that the application of features acquired from the autoencoder bottleneck layer in combination with a bidirectional LSTM improve the classification algorithm significantly and require fewer features in comparison to standard machine learning algorithms.

Keywords: Autoencoder · Deep learning · Feature fusion · LSTM · Signal processing

1 Introduction

Acoustic emissions of machines and industrial processes often contain information about the underlying system state [1]. Engineers with a high level of expertise are able to distinguish correct behavior from faulty behavior and can predict a potential system dropout by interpreting the emitted acoustic sound. This fact indicates that it should be possible to base an automatic condition monitoring system on the evaluation of psychoacoustic features.

A machine learning based approach for the classification of 5 different material types transported on a conveyor belt was described in [2]. This method did not consider the characteristic temporal variations of the extracted features between frames. However, for the acoustic classification of scenes it was shown in [3] that the application of Long Short-Term Memory neural networks (LSTMs) improved the overall classification accuracy in comparison to feedforward Deep Neural Networks. This contribution will hence investigate the application of LSTMs for the classification scenario in [2].

An important criterion for the success of classification methods is the proper choice of input features. Feature selection and reduction are therefore subject of undergoing intense study. One method recently investigated are autoencoders, which represent an unsupervised technique for dimensionality reduction using artificial neural networks [4].

© Springer Nature Switzerland AG 2020
R. Moreno-Díaz et al. (Eds.): EUROCAST 2019, LNCS 12014, pp. 44–51, 2020.
https://doi.org/10.1007/978-3-030-45096-0_6

Based on this approach the work reported in this paper will employ an autoencoder to achieve a reduction in the selected psychoacoustic feature set. This reduced feature set is applied to different LSTM configurations for the classification of the material transport processes. The remainder of this paper is organized as follows: Sect. 2 introduces the autoencoder structure used for feature fusion and Sect. 3 illustrates the classification decision structure and introduces the classifier. Subsequently Sect. 4 investigates the classification performance based on the test dataset.

2 Feature Fusion

It was found in [2] that for the investigated material transport process the Bark scale Power Spectral Density (BPSD) and Spectral Sharpness (SS) features achieved the highest classification accuracy. Consequently, these features are also used in this work. Additionally, the temporal variation (deltas) of the BPSD (DBPSD) and the temporal variation of the DBPSD (D2BPSD) are included in the feature vector x. This vector is then applied to an undercomplete autoencoder as shown in Fig. 1 in order to reduce the number of effective features used for training and classification.

The autoencoder applied in this scenario consists of three hidden layers, namely the precompression layer y, the bottleneck layer z and the reconstruction layer y'. The structure is chosen such that $D_y = D_{y'}$, where the notation $D_v = \dim(v)$ is used to describe the dimension of a vector v. Autoencoders are compressing the information in the bottleneck layer. Due to this constraint, features acquired from the bottleneck layer are more discriminative with respect to the single classes than the input features [5]. The choice of the appropriate structure and the required hyperparameters D_y and D_z strongly affects the activations of the hidden units and therefore the constructed new features.

To obtain the optimum widths of these three hidden layers the loss function L is chosen according to

$$L(X, X') = ||X - X'||_F^2 \tag{1}$$

where $||X - X'||_F^2$ is the squared Frobenius norm of the error between the original sample feature matrix $X = [x_1, \ldots, x_N]^T \in \mathbb{R}^{N \times D_x}$ and the matrix $X' = [x'_1, \ldots, x'_N]^T \in \mathbb{R}^{N \times D_{x'}}$ of the reconstructed feature vectors x' with N the number of feature sample vectors.

In order to find the optimum values of the two hyper-parameters of the autoencoder $D_y = D_{y'}$ and D_z a two stage process is employed where 20% of the training data was set aside as validation data for regularization to avoid overfitting. The sample feature matrix of the training data can be written as

$$X_T = [x_{T1}, \ldots, x_{TN_T}]^T \in \mathbb{R}^{N_T \times D_x} \tag{2}$$

where N_T is the number of feature vector samples x_n in the training set. Equally, sample feature matrices are defined for the decoded training data output $X'_T =$

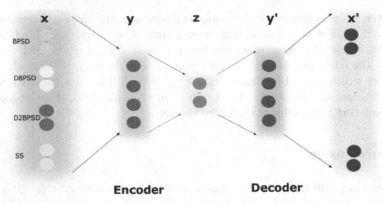

Fig. 1. Structure and input features of the undercomplete autoencoder used for feature fusion.

$\left[x'_{T1}, \ldots, x'_{TN_T}\right]^T$, the validation data $X_V = \left[x_{V1}, \ldots, x_{VN_V}\right]^T$ and the decoded validation data $X'_V = \left[x'_{V1}, \ldots, x'_{VN_V}\right]^T$.

In a first step the training data is used to find D_y according to

$$D_{y_{opt}} = \operatorname{argmin}_{D_y}(\min_{D_z}(\|X - X'\|_F^2)) \tag{3}$$

over a grid of $D_y \in \{50, 60, 70, 80\}$ as depicted in Fig. 2. A minimum loss was found for 60 hidden units in layer y.

In a second step $D_{y_{opt}}$ was kept fixed and the optimum value for D_z was found over a search using the validation data according to

$$D_{z_{opt}} = \operatorname{argmin}_{D_z}\left(\|X_V - X'_V\|_F^2\right)|D_y = D_{y_{opt}} \tag{4}$$

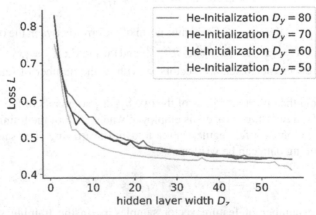

Fig. 2. Loss L on training data to determine the optimum hidden layer width of precompression and reconstruction layer.

Figure 3 illustrates the loss on training and validation data with a fixed precompression and reconstruction layer width of $D_y = 60$. It can be observed that the loss on the validation data is increasing for more than 47 hidden units. To prevent this overfitting tendency a hidden layer width of $D_{z_{opt}} = 47$ is hence used for further investigations.

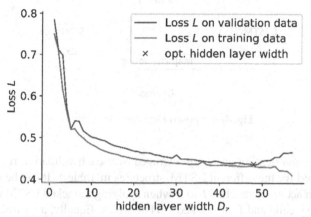

Fig. 3. Loss L on training and validation data to find the optimum width D_z of the bottleneck layer.

The autoencoder training was based on a dataset of 200 audio sequences with 40 sequences for each of the 5 material classes. Each sequence consists of 10 s of recorded data. The features were calculated on frames of 20 ms duration with a 10 ms overlap, which results in 999 feature vectors per sequence. The autoencoder was trained over 50 epochs. The ReLU-function was used as the activation function inside the single layers and the He Weight-Initialization method [6] was applied.

3   Decision Process

For classification the performance of a vanilla LSTM, a stacked LSTM and a bidirectional LSTM were compared. The input to the LSTM networks are the output activations of the compression layer z of the autoencoder. The required memory cells and stacked layer size of different LSTM-network configurations are chosen in order to prevent overfitting and to maximize the overall classification accuracy. The LSTM-network training is based on a 5-fold cross validation where the same dataset and feature vectors are used as for the autoencoder training.

It was shown in [2] that the recorded audio signals and the acoustic features were subject to strong variations due to the varying material feed rate. Therefore, to improve the decision robustness the classification was not based on the result of a single LSTM network, but the following method was applied instead. As depicted in Fig. 4 a 10 s sound recording sequence was divided in subsequences of 1 s each. The subsequences were input to 10 parallel LSTM-classification networks. The final classification decision for one sequence was obtained by majority voting of the 10 individual decisions.

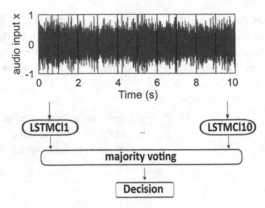

Fig. 4. Proposed Decision Algorithm

The overall classification accuracy averaged over each validation run as proposed in [2] is compared for the different LSTM-structures in Table 1. It can be observed that the classification accuracy reached 100% when applying a stacked LSTM configuration with 150 memory cells and four stacked LSTM layers. Equally, a bidirectional LSTM in combination with 150 memory cells also achieves an accuracy of 100% while 99% accuracy is achieved with 125 memory cells.

To further qualify the top scoring classifiers of Table 1 the precision P and recall R averaged over all five material classes as introduced in [2] are compared. As shown in Fig. 5, the best results are achieved with the bidirectional LSTM and 150 memory cells. Therefore this configuration was chosen for further evaluation and comparison on the test dataset.

Table 1. Averaged Classification Accuracy based on 5 fold cross validation.

Memory cells	Vanilla LSTM	2 Stacked LSTM	3 Stacked LSTM	4 Stacked LSTM	Bidirectional LSTM
1	44.5%	46%	65.5%	67%	85%
25	91.5%	92.5%	92.5%	92%	92%
50	93%	93%	93.5%	93%	93%
75	93.5%	93.5%	93.5%	93%	94%
100	93.5%	94%	94%	95%	96%
125	94%	93%	94%	97.5%	**99%**
150	94.5%	92.5%	95%	**100%**	**100%**
175	92%	92%	91%	92.5%	95%

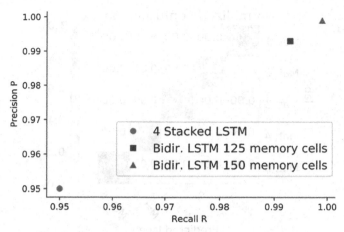

Fig. 5. Precision P and Recall R of different classifiers

4 Performance Evaluation

Table 2 compares the classification accuracy based on the test dataset. The test dataset consists of 100 audio sequences of 10 s duration with 20 sequences for each of the five material classes. In addition to the bidirectional LSTM with autoencoder and psychoacoustic features the table also lists the achieved accuracy as reported in [2]. On the test dataset the bidirectional LSTM with autoencoder bottleneck features performed better with respect to the overall classification accuracy reaching 96.6%. Without autoencoder an overall classification accuracy of 95.5% is achieved.

Table 2. Averaged overall Classification Accuracy for bidirectional LSTM with autoencoder and psychoacoustic features.

Bidirectional LSTM psychoacoustic	Bidirectional LSTM autoencoder features	FF-NN (from [2])
95.5%	**96.6%**	95.4%

The confusion matrix shown in Fig. 6 indicates that the system identified material classes 1, 3 and 4 without any misclassification. The other materials are correctly classified with an accuracy of 86 to 97%.

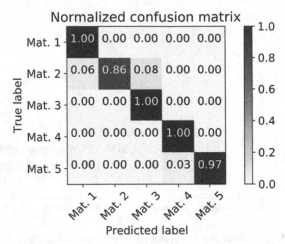

Fig. 6. Confusion matrix applied on test data.

The proposed autoencoder architecture with features acquired from the autoencoder's bottleneck layer provides robust features and good classification results on test data. The maximum misclassification rate of any material class was 14%. In comparison to the results reported in [2], the overall classification accuracy is improved, whereas the maximum misclassification rate of an individual material class is increased from 12% to 14%.

5 Conclusion

Autoencoders are a feature reduction and selection method widely applied in image processing. Within the context of this paper, it was used for feature fusion and compression, and applied to the BPSD, DBPSD, D2BPSD and SS-features.

The bidirectional LSTM architecture with 150 memory cells and ensemble decision process with the autoencoder bottleneck layer features provided robust classification results with respect to both precision P and recall R.

In [7], the application of convolutional neural networks to acoustic scene classification significantly improved the overall classification performance. Additionally, the combination of a convolutional neural network with a data augmentation method led to remarkable improvement of the classification method in [8]. Hence, future investigations will focus on data augmentation methods and the application of convolutional neural networks to the classification of material transport processes.

Acknowledgment. This work has been supported by the COMET-K2 "Center for Symbiotic Mechatronics" of the Linz Center of Mechatronics (LCM) funded by the Austrian federal government and the federal state of Upper Austria.

References

1. Berckmans, D., Janssens, K., Van der Auweraer, H., Sas, P., Desmet, W.: Model-based synthesis of aircraft noise to quantify human perception of sound quality and annoyance. J. Sound Vib. **311**(3–5), 1175–1195 (2008). https://doi.org/10.1016/j.jsv.2007.10.018
2. Husakovic, A., Pfann, E., Huemer, M.: Robust machine learning based acoustic classification of a material transport process. In: Proceedings of the 14 Symposium on Neural Networks and Applications (NEUREL), Belgrade, Serbia (2018). https://doi.org/10.1109/NEUREL.2018.8587031
3. Bae, S.H., Choi, I., Soo Kim, N.: Acoustic scene classification using parallel combination of LSTM and CNN, DCASE2016 challenge. Technical report, Budapest, Hungary (2016)
4. Han, K., Wang, Y., Zhang, C., Lee, C., Hu, C.: Autoencoder inspired unsupervised feature selection. In: Proceedings of the IEEE International Conference on Acoustics, Speech and Signal Processing (ICASSP), Calgary, Canada, pp. 2941–2945 (2018). https://doi.org/10.1109/ICASSP.2018.8462261
5. Huang, K., Wu, C., Yang, T., Su, M., Chou, J.: Speech emotion recognition using autoencoder bottleneck features and LSTM. In: Proceedings of the 2016 International Conference on Orange Technologies (ICOT), Melbourne, Australia, pp. 1–4 (2016). https://doi.org/10.1109/ICOT.2016.8278965
6. He, K., Zhang, X., Ren, S., Sun, J.: Delving deep into rectifiers: surpassing human-level performance on ImageNet classification. In: Proceedings of the 2015 IEEE International Conference on Computer Vision (ICCV), Santiago, Chile, pp. 1026–1034 (2015). https://doi.org/10.1109/ICCV.2015.123
7. Nguyen, T., Pernkopf, F.: Acoustic scene classification using a convolutional neural network ensemble and nearest neighbor filters. In: Proceedings of the Detection and Classification of Acoustic Scenes and Events 2018 Workshop (DCASE), Tampere, Finland, pp. 34–38 (2018)
8. Han, Y., Lee, K.: Acoustic scene classification using convolutional neural network and multiple-width frequency-delta data augmentation. arXiv preprint arXiv:1607.02383 (2016)

Requirement-Adapted Enhancement of a Faraday Rotation Magnetometer's Output

Ruben Piepgras[✉], Sebastian Michlmayr, and Bernhard Zagar

Institute for Measurement Technology, Johannes Kepler University Linz,
Altenberger Straße 69, 4040 Linz, Austria
ruben.piepgras@jku.at

Abstract. Magnetic microstructures are a useful tool to encode information. In order to repeatedly make use of this information a non-destructive measurement system is needed. Such a system would be applicable to many technical problems, however, within this contribution we discuss a method to analyse the magnetic pattern of the security thread used in banknotes specifically. In order to assess the quality of the threads' magnetic patterns during their production, a previous study used a Faraday Rotation Magnetometer (FRM). An FRM is a magneto-optical – and therefore non-destructive and non-contacting – setup based on the Faraday effect, which correlates the strength of a magnetic field with the rotation of polarised light. Albeit meeting the required specifications, this FRM's amplitude resolution wasn't sufficient to allow meaningful quantitative measurements. Hence, within this contribution we discuss the suitability and scope of an FRM for quantitative measurements of magnetic microstructures. We present a generalised version of the previous FRM and characterise it with regard to its amplitude, spatial, and temporal resolution. We point out ways to enhance the signal and show the limitations of such measures separately as well as comprehensively. From this we derive a way to estimate the feasibility of an FRM as a quantitative measurement device for a given set of parameters. Furthermore, this contribution may be used as a build and signal enhancement guideline for a similar setup.

Keywords: Non-destructive testing · Magneto-optics · Signal enhancement

1 Introduction and Theoretical Background

In order to prevent counterfeiting, central banks require banknotes to have a variety of security features. For instance, some banknotes may have a security thread woven in along the height. These threads usually are imprinted polyethylene foils cut to a width of a couple of millimetres. The imprints consist of stripes with magnetic patterns as well as additional masking agents to impede

© Springer Nature Switzerland AG 2020
R. Moreno-Díaz et al. (Eds.): EUROCAST 2019, LNCS 12014, pp. 52–58, 2020.
https://doi.org/10.1007/978-3-030-45096-0_7

a purely optical examination. The production of the threads and their magnetic patterns require a quality assessment – preferably as early as during the production. Therefore, a suitable measurement system should be non-destructive as well as sufficiently precise and fast. A potentially suitable measurement setup is the Faraday Rotation Magnetometer (FRM). An FRM is a magneto-optical setup based upon the Faraday effect. The Faraday effect states that the plane of polarisation of light passing a transparent medium is rotated when it is subjected to a magnetic field in direction of propagation. The rotational angle β is calculated according to

$$\beta = H \cdot d \cdot V',\tag{1}$$

where H is the magnetic field strength in direction of propagation, d is the thickness of the transparent medium, and V' is the so-called Verdet constant [1,2]. The Verdet constant is specific to a certain material. In order to maximise the magnetometer's sensitivity, materials with high Verdet constants (Faraday crystals) are used. The magnetic patterns to be analysed in the scope of this contribution are non-transparent. Therefore, the setup's Faraday crystal needs to be mirrored and thus, the polarised light passes the crystal twice in opposite directions. Due to birefrigence this doubles the rotation, i.e. $\beta^\dagger = 2\beta$. In conclusion, knowing the crystal's thickness d and Verdet constant V' as well as measuring the rotational angle β would allow to infer the external magnetic field H. However, it's not possible to measure the rotational angle directly. Instead, the polarised and rotated light passes an analysing filter and only its intensity $I_{\alpha,\beta^\dagger}$ is measured. For an initial intensity I_0, an angle α between polarising and analysing filter, and a Faraday rotation $\beta^\dagger$, the intensity $I_{\alpha,\beta^\dagger}$ can be calculated using Malus' Law [1,2], which states

$$I_{\alpha,\beta^\dagger} = I_0 \cdot \cos^2\left(\alpha + \beta^\dagger\right) = I_\alpha \cdot \frac{\cos^2\left(\alpha + \beta^\dagger\right)}{\cos^2\left(\alpha\right)}.\tag{2}$$

Here, I_α is the intensity after the polarising filter, which is more convenient to measure in the setup presented in Sect. 3.

2   Production Process, Setup Principle, and First Results

The principles of the production of the security threads used in banknotes and of the subsequent steps of quality assessment as presented in this paper are shown in Fig. 1.

The threads are produced in a roll-to-roll process. Here, a polyethylene foil with a thickness of $50\,\mu m$ is moved at a speed of up to $3\,m\,s^{-1}$. Upon this foil the magnetic stripes are printed. The stripes may have widths between one and five mm, a layer thickness of $500\,nm$, and contain a pattern with a structure size of approximately $50\,\mu m$. The differentiating criteria within the pattern are the printing materials or rather their magnetic properties. As of now, two materials are used with a coercitivity of $30\,mT$ and around $300\,mT$ respectively. Hereafter, some additional layers are added. These layers are non-magnetic and purely serve masking purposes against simple optical pattern analysis. The stripe that is woven in the banknotes then is gained by cutting the imprinted foil such that it is as long as the banknote, a couple of millimetres wide, and contains several pattern sections.

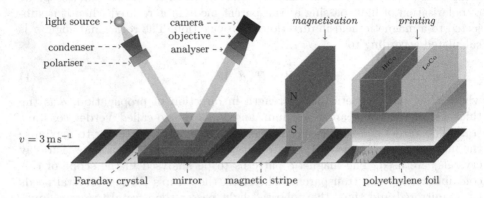

Fig. 1. Roll-to-roll process with printing, magnetisation, and Faraday Rotation Magnetometer

In order to assure the possibility of a timely intervention, an in-line quality assessment is required. The method proposed in this contribution is a two-step process and consists of the magnetisation of the pattern and the subsequent measurement with an FRM. Due to the non-transparent nature of the stripes this FRM needs to be adapted for usage from one side.

The first setup used yielded promising results [3]. The setup was built around a rare-earth substituted bismuth iron-garnet Faraday crystal produced by Matesy. Here, the Faraday active layer is 5 µm thick and deposited on one side of a glass block, while the other side has a mirror coating. The crystal's specified working range is around $\pm 2\,\mathrm{kA\,m^{-1}}$ or $\pm 4°$. The most stand out feature of this crystal is its extraordinarily high Verdet constant of about $2.5 \times 10^6\,\mathrm{rad\,T^{-1}\,m^{-1}}$. In comparison, this is four orders of magnitude higher than those of typically used crystals like terbium gallium garnet. The light incidence upon this crystal was non-orthogonal. This allowed to directly measure the reflected light without further use of mirrors. The measurement was then carried out by a high-speed Hamamatsu line-scan camera with a suitable resolution of 60 µm, which was followed by the data processing unit. In order to be able to record quadratic pixels at the maximum speed of the foil in the roll-to-roll process, the camera needed to perform 65 000 line scans per second. This necessity for high acquisition speed put great demands on many parts of the setup as it entailed poor illumination at the camera and high sustained data-rates in the data processing unit amongst many others. These difficulties notwithstanding, it was possible to record useful images at the required speed and for several hours of continuous measurement. An excerpt of such a measurement is shown in Fig. 2. In this image of a 4 mm wide stripe it is easily possible to distinguish the differentiating elements of the magnetic pattern.

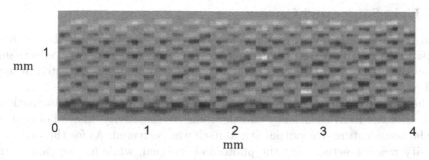

Fig. 2. Image of a 4 mm wide stripe recorded with the Faraday Rotation Magnetometer according to [3]

However, the possibility to distinguish the elements was largely down to the large differences in coercitivity. This setup is not well-suited for smaller differences or any kind of meaningful quantitative measurements. Nonetheless, it remains of interest if an FRM in general might be adapted to be able to do so. Therefore, a generalised version of the first setup was built with the purpose of characterisation, especially with regard to the limitations of amplitude, spatial, and temporal resolution.

3   Characterisation Setup and Signal Enhancement

The setup used for characterisation was largely similar to the one used before. However, it included some alterations that facilitated the characterisation. First, it allows the separation of the light after the polariser into a measurement and a reference path, which is achieved using a beamsplitter. Thus, the intensity I_α can be recorded with a photodiode and in turn this information can be used to correct for unwanted variations of the LED's intensity. Secondly, the magnetic probe was replaced by Helmholtz coils centred around the Faraday crystal. This allows to comparatively easily generate a well-defined magnetic excitation field H, which can be considered homogeneous over the volume of the Faraday active layer. Lastly, in lieu of the high-speed line-scan camera an Allied Vision Mako G223B was used. This camera records two-dimensional frames with a 5 μm × 5 μm resolution, albeit at a much lower frame rate of 49.5 fps. However, the insights gained using this camera may still be used to extrapolate for lower acquisition times.

First measurements performed with this setup revealed three main sources of error and therefore limiting factors to either amplitude, spatial, or temporal resolution. These components are the light source, the camera, and the Faraday crystal. In the following various methods to counteract those influences are presented. Their efficacy as standalone measures as well as their potential disadvantages are evaluated.

3.1 Light Source and Camera

Given that the LED and the camera work in conjunction towards the recorded intensity, it's not necessarily expedient to view possible detrimental effects separately but rather comprehensively. These detrimental effects consisted in temporal dependencies in the long-term behaviour as well as in noise.

The long term variations were mainly attributed to temperature fluctuations, which alter the LED's efficiency and the camera's sensitivity. Instead of controlling the temperature, the output signal itself was corrected. As for the LED, the intensity was corrected using the photodiode's signal, while for the camera the internal temperature sensor together with its temperature-sensitivity-chart was used. These measures effectively enhance the amplitude resolution and have no adverse effect on either temporal or spatial resolution.

Initially, noise took up nearly 40% of the working range making quantitative measurements impossible. However, the noise behaviour was approximately gaussian. Therefore, repeated measurements and a Moving Average Filter of length N reduce the noise by a factor of about $1/\sqrt{N}$. However, in most use cases this improvement in amplitude resolution has a significant detrimental effect on the temporal resolution.

3.2 Faraday Crystal

The magnetic behaviour of the Faraday crystal proved disadvantageous for two reasons. First, even within the specified working range the reaction to an external excitation was hysteretic. Given the resulting reduction in amplitude resolution,

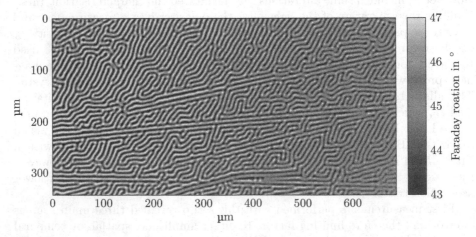

Fig. 3. Ferrimagnetic pattern of crystal at 0 A/m [4]

the working range was reduced to ±1.5 kA, where the remaining hysteresis was negligible.

Secondly, the crystal displayed ferrimagnetic behaviour, i.e. a magnetisation pattern rather than a homogeneous magnetisation. This is also true for zero excitation as shown in Fig. 3. Furthermore, for an increasing excitation field not only the mean magnetisation rises but also the pattern changes. This deteriorates the amplitude information gained by a pixel-wise evaluation. Given the regularity of the pattern however, spatial averaging over a cluster of neighbouring pixels can be used to improve amplitude resolution. In Fig. 4 the standard deviation of a set of randomly chosen quadratic clusters is plotted over their edge length. The trend of the standard deviation is equivalent to a damped oscillation according to the spatial repetition frequency of the pattern. At around 50 µm the effect of the pattern on the amplitude resolution is mostly suppressed and the resolution gain for a larger spatial average diminishes. Of course however, the spatial averaging deteriorates the spatial resolution.

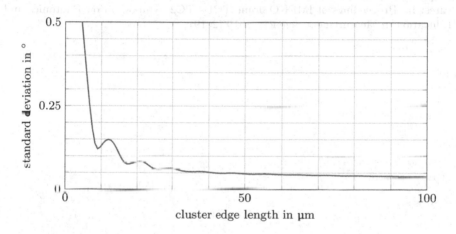

Fig. 4. Standard deviation depending on cluster size

4   Conclusion

The Faraday Rotation Magnetometer (FRM) showed good results for the qualitative evaluation of magnetic microstructures. In order to evaluate its suitability as a quantitative measurement device, a generalised version of the FRM was characterised. The main factors for a low amplitude resolution – and therefore poor quantitative performance – were singled out. In order to counteract those factors various signal enhancement methods were presented. Although these methods lead to a considerable increase in amplitude resolution, most of them had unfavourable effects on either spatial or temporal resolution. Consequently, the suitability of an FRM as a quantitative measurement device is highly dependent on other considerations like pattern structure size or required acquisition speed. This notwithstanding, this contribution should allow the prediction of the achievable amplitude resolution for given or required spatial and temporal resolutions. This should help to estimate whether a measurement with an FRM is an applicable method for a given quantitative measurement problem.

References

1. Pedrotti, F., Pedrottti, L., Bausch, W., Schmidt, H.: Introduction to Optics, 2nd edn. Pearson Education Company, London (1993)
2. Tumanski, S.: Handbook of Magnetic Measurements. CRC Press, Taylor & Francis Group, Boca Raton, Milton Park (2011)
3. Egger, J., Zagar, B.: In-line processing of Faraday-magnetometer scans. In: Proceedings of EUROCAST 2017 (2017)
4. Piepgras, R., Michlmayr, S., Zagar, B.: Optical analysis of magnetic microstructures. In: Proceedings of IMEKO Joint TC1 - TC2 Symposium on Photonics and Education in Measurement Sciences 2019 (2019)

Simultaneous Measurement of the Flow Velocities of Liquids and Gases

Michael Schwarz[1(✉)], Bernhard Uhl[1], Bernhard Zagar[1], and Michael Stur[2]

[1] Institute for Measurement Technology, Johannes Kepler University Linz,
Altenberger Straße 69, 4040 Linz, Austria
`michael.schwarz@jku.at`
[2] Sachverständigenbüro für Boden + Wasser GmbH, Hans-Zach-Straße 4,
4210 Gallneukirchen, Austria

Abstract. This contribution presents a measuring system for the simultaneous measurement of the flow velocity and direction of air and water in a partially filled pipe. A possible application for the presented system are drainage pipes in railway tunnels. A train passing a tunnel causes a strong pressure wave, depending on its speed. Under disadvantageous conditions, this can adversely affect the atmospheric environment of the tunnel drainage. Since railway tunnels usually have a very low gradient, the effect of the pressure wave can cause a critical reversal of the air flow direction, which can also reverse the flow direction of the water.

The presented measuring system is based on the ultrasonic transit time difference method and has a measuring uncertainty of less than 1 cm/s in air as well as in water. The setup of the measuring system and the applied signal processing are presented. The performance of the measuring system is evaluated using results obtained under laboratory conditions. Furthermore, the systems suitability for the use in drainage pipes of a railway tunnel is confirmed by results of a first test in a tunnel.

Keywords: Ultrasound · Flow measurement · Transit time difference method

1 Introduction

When a train passes a tunnel, an increased air pressure occurs in front of the vehicle and a lower air pressure behind it. Due to this pressure difference, there are often compression and suction effects in the tunnel. As a consequence, the atmosphere in the drainage system of the tunnel can change with regard to pressure and temperature depending on the kind of duct covers used. Various studies showed that under some circumstances even a flow reversal of the drainage water occurred. Thus, during the train passage, the intended outflow of the water through the drainage was impeded.

The authors gratefully acknowledge the financial support of this work by the Austrian Research Promotion Agency (FFG) under grant 864515.

R. Moreno-Díaz et al. (Eds.): EUROCAST 2019, LNCS 12014, pp. 59–66, 2020.
https://doi.org/10.1007/978-3-030-45096-0_8

These changes in the pressure and temperature conditions as well as the flow conditions of the water also affect the hydrochemical characteristics of the water in the drainages. This can lead to a shift of the hydrochemical equilibrium, especially of the carbonate balance, which in turn can lead to increased carbonate scaling. This scaling increases maintenance costs and may even endanger the tunnel structure itself.

In order to further investigate the flow reversal in the tunnel drainage, the measuring system presented in this contribution was designed. The system is able to simultaneously measure the flow velocities and directions of air and water with high temporal resolution. Besides, the system is able to measure the water level, the temperature, the air pressure, and the humidity in the pipe. This should help to determine if specific conditions favor a reversal of the water flow.

2   Measuring Principle

The measuring system utilizes the ultrasonic time-of-flight principle to measure the flow velocity of each medium. This principle is shown in Fig. 1. Two ultrasound transducers facing each other are positioned at a certain angle α to the flow with velocity v. The transmitted sound waves are carried along by the flowing medium. This leads to different sound propagation velocities with and against the flow direction and thus to different propagation times t_1 and t_2:

$$t_1 = \frac{L}{c + v\cos(\alpha)}, \tag{1}$$

$$t_2 = \frac{L}{c - v\cos(\alpha)}, \tag{2}$$

where L denotes the distance between the transducers and c the speed of sound [1–3]. If ultrasonic pulses are concurrently transmitted and received in both directions, the flow velocity can be calculated according to

$$v = \frac{t_2 - t_1}{t_1 t_2} \cdot \frac{L}{2\cos\alpha}. \tag{3}$$

However, the time difference $t_2 - t_1$ is typically very small. For example, for a chosen distance $L = 11$ cm the propagation time without flow is 321 µs in air and 74 µs in water, but the time difference $t_2 - t_1$ caused by a flow velocity $v = 1$ cm/s is only 13.2 ns in air and 0.7 ns in water. Thus, for the measurement of low flow velocities a time measurement with very high resolution is necessary.

3   Measuring System

The drainage pipes are surrounded by concrete. Periodically placed maintenance shafts are the only possible access. Consequently, the measuring system can only be positioned inside the pipe from the maintenance shaft. Hence, the measuring system must be compact in size and should be easy to slide into the pipe.

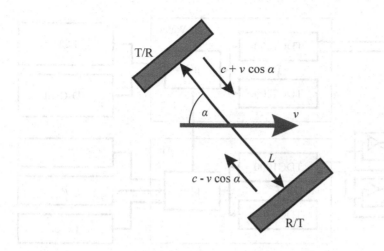

Fig. 1. Measuring principle [1,2]. Transmitter and receiver are labeled T and R

Furthermore, it has to be mechanically stable, water-resistant, and its influence on the flow should be as small as possible. Therefore, only the small sized ultrasound transducers are placed in the drainage pipe with the electronics located in the maintenance shaft.

In the following, the electronics of the measuring system will be described first. Subsequently, the signal processing will be discussed in more detail.

3.1   Electronics

In order to be able to resolve the small time differences mentioned in Sect. 2, the measuring system utilizes a time-to-digital converter (TDC) TDC7200 manufactured by *Texas Instruments* with a resolution of 55 ps and a standard deviation of 35 ps [4] to measure the sound propagation times. For the measurement in water and air respectively, an analog front-end TDC1000 likewise from *Texas Instruments* is used to generate and receive the signals of the ultrasound transducers. This front-end starts and stops the time measurement with the TDC. For both media, a microcontroller triggers the analog front-end to send and reads the measured propagation times from the TDC via SPI. For the measurement in air, the pulses generated by the analog front-end are additionally amplified by 21 dB in order to counter the expected higher attenuation. The amplifiers are switched off during receiving since they seem to cause interference caused by their switched power supply. A block diagram of the electronics of the measuring system is depicted in Fig. 2.

Furthermore, the measuring system has sensors for air temperature, air pressure, humidity, and water level. The microcontroller for the measurement in air reads in their data via I^2C and sends them along with the calculated air velocity via UART to the microcontroller, which performs the measurement in water. This microcontroller writes the received data and the calculated water

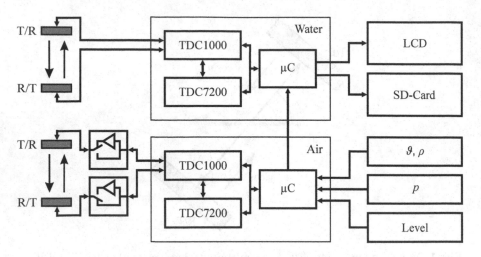

Fig. 2. Block diagram of the measuring system [5]. The ultrasound transducers, which are alternately operated as transmitter and receiver, are labeled T and R.

velocity to an SD-Card for further analysis. In addition, the measured values are displayed on an LCD to facilitate the start-up of the system.

3.2   Signal Processing

The electronics and transducers cause delays in the measured times compared to the actual sound propagation times. Because of this, biased values of the two propagation times t_1 and t_2 arise. Due to equal but not identical components used the delays are different for both media and also for the two directions. Their influence on the measurement can be circumvented by an appropriate calibration procedure with known flow velocities resulting in unbiased estimates of the flow velocities. Thus, each measured propagation time must be corrected according to the delay values before calculating the flow velocity v.

Furthermore, it is possible that due to external influences single ultrasonic pulses are detected incorrectly or cannot be detected at all. This would lead to erroneous values of the propagation times and consequently of the calculated flow velocity. Therefore, the microcontrollers store the results of 101 consecutive time measurements in both directions. They check each value for plausibility based on upper and lower bounds and perform a median filtering. This suppresses single propagation time values with large deviations from the mean, since these values cannot be correct, as the flow velocity cannot change as much in the time between two consecutive measurements, which is less than 7 ms. Subsequently, the flow velocity v is calculated according to Eq. 3 with the median values for both directions.

4   Results

This section presents calibration and measurement results. First, results for zero flow velocity are shown. Subsequently, results of calibration measurements with various flow velocities in the range of a few cm/s and of a first test of the measuring system in an actual tunnel follow.

4.1   Results with Zero Flow Velocity

For a first functional test, the transducers were exposed to a presumed zero velocity external flow to determine the measurement uncertainty of the measuring system. However, it is very difficult to completely prevent any flow, especially in air, since there are always air flows present, for example caused by temperature induced convection in the measuring volume. In order to analyze the inherent uncertainty of the measuring system the inevitable true flows must be suppressed by an appropriately designed high-pass filter. A histogram of the resulting data of a measurement of about 30 min is depicted in Fig. 3(a). The distribution is nearly Gaussian and has a standard deviation of about 0.1 cm/s, which is assumed to be the measurement uncertainty of the system.

Unlike in air, the unavoidable flow velocities in water are much lower. Therefore, high-pass filtering is not performed here. Figure 3(b) shows a histogram of a measurement of about 30 min without an external flow in water. The data seem to indicate a discrete probability density function and an additive Gaussian distribution. The distance between two adjacent peaks is about 0.1 cm/s. This corresponds to a time difference of 55 ps, which is the inherent resolution of the used time-to-digital converter TDC7200. Thus, the resolution of the TDC can be fully exploited in water.

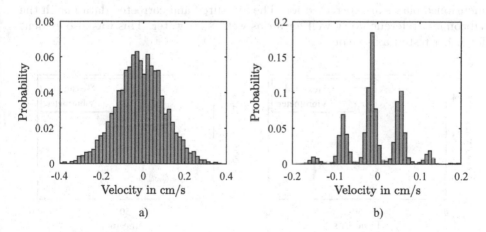

Fig. 3. Histogram of the high-pass filtered part of the results of a measurement of the flow velocity in air (a) and the result of a measurement of the flow velocity in water (b), each without external flow.

4.2   Results with Non-zero Flow Velocity

In this section results with flow velocities unequal $0\,\mathrm{cm/s}$ in the range of a few $\mathrm{cm/s}$ are presented. Due to the difficulty of producing a laminar flow to be analyzed, the transducers were moved through the static medium instead. For this purpose, a linear axis was placed over a water basin and the transducers were moved along the axis. In addition, an OFV-5000 vibrometer with an OFV-505 measuring head manufactured by *Polytec* was used as a reference.

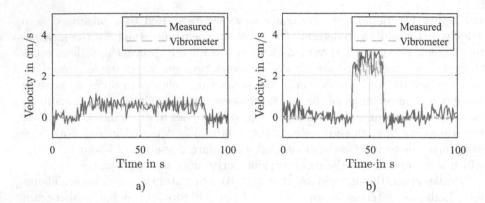

Fig. 4. Flow velocity and vibrometer reference measured in air at $v_{\mathrm{axis}} = 0.6\,\mathrm{cm/s}$ (a) and $v_{\mathrm{axis}} = 2.5\,\mathrm{cm/s}$ (b), respectively

The results collected in air at two different velocities of the axis $v_{\mathrm{axis}} = 0.6\,\mathrm{cm/s}$ and $v_{\mathrm{axis}} = 2.5\,\mathrm{cm/s}$ are displayed in Fig. 4. In Fig. 5 the results at the same axis velocities collected in water are shown. In these results all previously mentioned biases are corrected for. The measured and corrected data match the vibrometer reference very well for air as well as for water. This was also evident for other tested axis velocities.

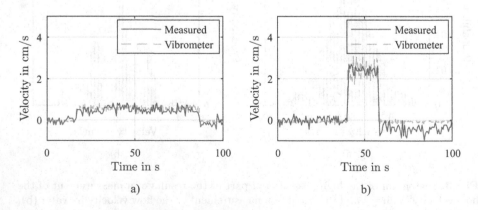

Fig. 5. Flow velocity and vibrometer reference measured in water at $v_{\mathrm{axis}} = 0.6\,\mathrm{cm/s}$ (a) and $v_{\mathrm{axis}} = 2.5\,\mathrm{cm/s}$ (b), respectively

4.3   Results of In Situ Measurements

In addition to the calibration measurements, a first test was carried out in a tunnel. The test took place in the Siebergtunnel on the railway line between Linz and Vienna in Austria. The transducers were mounted on a temporary rack and positioned in the maintenance shaft instead of the drainage pipe, as the actual mounting was not yet completed at the time of the measurement. The used measurement setup is shown in Fig. 6.

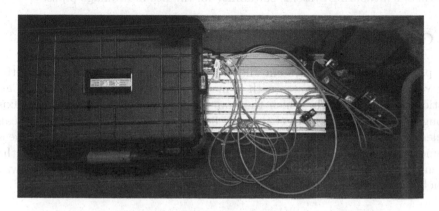

Fig. 6. Measurement setup used in the tunnel with a temporary transducer mount placed directly in the maintenance shaft

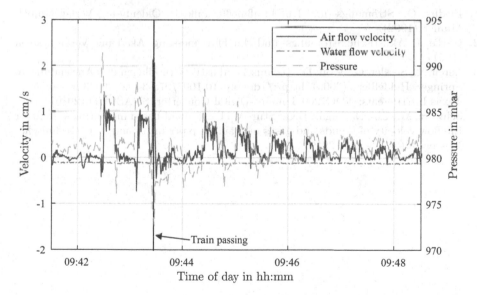

Fig. 7. Short excerpt of the results of a 24-h measurement in a tunnel

The main reason for a measurement in the tunnel with a temporary setup was to determine the suitability of the system. For operative reasons the measurements had to last about 24 h. Figure 7 shows a short excerpt from the captured data, which contains the moment of passing of a train at the measuring position. As expected, the pressure is higher before the train passes and lower afterwards. Additionally, the pressure varies slowly and the air flow velocity changes correspondingly. Furthermore, it can be seen that in this case the flow direction of the water is not affected by the passing train. The results of the 24-h measurement confirm the measuring systems suitability for the use in drainage pipes.

5   Conclusion

The presented measuring system allows the simultaneous measurement of the flow velocity of air and water with a measuring rate higher than 1.5/s. Calibration measurements in which the transducers were moved by a linear axis through static media showed that small flow velocities of less than 1 cm/s can be clearly distinguished from 0 cm/s in water as well as in air. Moreover, measurements with zero flow velocity revealed a measurement uncertainty of the system of 0.1 cm/s. Furthermore, a first test in a drainage pipe of a railway tunnel confirmed the systems suitability.

References

1. Fiedler, O.: Strömungs- und Durchflußmeßtechnik. R. Oldenbourg Verlag GmbH, Munich (1992)
2. Gätke, J.: Akustische Strömungs- und Durchflussmessung. Akademie-Verlag, Berlin (1991)
3. Lerch, R., Sessler, G., Wolf, D.: Technische Akustik: Grundlagen und Anwendungen. Springer, Heidelberg (2009). https://doi.org/10.1007/978-3-540-49833-9
4. Texas Instruments: TDC7200 Time-to-Digital Converter. SNAS647D (2016)
5. Schwarz, M., Uhl, B., Zagar, B.G., Stur, M.: Ultrasound-based measuring system for the flow velocity of liquids and gases in drainage pipes in tunnels. tm - Technisches Messen **86**(2), 93–103 (2019)

Counter-Based vs. Shift-Register-Based Signal Processing in Stochastic Computing

Werner Haselmayr[1]([✉]), Daniel Wiesinger[1,2], and Michael Lunglmayr[2]

[1] Institute for Communications Engineering and RF-Systems,
Johannes Kepler University Linz, Linz, Austria
werner.haselmayr@jku.at
[2] Insitute of Signal Processing,
Johannes Kepler University Linz, Linz, Austria
michael.lunglmayr@jku.at

Abstract. In this work, we investigate non-scaled adders for stochastic computing, an emerging computation paradigm that represents real numbers as random bit streams. In particular, we compare two different non-scaled adder implementations, the shift-register-based (SRB) and up/down-counter-based (UCB) approach, respectively. In the former approach, overflowing carry bits of the addition are shifted into a shift register while the latter method uses a binary counter for storing the carry bits. We provide a unified description of both approaches and analyze the expected number of errors in case of a single bit flip. We furthermore show bit-true simulations results describing the error behavior of both designs. These results show that the SRB approach significantly outperforms the UCB approach in terms of computation accuracy, while having similar complexity.

Keywords: Stochastic computing · Non-scaled adders · Fault tolerant computing

1 Introduction

Stochastic computing (SC) is a promising computation paradigm that encodes real-valued numbers into a stochastic bit stream [1]. In particular, the number is represented by the probability of observing a one-bit in the stream. This representation enables the implementation of basic arithmetic operations using only a few logic gates. For example, a multiplier or a (scaled) adder can be realized by an AND gate or a multiplexer. Moreover, compared to the binary radix implementation, SC has a high fault tolerance to circuit noise and bit flips [2].

Over the years, SC has been successfully applied to various areas, such as decoding of error correcting codes, control systems, image processing, filter design, and

© Springer Nature Switzerland AG 2020
R. Moreno-Díaz et al. (Eds.): EUROCAST 2019, LNCS 12014, pp. 67–75, 2020.
https://doi.org/10.1007/978-3-030-45096-0_9

neural networks (see for example, [3–7]). Many of the aforementioned applications require a large number of additions. However, the conventional approach using an adder tree with multiplexer-based scaled adders suffers from accuracy loss due to downscaling, which becomes even more severe as the number of additions increases. Recently, three different approaches have been proposed to overcome this issue: (i) adder tree with multiplexer-based adders using uneven weights [6]; (ii) adder tree with non-scaled adders [8]; (iii) sequential processing in a central accumulation unit realized as non-scaled adder [9]. The first approach suffers from complex computation of the weights and has still a precision loss in case of many additions due to the multiplexer-based adders. Although, the non-scaled adder approaches have higher complexity, they achieve a significantly higher accuracy. Moreover, the sequential processing approach increases the scalability compared to the adder tree approaches.

For the non-scaled adder two different implementations exist: (i) shift-register-based (SRB) non-scaled adder [9], shifting the generated carry bits into a shift register; (ii) up/down counter-based (UCB) non-scaled adder, where the carry bits are stored as a binary counter value [8].

The aim of this work is to provide a comprehensive comparison between the SRB and the UCB approach for the non-scaled adder using the TLB format[1]. Although an initial comparison has been provided in [10], a comparison in terms of fault tolerance and hardware costs is lacking in the literature. Hence, we derive an analytical expression for the expected number of errors in case of a bit flip in the carry shift register and carry counter, respectively. Moreover, we validate the theoretical results through bit-true simulation and discuss the tradeoff between the SRB and UCB design in terms of hardware costs.

The rest of the paper is organized as follows: In Sect. 2, we provide a brief overview of the different SC encoding formats. In Sect. 3, we first describe the principle of the non-scaled adder using either the SRB or the UCB approach. Then, we derive the expected number of errors for both approaches in case of a single bit flip in the carry shift register and carry counter, respectively. In Sect. 4, we evaluate the performance of the SRB and the UCB approach and validate the theoretical results using bit-true simulations. Finally, Sect. 5 provides concluding remarks.

2   Encoding Formats

In this section, we provide a brief overview on single- and two-line encoding formats used in SC. The former kind of format encodes a desired number in a single stochastic stream, while the latter format uses two streams.

---

[1] TLB is a promising two-line SC encoding format, which will be introduced in Sect. 2.

2.1 Single-Line Encoding Formats

Unipolar Format. In the unipolar format, the value of a deterministic number $x \in [0, 1]$ is encoded in a stochastic bit stream X of length K by [1]

$$x = \frac{1}{K} \sum_{k=1}^{K} X[k], \tag{1}$$

where $X[k] \in \{0, 1\}$ denotes the kth bit of the bit stream X. The precision (representation resolution) of the unipolar format is given by $1/K$. Based on this format, basic arithmetic operations can be implemented using simple logic gates (e.g., AND gate for multiplication) [1].

Bipolar Format. In contrast to the unipolar format, the bipolar format can also represent negative numbers. This is accomplished through a different interpretation of the stochastic stream. In this case, a number $x \in [-1, 1]$ can be represented by a bit stream X of length K by [1]

$$x = \frac{1}{K} \sum_{k=1}^{K} (2X[k] - 1). \tag{2}$$

The precision of the bipolar format is given by $2/K$, i.e. half the resolution of the unipolar format. Similar to the unipolar format, the circuits for basic arithmetic operations are very simple [1].

2.2 Two-Line Encoding Formats

Signed Magnitude Format. In the signed magnitude (SM) format, the sign and magnitude information of a number $x \in [-1, 1]$ is carried by the bit streams X_s and X_m, respectively. Hence, x can be represented as [11]

$$x = \frac{1}{K} \sum_{k=1}^{K} X^{\mathrm{SM}}[k], \tag{3}$$

with $X^{\mathrm{SM}}[k] = (1 - 2X_s[k]) X_m[k]$. The kth bit of the bit stream X_s and X_m is denoted by $X_m[k]$ and $X_s[k]$, respectively. The SM representation achieves the same resolution as the unipolar format, i.e. $1/K$, while maintaining the same range as the bipolar format. Although the hardware effort for basic arithmetic operations is higher compared to the unipolar and bipolar format [11], it enables an efficient implementation of a non-scaled adder [8]. Non-scaled adders[2] are very important if multiple successive additions are required (e.g., in an adder tree) since it avoids downscaling.

---

[2] To the best of our knowledge, so far no non-scaled adder has been proposed for the bipolar format.

Two-Line Bipolar Format. The two-line bipolar (TLB) format uses a different interpretation of the bit streams compared to the SM format. In particular, a number $x \in [-1,1]$ is interpreted as the difference between the numbers $x_p \in [0,1]$ and $x_n \in [0,1]$, which are encoded as unipolar bit streams X_p and X_n. Hence, x can be represented as [1]

$$x = \frac{1}{K} \sum_{k=1}^{K} X^{\mathrm{TLB}}[k], \tag{4}$$

with $X^{\mathrm{TLB}}[k] = X_p[k] - X_n[k]$. The kth bit of the bit stream X_p and X_n is denoted by $X_n[k]$ and $X_p[k]$, respectively. The resolution of the TLB format is given by $1/K$. Similar to the SM format, the circuits for the basic arithmetic operations are slightly more complex than for the unipolar and bipolar format [1], but the TLB format also enables an efficient non-scaled adder implementation.

3   Non-scaled Adder

In this section, we first describe the principle of an SRB non-scaled adder and a UCB non-scaled adder using the TLB format, respectively. Then, we derive the expected number of errors for both approaches in case of a single bit flip in the carry shift register and carry counter, respectively.

3.1   SRB Non-scaled Adder

The SRB non-scaled adder for the TLB format has been recently proposed in [9]. The circuit is shown in Fig. 1(a) and consists of an update logic and carry shift registers $\mathbf{p}_c$ and $\mathbf{n}_c$, each of size M. The update logic must consider many different cases, including the preservation and cancellation of carry bits in the carry shift registers. As an example, one might consider the numbers x, y and their sum z. These numbers can be represented as streams $X[k], Y[k], Z[k] \in \{-1, 0, 1\}$. However, since each element of the result $Z[k]$

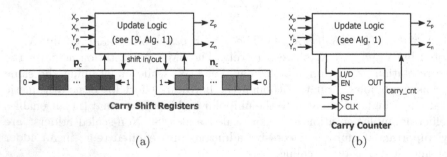

Fig. 1. Stochastic non-scaled adder using different methods for carry bit handling: (a) shift-register-based approach; (b) counter-based approach.

Algorithm 1. Update Logic for UCB Non-Scaled Adder

Input: $\{X[k]\}_{k=1}^{K}, \{Y[k]\}_{k=1}^{K}$

1: *Initialization:* carry_cnt = 0   ▷ Carry counter initialization
2: **for** $k = 1$ to K **do**
3:     **if** $X[k] + Y[k] = 2$ **then** $Z[k] \leftarrow 1$; *carry_cnt* ++
4:     **else if** $X[k] + Y[k] = 1$ **then**
5:         **if** *carry_cnt* < 0 **then** $Z[k] \leftarrow 0$; *carry_cnt* ++ **else** $Z[k] \leftarrow 1$
6:     **else if** $X[k] + Y[k] = -1$ **then**
7:         **if** *carry_cnt* > 0 **then** $Z[k] \leftarrow 0$; *carry_cnt* $--$ **else** $Z[k] \leftarrow -1$
8:     **else if** $X[k] + Y[k] = -2$ **then** $Z[k] \leftarrow -1$; *carry_cnt* $--$
9:     **else**
10:         **if** *carry_cnt* > 0 **then** $Z[k] \leftarrow 1$; *carry_cnt* $--$
11:         **else if** *carry_cnt* < 0 **then** $Z[k] \leftarrow -1$; *carry_cnt* ++
12:         **else** $Z[k] \leftarrow 0$
13: **return** $\{Z[k]\}_{k=1}^{K}$

---

can only be within the set $\{-1, 0, 1\}$, $Z[k]$ is not only the sum of $X[k]$ and $Y[k]$, but the effect of carry must be considered. If both $X[k]$ and $Y[k]$ are either 1 or -1, $Z[k]$ is either 1 or -1 and a carry 1 ($\mathbf{p}_c$ shift in) or -1 ($\mathbf{n}_c$ shift in) should be stored in the carry shift registers for the next calculation. However, it is also possible that the current carry bit cancels a stored carry bit from a previous calculation, e.g. a generated carry 1 cancels a stored carry -1 ($n_c[1] = 1$). The update logic takes all this different scenarios into account. Please refer to [9, Algorithm 1] for the detailed algorithm of the update logic.

3.2 UCB Non-scaled Adder

Although an UCB non-scaled adder has been proposed for the SM format in [8], to the best of our knowledge, no UCB non-scaled adder has been reported for the TLB format. The circuit is shown in Fig. 1(b) and consists of an update logic and a carry counter. Similar to the SRB non-scaled adder, the update logic must consider many different scenarios. For example, if either $X[k]$ or $Y[k]$ are 1 results in $Z[k] = 1$, if the current value of the carry counter is greater zero. However, if the counter value is smaller than zero gives $Z[k] = 0$ and the carry counter is incremented, i.e. the amount of negative carry bits is reduced. The detailed update logic, taking all different scenarios into account is given in Algorithm 1.

3.3 Fault Tolerance

In the following, we provide a theoretical analysis of the fault tolerance on bit flips for the SRB and UCB approach. In particular, we derive the expected number of errors in case of a single bit flip in the carry shift register and carry counter, respectively.

To keep the analysis simple, we consider the unipolar encoding format[3]. Moreover, we assume that a single bit is randomly flipped in the carry shift register or the carry counter with probability P_{flip}.

In the SRB approach, the carry bits in the carry shift register are equally weighted and, thus, the expected error for a single bit flip can be calculated as

$$E_{\text{SRB}} = \sum_{i=1}^{M} P_{\text{bit}} = M P_{\text{bit}}, \tag{5}$$

where M denotes the carry shift register length.

In the UCB approach, the number of required bits for the representation of the carry counter value is smaller than the corresponding shift register length, i.e. for a carry shift register of length M the size of the corresponding is given by $L = \lfloor \log_2 M + 1 \rfloor$. Moreover, the bits representing the counter value have different weights. Hence, the expected number of errors due to a single bit flip can be written as

$$E_{\text{UCB}} = \sum_{i=0}^{L-1} 2^i P_{\text{bit}} = \left(2^L - 1\right) P_{\text{bit}}. \tag{6}$$

Assuming that M carry bits should be stored (requires a carry shift register of size M), after deriving the corresponding counter size $L = \lfloor \log_2 M + 1 \rfloor$, two cases are especially of interest: (i) $(2^L - 1) = M$; (ii) $(2^L - 1) > M$. In the former case, the SRB and UCB approach provide the same error performance (see (5) and (6)). In the latter case, the SRB approach outperforms the UCB design. This is because, for the SRB approach the length of the carry shift register can be designed exactly as needed, while the binary storage has to be built using $\lfloor \log_2 M + 1 \rfloor$ bits. For the worst case scenario, consider a carry counter that needs to count up to $M = 2^L$ instead of $M = 2^L - 1$ and, thus, requires a counter size of $L + 1$ instead of L. Then, the expected number of errors due to a single bit flip is given by

$$E_{\text{UCB,wc}} = \sum_{i=0}^{L} 2^i P_{\text{bit}} = \left(2^{L+1} - 1\right) P_{\text{bit}} = (2M - 1) P_{\text{bit}}. \tag{7}$$

By comparing (5) and (7) we observe that the expected error of the UCB approach is almost twice the error of the SRB approach.

Please note that the aim of the above analysis was to provide first insights into the fault tolerance to bit flips of the SRB and UCB approach. Due to the limited space, more detailed investigations are left to be presented in future work. In such a future analysis, multiple bit flips and bit flips at the output streams should be considered. Additionally, for the TLB format the inherent compensation of bit flips must be taken into account.

---

[3] Please note that a non-scaled adder using the unipolar format requires only one carry shift register for the SRB design and has a slightly modified update logic compared to the TLB format.

4   Simulation Results

In this section, we provide a numerical performance evaluation of the presented SRB and UCB non-scaled adders. In particular, we compare the fault tolerance due to bit flips for the SRB and UCB design for the unipolar and TLB format using bit-true simulations. For this, we randomly flipped bit positions in the carry shift register and carry counter with probability P_{flip} (not necessarily resulting in only a single bit flip, as assumed by the simplified analysis above). Then we measured the computation accuracy of the non-scaled adder by the root mean square error (RMSE) given by RMSE $= \sqrt{\text{mean}|x - \hat{x}|}$, where x denotes the true result (double precision floating point) and $\hat{x}$ corresponds to the result of the stochastic implementation with bit flips. We chose a bit stream length of $K = 10^4$ and the results have been averaged over 1000 simulations per simulated flip probability P_{flip}.

For the unipolar format, we observe from Fig. 2 that the error performance for shift register length $M = 7$ and a counter bit width of $L = 3$ is similar. In case of $M = 8$ and $L = 4$, we observe approximately twice the error, which confirms the theoretical results in Sect. 3.3.

We observe from Fig. 3 that for the TLB format the UCB approach has an even lower fault tolerance compared to the SRB approach. In particular, the SRB design using two carry shift registers (see Fig. 1(a)) of length $M = 7$ has already a significantly higher fault tolerance to bit flips compared to the UCB design using a 4-bit counter (one additional bit due to the signed format). This gap becomes even larger when comparing the SRB design using two shift registers of length $M = 8$ with a UCB design using a 5-bit counter.

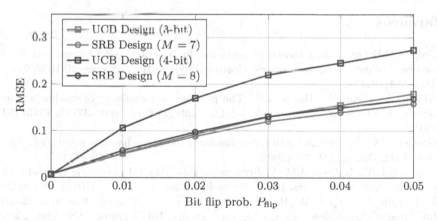

Fig. 2. Comparison of the fault tolerance of a unipolar non-scaled adder using the SRB or UCB approach, assuming a bit flip probability P_{flip}.

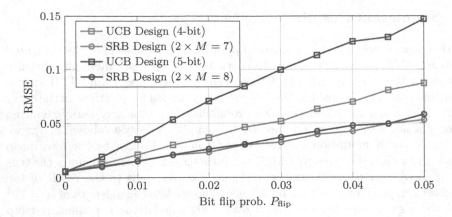

Fig. 3. Comparison of the fault tolerance of a TLB non-scaled adder using the SRB or UCB approach, assuming a bit flip probability P_{flip}.

5   Conclusions

In this work, we compared two different approaches for the implementation of stochastic non-scaled adders, the SRB and the UCB non-scaled adders. We presented a unified description of both approaches and provided a theoretical analysis of the fault tolerance to bit flips. Bit-true simulations confirmed the theoretical results and showed that the UCB approach is more sensitive to bit flips than the SRB approach.

References

1. Gaines, B.R.: Stochastic computing systems. In: Tou, J.T. (ed.) Advances in Information Systems Science. Springer, Boston (1969). https://doi.org/10.1007/978-1-4899-5841-9_2
2. Alaghi, A., Qian, W., Hayes, J.P.: The promise and challenge of stochastic computing. IEEE Trans. Comput. Aided Des. Integr. Circ. Syst. **37**(8), 1515–1531 (2018)
3. Gaudet, V.C., Rapley, A.C.: Iterative decoding using stochastic computation. Electron. Lett. **39**(3), 299–301 (2003)
4. Marin, S.L.T., Reboul, J.M.Q., Franquelo, L.G.: Digital stochastic realization of complex analog controllers. IEEE Trans. Ind. Electron. **49**(5), 1101–1109 (2002)
5. Li, P., Lilja, D.J., Qian, W., Bazargan, K., Riedel, M.D.: Computation on stochastic bit streams digital image processing case studies. IEEE Trans. VLSI Syst. **22**(3), 449–462 (2014)
6. Chang, Y., Parhi, K.K.: Architectures for digital filters using stochastic computing. In: 2013 IEEE International Conference on Acoustics, Speech and Signal Processing, pp. 2697–2701, May 2013
7. Brown, B.D., Card, H.C.: Stochastic neural computation. I. Computational elements. IEEE Trans. Comput. **50**(9), 891–905 (2001)

8. Yuan, B., Wang, Y., Wang, Z.: Area-efficient scaling-free DFT/FFT design using stochastic computing. IEEE Trans. Circ. Syst. II **63**(12), 1131–1135 (2016)
9. Haselmayr, W., Wiesinger, D., Lunglmayr, M.: High-accuracy and fault tolerant stochastic inner product design. IEEE Trans. Circuits Syst. II **67**(3), 541–545 (2019). arxiv.org/abs/1808.06500, accepted for publication
10. Ting, P., Hayes, J.P.: Stochastic logic realization of matrix operations. In: 2014 17th Euromicro Conference on Digital System Design, pp. 356–364, August 2014
11. Toral, S.L., Quero, J.M., Franquelo, L.G.: Stochastic pulse coded arithmetic. In: 2000 IEEE International Symposium on Circuits and Systems, vol. 1, pp. 599–602, May 2000

Artificial Intelligence and Data Mining for Intelligent Transportation Systems and Smart Mobility

Analyzing Network-Wide Effects of Cooperative Adaptive Cruise Control Without Traffic Signal Control at Intersections

Mehmet Ali Silgu[1,2,3]($\boxtimes$), Ismet Goksad Erdagi[1,2], and Hilmi Berk Celikoglu[1,2]

[1] Department of Civil Engineering, Technical University of Istanbul, Ayazaga Campus, 34469 Istanbul, Turkey
msilgu@itu.edu.tr
[2] ITS Research Lab, Faculty of Civil Engineering, Technical University of Istanbul, Ayazaga Campus, 34469 Istanbul, Turkey
[3] Bartin University, 74100 Bartin, Turkey

Abstract. In this paper, a problem to jointly optimize the performances of vehicular traffic flow, i.e., the total time spent, the number of stop-and-go movements, and the total emissions, is handled to investigate and discuss the effectiveness of the penetration rates of cooperatively controlled vehicles in mixed traffic. A simulation-based solution is sought over the SUMO micro-simulation environment considering three hypothetical road networks and varying demand profiles.

Keywords: Cooperative Adaptive Cruise Control · Traffic flow · Microscopic simulation · Smart mobility

1 Introduction

Advances in the vehicular technology, specifically on communication and control, have been fundamental to the increasing interest on the adaptive and cooperative control of road vehicles that extended the feature of the studies so to incorporate several disciplines. The current trend has therefore been questioning the consequences of the recent advances in real commuting life in terms of transport figures and traffic flow performances. In the present study, in order to evaluate a selected range of penetration rate for vehicles with Cooperative Adaptive Cruise Control (CACC) at network scale with varying demand profiles and road geometry, we have considered explicitly in our analyses three performance measures. In the literature on traffic flow control, it has been documented that the total time spent, the number of stop-and-go movements, and the total emissions strongly affect each other [1]. Given what the relevant literature suggests in addition to our findings on the emission effects of CACC in mixed traffic [2], we investigate in the present study the effectiveness of the CACC considering explicitly the number of stop-and-go movements, in addition to emission and travel time measures. Dependent on the level of complexity, as well as on our findings in [2], in which simulations are conducted over the two identical networks with signal control, we have chosen three hypothetical networks

© Springer Nature Switzerland AG 2020
R. Moreno-Díaz et al. (Eds.): EUROCAST 2019, LNCS 12014, pp. 79–86, 2020.
https://doi.org/10.1007/978-3-030-45096-0_10

for simulation-based analyses. We have used the open source microscopic simulation software Simulation of Urban MObility (SUMO) [3] for modeling.

In the following, after a brief review on related literature, we summarize the simulation setup and the discussion on the findings from the analyses conducted.

2 Literature Review

The literature about CACC can be divided into categories, i.e. effects on traffic flow, effects on safety, and effects on the environment. In this study, we focus primarily on the effects of CACC on traffic flow and environment as an extension of our previous studies [2]. In [4], two scenarios are generated for observing different penetration rates of CACC equipped vehicles. In the first scenario in [4], externally created disturbances are expected to be damped on a circular track by the harmonizing effect of CACC on traffic. In the second scenario, the disturbances caused the merging vehicles on a roadway segment are anticipated to be damped by the effect of CACC [4]. Authors mostly focus on the improvements in the density values, and it is shown that with a penetration rate of 30% significant improvements can be achieved, however, the penetration rate of CACC equipped vehicles should be 100% for a traffic flow without any disturbances [4]. In [5], varying penetration rates of CACC and Adaptive Cruise Control (ACC) equipped vehicles are analyzed at signalized intersections. A modified Intelligent Driver Model is adopted for the observation of the effects of reducing headways, distance to the leading vehicle and the reaction time [5]. At each penetration rate, authors achieve an improvement in traffic conditions [5]. As in the given summary of the relevant literature, we analyze the effect of varying penetration rates as well. In our analysis, the environmental effects of CACC have great importance while the existing studies are mostly focused on eco-routing for CACC and energy efficient driving maneuvers for CACC. In [6], energy efficient platooning maneuvers, i.e., platoon formation, gap regulating, splitting, and merging maneuvers, are proposed. However, simulations are conducted on a relatively quite small scale [6], which necessitates the proposed maneuvers to be tested on more significant scenarios in order to have a clear judgement about the effectiveness. Focusing on the effectiveness and potential of CACC on energy efficiency under different conditions, i.e., traffic conditions, lane change maneuvers, traffic control schemes, intersection control strategies, and road topology, a fruitful review of the relevant literature is presented in [7]. In [8], authors propose an algorithm, which uses the location information of vehicles from Vehicle-to-X communication and decides whether a vehicle should pass or should decrease its velocity to a defined minimum value for reducing or eliminating idling duration. The main objective of the proposed algorithm in [8] is to reduce the number of stop-and-go movements to achieve a fuel economy for the vehicles.

From the literature, it can be seen that at each penetration rate, different levels of improvements are achieved, but these improvements are valid only for the created scenarios, hence we cannot assert that CACC equipped vehicles can provide a de facto improvement for the traffic flows. It is shown that it is possible to obtain a reduction in emissions at each penetration rate, as well. In the present study, our primary focus is to obtain optimum penetration rates for traffic flowing over networks with different levels of complexity and discuss the effectiveness of CACC equipped vehicles on the networks without traffic signal control at their intersections. Main contributions we've obtained from the simulation-based modeling and analysis study summarized in the following is two-fold: a discussion about the transition process into a fully cooperative traffic environment; and, handling CACC as a possible sole control strategy at intersections, in contrast to signal control at highways [2, 9] and ramp control at freeways [10–12].

3 Methodology and Simulation Setup

We utilize the Eclipse SUMO as the microscopic traffic simulation environment. SUMO is open-source software, which is developed by German Aerospace Center (DLR). It has several internal tools to create road networks and define traffic flows. In our study, NETEDIT is utilized in order to obtain road networks. The properties of the road network, i.e. intersection control type, speed limits, road topology, is defined via NETEDIT. For defining traffic flows, we encoded the parameters of routes and vehicle types in a code-editor software in an understandable fashion for SUMO. For having a speed varying minimum gap algorithm, Traffic Control Interface (TRACI) of SUMO is used. It is an internal tool of SUMO, which needs to be encoded in Python language. With TRACI, it is possible to obtain speed values of each vehicle and using these values as an input parameter in a function to rearrange spacing between vehicles. In order to model Vehicle-to-Vehicle (V2V) communication, the Veins framework is used. Veins has the ability to model the parameters of the CACC equipped vehicles, and can connect to SUMO via TRACI. The V2V communication mentioned needs to be modeled in another software called Omnet++, which is a network simulator. Veins framework provides the needed mobility for the communicating nodes in Omnet++, at the same time, TRACI tool of SUMO connects to Veins and provides information flow between SUMO and Veins.

In terms of modeling V2V communication, we have utilized Veins and Omnet++ assuming that vehicles: are in a V2V communication in a range of 100 m radius; and, follow each other with the spacing that equals at least the stopping sight distance, which varies with the speed of vehicles. In the present study, we have alternated the penetration rate of CACC equipped vehicles by an increase of 10% at each simulation in order to observe the gradual effects of CACC on uninterrupted urban traffic flow.

3.1 Models of Motion and Emission in SUMO

In SUMO, the default car-following model is a modified version of the Krauss car-following model that is developed by Stefan Krauss in the year 1998 [13], in which the safe speed is computed as a function of: the speed of the leader vehicle, the spacing between leader and the follower vehicles, the speed of the follower vehicle, and the maximum deceleration and reaction time of the drivers. As the safe speed can exceed a speed limit or be beyond the speed that a vehicle can reach, the term 'desired speed' is defined as the minimum of the arguments: the accelerated speed, the safe speed, and the speed limit [2]. In order to realistically model driving behavior, an imperfection parameter, which is randomly chosen at each time step for each vehicle, is defined to account for spacing distribution. To prevent vehicles' moving backwards, another limit is defined as well [2].

As to figure out emissions, we use the Handbook Emission Factors for Road Transport (HBEFA) model in SUMO, which is based on the power demand calculation of Passenger Car and Heavy Duty Emission Model (PHEM). The PHEM model calculates power demand for different speed profiles and road topologies based on the vehicle dynamics and the actual engine speed for any vehicle combination. The fuel consumption and emissions are then interpolated from engine maps. The needed engine power demand in the PHEM model is calculated as a function of: the power demand to overcome the rolling resistance, the power demand to overcome the air resistance, the power demand for acceleration, the power demand to overcome the road gradient, the power losses in the transmission system, and the power demand from auxiliaries [2]. HBEFA emission factors are found in the connection between the calculated engine power demand, engine speed, and emissions from real-world measurements [14]. In our present study, we have considered the number of stop-and-go movements as a critical performance measure that determines total emissions since the relationship affects several power demand types.

3.2 Test Cases

In case of observing network-wide effects of CACC on urban road networks, we defined three hypothetical test networks, i.e., named as T1, T2, and T3. These networks are assumed to be a part of an urban road network, hence, a speed limit of 50 km/h is defined for each network containing 6 nodes, which are designed as unsignalized intersections. As shown in Fig. 1, each network has the identical number of intersections. However, the number of intersection legs is different. Each of the links of the networks has a length of 1 km. All the links of T1 and T2 have one direction, wherein T3 links have two directions. For providing the best possible V2V communication, there assumed no buildings or none obstacles, which can attenuate the V2V communication. In order to provide decentralized communication, Road Side Units are not placed in the networks.

The demand profiles loaded to networks are chosen as time-varying in order to model different traffic flow conditions. For T1 and T2, the vehicles are loaded from node "1" and destinated to node "8". In order to obtain the effect of having different conditions at the intersections, 5 different routes are defined for T1 and 4 different routes are defined for T2. For T3, the given demand profile is loaded 3 times from outer nodes for each node at the other side of the symmetry. We do not define any exact route for this network, thus, drivers/vehicles can decide the intermediate nodes on their routes.

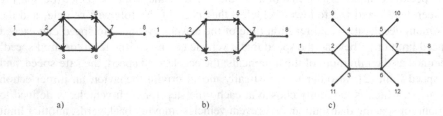

Fig. 1. Test Networks (a) T1, (b) T2, and (c) T3

Two vehicle types, i.e., Type-I and Type-II, are defined to represent vehicles with human drivers and CACC equipped vehicles, respectively. Although vehicle types are defined with identical parameters, i.e., vehicle mass equals 1200 kg, frontal areas are 2.5 m^2, drag coefficient is 0.32, air density is 1184 kN/m2, rolling resistance is 0.0015 and maximum acceleration and deceleration are 4.5 m/s^2 [15], Type-II vehicles are equipped with CACC, thus, they are in a V2V communication. For limiting the information flow and reducing the computational load for micro-simulation [16], the communication range of V2V is limited in a 100 m radius for each vehicle. Both of the vehicle types are modeled with a gasoline engine by Euro Norm 6. The minimum headways between cooperatively controlled vehicles are determined as stopping sight distances, which depend on the speed values of the vehicles.

The simulation duration is set to 3600 s. Each network is simulated with a penetration rate of 0% to 100% with an increase of 10% at each simulation. As aforementioned, three parameters chosen for the performance evaluation are Total Time Spent (TTS), Number of Stop-and-Go Movements (NSG), and Total Emissions (TE). For obtaining these parameters, different detector types, which are defined in SUMO, are utilized.

4 Results

In order to find an optimum penetration rate for CACC equipped vehicles for traffic-related problems and environmental problems in urban networks, we consider TTS, NSG, and TE values in comparison. Results we've obtained show that for T1 and T2, similar trends are observable. As shown in Figs. 2 and 4, around 50% of a penetration rate, minimum NSG values are obtained for our test case, however, improvements in TTS values are not satisfactory as expected. The Fig. 3 shows that 50% of penetration rate can be accepted as optimum from an environmental aspect.

As given in Fig. 5, for T3, NSG and TTS values are in an increasing trend with the increase of penetration rate, thus, we consider environmental effects for asserting an optimum penetration rate for T3. As shown in Fig. 5, TE values decrease with an increase of penetration rate, thus, the optimum penetration rate for T3 can be considered as 50%, as well.

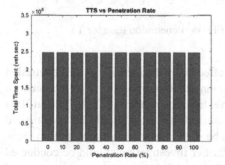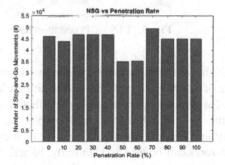

Fig. 2. TTS vs. Penetration Rate and NSG vs. Penetration Rate for T1

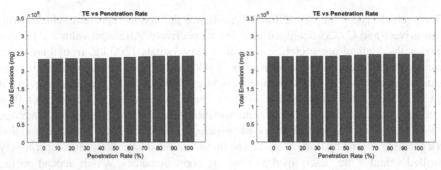

Fig. 3. TE vs. Penetration Rate for T1 and T2, respectively

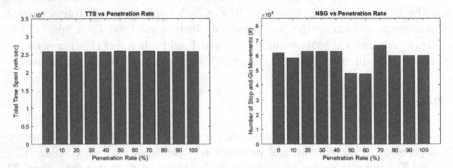

Fig. 4. TTS vs. Penetration Rate and NSG vs. Penetration Rate for T2

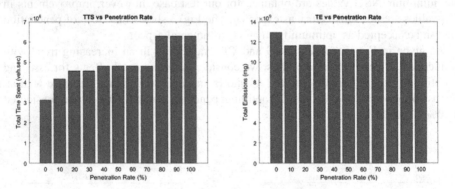

Fig. 5. TTS vs. Penetration Rate and TE vs. Penetration Rate for T3

The results show that similar networks are affected by the increase of the penetration rate of CACC equipped vehicles in a similar fashion and the complexity level of a network is also a defining parameter for the affection level from the penetration rate. TE and NSG values are not related as much as they are expected, hence, it should be investigated further. From the findings of this study, it can be seen that at several penetration rates, networks can be affected similarly, hence, a further investigation should be conducted for finding the exact relation between traffic flow conditions and penetration rates of

CACC equipped vehicles. By this mean, a fixed penetration rate of CACC equipped vehicles should be analyzed under different traffic flow conditions for a given network.

From an environmental aspect, the effectiveness of CACC can be reputed to be debatable. Emissions are not reduced for simple cases, however, in a more complex network with a denser traffic condition, the reductions in TE are significant. For a clear conclusion, several different networks should be analyzed under the same procedures.

5   Conclusion and Future Research

In the present study, we have sought an optimum penetration rate of CACC equipped vehicles for urban networks of different levels of complexity in environmental and traffic harmonization aspects, jointly. As a critical performance measure to justify the effects of emissions exhausted in considerable quantities as an extension to total emission figures studied in [2], we have investigated under uninterrupted flow scenarios at network scale the consequent effects on the number of stop-and-go movements with respect to variations in the penetration rate. In our case, it is asserted that a 50% penetration rate of CACC equipped vehicles can be an optimum value for networks, where no traffic signal control is applied at intersections. Our future research focuses on modeling more complex networks with similar scenarios seeking the network-wide fuel consumption optimization in order to increase the effectiveness of CACC for mixed traffic compositions.

References

1. Pasquale, C., Liu, S., Siri, S., Sacone, S., Schutter, B.D.: A new emission model including on-ramps for two-class freeway traffic control. In: 2015 IEEE 18th International Conference on Intelligent Transportation Systems (2015)
2. Erdagi, I.G., Silgu, M.A., Celikoglu, H.B.: Emission effects of cooperative adaptive cruise control: a simulation case using SUMO. In: Weber, M., Bieker-Walz, L., Hilbrich, R., Behrisch, M. (eds.) Proceedings of the SUMO User Conference 2019 – Simulating Connected Urban Mobility. EPiC Series in Computing, vol. 62, pp. 92–100 (2019)
3. Krajzewicz, D.: Traffic simulation with SUMO – simulation of urban mobility. In: Barceló, J. (ed.) Fundamentals of Traffic Simulation International Series in Operations Research & Management Science, vol. 145, pp. 269–293. Springer, New York (2010). https://doi.org/10.1007/978-1-4419-6142-6_7
4. Delis, A.I., Nikolos, I.K., Papageorgiou, M.: Simulation of the penetration rate effects of ACC and CACC on macroscopic traffic dynamics. In: 2016 IEEE 19th International Conference on Intelligent Transportation Systems (ITSC) (2016)
5. Askari, A., Farias, D.A., Kurzhanskiy, A.A., Varaiya, P.: Effect of adaptive and cooperative adaptive cruise control on throughput of signalized arterials. In: 2017 IEEE Intelligent Vehicles Symposium (IV) (2017)
6. Wang, Z., Wu, G., Hao, P., Boriboonsomsin, K., Barth, M.: Developing a platoon-wide Eco-Cooperative Adaptive Cruise Control (CACC) system. In: 2017 IEEE Intelligent Vehicles Symposium (IV) (2017)
7. Vahidi, A., Sciarretta, A.: Energy saving potentials of connected and automated vehicles. Transp. Res. Part C Emerging Technol. 95, 822–843 (2018)

8. Homchaudhuri, B., Vahidi, A., Pisu, P.: Fast model predictive control-based fuel efficient control strategy for a group of connected vehicles in urban road conditions. IEEE Trans. Control Syst. Technol. **25**, 760–767 (2017)

9. Akyol, G., Silgu, M.A., Celikoglu, H.B.: Pedestrian-friendly traffic signal control using Eclipse SUMO. In: Weber, M., Bieker-Walz, L., Hilbrich, R., Behrisch, M. (eds.) Proceedings of the SUMO User Conference 2019 – Simulating Connected Urban Mobility. EPiC Series in Computing, vol. 62, pp. 101–106 (2019)

10. Demiral, C., Celikoglu, H.B.: Application of ALINEA ramp control algorithm to freeway traffic flow on approaches to Bosphorus strait crossing bridges. Procedia Soc. Behav. Sci. **20**, 364–371 (2011)

11. Abuamer, I.M., Silgu, M.A., Celikoglu, H.B.: Micro-simulation based ramp metering on Istanbul freeways: an evaluation adopting ALINEA. In: 2016 IEEE 19th International Conference on Intelligent Transportation Systems (ITSC) (2016)

12. Abuamer, I.M., Sadat, M., Silgu, M.A., Celikoglu, H.B.: Analyzing the effects of driver behavior within an adaptive ramp control scheme: a case-study with ALINEA. In: 2017 IEEE International Conference on Vehicular Electronics and Safety (ICVES) (2017)

13. Krauss, S.: Microscopic modeling of traffic flow: investigation of collision free vehicle dynamics (1998)

14. Hausberger, S., Rexeis, M., Zallinger, M., Luz, R.: Emission Factors from the Model PHEM for the HBEFA Version 3 (2009)

15. Malikopoulos, A.A., Hong, S., Park, B.B., Lee, J., Ryu, S.: Optimal control for speed harmonization of automated vehicles. IEEE Trans. Intell. Transp. Syst. **20**, 1–13 (2018)

16. Celikoglu, H.B., Hudson, R.V., Blum, J.J., Ravi, V.K.: Introduction to parallelization of a quasi-anisotropic mesoscopic model for network traffic simulation. In: 2015 IEEE 18th International Conference on Intelligent Transportation Systems (2015)

Convolutional Gated Recurrent Units for Obstacle Segmentation in Bird-Eye-View

Luigi Musto[1]([⊠]), Francesco Valenti[3], Andrea Zinelli[1], Fabio Pizzati[2], and Pietro Cerri[3]

[1] University of Parma, Parma, Italy
{luigi.musto,andrea.zinelli1}@studenti.unipr.it
[2] University of Bologna, Bologna, Italy
fabio.pizzati2@unibo.it
[3] Vislab SRL, Parma, Italy
francesco.valenti@studenti.unipr.it, pietro.cerri@unipr.it

Abstract. Obstacle detection is a fundamental problem in autonomous driving. The most common solutions share the idea of modeling the free-space and marking as obstacles all the points that lie outside this model according to a threshold. Manually setting this threshold and adapting the model to the various scenarios is not ideal, whereas a machine learning approach is more suitable for this kind of task. In this work we present an application of Convolutional Neural Networks (CNNs) for the detection of obstacles in front of a vehicle. Our goal is to train a CNN to understand which patterns in this area are connected to the presence of obstacles. Our method does not require any manual annotation, since the training relies on a classification that comes from a LiDAR. During inference, our network requires as input a 3D point cloud generated from stereoscopic images. Moreover, we make use of recurrent units in our network, since they are able to exploit temporal information to provide more accurate results in case of occlusion. We compare different input configurations and show that our final selection is able to correctly predict the position of obstacles and to generalize well in unseen environments.

1 Introduction

Any mobile robot needs to regularly perform various high level tasks, like path planning and collision avoidance, in order to safely navigate in the environment. As a low level input, these tasks require to detect the presence of obstacles in the surrounding environment and to compute their position. Here we focus on a solution that is based on computer vision and employs only a stereo camera placed in front of a vehicle, even though some commercial solutions sometimes replace or combine cameras with LiDARs or Sonars. In particular, as discussed in Sect. 3.5, we use a LiDAR only for ground-truth collection, because of its precision and the possibility to distinguish each point as belonging to the road or to an object. Our solution, in fact, is based on a Recurrent Neural Network which needs as input only data from a stereo camera setup. This has various

© Springer Nature Switzerland AG 2020
R. Moreno-Díaz et al. (Eds.): EUROCAST 2019, LNCS 12014, pp. 87–94, 2020.
https://doi.org/10.1007/978-3-030-45096-0_11

advantages compared to other work, like the possibility of learning directly from data which do not include any manual annotation.

2   Related Work

Various methods have been proposed to detect obstacles in an automotive scenario using a stereoscopic camera. Such approaches differ in many aspects but they all share the same idea: obstacles are entities that can be distinguished from the drivable road surface. The problem can therefore be formulated as finding such surface and identifying as obstacles all the objects that do not belong to it.

One of the earliest solution is based on modeling the road surface using a V-disparity histogram image [1,10], implicitly assuming that the road is a flat but possibly inclined surface.

A possible improvement relies on the computation of a UV-disparity map [11], which can be used to directly detect large obstacles.

Another class of solutions represents the environment using Digital Elevation Models [12] and discriminates between free-space and obstacles based on the density of a certain area. These approaches also assume that the road is a planar surface, not necessarily flat, but can reach a finer level of detection if compared with a V-disparity approach.

Generic terrain mapping methods [2] do not make any fundamental assumption regarding the shape of the road and try to estimate a 3D model of the drivable surface. Obstacles are then identified as the outliers of the model.

A more recent solution has been proposed in [8], where obstacles are directly identified in the original image space. The core idea of this method lies in the computation of a Vertically Local Disparity Histogram (VLDH), defined as a disparity histogram computed in a vertically local neighborhood of each pixel. Making the reasonable assumption that the road surface is non-vertical, the computed quantity becomes large when obstacles exist at a given image position. Conversely, when the local histogram assumes low values, corresponding pixels are classified as road.

All these approaches share the idea of modeling the free-space by exploiting the disparity map and marking as obstacles all entities that lie outside the model. This can be done by setting a threshold that defines the minimum acceptable distance between an entity and the model, to still consider that point as an inlier to the model.

Such threshold can assume various meanings depending on the particular approach, but in general manually setting a single value is often a sub-optimal decision, due to different characteristics of each given scenario or situation, like the weather condition or the environment illumination.

Our work takes inspiration from the state of the art of deep learning approaches to object detection, while differing in the computational cost and in the sensor input. In MV3D [3] and AVOD [4] the problem is solved by regressing 3D bounding boxes from an aggregation of features extracted in Bird-Eye View and perspective view, but the 3D input is a LiDAR point cloud. Our network is more similar to the one in [6], where a lightweight object detector is trained on raw LiDAR input. Here, instead, we only rely on LiDAR during training, while we make use of a stereoscopic camera to generate the 3D point cloud needed as input.

3   Method

Our goal is to train a network to understand which patterns in the area in front of a vehicle are connected to the presence of obstacles.

3.1   World Model

The world is modeled as a 101×31 Bird-Eye View (BEV) grid, where the car is placed in the top-middle cell. Each cell represents a square of size $0.5\,m \times 0.5\,m$ in the world, which means that the grid is able to model an area of $50.5\,m \times 15.5\,m$. The input of the network is a 3D tensor of shape $16 \times 101 \times 31$ that encodes the grid information as follows:

- The first 3 channels are a projection of the perspective image to the BEV grid, denoted as $\mathcal{B}$.
- The fourth channel is the density of the points that fall into each cell, which is the number of points normalized by the theorical maximum. We will refer to this channel as $\mathcal{D}$ and show an example of it in Fig. 1a.
- The fifth channel is the maximum height found among the points that fall into each cell. We will refer to this channel as $\mathcal{H}$, which somehow encodes the slope information, since a rough change in height between one cell and the other may suggest the presence of an obstacle. We show an example of this in Fig. 1b.
- The other 11 channels encode a 3D occupancy grid, denoted as $\mathcal{G}$. Each channel is a 2D grid which represents a plane (parallel to the ground) at a different height. For each plane, we write 1 in a cell if there is a point in it and 0 otherwise.

This information is originated from a preprocessing step, which takes as input two stereo images and computes a 3D point cloud using Semi-Global Matching [7]. The points are then projected and accumulated in the corresponding BEV grid cell and used to generate the input tensor.

3.2   Architecture

The network architecture is inspired by [6] and is comprised of Convolutional Gated Recurrent Units [5] (CGRUs) given by the following equations:

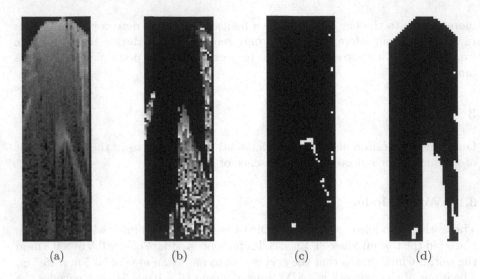

(a)   (b)   (c)   (d)

Fig. 1. Grid data used by the network. (a) Representation of $\mathcal{D}$. (b) Representation of $\mathcal{H}$. (c) Representation of the LiDAR readings (i.e. the ground truth of the network). (d) Representation of the occluded points mask.

$$z_t = \sigma(W_{xz} * x_t + W_{hz} * h_{t-1} + b_z) \qquad (1)$$
$$r_t = \sigma(W_{xr} * x_t + W_{hr} * h_{t-1} + b_r) \qquad (2)$$
$$\bar{h}_t = tanh(W_{xh} * x_t + r_t \circ W_{hh} * h_{t-1} + b_h) \qquad (3)$$
$$h_t = z_t \circ h_{t-1} + (1 - z_t) \circ \bar{h}_t \qquad (4)$$

where x_t is the input at step t, h_t and h_{t-1} are the hidden states after and before the update respectively, z_t is the update gate, r_t is the reset gate, $\bar{h}_t$ is the candidate activation. Here $*$ denotes a dilated convolution, while σ is a sigmoid activation function and $\circ$ is an element-wise multiplication.

The full architecture is given in Table 1 and is comprised of 3 CGRUs denoted as $\mathcal{C}$ with increasing dilation and number of channels. The hidden state of the last CGRU is fed to a final convolutional layer with a Sigmoid activation function that outputs the network prediction $\mathcal{P}$ in a single channel.

Table 1. Network architecture.

Input	Output	Input channels	Output channels	Kernel size	Dilation
$concat(\mathcal{B}, \mathcal{D}, \mathcal{H}, \mathcal{G})$	$h^{\mathcal{C}_1}$	16	32	3	1
$h^{\mathcal{C}_1}$	$h^{\mathcal{C}_2}$	32	64	3	2
$h^{\mathcal{C}_2}$	$h^{\mathcal{C}_3}$	64	128	3	3
$h^{\mathcal{C}_3}$	$\mathcal{P}$	128	1	3	1

In its final version, our network has 870000 parameters. The information to be processed is much simpler than the one contained in an high resolution perspective image, which may require a bigger model with more parameters.

3.3 Advantages of Recurrent Units

Since the network layers are recurrent, they are able to exploit temporal information. This gives the network great advantages. First, the network can refine the predictions frame by frame. Second, it has the power to track moving obstacles and distinguish them from static ones. Finally, the network has the possibility of tracking obstacles even when they get occluded [6], solving the ghosting phenomenon illustrated in Fig. 2.

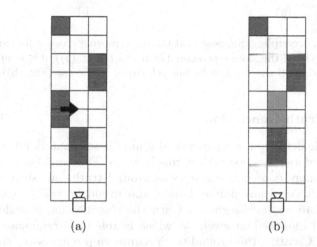

(a)   (b)

Fig. 2. Example of ghosting. Cells marked as red are occupied by obstacles, while white cells are free-space. At frame t (Fig. (a)), we have an obstacle that moves from a cell to another, which is occluded by another obstacle at frame t + 1 (Fig. (b)). (Color figure online)

3.4 Decoupling of Ego-Motion

Training a recurrent network with images taken from a moving vehicle comes with a problem. The difference between one frame and next, in fact, depends on both the movement of the ego-vehicle and the other objects of the scene. In order to avoid a training bias due to the particular movement of the vehicle in the sequences recorded, we decouple it from the other objects as in [6]. In particular, we make use of the car odometry to compute the relative transformation of the vehicle between two consecutive frames t and $t + 1$. Then we use it to project each hidden state of the network from frame t to frame $t + 1$. This has the effect of adjusting the network memory to the current frame, moving all the features of frame t to the position they should have at frame $t + 1$. A representation of this given in Fig. 3.

   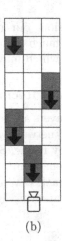

(a)   (b)

Fig. 3. Ego-motion decoupling. Suppose that the car is moving straight forward by one cell at each frame. Given the state represented at frame t (Fig. (a)), it gets updated at frame $t + 1$ by moving all the features by one cell closer to the car (Fig. (b)).

3.5   Ground-Truth Generation

We tackle obstacle detection as a supervised semantic segmentation task, where the commonly used loss function is the Cross Entropy. This would need obstacles annotations for many consecutive frames as ground truth, but such a kind of labels is not available in any public dataset and would be really expensive to annotate. Therefore we use as ground truth the classification provided by an Ibeo LUX LiDAR mounted on a vehicle, which is able to discriminate between road and objects. Creating this ground truth requires a preprocessing step, since the laser readings need to be synchronized with images, clustered and projected onto the corresponding grid cells. An example of the generated grid is given in Fig. 1c.

When preprocessing the laser readings, we also compute masks for the loss function, like the one in Fig. 1d. These masks are used during training to ignore two kinds of cells, since it would be useless or detrimental to train the network on them. First we mask all the cells that lie outside the camera FOV, where the network cannot make any prediction. Second we use a ray casting algorithm to mask the portion of the grid that is occluded by the obstacles.

4   Experiments and Results

4.1   Dataset Preparation

Since the dataset preparation does not need any manual annotation, we were able to create a very large training set. We recorded the stereo images, the LiDAR readings and the vehicle odometry with the respective timestamps, since they are needed for the synchronization. We collected a total of 69 sequences of 900 frames each in different environments, which were split into 60 for training and 9 for testing.

4.2 Training Procedure

The network was trained on sequences of 30 frames per iteration. We used the Adam [9] optimizer with default hyperparameters, a learning rate of 8.8×10^{-4} and a batch size of 16. In this configuration we stopped the training after 28 epochs, as the accuracy on the test set started to decrease (suggesting overfitting). In order to perform backpropagation through the whole sequence, the final loss is given by the sum of the loss for each frame. By doing so, at the end of each sequence, we update the network parameters and reset the network hidden states.

4.3 Evaluation

In order to evaluate our network, we computed the mean Intersection over Union (mIoU) over the 9 sequences kept for testing. Table 2 shows the network performance with different configurations of input, giving us the intuition that the height and density information are the most important to detect obstacles.

Table 2. Accuracy of the network with different input configurations. $\mathcal{B}$ is the Bird-Eye View projection of the perspective image, $\mathcal{D}$ is the density of points, $\mathcal{H}$ is the maximum height, while $\mathcal{G}$ is the 3D occupancy grid.

$\mathcal{B}$	$\mathcal{D}$	$\mathcal{H}$	$\mathcal{G}$	mIoU
✓	✓	✓	✓	**33.71**
✗	✓	✓	✓	33.51
✓	✓	✗	✓	33.44
✗	✗	✗	✓	32.28
✗	✓	✓	✗	31.64
✓	✓	✓	✗	31.20
✗	✗	✓	✗	25.64
✓	✗	✗	✗	5.58

5 Conclusion and Future Work

We presented an application of CNNs to solve the problem of obstacle detection. Our method allows training without the need of any manual annotation and consists of a fast and lightweight network which only requires information from a stereo camera (besides of the odometry). We note that the LiDAR employed to gather the ground truth is capable of perceiving very few points compared to the ones generated with stereo matching with cameras. Therefore an improvement to this method could be to gather a richer training set, where the ground truth does not come from a single firing of the LiDAR, but as the accumulation and alignment of the readings in multiple frames. Moreover, it could be possible to integrate information that comes directly from the perspective image, since the object appearance is an important feature for the task at hand which gets almost lost in the BEV projection.

References

1. Broggi, A., Caraffi, C., Fedriga, R.I., Grisleri, P.: Obstacle detection with stereo vision for off-road vehicle navigation. In: IEEE Computer Society Conference on Computer Vision and Pattern Recognition-Workshops, 2005. CVPR Workshops, pp. 65–65. IEEE (2005)
2. Broggi, A., Cardarelli, E., Cattani, S., Sabbatelli, M.: Terrain mapping for off-road autonomous ground vehicles using rational b-spline surfaces and stereo vision. In: Intelligent Vehicles Symposium (IV), 2013 IEEE, pp. 648–653. IEEE (2013)
3. Chen, X., Ma, H., Wan, J., Li, B., Xia, T.: Multi-view 3D object detection network for autonomous driving. In: Proceedings of the IEEE Conference on Computer Vision and Pattern Recognition, pp. 1907–1915 (2017)
4. Chen, X., Ma, H., Wan, J., Li, B., Xia, T.: Multi-view 3D object detection network for autonomous driving. In: IEEE CVPR, vol. 1, p. 3 (2017)
5. Chung, J., Gulcehre, C., Cho, K., Bengio, Y.: Empirical evaluation of gated recurrent neural networks on sequence modeling. In: NIPS 2014 Workshop on Deep Learning, December 2014 (2014)
6. Dequaire, J., Ondrúška, P., Rao, D., Wang, D., Posner, I.: Deep tracking in the wild: end-to-end tracking using recurrent neural networks. Int. J. Robot. Res. **37**(4–5), 492–512 (2018)
7. Hirschmuller, H.: Stereo processing by semiglobal matching and mutual information. IEEE Trans. Pattern Anal. Mach. Intell. **30**(2), 328–341 (2007)
8. Kakegawa, S., Matono, H., Kido, H., Shima, T.: Road surface segmentation based on vertically local disparity histogram for stereo camera. Int. J. Intell. Transp. Syst. Res. **16**(2), 90–97 (2018)
9. Kingma, D.P., Ba, J.: Adam: A method for stochastic optimization (2014). arXiv preprint arXiv:1412.6980
10. Labayrade, R., Aubert, D., Tarel, J.P.: Real time obstacle detection in stereovision on non flat road geometry through "v-disparit" representation. In: Intelligent Vehicle Symposium, 2002, IEEE. vol. 2, pp. 646–651. IEEE (2002)
11. Musleh Lancis, B., Escalera Hueso, A.d.l., Armingol Moreno, J.M.: Uv disparity analysis in urban environments (2011)
12. Oniga, F., Nedevschi, S.: Processing dense stereo data using elevation maps: road surface, traffic isle, and obstacle detection. IEEE Trans. Veh. Technol. **59**(3), 1172–1182 (2010)

Lane Detection and Classification Using Cascaded CNNs

Fabio Pizzati[1](✉), Marco Allodi[2], Alejandro Barrera[3], and Fernando García[3]

[1] University of Bologna, Viale Risorgimento 2, 40136 Bologna, BO, Italy
fabio.pizzati2@unibo.it
[2] University of Parma, Via delle Scienze, 181/a, 43124 Parma, PR, Italy
marco.allodi1@studenti.unipr.it
[3] Universidad Carlos III de Madrid,
Av. de la Universidad, 30, 28911 Leganés, Madrid, Spain
alebarre@pa.uc3m.es, fegarcia@ing.uc3m.es

Abstract. Lane detection is extremely important for autonomous vehicles. For this reason, many approaches use lane boundary information to locate the vehicle inside the street, or to integrate GPS-based localization. As many other computer vision based tasks, convolutional neural networks (CNNs) represent the state-of-the-art technology to indentify lane boundaries. However, the position of the lane boundaries w.r.t. the vehicle may not suffice for a reliable positioning, as for path planning or localization information regarding lane types may also be needed. In this work, we present an end-to-end system for lane boundary identification, clustering and classification, based on two cascaded neural networks, that runs in real-time. To build the system, 14336 lane boundaries instances of the TuSimple dataset for lane detection have been labelled using 8 different classes. Our dataset and the code for inference are available online.

Keywords: Lane boundary detection · Lane boundary classification · Deep learning

1 Introduction

In autonomous driving, a deep understanding of the surrounding environment is vital to safely drive the vehicle. For this reason, a precise interpretation of the visual signals is necessary to identify all the components essential for navigation. One of them of particular importance is lane boundary position, which is needed to avoid collisions with other vehicles, and to localize the vehicle inside the street. Besides easing localization, lane detection is employed in many ADAS for lane departure warning and lane keeping assist. As many others computer vision based tasks, lanes boundaries detection accuracy has been significantly

---

The GPU used has been donated by the NVIDIA corporation.

R. Moreno-Díaz et al. (Eds.): EUROCAST 2019, LNCS 12014, pp. 95–103, 2020.
https://doi.org/10.1007/978-3-030-45096-0_12

improved after the introduction of deep learning. The majority of recent systems, indeed, use convolutional neural networks to process sensorial data and infer high-level information relative to lanes. Some of them process LiDAR data to exploit differences in lane markings reflectivity [1,2]. However, LiDARs are extremely expensive, thus not always available on a vehicle. On the other hand, cameras are cheaper, and they make it possible to exploit chromatic differences on the road surface. Among the deep learning based lane detection approaches that rely solely on visual data, there is significant interest in lane marking detection [3–7]. In [4], a modified version of Faster R-CNN [8] is used to identify road patches that belong to lane markings. Many of those patches are then joined to obtain a complete representation of the marking. However, the system runs at approximately 4 frames per seconds, so it is not suitable for real-time elaboration, that is often a hard requirement for high-speed driving. In other works [6,7,9] lane markings detection and classification is achieved using fully-convolutional networks [10], and this enables more complex path planning tasks, where lane changes could be considered. Nonetheless, a comprehensive understanding of lane boundaries may be needed for path planning, so it may be necessary to join the detected markings with post processing algorithms. An alternative approach is to directly identify the boundaries, in order to reduce post-processing times. In [11–14], fully-convolutional networks are used to obtain a pixelwise representation of lane boundaries. A slightly different approach is proposed in [15], where a CNN is used to estimate polylines points, in order to solve fragmentation issues that often occurr in segmentation networks. They classify the obtained boundaries, but only in terms of position w.r.t. the ego vehicle, so no information regarding the lane boundary type (e.g. dashed, continuous) is extracted. Similarly to [15], Ghafoorian et al. [16] exploit adversarial training to reduce fragmentation. In [17], an end-to-end approach is proposed, where lane boundary parameters are directly estimated by a CNN. As lane boundaries position, also lane boundaries types could be exploited to achieve a high grade of scene understanding. For example, knowing if a lane is dashed is indispensable for a lane change. Nonetheless, there is little interest in literature for simultaneous lane boundary identification and classification using deep learning. This could be caused by the lack of datasets that contains both information. For this reason, we extended a lane detection dataset with lane class annotations. Then, we developed a novel approach, based on the concatenation of multiple neural networks, that is used to perform lane boundary instance segmentation and classification, in an end-to-end deep learning based fashion. Our system satisfy real-time constraints on a NVIDIA Titan Xp GPU. Code for inference and pretrained models are available online.

2   Method

Our method is composed by two main sections, as presented in Fig. 1. As a first step, we train a CNN for lane boundary instance segmentation. Then, we extract a descriptor for each detected lane boundary and process it with a second CNN.

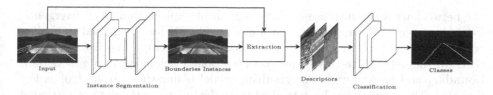

Fig. 1. System overview

2.1 Instance Segmentation

As discussed in Sect. 1, several state-of-the-art approaches employ pixelwise classifications in order to differentiate pixels belonging to lane boundaries and background. In our case, different approaches are possible, so several design guidelines have been defined. First of all, we train the CNN to recognize lane boundaries, rather than lane markings. Doing this, it is indeed avoidable to group different lane markings in a lane boundary, considerably saving processing times. For similar reasons, we perform instance segmentation on lane boundaries instead of semantic segmentation. In this way, it is possible to distinguish different lane boundaries without relying on clustering algorithms. The state-of-the-art network for instance segmentation is Mask R-CNN [18]. However, two-step networks like Mask R-CNN are tipically not amenable to use in real-time application, as they are typically slower than single-step ones. Furthermore, they are usually employed to detect objects easily enclosable in rectangular boxes. Being lane boundaries appearance heavily influenced by the perspective effects, other kinds of architectures should be preferred. Taking into account the previous assumptions, a fully-convolutional network has been trained.

We choose ERFNet [10] as our baseline model, as it is the model that, at the time of writing, has the best performances among real-time networks in the Cityscapes Dataset benchmark for semantic segmentation. As in all deep-learning based approaches, large amounts of images and annotations are crucial to achieve correct predictions and to avoid overfitting. For this reason, the TuSimple dataset for lane detection has been used. It is composed by 6408 1280 × 720 images, divided in 3626 for training, and 2782 for testing. 410 images extracted from the training set have been used as validation set during training. The main peculiarity in the TuSimple dataset is that entire lane boundaries are annotated, rather than lane markings. This makes the TuSimple dataset ideal for our needs. The lane boundaries are represented as polylines. In order to avoid clustering via post-processing, it is possible to make use of the loss function presented in [20], that is based on the Kullback-Leibler divergence minimization between the output probability distributions associated to pixels belonging to the same lane boundary instance. Please note that we do not address an unlimited number of possible instances for lane boundaries, as we decided to detect only the ego-lane boundaries, and the ones of the lanes on the sides of the ego-lane. Considering that two boundaries are shared for different lanes, we set a fixed maximum number of detected boundaries to 4. However, directly training the network with [20] ultimately leads to gradient explosion and loss divergence. For this reason, the curriculum learning strategy [21] has been used to achieve convergence. In fact, in a first step a binary cross entropy loss has been used to train the network to distinguish between points belonging to a generic lane boundary and background. The resulting model is fine-tuned using [20] as loss function. The network has been trained using the images in the dataset resized at 512×256 resolution, for 150 epochs. This resolution leaded to satisfying results, while keeping the computational cost low. In order to represent the ground truth data as images, the polylines in the dataset have been projected with a fixed width of 5px on semantic maps of size 512×256. We use the Adam optimizer, with learning rate $5 \cdot 10^{-4}$, and polynomial learning rate decay with exponent set to 0.9.

2.2   Classification

To the best of our knowledge, there are currently no publicly available datasets where entire lane boundaries with class-related information are annotated. For this reason, all the lanes in the TuSimple dataset have been manually classified using 8 different classes: *single white continuous, double white continuous, single yellow continuous, double yellow continuous, dashed, double-dashed, Botts' dots* and *unknown*. The obtained annotations are available online at https://github.com/fabvio/TuSimple-lane-classes.

Associating a class to each lane boundary detected could be addressed in several different ways. One possibility that has been considered in an early stage of the development was branching the instance segmentation network, to perform a pixel-wise classification of lane boundaries with dedicated convolutional layers, then fuse the outputs of the two branches. This approach has been discharged as it is memory intensive, because it requires two decoders in the same network, and it may generate inconsistencies between the detection of the two branches, that should be solved using post-processing algorithms. For example, there could be pixels classified as background from the instance segmentation branch, but classified as lane from the other branch. For this reason, we perform a classification for each lane boundary with another CNN, associating the detected boundaries to the ground truth. A problem with this approach is that each lane boundary is constituted by a different number of points in the input image. For this reason, it is difficult to extract a representation of them that is position-independent w.r.t. the ego vehicle. This may be essential to achieve a correct classification. Thus, we extract a descriptor for each boundary, sampling a fixed number of points from the input image which belong to the detected lane boundary. The points extracted in this way are then ordered following their index in the original image, and arranged in squared images, that are processed by the second neural network. In this way, a spatially normalized compact representation of lane boundaries is obtained, while preserving information given by visual clues such as lane markings. Furthermore, using this approach we are able to perform lane boundary instance segmentation and classification with only two inferences, in an end-to-end fashion. In fact, the descriptors of different lane boundaries detected could be grouped in batches and classified simultaneously. Examples of descriptors are shown in Fig. 2.

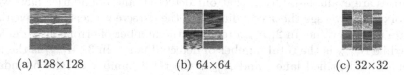

     (a) 128×128   (b) 64×64   (c) 32×32

Fig. 2. Descriptors of different sizes

The architecture we use for this task is derived from H-Net [11]. A detailed description of its structure is given in Fig. 3. We trained this network separately from the first one. To do that, the TuSimple dataset has been processed by the instance segmentation network. Each detected lane boundary is then compared with the ground truth, and it is associated to the corresponding class if the average distance between the detected points and the ground truth is under a threshold. This is needed to filter false positives generated by the first network. In fact, only lane boundaries that are effectively in the training set have a ground truth class, while others detected by the CNN should be excluded. As a result, we obtain a set of $\{descriptor, class\}$ objects that can be used to train the classification neural network. This has been trained with the same hyperparameters of the instance segmentation network. Examples of extracted descriptors are shown in Fig. 2. Code for inference, descriptor extraction and pretrained models are publicly available at https://github.com/fabvio/Cascade-LD.

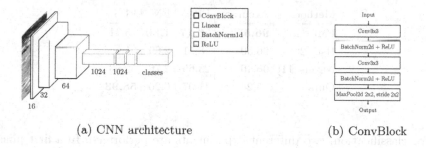

         (a) CNN architecture   (b) ConvBlock

Fig. 3. Classification network. Output channels are listed below each layer.

3 Results

In order to validate our method, we evaluate the performances of both networks separately. For lane boundary instance segmentation, the evaluation formula for the TuSimple benchmark is presented in Eq. 1. In it, C_i and S_i are the number of correctly detected points and ground truth points in image i, respectively. A point is defined as correctly detected if it has a distance w.r.t. a ground truth point under 20 pixels. Additionally, false positive and false negative lane boundaries are evaluated. Given that our detected lane boundaries have width over 1 pixel, we average the x coordinates of the detected pixels for a given row, to obtain a single value. In 2, F_{pred} refers to the number of erroneously detected lanes, while N_{pred} is the total number of detected lanes. In 3, M_{pred} is the total number of unidentified lanes, and N_{gt} is the total number of lane boundaries annotated.

$$accuracy = \frac{\sum_i C_i}{\sum_i S_i} \tag{1}$$

$$FP = \frac{F_{pred}}{N_{pred}} \tag{2}$$

$$FN = \frac{M_{pred}}{N_{gt}} \tag{3}$$

We compare our instance segmentation network with the top-three approaches in the TuSimple benchmark for lane detection. We do not evaluate lanes that are composed than less of three points, in order to filter false positives. Results are presented in Table 1. Inference times are evaluated on 512×256 images. Our network is slightly less accurate than the others. However, taking into account the computational times reduction, we found this tradeoff acceptable.

Table 1. TuSimple Lane detection metrics results and comparison.

Method	Accuracy	FP	FN	FPS
Pan [12]	**96.53**	**6.17**	**1.80**	5.31
Hsu [20]	96.50	8.51	2.69	55.55
Neven [11]	96.40	23.65	2.76	52.63
Ours	95.24	11.97	6.20	**58.93**

For classification, two different experiments are performed. In a first phase, we train the network to distinguish between two different classes: *dashed* and *continuous*. To do that, the *single white continuous, double white continuous, single yellow continuous, double yellow continuous* classes are mapped to the *continuous* class. On the other hand, *dashed, Botts' dots* and *double-dashed* are equally labelled as *dashed*. *Unknown* descriptors are ignored. In this way, it is possible to distinguish between lane boundaries that may or may not be crossed. In the second experiment, we treat the *double-dashed* class as indipendent. Doing this, we could identify also the boundaries of lanes that may be crossed only in specific conditions, as highway entry or exit. An ablation study regarding the descriptor size has been performed. We evaluate classification performances on the validation set, as the test set labels for lane boundaries are not publicly available. Results are reported in Table 2, and qualitative evaluation in Fig. 4. Inference times for the classification network are around 1 ms.

Fig. 4. Qualitative results on the test set. From top to bottom: original image, instance segmentation, classification. For instance segmentation, different colors represent different boundaries. For classification, green represents dashed lanes, yellow double-dashed, red continuous. (Color figure online)

Table 2. Ablation study on descriptor size.

Descriptor size	Acc. (two classes)	Acc. (three classes)
256 × 256	**0.9698**	**0.9600**
128 × 128	0.9596	**0.9600**
64 × 64	0.9519	0.9443
32 × 32	0.9527	0.9436
16 × 16	0.9359	0.9203

As it is visible, it is possible to achieve better performances increasing the descriptor spatial resolution. However, this leads to a major occupation of GPU RAM. On the other hand, our results demonstrate that it is possible to achieve satisfying accuracies with only 256 points.

4 Conclusions

In this work, we presented a novel approach to lane boundary identification and classification in a end-to-end deep learning fashion. With our method, it is possible to achieve high accuracy in both tasks, in real-time. We formalized a descriptor extraction strategy that is useful when it is needed to combine instance segmentation and classification without relying on two-step detection networks. Furthermore, we performed an ablation study on the descriptor size, in order to define the tradeoff between detection accuracy and needed GPU RAM.

References

1. Caltagirone, L., Scheidegger, S., Svensson, L., Wahde, M.: Fast lidar-based road detection using fully convolutional neural networks. In: 2017 IEEE Intelligent Vehicles Symposium (IV) (2017)
2. Bai, M., Mattyus, G., Homayounfar, N., Wang, S., Lakshmikanth, S.K., Urtasun, R.: Deep multi-sensor lane detection. In: 2018 IEEE/RSJ International Conference on Intelligent Robots and Systems (IROS) (2018)
3. Chen, P., Lo, S., Hang, H., Chan, S., Lin, J.: Efficient road lane marking detection with deep learning. CoRR abs/1809.03994 (2018)
4. Tian, Y., et al.: Lane marking detection via deep convolutional neural network. Neurocomputing **280**, 46–55 (2018)
5. Li, J., Mei, X., Prokhorov, D., Tao, D.: Deep neural network for structural prediction and lane detection in traffic scene. IEEE Trans. Neural Netw. Learn. Syst. **28**(3), 690–703 (2017)
6. Lee, S., et al.: VPGNet: vanishing point guided network for lane and road marking detection and recognition. In: ICCV (2017)
7. Zang, J., Zhou, W., Zhang, G., Duan, Z.: Traffic lane detection using fully convolutional neural network. In: APSIPA ASC. IEEE (2018)
8. Ren, S., He, K., Girshick, R., Sun, J.: Faster R-CNN: towards real-time object detection with region proposal networks. In: Advances in NIPS (2015)
9. John, V., Liu, Z., Mita, S., Guo, C., Kidono, K.: Real-time road surface and semantic lane estimation using deep features. Sig. Image Video Process. **12**(6), 1133–1140 (2018). https://doi.org/10.1007/s11760-018-1264-2
10. Long, J., Shelhamer, E., Darrell, T.: Fully convolutional networks for semantic segmentation. In: CVPR, pp. 3431–3440 (2015)
11. Neven, D., De Brabandere, B., Georgoulis, S., Proesmans, M., Van Gool, L.: Towards end-to-end lane detection: an instance segmentation approach. In: 2018 IEEE Intelligent Vehicles Symposium (IV), pp. 286–291. IEEE (2018)
12. Pan, X., Shi, J., Luo, P., Wang, X., Tang, X.: Spatial as deep: Spatial CNN for traffic scene understanding. In: 32nd AAAI Conference on Artificial Intelligence (2018)
13. Zhang, J., Xu, Y., Ni, B., Duan, Z.: Geometric constrained joint lane segmentation and lane boundary detection. In: Ferrari, V., Hebert, M., Sminchisescu, C., Weiss, Y. (eds.) ECCV 2018. LNCS, vol. 11205, pp. 502–518. Springer, Cham (2018). https://doi.org/10.1007/978-3-030-01246-5_30
14. Kim, J., Park, C.: End-to-end ego lane estimation based on sequential transfer learning for self-driving cars. In: Proceedings of the IEEE CVPR Workshops (2017)
15. Chougule, S., Koznek, N., Ismail, A., Adam, G., Narayan, V., Schulze, M.: Reliable multilane detection and classification by utilizing CNN as a regression network: In: Leal-Taixe, L., Roth, S. (eds.) ECCV 2018. LNCS, vol. 11133. Springer, Heidelberg (2018). https://doi.org/10.1007/978-3-030-11021-5_46
16. Ghafoorian, M., Nugteren, C., Baka, N., Booij, O., Hofmann, M.: EL-GAN: embedding loss driven generative adversarial networks for lane detection. In: Leal-Taixé, L., Roth, S. (eds.) ECCV 2018. LNCS, vol. 11129, pp. 256–272. Springer, Cham (2019). https://doi.org/10.1007/978-3-030-11009-3_15
17. Brabandere, B.D., Gansbeke, W.V., Neven, D., Proesmans, M., Gool, L.V.: End-to-end lane detection through differentiable least-squares fitting. CoRR
18. He, K., Gkioxari, G., Dollár, P., Girshick, R.: Mask R-CNN. In: Proceedings of the IEEE International Conference on Computer Vision (2017)

19. Romera, E., Alvarez, J.M., Bergasa, L.M., Arroyo, R.: Erfnet: efficient residual factorized convnet for real-time semantic segmentation. IEEE Trans. ITS **19**, 263–272 (2017)
20. Hsu, Y.C., Xu, Z., Kira, Z., Huang, J.: Learning to cluster for proposal-free instance segmentation, pp. 1–8 (2018)
21. Bengio, Y., Louradour, J., Collobert, R., Weston, J.: Curriculum learning. In: Proceedings of the 26th Annual International Conference on Machine Learning (2009)

CNNs for Fine-Grained Car Model Classification

H. Corrales, D. F. Llorca$^{(\boxtimes)}$, I. Parra, S. Vigre, A. Quintanar, J. Lorenzo,
and N. Hernández

Computer Engineering Department, Universidad de Alcalá, Alcalá de Henares, Spain
{hector.corrales,david.fernandezl,ignacio.parra,susana.vigre,
alvaro.quintanar,javier.lorenzod,noelia.hernandez}@uah.es

Abstract. This paper describes an end-to-end training methodology for CNN-based fine-grained vehicle model classification. The method relies exclusively on images, without using complicated architectures. No extra annotations, pose normalization or part localization are needed. Different full CNN-based models are trained and validated using CompCars [31] dataset, for a total of 431 different car models. We obtained a top-1 validation accuracy of 97.62% which substantially outperforms previous works.

Keywords: Vehicle model · Fine-grained classification · CNNs

1 Introduction

Fine-grained classification of cars, also known as model classification, has a great interest for a considerable number of applications such as traffic regulation, surveillance, tolls automation or parking monitoring. This task can be extremely challenging due to big similarities and subtle differences between related car models, differences that can be easily lost with changes in location, viewpoint or pose. Most of fine-grained classification methods make use of techniques such as pose normalization, part localization [8] and modeling [18] or additional annotations to accomplish this task. As a result complex models are obtained and a large amount of time is spent labelling datasets.

In this paper we propose an end-to-end training methodology for CNN-based fine-grained vehicle model classification (see Fig. 1). Our method relies exclusively on images, without using complicated architectures, extra annotations, pose normalization or part localization. Different full CNN-based models have been trained and validated using CompCars [31] dataset and with our methodology we substantially outperform previous works obtaining a top-1 validation accuracy of 97.62% for a total of 431 different car models.

© Springer Nature Switzerland AG 2020
R. Moreno-Díaz et al. (Eds.): EUROCAST 2019, LNCS 12014, pp. 104–112, 2020.
https://doi.org/10.1007/978-3-030-45096-0_13

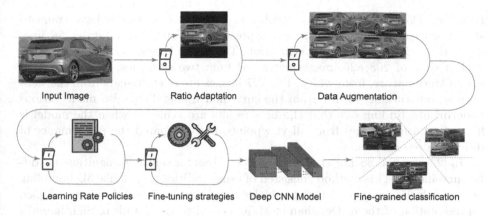

Fig. 1. General overview of the proposed methodology.

2   Related Work

Nowadays, there is a large amount of datasets of fine-grained categories, among which we can find birds [2,27,29], flowers [1,21], dogs [10,16], leaves [14], aircrafts [20,26] and cars [12,31]. Many approaches have been used in order to improve fine-grained classification tasks, like 3D object representations [12], pose normalization [3] or part localization [11,32].

Prior to the popularization of CNNs, classification tasks laid on hand-crafted features such as HOG [5], SIFT [19] or more recent visual word features like [4, 28,30] used together with classifiers like SVM. Thus, in December 2013, Krause et al. [12] proposed a method to extract 3D model based features. Jointly, they presented the ultra fine-grained BMW10 dataset and the cars196 dataset. In [3], Branson et al. proposed an architecture to normalize the pose of birds and extract features using CNNs that will be fed to a SVM classifier. Following this line, Zhang et al. [32] presented a method to semantically localize key parts of objects and extract the features from them. Krause et al. [11] also proposed a method to align the images through segmentation to extract the pose without part annotations, making the training process easier.

In [18], Llorca et al. presented a vehicle model recognition approach by modeling the geometry and appearance of car emblems from rear view images using a linear SVM classifier with HOG features. Classification is performed within the set of models of each car manufacturer, which is previously recognized by means of logo classification [17]. Lin et al. [15], instead of manually defining the parts of the objects from which the features will be extracted, used bilinear networks to automatically extract the features with two twin CNNs and multiplex its outputs to feed them to a SVM. In [8], Fang et al. developed a coarse-to-fine method in which they automatically detect discriminative regions and extract features to feed them to a one-versus-all SVM.

Since the appearance of AlexNet [13] in 2012 the use of CNNs has growth considerably. The appearance of other architectures like VGG [22], GoogLeNet/

Inception [25] or ResNet [9] as evolution confirms that CNNs have come to stay. For example, in [31], Yang et al. presented CompCars, a dataset for fine-grained car classification and verification. This is the largest car dataset to date, with a total of 208, 826 images extracted from two scenarios, web-nature and surveillance-nature, from which, 136, 727 images are of entire cars from the web-nature scenario and 44, 481 from the surveillance one. They also made various experiments, finding out that the best results are achieved when the model is fine-tuned using images from all viewpoints, and compared the performance of different deep models.

In [23] and [24] Sochor et al. proposed a system for vehicle recognition on traffic surveillance. This method consisted of using additional data like 3D bounding box of vehicles, with which the vehicles are "unpacked" to obtain an aligned representation of them. Dehghan et al. [6] described the details of Sighthound's vehicle make, model and color recognition system. As this is a private commercial solution they didn't showed the full system, but they tested it in multiple datasets like CompCars, which can be used for performance comparison purposes.

3   System Description and Results

As we have previously introduced we are going to use CompCars dataset. Specifically a subset of 431 different car models with a total of 52 083 images, 36 456 for training and 15 627 for validation.

In order to carry out the different experiments and compare their results, a basic architecture will be used on which modifications will be made. This basic architecture is an Imagenet [7] pretrained ResNet50 model fine-tuned for 50 epochs with a constant learning rate of 0.001 for all layers. The loss function used is cross entropy and stochastic gradient descent with 0.9 momentum as optimizer.

We have tried a variety of modifications over the data (data-augmentation), different models (ResNet50, ResNet101 and InceptionV3) and different fine-tuning approaches and learning rate policies.

The top-1 and top-5 validation accuracy achieved with this base configuration is 88.49% and 97.45%.

3.1   Ratio Adaptation

CompCars images come in a variety of sizes and aspect ratios. One problem of fully connected classification CNNs is that input images have to be of a given size (224 × 224 pixels for ResNet and 299 × 299 pixels for Inception). So, to feed these images into the CNN we need to resize them to fit the expected sizes. The problem is that all images that do not have a 1:1 aspect ratio will be deformed in the resizing process.

This could be an obstacle to the network learning. To discern if this is the case, we have developed an experiment: in the process of training each image is padded with two vertical or horizontal bands to adapt its ratio and prevent the deformation. An example of this operation can be seen in Fig. 2(b).

We found that the top-1 accuracy drops from 88.49% to 82.12% when the ratio is adapted. This is a 6.37% loss in accuracy. This could be explained by the fact that the net is losing generalization capacity because of the vertical/horizontal bands that are being introduced in the images provoking a reduction in the area with relevant information.

Moreover, even if the images are deformed, the network has the ability to learn and interpret the content. So, the ratio adaptation technique has been discarded.

3.2 Data-Augmentation

Data augmentation its a common tool used in deep learning to artificially increment datasets. Its use is compulsory when available data is limited as it helps to fight overfitting. Although in our case the dataset that we are going to use has a huge amount of images, we can get benefit from data augmentation. To do so, we have implemented the following data augmentation operations:

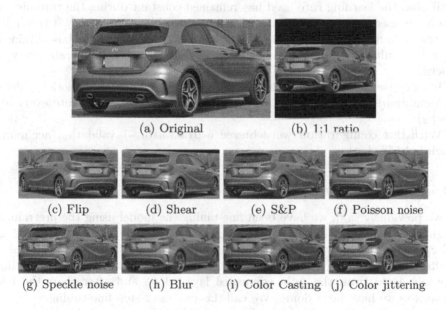

(a) Original   (b) 1:1 ratio

(c) Flip   (d) Shear   (e) S&P   (f) Poisson noise

(g) Speckle noise   (h) Blur   (i) Color Casting   (j) Color jittering

Fig. 2. Data augmentation and ratio adaptation examples

- *Horizontal Flip*: an horizontal flip (over y axis) with a probability of 50% is performed over the image.
- *Salt and Pepper*: each pixel of the image is set to 0 or 255 with a probability of 2%.

- *Poisson noise.*
- *Speckle noise.*
- *Bluring*: gaussian blur operation is performed over the image with a random kernel size between 3 and 11 and standard deviation of 6.
- *Color Casting.*
- *Color Jittering*: the image is converted to HSV color space and saturation and value are independently randomly modified.

An example of the previous described data augmentation operations can be seen in Fig. 2.

The process of data augmentation is as follows: in first place an horizontal flip its applied over the image, then, one of the other operations is randomly selected. This data augmentation process is computed online for each batch, therefore, all the images are slightly different in each epoch.

With this configuration we achieved a 95.48% top-1 validation accuracy, which is an improvement of 6.99% over the base model.

3.3 Learning Rate Policies

Until now, the learning rate used has remained constant during the training. A commonly used tool is to implement learning rate policies to modify it throughout the training. Of all those that have been tested, the one that has obtained the best results is the stepped one. This is, reduce the learning rate every n epochs.

In our case, we have added to the previous best model (base model + data augmentation) a 10-step policy rate (divide by 10 the learning rate every 10 epochs).

With this configuration we achieved a 97.03% top-1 validation accuracy, which is 1.55% better.

3.4 Fine-Tuning Process

As we previously said, we have been fine-tuning the model using the pretrained weights on Imagenet. As we have changed the last fully connected layers in order to adapt the network, this weights are randomly initialized, so, they have a difference in training compared with the rest of the network. An interesting approach is to train the fully connected layer alone and after that, the full network as we have been doing. We call this process 2-step fine-tuning.

After having tried multiple combinations of learning rate policies with 2-step fine-tuning the best results have been obtained when using constant learning rate in the fully connected training and 10-step in the full training.

With this configuration we achieved a 97.16% top-1 validation accuracy.

3.5   Other Models

So far Resnet50 has been used as the base model. In orther to achieve best results we have tried deeper models as Resnet101 and InceptionV3. After multiple trainings and configurations the best results for each model have been achieved with the 2-step fine-tuning process for both of them and constant+10-step learning rate policy in the case of Resnet101 and 10-step for InveptionV3.

With this configuration we achieved a 97.59% and 97.62% top-1 validation accuracy for Resnet101 and InceptionV3 respectively.

The best result was obtained with InceptionV3 with a top-1 validation accuracy of 97.62%.

A comparison of the different models can be seen in Table 1. Figure 3 shows some examples of the classification results with validation images.

Table 1. Results of the different configurations.

Model	Ratio/data-augmentation	Fine-tuning	Lr policy	Top-1/5 validation accuracy (%)
ResNet50 (base model)	✗/✗	Full	Constant	88.49/97.45
ResNet50	✓/✗	Full	Constant	82.12/92.21
ResNet50	✗/✓	Full	Constant	95.48/99.26
ResNet50	✗/✓	Full	Step-10	97.03/99.62
ResNet50	✗/✓	2-step	Constant+10-step	97.16/99.60
ResNet101	✗/✓	2-step	Constant+10-step	97.59/99.68
InceptionV3	✗/✓	2-step	Step-10	**97.62/99.64**
Yang et al. (CompCars)	–	–	–	91.20/98.10
Sighthound	–	–	–	95.88/99.53

Fig. 3. Fine-grained classification results. Three correct classifications (left) and one error (right).

4   Conclusions and Future Works

In this paper we have described an end-to-end training methodology for CNN-based fine-grained vehicle model classification. Compared to other methods, our proposal relies exclusively on images, without using complicated architectures or high time demanding datasets (pose normalization, part localization, extra info, etc.).

Data augmentation has been found to significantly improve performance, even with a large dataset. The use of 2-step fine-tuning and adaptive learning rate allows the system to reach the best results and by combining it with data augmentation we achieve 97.62% top-1 accuracy which outperform previous models like the one proposed by Yang et al. [31] or the private commercial solution from Sighthound [6].

As future work we have identified two promising lines. The first one is to adapt the system to track and reidentify vehicles in complex traffic scenes, which has a great potential in traffic surveillance. The second one is a classification reinforcement method based on pose and structural modeling in orther to achieve better results with an even wider variety of car models.

Acknowledgments. This work was supported in part by the Spanish Ministry of Science, Innovation and Universities under Research Grant DPI2017-90035-R, in part by the Community Region of Madrid (Spain) under Research Grant S2018/EMT-4362 and in part by the Electronic Component Systems for European Leadership Joint Undertaking through the European Union's H2020 Research and Innovation Program and Germany, Austria, Spain, Italy, Latvia, Belgium, The Netherlands, Sweden, Finland, Lithuania, Czech Republic, Romania and Norway, under Grant 73746.

References

1. Angelova, A., Zhu, S., Lin, Y.: Image segmentation for large-scale subcategory flower recognition. In: 2013 IEEE Workshop on Applications of Computer Vision (WACV), pp. 39–45, January 2013
2. Berg, T., Liu, J., Woo Lee, S., Alexander, M.L., Jacobs, D.W., Belhumeur, P.N.: Birdsnap: large-scale fine-grained visual categorization of birds. In: Proceedings of the IEEE Conference on Computer Vision and Pattern Recognition, pp. 2011–2018 (2014)
3. Branson, S., Van Horn, G., Belongie, S., Perona, P.: Bird species categorization using pose normalized deep convolutional nets. BMVC 2014 - Proceedings of the British Machine Vision Conference 2014 (2014)
4. Csurka, G., Dance, C., Fan, L., Willamowski, J., Bray, C.: Visual categorization with bags of keypoints. In: Workshop on Statistical Learning in Computer Vision. ECCV, pp. 1–22 (2004)
5. Dalal, N., Triggs, B.: Histograms of oriented gradients for human detection. In: 2005 IEEE Computer Society Conference on Computer Vision and Pattern Recognition (CVPR), vol. 1, pp. 886–893 (2005)
6. Dehghan, A., Masood, S.Z., Shu, G., Ortiz, E.G.: View independent vehicle make, model and color recognition using convolutional neural network. CoRR abs/1702.01721 (2017)
7. Deng, J., Dong, W., Socher, R., Li, L., Li, K., Fei-Fei, L.: Imagenet: a large-scale hierarchical image database. In: 2009 IEEE Conference on Computer Vision and Pattern Recognition (CVPR), pp. 248–255 (2009)
8. Fang, J., Zhou, Y., Yu, Y., Du, S.: Fine-grained vehicle model recognition using a coarse-to-fine convolutional neural network architecture. IEEE Trans. Intell. Transp. Syst. **18**(7), 1782–1792 (2017)

9. He, K., Zhang, X., Ren, S., Sun, J.: Deep residual learning for image recognition. In: 2016 IEEE Conference on Computer Vision and Pattern Recognition (CVPR), pp. 770–778 (2016)
10. Khosla, A., Jayadevaprakash, N., Yao, B., Fei-Fei, L.: Novel dataset for fine-grained image categorization. In: First Workshop on Fine-Grained Visual Categorization, IEEE Conference on Computer Vision and Pattern Recognition (2011)
11. Krause, J., Jin, H., Yang, J., Fei-Fei, L.: Fine-grained recognition without part annotations. In: 2015 IEEE Conference on Computer Vision and Pattern Recognition (CVPR), pp. 5546–5555 (2015)
12. Krause, J., Stark, M., Deng, J., Fei-Fei, L.: 3D object representations for fine-grained categorization. In: The IEEE International Conference on Computer Vision (ICCV) Workshops, pp. 554–561 (2013)
13. Krizhevsky, A., Sutskever, I., Hinton, G.E.: Imagenet classification with deep convolutional neural networks. In: Advances in Neural Information Processing Systems 25, pp. 1097–1105. Curran Associates, Inc. (2012)
14. Kumar, N., et al.: Leafsnap: a computer vision system for automatic plant species identification. In: Fitzgibbon, A., Lazebnik, S., Perona, P., Sato, Y., Schmid, C. (eds.) ECCV 2012. LNCS, vol. 7573, pp. 502–516. Springer, Heidelberg (2012). https://doi.org/10.1007/978-3-642-33709-3_36
15. Lin, T.Y., RoyChowdhury, A., Maji, S.: Bilinear CNN models for fine-grained visual recognition. In: 2015 IEEE International Conference on Computer Vision (ICCV), pp. 1449–1457 (2015)
16. Liu, J., Kanazawa, A., Jacobs, D., Belhumeur, P.: Dog breed classification using part localization. In: Fitzgibbon, A., Lazebnik, S., Perona, P., Sato, Y., Schmid, C. (eds.) ECCV 2012. LNCS, vol. 7572, pp. 172–185. Springer, Heidelberg (2012). https://doi.org/10.1007/978-3-642-33718-5_13
17. Llorca, D.F., Arroyo, R., Sotelo, M.: Vehicle logo recognition in traffic images using HOG and SVM. In: 16th International IEEE Conference on Intelligent Transportation Systems (ITSC), pp. 2229–2234 (2013)
18. Llorca, D.F., Colás, D., Daza, I.G., Parra, I., Sotelo, M.: Vehicle model recognition using geometry and appearance of car emblems from rear view images. In: 17th International IEEE Conference on Intelligent Transportation Systems (ITSC), pp. 3094–3099 (2014)
19. Lowe, D.G.: Distinctive image features from scale-invariant keypoints. Int. J. Comput. Vis. **60**(2), 91–110 (2004)
20. Maji, S., Rahtu, E., Kannala, J., Blaschko, M.B., Vedaldi, A.: Fine-grained visual classification of aircraft. CoRR abs/1306.5151 (2013)
21. Nilsback, M.E., Zisserman, A.: A visual vocabulary for flower classification. In: 2006 IEEE Computer Society Conference on Computer Vision and Pattern Recognition (CVPR), vol. 2, pp. 1447–1454. IEEE (2006)
22. Simonyan, K., Zisserman, A.: Very deep convolutional networks for large-scale image recognition. CoRR abs/1409.1556 (2015)
23. Sochor, J., Herout, A., Havel, J.: Boxcars: 3D boxes as CNN input for improved fine-grained vehicle recognition. In: 2016 IEEE Conference on Computer Vision and Pattern Recognition (CVPR), pp. 3006–3015 (2016)
24. Sochor, J., Spanhel, J., Herout, A.: Boxcars: improving fine-grained recognition of vehicles using 3-D bounding boxes in traffic surveillance. IEEE Trans. Intell. Transp. Syst. **20**, 97–108 (2019)
25. Szegedy, C., et al.: Going deeper with convolutions. In: 2015 IEEE Conference on Computer Vision and Pattern Recognition (CVPR), pp. 1–9 (2015)

26. Vedaldi, A., et al.: Understanding objects in detail with fine-grained attributes. In: Proceedings of the IEEE Conference on Computer Vision and Pattern Recognition, pp. 3622–3629 (2014)
27. Wah, C., Branson, S., Welinder, P., Perona, P., Belongie, S.: The caltech-UCSD birds-200-2011 dataset (2011)
28. Wang, J., Yang, J., Yu, K., Lv, F., Huang, T., Gong, Y.: Locality-constrained linear coding for image classification. In: 2010 IEEE Conference on Computer Vision and Pattern Recognition (CVPR), pp. 3360–3367 (2010)
29. Welinder, P., et al.: Caltech-UCSD birds 200 (2010)
30. Yang, J., Yu, K., Gong, Y., Huang, T.: Linear spatial pyramid matching using sparse coding for image classification. In: 2009 IEEE Conference on Computer Vision and Pattern Recognition (CVPR), pp. 1794–1801 (2009)
31. Yang, L., Luo, P., Change Loy, C., Tang, X.: A large-scale car dataset for fine-grained categorization and verification. In: Proceedings of the IEEE Conference on Computer Vision and Pattern Recognition, pp. 3973–3981 (2015)
32. Zhang, N., Donahue, J., Girshick, R., Darrell, T.: Part-based R-CNNs for fine-grained category detection. In: Fleet, D., Pajdla, T., Schiele, B., Tuytelaars, T. (eds.) ECCV 2014. LNCS, vol. 8689, pp. 834–849. Springer, Cham (2014). https://doi.org/10.1007/978-3-319-10590-1_54

License Plate Corners Localization Using CNN-Based Regression

D. F. Llorca[✉], H. Corrales, I. Parra, M. Rentero, R. Izquierdo,
A. Hernández-Saz, and I. García-Daza

Computer Engineering Department, University of Alcalá, Alcalá de Henares, Spain
{david.fernandezl,hector.corrales,ignacio.parra}@uah.es

Abstract. In this work, we tackle the problem of vehicle license plate localization in traffic images. Rather than modeling the appearance of the license plate, we propose to model the appearance of the corners of the license plate. Inspired by recent advances in human pose estimation, a CNN-based model trained to perform numerical regression is used to infer the location of the four corners that define the limits of the license plate. Coordinate regression is applied by means of Differentiable Spatial to Numerical Transform (DSNT) layer [1]. Preliminary results showed an average localization error of 0.3244 pixels which clearly supports the proposed methodology.

Keywords: License plate detection · CNNs · Numerical coordinate regression · DSNT

1 Introduction

Car license plate detection analyses an image to provide potential license plate bounding boxes. It is the first stage of most of the license plate recognition systems. License plate detection can be seen as a fast generic car detector since the license plate is always linked with a car. In addition, since the real dimensions of the license plate are known a priori, accurate license plate localization can be also used to accurately estimate the relative distance and speed of the surrounding vehicles [2].

Automatic car license plate localization has been studied over the last two decades [11]. Most of the existing approaches are focused on learning the appearance of the license plate using hand-crafted features such as gradients [6], color [12] or texture [13], and a classifier such as Adaboost or SVM. Other works pose the problem as a character detection task [8]. However, accurate license plate localization in the wild from arbitrary viewpoints, with partial occlusions and multiple instances remains as a challenging problem. Challenging scenarios have been considered (such as multi-directional license plate localization) using traditional methods [14] but with limited performance.

Recent works addressed the license plate detection problem using deep convolutional neural networks (CNNs), making use of the features extracted by the

© Springer Nature Switzerland AG 2020
R. Moreno-Díaz et al. (Eds.): EUROCAST 2019, LNCS 12014, pp. 113–120, 2020.
https://doi.org/10.1007/978-3-030-45096-0_14

Fig. 1. Change of paradigm: modeling the local appearance of the corners of the license plate instead of modeling the appearance of the whole license plate.

CNN instead of hand-engineered features of traditional methods, in an end-to-end learning fashion. Thus, in [3] a CNN-based approach is proposed to detect all characters in an image, and a second CNN classifier is used to remove false positives. In order to deal with highly rotated images, in [7], a CNN-based MD-YOLO framework is used to perform regression over the rotation angle. Still, previous approaches are prone to errors when extreme viewpoints or occlusions are present, and they have to be adapted to the appearance of each type of license plate depending on the country.

In this paper, we tackle the license plate localization problem as a keypoint detection problem, modeling the appearance of the four external corners (see Fig. 1) using a CNN-model adapted to perform coordinate regression by adding a differentiable spatial to numerical transform (DSNT) layer as proposed in [1] for human pose estimation. The main advantages are the simplicity of the method, which does neither require complex architectures nor big datasets, its potential to deal with highly rotated images and occlusions, and its feasibility to deal with license plates from different countries (different appearances, type of characters, etc.).

2   System Description

2.1   System Architecture

A ResNet50 [4] model pre-trained with Imagenet [5] dataset is used. The last two layers (average pooling and fully connected) are removed and a DSNT layer is attached instead of the last 2 layers. As suggested in [1], the DSNT layer allows a fully differentiable and spatially generalizable coordinate regression architecture with no trainable parameters. We manage the assumption that only one license plate is relevant at each iteration (the closest one), so the number of keypoints is four, representing the upper-left, upper-right, lower-right and lower-left corners of the license plate.

The DSNT layer is composed of two $m \times n$ matrices X and Y per each point to be detected (four points in this case), defined as follows:

$$X_{i,j} = (2j - (n+1))/n \qquad (1)$$

Fig. 2. Examples of the images contained in the dataset for training and validation (labeled).

$$Y_{i,j} = (2i - (m+1))/m \tag{2}$$

Then, the computation performed at this stage is given by:

$$DSNT(\hat{Z}) = \left[\left\langle \hat{Z}, X \right\rangle_F, \left\langle \hat{Z}, Y \right\rangle_F \right] \tag{3}$$

being F the Frobenius inner product of real values (scalar dot product of vectorized matrices) and $\hat{Z}$ the normalized heatmaps given by the CNN model using the L^1 norm.

Since the DSNT layer computes numerical coordinates, it is possible to use the 2D Euclidean distance as the loss function. The main advantage is that we directly optimize the distance between the predicted locations and the actual ones.

Other approaches to deal with numerical coordinate regression are the so-called heatmap matching, where a loss is directly applied to output heatmaps and synthetic heatmaps generated by rendering a 2D Gaussian center on the ground truth coordinates, or by adding a fully connected layer (with trainable weights) which produces numerical coordinates.

2.2 Dataset and Training

A specific dataset was created using images of different vehicles approaching a parking entry (see Fig. 2). A total of 557 images were manually labeled to generate the ground truth of the four license plate corners for each image. The input images size is 640 × 480 pixels.

Although the DSNT layer does not contain trainable parameters, the whole architecture (ResNet50+DSNT) is fine-tuned for training and validation using the dataset. An independent qualitative test is applied using non-labeled images from different camera points of view (see Fig. 3).

As suggested by [1], to force the heatmaps to resemble a 2D Gaussian, it is possible to minimize the divergence between the generated heatmap and an appropriate target normal distribution (similar to heatmap matching). A specific regularization term is introduced in the DSNT loss function using the Jensen-Shannon divergence.

Fig. 3. Examples of the images contained in the dataset for an independent qualitative test (non-labeled).

Table 1. Heatmap size depending on the number of dilated convolutions (input images 640×480) and corresponding batch size.

# dilated conv.	Heatmap size	Batch size
0	20×15	18
1	40×30	15
2	80×60	8
3	160×120	2

The standard heatmap size before the DSNT layer for the standard ResNet50 model is 20×15 pixels for input images of size 640×480. We find that higher heatmap resolutions increases the localization accuracy. In order to increase its size, the stride and dilation factors of last and second-to-last layers of the ResNet50 model can be adapted [9]. Depending on the number of dilated convolutions we can have different heatmap size, as described in Table 1. The costs of increasing the number of dilated convolutions are higher memory requirements and higher training time. The batch size has to be reduced as long as we increase the size of the heatmaps.

3   Results

We split our labeled dataset in 389 images for training and 168 images for validation (70/30). The initial learning rate was set to 10^{-4}, and the number of epochs defined to 50. The learning rate was reduced by a factor of 10 at epochs 20 and 40 (an epoch is considered as one complete pass over the training set). The different models were optimez with RMSProp [10]. A Maxwell-architecture NVIDIA Titan X GPU was used to perform the fine-tuning learning process.

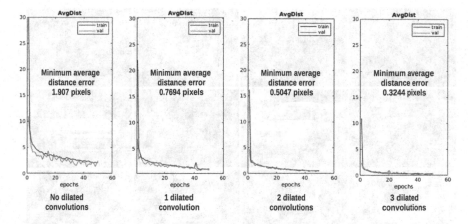

Fig. 4. Average distance training error evolution and minimum value depending on the number of dilated convolutions.

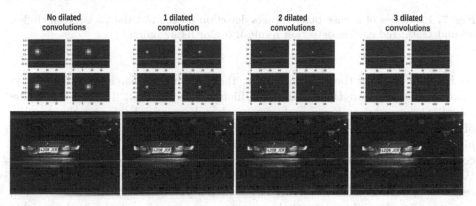

Fig. 5. Heatmaps resolution and accuracy depending on the number of dilated convolutions. Upper row: heatmaps for the four corners. Lower row: license plate corner detection results.

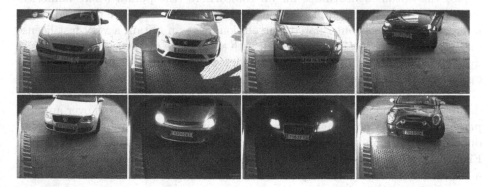

Fig. 6. Examples of license plate corners detection on the validation data set (green circles: ground truth; red circles: detection results). (Color figure online)

Fig. 7. Examples of license plate corners detection on the test data set (green circles: ground truth; red circles: detection results). (Color figure online)

Figure 4 depicts the training error, that is, the 2D Euclidean distance in pixels, depending on the number of dilated convolutions. The average value for all the corners is computed. As can be observed, the larger the number of dilated convolutions (or heatmap size), the better the accuracy of the license plate corners localization. Best results are obtained when applying 3 dilated convolutions, which provides a minimum average distance error of 0.3244 pixels. We have tested the use of fully connected layer to deal with numerical coordinates regression, with localization errors larger than 2 pixels. The moderate number of samples of the training dataset does not seem appropriate to learn the weights of the fully connected layer.

The effect of the dilated convolutions can be seen in Fig. 5. The upper row depict the obtained heatmaps for all the corners (the points where numerical coordinate regression is applied). The final detected corners are depicted in the lower row. Even without dilated convolutions we can obtain a very fast license plate (generic car) localization system with an average distance error lower than 2 pixels, which may be more than enough for performing further steps such as optical character recognition.

Figure 6 depicts some examples of the detection results from the validation dataset. The proposed approach has been also qualitatively tested over an independent dataset with images recorded with different cameras (traffic cameras, onboard forward and rear looking cameras, etc.). Some examples can be seen in Fig. 7. We can observed that the model has generalized appropriately, even with a low number of training samples.

4 Conclusions and Future Works

In this paper we have proposed a new paradigm to deal with license plate localization. We tackle this problem as a pose detection problem, learning the appearance of the four external corners of the license plate, instead of learning its whole appearance. This solution offers a more general approach more robust to occlusions and extreme viewpoints. The use of DSNT layers proved to be an efficient approach to deal with numerical coordinate regression. An average localization error of 0.3244 pixel was obtained when applying four dilated convolutions of the ResNet50 model.

As future works, we plan to improve the learning process and the experimental validation using a larger dataset, allowing its comparison with other data-dependent approaches. In addition, we plan to extend the proposed methodology to deal with vehicle pose estimation.

Acknowledgments. This work was supported in part by the Spanish Ministry of Science, Innovation and Universities under Research Grant DPI2017-90035-R, in part by the Community Region of Madrid (Spain) under Research Grant S2018/EMT-4362 and in part by the Electronic Component Systems for European Leadership Joint Undertaking through the European Union's H2020 Research and Innovation Program and Germany, Austria, Spain, Italy, Latvia, Belgium, The Netherlands, Sweden, Finland, Lithuania, Czech Republic, Romania, and Norway, under Grant 73746.

References

1. Nibali, A., He, Z., Morgan, S., Prendergast, L.: Numerical Coordinate Regression with Convolutional Neural Networks. CoRR, vol. abs/1801.07372 (2018)
2. Llorca, D.F., et al.: Two-camera based accurate vehicle speed measurement using average speed at a fixed point. In: IEEE 10th International Conference on Intelligent Transportation Systems (2016)
3. Li, H., Shen, C.: Reading Car License Plates Using Deep Convolutional Neural Networks and LSTMs. CoRR, vol. abs/1601.05610 (2016)
4. He, K., Zhang, X., Ren, S., Sun, J.: Deep Residual Learning for Image Recognition. CoRR, vol. abs/1512.03385 (2015)
5. Deng, J., Dong, W., Socher, R., Li, L.-J., Li, K., Fei-Fei, L.: ImageNet: a large-scale hierarchical image database. In: CVPR 2009 (2009)
6. Muhammad, J., Altun, H.: Improved license plate detection using HOG-based features and genetic algorithm. In: 24th Signal Processing and Communication Application Conference (2016)
7. Xie, L., Ahmad, T., Jin, L., Liu, Y., Zhang, S.: A new CNN-based method for multi-directionalcar license plate detection. IEEE Trans. Intell. Transp. Syst. **19**(2), 507–517 (2018)
8. Hamandi, L., Almustafa, K., Zantout, R., Obeid, H.: Using character recognition for plate localization. Int. J. Multimedia Appl. **4**(5), 39–50 (2012)
9. Yu, F., Koltun, V.: Multi-scale context aggregation by dilated convolutions. In: ICLR (2016)
10. Tieleman, T., Hinton, G.: Lecture 6.5-rmsprop: divide the gradient by a running average of its recent magnitude. COURSERA: Neural Netw. Mach. Learn. **4**(2), 26–31 (2012)

11. Anagnostopoulos, C.-N.E., Anagnostopoulos, I.E., Psoroulas, I.D., Loumos, V., Kayafas, E.: License plate recognition from still images and video sequences: a survey. IEEE Trans. Intell. Transp. Syst. **9**(3), 337–391 (2008)
12. Deb, K., Jo, K-H.: HSI color based vehicle license plate detection. In: International Conference on Control, Automation and Systems, pp. 687–691 (2008)
13. Rabee, A., Barhum, I.: License plate detection and recognition in complex scenes using mathematical morphology and support vector machines. In: 21st International Conference on Systems, Signals and Image Processing, pp. 59–62 (2014)
14. Hsu, G.-S., Chen, J.-C., Chung, Y.-Z.: Application-oriented license plate recognition. IEEE Trans. Veh. Technol. **62**(2), 552–561 (2013)

Analysis on Pedestrian Green Time Period: Preliminary Findings from a Case Study

Mehmet Ali Silgu[1,2(✉)], Gorkem Akyol[1], and Hilmi Berk Celikoglu[1]

[1] ITS Research Lab, Faculty of Civil Engineering, Technical University of Istanbul (ITU), Ayazaga Campus, 34469 Istanbul, Turkey
{msilgu,akyolgo,celikoglu}@itu.edu.tr, masilgu@bartin.edu.tr
[2] Faculty of Engineering, Department of Civil Engineering, Bartin University, 74100 Bartin, Turkey

Abstract. In the present study, we concentrate on the problem of optimization and the usage of green times for pedestrian traffic at crosswalks. We conduct a simulation based study that is calibrated with the field data collected. We propose a frame for the signal controllers in an adaptive fashion. Result from micro-simulation strengthens the finding that a trade-off between the pedestrian travel times and vehicles' delays has to be made.

Keywords: Pedestrian traffic · Adaptive traffic control · Micro-simulation · Smart mobility

1 Introduction

In the present paper, we focus on the cycle time optimization for successive traffic signals in one of the centers in the polycentric form of the City of Istanbul, Turkey, where the peak hour congestion has been extensively studied dominantly on urban freeways including [1–5] and rarely on interrupted urban road flows including [6, 7]. The case area, for which the analyses are conducted for, suffers from heavy congestion in the whole daily traffic due to the facts that the area accommodates several attractive functions the pedestrianized area is both bounded and divided by vehicular arterials. For the purpose of fully understanding the problem and deriving control measures, as well as collecting calibration data, data from two cameras mounted for the acquisition of pedestrian traffic scene is utilized. Processing the data followed by the simulation is done using VISSIM and VISWALK. The pedestrian specific simulation program, VISWALK, uses Helbing's Social Force Model [8] at both microscopic and mesoscopic scale, where the vehicular simulation is done adopting Wiedemann's car following model [9]. In order to optimize the system composed of vehicular and pedestrian conflicting movements in terms of adaptive signaling, coordination of the two successive signals is sought. When the approaching pedestrians' flow reaches to a critical volume, the related signal controller is actuated to adjust the pedestrian green time considering as well the vehicular traffic's volume information from the successive traffic lights to prevent vehicular congestion in

© Springer Nature Switzerland AG 2020
R. Moreno-Díaz et al. (Eds.): EUROCAST 2019, LNCS 12014, pp. 121–128, 2020.
https://doi.org/10.1007/978-3-030-45096-0_15

cases with low demands of pedestrian traffic. To obtain vehicle presence data, detectors are placed at the upstream of the intersections in the simulation environment.

In the following section, we summarize the relevant literature. Section 3 describes the methodology for the system we propose, case area's characteristics, and the simulation setup. In Sect. 4, results of the simulation trials and comparison between the current control strategy and the proposed system is given. Section 5 concludes the paper with remarks and future research topics.

2   Literature Review

Relevant literature on adaptive signal control and pedestrian green time optimization are summarized in this chapter. We take advantage from the extensive review on the literature for the theory behind pedestrian dynamics [10, 11] and models used for coupled car traffic and pedestrian flow [12]. We divide our literature review into four parts. Firstly, the effects of the bi-directional flow at the signalized intersections are explained. Secondly, different delay models are presented. Effects of pedestrians' crossing speed and estimation methods for pedestrians' average speed are given next. Finally, signal optimization methods for mixed traffic conditions are described.

2.1   Bi-directional Flow

Effects of the bi-directional flow at the crosswalks are studied by many researchers. Relationship between pedestrian speed and flow is examined in [13]. In [13], it is found that bi-directional flow can reduce the average crossing speed of pedestrians and thus, decrease in the efficient capacity can occur. The capacity of signalized crosswalks for different scenarios is examined in [14]. Several pedestrian compositions are tested in order to estimate the capacity and maximum reduction in capacity occurred when 50% directional split from both sides of the crosswalk. In [15], a Cellular Automata model is proposed to investigate the effects of the bi-directional flow. Three different bi-directional pedestrian flow is defined in [15]: divided directional flows; intersped flow and dynamic multi-lane flow.

2.2   Delay Models

Determination of pedestrian delay is attracting attention for researchers since there is generally high pedestrian demand in central business districts. A new model for estimating pedestrian delays is proposed in [16]. An experiment is conducted in two parts: first by observing one crosswalk with dividing its cycle length into 13 subphases, and second by examining 13 crosswalks by dividing the cycle times into 2 parts, i.e., green and non-green phases. The model proposed in [16] showed that pedestrians can experience delay even if their arrival is at the green phase for them. Another pedestrian delay model is presented in [17]. Three different delay types are chosen for comparison with existing delay models in [17]: waiting delay, crossing delay, and conflict delay. A case area study is conducted in China for evaluating different conflict scenarios between pedestrians and vehicular traffic at the crosswalks [18]. The model proposed in [18] showed that pedestrian detour is the main part of the pedestrian delay at the intersections. Different crosswalk attributes are simulated in VISSIM for the proposed model in [18].

2.3 Pedestrian Speed

Pedestrians' speed is an important indicator for assessing intersection safety and efficiency. Minimum green time for pedestrians is determined by either the average speed or 15th percentile speed of pedestrians. A study is conducted in Qatar [19] to investigate pedestrians' speed at signalized intersections. Three different speeds types at the intersections are defined (entry, crossing, exit) and measurements are taken at different phases such Pedestrian Green (PG), Pedestrian Flashing Green (PFG), and Red (R). In [19], main parameter that affects crossing speed is found to be crossing speed. Another case study for determining crossing speed in safety margins is done in [20]. Different parameters are defined to perform an evaluation for pedestrian speed. These parameters are age, gender, items carrying and group size. Most important founding of [20] is that the average design speed for crosswalks should be at most 1.3 m/s even through recommended design speed for pedestrians at signalized intersections is set to 1.4 m/s in Turkish Standards Institution [21]. To analyze pedestrian flow characteristics on different walking facilities, a field survey is conducted in Hong Kong [22]. Signalized crosswalks that have raised midblock have higher pedestrian speeds because midblocks helps pedestrians to analyze traffic conditions by standing on them.

2.4 Signal Optimization

Different signal optimization methods are presented for many decades in order to compensate stochastic nature of traffic demand. A convex programming method at signalized intersection is proposed in [23] for reducing delays for both vehicles and pedestrians. By using quadratic programming, it is shown that global optima can be found for pedestrian vehicle mixed objective function. In [24], coordination of signal controllers is formulated with mixed-integer-linear-programming. Proposed model is done by maximum green bandwidth model with offset calculation. While pedestrian delays increased slightly with presented model in [24], delay for vehicles is significantly reduced. A hybrid system is presented in [25] that considering both the coordination of signal controllers and signal priority. Vehicle to Infrastructure communication technology is used with the assumption for both pedestrians and vehicles. The model proposed in [25] is achieved 24.9% reduction in bus delays and 14% reduction in pedestrian delay.

Having been initiated with our study on pedestrian-friendly optimization of traffic signals using pedestrian [26, 27] and vehicular [28] motion models in SUMO [6], the novel contribution of our present study is prioritizing pedestrians in the signalized intersections with an adaptive fashion using VISSIM and VISWALK. Our main aim is to reduce pedestrian travel times in the network while satisfying the vehicular traffic demand by providing sufficient green times.

3 Methodology and Case Study

In order to achieve adaptive signal control at signalized intersections, VISual Vehicle Actuated Programming (VISVAP) – an add-on module from VISSIM– is adapted in our case. Using VISVAP, we create an actuation flow-chart for the controllers we propose. Details of the signal controller design is given in the following.

3.1 Signal Controller Design

We have developed an actuation program with VISVAP. Flow-chart for what the program executes is shown in Fig. 1. Actuation process is working in the following order: Firstly, the main timer is started at zero. If a pedestrian is detected at the curb and main timer passes a threshold value, the pedestrian phase is actuated. There is also a strict constraint that minimum green time for vehicles must be achieved before the phase switches. We have defined a timer that starts when the pedestrian phase is activated and it is named as "Ped timer". While the pedestrian phase is active, if a vehicle is detected on the road and Ped timer reaches a predetermined threshold, the vehicle phase is actuated. The strict constraint is valid here too: no phase actuation occurs before the minimum green time for pedestrians is reached.

Interphase lengths are chosen same with the current situation: 5 s all-red for each phase switch. Minimum green time for vehicles is chosen as 30 s for providing enough split time to pass. Minimum green time for pedestrians is determined from formulae presented in [29]:

$$G_p = 3.2 + \frac{L}{S_p} + \left(0.81 \frac{N_{ped}}{W_E} \right) \tag{1}$$

where G_p, L, S_p, N_{ped}, and W_E denote respectively the minimum pedestrian green time in seconds, cross-walk length in meters, walking speed of pedestrians, number of pedestrians crossing during an interval, and effective crosswalk width in meters. The constant value, 3.2, represents the pedestrian start-up time in seconds.

3.2 Case Study Area

Kadıköy, as the case area, is one of the central business districts in Anatolian side of Istanbul, which experiences high pedestrian demand most of the time. Pedestrians can reach the case area using several transport modes: private vehicles, ferry, subway, and

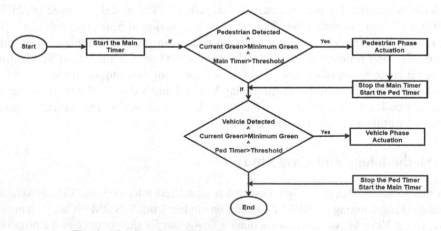

Fig. 1. The flowchart of signal actuation program in VISVAP

public buses. There is also a tram line, traversing in the same direction with the vehicular flow, in our case area.

In order to derive control measures, data is retrieved from camera recordings. Two video recorders are mounted to high rise buildings with a clear vision of the case area. Two intersections are observed during morning peak hours (07:00–10:00) and evening peak hours (16:00–19:00) on 26th of January, 2019. Data aggregation is processed manually.

Figure 2 shows the case area to our interested. Yellow polygon shows the inner area of Kadıköy, where pedestrians can find restaurants, shopping malls, historical places, and etc. Orange line indicates tram line and serves as a ring service between the coastline and the inner area of Kadıköy. The two traffic lights considered are pointed by red arrows. Black arrows show the ferry terminals location. Subway entry and exit points are shown by blue arrows.

In the real case, 105 s of cycle time is applied for both intersections. This cycle time is divided into four phases: 75 s green for vehicular traffic, 5 s all-red for clearance phase, 20 s for pedestrians to cross the street, and 5 s all-red.

Fig. 2. Case study area (Color figure online)

3.3 Simulation Environment

Modeling and simulations are done using VISSIM. The case area consists 48 sub-areas for pedestrians and 36 links for vehicles. Route definitions, vehicle and pedestrian flows are determined from video recordings. 6000 vehicles are loaded to the system from three origin points within 3600 s.

Pedestrian flow is aggregated at three main origin points in the case area: In order to model passengers from the ferry terminal, 15 min of cyclic inputs are used; 6 min of cyclic inputs are used to model the subway passengers traveling in the case area; and, Rest of the pedestrians that are counted manually using video recordings are input as well. 8190 pedestrians are assumed to walk in the system in 3600 s.

Simulations are repeated 10 times varying the random seeds to incorporate the stochastic nature of traffic demand.

4   Simulation Results

Simulations trials have shown that improvement on pedestrian travel times can be achieved by 11%, while vehicle delays increase by 10.5%. The increase in vehicle delay exists due to the fact that around three fourth of the cycle time is the green period for vehicles. Results illustrate the need to a trade-off between vehicle delay and pedestrian travel time. Since the case area is a central business district and high pedestrian demands occur at the signalized intersections, the trade-off is logic and it should be investigated in depth.

Simulation results for vehicle delays and pedestrian travel times are shown in Fig. 3.

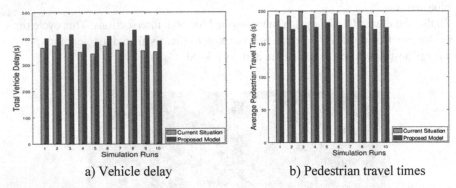

a) Vehicle delay   b) Pedestrian travel times

Fig. 3. Performance of simulations for current and proposed controls in terms of (a) vehicle delays, and (b) pedestrian travel times

Distribution of vehicle delays for each of the simulation runs are shown in Fig. 3a. Vehicle delays are measured at the two intersections considered. Figure 3b shows average pedestrian travel times per simulation run. Pedestrian travel times are measured at the two densely used areas that are pointed with red arrows in Fig. 2.

5   Conclusions and Future Research

In this paper, we summarize our findings from a real case study employing a fully actuated signal control program. Data gathered from the field are used to model and simulate the problem to our interest using PTV VISSIM. Simulations performed show that pedestrian travel times in the system can be reduced while vehicle delays are increased. One of the directions to our future research is to consider different control measures and employ different control methods.

Acknowledgements. Authors thank to PTV AG Group for providing VISSIM 10 license for academic purposes.

References

1. Celikoglu, H.B., Dell'Orco, M.: A dynamic model for acceleration behaviour description in congested traffic. In: 11th International IEEE Conference on Intelligent Transportation Systems (ITSC2008), pp. 986–991 (2008). https://doi.org/10.1109/itsc.2008.4732521
2. Demiral, C., Celikoglu, H.B.: Application of ALINEA ramp control algorithm to freeway traffic flow on approaches to Bosphorus strait crossing bridges. Procedia Soc. Behav. Sci. **20**, 364–371 (2011). https://doi.org/10.1016/j.sbspro.2011.08.042
3. Deniz, O., Aksoy, G., Celikoglu, H.B.: Analyzing freeway travel times within a case study: reliability of route traversal times. In: 16th International IEEE Conference on Intelligent Transportation Systems (ITSC 2013), pp. 195–202 (2013). https://doi.org/10.1109/itsc.2013. 6728233
4. Abuamer, I.M., Silgu, M.A., Celikoglu, H.B.: Micro-simulation based ramp metering on Istanbul freeways: an evaluation adopting ALINEA. In: 2016 IEEE 19th International Conference on Intelligent Transportation Systems (ITS), pp. 695–700 (2016)
5. Abuamer, I.M., Sadat, M., Silgu, M.A., Celikoglu, H.B.: Analyzing the effects of driver behavior within an adaptive ramp control scheme: a case-study with ALINEA. In: 2017 IEEE International Conference on Vehicular Electronics and Safety (ICVES), pp. 109–114 (2017)
6. Akyol, G., Silgu, M.A., Celikoglu, H.B.: Pedestrian-friendly traffic signal control using Eclipse SUMO. In: Weber, M., Bieker-Walz, L., Hilbrich, R., Behrisch, M. (eds.) Proceedings of the SUMO User Conference 2019 – Simulating Connected Urban Mobility. EPiC Series in Computing, vol. 62, pp. 101–106 (2019)
7. Erdagi, I.G., Silgu, M.A., Celikoglu, H.B.: Emission effects of cooperative adaptive cruise control: a simulation case using SUMO. In: Weber, M., Bieker-Walz, L., Hilbrich, R., Behrisch, M. (eds.) Proceedings of the SUMO User Conference 2019 – Simulating Connected Urban Mobility. EPiC Series in Computing, vol. 62, pp. 92–100 (2019)
8. Helbing, D., Molnár, P.: Social force model for pedestrian dynamics. Phys. Rev. E **51**, 4282–4286 (1995)
9. Wiedemann, R.: Simulation des Strassenverkehrsflusses. Schriftenreihe des Instituts für Verkehrswesen der Universität Karlsruhe, Band 8, Karlsruhe, Germany (1974)
10. Helbing, D., Molnár, P., Farkas, I.J., Bolay, K.: Self-organizing pedestrian movement. Environ. Plan. **28**(3), 361–383 (2001)
11. Kachroo, P.: Pedestrian Dynamics: Mathematical Theory and Evacuation Control. Taylor and Francis Group, Boca Raton (2009)
12. Borsche, R., Meurer, A.: Microscopic and macroscopic models for coupled car traffic and pedestrian flow. J. Comput. Appl. Math. **348**, 356–382 (2019)
13. Lam, W.H.K., Jodie, Y.S., Lee, Y.S., Chan, K.S.: A study of the bi-directional flow characteristics at Hong-Kong signalized walking facilities. Transportation **29**, 169–192 (2002)
14. Alhajyaseen, W., Nakamura, H., Asano, M.: Effects of bi-directional pedestrian flow characteristics upon the capacity of signalized crosswalks. Procedia Soc. Behav. Sci. **16**, 526–535 (2011)
15. Adler, J.L., Blue, V.J.: Cellular automata microsimulation for modeling bi-directional pedestrian walkways. Transp. Res. Part B: Methodol. **35**(3), 293–312 (2001)
16. Li, Q., Wang, Z., Yang, J., Wang, J.: Pedestrian delay estimation at signalized intersections in developing cities. Transp. Res. Part A Policy Pract. **39**, 61–73 (2005)
17. Marisamynathan, S., Vedagiri, P.: Modeling pedestrian delay at signalized intersection crosswalks under mixed traffic condition. Procedia Soc. Behav. Sci. **104**, 708–717 (2013)
18. Gao, L., Liu, Z., Xu, Q., Feng, X.: A delay model of pedestrian-vehicle system on two crossings. In: 5th Advanced Forum on Transportation of China (AFTC 2009), pp. 192–198 (2009)

19. Muley, D., Alhajyaseen, W., Kharbeche, M., Al-Salem, M.: Pedestrians' speed analysis at signalized crosswalks. Procedia Comput. Sci. **130**, 567–574 (2018)
20. Onelcin, P., Alver, Y.: The crossing speed and safety margin of pedestrians at signalized intersections. Transp. Res. Procedia **22**, 3–12 (2017)
21. Turkish Standards Institute: Urban Roads - Design Criteria on Sidewalks and Pedestrian Areas (2012)
22. Lam, W.H.K., Cheung, C.: Pedestrian speed-flow relationships for walking facilities in Hong Kong. J. Transp. Eng. **126**(4), 343–349 (2000)
23. Yu, C., Ma, W., Han, K., Yang, X.: Optimization of vehicle and pedestrian signals at isolated intersections. Transp. Res. Part B: Methodol. **98**, 135–153 (2017)
24. Ma, W., Yang, X.: Signal coordination models for midblock pedestrian crossing and adjacent intersections. In: 2009 Second International Conference on Intelligent Computation Technology and Automation. Changsha, Hunan, pp. 193–196 (2009)
25. He, Q., Head, K.L., Ding, J.: Multi-modal traffic signal control with priority, signal actuation and coordination. Transp. Res. Part C Emerg. Technol. **46**, 65–82 (2014)
26. Erdmann, J., Krajzewicz, D.: Modelling pedestrian dynamics in SUMO. In: SUMO 2015 - Intermodal Simulation for Intermodal Transport, vol. 28, pp. 103–118 (2015)
27. Lopez, P.A., et al.: Microscopic traffic simulation using SUMO. In: 21st International Conference on Intelligent Transportation Systems (ITSC), Maui, HI, 2018, pp. 2575–2582 (2018)
28. Krauss, S.: Microscopic Modeling of Traffic Flow: Investigation of Collision Free Vehicle Dynamics. Ph.D. thesis, Universität zu Köln (1998)
29. Mannering, F.L., Washburn, S.S.: Principles of Highway Engineering and Traffic Analysis, 5th edn. Wiley, Hoboken (2013)

Intelligent Longitudinal Merging Maneuver at Roundabouts Based on Hybrid Planning Approach

Carlos Hidalgo[1,2]([✉]), Ray Lattarulo[1], Joshué Pérez[1], and Estibaliz Asua[2]

[1] Tecnalia Research and Innovation, Parque Científico y Tecnológico de Bizkaia,
Geldo Auzoa, Edif. 700, 48160 Derio, Bizkaia, Spain
{carlos.hidalgo,rayalejandro.lattarulo,joshue.perez}@tecnalia.com
[2] University of the Basque Country, Sarriena, s/n, 48940 Leioa, Vizcaya, Spain
estibaliz.asua@ehu.eus

Abstract. Roundabout intersections promote a continuous traffic flow, with less congestion and more safety than standard intersections. However, there are several problems related to its entrance. In this way, the article presents a method to solve the roundabout merging combining a nominal trajectory generated with Bézier curves with a Model Predictive Control (MPC) to assure safe maneuvers. Simulation results using Dynacar are shown and the good performance of the approach under merging maneuvers is demonstrated.

Keywords: Bézier Curves · Model Predictive Control · Merging Maneuver

1 Introduction

In last years, more automation capabilities have been implemented on vehicles. However, there are a great number of unresolved scenarios that makes autonomous driving a distant reality. As an example, because of the multiple and complex actions that can be performed, the roundabouts are an interesting case of study.

The roundabouts are considered as a good alternative in comparison with other type of intersections [11]. However, bottlenecks and traffic accidents could be generated due to the driver inexperience, the roundabout geometry, and the signs and markings, among others [7].

In Australia, a study demonstrate that 50.8% of accidents take place at the entrance and 6.5% at the exit [1]. In other hand, in US a similar study shows that 40% of accidents happen at the entrance [3]. In Italy, [17] points the roundabout entrance as the most problematic element, with a total of 68% crashes.

Advanced Driver Assistance Systems (ADAS), are considered as a possible solution to the roundabout entrance problem. Trajectory planning [9] and control [18] are the main approaches to solve the problem with a single vehicle. Moreover,

© Springer Nature Switzerland AG 2020
R. Moreno-Díaz et al. (Eds.): EUROCAST 2019, LNCS 12014, pp. 129–136, 2020.
https://doi.org/10.1007/978-3-030-45096-0_16

connected and Automated Vehicles (CAVs) emerges as possible solution, involving the coordination of multiple vehicles to safely drive through the roundabout. Different coordination methods have been tested. In [4], an algorithm using fuzzy logic for roundabout intersection management has been proposed. In [6], a distributed maneuver planner based on an optimization method to create virtual vehicles managing the merging have been presented. In [2] employs a vehicular networks protocols, with Dedicated Short Range Communications (DSRC) and Wireless Access Vehicular Environment (WAVE) technologies to coordinate vehicles movement through roundabouts.

In this paper, the roundabout merging problematic is solved proposing a hybrid planning method which considers parametric curves of Bézier (nominal planner) and Model Predictive Control (dynamic planner). The separation in two different task allows to reduce the computational time with the benefits of each technique, e.g. comfort and smoothness of Bézier and dynamically fast computation of a linear MPC problem. Furthermore, the method provides and verifies safety and comfort during the maneuver execution.

The current work is organized as follows: Sect. 2 presents a description of the simulation environment employed for testing. In Sect. 3, the merging approach is detailed. In Sect. 4, the maneuver results are presented. Lastly, Sect. 5 shows the conclusions and future works.

2   Simulation Environment

The Dynacar is used for developing and validation of the algorithm [16]. It is an integrated solution for electrical and hybrid vehicle design which uses a multi-body formulation to model the vehicle's characteristics [5]. Furthermore, it includes a 3D interface for vehicle monitoring. This tool runs the modular control architecture presented in [10] (see Fig. 1).

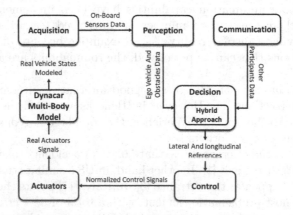

Fig. 1. Automated driving control architecture.

The architecture is divided in 6 blocks: acquisition, perception, communication, decision, control and actuation. In addition, a seventh block is added which depicts the multi-body representation of the vehicle. The acquisition module gathers information of the on-board sensors or the multi-body representation, such as reference system transformation and time stamping, among others. The perception module is responsible for the ego-vehicle representation, detection and obstacle classification, lane detection, etc.

Communication module provides information coming from external sources (vehicles, infrastructure and pedestrian). The decision block determines the trajectory and speed plan to be followed by the vehicle based on the hybrid approach presented in Sect. 3. The control module generates normalized control actions over the longitudinal and lateral actuators. Finally, the actuator module transforms the normalized control outputs to real action signals over the actuators (throttle, brake and steering) or the multi-body model.

3   Implemented Strategy

With the objective of solving the merging maneuver, a nominal trajectory is generated with Bézier curves, method that is easy to implement and has a great performance [9]. In parallel, projections all over the route of both vehicles are generated, verifying possible collisions with other participants every time step. With this purpose, Model Predictive Control (MPC) has proven to be a technique with acceptable results in vehicle predictions and collision avoidance [12,15].

In order to generate the projections, the vehicles must exchange their states information (speed, position, heading, acceleration, etc.). Using the time steps obtained with the MPC, a kinematic model and the information coming from communication, the projections of the vehicle inside the roundabout can be obtained.

3.1   Hybrid Approach

In Fig. 2, the block diagram of the hybrid approach is depicted. The nominal trajectory calculator uses the information related to the ego-vehicle and a map in order to generate the trajectory with the Bézier Curves. In addition, this block incorporates a double proportional feedback plus curvature feed-forward submodule that generates the references for the lateral and longitudinal controllers.

In parallel, the MPC references and boundaries are calculated using the information of the past iteration (longitudinal jerk and lateral acceleration) which are integrated in the MPC block obtaining the future states of the vehicle (acceleration, speed and distance for the longitudinal case, and speed and distance in the lateral case). These information is used to modify the control references generated by the nominal trajectory block.

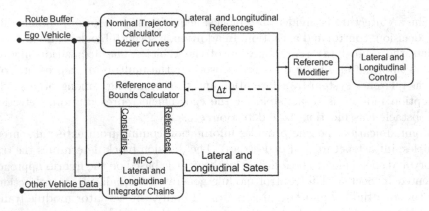

Fig. 2. Decision module: hybrid approach block diagram.

Bézier Curves: Bézier curves are a type of parametric curve that has been widely used in automated driving fields in the past few years [8]. These type of curves present geometrical (C^n) and curvature (G^n) continuity, low computational time and are easy to implement.

The nominal trajectory generation is done using the framework developed by [14]. Different types of road components such as intersections, roundabouts, lane changes, straight lines, among others are defined combining Bézier curves in segments along lines and arcs. The roundabouts, the following considerations are taken:

- The entrance and exit must be straight path (curvature equal 0).
- The entrance and exit segments must fit its inner part with curvature equal to the inverse radius.
- Bézier joining points angles must be the same of the circle arc angle.

Model Predictive Control: A linear model (point mass) with decoupled lateral and longitudinal dynamics is selected for the MPC design. An optimal solution with fast response time can be achieved with this model. The longitudinal motion is in a cartesian coordinates frame to easily combine with the Bézier curve planning. The longitudinal model used is based on a triple integrator chain of the longitudinal jerk (J_{lon}) component (1), that will provide different states, such as speed set points to a closed loop controller.

$$d_{lon} = \int \int \int J_{lon}(t)dt^3 \qquad (1)$$

The model can be represented as a linear differential equation system, that involves the longitudinal distance (d_{lon}), speed (v_{lon}), acceleration (a_{lon}) as state variables and jerk (J_{lon}) as control input, leading to the state space representation in (2).

$$\begin{bmatrix} \dot{d}_{lon} \\ \dot{v}_{lon} \\ \dot{a}_{lon} \end{bmatrix} = \begin{bmatrix} 0 & 1 & 0 \\ 0 & 0 & 1 \\ 0 & 0 & 0 \end{bmatrix} \begin{bmatrix} d_{lon} \\ v_{lon} \\ a_{lon} \end{bmatrix} + \begin{bmatrix} 0 \\ 0 \\ 1 \end{bmatrix} J_{lon} \qquad (2)$$

These variables are used as the optimization problem constrains. The relative distance between vehicles is used to prevent collision with other participants. The speed is set to limit the speed according the maximum road speed. The acceleration sets the maximum acceleration and deceleration that the system can achieve by design. Lastly, the jerk is used as comfort parameter, as the ones mentioned in the work [19].

The objective function $(J(x(t), u(t)))$ used in the optimization problem consists in the least squared error between the ego-vehicle speed (v_{lon}) and the reference speed generated by the MPC $(v_{lon_{ref}})$. The solution will be given using a Quadratic Problem (QP) formulation (3), with the variables L and M as weights, and the constrains explained above.

$$\Phi(x(\cdot), u(\cdot)) = min\{\int_{t_0}^{T} L(J(x(t), u(t)))dt + M(J(x(T), u(T)))\}$$

$$J(x(t), u(t)) = (v_{ref_{lon}} - v_{lon})^2$$

(3)

The ACADO toolkit [13] is used to solve the optimization problem presented. It is a self-contained library based on C++ which was designed to solve linear and no linear models under multi-objective optimization functions.

4   Results

A single lane roundabout is selected for the tests. In Fig. 3, an image sequence of the merging process is shown. The vehicle's projections (red rectangles represents the ego vehicle and black rectangles the inside vehicle) are shown in Fig. 3a, leading the vehicle to slow down (Fig. 3b) until braking, yielding the space to the other vehicle in the roundabout (Fig. 3c). Once it is safe to continue, the vehicle accelerates (Fig. 3d).

Figure 4 shows the detection of possible collision during the merging process, identifying it between seconds 12.21 and 13.3. In Fig. 5, the MPC boundaries and the trajectory planning speed reference are shown. In second 11.53 the vehicle slowing down is observed, until it brakes in second 13.70. In second 14.15, since there is no risk the vehicle accelerates.

In addition, Figs. 6 and 7 present the vehicle acceleration and jerk. Both variables stays under the limits defined, ensuring a safety and comfortable planning for the driver during the merge.

Tests show the good performance of the hybrid approach, combining the trajectory generation by a Bézier curve framework, with a fast linear MPC. This method ensures passenger safety and comfort, reducing the computational cost of resolving two problems in one module, since it splits the maneuver in two different task.

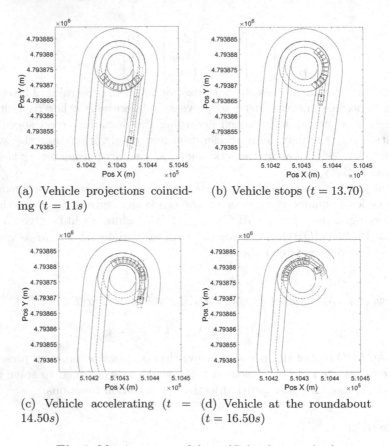

(a) Vehicle projections coinciding ($t = 11s$)

(b) Vehicle stops ($t = 13.70$)

(c) Vehicle accelerating ($t = 14.50s$)

(d) Vehicle at the roundabout ($t = 16.50s$)

Fig. 3. Merging at roundabout (Color figure online)

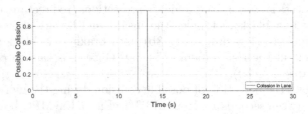

Fig. 4. Collision in lane indicator.

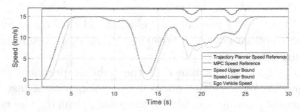

Fig. 5. Vehicle speed and references.

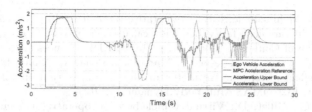

Fig. 6. Vehicle acceleration and references.

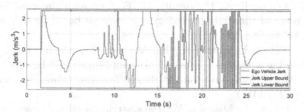

Fig. 7. Vehicle jerk and references.

5   Conclusion

This work presents the adaptation of a hybrid approach concept to the roundabout merging. In this approach a nominal trajectory is generated with a specific Bézier curve framework, which may be modified according the MPC predictions of the vehicles.

The results obtained using the approach are satisfactory. The vehicle safely enters the roundabout, yielding the other vehicle right to drive, ensuring safety and comfort during the entire maneuver. Future works will be carried out taking into account more vehicles, combining this technique with other maneuvers such as Cooperative Adaptive Cruise Control (CACC). In addition, the lateral component of the approach will be implemented to execute more complex maneuvers inside the roundabout.

Acknowledgment. This work was supported in part by the ECSEL Project ENABLE-S3 with grant agreement number 692455-2 and the Spanish Ministry of Economy, Industry and Competitiveness TEC2016-77618-R (AEI/FEDER, UE).

References

1. Arndt, O., Troutbeck, R.J.: Relationship between roundabout geometry and accident rates. Transp. Res. Circ, (E-C003), 28–1 (1998)
2. Azimi, R., Bhatia, G., Rajkumar, R., Mudalige, P.: V2v-intersection management at roundabouts. SAE Int. J. Passeng. Cars-Mech. Syst. **6**(2013–01–0722), 681–690 (2013)
3. Badgley, J., Condon, J., Rainville, L., Li, D., et al.: FHWA research and technology evaluation: roundabout research final report. Tech. rep., United States. Federal Highway Administration. Office of Corporate Research (2018)

4. Bosankić, I., Mehmedović, L.B.: Cooperative intelligence in roundabout intersections using hierarchical fuzzy behavior calculation of vehicle speed profile. In: MATEC Web of Conferences, vol. 81, p. 01008. EDP Sciences (2016)
5. Cuadrado, J., Vilela, D., Iglesias, I., Martín, A., Peña, A.: A multibody model to assess the effect of automotive motor in-wheel configuration on vehicle stability and comfort. ECCOMAS Multibody Dynamics (2013)
6. Debada, E.G., Gillet, D.: Virtual vehicle-based cooperative maneuver planning for connected automated vehicles at single-lane roundabouts. IEEE Intell. Transp. Syst. Mag. **104**, 35–46 (2018)
7. Distefano, N., Leonardi, S., Pulvirenti, G.: Factors with the greatest influence on drivers' judgment of roundabouts safety. An analysis based on web survey in Italy. IATSS Res. **42**(4), 265–273 (2018)
8. González, D., Pérez, J., Lattarulo, R., Milanés, V., Nashashibi, F.: Continuous curvature planning with obstacle avoidance capabilities in urban scenarios. In: 17th International IEEE Conference on Intelligent Transportation Systems (ITSC), pp. 1430–1435. IEEE (2014)
9. Gonzalez, D., Pérez, J., Milanés, V.: Parametric-based path generation for automated vehicles at roundabouts. Expert Syst. Appl. **71**, 332–341 (2017)
10. González, D., Pérez, J., Milanés, V., Nashashibi, F.: A review of motion planning techniques for automated vehicles. IEEE Trans. Intell. Transp. Syst. **17**(4), 1135–1145 (2016)
11. Hatami, H., Aghayan, I.: Traffic efficiency evaluation of elliptical roundabout compared with modern and turbo roundabouts considering traffic signal control. Promet-Traffic Transp. **29**(1), 1–11 (2017)
12. Heß, D., Lattarulo, R., Pérez, J., Schindler, J., Hesse, T., Köster, F.: Fast maneuver planning for cooperative automated vehicles. In: 2018 21st International Conference on Intelligent Transportation Systems (ITSC), pp. 1625–1632. IEEE (2018)
13. Houska, B., Ferreau, H.J., Diehl, M.: Acado toolkit-an open-source framework for automatic control and dynamic optimization. Optim. Control Appl. Methods **32**(3), 298–312 (2011)
14. Lattarulo, R., González, L., Martí, E., Matute, J., Marcano, M., Pérez, J.: Urban motion planning framework based on N-Bézier curves considering comfort and safety. J. Adv. Transp. **2018** (2018)
15. Lattarulo, R., Marcano, M., Pérez, J.: Overtaking maneuver for automated driving using virtual environments. In: Moreno-Díaz, R., Pichler, F., Quesada-Arencibia, A. (eds.) EUROCAST 2017. LNCS, vol. 10672, pp. 446–453. Springer, Cham (2018). https://doi.org/10.1007/978-3-319-74727-9_54
16. Lattarulo, R., Pérez, J., Dendaluce, M.: A complete framework for developing and testing automated driving controllers. IFAC-PapersOnLine **50**(1), 258–263 (2017)
17. Montella, A.: Identifying crash contributory factors at urban roundabouts and using association rules to explore their relationships to different crash types. Accid. Anal. Prev. **43**(4), 1451–1463 (2011)
18. Rastelli, J.P., Peñas, M.S.: Fuzzy logic steering control of autonomous vehicles inside roundabouts. Appl. Soft Comput. **35**, 662–669 (2015)
19. Villagra, J., Milanés, V., Pérez, J., Godoy, J.: Smooth path and speed planning for an automated public transport vehicle. Robot. Auton. Syst. **60**(2), 252–265 (2012)

Data Sources for Information Extraction in Automotive Forensics

Andreas Attenberger[✉]

Digital Forensics Research Unit,
Central Office for Information Technology in the Security Sector (ZITiS),
Munich, Germany
andreas.attenberger@zitis.bund.de

Abstract. In digital forensic analysis, it is not possible to pre-determine the exact nature of information relevant for a case. Subsequently, complete physical images of digital memory chips or devices are extracted. In the case of car forensics, it is thus crucial to have knowledge about the format, type and the logical and physical location of the information in a vehicle. Next to increasing utilization of electronics in vehicle control, the situation is further compounded by the introduction of so-called connected car or smart car solutions. In contrast to other areas like smartphone forensics, digital forensics in the automotive field is more complex as it encompasses a multitude of hardware- and software systems both in place and in remote locations, including smartphones themselves, in order to reach a complete view of relevant information. The article gives an overview of the different types of digital information stored in the respective areas. In the following, a separation of data sources is considered with data preserved inside the vehicle (front end and vehicle electronics) as well as outside of the vehicle (connected back end). For handling the increasing amount of data present in modern vehicles, a corresponding solution for data preservation and exchange is necessary. Finally to solve the problem of attributing collected data to individual drivers, pattern-recognition-based methods are presented.

1 Introduction and Related Work

With the introduction of the first production microprocessor-based engine control unit (ECU) in vehicles in 1977 and current low-end models containing at least 30 ECUs [1], forensic investigations started to extend to engine control units (ECUs) as additional sources of information in law enforcement. The proliferation of electronic devices in every day life in the shape of the internet of things and smart embedded systems added further data generation and storage modules. As a consequence, physical and digital evidence often need to be combined for successful investigations [2]. Previous work on automotive forensics generally focuses on individual aspects of digital forensics in the automotive sector, an area that so far has received a restricted amount of attention [3,4]. Most commonly, either the infotainment and navigation modules or the car area network

© Springer Nature Switzerland AG 2020
R. Moreno-Díaz et al. (Eds.): EUROCAST 2019, LNCS 12014, pp. 137–144, 2020.
https://doi.org/10.1007/978-3-030-45096-0_17

(CAN) bus are targeted [3–6] or yet-to-be-implemented future developments like smart cities are discussed [7]. This article proposes the consideration of all possible data points generated in automobiles along with a basic categorization of these information sources. For subsequent processing, the future requirements for format standardization and pattern-based data classification are presented. Avenues for future work in this field are given at the end of this paper.

2   Data Sources for Automotive Forensics

In the following, an overview and possible basic taxonomy of the logical and physical locations of digital automotive data is given. A distinction between front end modules for the end user, a back end exposing various connectivity services residing with the manufacturer and classic vehicle electronics in the form of ECUs is proposed.

2.1   Front End

The front end is considered the head unit or infotainment module with respective functionality for telecommunication, navigation and further services like web connectivity. Some commercial solutions exist for extraction from these modules for select car models [8]. However, the amount of data stored both in terms of detail and duration varies between module types. Examples of saved information are GPS location, routing information and vehicle events [9]. The major challenge in digital forensics considering the front end or infotainment modules is that manufacturers currently do not implement standardized interfaces for information extraction from these hardware components. Besides the commercial software suites mentioned above, there is only limited support for the forensic investigator. In the case of modules not supported by off-the-shelf solutions, extraction of data from the memory and storage chips contained in these components is more challenging. If there are no debug interfaces present on the corresponding circuit boards this typically involves chip-off procedures in order to remove the individual integrated circuit for further processing. The result of which is shown for an exemplary module in Fig. 1.

If connectivity options extend to bluetooth pairing or USB connection of smartphones, additional data can be present in the devices, for example phone messages and contact lists [5]. Furthermore, at least the connection information in terms of bluetooth pairing and possible further data points remain on the utilized mobile devices. This means that analysis should be extended to classic smartphone forensic approaches for the corresponding mobile devices. Individual software solutions exist for these cases [10]. The reverse is equally true, especially considering smartphone access protection. If the smartphone is not accessible, valuable information can be retrieved from the infotainment modules.

Fig. 1. Part of an infotainment module after chip-off with the blue circle in the left image indicating the original position of the extracted chip displayed on the right. (Color figure online)

2.2   Connected Back End

With the advent of smart car models, data is not exclusively generated, processed and stored on the individual vehicle. Instead, connected vehicles make use of back end solutions to transmit data to cloud servers for subsequent processing and further services tied to those back end systems. For example, connected car solutions record data points derived from vehicle usage like distance travelled, door status or fuel range. These are utilized for improving the user experience and there are various business models ranging from entertainment to insurance applications [11]. Further processing capabilities have been introduced with cloud services. As a consequence, machine learning methods with elevated processing power demands can be executed on the collected driving data [12]. At this moment, a number of different manufacturers offer car data solutions. A possible classification is between on-board and off-board services, of which the latter allow access to recorded driver data only from external devices like smartphones while on-board services expose information to the driver through built-in interfaces like the infotainment module. Some of these solutions offer more than 100 data points recorded during vehicle utilization [13]. Autonomous driving services as a recent technological advancement in modern vehicles can equally rely on data processing in the cloud. Furthermore, car data can also be transmitted to social media and other web services through a corresponding internet gateway. At the moment, standardization is underway to introduce Car-to-X communication[1]. Future vehicles will be equipped with the means to

---

[1] https://www.car-2-car.org/.

exchange messages with both other vehicles as well as infrastructural elements like intersections or traffics lights. For a complete view of vehicle data, these infrastructure elements also have to be taken into account.

2.3   Vehicle Electronics

Since the first integration of ECUs in cars, the amount of electronic components in automobiles has steadily been increasing. Many ECUs contain microcontrollers including memory banks which may log some of the activity of either the connected actuators and sensors or the bus communication present on the vehicle field buses. Just as for front end modules, gaining access to the memory content often requires chip-off procedures. For the communication buses in vehicles, widely utilized standards are CAN, MOST or FlexRay [14]. Transmitted information over the CAN bus includes safety-relevant information like brake activation or instrument panel control. There are various devices available to car drivers to record CAN bus information during driving for further personal use. Additionally, some insurance and rental companies install or supply customers with CAN bus dongles as a means to offer services similar to those made possible by car data collected for back-end services as described in the previous chapter [15].

3   Data Processing for Automotive Forensics

After relevant data has been collected from data sources in and outside the vehicle, it has to be edited, filtered and processed accordingly. Due to the lack of commercial solutions, this is often a process including a high number of manual tasks. With the increasing volume of data associated with automobiles both in terms of size and bandwidth, new approaches need to be introduced for structuring forensic case work. In the following two possible solutions to some of the issues in the field are discussed briefly. In order to yield data ready for both subsequent software-based processing as well as exchange with different national and international agencies and institutions, a common data format is needed. Additionally, with several terabytes of potentially relevant data, manual selection becomes increasibly infeasible. One solution is the utilization of machine learning methods in order to select the actual information pertaining to the subject of interest. Both of these approaches have potential applications in other digital forensic domains.

3.1   Forensic Data Standardization

Due to the wealth and disparity of the data present in the different components, connected devices and infrastructure, current automotive forensic data is often not stored in a standardized format or storage solution that extends beyond individual hex dump files for memory contents or seperate device file systems. While specialized forensic software utilizes various proprietary formats, there is currently no generally accepted exchangeable data format. The author advocates the introduction of a common exchange format as well as further standardization efforts for forensic data. One example for a forensic investigation format is the Cyber-investigation Analysis Standard Expression (CASE) standard[2], which is a preliminary standard founded in the Unified Cyber Ontology (UCO) ontology. Among the various needs in cyber-investigation that will be covered by CASE is digital forensic science with the standard focusing especially on interoperability.

3.2   Attribution of Forensic Data

One of the main challenges in automotive forensics is driver attribution to determine the person driving the car at a specific point of time. This is typically an issue in cases like car accidents, car theft and insurance fraud. While traditional forensic methods include dactyloscopy, digitally generated data in vehicles allow another way of driver identification through pattern-based analysis of driver data. If there is historic data about vehicle usage, this can be employed to attribute incident-related information to an individual previously driving the car. It is also possible to determine if a third party was implicated in the case. The general method for user attribution is to follow machine learning methods as utilized in supervised classification [16]. This process involves training an algorithm or pattern recognition method with training data in order to yield a classification model. Subsequentially, future data can automatically be attributed to a certain class of data, which corresponds to individual drivers. Often, input data is subjected to pre-processing like filtering as well as the extraction of characteristic feature data from the input in order to reduce the input data volume. In automotive forensics, an additional challenge is to achieve a complete data profile with a format fit for corresponding processing with data analysis tools. Possible sources have been mentioned above. Both the back end as well as the front end and vehicle electronics data points can be either directly processed in pattern recognition or filtered to yield feature data for classifier training. Figure 2 illustrates this process with optional pre- and post-processing steps, for example to reduce noise effects.

In a paper by Kwak et al. a driver data set was compiled with CAN bus data recorded from the on-board diagnostics 2 (OBD-II) interface [17]. The data set which is available on the web[3] contains 51 data points recorded per second during driving action from ten different drivers with a total driving time of 23 h and a distance of 46 km in a round trip. Kwak et al. employed the data set for developing an anti-theft system tuned to authorized drivers of a vehicle. Figure 3 contains preliminary results of a test to determine if an unknown driver as pertaining to the recorded CAN data can be distinguished from known drivers conducting the same vehicle. This corresponds to common use cases in law enforcement where the identification of the actual driver is often crucial to the solution of a case. In this example, a random forest model was trained with data from three different

---

[2] https://caseontology.org.

[3] http://ocslab.hksecurity.net/Datasets/driving-dataset.

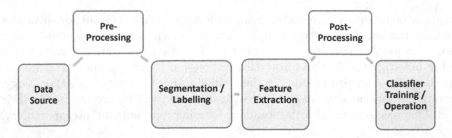

Fig. 2. The general classification process for supervised classification with labelling of source data for class attribution, feature extraction and classifier training and utilization. Pre- and post-processing steps are optional possibilities for improving class separation, for example through noise removal.

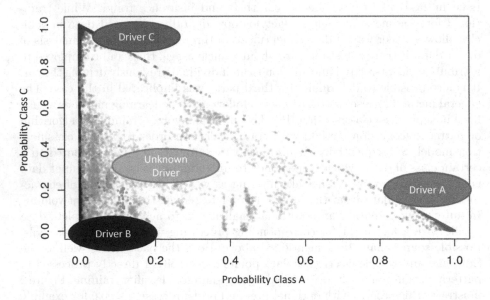

Fig. 3. Classification results with a classifier model trained on data from three different drivers when additional information about an unknown driver is input to the classifier. The graph shows that feature data points for the unknown driver do not cluster or center around the respective areas of the previously known drivers.

drivers. To test the possibility of detecting driving activity by an unknown third party, driving data of both the known driver was input to the classifier along with CAN bus information from another driver. Kwak et al. give a short overview of related work pertaining to CAN data [17]. In previous work, Bsouni et al. demonstrated an approach relying on a combination of CAN Bus, GPS and accelerometer sensor data to detect drunk driving. In their work, sensor data was pre-processed and subjected to feature extraction [18]. Further activities are underway to target specific law enforcement use cases. Additionally, a high amount of accuracy and field tests with a sufficient amount of drivers are necessary to verify statistical significance of these classification results. As in other areas where pattern recognition methods can be applied, new feature methods need to be developed for achieving maximum class separation.

4   Conclusion and Future Work

The above sections present a basic taxonomy of data sources for digital automotive forensics. As has been outlined, further efforts need to be directed both to standardization of data formats as well as the investigation of the reliability of user attribution methods. This includes the definition of reliable forensic process models, especially when handling memory modules with size-restricted or non-permanent storage technologies. General guidelines can be derived from other IT forensic process models, for example by the federal office for information security (BSI) in Germany [4]. Furthermore, current communication systems like the CAN bus and other connectivity solutions in modern cars are potentially subject to attacks impairing vehicle safety [19,20]. Specialists in digital automotive forensics need to be aware of these threats and develop adequate methods for detecting and investigating such manipulations.

References

1. Charette, R.N.: This car runs on code. IEEE Spectr. **46**(3), 3 (2009)
2. Nilsson, D.K., Larson, U.E.: Combining physical and digital evidence in vehicle environments. In: 2008 Third International Workshop on Systematic Approaches to Digital Forensic Engineering, pp. 10–14 (May 2008)
3. Le-Khac, N.A., Jacobs, D., Nijhoff, J., Bertens, K., Choo, K.K.R.: Smart vehicle forensics: challenges and case study. Future Gener. Comput. Syst. (2018)
4. Hoppe, T., Kuhlmann, S., Kiltz, S., Dittmann, J.: IT-forensic automotive investigations on the example of route reconstruction on automotive system and communication data. In: Ortmeier, F., Daniel, P. (eds.) SAFECOMP 2012. LNCS, vol. 7612, pp. 125–136. Springer, Heidelberg (2012). https://doi.org/10.1007/978-3-642-33678-2_11
5. Jacobs, D., Choo, K.R., Kechadi, M., Le-Khac, N.: Volkswagen car entertainment system forensics. In: 2017 IEEE Trustcom/BigDataSE/ICESS, pp. 699–705 (August 2017)
6. Mansor, H., Markantonakis, K., Akram, R.N., Mayes, K., Gurulian, I.: Log your car: the non-invasive vehicle forensics. In: 2016 IEEE Trustcom/BigDataSE/ISPA, pp. 974–982 (August 2016)
7. Feng, X., Dawam, E.S., Amin, S.: A new digital forensics model of smart city automated vehicles. In: 2017 IEEE International Conference on Internet of Things (iThings) and IEEE Green Computing and Communications (GreenCom) and IEEE Cyber, Physical and Social Computing (CPSCom) and IEEE Smart Data (SmartData), pp. 274–279 (June 2017)
8. Whelan, C.J., Sammons, J., McManus, B., Fenger, T.W.: Retrieval of infotainment system artifacts from vehicles using iVe. J. Appl. Digit. Evid. **1**(1), 30 (2018)
9. Bortles, W., McDonough, S., Smith, C., Stogsdill, M.: An introduction to the forensic acquisition of passenger vehicle infotainment and telematics systems data. In: SAE Technical Paper. SAE International (2017)

10. Cahyani, N.D.W., Martini, B., Choo, K.K.R., Al-Azhar, A.M.N.: Forensic data acquisition from cloud-of-things devices: windows smartphones as a case study. Concurr. Comput. Pract. Exp. **29**(14), e3855 (2017)
11. Barth, H.: Big data analytics für connected cars. Mobilität und digitale Transformation, pp. 137–151. Springer, Wiesbaden (2018). https://doi.org/10.1007/978-3-658-20779-3_9
12. Wiesbaden, S.F.: Personen + Unternehmen. ATZelektronik **12**(4), 6–7 (2017)
13. Knobloch, C.: Telematics systems available for 3rd Parties in comparison to OEMs telematics systems (2018). https://www.figiefa.eu/wp-content/uploads/Presentation.pdf
14. Kleberger, P., Olovsson, T., Jonsson, E.: Security aspects of the in-vehicle network in the connected car. In: 2011 IEEE Intelligent Vehicles Symposium (IV), pp. 528–533 (June 2011)
15. Fugiglando, U., et al.: Driving behavior analysis through can bus data in an uncontrolled environment. IEEE Trans. Intell. Transp. Syst. **20**(99), 1–12 (2018)
16. Theodoridis, S., Koutroumbas, K.: Pattern Recognition, 4th edn. Elsevier Inc., Amsterdam (2009)
17. Kwak, B.I., Woo, J., Kim, H.K.: Know your master: driver profiling-based anti-theft method. In: PST 2016 (2016)
18. El Basiouni El Masri, A., Artail, H., Akkary, H.: Toward self-policing: detecting drunk driving behaviors through sampling CAN bus data. In: 2017 International Conference on Electrical and Computing Technologies and Applications (ICECTA), pp. 1–5 (November 2017)
19. Hoppe, T., Kiltz, S., Dittmann, J.: Security threats to automotive CAN networks – practical examples and selected short-term countermeasures. In: Harrison, M.D., Sujan, M.-A. (eds.) SAFECOMP 2008. LNCS, vol. 5219, pp. 235–248. Springer, Heidelberg (2008). https://doi.org/10.1007/978-3-540-87698-4_21
20. Checkoway, S., et al.: Comprehensive experimental analyses of automotive attack surfaces. In: USENIX Security Symposium, San Francisco, vol. 4, pp. 447–462 (2011)

Autonomous Vehicle Architecture for High Automation

Miguel Ángel de Miguel[1]([✉]), Francisco Miguel Moreno[1], Fernando García[1], Jose María Armingol[1], and Rodrigo Encinar Martin[2]

[1] Intelligent System Lab, University Carlos III de Madrid, Leganés, Spain
{mimiguel,franmore,fegarcia,armingol}@ing.uc3m.es
[2] CESVIMAP/MAPFRE, Ávila, Spain
RENCIN1@cesvimap.com
http://www.uc3m.es/islab

Abstract. This work presents the new research platform of the Intelligent System Lab (LSI), a fully functional self driven vehicle that is used by this laboratory to research in the autonomous vehicles field. There exist many research works in perception, path planning and control, but software and hardware architecture is hardly mentioned. This paper is focused on the architecture design of this vehicle, focusing on making it very flexible and to allow testing and validating state of the art algorithms. Furthermore, all the elements needed for that automation are detailed: the modules and algorithms used and how they are connected between them, the sensors it uses, its locations and all the additional elements needed to set up an autonomous vehicle (low level control design, computers, network, ...). This platform is tested and showed in a public demonstration of an international conference, proving its flexible architecture and good performance.

Keywords: Autonomous vehicle · Self driving · Architecture

1 Introduction

Autonomous vehicles have been a research topic in growth in the last years, since they have several advantages: they can reduce the number of traffic accidents significantly, save time to users and reduce pollution [1].

Revising the literature, autonomous vehicles research is mainly focused on algorithms designed for specific tasks, like perception (obstacle detection, traffic signals and marks recognition, etc.), control or path planning, but it is hard to

Research supported by the Spanish Government through the CICYT projects (TRA2015-63708-R and TRA2016-78886-C3-1-R), and the Comunidad de Madrid through SEGVAUTO-TRIES (S2013/MIT-2713) and CESVIMAP/MAPFRE. We gratefully acknowledge the support of NVIDIA Corporation with the donation of the GPUs used for this research and Robosense for the donation of a the RS-LiDAR-32B unit.

R. Moreno-Díaz et al. (Eds.): EUROCAST 2019, LNCS 12014, pp. 145–152, 2020.
https://doi.org/10.1007/978-3-030-45096-0_18

find works describing the platform itself. Software or hardware configuration and architecture topics usually are not well covered. Which sensors to use, where to place them, all the extra components needed to set up an autonomous vehicle (batteries, network connections, low level control), in resume, how to set up an autonomous vehicle and how to put together all those algorithms to make everything work.

The purpose of this work is to present the new autonomous vehicle platform of the Intelligent Systems Lab and describe it. Based on the experience acquired in the previous platforms: IvvI [2] and IvvI 2.0 [3], two vehicles that incorporate advanced ADAS systems based mainly on vision algorithms and iCab [4], a fully autonomous vehicle that can navigate through the university campus without a driver, we have designed the architecture of our new autonomous vehicle. As we are working in a research laboratory, the main objective is to design a platform where new algorithms can be tested, so the main characteristic is that it has to be very flexible and it has to allow changing software modules to test new ones. This flexibility have to be present also in hardware, allowing the possibility of incorporating new sensors, or changing the position of the original ones without affecting the correct performance of the vehicle.

After this introduction, the content is organized as follows: Sect. 2 describes the hardware configuration of the vehicle, detailing each module, Sect. 3 describes the software architecture and some of the most relevant algorithms used, in Sect. 4 the results are presented and finally, Sect. 5 exposes the conclusions and future work.

2   Hardware Architecture

The first part of the hardware description is the vehicle itself. Unlike iCab platform, the proposed one has to be able to circulate in roads sharing traffic with real drivers, so the platform have to be able to drive in these environments. The vehicle chosen is a Mitsubishi iMiev. It is an electric vehicle which can be driven in roads up to 130 km/h and has an autonomy of 160 km. The specific model of the vehicle is not a critical factor as long as it meets a minimum speed and autonomy requirements. The only important considerations when choosing the vehicle are related to the modifications that have to be made in order to make it drive-by-wire, explained with more detail in Sect. 2.4. This vehicle is also equipped with different sensors, computers and communication devices to make it drive autonomously that will be described in the following sections.

2.1   Sensors

This is one of the most critical configuration as it supposes the main cost and it is essential for autonomous driving. The configuration have to include the minimum number of sensors that makes sure that all the elements surrounding the vehicle are correctly perceived, so it is completely secure and it follows all the driving rules (Fig. 1).

Fig. 1. Autonomous vehicle platform.

Based on our previous experience in similar projects, the most adequate sensors configuration that provides enough environment information consist on the following:

32 layers LiDAR: This sensor is mainly used to detect obstacles in the surroundings of the vehicle and get their 3D position. It is placed in the top of the vehicle and it has a non regular layer distribution, pointing more layers down, where most of the obstacles usually are. Also, odometry information can be obtained as shown in Sect. 3.3.

Monocular camera: It is used to classify these obstacles into different types (e.g. pedestrian, car, bike, etc.) and to get more information of the environment (road lanes, traffic signs, etc.). It has an optic chosen to have a 90° Horizontal Field of View, so most of the front area is covered.

RTK GPS and IMU: In order to have a precise localization of the vehicle a GPS with RTK corrections, fused with an IMU sensor is used. This system generates precise coordinates and orientation of the vehicle.

2.2 Processing

Every sensor produces a high amount of data that needs to be processed. Processing units can also be an expensive part of an autonomous vehicle. The exact amount of CPU's and GPU's have to be determined to being able to run algorithms in real time, so the computational charge of every algorithm have to be characterized. For our platform, three computers are used.

The perception computer: It receives and processes the images. It has a NVIDIA TITAN XP GPU in order to compute all the deep learning algorithms as they can run faster using GPU.

The localization computer: Is in charge of processing the pointclouds received by the LiDARs. This computer does not need any GPU, as it mainly generates LiDAR odometry.

The control computer: Manages all the low level control (CAN BUS) tha will be explained later, and the control and path planning algorithms that make the vehicle move.

2.3 Communication

All the amount of raw data provided by the sensors, and the processed data generated by the computers needs to be shared. Data from one sensor might be needed by more than one computer, or the processed data by an algorithm in one computer may be required by another computer. In order to share all this information, a STAR topology is adopted, where all the devices are connected to a switch device. The main advantage of this topology is that it is easily upgradeable if more sensors or computers are included, considering that the network will have only a few nodes with low network traffic, which this platform more than meets. Apart from computers and sensors, Internet connection is needed in order to provide GPS corrections, download maps or any other additional feature that may require it. For that purpose, a 4G router is connected to the switch, giving internet access to all the computers of the network.

2.4 Low Level Control

The low level control of the vehicle refers to the wire control of the three inputs of any vehicle: The steering wheel, the throttle and the brake pedal. In order to control these three elements of a commercial vehicle, there are some modifications that are needed. The easiest way of controlling these elements is by placing different electric actuators that move them. It allows a rapid control as the signals to control the vehicle are the same to control the actuators, but it shows some drawbacks, like having the need to create a support structure that may disturb the driver that is controlling the vehicle in manual mode. For the brake pedal, as it acts directly to the braking disks, an actuator is the only solution. The actuator pulls of the brake with a chain, making possible the driver to always press the pedal if needed for an emergency. Besides, the throttle pedal and steering wheel can be controlled by sending specific messages to the vehicle's CAN Bus as in our platform. CAN bus is an internal network of the vehicle where data like the position of the throttle or the steering wheel is published in between many other messages. By overriding these messages with the desired ones, the steering angle and acceleration can be controlled. This automation must not compromise the security of the vehicle and must have emergency systems to get manual control if necessary. The brake pedal, as it was explained before, allows always manual intervention, which means that the driver can always break if necessary. In order to stop the automatic steering and throttle, an emergency mushroom disconnects all the CAN devices giving immediate control to the driver.

2.5 Power

The last part of the hardware that the vehicle must include is the power. All the sensors and computer units have to be powered. Using the power of the electric vehicle battery can be dangerous due to the high voltage (more than 300 V), and this battery can be damaged as it is designed to only power the vehicle. An independent power supply has been chosen as the most adequate option. The main power source consists on three 12 V and 70 Ah batteries that, according to the measures of the system consumption, it can last up to three hours. The batteries are connected to an inverter that generates the appropriate 230 V alternating current needed by all the sensors and computers. The inverter output goes to an uninterruptible power supply (UPS), that allows continuous working of the system if any disconnection happens.

3   Software Architecture

Figure 2 shows a simplified diagram of all the software modules needed to make the vehicle move autonomously. The autonomous driving process starts with an user that wants to go somewhere (the goal point). The different modules (Odometry, perception, path planning, control, etc.) gets information from the sensors (GPS, Camera, LiDAR, etc.), and outputs processed information. The final output is a sequence of control signals for the steering wheel, throttle and brake pedal that will lead the vehicle to the desired goal.

In the following lines, the architecture framework used is explained so as some of the most relevant modules used in the vehicle.

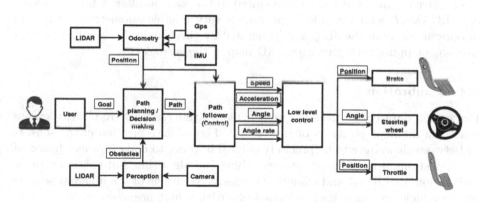

Fig. 2. Architecture of the autonomous vehicle's software.

3.1   ROS Architecture

The software architecture of the vehicle is ROS [5] based. ROS is a framework to develop robots software. It allows launching multiple algorithms in parallel (nodes) and implements communication between them with messages (topics). Using ROS adds flexibility to the system, making possible to replace an algorithm with a new one that uses the same messages types. It also helps balancing computing load as the computing resources used by each algorithm can be configured. Another advantage of using ROS is the software package suite. It includes different algorithms (path planning, control, perception, etc.), sensors drivers or different types of messages (Images, LiDAR pointclouds, odometry, etc.).

3.2   Image Obstacle Detection and Classification

Detecting obstacles is an essential task in autonomous driving. It can be performed with LiDAR or camera, but in order to get a better classification of that obstacle, camera images are needed. For this purpose, our platform uses [6], an image classification algorithm based on deep learning. This algorithm can reason simultaneously about the location of objects in the image and their orientations on the ground plane. It can classify between car, cyclist and pedestrian, but it can be trained to classify more obstacles like traffic signs or differentiate between different vehicles (trucks motorcycles, etc.). It also can perform all the inference tasks in real time, taking less than 90 ms to process an image.

3.3   LiDAR Odometry

The main localization source for our vehicle comes from the kalman filter fusion of the GPS and IMU data. However, GPS position can be inaccurate in some specific circumstances (tunnels or city roads surrounded by high buildings). An alternative odometry source is introduced to the kalman filter, a LiDAR odometry LOAM [7] which is able to produce a very reliable odometry in real time making use only of the 3D points generated by this sensor. It also allows simultaneous mapping that generates a 3D map of the scenario.

3.4   Calibration

Perception data comes from different sensors (cameras, LiDARs), but they are placed in different positions of the vehicle. The relative position of the sensors in between them have to be precisely defined in order to make a proper fusion of the detections from different sensors. Using the algorithm Automatic extrinsic calibration for LiDAR and camera [8], relative positions of the different sensors of the vehicle are calculated automatically with a high accuracy.

4   Results

The described architecture, was shown in a demonstration for the IROS conference in Madrid 2018. Here, multiple universities showed their research in autonomous driving and our platform was presented. Key features like localization, image classification, image segmentation or navigation were showed to the public on the conference (Fig. 3), proving the feasibility of the architecture and its flexibility to new changes by launching different perception algorithms changing between them.

Fig. 3. IROS 2018 demonstration.

5   Conclusions and Future Work

To conclude, the main objectives are accomplished, the new laboratory research platform is developed and fully functional with a high flexible architecture that makes possible changing both, software and hardware modules to test state of the art self driving algorithms. As the architecture of the vehicle is working, the main future work of the vehicle is focused on improving algorithms and sensors configuration. Two more LiDARs can be added in order to have more points on both sides of the vehicle, and more cameras can also be added to increase the visual filed of view. This increase of the number of sensors would require a higher computational capacity which would be easily managed with this architecture New software modules would need to be integrated in order to improve navigation and perception, such as tracking or more complex decision making and path planning algorithms that would make possible to the vehicle drive in more complex environments.

For future work, this vehicle will include the two more LIDARs mentioned before that will increase the pointcloud density, so as two more cameras that will increase the vision range. With this new sensors configuration that increase the perception range, new algorithms like tracking can be implemented. Also, more complex control and path planning modules will be tested and will make the platform achieve a more complex behaviour.

References

1. Fagnant, D.J., Kockelman, K.: Preparing a nation for autonomous vehicles: opportunities, barriers and policy recommendations. Transp. Res. Part A Policy Pract. **77**, 167–181 (2015)
2. Armingol, J.M., et al.: IvvI: intelligent vehicle based on visual information. Robot. Auton. Syst. **55**(12), 904–916 (2007)
3. Martín, D., et al.: IvvI 2.0: an intelligent vehicle based on computational perception. Expert Syst. Appl. **41**(17), 7927–7944 (2014)
4. Gomez, D., Marin-Plaza, P., Hussein, A., Escalera, A., Armingol, J.M.: Ros-based architecture for autonomous intelligent campus automobile (iCab). UNED Plasencia Revista de Investigacion Universitaria **12**, 257–272 (2016)
5. Quigley, M., et al.: ROS: an open-source robot operating system. In ICRA Workshop on Open Source Software, vol. 3, p. 5, Kobe (2009)
6. Guindel, C., Martin, D., Armingol, J.M.: Fast joint object detection and viewpoint estimation for traffic scene understanding. IEEE Intell. Transp. Syst. Mag. **10**(4), 74–86 (2018)
7. Zhang, J., Singh, S.: LOAM: lidar odometry and mapping in real-time. Robot. Sci. Syst. **2**, 9 (2014)
8. Guindel, C., Beltrán, J., Martín, D., García, F.: Automatic extrinsic calibration for lidar-stereo vehicle sensor setups. In: 2017 IEEE 20th International Conference on Intelligent Transportation Systems (ITSC), pp. 1–6. IEEE (2017)

A Mixed Integer Linear Programming Formulation for Green Vehicle Routing Problem: Case for Shuttle Services

Selin Hulagu$^{(\boxtimes)}$ (iD) and Hilmi Berk Celikoglu (iD)

Technical University of Istanbul (ITU), ITS Research Lab, 34467 Istanbul, Turkey
{hulaguselin,celikoglu}@itu.edu.tr

Abstract. In the present study, we focus on a two-stage Green Vehicle Routing Problem that we have formulated to investigate the shuttle routing plan for a relatively small and specific case. We seek in the latter stage the optimal speed profile for a route that is determined according to the shortest paths in the former stage. Our findings from the case, where two shuttles lines serve the internal area of a university campus, reveal that the two-stage formulation we propose is an efficient alternative to be utilized especially for practical applications in real life, where there is a smooth traffic with low speeds and no significant effect of the topography.

Keywords: Vehicle routing problem · Speed profile · Mixed Integer Linear Program

1 Introduction

Although the total CO_2 emissions have begun to decrease in years by 1990, and some sectoral CO_2 emissions have been trending downwards in such as industry, agriculture, and energy supply as well, sectoral CO_2 emissions from transportation have increased by 7.21% to 20.98% in total due to the fact that road transport that dominates the transportation sector in terms of CO_2 emissions is mainly based on internal combustion engine vehicles using fossils as fuel [1]. In addition to the emissions, this fact has another direct effect on the environment and public health as the exhausted gases increase the air pollution. In order to reduce the effects of road transport mentioned, both the industrial and the scientific efforts mainly focus on the de-carbonization of the fossil fuel based transport as much as possible. In this context, different vehicle technologies are introduced such as, hybrid, battery electric and fuel-cell electric vehicles, and infrastructures are consequently being developed to improve their market share. Meanwhile, considerable amount of researches have focused on vehicle routing, eco-routing, and eco-driving problems directly or indirectly in order to reduce fuel consumption of vehicles. Vehicle routing problem (VRP) handles the case of path generation to cover all the necessary nodes in a minimum traveled distance. Various variants or aspects that have been being inspired from real-world conditions are analyzed using VRP from the very first one introduced in [2] as classified in [3, 4]. Regarding the fact that a shortest path cannot

© Springer Nature Switzerland AG 2020
R. Moreno-Díaz et al. (Eds.): EUROCAST 2019, LNCS 12014, pp. 153–160, 2020.
https://doi.org/10.1007/978-3-030-45096-0_19

always provide the least fuel consuming path, the navigation concept, called eco-routing, aims to provide a route plan for a vehicle to reach its destination by tracking the least fuel consumption route considering the road characteristics [5–7]. Besides the routing problems, for a predefined route, eco-driving concept that proposes an optimal speed profile to reduce the fuel consumption of a vehicle, which can help to attain up to 25% of decrease in short term, is introduced [8]. A speed profile advisory system for a single vehicle is proposed by Bart and Boriboonsomsin [9], while Kundu and Kundu [10] focus on vehicle platoon for eco-driving control, Sciarretta et al. [11] handle the problem as an optimal control problem, Thibault et al. [12] and Padilla et al. [13] propose an eco-driving option to electric vehicles considering their limited driving ranges, and Oh and Peng [14] discuss about the applicability of eco-driving in real-world. As a variant of the VRP, Pollution Routing Problem (PRP) combines the perspectives mentioned above, and aims to minimize not only the total distance, but also the fuel consumption and emissions [15]. In this study, we focus on small and specific cases, where there is a smooth traffic with low speeds and no significant effect of the topography, such university campuses. We aim at providing a speed profile for a predetermined route according to the shortest path, in order to reduce the fuel consumption considering environmental and economic parameters.

2   Methodology

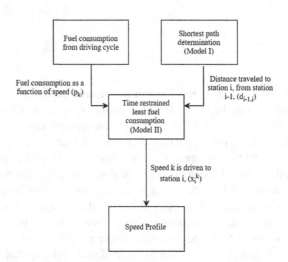

Fig. 1. Overall framework for routing method adopted.

In this study we focus on minimizing the fuel consumption of a university's shuttle services considering the higher number of their daily tours. In this context, we propose speed profiles for the shuttle services to drive covering the entire bus stops tracking the shortest path using two Mixed Integer Linear Programming (MILP) formulations. Our overall framework is summarized in Fig. 1. We have extracted the speed profiles using the Model II, where we seek the speed profile with the least fuel consumption respect to the time restrictions that has been fed with the fuel consumption function by the variation of speed, p_k, and the distance between two subsequent nodes $(d_{i-1, i})$, which are calculated respectively using a driving cycle and an MILP formulation, Model I.

2.1 Analyzing Fuel Consumption Change with Respect to Vehicle Speed

In order to propose a speed profile to minimize fuel consumption of shuttle services, we first analyze the change in fuel consumption with respect to the vehicle speed. In this context we use a simulation [16] to extract the fuel consumption and speed values of a vehicle from a driving cycle. The simulation conducted, in which the maximum speed is set to 40 km/h has revealed the excessive fuel consumption with speeds closer to 0 km/h, and the similar trends on increasing/decreasing rates for the similar speed changes. To capture the relationship between the fuel consumption and speed, we calculate the weighted average of fuel consumption values for each speed values ranging from 1 to 40 km/h, as we indicate in Fig. 2.

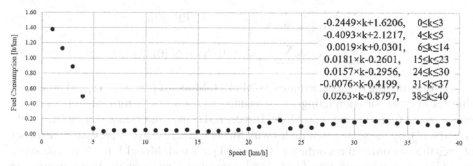

Fig. 2. Weighted average of fuel consumption values.

Having simulated the vehicle type we've considered for routing within driving cycle, we've proceeded by proposing a piecewise linear function to calculate the fuel consumption rate specific to the variance of speed, from 0 to 40 km/h, considering the speed limit areas, such university campuses, as we've focused on. The piecewise linear fuel consumption [l/km] function, p_k, written in terms of seven breakpoints and shown in Fig. 2 is determined applying linear regression.

2.2 Formulation for Mixed Integer Linear Programming Models

Although our main objective is minimizing total fuel consumption of shuttle services by proposing an optimal speed profile, routing the shuttle services considering the possible shortest path by visiting each of the bus stops should be the initial step to minimize fuel consumption. In this context we define our shortest path formulation, Model I, using a directed and complete graph $G = (N, A)$, where $N = \{0,1...n\}$ represents set of bus stop nodes in which departing and arriving depots are given respectively with $\{0\}$ and $\{n\}$, and A is set of arcs between two subsequent nodes, (i, j). The decision variable, x_{ij}, determines whether arc (i, j) is traveled or not, where the distance between two nodes is represented with d_{ij}. Model I is introduced below through the Eqs. (1) to (6), where the objective function seeks to minimize the total distance traveled (1) respecting a set of constraints given through (2) to (6). The total number of vehicles assigned for the shuttle service fleet is restricted by limiting the number of arcs leaving and arriving to the depots, as represented by (2) and (3), where m is the maximum number of vehicles that can be assigned. Constraints (4) and (5) ensure that each bus stop is visited exactly once. The flow conservation is guaranteed by (6).

$$\sum_{j \in N} \sum_{i \in N} x_{ij} \times d_{ij} \tag{1}$$

$$\sum_{j \in N \setminus \{0\} \cup \{n\}} x_{0,j} = m \tag{2}$$

$$\sum_{i \in N \setminus \{0\} \cup \{n\}} x_{i,n} = m \tag{3}$$

$$\sum_{i \in N \setminus \{n\}} x_{ij} = 1 \quad \forall j \in N \setminus \{0\} \cup \{n\} \tag{4}$$

$$\sum_{i \in N \setminus \{0\}} x_{ij} = 1 \quad \forall j \in N \setminus \{0\} \cup \{n\} \tag{5}$$

$$\sum_{j \in N} x_{ji} - \sum_{j \in N} x_{ij} = 0 \quad \forall i \in N \{0\} \cup \{n\} \tag{6}$$

Considering the route determined by Model I, Model II proposes a speed profile for shuttles to drive for completing a tour visiting all the stops in turn while targeting to minimize the fuel consumption. Model II is defined using a directed and complete graph, $G = (N, A')$, by the same set of nodes with Model I, where arc A' represents here the set of arcs that are ordered according to the routed path with Model I, $(i-1, i)$. The set of speed is represented with $V = \{1, 2 ..., v\}$ that is associated with the fuel consumption function, p_k, and the binary decision variable, x_i^k, that is used to decide whether speed k is used to drive to stop i or not, where $k \in V$. Objective function is given by (7), where parameter $d_{i-1,i}$ represents the distance traveled to node i, from node i-1. Constraint (8) forces to attain the appropriate speed value to be used to drive to the subsequent node. Time constraints that limit the duration for a complete tour, hence prevent selecting a low speed value corresponding to low fuel consumption that is likely to result in an excessive tour duration, are given in (9) and (10), where the arrival time at node i is represented with t_i, and the maximum time to finish each tour is restricted with T_{max}.

$$\min \sum_{k \in V} \sum_{i \in N} x_i^k \times p_k \times d_{i-1,i} \tag{7}$$

$$\sum_{k \in V} x_i^k = 1 \quad \forall i \in N \tag{8}$$

$$t_i \geq t_{i-1} + (\frac{d_{i-1,i}}{j} \times x_i^k) - T_{max}(1 - x_i^k) \tag{9}$$

$$t_i \leq T_{max} \tag{10}$$

3   Case Study and Results

We perform the MILP framework we propose for two shuttle service lines that serve to a university campus area in a daily basis, starting from 07:30 until 23:30. There is a great passenger demand in the campus to our interest for shuttle services, where one is expected to serve theoretically to 39300 students while other to 2052 academic staff, hence, a great number of daily tours is required to meet this demand that results in extensive amounts of fuel consumption. Shuttle lines that we call Shuttle 1 and Shuttle 2, serves respectively to eleven and nine bus stops in an 11.97 km long network piece, as shown in Fig. 3(a). We obtain the exact solution for Model I and Model II using IBM ILOG CPLEX 12.9.0 via Intel (R) Xeon (R) CPU E5-26500 processors each at 2.00 Ghz, and 32 GB of RAM.

3.1   Results of Model I

Aiming to find the shortest path possible to serve all bus stop nodes for each shuttle service, we perform Model I for given case area. Starting and ending in specific and different depots, models for Shuttle 1 and Shuttle 2 resulted respectively with 3.45 km and 2.78 km of total tour length. The paths to follow in present network by shuttles are shown in Fig. 3(b), where all the stops are visited.

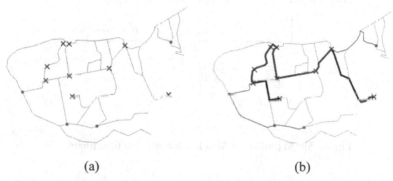

(a)   (b)

Fig. 3. (a) Network piece considered with bus stops of Shuttle 1 (see in grey squares) and Shuttle 2 (see in black cross), (b) Shortest paths for Shuttle 1 (see in grey line) and Shuttle 2 (see in black line).

3.2   Results of Model II

Considering the results of Model I, we obtain speed profiles for shuttles with the minimization of the fuel consumption via Model II. We set the distance between subsequent nodes, $d_{i-1,i}$, according to the order of bus stop nodes visited as the output of Model I. In order to decrease the computational times, we only consider the breakpoints of the piecewise linear function that we propose. The fuel consumptions, hence, the speed profiles are analyzed in three circumstances related with the time limit, T_{max}, as one of the main consideration criteria of this study. We consider in part 10, 12, and 15 min for T_{max}, for shuttles to finish their entire tours. Exact solutions of Model II returned the total fuel consumption values for: Shuttle 1 as 0.590 1, 0.375 1, and 0.336 1; and, Shuttle 2 as 0.280 1, 0.172 1, and 0.03 1 respectively from lowest to highest limit of T_{max}. Fuel consumptions increase as the time limit decreases, as expected, due to the need of driving in high speeds.

We obtain the speed profiles for two shuttle lines in different time limits using the output of Model II. As shown in Fig. 4, Shuttle 1 covers 95.7% and 4.3% of its route, driving respectively at 40 km/h and 37 km/h to complete its tour in 10 min, where it needs to drive at 37 km/h and 24 km/h respectively for the 47.2% and 52.8% of its route, in 12 min. When the time limitation is relaxed to the 15 min, Shuttle 1 covers the 69.8% of its route by driving at 24 km/h, and at 15 km/h for the rest of the tour.

Considering that Shuttle 2 has a shorter path compared to the path of Shuttle 1, a speed profile with lower speed values is proposed for all time limits accordingly, as given in Fig. 5. Results show that, for the time limit of 10 min, Shuttle 2 finishes its tour by driving at 37 km/h the 32.8% of its route, and 24 km/h the rest, where it needs to drive at 24 km/h the 71.5% of its route, and 15 km/h the rest, in the time limit of 12 min. For the last circumstance, Shuttle 2 completes its tour in 15 min by driving at 15 km/h to visit all bus stops nodes.

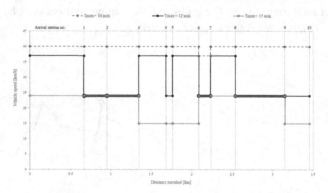

Fig. 4. Speed profiles of Shuttle 1 for different time limits.

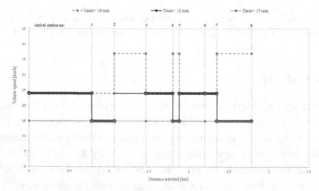

Fig. 5. Speed profiles of Shuttle 2 with different time limits.

4 Conclusions

In the present study, in conjunction with the motivation of our previous works on school bus routing [17] over a large scale road network experiencing extensive congestion in peak hours [18–24] and vehicle type selection [25] and alternative fuel vehicle routing [26] we concentrate on university shuttle services to minimize their fuel consumption to improve the air quality around campus and minimize the fuel expenses and the overall vehicle operating costs of the university, as well. We propose a piecewise linear function to the fuel consumptions for different speeds, in order to provide an optimal speed profile using the two-step MILP that minimizes the fuel consumptions for a path that is determined in terms of shortening the distance traveled. Based on the different time limits, three speed profiles have been obtained for two shuttle lines, for which the vehicles drive at least 25 tours daily.

References

1. European Environment Agency. https://www.eea.europa.eu/. Accessed 20 Nov 2018
2. Dantzig, G.B., Ramser, J.H.: The truck dispatching problem. Manage. Sci. **6**(1), 80–91 (1959)
3. Eksioglu, B., Vural, A.V., Reisman, A.: The vehicle routing problem: a taxonomic review. Comput. Ind. Eng. **57**(4), 1472–1483 (2009)
4. Braekers, K., Ramaekers, K., Nieuwenhuyse, I.V.: The vehicle routing problem: State of the art classification and review. Comput. Ind. Eng. **99**, 300–313 (2016)
5. Ericson, E., Larsson, H., Brundell-Freij, K.: Optimizing route choice for lowest fuel consumption-Potential effects of a new driver support tool. Transp. Res. Part C **14**, 369–383 (2006)
6. Boriboonsomsin, K., Barth, M.J., Zhu, W., Vu, A.: Eco-routing navigation system based on multisource historical and real-time traffic information. IEEE Trans. Intell. Transp. Syst. **13**(4), 1694–1704 (2012)
7. Sun, J., Liu, H.X.: Stochastic eco-routing in a signalized traffic network. Transp. Res. Part C **59**, 32–47 (2015)
8. Barkenbus, J.N.: Eco-driving: an overlooked climate change initiative. Energy Policy **38**(2), 762–769 (2010)
9. Barth, M., Boriboonsomsin, K.: Energy and emissions impacts of a freeway-based dynamic eco-driving system. Transp. Res. Part D Transp. Environ. **14**(6), 400–410 (2009)
10. Kundu, S., Kundu, S.: Flexible vehicle speed control algorithms for eco-driving. In: 2015 IEEE 82nd Vehicular Technology Conference (2015)
11. Sciarretta, A., De Nunzio, G., Ojeda, L.L.: Optimal ecodriving control: energy-efficient driving of road vehicles as an optimal control problem. IEEE Control Syst. Mag. **35**(5), 71–90 (2015)
12. Thibault, L., De Nunzio, G., Sciarretta, A.: A unified approach for electric vehicles range maximization via eco-routing, eco-driving, and energy consumption prediction. IEEE Trans. Intell. Veh. **3**(4), 463–475 (2018)
13. Padilla, G.P., Weiland, S., Donkers, M.C.F.: A global optimal solution to the eco-driving problem. IEEE Control Syst. Lett. **2**(4), 599–604 (2016)
14. Oh, G., Peng, H.: Eco-driving at signalized intersections: what is possible in the real-world? In: 21st International Conference on Intelligent Transportation Systems (2018)
15. Bektas, T., Gilbert, T.: The pollution-routing problem. Transp. Res. Part B Methodol. **45**(8), 1231–1250 (2011)

16. Silgu, M.A., Muderrisoglu, K., Unsal, A.H., Celikoglu, H.B.: Approximation of emission for heavy duty trucks in city traffic. In: 2018 IEEE International Conference on Vehicular Electronics and Safety (ICVES 2018) (2018)

17. Hulagu, S., Celikoglu, H.B.: An integer linear programming formulation for routing problem of university bus service. In: Daniele, P., Scrimali, L.(eds.) New Trends in Emerging Complex Real Life Problems. ASS, vol. 1, pp. 303–311. Springer, Cham (2018). https://doi.org/10.1007/978-3-030-00473-6_33

18. Celikoglu, H.B., Dell'Orco, M.: A dynamic model for acceleration behaviour description in congested traffic. In: 11th International IEEE Conference on Intelligent Transportation Systems (ITSC 2008), pp. 986–991 (2008)

19. Dell'orco, M., Celikoglu, H.B., Gurcanli, G.E.: Evaluation of traffic pollution through a dynamic link loading model. In: Li, S.C., Wang, Y.J., Cao, F.X., Huang, P., Zhang, Y. (eds.) Progress in Environmental Science and Technology, vol. II, Pts A & B, pp. 773–777 (2009). ISBN 978-7-03-024459-8

20. Demiral, C., Celikoglu, H.B.: Application of ALINEA ramp control algorithm to freeway traffic flow on approaches to Bosphorus strait crossing bridges. Procedia Soc. Behav. Sci. **20**, 364–371 (2011)

21. Deniz, O., Aksoy, G., Celikoglu, H.B.: Analyzing freeway travel times within a case study: reliability of route traversal times. In: 16th International IEEE Conference on Intelligent Transportation Systems (ITSC 2013), pp. 195–202 (2013)

22. Abuamer, I.M., Silgu, M.A., Celikoglu, H.B.: Micro-simulation based ramp metering on Istanbul Freeways: an evaluation adopting ALINEA. In: 2016 IEEE 19th International Conference on Intelligent Transportation Systems (ITSC 2016), pp. 695–700 (2016)

23. Sadat, M., Celikoglu, H.B.: Simulation-based variable speed limit systems modelling: an overview and a case study on Istanbul Freeways. Transp. Res. Procedia **22**, 607–614 (2017)

24. Abuamer, I.M., Sadat, M., Silgu, M.A., Celikoglu, H.B.: Analyzing the effects of driver behavior within an adaptive ramp control scheme: a case-study with ALINEA. In: 2017 IEEE International Conference on Vehicular Electronics and Safety (ICVES 2017), pp. 109–114 (2017)

25. Akti, S., Celikoglu, H.B.: An integrated decision making framework for vehicle selection in shuttle services: case of a university campus. In: Proceedings of the 6th International Conference on Models and Technologies for Intelligent Transportation Systems (MT-ITS 2019). IEEE Press (2019). ISBN 978-1-7281-2075-1

26. Hulagu, S., Celikoglu, H.B.: A multiple objective formulation of an electric vehicle routing problem for shuttle bus fleet at A University Campus. In: Proceedings of the 6th International Conference on Models and Technologies for Intelligent Transportation Systems (MT-ITS 2019). IEEE Press (2019). ISBN 978-1-7281-2075-1

An Integrated Decision-Making Framework for Shuttle Bus Selection Using DEMATEL and MULTIMOORA Methods

Sercan Akti[1]([⊠]) [iD] and Hilmi Berk Celikoglu[2] [iD]

[1] Faculty of Civil Engineering, Department of Civil Engineering,
Technical University of Istanbul (ITU), Ayazaga Campus, 34469 Istanbul, Turkey
aktis@itu.edu.tr
[2] Faculty of Civil Engineering, ITS Research Lab, Technical University of Istanbul (ITU),
Istanbul, Turkey
celikoglu@itu.edu.tr

Abstract. In the present study we integrate the Decision Making Trial and Evaluation Laboratory (DEMATEL) and the Multi-Objective Optimization by Ratio Analysis and Full Multiplicative Form (MULTIMOORA) methods to form a Multi-Criteria Decision Making process, in which we seek the solution for the problem of ranking the suitable options for vehicles types to be used in a shuttle bus fleet that serves the internal transport of a university campus.

Keywords: Multi-Criteria Decision Making · Environmental sustainability · Electric vehicles

1 Introduction

Providing people with freedom to travel both short and long distances, allowing them to contact each other easily, and increasing the opportunities for leisure activities, transport can be considered as a significant part of the modern world. As the transport makes people lives easier, demand for the transportation has a tendency to increase continuously. Figure 1 shows demand for both passenger and freight transport in Turkey between 2003 and 2017 [1]. It can be concluded from the figure that the demand for passenger transport in 2017 is almost twice the amount in 2003.

Beside its advantages, there is a significant concern about the road transport using fossil fuels, which is the severe effect of consequent air pollution on human health. The continuous increase in demand for transportation, and, consequently, the use of vehicles using conventional fuel types such as fossil fuels, causes serious problems on the environment. According to Künzli et al., ten thousands of people suffer from the diseases caused by road transport based air pollution [2]. Figure 2 demonstrates the rate of fuel types used in transportation sector [3]. According to the Turkish Statistical Institute, there are 3089626 vehicles (24.9% of total vehicles) with gasoline, 4568665 vehicles (36.8% of total vehicles) with diesel, 4695717 vehicles (37.9% of total vehicles) with LPG, 5367 vehicles (nearly 0.0% of total vehicles) with electric or hybrid and 38815 vehicles (0.3% of total vehicles) with unknown fuel type in 2018 [4].

© Springer Nature Switzerland AG 2020
R. Moreno-Díaz et al. (Eds.): EUROCAST 2019, LNCS 12014, pp. 161–169, 2020.
https://doi.org/10.1007/978-3-030-45096-0_20

	2003	2004	2005	2006	2007	2008	2009	2010	2011	2012	2013	2014	2015	2016	2017
Vehicle-km (Billion)	52,3	57,8	61,1	64,6	69,6	69,8	72,4	80,1	85,5	94,0	99,4	103,0	113,3	119,7	128,0
Passenger-km (Billion)	164,3	174,3	182,2	187,6	209,1	206,1	212,5	226,9	242,3	258,9	268,2	276,1	290,7	300,9	314,7
Tonne-km (Billion)	152,2	156,9	166,8	177,4	181,3	181,9	176,5	190,4	203,1	216,1	224,0	234,5	244,3	253,1	262,7

Fig. 1. Increase in transportation demand between 2003 and 2017 (Republic of Turkey Directory of Strategy Development)

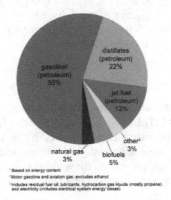

Fig. 2. U.S. Transportation Energy Sources/Fuels (U.S. Energy Information Administration, April 2018)

It is a well-known fact that the main reason of Green House Gas (GHG) emissions due to road transportation is vehicles with fossil fuels. These vehicles emit environmentally harmful gases, including carbon monoxide (CO), hydrocarbons (HC), and nitrogen oxides (NOx). In addition to the greenhouse effect caused by harmful gases, the leakage of harmful chemicals such as fuel or oil from road vehicles can also lead to water and soil degradation. The environmental pollution, air pollution, GHG emissions, global warming, and high oil prices have been the main motivation for the stakeholders of both the transport service and the vehicular industry on seeking environmentally friend transportation options. Therefore, the vehicles powered by alternative energy resources involving hybrid electric vehicles (HEVs) and electric vehicles (EVs) are introduced as alternatives to fossil - fueled vehicles in transport. Since there are many different brands producing EVs with different characteristics today, selecting the most suitable vehicle for their intended use is a challenging task for users.

In this study, as an extension of our ongoing study on vehicle type selection [5] in conjunction with an optimal routing and scheduling study [6, 7], with the ultimate motivation to aid the decision-making process for renewing the shuttle bus fleet -which currently consists of all internal combustion engine vehicles- serving a university campus, we focus on the problem of selecting the most suitable vehicle for the road network of a medium-scale settlement. Given the characteristics on shuttle operation in addition to the technical features of vehicles considered, we seek the solution to the problem integrating the Decision Making Trial and Evaluation Laboratory (DEMA-TEL) and the Multi-Objective Optimization by Ratio Analysis and Full Multiplicative Form (MULTIMOORA) methods to form a Multi-Criteria Decision Making (MCDM) process.

2   Problem Definition

In the present study, we focus on the problem of selecting the most suitable vehicle for the shuttle fleet serving over the road network of a medium-scale settlement. In view of the characteristics of shuttle operation besides the technical features of the vehicles taken into consideration, we seek the solution to the decision-making problem integrating the DEMATEL with the MULTIMOORA.

3   Problem Solution

In the decision-making process, the MULTIMOORA method allows making the best choice among alternatives using three different techniques including Ratio System, Reference Point Approach and Full Multiplicative Form, and the DEMATEL method gives the priorities of selected evaluation criteria. Using the DEMATEL method, the interdependency between elements in a complex system can be analyzed and this method can also investigate the cause and effect relationship between selected criteria [8]. In the decision process, the best alternative is determined based on the comparison of three ranking calculated with three different techniques, all of which are parts of the MULTIMOORA method [9]. In our study, while we utilize the DEMATEL method to determine the weights of the selected main and the sub criteria in terms of both qualitative and qualitative data, including economic, technical, and environmental measures as the main criteria and purchasing price, energy consumption, taxing, capacity, motor power, range, climbing ability, turning circle, vehicle weight, maximum speed, vehicle life, CO emission, NOx emission, HC emission, and the particulate emission measures as the sub-criteria, and the MULTIMOORA method to rank the selected alternatives from a total of six consisting of internal combustion, hybrid, and electric vehicles based on the calculated weights in the previous step.

In the following, we summarize the integrated structure of the overall MCDM frame we propose detailing the weight determining and the ranking methods.

3.1   Calculation of the Criteria Weights Using DEMATEL Method [10]

The calculation steps are followed to determine the priorities of selected evaluation criteria in DEMATEL method.

3.1.1   Construction of the Direct-Influence Matrix

For a decision-making problem, selected n-criteria are compared each other using N-scale pair-wise comparison scale, which forms the average matrix. The direct-influence matrices including the pair-wise comparison of sub-criteria with respect to the main criteria are given Figs. 3a, 3b, 3c and 3d.

SELECTION OF THE MOST APPROPRIATE VEHICLE FOR SHUTTLE BUS FLEET	Economical	Technical	Environmental	Total
Economical	0.00	2.00	1.00	3.00
Technical	2.00	0.00	1.00	3.00
Environmental	4.00	3.00	0.00	7.00
Total	6.00	5.00	2.00	
s	7.00			

Fig. 3a. Direct-influence matrix including pair-wise comparison of main criteria with respect to the goal

ECONOMICAL	Purchasing Price	Energy Consumption	Taxing	Total
Purchasing Price	0.00	3.00	4.00	7.00
Energy Consumption	1.00	0.00	2.00	3.00
Taxing	1.00	2.00	0.00	3.00
Total	2.00	5.00	6.00	
s	7.00			

Fig. 3b. Direct-influence matrix including pair-wise comparison of sub-criteria with respect to the Economical main criterion

TECHNICAL	Capacity	Motor Power	Range	Climbing Ability	Turning Circle	Vehicle Weight	Maximum Speed	Vehicle Life	Total
Capacity	0.00	3.00	1.00	2.00	2.00	3.00	4.00	1.00	16.00
Motor Power	1.00	0.00	1.00	1.00	1.00	2.00	3.00	1.00	10.00
Range	1.00	3.00	0.00	2.00	3.00	4.00	4.00	2.00	19.00
Climbing Ability	1.00	2.00	1.00	0.00	2.00	3.00	4.00	1.00	14.00
Turning Circle	1.00	2.00	1.00	1.00	0.00	2.00	3.00	1.00	11.00
Vehicle Weight	1.00	1.00	1.00	1.00	1.00	0.00	2.00	1.00	8.00
Maximum Speed	1.00	1.00	1.00	1.00	1.00	1.00	0.00	1.00	7.00
Vehicle Life	1.00	3.00	1.00	2.00	2.00	3.00	4.00	0.00	16.00
Total	7.00	15.00	7.00	10.00	12.00	18.00	24.00	8.00	
s	24.00								

Fig. 3c. Direct-influence matrix including pair-wise comparison of sub-criteria with respect to the Technical main criterion

ENVIRONMENTAL	CO Emission	NOx Emission	HC Emission	Particulate Matter Emission	Total
CO Emission	0.00	1.00	1.00	1.00	3.00
NOx Emission	4.00	0.00	2.00	1.00	7.00
HC Emission	4.00	2.00	0.00	1.00	7.00
Particulate Matter Emission	4.00	2.00	3.00	0.00	9.00
Total	12.00	5.00	6.00	3.00	
s	12.00				

Fig. 3d. Direct-influence matrix including pair-wise comparison of sub-criteria with respect to the Environmental main criterion

3.1.2 Calculation of the Normalized Direct-Influence Matrix

To compare the selected diverse criteria directly, the initial matrix should be normalized so that each value in the matrix will between 0–1.

For the normalization, the sum of each row and column are calculated and the highest sum value is determined. Then, each cell in the initial matrix is divided by this value;

$$X_{ij}^* = \frac{X_{ij}}{\max\left(\max_{1 \le i \le n}\left(\sum_{j=1}^{n} X_{ij}\right), \max_{1 \le i \le n}\left(\sum_{i=1}^{n} X_{ij}\right)\right)}, \quad i, j \in (1, 2, \ldots, n) \quad (1)$$

where, X_{ij} is the influence of ith criterion on j^{th} criterion, X_{ij}^* is the normalized value, n is the number of the criteria.

3.1.3 Construction of the Total-Influence Matrix

Enabling the expression of the relationship between the selected evaluation criteria, total influence matrix is calculated using Eq. (2).

$$T = X * (I - X) \quad (2)$$

where, T the total-influence matrix, X the initial direct-influence matrix and I the identity matrix.

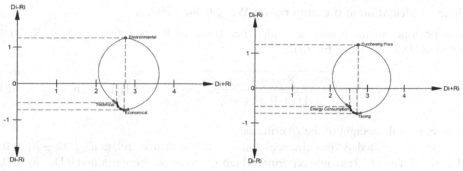

Fig. 4a. Total influential map for main criteria   **Fig. 4b.** Total influential map for cost related main criterion

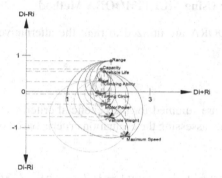

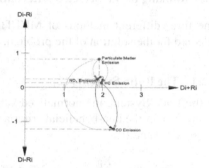

Fig. 4c. Total influential map for vehicle dynamics related main criterion

Fig. 4d. Total influential map for environment related main criterion

3.1.4 Drawing of the Influential Relation Map

The sum of each row (D) and column (R) are calculated;

$$D = [d_i]_{nx1} \left[\sum_{j=1}^{n} t_{ij} \right]_{nx1}, \quad i, j \in (1, 2, \ldots, n) \tag{3}$$

$$R = [r_j]_{1xn} \left[\sum_{i=1}^{n} t_{ij} \right]_{1xn} \tag{4}$$

where, d_i is the ith row sum in the matrix T, r_j is the jth column sum in the matrix T, t_{ij} is the each cell value in matrix T.

The influential relation maps drawn for pair-wise comparison matrices are given Figs. 4a, 4b, 4c and 4d.

3.1.5 Calculation of the Importance Weights for Criteria

The priorities of the criteria are calculated based on the prominence $(D_i + R_i)$ and relation $(D_i - R_i)$ using Eq. (5).

$$w_i = \frac{\sqrt{(D_i + R_i)^2 + (D_i - R_i)^2}}{\sum_{i=1}^{n} \sqrt{(D_i + R_i)^2 + (D_i - R_i)^2}}, \quad i = 1, 2, \ldots, n \tag{5}$$

where, w_i is the weight of the ith criterion.

$D_i + R_i$ is called as "prominence" and $D_i - R_i$ is called as "relation". If $D_i - R_i > 0$, the criterion is called as cause criterion, which affects all other criteria, and If $D_i - R_i < 0$, the criterion is called as effect criterion, which is affected by all other criteria [11].

3.2 Ranking of the Selected Alternatives Using MULTIMOORA Method

The three different methods of MULTIMOORA are utilized to rank the alternatives selected for the solution of the problem.

3.2.1 The Ratio System [12]

In the Ratio System, the normalized values are summed for the beneficial criteria and subtracted for the non-beneficial criteria while assessing the evaluation criteria based on the Eqs. (8) and (9).

$$X_{ij}^* = \frac{X_{ij}}{\sqrt{\sum_{i=1}^{m} X_{ij}^2}}, \quad (X_{ij}^* \in [0, 1]; \ i = 1, 2, \ldots, m; j = 1, 2, \ldots, n) \tag{6}$$

where, X_{ij} is the response of ith alternative on j^{th} criterion, X_{ij}^* is the normalized response of ith alternative on j^{th} criterion, m is the number of alternatives, n is the number of criteria.

After calculation of the normalization matrix, the normalized values are multiplied with the calculated criteria weights to obtain the weighted normalization matrix.

$$r_{ij} = w_j * X_{ij}^*, \quad (j = 1, 2, \ldots, n) \tag{7}$$

where, r_{ij} is the weighted normalized value, w_j is the weight of the jth criterion.

$$y_i^+ = \sum_{j \in \Omega_{max}} r_{ij} \qquad y_i = y_i^+ - y_i^- \tag{8}$$

$$y_i^- = \sum_{j \in \Omega_{min}} r_{ij} \tag{9}$$

where, y_i is the overall importance of ith alternative, y_i^+ is the overall importance of ith alternative based on the benefit criteria (to be maximized), y_i^- is the overall importance of ith alternative based on the cost criteria (to be minimized), Ω_{max} and Ω_{min} are the sets of benefit and cost criteria, respectively.

In the final ranking, the alternative with the highest y_i value is accepted as the best.

3.2.2 The Reference Point Approach

In the Reference Point Approach, while the maximum normalized value is accepted as the reference point for the beneficial criteria, the minimum normalized value is accepted as the reference point for the non-beneficial criteria. The ranking of alternatives are performed based on the deviation from the reference point using Eqs. (10) and (11) [13].

$$d_i^{max} = \max_j \left(w_j * \left| X_j^* - X_{ij}^* \right| \right) \tag{10}$$

where, d_i^{max} is the maximum distance of ith alternative to the reference point, X_j^* is the reference point for the jth criterion.

$$X_j^* = \begin{cases} \max_i X_{ij}^*, & j \in \Omega_{max} \\ \min_i X_{ij}^*, & j \in \Omega_{min} \end{cases} \tag{11}$$

In the final ranking, the alternative with the lowest d_i^{max} value is accepted as the best [12].

3.2.3 The Full Multiplicative Form

In Eq. (12) utilized in the Full Multiplicative Form, product of the weighted normalization values of beneficial criteria is represented by the numerator and the product of the weighted normalization values of non-beneficial criteria is represented by the denominator [14].

$$U_i = \frac{\prod_{j \in \Omega_{max}} r_{ij}^{w_j}}{\prod_{j \in \Omega_{min}} r_{ij}^{w_j}} \tag{12}$$

where, $\prod_{j \in \Omega_{max}} r_{ij}^{w_j}$ is the multiplication of the weighted normalization values of beneficial criteria, $\prod_{j \in \Omega_{min}} r_{ij}^{w_j}$ is the multiplication of the weighted normalization values of cost criteria.

In the final ranking, the alternative with the highest U_i value is accepted as the best.

The final decision is made based on the results obtained from these three methods. In the final ranking order, the alternative appearing mostly in the first positions on all ranking tables is accepted as the best alternative [12].

The decision matrix constructed for MULTIMOORA method including calculated weights by DEMATEL method, and the final ranking list obtained with three different methods are given in Figs. 5 and 6, respectively.

	Purchasing Price	Energy Consumption	Taxing	Capacity	Motor Power	Range	Climbing Ability	Turning Circle	Vehicle Weight	Maximum Speed	Vehicle Life	CO Emission	NOx Emission	HC Emission	Particulate Matter Emission
Unit	(TL)	(kWh/100 km)	(%)	(people)	(kW)	(km)	(%)	(m)	(kg)	(km/h)	(1-3)	(gr/km)	(gr/km)	(gr/km)	(gr/km)
Direction	↓ (min)	↓ (min)	↓ (min)	↑ (max)	↑ (max)	↑ (max)	↑ (max)	↓ (min)	↓ (min)	↑ (max)	↑ (max)	↓ (min)	↓ (min)	↓ (min)	↓ (min)
weights	0.049	0.009	0.017	0.075	0.021	0.098	0.033	0.033	0.012	0.008	0.054	0.285	0.151	0.093	0.052
A1 (ICV)	510770.00	101.88	9.00	29.00	107.00	1055.00	32.00	6.60	9000.00	109.00	3.00	0.50	0.08	0.17	0.01
A2 (ICV)	514737.00	101.88	9.00	29.00	140.00	830.00	37.40	6.45	9800.00	105.00	3.00	0.50	0.08	0.17	0.01
A3 (HEV)	1728512.50	240.89	2.25	22.00	146.40	400.00	18.00	8.53	9300.00	72.00	2.00	0.50	0.25	0.30	0.03
A4 (HEV)	3031545.00	145.46	2.25	32.00	176.27	810.00	18.00	10.83	19000.00	70.00	2.00	0.50	0.08	0.17	0.01
A5 (EV)	514010.86	130.00	2.25	26.00	180.00	250.00	15.00	12.00	19000.00	70.00	1.00	0.00	0.00	0.00	0.00
A6 (EV)	797775.00	130.00	2.25	23.00	180.00	217.00	17.00	9.17	13500.00	90.00	1.00	0.00	0.00	0.00	0.00
TOTAL	3688429.59	365.71	13.50	66.29	385.17	1651.55	59.87	22.43	34172.80	214.45	5.29	1.00	0.29	0.42	0.03

Fig. 5. The decision matrix constructed for MULTIMOORA method including calculated weights by DEMATEL method

	Ratio System	Reference Point Approach	Full Multiplicative Form	FINAL RANKING
A1	3	3	3	3
A2	4	3	4	4
A3	6	3	6	6
A4	5	3	5	5
A5	1	1	1	1
A6	2	2	2	2

Fig. 6. The final ranking list

4   Discussion and Conclusion

In the current study, DEMATEL and MULTIMOORA methods are used in an integrated way for the solution of the decision-making problem on determining the most suitable type of vehicles for the renewal of the shuttle bus fleet operated in a university campus.

For the solution of the decision-making problem, we have specified a number of criteria considering both alternative vehicle specifications and similar studies. While we have employed the DEMATEL method to calculate the priorities of the criteria, we've used the MULTIMOORA method to rank the alternatives.

In the solution process, the environmental effects of vehicles are determined as the main consideration. At the end of the study, Alternative 5, which is one of the electric vehicles, is determined as the solution of the decision-making problem based on the three different methods. The second best alternative is determined to be Alternative 6, which is also one of the electric vehicles. Although the internal combustion vehicles are more harmful for the environment than hybrid vehicles, hybrid vehicles - Alternative 3 and Alternative 4 - are determined to be the lattermost two solutions due to purchasing costs.

References

1. Transport, maritime and communication with statistics, Republic of Turkey Directory of Strategy Development. ISBN: 978-975-493-095-5 (2018)
2. Künzli, N., et al.: Public-health impact of outdoor and traffic-related air pollution: a European assessment. Lancet **356**, 795–801 (2000). https://doi.org/10.1016/S0140-6736(00)02653-2
3. https://www.eia.gov/energyexplained/index.php?page=us_energy_transportation
4. Turkish Statistical Institute: Distribution of vehicles registered to the traffic by vehicle type. http://www.turkstat.gov.tr/UstMenu.do?metod=temelist
5. Akti, S., Celikoglu, H.B.: An integrated decision making framework for vehicle selection in shuttle services: case of a university campus. In: Proceedings of the 6th International Conference on Models and Technologies for Intelligent Transportation Systems (MT-ITS 2019). IEEE Press (2019). ISBN: 978-1-7281-2075-1
6. Hulagu, S., Celikoglu, H.B.: A multiple objective formulation of an electric vehicle routing problem for shuttle bus fleet at a university campus. In: Proceedings of the 6th International Conference on Models and Technologies for Intelligent Transportation Systems (MT-ITS 2019). IEEE Press (2019). ISBN: 978-1-7281-2075-1
7. Hulagu, S., Celikoglu, H.B.: A mixed integer linear programming formulation for green vehicle routing problem: case for shuttle services. In: Moreno-Díaz, R., Pichler, F., Quesada-Arencibia, A. (eds.) EUROCAST 2019. LNCS, vol. 12014, pp. 153–160. Springer, Heidelberg (2020)
8. Si, S.L., You, X.Y., Liu, H.C., Zhang, P.: DEMATEL technique: a systematic review of the state-of-the-art literature on methodologies and applications. Math. Probl. Eng. **2018** (2018). https://doi.org/10.1155/2018/3696457
9. Aytac Adali, E., Tus Isik, A.: The multi-objective decision making methods based on MULTIMOORA and MOOSRA for the laptop selection problem. J. Ind. Eng. Int. **13**, 229–237 (2017). https://doi.org/10.1007/s40092-016-0175-5
10. Ren, J.: New energy vehicle in China for sustainable development. analysis of success factors and strategic implications. Transp. Res. Part D Transp. Environ. **59**, 268–288 (2018). https://doi.org/10.1016/j.trd.2018.01.017
11. Wu, W.W.: Choosing knowledge management strategies by using a combined ANP and DEMATEL approach. Expert Syst. Appl. **35**, 828–835 (2008). https://doi.org/10.1016/j.eswa.2007.07.025
12. Stanujkic, D., Zavadskas, E.K., Smarandache, F., Brauers, W.K.M., Karabasevic, D.: A neutrosophic extension of the MULTIMOORA method. Informatica **28**(1), 181–192 (2017). https://doi.org/10.15388/Informatica.2017.125
13. Li, Z.H.: An extension of the MULTIMOORA method for multiple criteria group decision making based upon hesitant fuzzy sets. J. Appl. Math. **2014**, 1–16 (2014). https://doi.org/10.1155/2014/527836
14. Hafezalkotob, A., Hafezalkotob, A., Sayadi, M.K.: Extension of MULTIMOORA method with interval numbers: an application in materials selection. Appl. Math. Model. **40**, 1372–1386 (2016). https://doi.org/10.1016/j.apm.2015.07.019

Floating Car Data: Comparison of Smartphone and On-Board Diagnostics (OBD)

Erum Naz[1], Franz Kopica[2] (iD), and Cristina Olaverri-Monreal[2(✉)] (iD)

[1] Institute of Software Technology and Interactive Systems, Technische Universität Wien,
Vienna, Austria
erum.naz@ectuwien.ac.at
[2] Chair Sustainable Transport Logistics 4.0., Johannes Kepler University Linz, Linz, Austria
{franz.kopica,cristina.olaverri-monreal}@jku.at

Abstract. On-board diagnostic (OBD) devices are able to extract information in vehicles to determine traffic flow patterns through localization data, speed, and direction of travel and time. An alternative, low-cost, ubiquitous custom-built mobile application, "SmartDriving" (SD) is presented in this paper. The resulting data from the mobile application was compared with data collected through OBD. Results showed that the collected data was satisfactory regardless of the device used and therefore the mobile application was validated as data collection tool.

Keywords: OBD · Smartphones · Sensors · Driving behavior

1 Introduction

Applications that provide information regarding the monitoring of mobility patterns are of particular interest for the transportation sector, as they can be used to study driving behavior that affect traffic flow and road safety [1]. For example data related to travel time can be used to measure congestion [2] and data-based applications that adhere to sensor technology are able to advance transportation through real time transport services that promote a of low environmental impact. In line with this, the driving style known as eco-driving was defined in the mid '90s and in the last decade it has been the subject of some initiatives and projects at European level. The growth of the eco-driving awareness is also testified by the many websites promoting this driving style in the U.S. and worldwide [3].

Due to the large number of electronic systems, modern vehicles are becoming an invaluable source of information that can be used for different purposes. With the help of these data a variety of applications can be developed to assist the driver. For example, to monitor the vehicle health, analyze driving behavior, for vehicle fault detection, and driving style evaluation criteria's. As a result of the analysis of the gathered information driving patterns can be improved and fuel consumption decreased contributing thus to reduce the environmental impact of traffic.

Accurate and timely information regarding traffic is decisive to minimize congestion and reduce travel times, being thus road and vehicle monitoring crucial for road safety

© Springer Nature Switzerland AG 2020
R. Moreno-Díaz et al. (Eds.): EUROCAST 2019, LNCS 12014, pp. 170–176, 2020.
https://doi.org/10.1007/978-3-030-45096-0_21

and efficiency of transport. To this end the European Commission has introduced a unit known as European On-board diagnosis (EOBD) that is in charge of monitoring the emissions of vehicles [4].

Several systems have been developed to acquire data related to driving patterns using smart phones. Their embedded sensors (i.e. accelerometer, digital compass, gyroscope, GPS, microphone, camera) make them cost efficient devices to gain information related to traffic or road conditions. For example, tri-axis acceleration signals can be analyzed to extract road surface anomaly information by using similar techniques to those applied in the classification of driver styles [5].

The tracking and localization of data related to vehicles can also be facilitated by OBD data loggers. Several solutions from different vendors for fleet management and tracking already exist that include telematics platforms for vehicle health monitoring or to track stolen vehicles [6–9].

2 Implementation

In this paper, we present a method to collect and integrate data from OBD II and smart devices. We aim at determining which device provides a more efficient and cost effective solution with regards to a real-time assistance for drivers based on their driving behavior. Data is collected from two different sources via the telecommunication system 3G or LTE, and stored in a MySQL database for later retrieval via multiple queries and a subsequent analysis and visualization.

The system architecture was designed for open source software. We used the LAMP stack which consists of the four components Linux (operating system), Apache (web server), MySQL (database system) and PHP (server-side script interpreter).

A Web interface was also developed to monitor and display all the collected data in a user-friendly manner. Figure 1 represents the data acquisition and integration method. Data analysis takes place based on input from sensors. Relevant notifications regarding unsafe or inefficient driving behavior are then sent to the driver via Application Programming Interfaces (API).

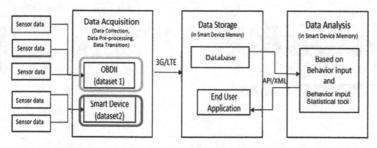

Fig. 1. Conceptual diagram to acquire and analyze the collected data.

2.1 OBD Data Collection

Data was acquired through an OBD device by using the advanced plug and track real-time tracking terminal with GNSS, GSM and Bluetooth connectivity, TELTONIKA FMB001. The device is able to collect device coordinates and other useful data including vehicle onboard computer data to transfer them via GSM network to the server.

In case of a loss of connection to GNSS satellites, it continues to acquire data that is logged under the last known coordinates. Data are stored in a SD memory card for later transmission to the server via GPRS.

This device is suitable for applications where location of remote objects is needed: fleet management, car rental or taxi companies, personal vehicles, etc. The TELTONIKA FMB001 connects directly to the car OBD-II and is able to read up to 32 vehicle onboard parameters. Data monitoring and visualization can be performed through a desktop and web-based application. Figures 2 and 3 illustrate the data collection process and the web interface respectively.

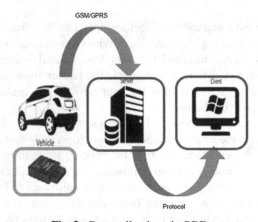

Fig. 2. Data collection via OBD.

Fig. 3. ODB Web interface from Teltonika.

2.2 Smart Phone Data Collection and Analysis

To collect mobile phone-related data we developed an Android application that we called *SmartDriving (SD)*. The application is capable of monitoring driving behavior by using mobile sensors such as GPS, Bluetooth and accelerometer.

The application provides an interface to create an administrator account. After successful registration, the administrator can manage different users (i.e. drivers) and add vehicles. The location of the driver's vehicle is shown on a map. When the driver activates the "start trip" button, the parameters below are captured and stored in a MYSQL database:

- Vehicle's coordinates
- Altitude
- Current Time
- Speed of vehicle (m/s)
- Acceleration of vehicle (m/s^2)
- Deceleration of vehicle (m/s^2)
- Bluetooth

    - Number of Bluetooth devices found near or in the range of the driver's smart phone with time stamp
    - Signal strength (low, medium, high)
    - Bluetooth MAC address

Fig. 4. *SmartDriving* application. The image on the left shows the login interface. The image on the right shows one of the trips that were taken.

- Angular velocity
- Temperature (Celsius)

The "End Trip" button stops the recording process. All the travels performed are plotted on Google Maps (for a real time driving monitoring the respective API were used) as polylines via latitude/longitude coordinates. The administrator can see the list of drivers, registered vehicles and all the trips that are incomplete (in process) or have been already completed. Users can also update their information and change their passwords. The *SmartDriving* application works with sensors of the Android device, which is why it requires certain permissions. Figure 4 shows its user interface. Figure 5 shows the flow diagram that illustrates the major components of the developed smart phone application.

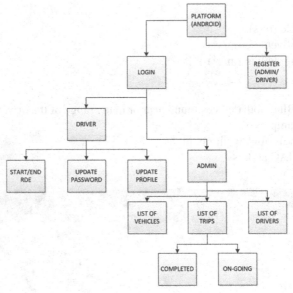

Fig. 5. Flow diagram illustrating the major components of the developed *SmartDriving* application

The logical database design was implemented in MySQL. Figure 6 shows the entity relationship diagram. The data collection steps of both the *SmartDriving* and the OBD are illustrated in the flow diagram in Fig. 7. Travel data such as origin and destination were visualized on Google Maps.

Data from 5 trips of 15 min each was collected for 5 consecutive days using a OBD device and the smart phone application both in the same trip. 18,000 records were analyzed and their differences regarding both collection methods evaluated by plotting the trips on maps and calculating the difference between the two data sets.

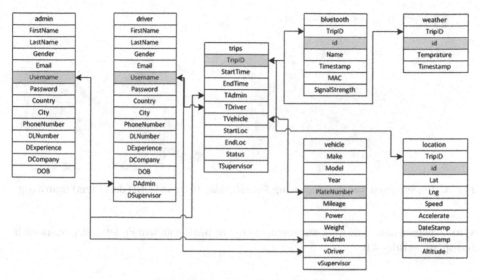

Fig. 6. Entity relationship diagram.

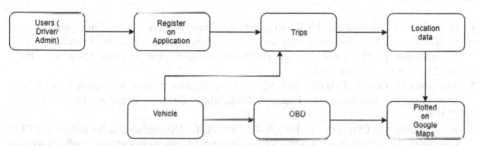

Fig. 7. Flow diagram illustrating the developed *SmartDriving* smart phone application and the data collected by using an OBD device

3   Results

Location data comparison occurred based on differences between distances at a particular location. Results showed a good performance of the developed application as illustrated in Fig. 8 by an example of the data collected using the *SmartDriving* application and the data collected from OBD.

Trip ID : 180929162923 Map Details

Fig. 8. Implemented web portal showing *SmartDriving* (left) and OBD data (right) from a trip.

Acknowledgments. This work was supported by the BMK endowed Professorship Sustainable Transport Logistics 4.0.

References

1. Gonçalves, J., Gonçalves, J.S.V., Rossetti, R., Olaverri-Monreal, C.: Smartphone sensor platform to study traffic conditions and assess driving performance. In: Proceedings 17th International IEEE Conference on Intelligent Transportation Systems, Qingdao, China, pp. 2596–2601, October 2014
2. Margiotta, R., Lomax, T., Hallenbeck, M., Dowling, R., Skabardonis, A., Turner, S.: Analytical procedures for determining the impacts of reliability mitigation strategies, Technical report (2013)
3. Alessandrini, A., Cattivera, A., Filippi, F., Ortenzi, F.: Driving style influence on car CO2 emissions. http://www3.epa.gov/ttnchie1/conference/ei20/session8/acattivera.pdf. Accessed 22 Feb 2016
4. VW, European On-Board Diagnosis. http://www.volkspage.net/technik/ssp/ssp/SSP_315.PDF. Accessed 21 Sept 2016
5. Meiring, G., Myburgh, H.: A Review of intelligent driving style analysis systems and related artificial intelligence algorithms. Sensors **12**, 30653–30682 (2015)
6. Ulbotech. http://www.ulbotech.com/. Accessed 23 Nov 2016
7. Teltonika.   http://teltonika.lt/products/products-and-solutions/autonomous-gps-trackers/. Accessed 23 Nov 2016
8. Jheng-Syu, J., Shi-Huang, C., Wu-Der, T., Mei-Chiao, L.: The Implementation of OBD-II vehicle diagnosis system integrated with cloud computation technology. In: Second International Conference on Robot, Vision and Signal Processing, Kitakyushu (2014)
9. Lian-Bi, C., Hong-Yuan, L., Wan-Jung, C., Jing-Jou, T., Shu-Min, L.: An intelligent vehicular telematics platform for vehicle driving safety supporting system. In: International Conference on Connected Vehicles and Expo (ICCVE), Shenzhen (2015)

Promotion of Sustainable Transport by a Tracking System for Bicycles

Daniel Braunauer[1], Franz Kopica[2] (ID), and Cristina Olaverri-Monreal[2](✉) (ID)

[1] Nast Consulting ZT GmbH für Verkehr- Umwelt- und Infrastrukturplanung, Lindengasse 38, 1070 Vienna, Austria
daniel@braunauer.at
[2] Chair Sustainable Transport Logistics 4.0., Johannes Kepler University Linz, Altenberger Straße 69, 4040 Linz, Austria
{franz.kopica,cristina.olaverri-monreal}@jku.at

Abstract. The trend of delivering items by bicycle is getting more and more attractive for companies, particularly if they are based on metropolitan areas. Cities around the globe are already promoting and popularizing bikes and e-bikes as an efficient and ecological delivery and commuting option that can replace conventional motorized vehicles. Unfortunately, a side effect of encouraging the use of bicycles is the rate of bicycle theft.

To promote the use of bicycles for personal mobility or as mean for transport supply we propose a low-cost system to track stolen or vandalized and abandoned bicycles. Location data are displayed on Google Maps using markers.

Keywords: Tracking · ICT · Sensors · Wireless communication

1 Introduction

The trend of delivering items by bicycle is getting more and more attractive for companies, particularly if they are based on metropolitan areas. The main advantage of this kind of delivery service is that bicycles can easily avoid road congestion and therefore collect and distribute packages or mail quickly throughout the city [1]. Additionally the costs for companies that rely on fleet of bicycles are much lower compared to the costs derived from conventional van- or truck transport. In line with this cities around the globe are already rethinking mobility systems by promoting and popularizing bikes and e-bikes as an efficient and ecological delivery and commuting option, that can replace the conventional motorized vehicles.

Unfortunately, a side effect of encouraging the use of bicycles is the rate of bicycle theft that has increased in recent years. In Austria 28.018 bicycles were stolen only in 2015. This number corresponds to the cases that were reported to the police, but the real number is estimated to be eight times higher with 22.0000 stolen bicycles per year. With around 6.224.000 bicycles, one bicycle out of 28 is stolen [2].

As this fact might undermine further efforts to promote biking we propose in this work a system relying on connected Information and Communication Technologies

R. Moreno-Díaz et al. (Eds.): EUROCAST 2019, LNCS 12014, pp. 177–181, 2020.
https://doi.org/10.1007/978-3-030-45096-0_22

(ICT) that makes it possible to collect data on mobility behavior to assess for example environmental impact or to localize bicycles in case of theft. A bicycle GPS tracker is also attractive to reduce insurance costs and to find a particular parked bike among others in huge parking lots.

2 Related Work

There are currently several products for tracking bicycles, which are already available to customers. As an example, we describe 3 devices that have a GPS module and a GSM module installed. The acquired location data can be transmitted through the following options:

(a) via a text message over the Global System for Mobile (GSM) communications that describe the protocols for second-generation (2G) digital cellular networks used by mobile devices such as mobile phones and tablets.
(b) via a web-application over the General Packet Radio Service (GPRS) standard for mobile phones.

Velocate offers a rear light for bicycles, which allows tracking by using a pre-installed application that is available for smartphones with the Android and iPhone operative systems. The rear light contains the necessary hardware that consists of a battery, Bluetooth, a GPS module and a GSM module. The module has a motion detector. The application transmits the location information as soon as a theft or movement is detected [3].

An additional GPS antitheft tracker for bicycles is the Sherlock box that contains the same components as the rear light by Velocate but it is shaped in a different design. Here the device is manufactured in an elongated, cylindrical shape so that it can be placed it in the frame or handlebar of the bicycle [4].

The GPS tracker by Spy Lamp 2 is hidden inside a bicycle tail light. It consists of a motion sensor, a GPS module and a GSM module. If a movement is detected, the location data is sent by SMS. The movement history and the live location can be seen on the manufacturer's website [5].

3 Technical Implementation

We propose in this paper a low-cost system to acquire mobility data and represent it in a map. To this end, we use a GPS module. To run dynamic web sites or servers the software bundles Apache, MySQL, PHP and Python are used. A Raspberry Pi reads the information and sends it wirelessly to a server in which it is stored for its later graphical representation in a map. The prototype uses the following standard components:

- Raspberry Pi 3 Model B
- Adafruit Ultimate GPS Breakout
- USB-TTL cable
- External battery
- Box for the Raspberry Pi
- Micro SD memory card
- Mobile WLAN router

3.1 Hardware

The Raspberry Pi is the core of the prototype. It has a processor with 4 cores each with 1.2 GHz computing power, a main memory with 1 GB, modules for Bluetooth and Wireless Local Area Network (WLAN) are also accommodated on the board and it offers four USB 2.0 ports as well as a Local Area Network (LAN) port. The power supply is provided by a Micro-USB socket [6].

The GPS Adafruit Ultimate GPS Breakout module is connected to the Raspberry Pi using a USB TTL cable. This connection supplies the module with power so that it can immediately start searching for the signals from the GPS satellites. If a signal can not be detected by the GPS and an exact position can not be determined, a red LED flashes once per second. As soon as a position can be calculated and read by the software, the red LED flashes only every 30 s [7]. The use of GPS for position determination allows accuracies of 13 m horizontally and 22 m in height [8].

A mobile Wi-Fi-router dials into the 4G network via a SIM card and establishes a connection to the Internet. This enables the Raspberry Pi to communicate permanently with the web server. The used battery has a capacity of 10,000 mAh. This battery supplies the Raspberry Pi with power via its USB output using a micro-USB cable.

3.2 Software

The Raspbian Stretch computer operating system for Raspberry Pi is installed on the SD memory card. The GPS coordinates are sent in a permanent stream via the USB TTL cable from the GPS breakout to the Raspberry Pi. A Python program takes the longitude and latitude values from the stream once a second and writes them into the local database.

The system is equipped with an Apache web server and a MySQL database. Furthermore, the scripting language PHP allows the execution of embedded HTML code. The GPS coordinates are stored in the database. In addition to the values of longitude and lattitude, a location point and a timestamp of the recording time are added. If there is a connection to the Internet, the locally stored data is sent to a web server. Figure 1 shows a section of the SQL-code to write the GPS values into the database.

The data is transferred using client for Uniform Resource Locator (cURL), a program library for transferring files in computer networks. After the data is read from the local database of the Raspberry Pi, each record is converted into a double, integer or timestamp string using Typecast and writes the values in the database of the Web server.

```
try:
        # Execute the SQL command
        #pnr=21
        time='{:%Y-%m-%d %H:%M:%S}'.format(datetime.datetime.now())
        fid=1
        lat=latte
        lng=longe
        cursor.execute("INSERT INTO tbltrack VALUES (%s,%s,%s,%s,%s)", (pnr,time,fid,lat,lng))
        # Commit your changes in the database
        db.commit()
        pnr+=1
except:
        # Rollback in case there is any error
        db.rollback()
```

Fig. 1. Section of the SQL-code that writes the GPS values into the database.

The code in Fig. 2 shows the PHP script code for inserting data into the MySQL database.

In case of an interruption in the transmission of the data the highest number, which the Web server has received is written in the text file, that is stored on the Web server. In case of a retransmission the text file will be read and the remaining values will be transferred to the Web server. To reduce the volume of data and at the same time being able to achieve a sufficient density, only one thirtieth point is transmitted to the Web server.

The Google Maps Application Programming Interface (API) was used to visualize the data. As Google maps are already pre-installed on many mobile devices and Google provides HTML code to place markers on them [9].

```
$pnr = (int)$_POST['pnr'];
$lat = (double)$_POST['lat'];
$lng = (double)$_POST['lng'];

$query = "INSERT INTO tbltrack set pnr='$pnr', lat='$lat', lng='$lng'";
$db->query($query);
```

Fig. 2. PHP script for inserting data into the MySQL database.

4 Results

Figure 3 shows an excerpt from inserted data into the MySQL database. This dataset consists of the location point, the recording date, the bicycle ID and the latitude- and longitude information. Figure 4 visualizes the collected data through markers indicating a route on the map.

LocPoint	TimeStamp	BicycleID	Latitude	Longitude
2606	2019-02-17 13:27:34	1	48.341826	16.330477
2607	2019-02-17 13:27:35	1	48.341827	16.330478
2608	2019-02-17 13:27:36	1	48.341828	16.330479
2609	2019-02-17 13:27:37	1	48.341829	16.330480

Fig. 3. Excerpt from the MySQL database.

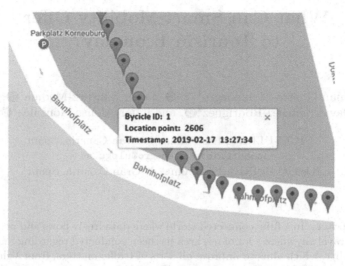

Fig. 4. Graphic visualizing the collected data through markers indicating a route on the map.

Acknowledgments. This work was supported by the BMK endowed Professorship Sustainable Transport Logistics 4.0.

References

1. Maes, J., Vanelslander, T.: The use of bicycle messengers in the logistics chain, concepts further revised. Procedia Soc. Behav. Sci. **39**, 409–423 (2012)
2. Bundesministerium für Verkehr, Innovation und Technologie, "bmvit.gv.at". https://www.bmvit.gv.at/service/publikationen/verkehr/fuss_radverkehr/downloads/fahrraddiebstahl.pdf. Accessed 18 Jan 2018
3. PSP Pauli Services & Products GmbH. https://velocate.com/produkte/vcone/#1486144711310-d94aa6ed-b72f. Accessed 18 Jan 2018
4. Sherlock, the ultimate GPS anti-theft device for bikes. https://www.sherlock.bike/en/. Accessed 06 Jan 2018
5. Integratedtrackers. http://www.spybike.com/index.php?route=product/product&product_id=50#view-technical. Accessed 06 Jan 2018
6. Raspberry Pi Foundation. https://www.raspberrypi.org/about/. Accessed 06 Jan 2018
7. Adafruit Ultimate GPS. https://cdn-learn.adafruit.com/downloads/pdf/adafruit-ultimate-gps.pdf. Accessed 06 Jan 2018
8. Kahmen, H.: Vermessungskunde. Walter de Gruyte, Wien (2006)
9. Google Cloud. https://cloud.google.com/blog/products/maps-platform/introducing-google-maps-platform. Accessed 18 Jan 2018

What Can Smart Mobility Offer to Tourism Economy?

Juan Guerra-Montenegro[1]([⊠]) [iD], Javier Sánchez-Medina[1][iD],
David Sánchez-Rodríguez[2][iD], and Itziar Alonso-González[2][iD]

[1] CICEI-ULPGC, Las Palmas de Gran Canaria, Spain
juanantonio.montenegro@ulpgc.es
[2] IDeTIC-ULPGC, Las Palmas de Gran Canaria, Spain

Abstract. In a fully connected world where data freely flows and people can travel anywhere a lot of research has been conducted regarding Smart Mobility, which aims to improve all sorts of traffic matters, from Vehicle Data to Traffic flow management. However, it is also surprising how this topic has been applied in such a small extent to Tourism, an area that can benefit from this kind of research. This paper summarizes the current state of the art regarding Smart Mobility, and exposes useful insights about how this topic might be applied to tourism in order to improve various kinds of tourism services by using Smart Mobility.

Keywords: Smart · Mobility · Tourism · Economy

1 Introduction

It is undeniable that mobility is changing. Transportation is converging with the digital industry and shifting into what is commonly called as "Smart Mobility" [6]. Smart mobility refers to the use of ICTs (Information and Communication Technologies) in modern transport technologies to improve urban traffic, and is one of the main components of a smart city [2]. Additionally, it is stated that "Smart Tourism" involves multiple components and layers of "smart" that are supported by ICTs (Smart Experience, Smart Business Ecosystem and Smart Destination), and that Smart Destinations are a special case of Smart Cities [4]. In this paper, a relation between Smart Mobility and Smart Tourism will be exposed in Sect. 2, along with a research distribution of Smart Mobility applied to the tourism industry in Sect. 3. Finally, in Sect. 4 conclusions of this study will be presented along suggestions for further research about this topic.

This work has been partially funded by the ACIISI and the EU FSE, Programa Operativo Integrado de Canarias 2014–2020, and by the Consejería de Economía, Industria, Comercio y Conocimiento del Gobierno de Canarias (CEI2018-16).

R. Moreno-Díaz et al. (Eds.): EUROCAST 2019, LNCS 12014, pp. 182–189, 2020.
https://doi.org/10.1007/978-3-030-45096-0_23

2   Smart Cities and Smart Tourism

In the recent times, there has been a noticeable increase in the use of online services and applications. These applications provide access to a wide variety of services by using different devices, such as computers or smartphones. Actually, governments and enterprises are creating their own applications for citizens and/or clients in order to have access to their services in an easy way. However, making a city "smart" is not an easy task because of its difficulty in terms of organization, and transportation is not an exception to this. According to [5] "A smart city is an urban area that uses different types of digital data collection sensors to supply information which is used to manage assets and resources efficiently." This makes ICTs of paramount importance, as they take the role of collecting and supplying information in order to create an efficient smart city.

2.1   Smart Cities and Smart Mobility

According to a study published by Navigant Research [1], we can see in Figs. 1 and 2 that the number of smart city projects has increased notably from 252 to 355 (nearly a 29% more) in just a year. This showcases how governments are embracing the smart city paradigm, with Europe as a leader in number of projects and in depth of multi-sector integration. Additionally, we can see that Smart Transportation is one of the areas that is being researched, and that Smart Cities are starting to be a hot topic around the world.

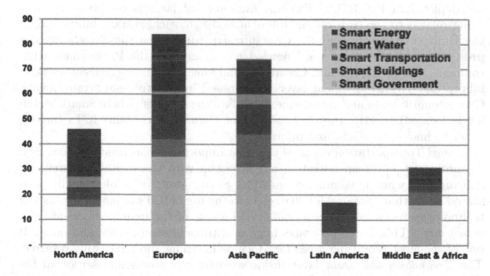

Fig. 1. Worldwide smart city Projects (2017). Source: *Navigant Research - Smart city Tracker Q1 2017/Q1 2018*

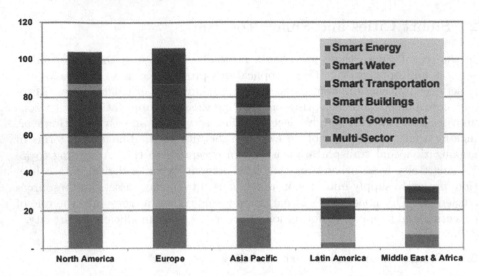

Fig. 2. Worldwide smart city Projects (2018). Source: *Navigant Research - smart city Tracker Q1 2017/Q1 2018*

At a steady pace, cities are adding "smartness" into all their services and infrastructures. It was already shown that technology and data are important components of a smart city, but there are other parts that must be taken into account. According to [3], a smart city is composed by different layers, which are depicted in Fig. 3. The *Physical Environment* layer is composed by anything related to the Natural environment and Ecological sustainability, and by the Built environment and the City infrastructure. Then the *Society* layer is presented, which contains the Knowledge economy and the Pro-business environment, Human capital and Creativity, and Governance, engagement and collaboration. The *Government* layer is composed by Institutional arrangements, City administration and management, and Public services (where Smart Mobility is located). Lastly, the *Technology and Data* layer contains ICTs (among other technologies), Data and Information.

Smart Transportation is one of the most important areas inside a smart city. According to [6] "Transportation is converging with the digital industry and shifting into what is commonly called as Smart Mobility". Additionally, it is stated by [2] that "Smart Mobility refers to the use of ICTs in modern transport technologies to improve urban traffic, and is one of the main components of a smart city". This sector generates huge quantities of sensor data, and makes it one of the most promising areas for Machine Learning and forecasting research. The *Technology and Data* layer inside a smart city stores and serves all the necessary information using ICTs.

As it has been exposed, cities are getting "smarter" and all of their services are shifting to the smart city paradigm, but we must also talk about how tourism is getting "smarter" too.

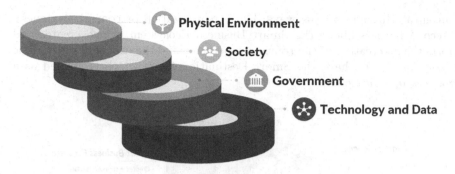

Fig. 3. Smart city Layer composition

2.2 Smart Tourism

Each year that passes, more tourists around the globe use their smart devices not only to plan their trips, but also to search real-time information about various topics, such as public services or traffic conditions. According to the research *Multi-National travel trends in the tourism industry (2017)* published by the Expedia Group [7], it is clear that the smartphone is one of the most used tools in any trip. In Fig. 4, the use of a smartphone in various moments of a trip is depicted. Smartphones are somehow more or less used when looking for inspiration or research on where to travel, and less used when booking the travel itself. However, it is clear that smartphones are a very used device during travels.

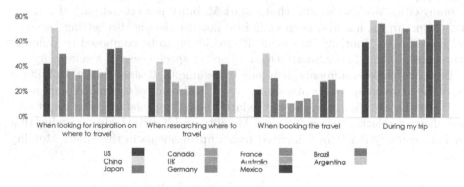

Fig. 4. Smartphone use in a journey. Source: *Expedia group - Multi-national travel trends in the tourism industry (2017)*

According to [4], "Smart Tourism involves multiple components and layers of *smart* that are supported by ICTs". This is not very different from the definition of a smart city. In fact, it is also stated in [4] that Smart Tourism is composed by three specific layers, as depicted in Fig. 5. The first layer is the Smart Experience, which is composed by technology-mediated experiences and their enhancement through various ways, like personalization or context-awareness. The second layer is about the Smart Business Ecosystem, which creates and supports the co-creation of the tourism experience and the exchange of touristic resources. Lastly, we have the Smart Destination layer, which is defined as a *special case of smart city*.

Smart Experience
- Technology-mediated experiences.

Smart Business Ecosystem
- Creates + supports exchange of touristic resources.

Smart Destination*
- Special case of Smart City.

Fig. 5. Smart Tourism layers

A Smart Destination applies smart city principles to rural or urban areas, considering residents and tourists. It efforts to support resource availability and allocation, quality of life, sustainability and, of course, mobility.

2.3   Relations Between Smart Mobility and Smart Tourism

In this paper, it has been exposed that the smart city paradigm is being adopted by many cities worldwide, and that Smart Mobility is a crucial part of a smart city's structure. It has also been explained how tourism is also getting "smart", and how "Smart Tourism" has been defined by [4] to be composed by different layers, one of them being Smart Destinations, a special case of a smart city.

Based on these statements, it is safe to assume that, since Smart Mobility is one of the main components of a smart city, it is also one of the main components of a Smart Destination, because of the latter being a special case of a smart city. This shows a relation between Smart Mobility and Tourism, also exposing that tourism economy might be benefited from improvements in the Smart Mobility area.

3   Research Areas and Distributions

Additionally, a recent State of the art revision has been made to showcase how the research efforts on Smart Mobility are being distributed. With 62 papers on the matter in 8 years and 18 research publications in 2018, Smart Mobility has risen to be a current research topic. Eight Smart Mobility research areas were identified, which are depicted in Fig. 6. It is noticeable that most of the research efforts have been conducted in *Sustainability*, followed by *Data Management*. Other areas like *Service Management* and *Traffic Flow Management* are also being researched in a lesser way. Lastly, *Vehicle Tracking, Energy Management* and *Fleet Management* seem to be unexploited research niches. However, it is surprising to see how the relations between *Smart Mobility* and *Smart Tourism* are not given proper attention.

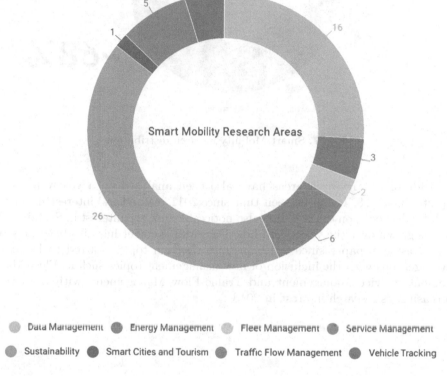

Fig. 6. Smart Mobility research topics

This study has also uncovered how unbalanced the research efforts have been in this area. As depicted in Fig. 7, Data Management and Sustainability comprise a sixty-eight per cent of the entire Smart Mobility research topic, with the other six areas (Service Management, Traffic Flow Management, Vehicle Tracking, Energy Management, Fleet Management, and Smart Cities and Tourism) portraying the other sixty-two per cent.

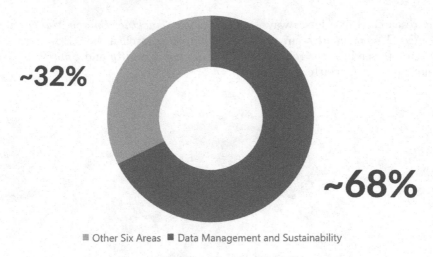

Fig. 7. Smart Mobility research distribution

Additionally, research areas have also been analyzed on a yearly basis as depicted in Fig. 8. It can be seen that since 2011 researchers' interest in Smart Mobility has been on the rise. It is also noticeable how the interest in Sustainability has grown over the years, and how Data Management has also been present in at least one paper since 2012. In 2016 research topics started to be more heterogeneous with the inclusion of new management topics such as Fleet Management, Service Management and Traffic Flow Management, with the latter increasing its research interest in 2018.

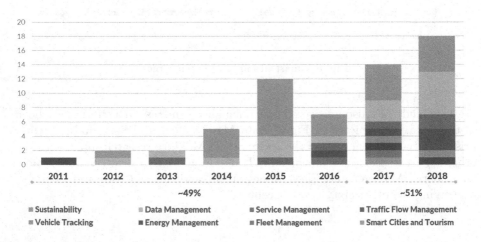

Fig. 8. Smart Mobility yearly research distribution

4 Conclusion

This paper exposes a relation between Smart Mobility and Tourism Economy in Smart Tourism, and important research gaps in the Smart Mobility topic. Although this area is an important part of Smart Destinations, little research effort has been conducted in applying this topic over tourism areas to generate knowledge in the Smart Tourism field. It has also been proven that there is a growing interest in Smart Mobility and it was found that the main research effort on this area is focused on *Sustainability* and *Data management*, exposing that there are many different areas where further researches can be conducted which might yield fruitful results for the Smart Mobility research panorama.

References

1. Smart City Tracker 1q18. https://www.navigantresearch.com/reports/smart-city-tracker-1q18
2. Albino, V., Berardi, U., Dangelico, R.M.: Smart cities: definitions, dimensions, performance, and initiatives. J. Urban Technol. **22**(1), 3–21 (2015). https://doi.org/10.1080/10630732.2014.942092
3. Gil-Garcia, J.R., Pardo, T., Nam, T.: What makes a city smart? Identifying core components and proposing an integrative and comprehensive conceptualization. Inf. Polity **20**, 61–87 (2015). https://doi.org/10.3233/IP-150354
4. Gretael, U., Sigala, M., Xiang, Z., Koo, C.: Smart tourism: foundations and developments. Electron. Markets **25**(3), 179–188 (2015). https://doi.org/10.1007/s12525-015-0196-8
5. Mclaren, D., Agyeman, J.: Sharing cities: a case for truly smart and sustainable cities (2015)
6. Noy, K., Givoni, M.: Is 'Smart Mobility' sustainable? Examining the views and beliefs of transport's technological entrepreneurs. Sustainability **10**(2), 422 (2018). https://doi.org/10.3390/su10020422
7. EGM Solutions: Multi-National Travel Trends in the Tourism Industry. https://info.advertising.expedia.com/multi-national-travel-trends-in-the-tourism-industry

Traffic Predictive Analysis Through Data Stream Mining

Juan Guerra-Montenegro$^{(\boxtimes)}$ and Javier Sánchez-Medina

CICEI-ULPGC, Las Palmas de Gran Canaria, Spain
{juanantonio.montenegro,javier.sanchez}@ulpgc.es

Abstract. With a huge increase in computational power, Traffic Predictive Analysis has seen various improvements in the recent years. Additionally, this field is experimenting an increase in available data, which allows to produce more precise forecasting and classification models. However, this means that the available data has also seen a huge increase in terms of storage size. Data Stream Mining provides a brand new approach to data processing, allowing to create adaptive, incremental models that do not need huge amounts of storage size, as the data is processed as it is received. In this communication, we will explore the state of the art and the first research efforts that can be found in this direction.

Keywords: Traffic modeling · Predictive analysis · Data Stream Mining · Data Science

1 Introduction

Traffic predictive analysis is one of the most important and classic topics in Intelligent Transportation Systems. In the last years the field is moving decidedly to data centered research developments because of the overabundance of Data, alongside the ever rising computing power availability. As stated by [3], "in modern ITS, the popular introduction of advanced data management systems has made tremendous quantities of traffic variable data available". As a matter of fact, with such quantities of data the actual risk resides in how to handle its huge volumes, since Big Data is the current situation for almost any traffic modeling and management problem, along with real-time processing of big spatiotemporal traffic data because of compliance with anticipated service quality requirements [4]. This is where Data Stream Mining (DSM), a brand new different approach to Data Science is expected to play a role.

In this new approach, data is consumed as it comes, meaning the required knowledge is mined on the fly instead of the common setup of storing and later

Work cofinanced by the Agencia Canaria de Investigación, Innovación y Sociedad de la Información from Consejería de Economía, Industria, Comercio y Conocimiento and by the European Social Fund (ESF), Programa Operativo Integrado de Canarias 2014–2020, Eje 3 Tema Prioritario 74 (85%).

© Springer Nature Switzerland AG 2020
R. Moreno-Díaz et al. (Eds.): EUROCAST 2019, LNCS 12014, pp. 190–196, 2020.
https://doi.org/10.1007/978-3-030-45096-0_24

mining enormous amounts of data. The benefits are obvious: no need for complex and expensive data warehousing infrastructures, and adaptive models to cope with the so called concept-drift, which is omnipresent due to the stochastic instability of traffic related processes. However, the main difficulty of this kind of approximation lies in it means a denial of classic machine learning paradigms, as an extensive training set and an independent test set to learn and evaluate the required models will not be available. These models need to be learned incrementally, as new data comes. Therefore, there is not enough literature and methodologies yet for many cases, meaning that there is a big pristine land to new knowledge about this topic.

Additionally, a brief survey was took to overview the current state of the art regarding the Real-Time traffic forecasting panorama, uncovering that, although DSM is used in various articles, it is rarely used to generate adaptive models but only real-time forecasting models that cannot adapt to the concept-drift. It should be also noted that the main focus on this research area lies in Traffic Conditions forecasting, but there is also room for additional research areas that are heavily linked with the original topic, namely Travel Time Prediction, Crash Risk Evaluation, Vehicle Platoon Management, Road Traffic Management, Vehicle Speed Prediction or even Fuel Efficiency forecasting.

2   Computational Improvements and Big Data

According to a research [1] published by Top500 in Fig. 1, which showcases the first and the 500th most powerful supercomputers in the world, supercomputers have evolved from computing one PetaFLOPS at most to a hundred PetaFLOPS. This increment comes in a logarithmic fashion and this trend seems to be stable for the coming years. Each year that passes, new powerful computers are available to analyze Big Data or to compute new predicting models in a lesser time. We can extract from this chart that the most powerful supercomputer as of the last register taken in 2018 surpasses the 100 PetaFLOPS barrier (triangle), and the less powerful one almost reaches 1 PetaFLOPS in computing power (square). If the computational power of all of the five hundred analyzed supercomputers were to be combined (circle), their computational power would surpass the ExaFLOP barrier.

As stated by [3] "In modern Information Technology Systems, the popular introduction of advanced data management systems has made tremendous quantities of traffic data available". Having a great computational power is useless if we do not have data to analyze at all, and if we have them we will also have to manage these huge quantities of data. Having these tremendous data banks, we can train and deploy more accurate traffic prediction models. However, it is worth noting that having prediction systems integrated as subsystems of ITS is of a great importance if we want to produce accurate future or real-time traffic data, as was also stated by [3].

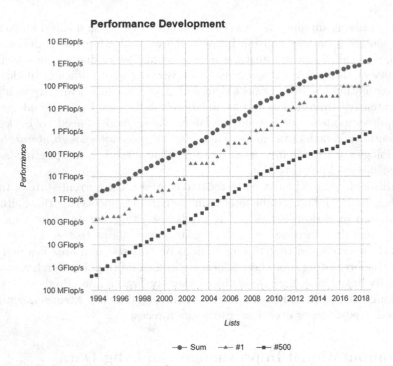

Fig. 1. Performance development - *Source: Top500* (https://www.top500.org/statis tics/perfdevel/)

Additionally, in Fig. 2 we can see how the number of passenger cars has drastically increased in Europe since 2012. If every single car was to generate data related to various factors such as origin, route, velocity etc. the amount of data that might be potentially generated would be of dire importance to generate accurate traffic forecasting methods.

According to the facts exposed earlier in this paper, it is undeniable that we have huge amounts of data with lots of potentially useful knowledge inside waiting for it to be discovered. In fact, as [4] exposed, "There is so much data that the actual risk is how to handle its huge volumes", meaning that the difficulty is now focused on "how" to process these amounts of data. An added difficulty on this matter is that traffic forecasting's usefulness relies on generating future predictions in real-time, something that [4] also mentions on its investigation ("[...] compliance with anticipated service quality requirements mandates consistent real-time processing of big spatio-temporal traffic data"). Traffic data might present different kinds of evolution depending on the traffic topology, an actual, precise prediction model might be outdated in a matter of years or even months, creating the need of a new forecasting model which is trained by using new huge data banks that might pose a challenge in terms of storage and handling. Since these models usually take long times to be trained, it is not possible to get them in a real-time fashion.

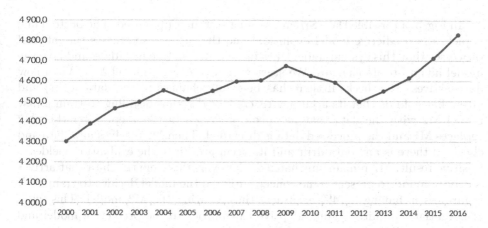

Fig. 2. Passenger cars in passenger-kilometer (PKM) *Source: European Commission - Directorate General for Mobility and Transport (Statistical Pocketbook 2018)*

3   Data Stream Mining Applied to Traffic Forecasting

As stated by Albert Bifet in 2009 [2], in many organizations digital data can limitlessly grow at a high rate of millions of data items each day. This means that there is a consistent number of continuous samples that are generated by many sources, a behaviour similar to traffic forecasting, where thousands of cars generate all kinds of data in a single day. Since there is a lot of data it is unfeasible to treat it all in a single run, but it is possible to process this data in lesser quantities as it comes to generate updated prediction models in real-time. Data Stream Mining proves to be the perfect tool to get this job done. However, before speaking about Data Stream Mining it is important to address a well-known fact in the data mining world: There is no universal methodology or algorithm. Here one of the many ways a Data Stream Mining system might be organized will be shown, but it is not the only way to organize these kind of systems.

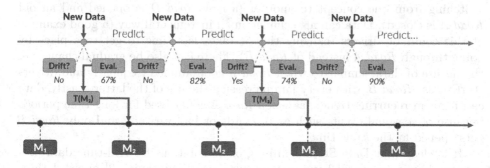

Fig. 3. Possible layout of a Data Stream Mining system. *Source: Own elaboration.*

In Fig. 3, a possible Data Stream Mining system is presented. The bottom line depicts the predictive model evolution, and the top one showcases the internal processes that this system undertakes in order to analyze new data and how the model adapts to its changes. We start with a predictive model M1. When new data arrives, M1 checks if there has been any changes in the data (drift) and after that it finds that its accuracy reaches a 67%, thus deciding to train a new model M2 with the data that has been processed in this step. After this, M2 replaces M1 and the processed data is discarded. Then M2 receives new data and checks if there is any data drift and its accuracy. Since the evaluation yielded a positive result, M2 remains unchanged. However, this time the data that arrives has been found to present some concept drift, so the model decides to train itself regardless it having a 74% accuracy, thus creating the M3 model. This cycle is potentially infinite, giving adaptive capabilities to the predictive model and making it resilient to the wear of time.

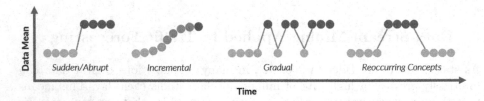

Fig. 4. Concept Drift Types. *Source: Gama et al. (2014)*

Additionally, to understand why Data Stream Mining is useful for traffic forecasting we must talk about data concept drift, something that usually affects evolving data streams. Concept Drift is a change in the nature of data, and because of it high accuracy models can get obsolete in years or months. Gama et al. [5] stated that "The real concept drift refers to changes in the conditional distribution of the output (i.e., target variable) given the input (input features), while the distribution of the input may stay unchanged", and classified this concept in four types that can be seen in Fig. 4. Data can suddenly change, switching from one concept to another (a new *Road D* is opened and an old *Road A* is closed). Data can also change in an incremental way (a good example of this could be drivers realizing that it takes less time to get to a place by going through *Road A* instead of *Road B*). There can also be gradual changes in the nature of data, similar to when *Road A* gets jammed frequently and drivers start to use *Road B*, with every jam increasing the use of the latter. Lastly, data can incur in recurring trends, as when *Road A* gets closed for long time periods because of seasonal events such as blizzards or bad weather, and only *Road B* gets opened at the same time.

It is clear that Data Stream Mining offers solutions for real-time data processing, but it does still have certain rules and limitations. [2] exposed three constraints of Data Stream Mining: The first one is that "The amount of data that has arrived and will arrive in the future is potentially infinite. Thus, it is impossible to store it all.", meaning that, since the model will be handling endless amounts of data, it will not be able to store this data for later processing. The second one is closely tied to the first one. and enunciates that "The speed of arrival is large, so that each particular element has to be processed essentially in real time, and then discarded.", which means that, since it is impossible to store infinite data it has to be processed in real time and then it will be lost forever. Lastly, and as it was seen in the previous paragraph, the third constraint exposes that "The distribution generating the items can change over time. Thus, data from the past may become irrelevant, or even harmful, for the current summary.", demonstrating that since data streams are usually affected by Concept Drift problems, past instances of data may lower the precision of a real-time predictive model.

4   Traffic Prediction's State of the Art

Additionally, in this paper a brief survey of the state of the art regarding the traffic forecasting topic has been done. This survey analyzed the last two years with 40 papers on the matter, exposing that Data Stream Mining is not being extensively applied to this area.

As can be seen in Fig. 5, the majority of the research efforts are clearly centered on Road Traffic Prediction. There are other areas, such as *Travel Time Prediction*, *Road Traffic Management* and *Speed Prediction* which are also being developed in a small extent, closely followed by other topics, namely *Crash Risk Evaluation*, *Fuel Efficiency* and *Platoon Management*.

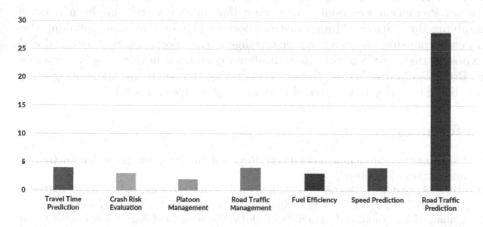

Fig. 5. Travel Prediction Research Area Distribution - *Source: Own Elaboration*

This means that an impressive 58% of the research efforts are being focused on *Road Traffic Prediction*, as portrayed in Fig. 6, proving that the other previously mentioned six areas present research opportunities which might yield interesting results in the future.

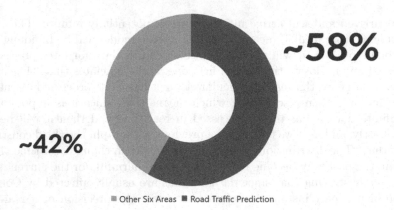

Fig. 6. Travel Prediction Research Percentages - *Source: Own Elaboration*

5   Conclusion

This communication exposes a new research area based on Data Stream Mining methodologies. Processing data in streams has proven to be more efficient for real-time purposes, and it can be additionally used to create models that adapt over time, which by definition will yield a greater forecasting accuracy than their previously trained counterparts. DSM allows predictive models to be trained incrementally, meaning that if new data arrives this model will adapt in real-time to new trends and also reducing the storage space needed for traditional Machine Learning Methodologies. Additionally, a brief survey about Travel Prediction was done, uncovering that little research has been done in applying Data Stream Mining methodologies to traffic forecasting, making this a new, promising research area for Intelligent Transportation Systems, and also exposing that a 58% of the research efforts conducted in this area are centered in Road Traffic Prediction, thus demonstrating that there are many other areas not being extensively researched that might yield fruitful results.

References

1. Performance Development–TOP500 Supercomputer Sites. https://www.top500.org/statistics/perfdevel/
2. Bifet, A.: Adaptive learning and mining for data streams and frequent patterns. SIGKDD Explor. **11**, 55–56 (2009). https://doi.org/10.1145/1656274.1656287
3. Chang, H.H., Yoon, B.J.: High-speed data-driven methodology for real-time traffic flow predictions: practical applications of ITS. J. Adv. Transp. **2018** (2018). https://doi.org/10.1155/2018/5728042
4. Chindanur, N., Sure, P.: Low-dimensional models for traffic data processing using graph Fourier transform. Comput. Sci. Eng. **20**(2), 24–37 (2018). https://doi.org/10.1109/MCSE.2018.110111913
5. Gama, J., Žliobaitė, I., Bifet, A., Pechenizkiy, M., Bouchachia, A.: A survey on concept drift adaptation. ACM Comput. Surv. **46**, 44:1–44:37 (2014)

Smart Recommender for Blue Tourism Routing

José A. Moreno-Pérez, Julio Brito Santana, Agustín Santana Talavera,
Dagoberto Castellanos Nieves, Iradiel García Pérez,
and Airam Expósito Márquez[(⊠)]

Universidad de La Laguna, Tenerife, Spain
{jamoreno,jbrito,asantana,dcastell,igarciap,aexposim}@ull.edu.es

Abstract. This work describes the research and preliminary results for
the development of an intelligent planning and recommendation system
for the marine tourism sector. The application of technology and its rapid
advance offers users the opportunity to use geo-location at all times, giving rise to a new range of personalized products and services, thereby
generating a set of favorable impacts in the economic and social field. We
describe the generation of knowledge developed on the services of marine
tourism and their characteristics and the selection of technological tools
for the construction of the recommender system. The system will generate recommended routes based on the traveler preferences profile. It also
provides information on resources and tourist services, including mobility, and a system to help in the dynamic and optimal planning of tourist
itineraries.

Keywords: Blue tourism · Tourist recommender · Route planning

1 Introduction

The coastal and maritime tourism sector (or blue tourism sector) is part of the
European strategy to promote the objectives of smart, sustainable, and inclu-
sive growth strategy of EUROPE 2020. The diversification of marine and coastal
tourism products as well as the development of markets, and innovative solutions using information technology are proposed in the action plan. The strategy
of smart specialization of the Canary Islands (RIS3) establishes among its priority axes Intelligent Tourism Leadership for the consolidation of its current
position as a destination, the strengthening of other sectors, and the diversification of the economy. This strategy includes measures to develop new for-
mulas to promote tourist products and relationships with customers, where the
development of technological applications are facilitating elements. It also proposes to respond to the demands and challenges found in the tourism sector to
improve the tourist experience at destination, facilitating access to information
and resources through systems and mobile, interactive, intelligent and accessible devices. Innovative information, planning and organization tools in tourist

R. Moreno-Díaz et al. (Eds.): EUROCAST 2019, LNCS 12014, pp. 197–204, 2020.
https://doi.org/10.1007/978-3-030-45096-0_25

destinations will contribute to the growth of the sector. The conditions of the tourist market have changed with the increasing importance of the travelling, the diversification of tourist interests and the rapid evolution of information and communication technologies.

Tourists demand information adapted to their preferences to plan and organize their trips. Search engines and/or specialized portals help tourists who want to plan their trip beforehand. The internet contains such information, however the user may not know where or how to look for it, since it first must be filtered before selecting a useful site. Therefore the need for intelligent tourism recommender systems arises [1].

The utilization of intelligent and expert recommender systems plays a decisive role in tourist satisfaction and these systems are specially applicable to tourism services. Broadly speaking, these systems perform two fundamental tasks: recommendations of points of interest (POI) and route generation. These two services usually are performed by Personalized Electronic Tourist Guides (PETs) which are hand-held devices with limited computing performance. An extensive review of PETs can be found in [3] and [4].

Recommender systems (RS) are a technology whose development coincides with the emergence of content filtering in the mid-1990s [6]. The management and processing of input data from their user allows them to make predictions and offer recommendations about a certain subject or set of subjects [7]. RS are divided into two main approaches: collaborative filtering (CF) and content-based filtering (CBF) [8]. The collaborative approach makes recommendations based on comparisons of user behaviour to others with similar patterns. The content-based approach, on the other hand, it is more focused on a set of attributes and object-related characteristics that the user directly mark as liked when elaborating its suggestions.

There are disadvantages in each approach used in RS. Collaborative filtering has issues with "cold start" (the lack of information for new users to elaborate recommendations for them) while "overspecialization" is a concern in CBF (the system always recommends the same type of contents the user already liked before). Some RS combine both approaches, thereby avoiding these difficulties and providing the smartest recommendations. A knowledge-based approach in RS is also gaining acceptance, where the user profile is modeled to identify the correlation between its preferences and existing products, services or content through inference algorithms [9].

Recommender systems offer the tourist a way to find the proper resources for his characteristics and preferences through a filtered and ordered POI relation. Tourism recommender systems with different AI techniques have recently been created [1]. RS such as Turist@ [10] are based on intelligent autonomous agents that analyze user behavior and learn all profile information to provide recommendations based on context. The automated planning of scheduled recommendations through multiple day and route itineraries is one feature found in many RS since the introduction of City Trip Planner [11]. Some RS even take into account the opening and closing times of the attractions and offer detailed timetables of the routes through the employment of optimization heuristics [12]. Other RS that have been developed follow innovative approaches such as automated clustering by tourists groups [13] and approximate reasoning [14].

The main purpose of this work is to present the development of an intelligent planning and recommendation system which integrates the capture of the traveler preferences profile, resource information and tourist services at destination, including information for mobility, to help the dynamic and optimal planning of tourist itineraries with inaccurate information. The following objectives are needed to design and develop the recommender system:

- Acquire, specify and structure knowledge about the destination, supply and demand, including user behavior and experience.
- Provide adequate optimization models and procedures to plan times and itineraries in the destination, providing a selection of realistic alternatives to decision makers in dynamic contexts of uncertain preferences.
- Design and develop search, filter and recommendation tools based on hybrid and contextual mechanisms that allow the customization of preferences for the preparation of tourist itineraries.
- Evaluate the proposed approach, creating a proof of concept associated with the available information of the marine-coastal tourism product.

2 System Architecture

In this section the main structure and basic architecture of the system are described. Figure 1 shows the architecture and high-level data flow through the recommendation component, route generation component, and user interface.

The recommender system is fed with user profile information, contextual parameters about sightseeing, and POI knowledge, regarding user preferences and POI ratings. The recommendation component then processes the information and generates the set of recommended POIs for a specific tourist. This set of POIs with associated information is the input for the route generation component.

The route generation component uses the set and parameters about sightseeing to design the recommended tourist route for the specific profile. The proposed routes are sent to the tourist via user interfaces, which address tourist changes regarding the proposed itinerary. The route generation component must be able to reschedule the recommended itinerary in a short period of time based on tourist changes.

Tourists, and in general users, interact with the planning and recommendation system through the user interface which includes a web platform and app for mobile devices.

3 Recommendation Component

The recommender system has a knowledge base with information of the POIs at its disposal. An exploratory online approach was needed to elaborate a meaningful proposal which incorporated a POI knowledge database. A requirement

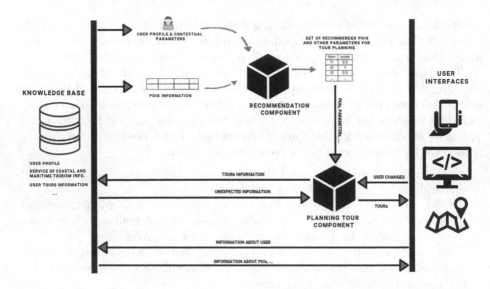

Fig. 1. System architecture

for this approach was a tourist site with tremendous diversity of target resources and products. The coastal area on the island of Tenerife fulfilled these needs and was chosen as the tourist market. A revision of secondary sources was also carried out to improve the information and location of the online approach. Direct contact with staff of POIs was then made together with informal interviews of businessmen and other relevant actors in the field in order to get reliable information. The information was then stored, organized, and systematized according to the characteristics and particularities of the tourist resources in order to build a knowledge database for the recommender system.

Based on this background, the implementation of filtering software modules, search and categorization of profiles and resources were addressed to allow the development of techniques and recommendation mechanisms that provide personalized itineraries to users. Figure 2 shows subsequent steps that can be identified in the internal information flow of the recommendation component. These steps are described in more detail below:

1. *User query.* In this step, the tourist selects their personal interests regarding POIs in blue tourism and specifies the parameters about their stay in the destination.
2. *Pre-filtering.* The POIs storage in database are filtered based on personal interests and stay parameters of the tourist.
3. *Rating calculation.* Personal interests, information about POIs, and historic information about previous touristic routes carried out by the tourist, are used to calculated a rating for each POI selected in the pre-filtering step.
4. *Recommendation.* The destinations with the highest rating are then sent to the route generation component.

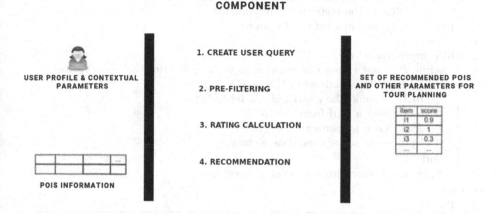

Fig. 2. Recommendation component

4 Routes Generation Component

The design of tourist routes is a complex task involving several constraints such as opening and closing times in POIs, visiting times for each POI, travel times among POIs, and a maximum time for sightseeing for each route or day of stay. A metaheuristic approach is proposed to deal with the computational complexity of route generation.

4.1 The Route Generation Problem

In this section we focus on route generation, and more specifically, on the route design problem description. In the literature this route design problem is known as the Tourist Trip Design Problem (TTDP) [2].

The problem consists in route planning for tourist tours visiting a set of POIs that have a score related with the satisfaction or preferences of the tourist. Each POI i is associated with a score p_i, and a time window $[e_i, l_i]$, where e_i is the opening or earliest time, and l_i is the closing or latest time. The index $i = 0$ describes the starting and ending point. This point generally corresponds to the accommodation of the tourist.

The target of the problem is to obtain a set of K routes, a route for each day of the tourist stay, that maximizes the total score. The total score is given by the sum of the profit or score p_i of all i visited POIs:

$$\sum_{k \in K} \sum_{i \in I} p_i Y_i^k \tag{1}$$

The POIs are treated as nodes of a connected graph, taking into account that each POI can be included in at most one route. Travel times are known, for each two nodes i and j, the travel time is t_{ij}. The problem considers t_{ij} may be

---

Input : P. Set of recommended POIs that can be visited
          κ. Size of the restricted candidate list
Output: r. Recommended tourist route
1 $r \leftarrow (s, e)$
2 **while** *improvement* **do**
3   **while** *P is not empty and constraints are satisfied* **do**
4   Evaluate the candidate POIs in P
5   RCL $\leftarrow$ Build the restricted candidate list
6        $p \leftarrow$ Select a POI from the RCL
7   Add POI p to route r
8   Update the set of candidate elements
9   **end**
10   Apply local search improvement strategy to r
11 **end**
12 return r

Algorithm 1. Pseudo-code of GRASP solution approach

different from t_{ji}, hence, the graph is considered directed. The constraints of the problem are related to times between POIs, opening and closing times of each POI, visit time for each POI, and a T_{max} maximum time of the sightseeing on a day. The time of the route is calculated considering the sum of the corresponding travel times plus the visit times of the POIs in the route.

4.2 Routes Generation Solution Approach

In order to solve the optimization problem introduced in Subsect. 4.1, we propose a solution approach based on the GRASP (Greedy Randomized Adaptive Search Procedure) metaheuristic. The GRASP is a multistart two-phase metaheuristic for combinatorial optimization [5]. This iterative process is composed of a construction phase and a improvement phase. In the construction phase a feasible touristic route is designed. Afterwards, the touristic route is improved by a local search, where the neighborhood of the solution is explored until a local optimum is found. Figure 1 depicts the GRASP approach pseudo-code, lines 3–9 represent the construction phase, and the local search corresponds to line 10.

The GRASP receives the set of POIs that can be visited by the tourist. Each route is here defined as a sequence of POIs to be visited by the tourist. The GRASP starts building a route, r, with only the s starting and e ending locations and with no POIs (line 1). Next, at line 4, the objective function value when a POI is included in each potential position of the route is calculated. In line 5, a Restricted Candidate List (RCL) with POIs and position in the route with the highest increment of the objective function value is built. The RCL is sorted according to the objective function value, thus, the POIs with the highest objective function value are more likely to be selected in order to be part of the route. The input parameter κ is selected by the user and indicates the size of the RCL. In the next step, a POI p is selected from RCL (line 6). Our GRASP approach included alternative solution construction mechanisms and techniques to improve the search of solutions. Some of these mechanisms introduce several ways to guide the selection of POIs to be part of the touristic routes. In line 7, the POI p is added to the partial route under construction, and the set of candidates elements is updated (line 8). The steps described above are repeated until no POI can be added to the partial route considering the constraints of the optimization problem described in Subsect. 4.2.

5   Software Developed and Technologies

Several software technologies have been combined for the technical development of the system. The system was deployed in the cloud to provide a Software as a Service (SaaS) distribution model that facilitates the tool access of tourists. The main software technologies used in the development of the system are NodeJS, Angular framework, The Firebase suite and Google Map Platform.

The platform where our recommendation system is deployed is shown in Fig. 3. The figures show the user interaction, and how information is retrieved from user behavior in order to feed our recommendation system.

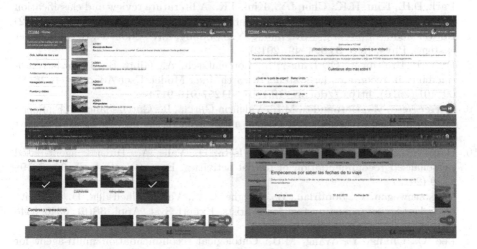

Fig. 3. User interface of recommendation system

6   Conclusions

The present day tourism market requires providing recommendation systems for the marine-coastal sector based on geolocation and technological advances. Current technological tools allow the design and development of a prototype for Tenerife. The state of development of the system confirms the technological viability of the proposal through the integration of different available technologies.

Acknowledgment. This work has been partially funded by Gobierno de Canarias with FEDER 2014–2020 funds in its program of priority areas RIS-3 through the project "Inteligencia turística para un turismo marino responsable" (Ref. ProdID 2017010128), and by Fundación Cajacanarias through the project "Planificación Inteligente de Actividades en Turismo Marino apoyadas en la Geolocalización y las TICs" (2016TUR19).

References

1. Borrás, J., Moreno, A., Valls, A.: Intelligent tourism recommender systems: a survey. Expert Syst. Appl. **41**(16), 7370–7389 (2014)
2. Vansteenwegen, P., Oudheusden, D.V.: The mobile tourist guide: an or opportunity. OR Insight **20**(3), 21–27 (2007)
3. Vansteenwegen, P.: Planning in tourism and public transportation. Ph.D. dissertation, Centre for Industrial Management, Katholieke Universiteit Leuven (2008)
4. Souffriau, W.: Automated tourist decision support. Ph.D. dissertation, Centre for Industrial Management, Katholieke Universiteit Leuven (2010)
5. Feo, T.A., Resende, M.G.C.: Greedy randomized adaptive search procedures. J. Glob. Optim. **6**(3), 109–133 (1995)
6. Park, D.H., Kim, H.K., Choi, I.Y., Kim, J.K.: A literature review and classification of recommender systems research. Expert Syst. Appl. **39**(11), 10059–10072 (2012)
7. Lu, L., Medo, M., Yeung, C.H., Zhang, Y.C., Zhang, Z.K., Zhou, T.: Recommender systems. Phys. Rep. **519**, 1–49 (2012)
8. Beel, J., Breitinger, C., Langer, S., Lommatzsch, A., Gipp, B.: Towards reproducibility in recommender-systems research. User Model. User-Adap. Inter. **26**(1), 69–101 (2016). https://doi.org/10.1007/s11257-016-9174-x
9. Carrer-Neto, W., Hernández, M.L., Valencia-García, R., García-Sanchez, F.: Social knowledge-based recommender system application to the movies domain. Expert Syst. Appl. **39**, 10990–11000 (2012)
10. Batet, M., Moreno, A., Sánchez, D., Isern, D., Valls, A.: Turist@: agent-based personalised recommendation of tourist activities. Expert Syst. Appl. **39**, 7319–7329 (2012)
11. Vansteenwegen, P., Souffriau, W., Berghe, G.V., Van Oudheusden, D.: The city trip planner: an expert system for tourists. Expert Syst. Appl. **38**(6), 6540–6546 (2011)
12. Lee, C., Chang, Y., Wang, M.H.: Ontological recommendation multi-agent for tainan city travel. Expert Syst. Appl. **36**, 6740–6753 (2009)
13. Gavalas, D., Kenteris, M.: A web-based pervasive recommendation system for mobile tourist guides. Pers. Ubiquit. Comput. **15**, 759–770 (2011)
14. Lamsfus, C., Alzua-Sorzabal, A., Martin, D., Smithers, T.: An evaluation of a contextual approach to visitor information system. In: Proceeding of the ENTER Conference, Austria, pp. 179–189 (2011)

Computer Vision, Machine Learning for Image Analysis and Applications

Hand Gesture Recognition Using Computer Vision Applied to Colombian Sign Language

I. C. Triviño-López, C. H. Rodríguez-Garavito$^{(\boxtimes)}$, and J. S. Martinez-Caldas

Automation Engineering, Universidad de La Salle, Bogotá D.C., Colombia
{itrivino07,cerodriguez,juansmartinez21}@unisalle.edu.co

Abstract. In this document we describe a hand gesture classification system of the Colombian Sign Language for both dynamic and static signs, based on Computer Vision and Machine learning. The proposed processes sequence is divided in four stages: acquisition of RGB-D image, extraction of the blob closest to the sensor, detection and validation of the hand, and classification of the sign entered. The results obtained are for multi-class classifiers with a self-captured dataset of 3.600 samples. As a conclusion we found that the best choice for descriptor-classifier according to sign type are HOG-SVM for static signs with an accuracy of 98%, and SVM classifier besides the trajectory-based descriptor with an accuracy of 94%.

Keywords: Machine learning · Computer vision · HOG · U-LBP · Contour signature

1 Introduction

One of the main aims of the automation era has been looking for natural interaction human-machine, due to the fact that robots will develope complex tasks not only at industries but also at home. In this research field, the information extraction from the body expression is an important part of the language, and it has been one of the great challenges of the last decades, especially because it involves head pose recognition, hands signs recognition, torso pose detection and face gestures identification [8]. This problem has been specifically addressed by the recognition of the sign language, each country and region have a particular code. Around this challenge, multiple approaches have been proposed to deal with automatic recognition of sign language [9,10].

Chronologically, it is possible to locate works based on instrumented gloves for motion detection, which use 1D information [11–13]. Later, different proposals based on 2D computer vision, have been developed. All of these have as a comon framework the use of a suitable features as a descriptor for detection and tracking hands. Local features such as SIFT [14,15], Wavelet moments [16], Gabor filters [17,18] among others, were used to perform recognition based on

© Springer Nature Switzerland AG 2020
R. Moreno-Díaz et al. (Eds.): EUROCAST 2019, LNCS 12014, pp. 207–214, 2020.
https://doi.org/10.1007/978-3-030-45096-0_26

multiclass classification, a technique known as a Machine Learning. In recent years, the use of 3D information [19,20], from RGB-D sensors or stereo cameras, has been employ to train convolutional neural networks with high performance even in complex background [21]. Tthis type of proposal has the disadvantage, however, of requiring large volumes of training data with consequent long trainning times and the need for robust hardware.

This work presents the exploration of different hand signal descriptors such as BLP, contour signature, HOG and trajectories angles together with a set of classic and modern classifiers trained with a small set of data training in a feasible time.

For the design of the system, the first stage of the baseline proposed by [1] and [2] was taken as reference, using a different preprocessing and validation of the hand. Initially, the depth map and the RGB image of the scene are captured using a Microsoft Kinect sensor to get a three-dimensional representation of the environment, then the nearest blob to the sensor is extracted and the preprocessing described in [3] is performed and evaluated with a pre-trained Haar Cascade classifier in search of a hand. If a hand is found in the blob, it is then proceeded to extract its fundamental features using its centroid, its convex hull and its defects. The furthest points away from the centroid correspond to the fingers in an outstretched hand, and the points closest to the centroid correspond to the intersection between fingers; for a hand to be validated correctly, the angle between two consecutive fingers and their corresponding defect can not be greater than 90°; in addition, it must has 5 extreme points along with 3–4 defect type points. On the segmented hand the HOG, U-LBP and Contour Signature descriptors are extracted for the static signs and a trajectory descriptor based on [4] for the dynamic signs; further, the PCA algorithm is applied to reduce the dimensionality of the descriptor vectors, which are used as inputs of the Naive Bayes, SVM, ANN, KNN and Random Forest classifiers, and from their results are extracted the accuracy indexes.

As a result, the best performance was obtained with the HOG-SVM pair, with an accuracy of 0,9806 for the static signs, and an accuracy of 0,9400 with the SVM classifier for the dynamic signs.

The article is divided into the following sections: Sect. 2 presents the hand gesture recognition, Sect. 3 shows and analyzes the final recognition results and conclusions are summarized in Sect. 4. Finally, Sect. 4.1 presents the future work.

2   Gestures Recognition

In the Fig. 1 is shown the flow diagram of the process which interact to recognize signs in the context of Colombian Sign Language. The sections below will explain the processes in.

2.1   Pre-processing and Detection

The pre-processing of the scene is done by removing all the elements at a distance greater than 0,8 m and obtaining the closest blob to the sensor, the extracted

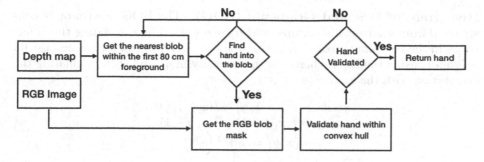

Fig. 1. Flow diagram of the application.

blob is evaluated using a pre-trained Haar-Cascades classifier that recognize the hand in five different positions, which only the fully extended hand is taken into account; if a hand is found, a validation process is applied, it consists of finding the convex hull of the hand, obtaining the points of the fingers corresponding to the inflection points of the convex hull and its defects (which are the points furthest on the contour), they are used for find the angle between two consecutive fingers. Only the defects found in the middle of two fingers must be taken as valid and for a defect to be taken as the point of union between two fingers, the angle between them should not be greater than 90°.

2.2   Feature Description

As a previous step to object detection is needed represent each object as a set of features. We have used the descriptor presented as follow.

Local Binary Patterns (LBP). The LBP is a texture descriptor, constructed from a histogram of patterns that are calculated over a region by the relative gray levels of the neighboring pixels [6].

The LBP is calculated by splitting the image into cells where each pixel inside the cell is compared with its neighbors within a radius of 1 to $n \in \mathbb{N}^+$ with $n < size(image)$; if the central pixel is greater than the neighbor, a value of 0 is taken, otherwise value is 1, the previous step generates a byte that is represented in decimal base, which replaces the value of the central pixel; the resulting histogram of each cell is normalized and concatenated to create the descriptor (see Eq. 1).

$$LBP_{R,N}(x,y) = \sum_{i=0}^{N-1} s(n_i - n_c)2^i, s(x) = \begin{cases} 1, & x \geq 0 \\ 0, & otherwise \end{cases} \qquad (1)$$

Where n_c corresponds to the value of the central pixel and n_i corresponds to the gray level of the neighborhood pixels in the radius R.

Histogram of Oriented Gradients (HOG). The HOG descriptor is constructed from gradient histograms, which are obtained by calculating the differences in the coordinate axes comparing the intensity value of a pixel against its neighbors using the Eq. 2 where I is the intensity map, and then calculating the orientation with the gradients.

$$dx = I(x+1, y) - I(x-1, y)$$
$$dy = I(x, y+1) - I(x, y-1)$$
$$\theta(x, y) = tan^{-1}\left(\frac{dy}{dx}\right)$$
(2)

For calculate the image descriptor, the intensity map is splitted into a fixed number of cells and for each cell, a histogram of the gradient orientations is obtained and finally all the histograms are put together to create the object descriptor [5].

Signature Descriptor. A signature is a one-dimensional vector representation of a contour, where each element consist of the distance from the centroid of the object to the contour and its angle is represented by the arrangement position. The centroid of the object is obtained by making use of the moments of order $p + q$ of the image $I(x, y)$, described by the Eq. 3.

$$M_{p,q} = \sum_{x=1}^{N}\sum_{y=1}^{M} x^p y^q I(x, y)$$
(3)

Trajectory-Based Descriptor. In this work, the trajectory was taken as a descriptor of the dynamic signs, capturing points for four seconds and applying a resampling process to normalize the vectors.

The process of resampling is done by calculating the length M of the points of the original trajectory and dividing the number of points by $N - 1$, where N is the normalized number of points. Once the path is resampled, its center is calculated and transferred to the origin of the coordinate plane X - Y, making the descriptor invariant to translations. Finally, a descriptor is constructed by calculating the angular relationship between the point N and the point $N + 1$, where X is the main axis (see Eq. 4).

$$\theta_t = arctan\left(\frac{y_{t-+1} - y_t}{x_{t+1} - x_t}\right), \quad t = 1, 2, ..., T - 1$$
(4)

2.3 Tracking Procedure Description

Two methods of segmentation of the hand were evaluated, the first by skin color consisting of 3 stages: color model mapping to YCrCb color space [7], background extraction and skin segmentation within the scene. The second method is based on Region Growing, whose process is observed in the pseudocode of the Algorithm 1.

Input: threshold, depthMap, window
seed = window.center;
meanDepth = depthMap[seed.x, seed.y];
queue = depthMap.resize(1, depthMap.width*depthMap.height);
while *length(queue) != 0* **do**
 item = getFirstElementInTheQueue(queue);
 dropFirstElementInTheQueue(queue);
 neighbors = getNeighbors(item);
 for *neighbor in neighbors* **do**
  if *isMember(neighbor, meanDepth)* **then**
   region.add(neighbor);
  end
 end
end
Output: region

Algorithm 1. Pseudocode of the Region Growing algorithm.

The Region Growing algorithm was selected, since it allows to obtain directly the segmented region of the scene and is invariant to the illumination when working only on the depth map. After having the segmented region, a Meanshift algorithm is used to track the hand.

3   Results and Analysis

3.1   Static Signs

For the Naive Bayes classifier, high accuracy is obtained with the U-LBP descriptor; however, the value obtained does not exceed the threshold of 0,86. On the other hand, for the SVM, ANN and KNN classifiers, superior results are obtained with both the HOG descriptor and the U-LBP descriptor. Discarding the Contour Signature descriptor and the Naive Bayes classifier for their low results, the average accuracy of the HOG descriptor is 0,98 for the SVM classifier and the descriptor U-LBP is 0,91; for the ANN classifier the average accuracy of the HOG descriptor is 0,91 and with the descriptor U-LBP is 0,84; for the KNN classifier the average accuracy of the HOG descriptor is 0,94 and with the descriptor U-LBP is 0,89 (see Fig. 2).

The lowest accuracy is 0, 84 for the U-LBP descriptor with the ANN classifier and the highest accuracy is 0, 98 for the HOG descriptor with the SVM classifier.

3.2   Dynamic Signs

According with the results of classification, the four classifiers present similar results, for the Random Forest classifier 0,805, for the SVM classifier 0,940, for the KNN classifier 0,880 and for the Naive Bayes classifier 0,885 for accuracy.

As a result, it is evident that the SVM classifier has a higher accuracy over the other three classifiers.

As in the case of static signs, it is obtained that the SVM classifier has a higher classification accuracy with a score of 0,9400 compared to the other classifiers that have an accuracy of 0,8050, 0,8800 and 0,8850 for Random Forest, KNN and Naive Bayes respectively; so that the SVM classifier is selected.

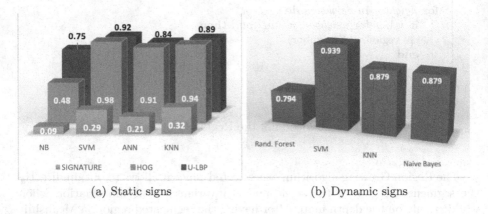

(a) Static signs   (b) Dynamic signs

Fig. 2. Accuracy for the classifiers.

4   Conclusions

Two techniques were evaluated for the segmentation of the hand, one based on segmentation of skin color and another based on segmentation of regions using a *Region Growing* algorithm. The segmentation algorithm by skin color proved to be highly dependent on illumination and it filters regions that do not correspond to the hand, which makes necessary an additional segmentation process; on the other hand, the algorithm of *Region Growing* proved to have better performance since it segments local regions and is not dependent on lighting; therefore, the *Region Growing* algorithm was selected.

For the description of static signs, the descriptors HOG, U-LBP and Contour Signature were analyzed together with the classifiers SVM, ANN, KNN and Naive Bayes, obtaining the highest precision results with the HOG descriptor and the highest accuracy with the HOG-SVM pair, with a value of 0,9806; for the dynamic signs, the trajectory-based descriptor was analyzed together with the SVM, Random Forest, KNN and Naive Bayes classifiers, obtaining the highest accuracy with the SVM classifier with a value of 0,9400. According to the above, for the static signs, the HOG classifier was chosen together with the SVM classifier and for the dynamic signs, the path descriptor was used together with the SVM classifier.

4.1 Future Work

It is suggested to increase the size and diversity of the data sets in order to improve the performance of the classification system; also, it is recommended to use Deep Learning algorithms to obtain better results, sacrificing the computational cost.

The HOG descriptor gave better results against the other descriptors, although it is not invariant to the lighting and also the Microsoft Kinect sensor can not be used outdoors, so to use a more robust sensor and propose a descriptor based only on three-dimensional data will improve the performance of the application in any environment, sacrificing computational cost.

References

1. Plouffe, G., Cretu, A., Payeur, P.: Natural Human-Computer Interaction Using Static and Dynamic Hand Gestures. IEEE (2015). ISBN 978-1-4673-9175-7
2. Yeo, H., Lee, B., Lim, H.: Hand tracking and gesture recognition system for human-computer interaction using low-cost hardware. Multimedia Tools Appl. **74**, 2687–2715 (2013). https://doi.org/10.1007/s11042-013-1501-1
3. Song, W., Le, A., Yun, S., Jung, S.: Hole filling for Kinect V2 depth images (2014)
4. Meng, H., Furao, S., Jinxi, Z.: Hidden Markov models based dynamic hand gesture recognition with incremental learning method (2014)
5. López, P., Antonio, Valveny, E., Vanrell, M.: Detección de objetos (2015)
6. Heikkilä, M., Pietikäinen, M., Schmid, C.: Description of interest regions with local binary patterns. Pattern Recogn. **42**, 425–436 (2009)
7. Khamar, S., Ganesan, P., Kanlist, V., Sathish, B.S., Merlin, J.: Comparative study of skin color detection and segmentation in HSV and YCbCr color space. Procedia Comput. Sci. **57**(12), 41–48 (2015)
8. Cooper, H., Holt, B., Bowden, R.: Sign language recognition. In: Moeslund, T., Hilton, A., Krüger, V., Sigal, L. (eds.) Visual Analysis of Humans, pp. 539–562. Springer, London (2011). https://doi.org/10.1007/978-0-85729-997-0_27
9. Dong, C., Leu, M.C., Yin, Z.: American sign language alphabet recognition using Microsoft Kinect. In: Proceedings of the IEEE Conference on Computer Vision and Pattern Recognition Workshops, pp. 44–52 (2015)
10. Majid, M.B.A., Zain, J.B.M., Hermawan, A.: Recognition of Malaysian sign language using skeleton data with neural network. In: 2015 International Conference on Science in Information Technology (ICSITech), pp. 231–236. IEEE, October 2015
11. Kushwah, M.S., Sharma, M., Jain, K., Chopra, A.: Sign language interpretation using pseudo glove. In: Singh, R., Choudhury, S. (eds.) Proceeding of International Conference on Intelligent Communication, Control and Devices, pp. 9–18. Springer, Singapore (2017). https://doi.org/10.1007/978-981-10-1708-7_2
12. Oz, C., Leu, M.C.: Recognition of finger spelling of american sign language with artificial neural network using position/orientation sensors and data glove. In: Wang, J., Liao, X.-F., Yi, Z. (eds.) ISNN 2005. LNCS, vol. 3497, pp. 157–164. Springer, Heidelberg (2005). https://doi.org/10.1007/11427445_25
13. Oz, C., Leu, M.C.: Linguistic properties based on American sign language recognition with artificial neural networks using a sensory glove and motion tracker. In: Cabestany, J., Prieto, A., Sandoval, F. (eds.) IWANN 2005. LNCS, vol. 3512, pp. 1197–1205. Springer, Heidelberg (2005). https://doi.org/10.1007/11494669_147

14. Gurjal, P., Kunnur, K.: Real time hand gesture recognition using SIFT. Int. J. Electron. Electr. Eng. **2**(3), 19–33 (2012)

15. Dardas, N.H., Georganas, N.D.: Real-time hand gesture detection and recognition using bag-of-features and support vector machine techniques. Instrum. Meas. **60**, 3592–3607 (2011)

16. Chen, K., Guo, X., Wu, J.: Gesture recognition system based on wavelet moment. In: Applied Mechanics and Materials, vol. 401–403, pp. 1377–1380 (2013)

17. Pugeault, N., Bowden, R.: Spelling it out: real-time ASL fingerspelling recognition. In: IEEE Workshop on Consumer Depth Cameras for Computer Vision (2011)

18. Amin, M.A., Yan, H.: Sign language finger alphabet recognition from Gabor-PCA representation of hand gestures. In: Machine Learning and Cybernetics, vol. 4, pp. 2218–2223 (2007)

19. Chai, X., Li, G., Chen, X., Zhou, M., Wu, G., Li, H.: Visualcomm: a tool to support communication between deaf and hearing persons with the Kinect. In: Proceedings of the 15th International ACM SIGACCESS Conference on Computers and Accessibility, p. 76. ACM, October 2013

20. Geng, L., Ma, X., Wang, H., Gu, J., Li, Y.: Chinese sign language recognition with 3D hand motion trajectories and depth images. In: Proceeding of the 11th World Congress on Intelligent Control and Automation, pp. 1457–1461. IEEE, June 2014

21. Ravi, S., Suman, M., Kishore, P.V.V., Kumar, K., Kumar, A.: Multi modal spatio temporal co-trained CNNs with single modal testing on RGB-D based sign language gesture recognition. J. Comput. Lang. **52**, 88–102 (2019)

Jupyter Notebooks for Simplifying Transfer Learning

Manuel García-Domínguez$^{(\boxtimes)}$, César Domínguez, Jónathan Heras, Eloy Mata, and Vico Pascual

Department of Mathematics and Computer Science,
University of La Rioja, Logroño, Spain
{manuel.garcia,cesar.dominguez,jonathan.heras,eloy.mata,
vico.pascual}@unirioja.es

Abstract. Nowadays, the use of transfer learning, a deep learning technique, is growing to solve imaging problems in several contexts such as biomedicine where the amount of images is limited. However, applying transfer learning might be challenging for users without experience due to the complexity of the deep learning frameworks. To facilitate the task of creating and using transfer learning models, we developed FrImCla, a framework for creating image classification models. In this paper, we have developed a set of Jupyter notebooks that use FrImCla to facilitate the task of creating and using image classification models for users without knowledge in deep learning frameworks and without any special purpose hardware.

Keywords: Deep learning · Transfer learning · Image classification

1 Introduction

Transfer learning is a deep learning method that has been successfully applied in computer vision to solve several problems [3,4,6,10,11]. This technique consists in re-using a neural network model that has been trained in a source task in a new target task, and it can be applied in different ways [12]. Namely, given a pre-trained model, we can distinguish three approaches for applying transfer learning: (1) use the architecture and the weights of the pre-trained model as the starting point to train a new model; (2) freeze the weights of some layers of the model and train the rest of the layers; and, (3) use the output of the pre-trained network as "off-the-shelf" features to train a completely new classifier for the target task. The first two approaches are data-demanding and require a lot of computational power; on the contrary, the last approach can be employed with small datasets and does not require special purpose hardware (like GPUs). In this work, we focus on the last approach.

Partially supported by Ministerio de Industria, Economía y Competitividad, project MTM2017-88804-P; Agencia de Desarrollo Económico de La Rioja, project 2017-I-IDD-00018; and FPI Grant of the Comunidad Autónoma de La Rioja.

© Springer Nature Switzerland AG 2020
R. Moreno-Díaz et al. (Eds.): EUROCAST 2019, LNCS 12014, pp. 215–221, 2020.
https://doi.org/10.1007/978-3-030-45096-0_27

Using pre-trained networks as feature extractors presents several challenges for non-expert users. First of all, there are several source models (for instance, DenseNet [8], GoogleNet [13], or Resnet 50 [7]) that can be employed for feature extraction, and their use differ from one to another. Moreover, those feature extractors must be combined with different machine learning algorithms to search for the best combination. Finally, once a model is trained following this approach, the developer must provide an interface for the model that can be employed by the final users.

To solve these problems, we developed FrImCla. This framework takes advantage of transfer learning features and helps users to create and train classification models. However, the interaction with the FrImCla library is provided by means of the command line interface. To simplify the interaction with FrImCla, we have created a set of Jupyter notebooks that allows users without knowledge in deep learning to employ this technology, see Sect. 2. With this approach users do not have to write a single line of code to create classifications models, as shown in Sect. 3. The paper ends with a conclusions and future work section.

2   Jupyter Notebooks for FrImCla

FrImCla [5] is an open source Python library for image classification. This framework provides algorithms to help the user in each step of the construction of machine learning models for image classification using both traditional and deep learning features. The workflow of FrImCla can be summarized in five different steps. First of all, the user selects the input that it is composed by the path of a dataset of images and some configuration parameters that include the feature extractor and classification algorithms. Then, FrImCla goes through the dataset collecting the features of the images using the feature extractor methods given by the user. For each feature extractor, FrImCla generates a dataset of features. From those dataset of features, FrImCla trains the classification algorithms. Another parameter is the list of machine learning algorithms that FrImCla uses to train the classifiers. Finally, a statistical analysis is employed to select the best combination of features and machine learning algorithm. The best combination is used to create a model for further use.

Even if FrImCla users only need to provide the path of the dataset of images and some configuration options, some users might find difficult to use this framework. This complexity is due to the fact that the configuration parameters must be provided by means of a JSON file and the framework is invoked from the command line. For this kind of users, we have developed Jupyter notebooks.

A Jupyter Notebook [9] is an interactive environment that allows users to develop and interact with Python code dynamically. It allows developers to integrate fragments of text, graphics or images along with the code to document it. We have developed a set of Jupyter notebooks that explain to non-expert users how to create and use their own classification models by applying transfer learning thanks to FrImCla. Even more, FrImCla can be used without any installation on the user computer. We have made accessible the Jupyter notebooks through Google colaboratory [2], a tool that allows users to construct models using FrImCla in the cloud in any computer with access to the Internet.

In the notebooks, there is a detailed explanation of the process of execution of FrImCla. In particular, the user only has to fix four parameters (see Fig. 1): the path of the dataset of images, the feature extractors (the user can select among eight deep feature extractors based on transfer learning and seven traditional computer vision methods), the supervised algorithms (among others, Neural Networks and Random Forest [1]) and the measure (currently, there are available metrics such as accuracy or AUROC). Then, the notebook connects with FrImCla and explores the different combinations of feature extractors and classification algorithms to obtain the best model for the given dataset. This process is carried out without any user interaction as shown in Fig. 2.

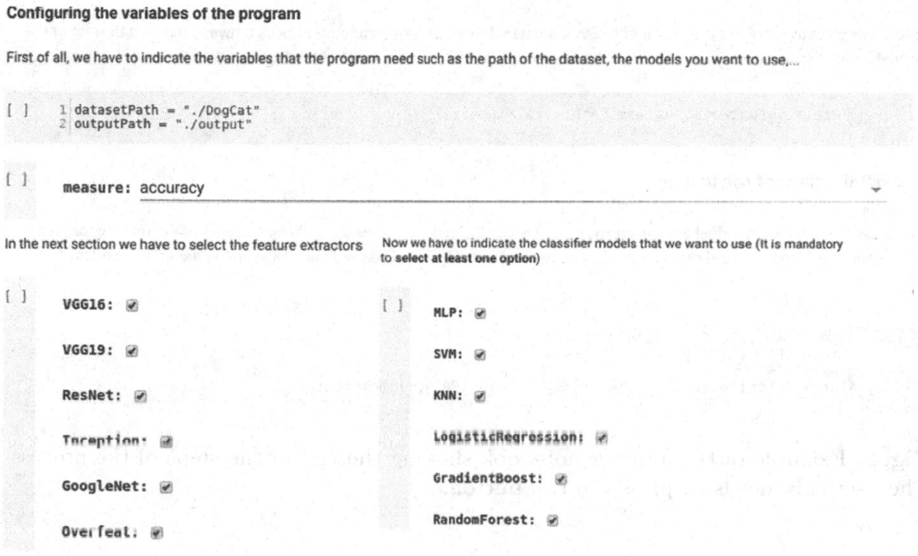

Configuring the variables of the program

First of all, we have to indicate the variables that the program need such as the path of the dataset, the models you want to use,...

```
[ ]    1 datasetPath = "./DogCat"
       2 outputPath = "./output"
```

[ ]   **measure:** accuracy ▾

In the next section we have to select the feature extractors   Now we have to indicate the classifier models that we want to use (It is mandatory to select at least one option)

[ ]   **VGG16:** ☑   [ ]   **MLP:** ☑

    VGG19: ☑   **SVM:** ☑

    ResNet: ☑   **KNN:** ☑

    Inception: ☑   **LogisticRegression:** ☑

    GoogleNet: ☑   **GradientBoost:** ☑

    OverFeat: ☑   **RandomForest:** ☑

Fig. 1. Example of the Jupyter notebook showing the configuration options.

3   Case Study

In order to show the feasibility of constructing models using FrImCla, we have used a dataset of dogs and cats that contains 600 images, 300 images for dogs and 300 images for cats for training the models. For testing we have used a dataset of 100 images to know the performance of the framework. Using FrImCla, we have performed a thorough study combining all the available feature extractors and machine learning models. Namely, we employed as featured extractors: VGG16,

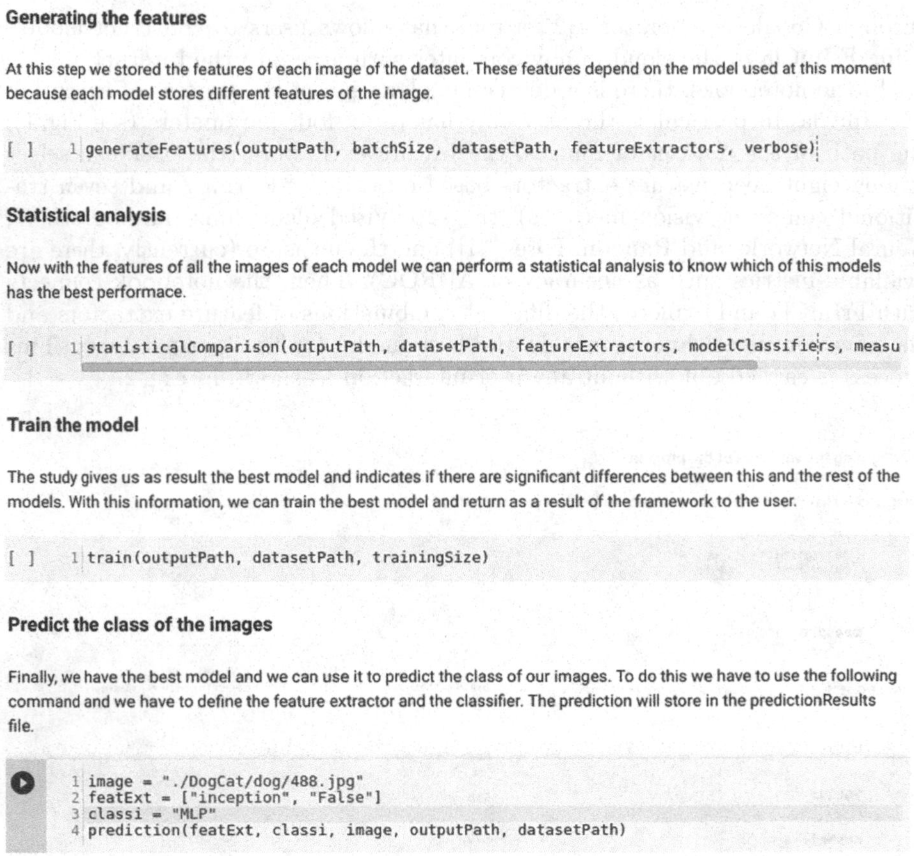

Generating the features

At this step we stored the features of each image of the dataset. These features depend on the model used at this moment because each model stores different features of the image.

```
[ ]    1 generateFeatures(outputPath, batchSize, datasetPath, featureExtractors, verbose)
```

Statistical analysis

Now with the features of all the images of each model we can perform a statistical analysis to know which of this models has the best performace.

```
[ ]    1 statisticalComparison(outputPath, datasetPath, featureExtractors, modelClassifiers, measu
```

Train the model

The study gives us as result the best model and indicates if there are significant differences between this and the rest of the models. With this information, we can train the best model and return as a result of the framework to the user.

```
[ ]    1 train(outputPath, datasetPath, trainingSize)
```

Predict the class of the images

Finally, we have the best model and we can use it to predict the class of our images. To do this we have to use the following command and we have to define the feature extractor and the classifier. The prediction will store in the predictionResults file.

```
1 image = "./DogCat/dog/488.jpg"
2 featExt = ["inception", "False"]
3 classi = "MLP"
4 prediction(featExt, classi, image, outputPath, datasetPath)
```

Fig. 2. Example of the Jupyter notebook showing the rest of the steps of the process. The user only needs to press the run button.

VGG19, Resnet, Inception, GoogleNet, Overfeat, Xception, DenseNet, LAB444, LAB888, HSV444 and HSV888 (LABXYZ and HSVXYZ are respectively LAB and HSV histograms using X,Y,Z bins per chanel); and as machine learning algorithms: SVM, KNN, Multilayer perceptron (MLP), Gradient Boost (GB), Logistic Regression (LR) and Random Forest (RF). The results are presented in Table 1 and Fig. 3. In order to compare all the possible combinations, we analyse the statistical study performed by FrImCla. Using transfer learning features we can easily obtain an accuracy higher than 85% but only with a few of them we can achieve an accuracy over 95%, see Fig. 3. On the contrary, models trained using traditional features are far from the 80% accuracy. This shows the importance of trying different models.

As a result of the analysis, we see that the best combination of feature extractor and machine learning algorithm is *DenseNet* with *MLP* (although similar results are obtained with other methods) with an accuracy of 99.0%. The result with the test set is a 96.0% accuracy.

Table 1. Mean (and standard deviation) of the different studied models for the dogs and cats dataset. The best result for each model in *italics*, the best result in **bold** face. $^*p < 0.05$; $^{**}p < 0.01$; $^{***}p < 0.001$; >: there are significant differences; $\simeq$: there are not significant differences.

Network	KNN	LR	MLP	RF	SVM	GB	Test (ANOVA or Friedman)	After post-hoc procedure
VGG16	89.5 (0.04)	95.8 (2.0)	95.3 (3.0)	*96.7 (2.2)*	96.0 (2.1)	95.5 (2.5)	5.84***	RF ≃SVM, LR, MLP, GB; RF> KNN
VGG19	92.2 (3.8)	95.2 (3.3)	95.5 (3.2)	*96.0 (2.5)*	96.0 (2.9)	95.2 (2.2)	2.37	RF≃ SVM, LR, GB, KNN, MLP
Xception	90.8 (5.5)	98.8 (1.3)	*98.8 (1.1)*	98.5 (1.2)	97.0 (2.6)	98.1 (2.1)	5.81***	MLP ≃ LR, GB, RF, SVM; MLP >KNN
Resnet 50	87.5 (2.4)	95.5 (1.8)	95.8 (1.7)	95.0 (3.1)	94.7 (2.4)	*95.7 (3.0)*	7.89***	GB ≃ MLP, LR, RF, SVM; RF > KNN
Overfeat	70.2 (7.5)	92.8 (3.0)	93.0 (3.9)	91.7 (4.2)	*93.3 (1.8)*	91.0 (2.4)	8.36***	SVM ≃ MLP, LR, RF, GB; SVM > KNN
Inception v3	80.1 (8.1)	*91.9 (3.8)*	67.7 (11.9)	87.8 (4.1)	91.9 (5.1)	85.8 (4.0)	22.59***	LR ≃ SVM, RF; LR > GB, KNN, MLP
DenseNet	92.3 (4.3)	98.7 (1.0)	**99.0 (1.3)**	96.7 (2.2)	98.5 (2.2)	96.7 (2.9)	5.64***	MLP ≃GB, RF, SVM, LR; MLP> KNN
GoogleNet	96.2 (1.4)	96.4 (1.4)	*96.8 (1.7)*	95.0 (3.7)	96.5 (1.6)	94.8 (3.1)	1.11	MLP≃ RF, SVM, LR, GB, KNN
LAB888	54.5(4.5)	*55.5 (9.5)*	55.5 (6.8)	56.5 (6.3)	54.2 (6.6)	56.7 (7.6)	0.19	GB ≃ LR, RF, SVM, KNN, MLP
LAB444	*54.6 (8.9)*	54.2 (6.2)	52.5 (6.2)	53.2 (8.0)	53.8 (6.4)	54.3 (5.3)	0.12	KNN ≃ SVM, GB, LR, RF, MLP
HSV888	55.2 (3.7)	56.7 (8.7)	50.5 (7.5)	*59.3 (6.5)*	57.3 (8.7)	61.8 (5.3)	2.8*	GB ≃ RF, LR, SVM, KNN; GB > MLP
HSV444	54.0 (7.8)	56.7 (5.3)	55.3 (4.8)	57.7 (6.9)	56.8 (4.8)	*58.7 (7.5)*	0.62	GB ~ RF, KNN, SVM, LR, MLP

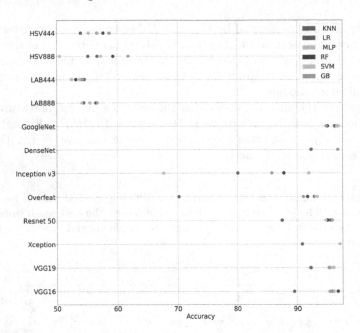

Fig. 3. Scatter plot diagram of the models constructed for the cats and dogs dataset.

4   Conclusions and Further Work

To conclude, Jupyter notebooks can be a really good tool to bring difficult technologies like transfer learning closer to non-expert users. This tool allows developers to combine code with it explanation. In this way, non-expert users can understand the process of the code that they are going to execute without write a single line of code. We have combined Jupyter notebooks with FrImCla, a tool that facilitates the task of creating and using transfer learning models. Using FrImCla, we can create accurate models for classification without any knowledge in machine learning and without any special purpose hardware.

Availability

- Project name: FrImCla notebooks.
- Project home page: https://github.com/ManuGar/FrImCla.
- Operating system(s): Platform independent.
- Programming language: Python.
- Other requirements: None.
- License: MIT.

References

1. Breiman, L.: Random forests. Mach. Learn. **45**(1), 5–32 (2001)
2. Carneiro, T., Da Nóbrega, R.V.M., Nepomuceno, T., Bian, G., De Albuquerque, V.H.C., Filho, P.P.R.: Performance analysis of google colaboratory as a tool for accelerating deep learning applications. IEEE Access **6**, 61677–61685 (2018). https://doi.org/10.1109/ACCESS.2018.2874767
3. Christodoulidis, S., et al.: Multisource transfer learning with convolutional neural networks for lung pattern analysis. IEEE J. Biomed. Health Inf. **21**(1), 76–84 (2017)
4. Domínguez, C., Heras, J., Mata, E., Pascual, V.: DecoFungi: a web application for automatic characterisation of dye decolorisation in fungal strains. BMC Bioinform. **19**(1), 66 (2018)
5. García-Domínguez, M., et al.: FrImCla: A Framework for Image Classification using Traditional and Transfer Learning Techniques. Preprint (2019). https://github.com/ManuGar/FrImCla
6. Ghafoorian, M., et al.: Transfer learning for domain adaptation in MRI: application in brain lesion segmentation. In: Descoteaux, M., Maier-Hein, L., Franz, A., Jannin, P., Collins, D.L., Duchesne, S. (eds.) MICCAI 2017. LNCS, vol. 10435, pp. 516–524. Springer, Cham (2017). https://doi.org/10.1007/978-3-319-66179-7_59
7. He, K., et al.: Deep residual learning for image recognition. In: Proceedings of IEEE Conference on Computer Vision and Pattern Recognition (CVPR 2016), pp. 770–778. IEEE Computer Society, IEEE (2016)
8. Huang, G., Liu, Z., van der Maaten, L., Weinberger, K.Q.: Densely connected convolutional networks. In: Proceedings of the IEEE Conference on Computer Vision and Pattern Recognition (CVPR 2017), pp. 2261–2269 (2017)
9. Kluyver, T., et al.: Jupyter notebooks – a publishing format for reproducible computational workflows. In: Proceedings of the 20th International Conference on Electronic Publishing, pp. 87–90. IOS Press (2016)
10. Menegola, A., Fornaciali, M., Pires, R., Dittencourt, F.V., Avila, S., Valle, E.: Knowledge transfer for melanoma screening with deep learning. In: 2017 IEEE 14th International Symposium on Biomedical Imaging (ISBI 2017), pp. 297–300, April 2017. https://doi.org/10.1109/ISBI.2017.7950523
11. Pan, S.J., Yang, Q.: A survey on transfer learning. IEEE Trans. Knowl. Data Eng. **22**(10), 1345–1359 (2010)
12. Razavian, A.S., et al.: CNN features off-the-shelf: an astounding baseline for recognition. In: Proceedings of IEEE Conference on Computer Vision and Pattern Recognition Workshops (CVPRW 2014), Columbus, Ohio, USA, pp. 512–519. IEEE Computer Society, IEEE (2014)
13. Szegedy, C., et al.: Going deeper with convolutions. In: Proceedings of IEEE Conference on Computer Vision and Pattern Recognition (CVPR 2015), pp. 1–9. IEEE Computer Society, IEEE (2015)

Impact of the Circular Region of Interest on the Performance of Multimodal Reconstruction of Retinal Images

Álvaro S. Hervella[1,2(✉)], José Rouco[1,2], Jorge Novo[1,2], and Marcos Ortega[1,2]

[1] CITIC-Research Center of Information and Communication Technologies,
Universidade da Coruña, A Coruña, Spain
{a.suarezh,jrouco,jnovo,mortega}@udc.es
[2] Department of Computer Science, Universidade da Coruña, A Coruña, Spain

Abstract. Recently, the multimodal reconstruction between complementary imaging modalities has been proposed as a self-supervised task for neural networks, that allows learning relevant data patterns without manual annotations. This idea can be easily applied to retinal imaging due to the common use of complementary image modalities in ophthalmology. However, the retinal fundus images typically depict the eye fundus in a limited circular region. This special characteristic of the retinal images may have an impact in the performance of the multimodal reconstruction due to different factors. For instance, less contextual information is available for the pixels near the border of the circular region of interest. Moreover, image acquisition defects are more prone to happen in these same regions.

In this work, experiments are performed to study the impact of the circular region of interest in the multimodal reconstruction between retinography and fluorescein angiography.

Keywords: Deep learning · Retinal imaging · Self-supervised learning · Multimodal

1 Introduction

Automated methods for retinal image analysis represent a promising tool for screening programs and common diagnostic procedures. In clinical practice, retinal imaging techniques are essential for the diagnosis of both ocular and systemic diseases with retinal manifestations [1]. Retinography, in particular, is a relatively affordable and broadly available retinal image modality that consists in a color photography of the eye fundus. The ease of producing this image modality, together with its relevance as diagnostic tool in ophthalmology, has motivated the development of numerous algorithms for the analysis of retinography. The applications of these algorithms range from the detection and extraction of anatomical structures and lesions in the retina [2] to the direct estimation of the patient's condition [1].

© Springer Nature Switzerland AG 2020
R. Moreno-Díaz et al. (Eds.): EUROCAST 2019, LNCS 12014, pp. 222–230, 2020.
https://doi.org/10.1007/978-3-030-45096-0_28

Nowadays, the automatic analysis of retinography is commonly approached using deep neural networks (DNNs). The emergence of deep learning has led to a better performance in comparison with traditional techniques. However, deep learning techniques require the use of a large amount of annotated data for training the networks. In the case of retinography, the manual labeling of the images should be performed by expert clinicians, which limits the number of available labels [3].

The scarcity of annotations for the use of DNNs is a widespread concern that affects many application domains. This has motivated the development of alternative methods to train neural networks using unlabeled or weakly labeled data. In this regard, a recent trend is the use of self-supervised learning techniques, which consist in training complementary tasks without manual annotations, with the objective of learning useful data representations. In particular, the self-supervised tasks typically consist in the prediction of hidden or complementary data [4].

Regarding the retinal images, we have recently proposed the multimodal reconstruction between retinography and fluorescein angiography as complementary task for improving the training of DNNs in the automatic analysis of retinography [5]. This multimodal reconstruction can be performed with unpaired or paired data samples [6]. In contrast with other domains, the multimodal pairs can be easily obtained in medical imaging.

The main difference between retinography and angiography is that the latter requires the injection of fluorescein contrast dye to the patients. The injected contrast dye provides additional information about the retinal vasculature. However, the more invasive procedure makes the angiography a less commonly used image modality [2]. A representative example of retinography and angiography for the same eye is depicted in Fig. 1. It can be observed that the retinal vessels are highlighted in the angiography due to the effect of the injected fluorescein. This property of the angiography can be directly exploited for the segmentation of the retinal vasculature [7]. Nevertheless, for representation learning purposes, training the prediction of angiography from retinography should lead to learn relevant patterns related to the whole retinal anatomy.

One distinctive characteristic of the retinal fundus images is that the representation of the retina is limited to a circular region of interest (ROI), which can be observed in Fig. 1. This particularity of the retinal images may have an effect in the multimodal reconstruction due to several reasons. As an immediate effect, the convolutions of the neural networks will produce a response derived from the high contrast ROI boundaries. Thus, the networks will have to learn how to correct this response in order to avoid artifacts in the predicted output. Additionally, the retinal regions near to the ROI boundary have less contextual information available around them, given that part of their neighborhood correspond to the blank background. This reduces the visual cues available for the network in order to predict the output for these regions. Another particularity of the regions near to the boundary is that they typically present a higher degree of artifacts derived from the image capturing process, such as, e.g., discoloration.

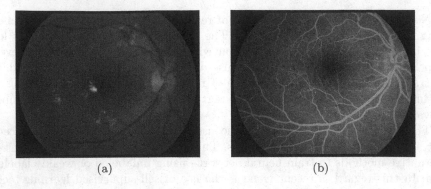

(a)   (b)

Fig. 1. Example of (a) retinography and (b) angiography from the same eye.

In this work, we analyze the effect of the circular ROI in the multimodal reconstruction between retinography and fluorescein angiography using paired data samples. In particular, we perform experiments to analyze the performance of the multimodal reconstruction near the ROI border in comparison with the rest of the image. This allows to evaluate the impact of the circular ROI.

2   Methodology

2.1   Self-supervised Multimodal Reconstruction

The multimodal reconstruction between retinography and fluorescein angiography is approached following the methodology proposed in [5]. In particular, a neural network is trained in the multimodal reconstruction task using paired and aligned retinographies and angiographies. The use of paired and aligned images facilitates the network training, which can be performed with common supervised methods despite the lack of manual annotations, hence the self-supervised approach.

The multimodal alignment of each retinography-angiography pair is performed following the methodology proposed in [8]. This methodology takes advantage of the retinal vasculature in both images modalities to perform a two-step registration. In an initial step, vessel crossings and bifurcations are extracted from both modalities and are used as landmarks for a point matching registration. In a second step, the retinal vasculature is enhanced in both modalities by means of a Multiscale Laplacian operation [8]. Then, the registration is refined optimizing a similarity measure between the vessel-enhanced images.

For the multimodal reconstruction, U-Net [9] is used as network architecture. The network training is performed with the aligned multimodal data using the retinographies as input to the network and their corresponding angiographies as target. The negative Structural Similarity (SSIM) [10] between the network output and the target is used as training loss. Given that the images are spatially transformed to align their contents, the ROIs of the aligned image pairs do not completely overlap. Thus, the training loss is only computed for the pixels within the intersection of the retinography and angiography circular ROIs.

Regarding the network training, the He et al. method [11] is applied to initialize the network parameters and the Adam algorithm [12] is used for the optimization. The learning rate is set to an initial value of $\alpha = 1e - 4$ and it is reduced by a factor of 10 when the validation loss does not improve during 25 epochs. The training is stopped after 100 epochs without improvement in the validation. Additionally, data augmentation is applied in the form of random spatial and color transformations.

As training data, we use the public dataset Isfahan MISP [13], which consists of 59 retinography-angiography pairs. Specifically, half of the image pairs correspond to patients diagnosed with diabetic retinopathy whereas the other half correspond to healthy cases. The images present a resolution of 720×576 pixels.

2.2 Experimental Analysis of the Circular ROI

If the presence of a circular ROI on the retinal images has an effect on the multimodal reconstruction, this should be especially reflected in the pixels close to the ROI border. Thus, in order to analyze the effect of the circular ROI, the performance of the multimodal reconstruction is evaluated over alternative ROIs that discard part of the outer pixels within the retinal region. This will evidence if there is a difference in performance between the area near to the ROI border and the rest of the retina.

The performance of the multimodal reconstruction is evaluated quantitatively following the same approach as [5]. In brief, a relevant property of the angiography is that the retinal vasculature is highlighted. If the multimodal reconstruction is successfully performed, the generated angiographics should also keep this property. This can be evaluated by means of a rough vasculature segmentation applying a global threshold over the images. The enhancement of the retinal vasculature in an angiography improves the performance of this segmentation with respect to the retinography. Thus, it is expected that the pseudo-angiography generated from the retinography also behaves in this manner. The assessment of the proposed vasculature segmentation, which is a binary classification problem, is performed with Receiver Operator Characteristic (ROC) and Precision-Recall (PR) analyses. In both cases, the required metrics are computed for several values of the applied global threshold. The resulting set of measurements is used to create a curve where each point corresponds to a particular decision threshold. In the case of a ROC curve, True Positive Rate (TPR) is plotted against False Positive Rate (FPR), whereas for a Precision-Recall curve, Precision is plotted against Recall, i.e., TPR. These measurements are computed as:

$$Precision = \frac{TruePositives}{TruePositives + FalsePositives} \tag{1}$$

$$TPR = \frac{TruePositives}{TruePositives + FalseNegatives} \tag{2}$$

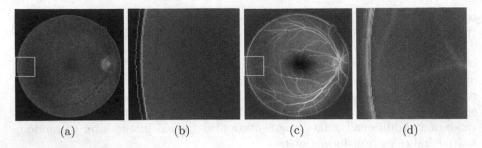

(a)   (b)   (c)   (d)

Fig. 2. Example of (a) retinography from the DRIVE dataset together with (c) the corresponding generated angiography and cropped regions in detail: (b) from (a) and (d) from (c). The red line represents the original ROI whereas the green line represents the redefined ROI.

$$FPR = \frac{FalsePositives}{FalsePositives + TrueNegatives} \tag{3}$$

In the performed experiments, these metrics are computed considering only the pixels within the circular ROI. Additionally, the performance according to ROC and PR analyses is summarized using the Area Under Curve (AUC) value.

As evaluation data, we use the public datasets DRIVE [14] and STARE [15], which are two reference datasets for vasculature analysis in retinography. These datasets contain retinographies with manually annotated vasculature segmentations. In particular, DRIVE consists of 40 retinographies with a resolution of 565×584 pixels whereas STARE consists of 20 retinographies with a resolution of 700×605 pixels.

The DRIVE dataset includes a binary mask defining the ROI for each image. However, in some cases, the provided masks are not properly adjusted to the retinal region, and some background pixels are included within the ROI (see Fig. 2(a)(b)). As this can interfere with the proposed experimentation, we redefine the ROI using a circular binary mask that perfectly matches the retinal region border. An example of original and redefined ROI are depicted in Fig. 2. Additional experiments are conducted to study the effect of using one or other ROI for the quantitative evaluation.

3   Results and Discussion

Figure 3 depicts examples of generated angiographies using a neural network trained for the self-supervised multimodal reconstruction. The examples correspond to the different training and evaluation datasets. The reconstruction of the different retinal structures is similar for all the datasets, which demonstrates an adequate generalization of the trained network. The generated angiographies depicted in Fig. 3 present a blank background because the adequate binary masks were applied to them. In contrast, an example of raw generated angiography is depicted in Fig. 2.

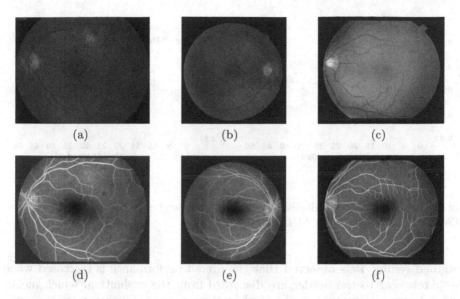

(a)   (b)   (c)

(d)   (e)   (f)

Fig. 3. Examples of (1st row) retinographies and (2nd row) corresponding generated angiographies. (a)(d) Example from the training dataset Isfahan MISP. (b)(e) Example from the DRIVE test set. (c)(f) Example from the STARE test set.

Table 1. Results of the quantitative evaluation for the original and redefined ROIs in DRIVE.

	AUC-ROC (%)	AUC-PR (%)
Original ROI	84.51 ± 0.40	60.11 ± 1.52
Redefined ROI	84.99 ± 0.51	64.43 ± 1.24

Table 1 shows the results of the quantitative evaluation for the original and redefined ROI in the DRIVE dataset. The redefined ROI results in better performance, specially when measured in terms of AUC-PR. This indicates that the evaluation with the original ROI produces a higher number of false positives. The results are explained by the additional background pixels that are included in the original ROI. Since the multimodal reconstruction is trained using perfectly matched ROIs, it can produce arbitrary intensity values outside the retinal region. In particular, in this case, it produces a bright response due to the border of the retinal region, as it is depicted in Fig. 2. The inclusion of these pixels for the evaluation inappropriately penalizes the performance. This fact should be considered for the self-supervised multimodal reconstruction but also for any other case where different ROI definitions could be used for training and evaluation.

Figure 4 depicts the quantitative results with varying ROI sizes for both DRIVE and STARE datasets. In the case of DRIVE, we use the redefined ROI to discard the inclusion of background pixels as a contribution factor in the

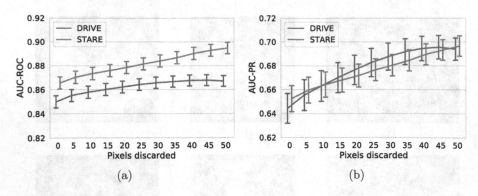

Fig. 4. Results of the quantitative evaluation with varying ROI sizes for DRIVE and STARE. (a) AUC-ROC. (b) AUC-PR.

obtained results. It is observed that the overall performance is increased when the pixels near to the border are discarded from the evaluation, which means that a lower performance is obtained in these regions. Furthermore, the same effect is observed when evaluating in terms of AUC-ROC and AUC-PR. This indicates that the characteristic circular ROI of the retinal images has a negative impact on the performance of the multimodal reconstruction, at least in terms of vasculature reconstruction. A possible cause of this is the lesser contextual information that is included within the neighborhood of each pixel near the ROI border. Additionally, pixels near the border are more likely to present defects like discoloration. The use of color augmentation during training can provide additional artificially discolored samples to the network, however, this does not necessarily leads to the same performance among regions with different image quality.

4   Conclusions

In this work, we have studied the impact that the circular region of interest of the retinal images have in a deep learning-based multimodal reconstruction between retinography and fluorescein angiography. This multimodal reconstruction has been recently proposed as an alternative to learn relevant retinal patterns without manual labels. However, the effect of the circular region of interest had not been studied yet.

The conducted experiments demonstrate that the circular region of interest affects the multimodal reconstruction, which is evidenced by the lesser performance near the border of the circular region. Furthermore, we also demonstrate that small differences in the definition of this circular region may produce significant variations in the evaluation of the studied multimodal setting.

Acknowledgments. This work is supported by the MINECO, Government of Spain, through the DPI2015-69948-R research project. The authors of this work also receive financial support from the ERDF and ESF of the EU, and the Xunta de Galicia through Centro Singular de Investigación de Galicia, accreditation 2016–2019, ref. ED431G/01 and Grupo de Referencia Competitiva, ref. ED431C 2016-047 research projects, and the predoctoral grant contract ref. ED481A-2017/328.

References

1. Cole, E.D., Novais, E.A., Louzada, R.N., Waheed, N.K.: Contemporary retinal imaging techniques in diabetic retinopathy: a review. Clin. Exp. Ophthalmol. **44**(4), 289–299 (2016)
2. Besenczi, R., Tóth, J., Hajdu, A.: A review on automatic analysis techniques for color fundus photographs. Comput. Struct. Biotechnol. J. **14**, 371–384 (2016)
3. Litjens, G., et al.: A survey on deep learning in medical image analysis. Med. Image Anal. **42**, 60–88 (2017)
4. Doersch, C., Zisserman, A.: Multi-task self-supervised visual learning. In: International Conference on Computer Vision (ICCV) (2017)
5. Hervella, Á.S., Rouco, J., Novo, J., Ortega, M.: Retinal image understanding emerges from self-supervised multimodal reconstruction. In: Frangi, A.F., Schnabel, J.A., Davatzikos, C., Alberola-López, C., Fichtinger, G. (eds.) MICCAI 2018. LNCS, vol. 11070, pp. 321–328. Springer, Cham (2018). https://doi.org/10.1007/978-3-030-00928-1_37
6. Hervella, A.S., Rouco, J., Novo, J., Ortega, M.: Deep multimodal reconstruction of retinal images using paired or unpaired data. In: International Joint Conference on Neural Networks (IJCNN) (2019)
7. Hervella, A.S., Rouco, J., Novo, J., Ortega, M.: Self-supervised deep learning for retinal vessel segmentation using automatically generated labels from multimodal data. In: International Joint Conference on Neural Networks (IJCNN) (2019)
8. Hervella, A.S., Rouco, J., Novo, J., Ortega, M.: Multimodal registration of retinal images using domain-specific landmarks and vessel enhancement. In: International Conference on Knowledge-Based and Intelligent Information and Engineering Systems (KES) (2018)
9. Ronneberger, O., Fischer, P., Brox, T.: U-net: convolutional networks for biomedical image segmentation. In: Navab, N., Hornegger, J., Wells, W.M., Frangi, A.F. (eds.) MICCAI 2015. LNCS, vol. 9351, pp. 234–241. Springer, Cham (2015). https://doi.org/10.1007/978-3-319-24574-4_28
10. Wang, Z., Bovik, A.C., Sheikh, H.R., Simoncelli, E.P.: Image quality assessment: from error visibility to structural similarity. Trans. Image Process. **13**(4), 600–612 (2004)
11. He, K., Zhang, X., Ren, S., Sun, J.: Delving deep into rectifiers: Surpassing human-level performance on imagenet classification. In: International Conference on Computer Vision (ICCV) (2015)
12. Kingma, D.P., Ba, J.: Adam: a method for stochastic optimization. In: International Conference on Learning Representations (ICLR), May 2015
13. Alipour, S.H.M., Rabbani, H., Akhlaghi, M.R.: Diabetic retinopathy grading by digital curvelet transform. Comput. Math. Methods Med. **2012** (2012)

14. Staal, J., Abramoff, M., Niemeijer, M., Viergever, M., van Ginneken, B.: Ridge based vessel segmentation in color images of the retina. Trans. Med. Imaging **23**(4), 501–509 (2004)
15. Hoover, A.D., Kouznetsova, V., Goldbaum, M.: Locating blood vessels in retinal images by piecewise threshold probing of a matched filter response. Trans. Med. Imaging **19**(3), 203–210 (2000)

Google Colaboratory for Quantifying Stomata in Images

Ángela Casado-García[1]([✉]), Jónathan Heras[1], and Alvaro Sanz-Sáez[2]

[1] Department of Mathematics and Computer Science,
University of La Rioja, Logroño, Spain
{angela.casado,jonathan.heras}@unirioja.es
[2] Department of Crop, Soil, and Environmental Sciences,
Auburn University, Auburn, USA
sanz@auburn.edu

Abstract. Stomata are pores in the epidermal tissue of plants formed by specialized cells called occlusive cells or guard cells. Analyzing the number and behavior of stomata is a task carried out by studying microscopic images, and that can serve, among other things, to better manage crops in agriculture. However, quantifying the number of stomata in an image is an expensive process since a stomata image might contain dozens of stomata. Therefore, it is interesting to automate such a detection process. This problem can be framed in the context of object detection, a task widely studied in computer vision. Currently, the best approaches to tackle object detection problems are based on deep learning techniques. Although these techniques are very successful, they might be difficult to use. In this work, we face this problem, specifically for the detection of stomata, by building a Jupyter notebook in Google Colaboratory that allows biologists to automatically detect stomata in their images.

Keywords: Object detection · YOLO · Stomata images · Google Colaboratory

1 Introduction

Stomata (singular "stoma") are pores on a plant leaf, see Fig. 1, that allow the exchange of gases, mainly CO_2 and water vapor, between the atmosphere and the plant. Stomata respond to changes in the environment and regulate the photosynthesis of plants, and thus their productivity. Due to these facts, scientists have studied the number, density, size, and behavior of stomata to model CO_2 dynamics in the atmosphere and predict future carbon and water cycles [10]; and, also, in crop breeding and crop management programs [3,11].

Partially supported by Ministerio de Industria, Economía y Competitividad, project MTM2017-88804-P; and Agencia de Desarrollo Económico de La Rioja, project 2017-I-IDD-00018. We also acknowledge the support of NVIDIA Corporation with the donation of the Titan Xp GPU used for this research.

© Springer Nature Switzerland AG 2020
R. Moreno-Díaz et al. (Eds.): EUROCAST 2019, LNCS 12014, pp. 231–238, 2020.
https://doi.org/10.1007/978-3-030-45096-0_29

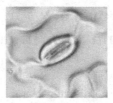

Fig. 1. Example of a stoma

In order to analyze stomata of plant leaves, plant biologists take microscopic images of leaves, and manually measure the stomata density, individual stomata opening, and morphological traits like the size and shape of the stomata guard cells (a pair of cells that surround each stoma). Those measurements are repeated over hundreds of images from different plant varieties. This is a tedious, error-prone, time-consuming and subjective task due to the large number of stomata in each image, see Fig. 2; but, it can be automatized by means of detection and imaging techniques. In this work, we present a first step towards such an automatization. Namely, using deep learning techniques, we have created a tool that automatically detects stomata in an image. The process to develop that kind of tool can be applied to other problems, and consists of two steps: training a detection model (see Sect. 2), and creating a graphical interface, in our case a Google colaboratory notebook, see Sect. 3.

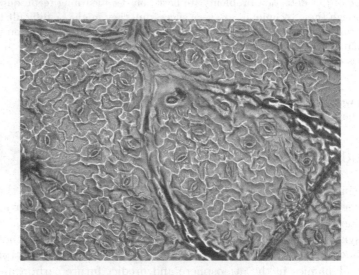

Fig. 2. Example of stomata detection

2 Training a Stomata Detection Model

In this section, we present the common workflow to create a deep learning-based object detector (see Fig. 3), the challenges that are faced on each stage of the workflow, the alternatives that can be employed to face those problems, and the concrete solutions given for the stomata case.

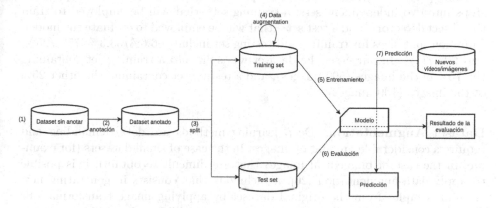

Fig. 3. Workflow of object detection projects

Nowadays, there are several algorithms and libraries that allow the creation of object detection models. Although each of them is different, the process to build a model is independent and always consists of the same 6 steps: dataset acquisition, dataset annotation, dataset split, dataset augmentation, model training and model evaluation.

Dataset Acquisition. The starting point of any image detection project is the acquisition of a dataset of images. This is an important step since the dataset must be representative of what the model will later find when deployed in the real world. Different alternatives can be used to obtain a dataset of images. For example, using open datasets, web scrapping images with the appropriate license, using images provided by a client, or using special purpose devices to capture the images. In our case, stomata images are acquired with a microscope, and this kind of image in not usually freely available. Therefore, we created our own dataset of images. Namely, our dataset consists of 500 stomata images of soy plants captured with a Leica microscope.

Dataset Annotation. The second step of the process consists in annotating the dataset; that is, indicating the position of the objects in the images. This is a time-consuming stage that might require the intervention of expert users. To simplify this task, there are graphical interactive tools, like LabelImg [22] or

YOLO mark [1], that help in the generation of the annotation files. Unfortunately, there is not a standard annotation format and, in fact, the format varies among object detection frameworks and annotation tools. In our case, the images were annotated using LabelImg by expert biologists.

Dataset Split. After annotating the images, and, As in any other machine learning project, it is instrumental to split the dataset obtained in the previous steps into two independent sets: a training set—that will be employed to train the object detector—and a test set—that will be employed to evaluate the model. Common split sizes for training and testing set include 66.6%/33.3%, 75%/25%, and 90%/10%. In our case, the dataset was split into a training set containing the 75% of the images (500 images), and a testing set containing the other 25% of the images (100 images).

Dataset Augmentation. Deep learning methods are data demanding and require a considerable amount of images. In the case of small datasets (for example, in the case of biomedical images that are difficult to obtain), it is posible to apply data-augmentation [20], a technique that consists in generating new training samples from the original dataset by applying image transformations (for instance, applying flips, rotations, filters or adding noise). This approach has been applied in image classification problems [20,21], and there are several libraries implementing this method (for instance, Augmentor [2] or Imgaug [12]). However, those libraries cannot be applied in the context of object detection since they do not alter the annotation (note that if we flip an image, the position, and hence the annotation, of the objects change). In our case, we employed CLODSA [9] a library that not only generates new images by applying data-augmentation but also creates the corresponding annotations. By employing this library, the training dataset of 500 images was augmented using flips, rotations, filters or adding noise, obtaining a final dataset of 4500 images.

Model Training. Currently there are two types of deep learning algorithms used to build object detection models: two-phase and one-phase algorithms. The two-phase detection algorithms have two components: the first is responsible for proposing regions of interest that are used by the second component to decide the position of the objects. These algorithms are usually accurate but slow at runtime, so they can not be used in real-time applications. Examples of algorithms of this type are R-CNN [8], Fast R-CNN [7] and Faster R-CNN [17]. The second type of detection algorithms are the one-phase algorithms, that are trained from start to end to make the detections. These algorithms are fast but not so precise as two-phase algorithms, although most of these algorithms are introducing improvements that increase their accuracy without affecting their response times, see Table 1. Among these algorithms we can find SSD [15], RetinaNet [14] or YOLO [16]. Recently the YOLO algorithm, a one-phase algorithm, has reached a precision comparable to that of two-phase algorithms, but keeping the processing in real time. This is why we have chosen this algorithm for our work. The YOLO algorithm was trained during 200.000 iterations using the default settings of this algorithm.

Table 1. Precision and detection time of algorithms in the Pascal Voc dataset [6]

Detection framework	mAP	FPS
Faster RCNN - VGG16	73.2	7
Faster RCNN - ResNet	76.4	5
YOLO v1	63.4	45
SSD 500	76.8	19
YOLO (416×416 image size)	76.8	67
YOLO (480×480 image size)	77.8	59

Model Evaluation. Finally, after training a model, we need to evaluate it to assess its performance. Namely, the images in the testing set, are presented to the model and ask it to detect the objects in those images. Those detections are compared to the ground-truth provided by the annotations of the testing set, and the result of the comparison is evaluated using metrics such as the IoU [18], the mAP [18], the precision, the recall or the F1-score [6]. A problem that might arise during the evaluation is the overfitting of the object detection model; that is, the model can detect objects on images from the training dataset, but it cannot detect objects on any other image. In order to avoid this problem, early stopping [19] can be applied by comparing the results obtained by the models after different numbers of iterations. Using this technique, in our stomata detection model, we built a model with a mAP of 90.91% and a precision of 98% in the testing set.

The complete workflow to train the stomata detection model is available at github https://github.com/ancasag/YOLONotebooks; and such a workflow can be generalized to other problems as explained in [4]. Finally, the model is ready to be employed in images that neither belong to the training set nor to the testing set.

3   A Google Colaboratory Notebook

Using a detection model with new images is usually as simple as invoking a command with the path of the image (and, probably, some additional parameters). However, this requires the installation of several libraries and the usage of a command line interface; and, this might be challenging for non-expert users like biologists. Therefore, it is important to create simple and intuitive interfaces that might be employed by different kinds of users; otherwise, they will not be able to take advantage of the object detection model.

▼ Detection

In this step, we invoke the *predict* function that returns the uploaded image with the detected stomata.

```
[4]  predict(imagePath)
```

Now, we show the result inside the notebook.

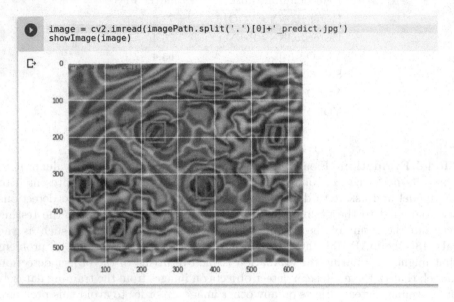

Fig. 4. Notebook to automatically detect stomata in images

To disseminate our detection model, we have created a Jupyter notebook, see Fig. 4, that allows users to detect stomata in their images. Jupyter notebooks [13] are documents for publishing code, results and explanations in a form that is both readable and executable; and, they have been widely adopted across multiple disciplines, both for its usefulness in keeping a record of data analyses, and also for allowing reproducibility. The drawback of Jupyter notebooks is that they require the installation of several libraries. Such a problem has been overcome in our case by providing our notebook in Google Colaboratory [5], a free Jupyter notebook environment that requires no setup and runs entirely in the cloud avoiding the installation of libraries in the local computer. The notebook is available at https://github.com/ancasag/Stomata.

4   Conclusions and Further Work

In this work, we have developed a tool that allows biologists to automatically detect stomata in images. To build this tool, it has been necessary to create a object detection model using the YOLO algorithm. In addition, since using models directly in the framework that provides YOLO models might be difficult for biologist we have developed a simple-to-use interface by means of a Jupyter notebook available in Google Colaboratory.

Several tasks remain as further work. First of all, we are planning to train a model with stomata images from several varieties of plants since the current model was built only soy plants. Moreover, we will develop a tool that allows users to interact with the result produced by the detection model; and not only obtain stomata density, but also other useful information.

References

1. Alexey, A.B.: YOLO mark (2018). https://github.com/AlexeyAB/Yolomark
2. Bloice, M.D., Stocker, C., Holzinger, A.: Augmentor: an image augmentation library for machine learning. J. Open Source Softw. **2**, 432 (2017)
3. Buttery, B.R., Tan, C.S., Buzzell, R.I., Gaynor, J.D., MacTavish, D.C.: Stomatal numbers of soybean and response to water stress. Plant Soil **149**(2), 283–288 (1993). https://doi.org/10.1007/BF00016619
4. Casado-García, A., Heras, J.: Guiding the creation of deep learning-based object detectorss. In: Proceedings of the XVIII Conferencia de la Asociacion Española para la Inteligencia Artificial (CAEPIA 2018), session DEEPL 2018 (2018)
5. Colaboratory Team: Google Colaboratory (2017). https://colab.research.google.com
6. Everingham, M., et al.: The pascal visual object classes challenge: a retrospective. Int. J. Comput. Vis. **111**(1), 98–136 (2015)
7. Girshick, R.: Fast R-CNN. In: 2015 IEEE International Conference on Computer Vision (ICCV), pp. 1440–1448 (2015)
8. Girshick, R., Donahue, J., Darrell, T., Malik, J.: Rich feature hierarchics for accurate object detection and semantic segmentation. In: 2014 IEEE Conference on Computer Vision and Pattern Recognition, pp. 580–587 (2014)
9. Heras, J., et al.: CLoDSA: an open-source image augmentation library for object classification, localization, detection and semantic segmentation (2018). https://github.com/joheras/CLoDSA
10. Hetherington, A.M., Woodward, F.I.: The role of stomata in sensing and driving environmental change. Nature **424**(6951), 901–908 (2003)
11. Hughes, J., et al.: Reducing stomatal density in barley improves drought tolerance without impacting on yield. Plant Physiol. **174**(2), 776–787 (2017)
12. Jung, A.: Imgaug: a library for image augmentation in machine learning experiments (2017). https://github.com/aleju/imgaug
13. Kluyver, T., et al.: Jupyter notebooks – a publishing format for reproducible computational workflows. In: Proceedings of the 20th International Conference on Electronic Publishing, pp. 87–90. IOS Press (2016)
14. Lin, T., Goyal, P., Girshick, R., He, K., Dollar, P.: Focal loss for dense object detection. IEEE Trans. Pattern Anal. Mach. Intell. **39**, 2980–2988 (2017). abs/1708.02002

15. Liu, W., et al.: SSD: single shot MultiBox detector. In: Leibe, B., Matas, J., Sebe, N., Welling, M. (eds.) ECCV 2016. LNCS, vol. 9905, pp. 21–37. Springer, Cham (2016). https://doi.org/10.1007/978-3-319-46448-0_2
16. Redmon, J., Farhadi, A.: YOLOv3: An Incremental Improvement. CoRR abs/1804.02767 (2018). http://arxiv.org/abs/1804.02767
17. Ren, S., He, K., Girshick, R., Sun, J.: Faster R-CNN: towards real-time object detection with region proposal networks. In: Advances in Neural Information Processing Systems, vol. 28, pp. 91–99 (2015)
18. Rosebrock, A.: Deep Learning for Computer Vision with Python. PyImageSearch (2018). https://www.pyimagesearch.com/
19. Sarle, W.S.: Stopped training and other remedies for overfitting. In: Proceedings of the 27th Symposium on the Interface of Computing Science and Statistics, pp. 352–360 (1995)
20. Simard, P., Steinkraus, D., Platt, J.C.: Best practices for convolutional neural networks applied to visual document analysis. In: Proceedings of the 12th International Conference on Document Analysis and Recognition (ICDAR 2003), vol. 2, pp. 958–964 (2003)
21. Simard, P., Victorri, B., LeCun, Y., Denker, J.S.: Tangent prop - a formalism for specifying selected invariances in an adaptive network. In: Proceedings of the 4th International Conference on Neural Information Processing Systems (NIPS 1991). Advances in Neural Information Processing Systems, vol. 4, pp. 895–903 (1992)
22. Tzutalin, D.: LabelImg (2015). https://github.com/tzutalin/labelImg

Unsupervised Anomaly Map
for Image-Based Screening

Shaon Sutradhar[1,2], José Rouco[1,2(✉)], and Marcos Ortega[1,2]

[1] CITIC - Research Center of Information and Communication Technology,
University of A Coruña, A Coruña, Spain
{shaon.sutradhar,jrouco,mortega}@udc.es
[2] Department of Computer Science, University of A Coruña, A Coruña, Spain

Abstract. Computer-aided screening methods can reduce the burden of manual grading. However, manual grading is still required to provide datasets with annotated pathologies that are used for the development of supervised machine learning based systems of the kind. In this paper we demonstrate a different method, based on unsupervised anomaly detection techniques, that can be exploited to detect and localize pathologies at the pixel-level in retinal images. We introduce a new reconstruction-based model architecture, trained with only healthy retinal images, and leverage it to generate anomaly maps from where the anomalous patterns can be located, which allows to automatically discover the image locations that can potentially be pathological lesions.

Keywords: Anomaly detection · Image reconstruction · Screening

1 Introduction

Diabetes mellitus (DM) is a severe health-threatening disease affecting 422 million adults globally [18]. A retinal microvascular complication of DM is known as diabetic retinopathy (DR). Approximately one-third of the DM patients are also diagnosed with DR and, if not detected early, DR can further cause irreversible vision loss [6]. For the early detection of DR, it is essential to establish systematic DR screening programs worldwide since such programs have been found effective to reduce the threat of visual impairment [6].

In a DR screening program, retinal images are analyzed to provide grading of the DR progression. This image analysis process is generally approached with manual assessment by expert clinicians or through the use of computer-aided systems. A manual grading system relies on highly skilled and expensive personnel. Moreover, such approach is very arduous, subjective and time-intensive. Also, with the rapidly increasing prevalence of DM, the manual approach may not cope with the increasing screening demand [9]. On the other hand, computer-aided screening (CAS) systems are automatic and can provide a fast, reliable and repeatable assessment.

© Springer Nature Switzerland AG 2020
R. Moreno-Díaz et al. (Eds.): EUROCAST 2019, LNCS 12014, pp. 239–246, 2020.
https://doi.org/10.1007/978-3-030-45096-0_30

The development of CAS systems is an extensive research field. Various kinds of methodologies, including classical image processing techniques, data-driven machine learning methods or recently popularized deep learning algorithms, are exploited in the development of such systems. Data-driven supervised machine learning methods are commonly used, but they require extensive lesion-annotated retinal image datasets for training. The lesion annotation of the retinal images needs to be meticulously carried out by several manual graders. However, it should be noted that the precise pixel-wise manual marking of the lesions within the image is a much more labor intensive task than providing a global disease grade for each whole image. Furthermore, on the one hand, it is usually easier to gather healthy cases than pathological and, on the other hand, pathological cases present a higher variability in the relevant image patterns that should be taken into account for the diagnosis. This results in either unbalanced datasets due to the former, or in scarce annotated datasets not representing the intra-class variability of pathological cases, cause of the latter.

In such scenario, unsupervised approaches that can take advantage of the abundant healthy data are encouraged, especially if a disease/no-disease decision is primarily important. Therefore, in this research, we propose a DR screening system based on unsupervised anomaly detection approaches which complementarily provides location information of the potential lesions that are present in the image. This approach has the advantage of being able to discover anomalies on the pixel level, associated with potential pathologies, without the need of explicitly labelling them.

Anomaly detection in biomedical imaging is a very important research field which primarily studies different techniques to distinguish pathologies, e.g. cancerous cells in blood, tumors in breast, cysts in retina, etc. [14]. Commonly applied anomaly detection techniques in medical images comprise statistical methods [8], supervised and unsupervised machine learning techniques [4,16], and deep learning algorithms [12]. Reconstruction-based unsupervised machine learning methods are particularly approached when there is a scarcity of labelled data for training, which is the case in biomedical imaging domain. These methods are exploited mainly to learn the structural variabilities of normal images by training a reconstructor model using the healthy data, with the aim that the model will not accurately reconstruct the pathological samples.

Autoencoders (AEs) are the common types of reconstructors which are found efficient in anomaly detection, particularly within the domain of natural images [10,15,19]. These reconstructors, however, are unable to accurately discriminate normal and anomalous samples in some applications within medical imaging domain [2,13]. In these cases, they did not learn high level discriminative features of the input distribution and only added blurring to the reconstructed output. Other complex and advanced types of reconstructors are some recent generative models, like the Generative Adversarial Networks (GAN) [11], and their different variations [2]. These models have been demonstrated as very effective for the anomaly detection in different medical images and do not suffer from the blurry reconstructions [2]. Generative models are, however, hard to train and cannot

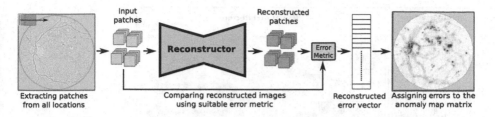

Fig. 1. Proposed anomaly map generation method using image reconstructor.

provide a guarantee of learning the whole input distribution [1]. Alternatively, in our previous work, we proposed a different architecture for a reconstructor model using convolutional neural networks, the Blind-Spot Network (BSNet) [13], which evidenced that the model was clearly able to discriminate healthy and pathological samples with higher accuracy while compared with AEs. The BSNet reconstructor did not reconstruct the pathological patterns and produced significantly higher reconstruction error showing its potential as a reconstruction-based anomaly detection model. In the work herein described, we use the BSNet for the detection of anomalies in retinal fundus images and consequently present a novel technique for generating anomaly maps on full-size images by automatically labelling the anomalies on pixel-level.

Reconstruction-based unsupervised anomaly detection methods are generally exploited to perform global labelling of normal and anomalous samples using the reconstruction error. The reconstruction error can also be used for the pixel-level classification of anomalies. The pixel-level anomaly classification provides the location information of the anomalies which can be significantly useful when applied to medical images for locating different types of pathologies. With this motivation, in this research we propose a novel method of generating anomaly maps using image reconstructor that provides pixel-wise labelling of anomalies in images. Schlegl et el. [11] and Baur et el. [2] demonstrated pixel-level anomaly detection methods using unsupervised reconstruction-based models. Schlegl et el. performed patch based model training and visualized anomalies on patches, where Baur et el. trained their model with full-size images and localized anomalies on whole images. In contrast to their methods, we train our model with patches and generate anomaly maps on whole images.

2   Methodology

The working principle of the proposed anomaly map generation method using reconstruction-based unsupervised anomaly detection technique is depicted in Fig. 1. The system consists of a reconstructor which reconstructs patches of all locations from a full-size image. Afterwards, each of the reconstructed patches is compared with the original patch using an error metric and the average reconstructed error is computed. This gives a vector of reconstruction errors for all

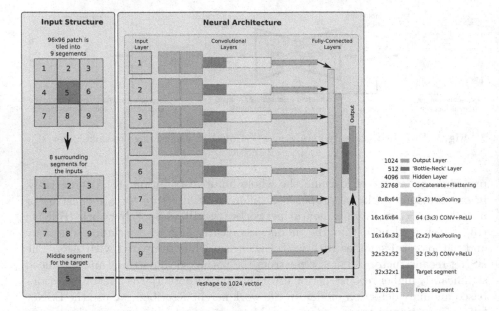

Fig. 2. The architecture of the Blind-Spot Network (BSNet) reconstructor.

the patches, from which a mapping of the errors to their original patch locations is built to form the anomaly map matrix.

The reconstructor is trained with healthy images so that it learns the high level structural features of the healthy retina by minimizing the reconstruction error on the healthy dataset. In consequence, the trained model is likely to reconstruct pathological samples with higher reconstruction error than the healthy samples. Thus, the reconstruction error can be used to identify anomalous samples.

The quality of the reconstructed images can be measured using different image quality metrics. In this study, we leverage the mean absolute error (MAE), the mean squared error (MSE) and the Structural Similarity Index (SSIM) [17] as the error metrics to generate the anomaly map, which yields three maps for each input image.

2.1   The Blind-Spot Network Architecture

The general working principle of an autoencoder model consists of compressing the input into a lower dimensional bottle-neck layer, then reconstructing the input from it. The bottle-neck layer holds the intrinsic information of the input data from where the same input is reconstructed. In other words, the autoencoder always sees in the input that it aims to reconstruct during the training of the model. In contrast to a such conventional types of reconstructor, our proposed BSNet reconstructor does not reconstruct the same input. It takes the surrounding segments of an image patch as the input and reconstructs the unseen middle segment, i.e. it never sees in the input what is has to reconstruct, as it is 'blind' to the center part of the image patch. And, since an unseen region has to be extrapolated from an input, therefore, the network is enforced to learn higher level discriminative features of the input data. Our previous experiments [13] showed that the BSNet performed significantly better than autoencoder-based reconstructor in the detection of pathological samples of retinal fundus images. We, therefore, utilize the BSNet as the reconstructor in this work for the generation of anomaly maps.

The architecture of the BSNet is shown in Fig. 2. A gray-scale image patch of 96×96 pixels is tiled into 9 equal segments, each with 32×32 pixels, where the middle segment is the target and the 8 surrounding segments are the inputs of the BSNet. Each input segment is connected with independent convolutional neural networks, and then their outputs are concatenated and flattened to further connect with a fully-connected neural network. The fully-connected neural network has encoding and decoding parts. The flattened layer is encoded to a bottle-neck layer of size 512 neurons and then decoded to 1024 neurons, which is the output of the BSNet. The output layer of the network has linear activation and the rest of the layers use ReLU.

3   Results and Discussion

We use the public Messidor [3] database in our experiments. The dataset has 1200 color fundus images with three different image sizes, 212 images of size 2304×1536, 588 images of size 1440×960 and 400 images of size 2240×1488. The Messidor database also provides DR grading in a scale of 0 to 3, which can be denoted as DR0 and DR123 grades, where DR0 represents healthy retina (absence of any DR signs) while DR123 represents pathological retina (having DR signs of different degrees). The dataset has 547 and 653 images labeled as DR0 and DR123 respectively.

In our experiments, we train the BSNet only with the 2240×1488 sized DR0 images. We randomly select 27 DR0 images and extract 13900 patches of three different sizes (96×96, 144×144 and 48×48 pixels) by covering the macula, optic disk and blood vessels regions. We further apply a data augmentation process. We rotate the 96×96 patches with $90°$, $180°$ and $270°$ angles and scale the 144×144 and 48×48 patches with 0.5 and 1.5 factors respectively to comprise the training dataset with a total of 83400 patches. We use the same process to prepare the validation dataset of 3135 patches collected from another 13 randomly chosen DR0 images. All the patches are converted to gray-scale and normalized dividing by 255. For the generation of anomaly maps to be presented in this paper, we select two healthy (which are not used in the training) and two pathological images.

We initialize the BSNet using the Glorot [5] method. The used loss function is MAE, which is minimized by the Adam [7] optimizer with a learning rate of 1e-5. We train the network by scheduling an early stopping criteria with a minimum change in the validation loss of 1e-7 and 500 epochs of patience.

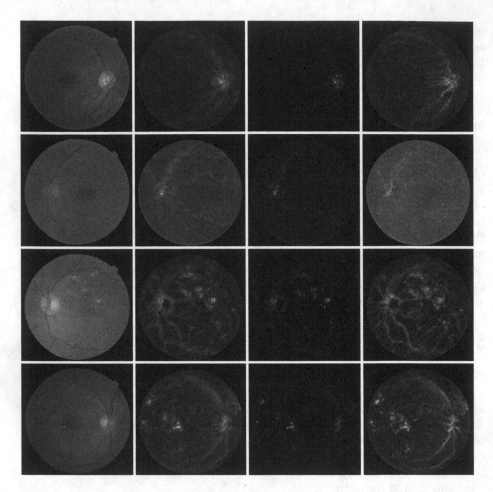

Fig. 3. Example of anomaly maps on three metrics. Each row contains original image followed by the error maps of MAE, MSE and SSIM metrics. First two rows contain the healthy examples and last two rows show pathological examples.

We generate anomaly maps by employing the BSNet reconstructor and three error metrics - MAE, MSE and SSIM. Examples of the generated maps for healthy and pathological retinal images are shown in the Fig. 3. The figure illustrates that the regions with pathological lesions result in higher error (brighter in appearance) than the healthy regions. Therefore, a pixel-level localization of the pathological signs is clearly observed from these anomaly maps. Furthermore, the MAE and SSIM maps illustrate overall higher contrast than the MSE map. We also notice that regions with complex structures like the optic disk regions and the vessel edges produce higher error for all the metrics, which is a downside of this mapping method. The reason for this is that the BSNet has not learnt to reconstruct these complex patterns from the healthy samples. This motivates future work on improving the used reconstructor model.

4   Conclusions

In this work we have proposed a new method to generate anomaly maps using reconstructor models that are trained on healthy images only. The generated image anomaly maps provide additional information about the pixel-level location of the pathologies that can be useful in the screening of diabetic retinopathy. We have demonstrated the anomaly map generation process for retinal fundus image by exploiting the Blind-Spot Network [13], which is an unsupervised image reconstructor, and leveraging three different image quality metrics, MAE, MSE and SSIM. The generated error maps show higher error near pathological regions, while lower error on healthy regions. This demonstrates the potential of our proposed anomaly mapping method for the localization of pathological signs in retinal fundus images on pixel-level.

Acknowledgement. This research is supported by the Instituto de Salud Carlos III, Government of Spain and the ERDF of the EU through the DTS15/00153 research project. The authors also receive financial support from the ERDF and ESF of the EU, and Xunta de Galicia through the Centro Singular de Investigacin de Galicia, accreditation 2016–2019, ref. ED431G/01 and Grupos de Referencia Competitiva, ref. ED481A-2017/328 research project.

References

1. Arora, S., Risteski, A., Zhang, Y.: Do GANs learn the distribution? Some theory and empirics. In: International Conference on Learning Representations (2018). https://openreview.net/forum?id=BJehNfW0-
2. Baur, C., Wiestler, B., Albarqouni, S., Navab, N.: Deep autoencoding models for unsupervised anomaly segmentation in brain MR images. In: Crimi, A., Bakas, S., Kuijf, H., Keyvan, F., Reyes, M., van Walsum, T. (eds.) BrainLes 2018. LNCS, vol. 11383, pp. 161–169. Springer, Cham (2019). https://doi.org/10.1007/978-3-030-11723-8_16
3. Decencière, E., Zhang, X., Cazuguel, G., Lay, B., et al.: Feedback on a publicly distributed database: the messidor database. Image Anal. Stereol. **33**(3), 231–234 (2014)
4. Erfani, S.M., Rajasegarar, S., Karunasekera, S., Leckie, C.: High-dimensional and large-scale anomaly detection using a linear one-class SVM with deep learning. Pattern Recogn. **58**, 121–134 (2016)
5. Glorot, X., Bengio, Y.: Understanding the difficulty of training deep feedforward neural networks. In: Proceedings of the Thirteenth International Conference on Artificial Intelligence and Statistics, pp. 249–256 (2010)
6. Goh, J., Cheung, C., et al.: Retinal imaging techniques for diabetic retinopathy screening. J. Diab. Sci. Technol. **10**(2), 282–294 (2016)
7. Kingma, D.P., Ba, J.: Adam: a method for stochastic optimization. arXiv:1412.6980 (2014)

8. Nguyen, L.H., Goulet, J.A.: Anomaly detection with the switching kalman filter for structural health monitoring. Struct. Control Health Monit. **25**(4), e2136 (2018)
9. Nørgaard, M., Grauslund, J.: Automated screening for diabetic retinopathy-a systematic review. Ophthalmic Res. **60**(1), 9–17 (2018)
10. Sabokrou, M., Fathy, M., Hoseini, M.: Video anomaly detection and localisation based on the sparsity and reconstruction error of auto-encoder. Electron. Lett. **52**(13), 1122–1124 (2016)
11. Almao, E.C., Golpayegani, F.: Are mobile apps usable and accessible for senior citizens in smart cities? In: Zhou, J., Salvendy, G. (eds.) HCII 2019. LNCS, vol. 11592, pp. 357–375. Springer, Cham (2019). https://doi.org/10.1007/978-3-030-22012-9_26
12. Schlegl, T., et al.: Fully automated detection and quantification of macular fluid in OCT using deep learning. Ophthalmology **125**(4), 549–558 (2018)
13. Sutradhar, S., Rouco, J., Ortega, M.: Blind-spot network for image anomaly detection: a new approach to diabetic retinopathy screening. In: 27th European Symposium on Artificial Neural Networks, Computational Intelligence and Machine Learning, pp. 541–546 (2019)
14. Taboada-Crispi, A., Sahli, H., Hernandez-Pacheco, D., et al.: Anomaly detection in medical image analysis. In: Handbook of Research on Advanced Techniques in Diagnostic Imaging and Biomedical Applications, pp. 426–446. IGI Global (2009)
15. Tan, C.C., Eswaran, C.: Reconstruction and recognition of face and digit images using autoencoders. Neural Comput. Appl. **19**(7), 1069–1079 (2010)
16. Vidal, P.L., de Moura, J., Novo, J., Penedo, M.G., Ortega, M.: Intraretinal fluid identification via enhanced maps using optical coherence tomography images. Biomed. Opt. Express **9**(10), 4730 (2018)
17. Wang, Z., Bovik, A., Sheikh, H., Simoncelli, E.: Image quality assessment: from error visibility to structural similarity. IEEE Trans. Image Process. **13**(4), 600–612 (2004)
18. World Health Organization: Global report on diabetes (2016)
19. Xia, Y., Cao, X., Wen, F., Hua, G., Sun, J.: Learning discriminative reconstructions for unsupervised outlier removal. In: Proceedings of the IEEE International Conference on Computer Vision, pp. 1511–1519 (2015)

Automatic Identification of Diabetic Macular Edema Biomarkers Using Optical Coherence Tomography Scans

Joaquim de Moura[1,2(✉)], Gabriela Samagaio[1,2], Jorge Novo[1,2], Pablo Charlón[3],
María Isabel Fernández[4,5,6], Francisco Gómez-Ulla[4,5,6], and Marcos Ortega[1,2]

[1] Department of Computer Science, University of A Coruña, A Coruña, Spain
{joaquim.demoura,gabriela.samagaio,jnovo,mortega}@udc.es
[2] CITIC - Research Center of Information and Communication Technologies,
University of A Coruña, A Coruña, Spain
[3] Instituto Oftalmológico Victoria de Rojas, A Coruña, Spain
pcharlon@sgoc.es
[4] Instituto Oftalmológico Gómez-Ulla, Santiago de Compostela, Spain
{maribelfernandez,franciscogomez-ulla}@institutogomez-ulla.es
[5] Department of Ophthalmology, Complejo Hospitalario Universitario de Santiago,
Santiago de Compostela, Spain
[6] University of Santiago de Compostela, Santiago de Compostela, Spain

Abstract. Optical Coherence Tomography (OCT) imaging has revolutionized the daily clinical practice, especially in the field of ophthalmology. Diabetic Macular Edema (DME) is one of the most important complications of diabetes and a leading cause of preventable blindness in the developed countries. In this way, a precise identification and analysis of DME biomarkers allow the clinical specialists to make a more accurate diagnosis and treatment of this relevant ocular disease.

Thus, in this work, we present a computational system for the automatic identification and extraction of DME biomarkers by the analysis of OCT scans, following the clinical classification of reference in the ophthalmological field. The presented method was validated using a dataset composed by 40 OCT images that were retrieved from different patients. Satisfactory results were obtained, providing a consistent and coherent set of different computational biomarkers that can help the clinical specialists in their diagnostic procedures.

Keywords: Computer-Aided Diagnosis · Optical Coherence
Tomography · Diabetic Macular Edema · Biomarkers

1 Introduction

Diabetic Macular Edema (DME) represents a leading cause of visual impairment and blindness among the working-age individuals in the developed countries [1]. DME is one of the most common eye diseases that is associated with diabetes

© Springer Nature Switzerland AG 2020
R. Moreno-Díaz et al. (Eds.): EUROCAST 2019, LNCS 12014, pp. 247–255, 2020.
https://doi.org/10.1007/978-3-030-45096-0_31

mellitus, affecting the 12% of type 1 and the 28% of type 2 diabetic patients [2]. This relevant disease is characterized by an abnormal retinal thickness produced by intraretinal fluid accumulations, also called Macular Edemas (MEs), within the retinal tissues. In this context, the use of Computer-Aided Diagnosis (CAD) systems is crucial, as it provides useful information for the clinical specialists to assess the severity of the DME pathology. In particular, in ophthalmology, Optical Coherence Tomography (OCT) has become an important clinical tool that is commonly used for the analysis and interpretation of many retinal structures and ocular disorders [3–5].

OCT is a well-established medical imaging technique that is capable of providing high-resolution cross-sectional tomographic images of biological tissues by measuring the intensity of the back-scattered light [6]. In this way, these images are widely used by the clinical specialists in the diagnosis and monitoring of the DME disease, permitting a complete analysis of the retinal morphology and their histopathology properties in real time and non-invasively.

Using the OCT image modality as reference, Otani *et al.* [7] proposed a clinical classification of the MEs associated with DME into 3 pathological types: Serous Retinal Detachment (SRD), Cystoid Macular Edema (CME) and Diffuse Retinal Thickening (DRT). This clinical classification is based on the different fluid accumulation patterns derived from the DME disease and that can be differentiated in the OCT images. Figure 1 presents an illustrative example of an OCT image with the simultaneous presence of the 3 defined types of the DME disease.

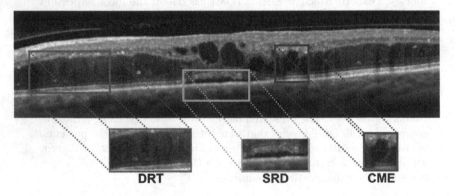

Fig. 1. Example of an OCT image with the simultaneous presence of the 3 defined types of DME: DRT, SRD and CME.

Posteriorly, Panozzo *et al.* [8] complemented the Otani classification using the presence of the Epiretinal Membrane (ERM) to better characterize the DME disease in the OCT images. Hence, ERM is a relevant disorder of the vitreoretinal interface that is also associated with DME disease. In particular, the ERM presence is defined by a response of the immune system to protect the retina from changes of the vitreous humour. Consequently, this response provokes that the cells of the retina converge on the inner retinal surface, producing a translucent membrane, which can thicken or contract. Figure 2 shows an illustrative example of an OCT image with the presence of the ERM membrane.

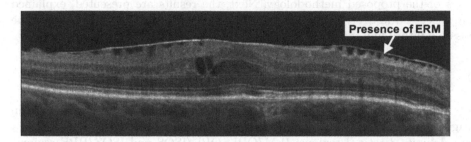

Fig. 2. Example of an OCT image with the presence of the ERM membrane.

In this context, an automatic system for the identification and analysis of different computational biomarkers of the DME disease facilitates the work of the clinical specialists, reducing the costs of medical care and improving the quality of life of patients.

Given the relevance of this ocular pathology, some computational proposals were presented focusing their studies in the automatic identification of the presence of DME cases using the OCT scans as source of information. As reference, Sidibé *et al.* [9] employed a Gaussian Mixture Models (GMM) for the identification of patients with DME using OCT images. In particular, the method models the appearance of normal OCT images with a GMM model and detects pathological OCT images as outliers. Quellec *et al.* [10] proposed a methodology using a set of texture features that were extracted to characterize different retinal tissues. Then, a learning strategy was applied using a k NN classifier for the identification of CME edemas in the macular region. Wilkins *et al.* [11] developed a method for the identification of the ERM presence through manual labeling in the OCT images performed by the clinical specialist, which allowed the computer tool to measure the retinal thickness around the labeled region. As we can observe, the presented methods only aimed at the partial identification of DME cases without addressing the problem of the extraction of relevant computational biomarkers for their clinical utility in predictive, preventive and personalized medicine.

Thus, in this work, we present a fully automatic system for the identification and extraction of DME biomarkers using OCT scans, following the clinical classification of reference in the ophthalmological field [7,8]. To achieve this, firstly, the system segments the main retinal layers to delimit 3 retinal regions in the OCT scan. Then, the system identify the presence of ME (SRD, CME and DRT) and ERM cases within the corresponding retinal region. To do so, the system combines and exploits different clinical knowledge (position, dimension, shape and morphology) with image processing and machine learning strategies. Finally, using these localizations as source of information, the system derives different computational biomarkers that can help the clinical specialists in their diagnostic procedures.

This paper is organized as follows: Sect. 2 includes the detailed character-istics of the proposed methodology. Next, the results are presented, explained and discussed in Sect. 3. Finally, Sect. 4 depicts the general conclusions and the possible future lines of work.

2   Methodology

As illustrated in Fig. 3, the designed methodology is divided into 4 main stages. Firstly, the system segments the main retinal layers. Posteriorly, the sys-tem delimits 3 retinal regions: ILM/OPL, OPL/ISOS and ISOS/RPE regions. Regarding the MEs, the system localizes and extracts the relevant biomarkers of each ME type within these retinal regions. Regarding the ERM, a complemen-tary strategy was implemented for the identification and subsequent extraction of the corresponding computational biomarkers.

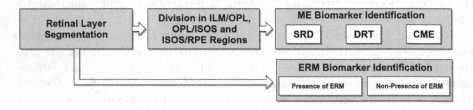

Fig. 3. Main structure of the proposed methodology.

2.1   Retinal Layer Segmentation

In this work, 4 main retinal layers were identified, since they provide the correct delimitation of the retinal regions where the different types of ME and ERM usually appear. These retinal layers are: the Inner Limiting Membrane (ILM), the Retinal Pigment Epithelium (RPE), the junction of the Inner and Outer Segments (ISOS) and the Outer Plexiform Layer (OPL). In particular, to extract the ILM, RPE and ISOS layers, we follow the work proposed by González-López *et al.* [12]. To do that, the method employs an active contour-based model to segment these retinal boundaries. For the OPL layer, we designed a different strategy based on a region growing approach to obtain the corresponding region with similar intensity properties [13]. As result of this strategy, the upper limits of the extracted region represents the OPL layer. Figure 4 shows a representative example of OCT image with the segmentation of the aimed retinal layers.

Fig. 4. Example of an OCT image with the segmentation of the aimed 4 retinal layers: ILM, OPL, ISOS and RPE.

2.2 Division in ILM/OPL, OPL/ISOS and ISOS/RPE Regions

Using the previous retinal layer identifications, 3 representative regions of interest are identified and extracted: ILM/OPL, OPL/ISOS and ISOS/RPE regions, as illustrated in Fig. 5. Generally, the SRD edemas appear as a dome-shape area in the ISOS/RPE region. DRT edemas usually appear in the OPL/ISOS region whereas CME edemas are frequently present in the ILM/OPL region. In more severe stages of the DME disease, CME edemas can also proliferate in the OPL/ISOS region.

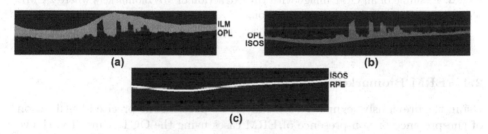

Fig. 5. Illustrative example of the division of the regions of interest. (a) Delimitation of the ILM/OPL region. (b) Delimitation of the OPL/ISOS region. (c) Delimitation of the ISOS/RPE region.

2.3 ME Biomarker Identification

The proposed methodology includes different strategies to perform a simultaneous identification of each type of ME (SRD, CME and DRT) within the corresponding retinal region. To do that, we follow the work proposed by Samagaio *et al.* [13], given their adequate results for this issue. For the SRD and CME cases, we apply an adaptive multilevel thresholding algorithm, whereas for the DRT case a machine learning strategy was implemented. Then, a list composed of different clinical knowledge (position, dimension, shape and morphology) is used to reduce the set of possible false identifications. As output, the method provides a labeled OCT image with the precise identification of each ME type for a better characterization of the present DME disease. Finally, the method extracts and analyzes different ME biomarkers according to their relative position within the OCT scans. These ME biomarkers are: number of SRDs, number of CMEs, number of DRT columns, relative position of SRDs, relative position of CMEs and relative position of DRTs. As we can see in Fig. 6, these ME biomarkers are extracted in the foveal region (1.0 mm diameter central circle area), parafoveal region (ring area between 1.0 and 3.0 mm in diameter) and perifoveal region (ring area between 3.0 and 6.0 mm in diameter). These regions were established according to clinical criteria [14].

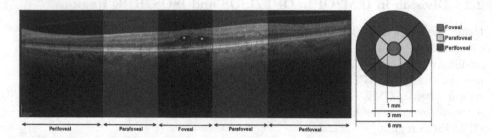

Fig. 6. Example of an OCT image with the extraction of ME biomarkers where 2 CME regions were identified in the foveal region.

2.4 ERM Biomarker Identification

Using the previously segmented ILM layer, we perform the precise identification of the presence or non-presence of ERM cases using the OCT scans. To achieve this, we based our proposal in the work of Baamonde *et al.* [15]. Firstly, the system extracts a set of relevant features from the search space, including intensity, texture and domain-related clinical features. Then, a machine learning strategy is used to train and test the potential of discrimination of the presented method. Using these identifications, the system derives different ERM biomarkers considering its relative position within the OCT scans, as seen on Fig. 7. In particular, these ERM biomarkers imply: absolute and relative number of ERM columns and relative position of ERMs.

3   Experimental Results

The proposed system was validated using a dataset consisting of 40 OCT images retrieved from different patients, being 20 acquired with a Spectralis OCT confocal scanning laser ophthalmoscope from Heidelberg Engineering and 20 obtained with a CIRRUS OCT from Carl Zeiss Meditec. Each OCT image was labeled by an expert clinician, identifying regions with the presence of ME as well as ERM.

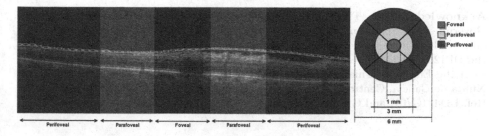

Fig. 7. Example of an OCT image with the extraction of ERM biomarkers where the presence of ERM was identified in all regions of the retina.

To measure the efficiency of the proposed method, we evaluated the identification of the different DME biomarkers according to their relative localization within the OCT scans, as show in Table 1. As we can see, the method achieved satisfactory results, returning in a coherent way the values of the DME identifications for the foveal, parafoveal and parafoveal retinal regions.

Table 1. Performance of the method for the identification of DME biomarkers.

	(%) SRDs	(%) CMEs	(%) DRT columns	(%) ERM columns
Foveal	100%	34.28%	22.43%	9.92%
Parafoveal	0%	54.28%	47.77%	28.01%
Perifoveal	0%	11.42%	29.79%	62.05%

4 Discussion and Conclusions

OCT has proven to be a robust medical imaging modality that provides cross-sectional tomographic scans that are commonly used for clinical specialists in the analysis and evaluation of DME. This relevant ocular disease is one of the most common causes of blindness in individuals with diabetes. In this context, we presented a fully automatic system for the identification and extraction of DME biomarkers using OCT scans, following the clinical classification of reference in the ophthalmological field. To do that, the presented method exploits different image processing and machine learning strategies to identify the presence of ME (SRD, CME and DRT) and cases of ERM from patients with DME disease. Subsequently, the system derives different computational biomarkers that may lead to the early diagnosis and treatment of this relevant ocular disease. The validation was performed using 40 OCT images from two representative ophthalmological devices. The presented system achieved satisfactory results, demonstrating its suitability to be used in real clinical scenarios.

Acknowledgments. This work is supported by the Instituto de Salud Carlos III, Government of Spain and FEDER funds through the DTS18/00136 research project and by the Ministerio de Economía y Competitividad, Government of Spain through the DPI2015-69948-R research project. Also, this work has received financial support from the European Union (European Regional Development Fund - ERDF) and the Xunta de Galicia, Centro singular de investigación de Galicia accreditation 2016-2019, Ref. ED431G/01; and Grupos de Referencia Competitiva, Ref. ED431C 2016-047.

References

1. Lee, R., Wong, T.Y., Sabanayagam, C.: Epidemiology of diabetic retinopathy, diabetic macular edema and related vision loss. Eye Vis. **2**(1), 17 (2015)
2. Romero-Aroca, P.: Managing diabetic macular edema: the leading cause of diabetes blindness. World J. Diabetes **2**(6), 98 (2011)
3. de Moura, J., Novo, J., Charlón, P., Barreira, N., Ortega, M.: Enhanced visualization of the retinal vasculature using depth information in OCT. Med. Biol. Eng. Comput. **55**(12), 2209–2225 (2017). https://doi.org/10.1007/s11517-017-1660-8
4. de Moura, J., Novo, J., Rouco, J., Penedo, M.G., Ortega, M.: Automatic identification of intraretinal cystoid regions in optical coherence tomography. In: ten Teije, A., Popow, C., Holmes, J.H., Sacchi, L. (eds.) AIME 2017. LNCS (LNAI), vol. 10259, pp. 305–315. Springer, Cham (2017). https://doi.org/10.1007/978-3-319-59758-4_35
5. de Moura, J., Novo, J., Penas, S., Ortega, M., Silva, J., Mendonça, A.M.: Automatic characterization of the serous retinal detachment associated with the subretinal fluid presence in optical coherence tomography images. Procedia Comput. Sci. **126**, 244–253 (2018)
6. Schmitt, J.: Optical coherence tomography (OCT): a review. IEEE J. Sel. Top. Quantum Electron. **5**(4), 1205–1215 (1999)
7. Otani, T., Kishi, S., Maruyama, Y.: Patterns of diabetic macular edema with optical coherence tomography. Am. J. Ophthalmol. **127**(6), 688–693 (1999)
8. Panozzo, G., et al.: Diabetic macular edema: an OCT-based classification. In: Seminars in Ophthalmology, vol. 19, pp. 13–20. Taylor & Francis (2004)
9. Sidibé, D., et al.: An anomaly detection approach for the identification of DME patients using spectral domain optical coherence tomography images. Comput. Methods Programs Biomed. **139**, 109–117 (2017)
10. Quellec, G., Lee, K., Dolejsi, M., Garvin, M., Abramoff, M., Sonka, M.: Three-dimensional analysis of retinal layer texture: identification of fluid-filled regions in SD-OCT of the macula. IEEE Trans. Med. Imaging **29**(6), 1321–1330 (2010)
11. Wilkins, J., et al.: Characterization of epiretinal membranes using optical coherence tomography. Ophthalmology **103**(12), 2142–2151 (1996)
12. González-López, A., de Moura, J., Novo, J., Ortega, M., Penedo, M.G.: Robust segmentation of retinal layers in optical coherence tomography images based on a multistage active contour model. Heliyon **5**(2), e01271 (2019)
13. Samagaio, G., Estévez, A., de Moura, J., Novo, J., Fernández, I., Ortega, M.: Automatic macular edema identification and characterization using OCT images. Comput. Methods Programs Biomed. **163**, 47–63 (2018)

14. Othman, S., Manan, F., Zulkarnain, A., Mohamad, Z., Ariffin, A.: Macular thickness as determined by optical coherence tomography in relation to degree of myopia, axial length and vitreous chamber depth in malay subjects. Clin. Exp. Optom. **95**(5), 484–491 (2012)

15. Baamonde, S., de Moura, J., Novo, J., Ortega, M.: Automatic detection of epiretinal membrane in OCT images by means of local luminosity patterns. In: Rojas, I., Joya, G., Catala, A. (eds.) IWANN 2017. LNCS, vol. 10305, pp. 222–235. Springer, Cham (2017). https://doi.org/10.1007/978-3-319-59153-7_20

DeepCompareJ: Comparing Image Classification Models

A. Inés^(✉), C. Domínguez, J. Heras, E. Mata, and V. Pascual

Department of Mathematics and Computer Science,
University of La Rioja, Logroño, Spain
{adrian.ines,cesar.dominguez,jonathan.heras,eloy.mata,
vico.pascual}@unirioja.es

Abstract. Image classification is a computer vision task that has several applications in diverse fields like security, biology or medicine; and, currently, deep learning techniques have become the state-of-the-art to create image classification models. This growing use of deep learning techniques is due to the large amount of data, the fast increase of the computer processing capacity, and the openness of deep learning tools. However, whenever deep learning techniques are used to solve a classification problem, we can find several deep learning frameworks with their own peculiarities, and different models in each framework; hence, it is natural to wonder which option fits better our problem. In this paper, we present DeepCompareJ, an open-source tool that has been designed to compare, with respect to a given dataset, the quality of deep models created using different frameworks.

Keywords: Deep learning · Image classification · Integration

1 Introduction

Image classification is an instrumental tool to solve several problems in diverse fields like security, biology or medicine; and, deep learning techniques have become the state-of-the-art approach to deal with them. Just to name a few examples, deep learning techniques have been applied for classifying objects within X-ray baggage [1], for detecting parasite malaria in thin blood smear images [16], for classifying breast cancer histology images [2], or for classifying skin cancer images [8].

The reason for the success of deep learning techniques is threefold: the fast increase of the computer processing capacity, the large amount of data, and the openness of deep learning methods. Namely, deep learning frameworks—such as Keras [4], Caffe [11] or MxNet [3]—are open-source libraries, and most of the models built with them are freely distributed [14]. Due to its open nature,

Supported by Ministerio de Industria, Economía y Competitividad, project MTM2017-88804-P; Agencia de Desarrollo Econmico de La Rioja, project 2017-I-IDD-00018; and FPU Grant 16/06903 of the Spanish MEC.

© Springer Nature Switzerland AG 2020
R. Moreno-Díaz et al. (Eds.): EUROCAST 2019, LNCS 12014, pp. 256–262, 2020.
https://doi.org/10.1007/978-3-030-45096-0_32

whenever we want to use a deep learning model to solve an image classification problem, we can find several models that can be adapted to solve the same task; hence, it is natural to wonder which model better fits to our dataset; or whether a new model that we have trained is more accurate than the existing ones. However, each deep learning framework has its own peculiarities, for instance, most frameworks can be used from different programming languages like Python or C++. However, as we can expect, a common language for all the deep learning frameworks does not exists. Hence, we have to pay attention to which programming languages support the framework we want to use. Also, the representation of the images depends on the framework, some frameworks represent the images with an image class like PIL, others for example represent the images with arrays or tensors. In addition, the representation of the layers differs from one framework to another, or even not all the frameworks have implemented all the kinds of layers. Because of this, some models can not be implemented in all the frameworks. These are some examples of the differences we can find among different deep learning frameworks. Therefore, it is difficult to work with several deep learning frameworks at the same time or even compare the quality of several models from different frameworks.

In this work, we have tackled this problem by developing DeepCompareJ, an open-source tool, built on top of DeepClas4Bio, that allows users to easily compare models from different deep learning frameworks without worrying about the particularities of each library.

2   DeepClas4Bio and DeepCompareJ

DeepClas4Bio [10] is an extensible API that provides a common access point for classification models of several deep learning frameworks. This API allows users to work with those deep learning frameworks and models easily and transparently for them. Namely, the DeepClas4Bio API provides five public methods, as shown in Fig. 1.

The method called listFrameworks allows users to know the frameworks included in the API. Currently, the API gives support for Keras [4], Caffe [11], DeepLearning4J [7], PyTorch [15] and MxNet [3]. In addition, for each framework in the API, we can find several models using the method listModels, that provides the available deep models for a particular framework; for instance, the networks VGG [17], AlexNet [13], ResNet [9] and GoogleNet [18], trained for the ImageNet challenge [6], are available in Keras. Also, the API allows users to classify an image or a batch of images given a specific model and framework using respectively the predict or the predictBatch method. Finally, we can find a method called evaluate, that can be used to compare the quality of several models with respect to a dataset using different measures (accuracy, rank5, precision, recall, F1-score, Jaccard Index, Matthews Correlation and AUROC are available).

DeepClas4Bio API has several applications: classifying images or a batch of images (several examples can be seen in the project webpage), evaluating the

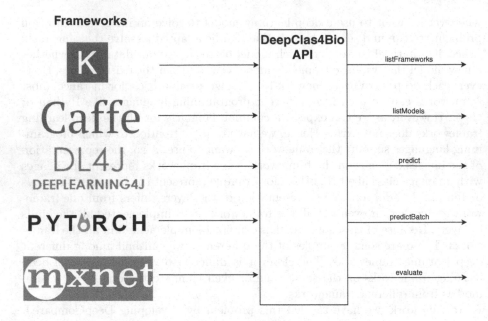

Fig. 1. Structure of the DeepClas4Bio project.

quality of a model; or comparing the quality of several models. In this paper, we focus on the latter application. In particular, we have developed DeepCompareJ, an open-source Java application built on top of DeepClas4Bio.

In order to compare image classification models using DeepCompareJ, the user must select: (1) the models to compare; (2) the measures to evaluate the models; and, (3) the dataset of images. DeepCompareJ offers several models from different deep learning frameworks, several measures and several procedures to load an annotated dataset of images (by default, the API loads datasets from a folder where each class has its corresponding folder of images). All this information can be selected from the interface of Fig. 2, and it is obtained from the DeepClas4Bio API.

The workflow of DeepCompareJ is straightforward. When DeepCompareJ starts, the application connects with the DeepClas4Bio API to obtain all the models, measures and ways of loading datasets available in the system. Then, the users select the most suitable options for their problems; and, finally, Deep-CompareJ connects with the DeepClas4Bio API to compare the selected models and shows the result in a table.

3   Case Studies

In this section, we show a couple of examples of the usage of DeepCompareJ. In the first example, we compare several models trained in the Imagenet challenge [6]. And, in the second example, we compare models trained in the Kvasir dataset [12], a gastrointestinal disease dataset.

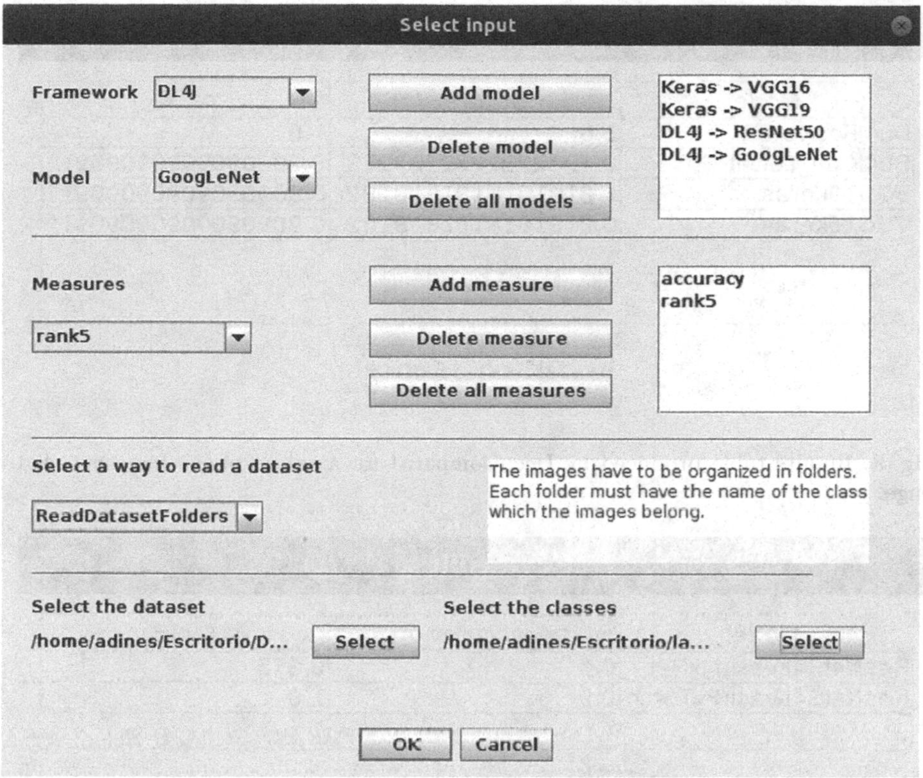

Fig. 2. Interface of DeepCompareJ.

Namely, in the first example we have compared the quality of four models trained in the Imagenet dataset. The four models used in this example are ResNet50 and GoogleNet from DeepLearning4J—a Java framework for deep learning—and VGG16 and VGG19 from Keras—an open source neural network library written in Python, capable of running on top of TensorFlow, CNTK, or Theano. The measures selected to compare these models are accuracy and rank5. Finally, the dataset used to compare these models is a subset of the Imagenet dataset. The result of this experiment is shown in Fig. 3.

In the second example, we have compared the quality of two models trained in the Kvasir dataset. The models used in this example are ResNet34 trained in the MxNet framework—a deep learning framework that gives support for several programming languages, namely Python, Scala, R, Julia and Perl—and also ResNet34 trained in the PyTorch framework—a Python deep learning framework based on the Torch library [5]. The measures selected to compare these models are accuracy and rank5. The results of this experiment are shown in Fig. 4.

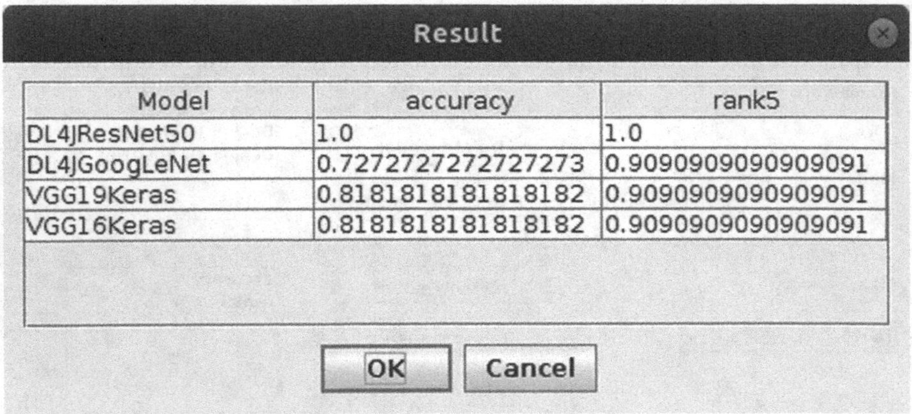

Model	accuracy	rank5
DL4JResNet50	1.0	1.0
DL4JGoogLeNet	0.7272727272727273	0.9090909090909091
VGG19Keras	0.8181818181818182	0.9090909090909091
VGG16Keras	0.8181818181818182	0.9090909090909091

Fig. 3. Results table produced by DeepCompareJ for a subset of the Imagenet challenge.

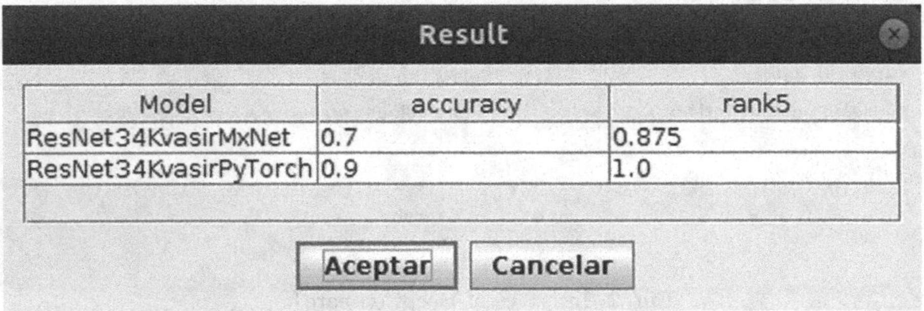

Model	accuracy	rank5
ResNet34KvasirMxNet	0.7	0.875
ResNet34KvasirPyTorch	0.9	1.0

Fig. 4. Results table produced by DeepCompareJ for a subset of the Kavasir dataset.

4 Conclusions

In this paper, we have presented DeepCompareJ, an open source tool that can be used to easily compare the quality of several deep classification models. This tool solves the problem of comparing models from different deep learning frameworks using the same dataset thanks to the DeepClas4Bio API.

Another problem solved by DeepCompareJ and DeepClas4Bio is the task of working with different frameworks at the same time. This is due to the fact that deep learning frameworks can have several differences, for example, the programming language, the supported layers or the way to load an image. DeepClas4Bio and DeepCompareJ abstract these particularities and hide these difficulties to the user improving the usability of different deep learning frameworks.

5   Availability and Requirements

- Project name: DeepCompareJ.
- Project home page: https://github.com/adines/DeepCompareJ.
- Operating system(s): Platform independent.
- Programming language: Java.
- License: GNU GPL 3.0.
- Any restrictions to use by non-academics: None.
- Dependencies: DeepClas4Bio (https://github.com/adines/DeepClas4Bio).

The project home page contains the installation instructions and usage examples.

References

1. Akay, S., Kundegorski, M.E., Devereux, M., Breckon, T.P.: Transfer learning using convolutional neural networks for object classification within X-ray baggage security imagery. In: 2016 IEEE International Conference on Image Processing (ICIP), pp. 1057–1061 (2016)
2. Araújo, T., Aresta, G., Castro, E., Rouco, J., Aguiar, P., Eloy, C., et al.: Classification of breast cancer histology images using convolutional neural networks. PLoS ONE **12**(6), e0177544 (2017)
3. Chen, T., et al.: MxNet: a flexible and efficient machine learning library for heterogeneous distributed systems. In: Proceedings of Neural Information Processing Systems (NIPS 2015) - Workshop on Machine Learning Systems (2015)
4. Chollet, F.: Keras: the Python deep learning library (2015). https://keras.io
5. Collobert, R., Bengio, S., Mariéthoz, J.: Torch: a modular machine learning software library. Technical report, IDIAP (2002)
6. Deng, J., Dong, W., Socher, R., Li, L.J., Li, K., Fei-Fei, L.: ImageNet: a large-scale hierarchical image database. In: 2009 IEEE Conference on Computer Vision and Pattern Recognition, pp. 248–255 (2009)
7. Eclipse Deeplearning4j Development Team: Deeplearning4j: Open-source, distributed deep learning for the JVM (2018). https://deeplearning4j.org/
8. Esteva, A., et al.: Dermatologist-level classification of skin cancer with deep neural networks. Nature **542**, 115–118 (2017)
9. He, K., Zhang, X., Ren, S., Sun, J.: Deep residual learning for image recognition. In: 2016 IEEE Conference on Computer Vision and Pattern Recognition (CVPR 2016), pp. 770–778 (2016)
10. Inés, A., Domínguez, C., Heras, J., Mata, E., Pascual, V.: DeepClas4Bio: connecting bioimaging tools with deep learning frameworks for image classification. Comput. Biol. Med. **108**, 49–56 (2019)
11. Jia, Y., Shelhamer, E., Donahue, J., Karayev, S., Long, J., Girshick, R., Guadarrama, S., Darrell, T.: Caffe: convolutional architecture for fast feature embedding. In: Proceedings of the 22nd ACM International Conference on Multimedia. ACM (2014)
12. Pogorelov, K., Randel, K.R., Griwodz, C., Eskeland, S.L., de Lange, T., Johansen, D., et al.: KVASIR: a multi-class image dataset for computer aided gastrointestinal disease detection. In: Proceedings of the 8th ACM on Multimedia Systems Conference, MMSys 2017, pp. 164–169. ACM, New York (2017). https://doi.org/10.1145/3083187.3083212

13. Krizhevsky, A., Sutskever, I., Hinton, G.E.: ImageNet classification with deep convolutional neural networks. In: Pereira, F., Burges, C.J.C., Bottou, L., Weinberger, K.Q. (eds.) Advances in Neural Information Processing Systems 25, pp. 1097–1105. Curran Associates, Inc. (2012)
14. ModelZoo: Model Zoo: Discover open source deep learning code and pretrained models (2018). https://modelzoo.co/
15. Paszke, A., et al.: Automatic differentiation in PyTorch. In: Proceedings of Neural Information Processing Systems (NIPS 2017) - Workshop (2017)
16. Rajaraman, S., et al.: Pre-trained convolutional neural networks as feature extractors toward improved malaria parasite detection in thin blood smear images. PeerJ (2018). https://lhncbc.nlm.nih.gov/system/files/pub9752.pdf
17. Simonyan, K., Zisserman, A.: Very deep convolutional networks for large-scale image recognition. In: Proceedings of International Conference on Learning Representation (ICLR 2015) (2015)
18. Szegedy, C., et al.: Going deeper with convolutions. In: 2015 IEEE Conference on Computer Vision and Pattern Recognition (CVPR 2015), pp. 1–9 (2015)

Applying SSD to Real World Food Production Environments

Tilman Klaeger[(✉)] [ID], Moritz Schroth, Andre Schult, and Lukas Oehm [ID]

Division Processing Technology, Fraunhofer Institute for Process Engineering
and Packaging IVV, Heidelberger Straße 20, 01189 Dresden, Germany
{tilman.klaeger,moritz.schroth,andre.schult,
lukas.oehm}@ivv-dresden.fraunhofer.de
https://www.ivv.fraunhofer.de

Abstract. To reduce the number of unplanned machine stops in packaging machines the root cause of the short but frequent interruptions has to be found. To assist operators in trouble shooting the current setting has to be automatically described to be able to link it with suitable knowledge bases.

To start building the system the applicability of object detection using the deep learning architecture "Single Shot Detector" (SSD) is analyzed under real world conditions on a form-, fill- and sealing-machine. The objective is to have suitable coordinates of packaging goods and machine components to later calculate trajectories and doing anomaly detection on those trajectories to identify and distinguish different break downs.

Keywords: Single Shot Detector (SSD) · Artificial neural network (ANN) · Machine learning · Object detection · Small data · Packaging machinery

1 Introduction

The process of packaging food is characterized by many but short interruptions caused by, often immeasurable, deviations in the properties of the packaging goods and materials [1]. The number and impact of these interruptions can only be limited but not excluded by automation. One solution can be assisting operators in error detection using assistance systems [2,3]. To assist operators in finding lasting solutions advanced technologies for error detection are necessary going further than explicitly programmed error codes in the PLC to allow for finer granularity. One solution to detect errors currently undetected by the machine and its PLC may be the application of image recognition technologies.

The objective is to use trajectories of packing goods and machine components to detect anomalies in the movement. Classifications of specific anomalous movements may later be combined with hints for the operator to solve the problem. Classifying detected situations as a whole or classifying detected objects like smashed yogurt cups may also work. This will most likely end in less generalization as each used printing on the package may have to be trained separately.

© Springer Nature Switzerland AG 2020
R. Moreno-Díaz et al. (Eds.): EUROCAST 2019, LNCS 12014, pp. 263–269, 2020.
https://doi.org/10.1007/978-3-030-45096-0_33

As a first step for calculation of the trajectories objects in the picture need to be tracked. There have been many studies on object tracking in the past using object detection, classification or direct tracking methods like optical flow [4]. Recent research has mainly focused on using different architectures of deep artificial neural networks (deep learning, ANN) to solve object detection tasks, which may also be used for tracking objects. Among these architectures very good results were accomplished using Faster R-CNN [5], YOLO ("You only look once") [6] and SSD [7]. In general there are two architectures, both being under continuous improvement using either a 1-stage-detector or a 2-stage-detector. By using two stages in general a higher precision is possible whereas 1-stage or single-shot detectors tend to be faster [8,9]. For both types of architectures many improvements have been made since the first versions where published. SSD are optimized for smaller objects [10], YOLOv3 has improved the detection speeds [11] and RetinaNet tries to archive performance of 2-stage detectors using only one stage [12].

Many of these designs have been developed and tested on popular and large data sets like the PASCAL VOC [13] or the COCO data set [14]. Most of the pictures in these data sets are taken from typical environments like at home or outdoors having good lighting conditions and sufficient contrast.

Working with pictures from industrial sites may result in different challenges to be solved, e.g. many reflections on stainless steel or wet surfaces, changing light conditions, usually with very few shades and comparable small objects if the camera is positioned to monitor complete machines.

The aim of this paper is therefore to apply an SSD network as state of the art to pictures taken in an environment for food packaging. To this the influence of the number of samples per class used for training on the performance of object detection is investigated and discussed in relation to the current state of the art.

2   Materials and Methods

To achieve high prediction speeds an SSD net was chosen using MobileNet as feature extractor as detection speed is relevant for live detection and tracking for objects. To improve learning speed transfer learning was used with weights pretrained on the COCO data set.

The SSD network is trained using pictures of the machine packing ham, salami and cheese. These three products are differentiated for this paper to find possible weaknesses of the trained model. In real world scenarios it should usually be sufficient to find one class called "product". The three types of food have different specific challenges like little contrast to the packaging material and the stainless steel body of the machine for ham. Both ham and cheese are little to big for their shell resulting in bent forms and thus making it harder for feature extractors to detect by shape. The typical holes in the cheese may be an additional challenge. The little texture of the salami will be total equalized by the image scaling for the ANN. Thus the texture will not effect the precision.

For real world problems, it is essential to cut down on the number of manually labeled data sets required for the training of the network. If thousands of labeled images have to be provided, a profitable launch of assistance systems for new machines or new types of products is impossible. Thus, an analysis of the actual required data is made. We cut down the number of images used for training from 75 images in steps to the lowest value of only five images resulting in 230 objects per class to only 14 objects per class. The objects for each class are evenly spread. The number of total objects used for training is presented in Table 1.

In addition, an analysis of effects of changing lighting conditions is made to ensure the system continues working if the lighting changes between training and real production.

To ensure blur free pictures of fast moving objects expensive fast lenses and cameras are needed. To save on investment for new setups also cheaper surveillance cameras may be an option being water resistant and easy to mount. As longer apertures are necessary using cheaper hardware a motion blur can be expected. To simulate this the testing data set was artificially endowed with motion blur of different lengths ranging from 10 (only very little motion blur) to 40. For resulting effects see Fig. 1.

Fig. 1. Sample image of the form-, fill- and sealing-machine (FFS) taken from the testing data set without blur (left) and with motion blur of distance 10, 20 and 40 (left to right)

3   Results

At 12 000 training steps, an initial learning rate of 0.004 and a batch size of 32 taking all images into account an mean average precision (mAP) of 55% could be achieved. For calculation the common metrics mAP and mAR are used [15], well known by the Coco-Detection challenge [14]. The recall in this setting with all available training objects was calculated at 32%. Using less training objects the mAP and Recall gradually decreased following approximately the progression of an Exponential-function. A visual descent is visible using about 89 pictures per class. With an average of 132 objects per class an mAP of 51% is possible, with an training set of 89 objects per class the mAP drops to 46%. It continuous descending to an mAP of 19% when finally only 14 objects per class are used for training.

The Recall follows in a similar manner even though the gradient is not as steep as for the mAP as can be seen in Fig. 2.

Adding only little motion blur to the images there is no significant change in performance. For a set with 132 objects per class little motion blur (length 10) even results in a slight increase of performance by 1% point, which may as well be seen as statistical noise. Adding more motion blur (blur lengths set to 20 and 40) in the training data the performance of the models decreases to 52% mAP and finally down to 44%. For these experiments again the complete training data set was used. The results with the reduced training data set (132 objects per class) are similar.

For the complete results you also may consult Table 1.

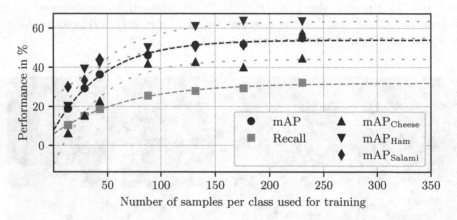

Fig. 2. mAP (total and for each class) and Recall over the number of samples per class used to train the network. An extrapolation for the determined values is shown using a fitted *e*-function.

4   Discussion

As the trajectory processing is still under ongoing research a final statement on the achieved performance is not possible at the moment. But an mAP of 55% is within any good standards accomplished by object detection researches on various data sets [9]. Looking at the results manually we could not detect many false positives which is positive as those will most probable cause unwanted anomalies in the calculated trajectories. Missed objects in single frames will only cause trajectories to have a smaller resolution. For a linear motion this will not change the result, for nonlinear object movements this will cause a smoother calculated trajectory.

Table 1. Used training sets and their respective mAP@IOU.5

Obj. per class	mAP	mAP			Recall
		Cheese	Ham	Salami	
14	18.8%	6.2%	20.2%	30.0%	10.4%
29	29.3%	15.2%	39.2%	33.3%	15.1%
44	36.3%	22.6%	42.2%	44.2%	18.6%
89	46.1%	41.8%	50.2%	46.4%	25.5%
132	51.5%	42.7%	61.0%	50.7%	27.9%
176	51.7%	40.0%	63.7%	51.5%	29.3%
230	54.9%	44.6%	63.5%	56.7%	32.2%
With motion blur					
Blur 10@230	54.9%	46.5%	62.1%	56.2%	31.3%
Blur 20@230	51.9%	42.7%	59.8%	53.3%	28.7%
Blur 40@230	43.9%	36.9%	50.4%	44.2%	24.3%
Blur 10@132	52.3%	42.0%	57.7%	57.3%	29.4%
Blur 20@132	44.8%	37.2%	49.0%	48.1%	25.1%
Blur 40@132	39.1%	33.1%	39.9%	44.3%	20.3%

If further research calls for higher performance there is still chance for improvement. Both values for learning rate and batch size may be adjusted as well as many other parameters of feature extraction and object detection. Looking at the feature extraction the initial goal was to have a fast process. If more precision is needed a more accurate but slower feature extractor may be used always causing some speed-accuracy trade-offs. Not only in feature extraction but also in object detection there are still possibilities for improvement using different detectors if needed. Especially two-stage detectors may cause a higher accuracy with the cost of longer calculation times.

5 Conclusion and Perspective

Object detection with current state of the art technologies is working well for situations in food production using pretrained networks and a reasonable small training set. Expected difficulties for the artificial neural network like reflections on low contrasts did not occur as expected. Building an assistance system on basis of this object detection is promising and will result in further research.

The assistance system will after completion be part of complex operator assistance system containing various components to work on low- and high-frequency machine data [16,17], interact with the user in a dialog system [3] and use cameras (this paper) to detect breakdowns and assist in solving them using stored expert knowledge. A first version, not yet containing all modules will be available to customers soon, whereas more complex modules like the one described here will still take some time till market readiness.

Acknowledgments. This research and the following development of the assistance system is made possible by funding from the European Regional Development Fund (ERDF) for Saxony, Germany.

Europa fördert Sachsen.

EFRE

Europäischer Fonds für
regionale Entwicklung

Europäische Union

References

1. Schult, A., Beck, E., Majschak, J.P.: Steigerung der Effizienz von Verarbeitungs- und Verpackungsanlagen durch Wirkungsgradanalysen. Pharma+Food **18**(7), 66–68 (2015)
2. Majschak, J.P., Mauermann, M., Müller, T., Richter, C., Wagner, M., Reinhart, G.: Verarbeitungsanlagen und Verpackungsmaschinen. In: Handbuch Industrie 4.0, pp. 379–427, 1 auflage edn. Carl Hanser, München, April 2017
3. Rahm, J., et al.: KoMMDia: dialogue-driven assistance system for fault diagnosis and correction in cyber-physical production systems. In: 2018 IEEE 23rd International Conference on Emerging Technologies and Factory Automation (ETFA), vol. 1, pp. 999–1006, September 2018. https://doi.org/10.1109/ETFA.2018.8502615
4. Parekh, H.S., Thakore, D.G., Jaliya, U.K.: A survey on object detection and tracking methods. Int. J. Innov. Res. Comput. Commun. Eng. **2**(2), 2970–2979 (2014)
5. Girshick, R., Donahue, J., Darrell, T., Malik, J.: Rich feature hierarchies for accurate object detection and semantic segmentation. arXiv:1311.2524 [cs], November 2013
6. Redmon, J., Farhadi, A.: YOLO9000: better, faster, stronger. arXiv:1612.08242 [cs], December 2016
7. Liu, W., et al.: SSD: single shot multibox detector. In: Leibe, B., Matas, J., Sebe, N., Welling, M. (eds.) ECCV 2016. LNCS, vol. 9905, pp. 21–37. Springer, Cham (2016). https://doi.org/10.1007/978-3-319-46448-0_2. arXiv:1512.02325 [cs]
8. Huang, J., et al.: Speed/accuracy trade-offs for modern convolutional object detectors. In: 2017 IEEE Conference on Computer Vision and Pattern Recognition (CVPR), pp. 3296–3297, July 2017. https://doi.org/10.1109/CVPR.2017.351
9. Peng, C., et al.: MegDet: a large mini-batch object detector. arXiv:1711.07240 [cs], November 2017
10. Xie, X., Cao, G., Yang, W., Liao, Q., Shi, G., Wu, J.: Feature-fused SSD: fast detection for small objects. In: Yu, H., Dong, J. (eds.) Ninth International Conference on Graphic and Image Processing (ICGIP 2017). SPIE, Qingdao, China, p. 236, April 2018. https://doi.org/10.1117/12.2304811
11. Redmon, J., Farhadi, A.: YOLOv3: an incremental improvement. arXiv:1804.02767 [cs], April 2018
12. Lin, T.Y., Goyal, P., Girshick, R., He, K., Dollár, P.: Focal loss for dense object detection. arXiv:1708.02002 [cs], August 2017
13. Everingham, M., Van Gool, L., Williams, C.K.I., Winn, J., Zisserman, A.: The PASCAL visual object classes (VOC) challenge. Int. J. Comput. Vis. **88**(2), 303–338 (2010). https://doi.org/10.1007/s11263-009-0275-4
14. Lin, T.Y., et al.: Microsoft COCO: common objects in context. arXiv:1405.0312 [cs], May 2014

15. Hosang, J., Benenson, R., Dollár, P., Schiele, B.: What makes for effective detection proposals? IEEE Trans. Pattern Anal. Mach. Intell. **38**(4), 814–830 (2016). https://doi.org/10.1109/TPAMI.2015.2465908
16. Klaeger, T., Schult, A., Majschak, J.P.: Lernfähige Bedienerassistenz für Verarbeitungsmaschinen. Industrie 4.0 Manag. **33**, 25–28 (2017)
17. Klaeger, T., Schult, A., Oehm, L.: Using anomaly detection to support classification of fast running packaging processes (Accepted). In: IEEE International Conference on Industrial Informatics, INDIN 2019, Helsinki-Espoo, Finland, July 2019

Intuitive and Coherent Intraretinal Cystoid Map Representation in Optical Coherence Tomography Images

Plácido Vidal[1,2]([✉]), Joaquim de Moura[1,2], Jorge Novo[1,2],
Manuel G. Penedo[1,2], and Marcos Ortega[1,2]

[1] Department of Computer Science, University of A Coruña, A Coruña, Spain
{placido.francisco.lizancos.vidal,joaquim.demoura,jnovo,
mgpenedo,mortega}@udc.es
[2] CITIC - Research Center of Information and Communication Technologies,
University of A Coruña, A Coruña, Spain

Abstract. Fluid accumulations in between the retinal layers represent one of the main causes of blindness in developed countries. Currently, these fluid accumulations are detected by means of a manual inspection of Optical Coherence Tomography images, prone to subjective and non-quantifiable diagnostics. For this reason, numerous works aimed for an automated methodology. Nonetheless, these systems mostly focus on obtaining a defined segmentation, which is not always possible. For this reason, we present in this work a fully automatic methodology based in a fuzzy and confidence-based visualization of a regional analysis, allowing the clinicians to study the fluid accumulations independently of their distribution, complications and/or other artifacts that may complicate the identification process.

Keywords: Computer-aided diagnosis · Optical Coherence
Tomography · Macular edema · Regional analysis · Visualization

1 Introduction

The retina represents the neurosensory part of the human eye. This structure comprises both an extension of the nervous and the vascular systems [6], reflecting changes that may appear in any of them in its sensitive structures. For this reason, the retina has become the focus of many Computer-aided diagnosis (CAD) systems, as it allows to obtain information about a wide-range of internal processes.

This work is supported by the Instituto de Salud Carlos III, Government of Spain and FEDER funds of the European Union through the DTS18/00136 research projects and by the Ministerio de Economía y Competitividad, Government of Spain through the DPI2015-69948-R research project. Also, this work has received financial support from the European Union (European Regional Development Fund - ERDF) and the Xunta de Galicia, Centro singular de investigación de Galicia accreditation 2016-2019, Ref. ED431G/01; and Grupos de Referencia Competitiva, Ref. ED431C 2016-047.

© Springer Nature Switzerland AG 2020
R. Moreno-Díaz et al. (Eds.): EUROCAST 2019, LNCS 12014, pp. 270–278, 2020.
https://doi.org/10.1007/978-3-030-45096-0_34

The main way of studying the retina is by the inspection of a medical imaging technique called Optical Coherence Tomography (OCT). This imaging modality is capable of providing a cross-sectional representation of the retinal layers in a non-invasive way. Currently, one of the most common uses for this technique is the study of intraretinal fluid accumulations. These accumulations, consequence of pathologies like the Age-Related Macular Degeneration (AMD) and the Diabetic Retinopathy (RD), are among the main causes of blindness in developed countries.

Frequently, these images are being manually analyzed by the expert ophthalmologist, assessing the severity of the pathology and its evolution by using only its expertise and experience (which may be subject to subjective variables, inter-expert discrepancy and even inter/intra device variations). For this reason, several methodologies arose trying to offer an improved alternative to this issue. These works follow a similar archetype to the one established by Wilkins *et al.* [13], mainly based on an image processing to enhance the features of the image, an initial candidate segmentation and a final false positive (FP) filtering. In the particular case of Wilkins *et al.*, this image processing is characterized by a denoising step, candidate segmentation by a fixed thresholding and candidate filtering by using shape and size rules. As an example of this tendency, Girish *et al.* [2] improved this work by using a watershed algorithm to the initial candidate listing, Chiu *et al.* [1] changed the classification to a kernel regression strategy and the FP filtering to a graph theory and dynamic programming strategy and Wang *et al.* [12] generated a 3D segmentation using subsequent OCT scans and a fuzzy C-means algorithm, but still maintaining the posterior FP filtering. Additionally, some works (like the proposal of Samagaio *et al.* [9]) have extended the segmentation approach to a characterization of these fluid accumulations into the different clinical types of macular edema.

Finally, some works focused on obtaining these segmentations using deep learning strategies. Most of these works follow an approach derived from the original (and commonly used in the analysis of medical images for obtaining a precise segmentation) U-Net architecture proposed by Ronnenberger *et al.* [8]. As an example of this, we find the works of Lee *et al.* [3], Venhuizen *et al.* [10] or Lu *et al.* [4] (albeit this last work focused in a multiclass fluid identification).

All these works present satisfactory results in the segmentation domain, but these fluid accumulations do not appear always with a defined region to segment, nor one that different experts would agree on. An example of fluid regions with confusing limits can be seen in Fig. 1. As shown, these fluid regions are mixed with other pathologies, artifacts product of the imaging technique, and with normal retinal tissue. Such is this variability that establishing a common ground truth with different experts would also carry an astonishing variability, thus making it unreliable as accurate baseline.

As an alternative, de Moura *et al.* [5,7] established other way of studying these accumulations. This approach does not look for a precise segmentation nor a full image classification. Instead, it merges both ideas to perform a regional analysis. This analysis is centered in classifying individual samples as patholog-

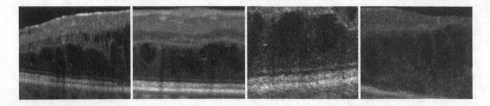

Fig. 1. Samples with diffuse fluid accumulations from OCT images that were captured by a Spectralis device and a Cirrus device.

ical or healthy regions. With this strategy as foundation [11], in this work, we present a visualization that takes advantage of the resilience of this method in the fluid problematic areas to create intuitive detections to be analyzed by the expert clinician. Down below we will proceed to further explain each of the steps followed during this process.

2   Methodology

2.1   Retinal Layer Segmentation

The first step of the strategy consists in delimiting the region of interest (ROI). In particular, we focused on two differentiated retinal layers: the Inner Limiting Membrane (ILM) and the Retinal Pigment Epithelium (RPE), both representing the innermost and outermost layers of the retina, respectively.

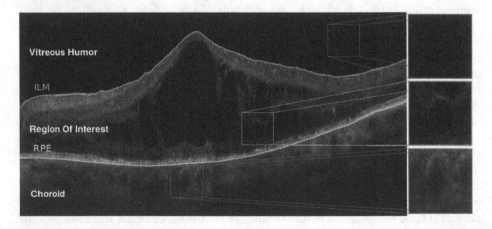

Fig. 2. Different regions considered in an OCT image and three confusing samples from each one of them. From top to bottom: choroid sample, fluid region inside the ROI and vitreous humor sample.

Just next to the ILM, we can find the vitreous humor (the fluid inside the eye); and next to the RPE, the choroid region (the vascular layer that nourishes the outermost layers of the retina). In Fig. 2, these main regions are shown with representative samples of each one of them that will illustrate and motivate why the extraction of the ROI is made. As the reader can see, the sample from the choroid and the sample from the vitreous humor can perfectly be visually confused as intraretinal fluid. The vitreous humor, being a liquid region, presents the same characteristics as the fluid leakages inside the retinal layers. The choroid, on the other hand, is a vascular network with circular diffuse patterns that perfectly mimic the ones also present in the fluid leakages. Finally, the fluid sample from the ROI shows a pattern that could be present in the retina, the vitreous humor and as well as in the choroid. For this reason, to diminish the pattern load the classifier has to learn, these regions are omitted in the posterior analysis.

2.2   Image Sampling and Subsample Extraction

After the ROI is extracted, the image is divided in a series of overlapping samples. To extract these overlapping samples, each axis of the ROI is divided in rows and columns spaced by *Window size - Established overlap* pixels. That way, the points where these rows and columns meet, a sample center is positioned. Finally, for each one of these points, a window is extracted.

The regional analysis used in this work bases itself in the study of texture features. These features describe statistically how the pixel gray levels are spatially organized in a given sample. Nonetheless, the image sampling extracts squared samples from an irregularly-shaped ROI, resulting in some samples partially falling outside the ROI and thus containing non-relevant information that must be discarded.

As this spatial information has to be maintained and the matrices have to be rectangular, we cannot simply remove the external pixels from a resulting array. For this reason, we devised an algorithm to find the biggest rectangle inside a given sample that contains only valid pixels. Additionally, to ensure a minimum size of this subsample, only those that are centered inside the ROI will be considered. If a sample does not meet this criteria, it is simply discarded and not counted towards the final vote.

To extract the subsample, we first find all the possible corners these subrectangle could have (Fig. 3a–b). For this, we use the *hit-or-miss* transform. This

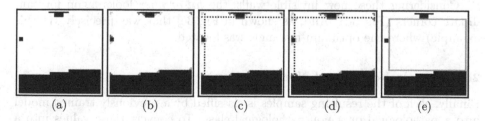

Fig. 3. Steps to extract the biggest subsample from the relevant region (in *white*). *Red: NE, Yellow: NW, Blue: SW, Green: SE, Magenta: S* and *Light Blue: E* (Color figure online)

morphological operation allows us to find points in an image that match both a pattern in the background of the image as well as the foreground. More precisely, we use the masks defined in Eq. 1. Each of these masks will return a series of different points where the ROI pixels (represented in the mask by 1s) and the non-ROI pixels (represented in the mask by -1s) match those patterns. That way, the NE mask will signal the north-east facing corners, the NW mask will signal the north-west facing corners, SE the south-east ones and, finally, the SW will mark the south-west ones.

$$NE = \begin{pmatrix} 0 & -1 & -1 \\ 1 & 1 & -1 \\ 0 & 1 & 0 \end{pmatrix} NW = \begin{pmatrix} -1 & -1 & 0 \\ -1 & 1 & 1 \\ 0 & 1 & 0 \end{pmatrix} SE = \begin{pmatrix} 0 & 1 & 0 \\ 1 & 1 & -1 \\ 0 & -1 & -1 \end{pmatrix} SW = \begin{pmatrix} 0 & 1 & 0 \\ -1 & 1 & 1 \\ -1 & -1 & 0 \end{pmatrix}$$
$$(1)$$

After these corners are found, all the possible rectangles formed by any combination of the opposing corners are studied. That is, NE with SW and NW with SE (and only if they are facing each other). If the area within a pair of corners contains any pixel from the non-ROI area, that candidate is also discarded. Finally, once we have all the valid candidates, the one with the biggest area is chosen and extracted from the original sample.

In some cases, the optimum rectangle would have corners in a region without valid paired candidate corner points. That is, for example, it would have an SE corner but not a corresponding NW (represented in Fig. 3 as the bottom right green corner without a matching NW). For this reason, to the previous set of detected corners, an additional set is added considering also artifacts that may create an invisible barrier. To find these candidates, the *hit-or-miss* transform is also used, but with the masks shown in Eq. 2 (Fig. 3c). Additionally, as these masks would return multiple detections in flat surfaces, only one of the pixels is considered per orientation and row/column. Also, as some of these regions are already covered by a previous detected corner, rows and corners with an existing previous corner will also be ignored.

$$N = \begin{pmatrix} 0 \\ 1 \\ -1 \end{pmatrix} S = \begin{pmatrix} -1 \\ 1 \\ 0 \end{pmatrix} E = \begin{pmatrix} -1 & 1 & 0 \end{pmatrix} W = \begin{pmatrix} 0 & 1 & -1 \end{pmatrix}$$
$$(2)$$

Considering these new invisible walls, the *hit-or-miss* looks again for candidate corners (Fig. 3d). And, as shown in Fig. 3e, that was precisely (in this example) where the optimum rectangle was located.

2.3 Sample Voting and Normalization

Finally, each of the resulting samples is classified by a previously trained model into a pathological or a non-pathological class. To convert these values into a confidence indicator, we use a voting strategy. The confidence of a given pixel is determined by the number of windows classified into the pathological class that in the original image contained that same pixel. Thanks to using this strategy, the confidence is calculated not only by one classification, but also using the information from the neighboring samples that cover an extended region.

Nonetheless, in the ROI areas close to the borders, the number of windows that overlap the region is sensibly lower than in the internal ones. Additionally, depending on the ROI shape and size, rounding errors when calculating the sample centers will cause a lattice pattern to appear (as some pixels, product of this rounding, will be overlapped by less windows in their frontier zones). To solve this issue, the number of pixels is divided by the number of windows that overlapped that pixel. This way, the confidence is stated as the relative percentage of windows that, overlapping that given pixel, were considered as pathological. Figure 4 shows a representation of these two issues in a map where the window overlap density is represented.

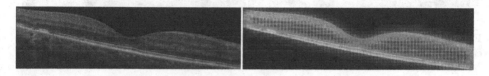

Fig. 4. Original healthy OCT image ROI and a representation over it of the vote density (overlap of 50 px between samples).

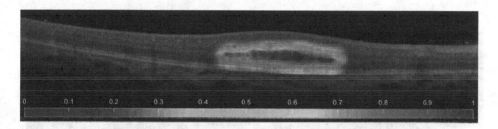

Fig. 5. Map with the corresponding color scale indicating the relationship between the color that is shown in the map and the confidence assigned by the system.

2.4 Intuitive Color Mapping

Finally, an intuitive color map is constructed to represent the final detection; being merged with the original image. The color map presents a cold-hot scale with several and progressive hue changes. This pattern allows the expert clinician to assess the severity of a pathology and know, with a quick look, the confidence metric established by the system. Figure 5 shows a finished confidence map. As shown, with a simple gaze, a human examiner can quickly assess the confidence thanks to the proposed color scale.

3   Results and Conclusions

The map generation strategy hereby presented and the resulting visualization are able to create, from an individual OCT image, a complete and intuitive representation of the fluid regions. Moreover, these detections are able to work even when the fluid accumulations do not present a defined border that can be segmented due to its diffuse nature.

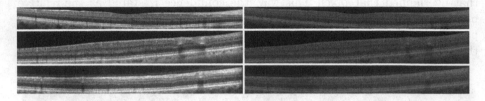

Fig. 6. Examples of healthy ROI regions without fluid leakages and their corresponding confidence maps.

Figure 6 shows an example of healthy OCT images without fluid accumulations. Even confusing artifacts like shadows that are generated by vessels or slight darkened regions product of the OCT device are explicitly and correctly identified as non-pathological.

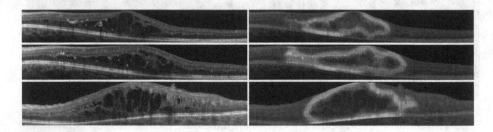

Fig. 7. Examples of ROI regions with complex fluid leakages and their corresponding confidence color maps.

On the other hand, Fig. 7 presents three complex cases of fluid accumulations mixed with other pathologies and healthy tissue. The reader can easily see how, comparing with Fig. 6, an expert clinician that analyzes both images could easily tell, without much inspection, which patients present relevant leakages and which ones are healthy. Additionally, this methodology is not limited to fluid accumulations or even to OCT images. By changing the classifier, the system could easily be used to detect other pathological complications in this or other different image modality (in most medical imaging systems, the ROI extraction phase can be omitted if there is no danger of confusing texture patterns between structures). Finally, we would like to remark that adapting this method also does not require a precise ground truth like a segmentation would. This model is trained by means of a binary classification of square samples, easier to do for a human expert and more robust than a segmentation-based one. That is, with vague classifications that tolerate the human margin of error we can create a coherent, intuitive and defined representation of the pathological regions.

References

1. Chiu, S.J., Allingham, M.J., Mettu, P.S., Cousins, S.W., Izatt, J.A., Farsiu, S.: Kernel regression based segmentation of optical coherence tomography images with diabetic macular edema. Biomed. Opt. Express **6**(4), 1172–1194 (2015)
2. Girish, G., Kothari, A.R., Rajan, J.: Automated segmentation of intra-retinal cysts from optical coherence tomography scans using marker controlled watershed transform. In: 2016 IEEE 38th Annual International Conference of the Engineering in Medicine and Biology Society (EMBC), pp. 1292–1295. IEEE (2016)
3. Lee, C.S., Tyring, A.J., Deruyter, N.P., Wu, Y., Rokem, A., Lee, A.Y.: Deep-learning based, automated segmentation of macular edema in optical coherence tomography. Biomed. Opt. Express **8**(7), 3440–3448 (2017)
4. Lu, D., et al.: Deep-learning based multiclass retinal fluid segmentation and detection in optical coherence tomography images using a fully convolutional neural network. Med. Image Anal. **54**, 100–110 (2019)
5. de Moura, J., Novo, J., Rouco, J., Penedo, M.G., Ortega, M.: Automatic identification of intraretinal cystoid regions in optical coherence tomography. In: ten Teije, A., Popow, C., Holmes, J.H., Sacchi, L. (eds.) AIME 2017. LNCS (LNAI), vol. 10259, pp. 305–315. Springer, Cham (2017). https://doi.org/10.1007/978-3-319-59758-4_35
6. de Moura, J., Novo, J., Ortega, M., Barreira, N., Charlón, P.: Automatic retinal vascularity identification and artery/vein classification using near-infrared reflectance retinographies. In: Cláudio, A.P., et al. (eds.) VISIGRAPP 2017. CCIS, vol. 983, pp. 262–278. Springer, Cham (2019). https://doi.org/10.1007/978-3-030-12209-6_13
7. de Moura, J., Vidal, P., Novo, J., Rouco, J., Ortega, M.: Feature definition, analysis and selection for cystoid region characterization in optical coherence tomography. In: Knowledge-Based and Intelligent Information & Engineering Systems: Proceedings of the 21st International Conference KES-2017, Marseille, France, 6–8 September 2017, pp. 1369–1377 (2017)
8. Ronneberger, O., Fischer, P., Brox, T.: U-Net: convolutional networks for biomedical image segmentation. In: Navab, N., Hornegger, J., Wells, W.M., Frangi, A.F. (eds.) MICCAI 2015. LNCS, vol. 9351, pp. 234–241. Springer, Cham (2015). https://doi.org/10.1007/978-3-319-24574-4_28
9. Samagaio, G., Estévez, A., de Moura, J., Novo, J., Fernández, M.I., Ortega, M.: Automatic macular edema identification and characterization using OCT images. Comput. Methods Programs Biomed. **163**, 47–63 (2018)
10. Venhuizen, F.G., et al.: Deep learning approach for the detection and quantification of intraretinal cystoid fluid in multivendor optical coherence tomography. Biomed. Opt. Express **9**(4), 1545–1569 (2018)
11. Vidal, P., de Moura, J., Novo, J., Penedo, M.G., Ortega, M.: Intraretinal fluid identification via enhanced maps using optical coherence tomography images. Biomed. Opt. Express **9**(10), 4730–4754 (2018)

12. Wang, J., et al.: Automated volumetric segmentation of retinal fluid on optical coherence tomography. Biomed. Opt. Express **7**(4), 1577–1589 (2016)
13. Wilkins, G.R., Houghton, O.M., Oldenburg, A.L.: Automated segmentation of intraretinal cystoid fluid in optical coherence tomography. IEEE Trans. Biomed. Eng. **59**(4), 1109–1114 (2012)

Computer and Systems Based Methods and Electronic Technologies in Medicine

Autoencoder Features for Differentiation of Leukocytes Based on Digital Holographic Microscopy (DHM)

Stefan Röhrl[1]([✉]), Matthias Ugele[2], Christian Klenk[2], Dominik Heim[2], Oliver Hayden[2], and Klaus Diepold[1]

[1] Chair for Data Processing, Department of Electrical and Computer Engineering, Technical University of Munich, Arcisstr. 21, 80333 Munich, Germany
stefan.roehrl@tum.de

[2] Heinz-Nixdorf-Chair of Biomedical Electronics, Department of Electrical and Computer Engineering, TranslaTUM, Campus Klinikum rechts der Isar, Technical University of Munich, Ismaningerstr. 22, 81675 Munich, Germany

Abstract. The differentiation and counting of leukocytes is essential for the diagnosis of leukemia. This work investigates the suitability of Deep Convolutional Autoencoders and Principal Component Analysis (PCA) to generate robust features from the 3D image data of a digital holographic microscope (DHM). The results show that the feature space is not trivially separable in both cases. A terminal classification by a Support Vector Machine (SVM) favors the uncorrelated PCA features.

Keywords: Blood cell analysis · Autoencoder · Convolutional neural networks · Digital holographic microscopy · Phase images

1 Motivation

Blood delivers a variety of insights into health conditions of an organism, especially in the field of in-vitro diagnostics. Therefore, hematological analysis such as complete blood count (CBC) represent a high share of laboratory tests in the health care sector. Despite the availability of largely automated analyzers, the gold standard for the routine diagnosis of hematological disorders is the tedious Giemsa stained blood smear [2] which suffers from inter-observer variations. Further drawbacks of current approaches are a high effort for sample preparation, material expenses, a long processing time or missing clinical relevance [5].

To overcome the mentioned issues and specially to reduce time-consuming manual intervention, the CellFACE project was created. Flow cytometry in combination with digital holographic microscopy (DHM) [9] enables researchers to record 3D images of each single cell, while sustaining a high-throughput stream of blood cells. The overall goal is to establish this label- and reagent-free [3,4] approach as a platform technology for automated blood cell diagnosis.

© Springer Nature Switzerland AG 2020
R. Moreno-Díaz et al. (Eds.): EUROCAST 2019, LNCS 12014, pp. 281–288, 2020.
https://doi.org/10.1007/978-3-030-45096-0_35

Following the statisitics of Siegel et al. [17] and Malvezzi et al. [12], partially displayed in Table 1, there were almost 70.000 cases of death due to Leukemia in the European Union and the United States combined. Therefore, we focus on the differentiation of leukocytes, which is an essential aspect in the diagnosis and treatment of Leukemia.

Table 1. Excerpt of cancer statistics of Leukemia in the EU and USA in 2018

2018	European Union [12]		United States [17]	
	Women	Men	Women	Men
Estimated deaths	19.800	24.700	10.100	14.270
Estimated new cases			25.270	35.030

2   State of the Art

Today, many diseases like Leukemia or other myeloproliferative neoplasms, which directly affect the composition of the blood or the morphology of blood cells, are analyzed with the mentioned blood smear technique. Here, the blood sample is spread to a thin film and then stained chemically [13]. A microscopist then has to classify and count the cells manually to get a diagnosis, which can be time consuming and is prone to human errors [2]. Modern hematology analyzers have partly automatized this process. Such devices can be used to perform a five-part differential of white blood cells which may indicate an unhealthy distribution of leukocyte sub-types. Further analysis, e.g. on a morphological level, is not possible with these devices due to the inflexibility of this method [2]. An even higher amount of detail is obtained by fluorescence-activated cell sorting (FACS). Here, cells can be marked with fluorescent antibodies and therefore clearly identified and counted. Though this method only works for the major cell types but not for degenerated cell populations and is additionally very cost intensive [5].

Statistical significance and a high certainty play major roles in a clinical surrounding. By using a microfluidic channel in combination with a phase microscope, it is possible to capture images of a vast number of cells in only a few minutes which contain a high degree of detail. Based on in-line differential holography, it is even possible to perceive information of the internal structures e.g. the nucleus of the cell. Figure 1 shows the simplified principle of operation of a digital holographic microscope. The Center for Translational Cancer Research (TranslaTUM) hosts a specifically manufactured DHM setup, which can take hundred phase images per second and provides a high-quality resolution over the whole image plane. A detailed description of the microscope, the alignment process and the sample handling is given in [18]. On the left side of Fig. 4, you can see a reconstructed phase image from DHM containing the three-dimensional relief of each blood cell. Since this approach is label-free, there are no markers attached to cells, which would allow

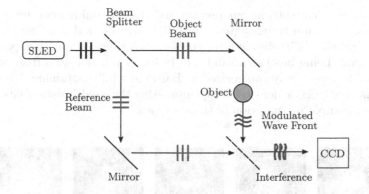

Fig. 1. Principle of operation of a digital holographic microscope

an easy differentiation of the distinct cell types. So, the classification and characterization of each cell only from the captured topology becomes a challenging task [14]. To get a visual impression, Fig. 2 contains five representative phase images of different leukocytes. Several approaches were proposed, which directly work on the morphological cell features to enable label-free differentiation of white blood cells. For three-part differentials of leukocytes Li et al. [11] used Linear Discriminant Analysis (LDA) to select features according to their importance and subsequently trained a Support Vector Machine (SVM) for classification. Vercruysse et al. [19] obtained similar results, but still could not reach the performance of modern haematology analyzers. Amir et al. [1] used t-Distributed Stochastic Nearest Neighbor Embedding in their tool viSNE, to reduce the high dimensional parameter space to two dimensions while preserving similar clusters. Roitshtain [15] and Ugele et al. [18] showed the advantages of Principal Component Analysis (PCA) for dimensionality reduction of the feature space. These analysis tools indicate a broad clinical applicability to overcome the limitations of today's standard methods for the routine diagnosis of hematological disorders and make the proposed goal seem achievable [18,20].

3   Data Set

For data generation, we use the combination of differential holographic microscopy with microfluidic alignment of the cells presented by Ugele et al. [18]. This allows robust imaging with high quality over the whole image plane. As displayed in Fig. 4, the re-constructed phase images from DHM contain the three-dimensional relief of each blood cell. The five subtypes of leukocytes (Basophil, Eosinophil, Lymphocyte, Monocyte and Neutrophil) were isolated originating from different blood samples of healthy donors. After rejecting obvious deviations of cells using morphological filters, such as size and circularity measures as described by Ugele et al., the recorded phase images still contain over 400.000 samples. Since most of them are Eosinophil we randomly select 12.000 representatives of every subtype and achieve a balanced data set with 60.000 cells.

From those, we pick 5.000 as our test set and the remaining ones are used in a 5-fold cross validation training procedure. It has to be said that the labeling is not totally reliable. The simple filter rules cannot prevent other components of the blood from being label as a valid cell. In Fig. 3 you can see a fraction of the images which were falsely categorized as Basophil while containing debris, doublets of smaller cells or defocused captures. Also the used isolation kits cannot guarantee a complete separation of the subtypes.

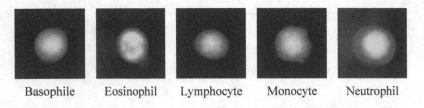

  Basophile   Eosinophil   Lymphocyte   Monocyte   Neutrophil

Fig. 2. Representative cell from each leukocyte subtype

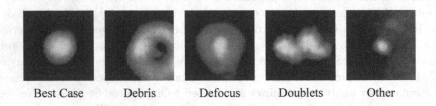

  Best Case   Debris   Defocus   Doublets   Other

Fig. 3. Different examples contaminate the ground truth

4   Autoencoder and Principal Component Analysis

As shown in the past [11,15,18], few features contributed significantly to the differentiation of white blood cells. Described in the previous chapter, the composition and the limited usability of the ground truth for supervised training imply the focus on unsupervised methods until this shortcomings are overcome. Hence, we train different Deep Convolutional Autoencoders [7] to generate a small number of data-driven features, which we consider to be a representation with a higher classification power. To keep the results comparable to [18], the latent feature space is designed eight dimensional. An extensive grid search lead to a symmetrical network with four hidden encoder and decoder layers containing respectively 64, 32, 16 and 8 filters with a kernel size of 3 by 3 followed by a ReLU activation function [6] and subsequent maximum pooling. The training process performs best in terms of reconstruction with the Adam optimizer using the recommended settings from Kingma and Ba [10]. The best reconstruction accuracy was 81%.

Whereas [15,18] used Principal Component Analysis (PCA) to compress the morphological features, this work applies PCA directly on the image pixel data in order to keep the process as automated as possible. This dimensionality reduction approach is used as a bench mark for the Autoencoder. Allowing PCA to use eight components, it was possible to achieve 73% reconstruction accuracy.

Finally, we provide both representations – Autoencoder and PCA features – to a Support Vector Machine (SVM) as in [11,15,18]. This large margin classifier should give a reliable statement about the separability and the encoding performance of the presented approaches.

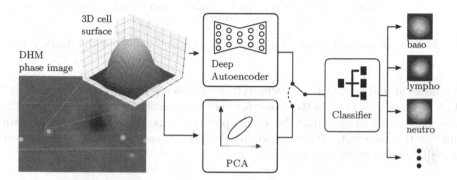

Fig. 4. Data Processing Pipeline: 3D cell morphology is encoded by handcrafted as well as data-driven features. A classifier is trained to assign a class to each cell.

5   Experiments

Since the training is conducted in an unsupervised manner, there is no way to optimize the result for classification accuracy. The presented approaches solely aim for the best reconstruction accuracy. In order to find a decent Autoencoder setup, a grid search within a reasonable scope is executed to find the architecture with the best reconstruction performance. We use 5-fold cross validation to achieve a well trained model, which shows a reconstruction error of 19%. The PCA is also computed on the same training fold as the Autoencoder and restricted to eight components resulting in a reconstruction error of 27%. Nevertheless, the analysis of both of the latent feature spaces showed that a trivial separation of clusters is not possible. By pairwise plotting all features against each other, none of the two dimensional subspaces shows any obvious clustering. The subspace with the highest inter-class distance is drawn in Fig. 5. To get an indicator for the separability of the features by the desired subtypes of leukocytes, a radial basis SVM is prepared on the encoded training data, once by the ones of the Autoencder and the PCA. The evaluation on the test set is displayed

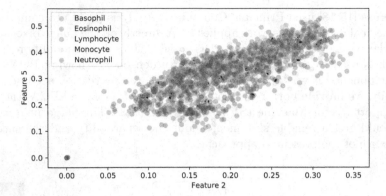

Fig. 5. Two dimensional plot of the autoencoder features 2 and 5 with arbitrary units

as confusion matrices in Fig. 6, where it is easy to see on the right side that the PCA features provide a better basis for classification. Both approaches have the most difficulties in encoding the Eosinophil (E) cells, since their share of data contains the most impurities. Removing this class from the data set leads to just a small increase of accuracy.

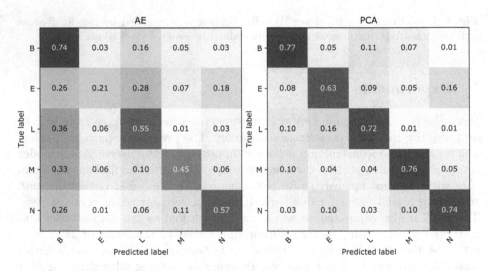

Fig. 6. Confusion matrices of SVMs based on autoencder (left) and PCA (right) features: the prediction frequency of each cell type is displayed in %.

6 Conclusion

The experiments show that none of the chosen approaches was able to achieve a simple clustering from data inherent patterns or correlations and it was not possible to reproduce the results of [18]. Due to the decorrealtion properties of the PCA, the features of this approach were more suitable to be used in a SVM for classification. Overall, the pre-processing and the data collection process has to be improved to generate a reliable ground truth. Not only the classification performance can be measured more accurately, but also the stable training of classifiers is improved by this step. Currently, both approaches are unsuitable for the use in a clinical system.

In future work, we will bring the advantages of both proposed approaches together and examine methodologies like kernel PCA [16] and Variational Autoencoders [8]. Here, PCA is enabled to handle non-linear relations whereas Variational Autoencoders can be forced to decorrelate the feature space.

References

1. Amir, E.A.D., et al.: viSNE enables visualization of high dimensional single cell data and reveals phenotypic heterogeneity of leukemia. Lab Chip **31**(6), 545–552 (2013)
2. Barcia, J.J.: The Giemsa stain: its history and applications. Int. J. Surg. Pathol. **15**(3), 292–296 (2007)
3. El-Schich, Z., Kamlund, S., Janicke, B., Alm, K., Wingren, A.: Holography: the usefulness of digital holographic microscopy for clinical diagnostics. In: Holographic Materials and Optical Systems, pp. 319–333. Intech (2017)
4. El-Schich, Z., Mölder, A.L., Wingren, A.: Quantitative phase imaging for label-free analysis of cancer cells focus on digital holographic microscopy. Appl. Sci. **8**, 1027 (2018)
5. Filby, A.: Sample preparation for flow cytometry benefits from some lateral thinking. Cytom. Part A: J. Int. Soc. Anal. Cytol. **89**, 1054–1056 (2016)
6. Glorot, X., Bordes, A., Bengio, Y.: Deep sparse rectifier neural networks. In: Gordon, G., Dunson, D., Dudík, M. (eds.) Proceedings of the Fourteenth International Conference on Artificial Intelligence and Statistics. Proceedings of Machine Learning Research, vol. 15, pp. 315–323 (2011)
7. Hinton, G.E., Salakhutdinov, R.R.: Reducing the dimensionality of data with neural networks. Science **313**(5786), 504–507 (2006)
8. Hou, X., Shen, L., Sun, K., Qiu, G.: Deep feature consistent variational autoencoder. In: 2017 IEEE Winter Conference on Applications of Computer Vision (WACV), pp. 1133–1141. IEEE (2017)
9. Jo, Y., et al.: Quantitative phase imaging and artificial intelligence: a review. IEEE J. Sel. Top. Quantum Electron. **25**, 1–14 (2018)
10. Kingma, D., Ba, J.: Adam: a method for stochastic optimization. In: International Conference on Learning Representations (2014)
11. Li, Y., et al.: Accurate label-free 3-part leukocyte recognition with single cell lens-free imaging flow cytometry. Comput. Biol. Med. **96**, 147–156 (2018)
12. Malvezzi, M., et al.: European cancer mortality predictions for the year 2018 with focus on colorectal cancer. Ann. Oncol. **29**(4), 1016–1022 (2018)

13. Prieto, S., Powless, A., Boice, J.W., Sharma, S., Muldoon, T.: Proflavine hemisulfate as a fluorescent contrast agent for point-of-care cytology. PLoS ONE **10**, e0125598 (2015)
14. Rinehart, M., Sang Park, H., Wax, A.: Influence of defocus on quantitative analysis of microscopic objects and individual cells with digital holography. Biomed. Opt. Express **6**(6), 2067–2075 (2015)
15. Roitshtain, D., Wolbromsky, L., Bal, E., Greenspan, H., Satterwhite, L.L., Shaked, N.T.: Quantitative phase microscopy spatial signatures of cancer cells. Cytom. Part A: J. Int. Soc. Anal. Cytol. **91**, 482–493 (2017)
16. Schölkopf, B., Smola, A., Müller, K.R.: Nonlinear component analysis as a kernel eigenvalue problem. Neural Comput. **10**(5), 1299–1319 (1998)
17. Siegel, R.L., Miller, K.D., Jemal, A.: Cancer statistics, 2018. CA Cancer J. Clin. **68**(1), 7–30 (2018)
18. Ugele, M., et al.: Label-free high-throughput leukemia detection by holographic microscopy. Adv. Sci. **5**, 1800761 (2018)
19. Vercruysse, D., et al.: Three-part differential of unlabeled leukocytes with a compact lens-free imaging flow cytometer. Nat. Biotechnol. **15**, 1123–1132 (2013)
20. Yoon, J., et al.: Identification of non-activated lymphocytes using three-dimensional refractive index tomography and machine learning. Sci. Rep. **7**(1), 6654 (2017)

Automatic ECG Screening as a Supporting Tool on a Telemedicine Framework

V. Mondéjar-Guerra[1,2]([✉]) [iD], J. Novo[1,2] [iD], J. Rouco[1,2] [iD], M. Ortega[1,2] [iD], and M.G. Penedo[1,2] [iD]

[1] Department of Computer Science, University of A Coruña,
A Coruña, Spain
v.mondejar@udc.es
[2] CITIC-Research Center of Information and Communication Technologies,
University of A Coruña, A Coruña, Spain

Abstract. ECG screening is an important prevention practice employed for the early detection of several cardiovascular diseases. There are many scenarios and emergency situations in which an expert that can interpret the ECG is not available. Aiming to make the connection between the specialists from the healthcare centers with the patients at underserved rural areas easier, telemedicine solutions are increasing in popularity every year. In this work, an automatic tool for ECG screening, which is able to classify up to four arrhythmia classes is presented. In addition, this tool is included as part of a multidisciplinary telemedicine framework, which is called eDSalud.

Keywords: Electrocardiogram (ECG) · Telemedicine · Automatic ECG screening

1 Introduction

Cardiovascular diseases (CVDs) are the number 1 cause of death in the world. Near to 17.9 million people die each year from CVDs, an estimated 31% of all deaths worldwide according to studies reported by the World Health Organization (WHO). It is also noticeable that more than 75% of CVD deaths occur in low-income and middle-income countries.

Electrocardiograms (ECGs) are a noninvasive and inexpensive technique widely used as a clinical practice for early identification of many CVDs and prevention for patients at risk of sudden cardiac death [8]. The ECGs measure the electrical activity of the heart over a period of time, allowing the detection of arrhythmia signs. For a routine analysis of the heart's electrical activity, an ECG recorded from 12 separate leads is typically used. The 12-lead ECG consists of three bipolar limb leads (I, II, and III), the unipolar limb leads (AVR, AVL, and AVF), and six unipolar chest leads, also called precordial or V leads, (V1, V2,

R. Moreno-Díaz et al. (Eds.): EUROCAST 2019, LNCS 12014, pp. 289–296, 2020.
https://doi.org/10.1007/978-3-030-45096-0_36

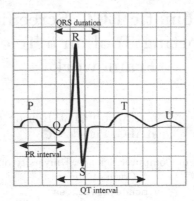

Fig. 1. Example of an ECG lead II indicating their waves.

V3, V4, V5 and V6). Each lead represents a view of the electrical activity of the heart from a particular angle across the body.

The record contains approximately 2.5 s of duration for each lead. Additionally, to accurately assess the cardiac rhythm, a prolonged recording from one lead is used to provide a rhythm strip of 10 s. Lead II, which usually gives a good view of the most important waves: P, Q, R, S and T (see Fig. 1), is the most commonly lead employed for the rhythm strip. Each beat of the heart contains a series of deflections away from the baseline on the ECG, or waves, which reflect the time evolution of electrical activity in the heart. P-wave is a small deflection caused by atrial depolarisation, Q, R, and S waves are usually considered as a single event known as the QRS-complex, which is the largest amplitude portion of the ECG, being caused by ventral depolarisation. T wave is caused by ventral repolarization. Finally, in some cases, an additional U wave may follow the T wave. Through the analysis of the changes that appear on these waves, different types of arrhythmias can be detected.

As was mentioned, the ECG screening is a common and widely used practice for the detection of the first symptoms of many CDVs. However, there are many circumstances in which an expert that can properly interpret the ECG signals may not be available, such as outreach clinics in rural areas or in emergency situations. In above cases, telemedicine approaches have proved to be a good solution, allowing the possibility that an expert cardiologist performs the diagnosis remotely. In recent years, there has been a growing interest in cloud computing and telemedicine [3]. Besides, in general, telemedicine systems also offer other utilities related to the storage, sharing, security and representation of the information, including even some automatic processing of the data.

On the other hand, a huge amount of works focused on the development of fully automatic systems for ECG classification have been proposed during the last decades [9]. These solutions provide an objective diagnosis in almost anywhere, allowing to alleviate the workload of the experts, and supporting their diagnostics.

In this work, a tool for automatic ECG screening is presented. In addition, this tool is included as part of a wider and multidisciplinary telemedicine framework, which is called eDSalud.

2   Telemedicine Framework eDSalud

Telemedicine has emerged as a feasible instrument to improve the sustainability of the actual health care systems, promoting universality and a greater efficiency at the care level. In developed countries, telemedicine is playing an important role, while for developing countries it is an absolute need. Nowadays, there already exist different telediagnostic services for customised advice and patient monitoring. However, there is a lack of telediagnostic services in which the specialist is directly involved, embracing more than one medical speciality, *i.e.*, multidisciplinary telemedicine frameworks that allow the integration of different diagnostic teams and include diagnostic support tools. To cover this need, the next goals are considered for the development of the telemedicine framework, eDSalud:

- Multidisciplinary and modularity: it is developed with the modules of cardiology, dermatology, ophthalmology and radiology. But the framework must also be modular, allowing the addition of new services in the future, and at the same time allowing information sharing between the different modules.
  Historical records integration: it must cover the management aspects, storage and standardisation of medical history, allowing the specialist to have an easy access to the previous records of the patients.
- Collaborative platform: it should allow an easy sharing and discussion between different specialists, allowing the request of second opinion diagnosis.
- Software support tools: it must display all the information clearly to the specialists easing their diagnostics. These tools may include an ECG viewer, a cardio/radio image viewer for ecography, SIRIUS (System for the Integration of Retinal Images) [6], among others. Furthermore, these tools should incorporate additional features that support the diagnosis of the specialists. For example, an automatic heartbeat segmentation that directly provides the specialists the beats per minute (bpm) rate for the ECG analysis, or the computation of the arteriolar-to-venular ratio (AVR) in the case of retinal images.

3   ECG Supporting Tool

Figure 2 shows an overview of the full ECG support tool included in the framework. First, the ECG signal of the patient is captured by the acquisition hardware. The module is hardware-independent and it currently supports the models EKG-200BT and IGReD from NDV, both working at 200 Hz. Next, the signal is sent to the client-side application through Bluetooth, or USB connection. The client application can be run on different operating systems (Linux distributions, Android, Windows). Once the signal is received by the client-side, it can

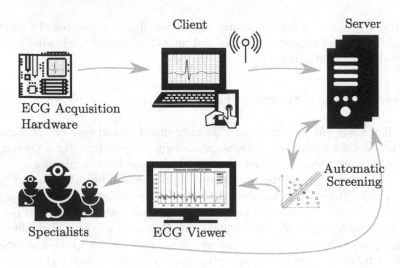

Fig. 2. Overview of the ECG support tool.

be immediately transmitted to the server. In the server-side there are different options for handling the ECG signal. In first place, there is an automatic screening module that performs an initial diagnosis of the signal, computing the heartbeat rate and identifying arrhythmias through an analysis that relies on morphological and temporal features. Next, this information along with additional personal data about the patient, like gender, age or blood pressure (BP), are showed to the specialists trough an ECG viewer GUI. All the information generated during the different stages, and the comments and diagnosis reported by the different specialists are stored on the server database.

A sketch of the ECG viewer GUI for the server-side application is showed on Fig. 3. It shows the personal information about the patient (age, sex, weigth, height, blood pressure), the date of the data acquisition, the different leads that compose the ECG signal, and the automatic diagnosis generated by the automatic tool. The automatic diagnosis includes the heartbeat rate and the percentage of the heartbeats among the total that belong to five different classes: Normal (N), Supraventricular (SVEB), Ventricular (V), Fusion (F) and Unknown (Q). The class N represents the healthy condition, while the $SVEB$, VEB, and F represent different groups of arrhythmias following the Association for the Advancement of Medical Instrumentation (AAMI) [1], finally the class Q is employed to represent noise or distorted heartbeats that can not be classified by the tool.

3.1 Automatic Screening of ECGs

In this section, the workflow of the automatic ECG classification is explained with more detail. Specifically, our automatic screening ECG tool is based on the method proposed by Mondéjar-Guerra *et al.* [4]. Figure 4 shows a diagram

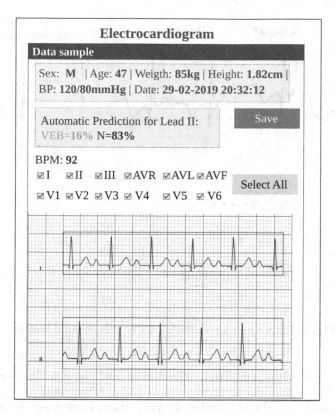

Fig. 3. Example of the GUI in the server-side application for ECG diagnostic.

with the required steps that compose the automatic screening tool. First, a pre-processing step is applied in order to remove some high-frequency noise and normalize the amplitude levels of the raw signal. To compute the baseline of the signal, two consecutive median filters of 200 ms and 600 ms are applied on it. Then, the computed baseline is subtracted from the original signal, producing the baseline corrected ECG signal (Fig. 4(b)). Next, a QRS detection method is employed to segment the signal at heartbeat level (Fig. 4(c)). Here, specifically, an implementation of the well-known algorithm proposed by Pan and Tompkins [7] is employed. Note, that using the average of the RR distance between consecutive beats, the heart rate at beats per minute (bpm) can be computed. Once the signal is segmented, different morphological and temporal feature descriptors are computed centered on the R-peak of each beat. These features aim to extract the required information to discriminate between four different classes of arrhythmias: N, $SVEB$, V, and F. Then, these descriptors feed a trained classifier that returns the output for each beat. Concretely, this method relies on an ensemble of SVMs, in which each single SVM is trained with a specific feature descriptor and then, their outputs are combined with the product rule.

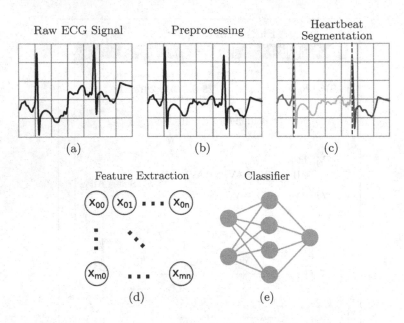

Fig. 4. Diagram of an automatic ECG classification system.

More detail of the computed feature descriptors and the classification algorithm can be found on [4].

The method has been validated with the Massachusetts Institute of Technology-Beth Israel Hospital (MIT-BIH) arrhythmia database [5]. This database contains 48 ECG records of about 30 min, approximately 110,000 beats, sampled at 360 Hz with 11-bit resolution. The ECG records were captured from 47 different patients. Each beat was independently annotated by two or more expert cardiologists and the disagreements were resolved.

The classifier method was trained and validated on the MIT-BIH database. However, in order to properly evaluate the extrapolation capabilities of the classifier, an inter-patient division [2] was employed. In this manner, the database was divided in two datasets, one for training (DS1) and other for testing (DS2), ensuring that no record of the same patient be mixed between both datasets.

Table 1 shows the confusion matrix obtained by the employed classifier on the DS2 dataset from MIT-BIH. In general, the method achieves a good performance on the major classes (N, V, S). Many false negatives are produced on the class F, misclassifying as class N and V. However, note also that the MIT-BIH database is highly imbalanced, and the data samples from F class correspond only with a 1% of the total samples.

Figure 5 shows an example of the automatic ECG screening: the signal is preprocessed (baseline and high frequency noise are removal), the dashed lines represents the beat segmentation, and each beat is colored according to the output class returned by the classification algorithm.

Table 1. Confusion matrix on MIT-BIH (DS2) of our automatic screening method.

Reference	Algorithm				
	n	s	v	f	Total
N	42244	1540	99	150	44033
S	427	1601	21	1	2050
V	90	75	3051	4	3220
F	256	2	82	48	388
Total	43017	3218	3253	203	49691

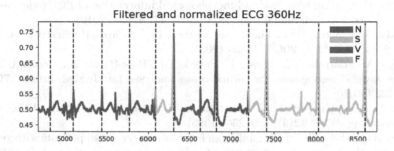

Fig. 5. Example of automatic ECG classification between four possible classes (Normal (N), Supraventricular (S), Ventricular (V) and Fusion (F)).

4 Discussions

In this work, an ECG screening tool for automatic diagnostic is presented. The presented tool performs a classification between four different arrhythmias at heartbeat level, supporting the diagnosis of the experts. In addition, this tool is included in a currently operative telemedicine framework, eDSalud. This framework is multidisciplinary, including specific modules for cardiology, dermatology, ophthalmology and radiology specialities. The use of this telemedicine framework enables some interesting future contributions. First, clinical population studies could be developed, employing the acquired information from the different specialities modules whilst also considering the personal information of the patients, sex, age, and demographic data. Second, a vast amount of ECG signals from many patients labelled by different specialists can be acquired, this allows the possibility to train better classification models, since machine learning methods are quite dependent on the quality and variability of the data employed during their training.

Acknowledgement. This work was partially supported by the Research Project RTC-2016-5143-1, financed by the Spanish Ministry of Economy, Industry and Competitiveness and the European Regional Development Fund (ERDF).

References

1. Testing and reporting performance results of cardiac rhythm and ST segment measurement algorithms. Association for the Advancement of Medical Instrumentation (1998)
2. de Chazal, P., O'Dwyer, M., Reilly, R.B.: Automatic classification of heartbeats using ECG morphology and heartbeat interval features. IEEE Trans. Biomed. Eng. **51**(7), 1196–1206 (2004)
3. Griebel, L., et al.: A scoping review of cloud computing in healthcare. BMC Med. Inform. Decis. Making **15**(1), 17 (2015)
4. Mondéjar-Guerra, V., Novo, J., Rouco, J., Penedo, M.G., Ortega, M.: Heartbeat classification fusing temporal and morphological information of ECGs via ensemble of classifiers. Biomed. Signal Process. Control **47**, 41–48 (2019)
5. Moody, G.B., Mark, R.G.: The impact of the MIT-BIH arrhythmia database. IEEE Eng. Med. Biol. Mag. **20**(3), 45–50 (2001)
6. Ortega, M., Barreira, N., Novo, J., Penedo, M., Pose-Reino, A., Gómez-Ulla, F.: Sirius: a web-based system for retinal image analysis. Int. J. Med. Inform. **79**(10), 722–732 (2010)
7. Pan, J., Tompkins, W.J.: A real-time QRS detection algorithm. IEEE Trans. Biomed. Eng. BME **32**(3), 230–236 (1985)
8. Priori, S.G., et al.: 2015 ESC guidelines for the management of patients with ventricular arrhythmias and the prevention of sudden cardiac death: the task force for the management of patients with ventricular arrhythmias and the prevention of sudden cardiac death of the European Society of Cardiology (ESC) endorsed by: Association for European Paediatric and Congenital Cardiology (AEPC). Eur. Heart J. **36**(41), 2793–2867 (2015)
9. da Luz, E.J.S., Schwartz, W.R., Cámara-Chávez, G., Menotti, D.: ECG-based heartbeat classification for arrhythmia detection: a survey. Comput. Methods Programs Biomed. **127**(Supplement C), 144–164 (2016)

Adaptive Robotic Platform
as an Inclusive Education Aid
for Children with Autism Spectrum
Disorder

Diana Lancheros-Cuesta(✉) ⓘ, Jorge Elicer Rangel ⓘ, Jose Luis Rubiano ⓘ,
and Yenny Alexandra Cifuentes ⓘ

Grupo de Investigación AVARC, Universidad de La Salle, Bogotá, Colombia
{dilancheros,jorangel,jorubiano,maick.marin}@unisalle.edu.co

Abstract. Abstract Language is the means by which a human being
understands and transmits ideas, feelings, and thoughts verbally or in
writing with other human beings. However, some people have difficulties in performing these activities, for example, in the case of autism.
High-functioning autism spectrum disorder (ASD) is a chronic, life long
condition characterized by social communication and social interaction
deficits during the educational process. The development of computational tools, that combine hardware and software, helps to overcome
these difficulties. This paper shows the development and implementa
tion of an adaptive robotic platform that aimed to construct robots to
establish a communication process with children at an educational level.

Keywords: Educational robotics · Technological platform ·
Technology · Education · Communication

1 Introduction

Autism spectrum disorder (ASD) is described as a mild or less severe type of
autism, which differs from other generalized developmental disorders, in the non-
presence of delayed language development and having IQ within normal ranges [7].
While symptoms can vary widely among individuals, autism symptoms begin to
manifest during the first 3 years of life; usually parents are the first to detect inappropriate behavior and, not according to age. Symptoms range from a poor verbal
communication, where child is unsociable and lonely or may also show no interest
in identifying objects or attracting parent's attention. In Colombia, the Ministry
of Health has withdrawn autism therapies for children from the health system [12].
Therefore, in most cases, therapies performed are isolated and do not have an adequate follow up. In addition, although the classroom environment should allow the
integration, they present many difficulties during the learning process. In this way,

Supported by Universidad de La Salle.

the development and implementation of devices allow inclusion of ASD students into the mainstream classroom [1,10]. Similarly, it is important to note that educational robotics is defined as "the activity of conception, creation and operation, with pedagogical purposes of physical and electronic technical objects" [2] Accordingly. three main stages should be taken into account when technological projects are developed in educational robotics [4].

- Conception stage: in this stage, the person or group proposes an idea or solution to a given problem, and generates on this basis a drawing or a first model which will support the implementation.
- Construction stage: according to results obtained in the previous stage, construction of the prototype is initiated by the integration of the different mechanisms and sensors selected for the device operation.
- Implementation stage: finally, in this phase the mechanism and the programming involved are tested verifying the effectiveness of the proposed models and prototypes.

In this regard, the design and implementation of a computational platform, which includes a diagnostic system and a Lego robot to facilitate the children communication, is proposed. This paper is organized as follows. Section 2 summarizes the studies in the field. Sections 3 and 4 describes the platform and Lego Robot development, respectively. Finally, in Sect. 5, the description of the case study and conclusions are presented.

2   Related Work

A review of related works is performed, focusing on two areas of research: platforms oriented to the diagnosis, monitoring and control at the educational level and educational robotics. Therefore, regarding to the first approach, Kamaruzaman et al. [9] proposed a math learning application for children with autism. The system is oriented to autistic children based on innovative interactive technologies; this platform consists of three sections: (1) Learning and discovering the numbers, (2) Numbers tracking by using images with points and (3) Learning and solving an addition problem. Lorenzo et al. [6] designed an application aimed at elementary students from 7 to 12 years old, who have a confirmed diagnosis of autistic spectrum disorder. The application is used through a virtual system, which has two objectives: to update social situations, taking into account the emotional mood of the student, and to confirm, automatically, if the child's behavior is in accordance to the social situation.

Simoes et al. [18] show that recent studies are oriented to repetitive tasks of daily life, focusing on social cognition and learning adaptive behavior. They present the high cost associated to the therapies and claim that improvements could take longer. Accordingly, they designed a web interface that allows access to the patient information monitoring, their progress and the platform use over time. The platform includes some tools based on virtual reality.

On the other hand, Carrillo et al. [3] implemented a platform with two purposes: easy access and fun for children. The platform includes 3D video games, which facilitate learning, in order to have a better follow-up and control of the activities, controlled by the therapist and the parents. In the same way, Herrera et al. [5] developed a video game based program oriented to autistic children with an emphasis on music and structured learning. Through virtual reality, children interact with the system achieving experience-based learning. Lozano et al. [8] developed teaching processes to improve emotional competences based on educational software. The implemented system showed a better performance when children developed tasks that assess the ability to understand and recognize emotions. After experimental tests, it was possible to demonstrate a development in the communicative skills of children.

Regarding to educational robotics in children with special needs, Ziaeefard et al. [14] conducted an investigation to establish the effect of learning contexts by using two robots that work with people (co-robots) to keep the commitment of university students. Evaluation results show that student's interest, in activities related to robotics, depends on their difficulty perception and their level of confidence. Strategies must be conceived in order to break down barriers and define tasks as fun activities. Similarly, Schneider et al. [16] developed a pedagogical framework oriented to work with robots in learning environments. They used robots to improve motor skills and perform physical tasks. As a contribution, they present the advantages of the interactive work with robots showing the improvement in motivation and attention during different tasks.

Malik et al. [13], on the other hand, conducted an investigation using robots for rehabilitation therapies in children with cerebral palsy. Experiments were carried out with the therapists support and showed the advantages of educational mobile robotics. Sergey et al. [17] present in their research the use of educational robotics in the classroom. Main contributions are oriented to the high motivation that students acquire when interacting with robots. Nowadays, strategies to increase motivation in students, in the classroom, include competences, processes of imitation, programming and the use of legos. Additionally, taking into account the disabilities that can occur in the classroom, Sartorato et al. [15] states that social robots are increasingly used as therapeutic tools for ASD children, in order to improve social and communication skills. In the research conducted, they demonstrated that robots generate a series of social and behavioral benefits in children with ASD. Di Lieto et al. [11] conducted a study in order to assess short-term effects in preschool children of an intensive training of educational robotics in executive functions. A sample of 12 children (age range: 5–6 years) participated in an intensive ER-Lab during 13 sessions (6 weeks) by using a bee-shaped robot, called Bee-Bot. The children were evaluated three times (baseline, pre and post) with a neuro psychological battery. The main result was a significant improvement in the visuo spatial working memory and a significant effect in robot programming skills. Yun et al. [19] developed a robot-assisted intervention system to improve social skills in ASD children through the human-robot interaction architecture (HRI). In addition, the proposed system allows teaching the reading of emotions in ASD children. As a result, it was possible to verify that proposed system can induce a positive response from ASD children, which allows the integration of this population in teaching and learning processes. Based on the aforementioned, it is important to implement educational computational platforms based on robotics to support children with special needs. The computational platform proposed in this work consists of two modules: a diagnostic system to establish the child's attention levels and the instructions and assembly of the robot. The development of the platform is detailed below.

3   Development of Diagnostic Module

The diagnostic module has a database that can be consulted by evaluators, where the classification of each of the children, in terms of attention, is verified. Taking into account the autism level, the platform shows activities to allow the child to develop cognitive skills such as attention, interpretation and memory.

Based on the selection, patients can login or register as a new user. If they are not registered, the specialist can create a new register for the patient.

When selecting the user's age, a diagnostic test will be automatically displayed, consisting of different questions. Once the test is completed, the system will indicate if the activities on the platform are adequate for the patient. The platform will indicate if the child can perform the activities, meaning that the patient has a high cognitive development. When the child or patient logins the platform, two options will be shown: spanish and math areas.

Options for the specialist: initially, in order to login in the platform, specialists must have their email and password. Then, they will be able to register users, upon entering you can register users, perform tests, and may also recommend patient treatments. The specialist can review test reports, treatment reports, developed activities, time spent to perform them and number of attempts. In statistics reports option, the specialist will have two options where test and treatment reports can be consulted. In test report option, specialists will find the patients evaluated and they will be able to review the diagnosis (YES/NO answers) as well as edit and remove it. Treatment report option will show the information of every patient. In addition, the specialist can review the general information, which includes the total number of patients on the platform, total active patients and time spent in performing the activities. For each patient, the specialist will be able to review the information of each topic, the proposed activities, number of misses and time spent to solve them correctly. Patient information allows to qualitatively evaluate the follow-up of patients/children and their evolution in the skills development. Hits numbers and time spent are analyzed in the same way to establish attentional patterns.

4 Development of Robots Module

During the construction of the robots, design criteria taken into account include lego-type mobile platform and ease of assembling for children, in order to establish an assertive communication with them. The communication is achieved when the child assembles the robot and selects, on a tablet or computer, a face that indicates his/her mood. With this information the robot performs an action (walks forward, back or lights up). These activities allow determining the state of mind of children, and attract their attention when assembling the robot.

The mechanism implemented was the Theo Jansen: this mechanical system is inspired by a horse robot and operates under the mechanism principle developed by Theo Jansen. In order to verify the adequate functioning of the mechanism, in terms of locomotion, and ensure its integrity during the movement, a dynamic analysis was performed using SolidWorks Fig. 1.

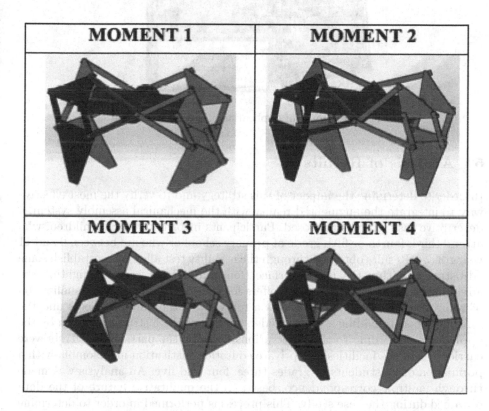

Fig. 1. Simulation results showing displacements of Theo Jansen mechanism

Instructions system is designed, using augmented reality, to guide the child during the robot assembly. When children select the piece to be assembled, they move it to the corresponding place within the mechanism, showing on the right side of the screen the result obtained. Figure 2 shows the procedure.

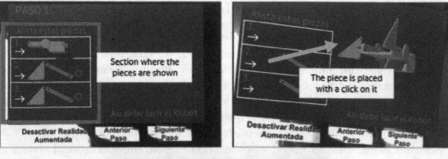

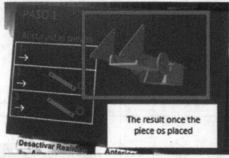

Fig. 2. Example of application of assembly tutorial

5   Analysis of Results

In order to determine the impact of this strategy and to verify the most effective way to integrate the augmented reality with the mechanical assembly system, a descriptive case study is proposed. Participants involved are ASD children, who attend third, fourth or fifth grade of primary school or who are between 9 and 11 years of age. Results obtained through the usability test allowed to establish some adjustments within the user interface (font and screen size), highlighting the advantage that augmented reality offers for the three-dimensional visualization of robot assemblies. This tool shows a full view of the different pieces and the finished robot, providing a better understanding of the instructions given by the application, according to the observations made by the participants. Tests were carried out in the facilities of a private education institution in Colombia with a population of 24 students of grades three, four and five. An analysis was made through multiple correspondence, based on the qualitative nature of the data obtained during the case study. This process is performed in order to determine the relationship and dependence between the different factors and categories and in this way, to validate the effectiveness of the implemented project. In most cases, students perceived the mechanical systems easy to assemble and the number of misses, during the execution of the instructions (regardless if instructions were in software or in a printed manual), were null or unitary in almost all tests. Likewise, the estimated time for assembling the robots was in a range from 10 to 15 min.

Based on test results, it is possible to conclude that: (a) Greatest number of misses was related to the Klann mechanism when it was assembled with the written instructor. (b) Participants between 10 and 11 years of age showed a higher level of difficulty when assembling the Klann mechanism using the written instructor. (c) Lowest number of failures was related to the assembly of the Jansen mechanism using the software as an instructor. (d) Participants between 8–10 years of age expressed greater ease when performing the assembly through the software instructor. (11) The average of assembly time for both, the Klann mechanism and the Jansen mechanism, was between 10 and 15 min, using either of two instructors.

6   Conclusions and Future Work

During the validation tests, it was evident that the robot assembling attracted children attention, which can be used in a future work to teach different concepts. Finally, according to the survey results, it was evident that the best way to integrate the augmented reality, as an assembly instructor of a mechanical system, is by using several markers. This option allows presenting the most relevant information and the user is not limited to the progressive monitoring in a certain number of steps, adapting in a better way to the work rhythm of the student.

In order to give greater coverage to this type of alternatives, during the teaching process, the range of ages of test participants could be extended. This option would allow to verify the relation between the strategies of augmented reality in robotics and the cognitive development according to the age.

References

1. Lancheros, D.J.: Diseño e implementación de un módulo didáctico para el aprendizaje en la construcción, implementación y manipulación de robots. Formación universitaria **3**(5), 3–8 (2010)
2. Denis, B. (ed.): Control Technology in Elementary Education. Nato ASI Subseries F. Springer, Heidelberg (1993). https://doi.org/10.1007/978-3-642-58026-0
3. Zambrano, E.C., Meneses, C.M.P.: Creación, diseño e implantación de plataforma e-learning utilizando mundos 3d para los niños con trastorno del espectro autista tea. Revista Educación y Desarrollo Social (2011)
4. Ruiz Velasco Sánchez, E.: Educatrónica: innovación en el aprendizaje de las ciencias y la tecnología. UNAM (2018)
5. Herrera, G., et al.: Pictogram room: Aplicación de tecnologías de interacción natural para el desarrollo del niño con autismo. Anuario de psicología clínica y de la salud = Annu. Clin. Health Psychol. **8**, 41–46 (2012)
6. Lorenzo, G., Lledó, A., Pomares, J., Roig, R.: Design and application of an immersive virtual reality system to enhance emotional skills for children with autism spectrum disorders. Comput. Educ. **98**, 192–205 (2016). https://doi.org/10.1016/j.compedu.2016.03.018

7. Hagberg, B., Billstedt, E., Nydén, A., Gillberg, C.: Asperger syndrome and non-verbal learning disabilities. Learning Disabilities Association of Ontario - LDAO (2018)
8. Lozano-Martínez, J., García, S.A.: Software educativo para la enseñanza de competencias emocionales en alumnado con trastornos del espectro autista. Educación XX1 **14**(2) (2011). https://doi.org/10.5944/educxx1.14.2.250
9. Kamaruzaman, M., Mohd Rani, N., Md Noor, H., Azahari, M.: Developing user interface design application for children with autism. Procedia - Soc. Behav. Sci. **217**, 887–894 (2016). https://doi.org/10.1016/j.sbspro.2016.02.022
10. Lancheros-Cuesta, D.J., Carrillo-Ramos, A., Pavlich-Mariscal, J.A.: Content adaptation for students with learning difficulties: design and case study. Int. J. Web Inf. Syst. (2014). https://doi.org/10.1108/ijwis-12-2013-0040
11. Di Lieto, M.C., et al.: Educational robotics intervention on executive functions in preschool children: a pilot study. Comput. Hum. Behav. **71**, 16–23 (2017). https://doi.org/10.1016/j.chb.2017.01.018
12. Marulanda, O.P.R.: Conozca los 44 servicios de salud que ya no tendrá el POS. el colombiano (2018)
13. Malik, N.A., Yussof, H., Hanapiah, F.A.: Interactive scenario development of robot-assisted therapy for cerebral palsy: a face validation survey. Procedia Comput. Sci. **105**, 322–327 (2017). https://doi.org/10.1016/j.procs.2017.01.229
14. Ziaeefard, S., Miller, M.H., Rastgaar, M., Mahmoudian, N.: Co-robotics hands-on activities: a gateway to engineering design and STEM learning. Robot. Auton. Syst. **97**, 40–50 (2017). https://doi.org/10.1016/j.robot.2017.07.013
15. Sartorato, F., Przybylowski, L., Sarko, D.K.: Improving therapeutic outcomes in autism spectrum disorders: enhancing social communication and sensory processing through the use of interactive robots. J. Psychiatr. Res. **90**, 1–11 (2017). https://doi.org/10.1016/j.jpsychires.2017.02.004
16. Schneider, S., Goerlich, M., Kummert, F.: A framework for designing socially assistive robot interactions. Cogn. Syst. Res. **43**, 301–312 (2017). https://doi.org/10.1016/j.cogsys.2016.09.008
17. Filippov, S., Ten, N., Shirokolobov, I., Fradkov, A.: Teaching robotics in secondary school. IFAC-PapersOnLine **50**, 12155–12160 (2017). https://www.sciencedirect.com/science/article/pii/S2405896317328124
18. Simões, M., Mouga, S., Pedrosa, F., Carvalho, P., Oliveira, G., Branco, M.C.: Neurohab: a platform for virtual training of daily living skills in autism spectrum disorder. Procedia Technol. **16**, 1417–1423 (2014). https://doi.org/10.1016/j.protcy.2014.10.161
19. Yun, S.S., Kim, H., Choi, J., Park, S.K.: A robot-assisted behavioral intervention system for children with autism spectrum disorders. Robot. Auton. Syst. **76**, 58–67 (2015). https://doi.org/10.1016/j.robot.2015.11.004

Smart Sensors and Communication Technologies for Triage Procedures

Maciej Nikodem[1], Jan Nikodem[1]([✉]), Ryszard Klempous[1],
Paweł Gawłowski[2], and Marek A. Bawiec[1]

[1] Faculty of Electronics, Wrocław University of Science and Technology,
Wrocław, Poland
{maciej.nikodem,jan.nikodem,ryszard.klempous,marek.bawiec}@pwr.edu.pl
[2] Department of Emergency Medical Service, Wrocław Medical University,
Wrocław, Poland
pawel.gawlowski@umed.wroc.pl

1 Introduction

This article presents various triage methods, low-power sensors and communication technologies that can be used in future wearable devices for triage. Type of devices used by rescuers during mass scale incidents to support triaging and enable more accurate and real-time examination of victim status during whole rescue action are presented.

A mass casualty incident is a sudden event with a large number of wounded people, where the capabilities of the local rescue system are insufficient. Due to the large number of victims in mass casualty incident and disasters, there is a need for medical segregation (triage) [3,5,7], which aims to determine the priorities of medical assistance and evacuation.

In mass-scale incidents it is usually the case that the number of on-site medical staff is always limited. The above mentioned issue has already attracted quite a lot of attention in recent years, as researchers were searching for a technological means to improve triage procedures [1,2,10,11].

2 First Response at the Mass Casualty Incidents

Rescue operations during a mass casualty incident consist of three levels:

- **Strategic Level** - the highest level of rescue operations covers the activity of the crisis management center staff. The task of the crisis staff is to provide all emergency services with the necessary number of forces and resources that are needed for good organization and operation at the scene of an accident.
- **Tactical Level** is the coordination of the first responder staff action. The main tasks on this level are to control the work of medical services at the scene, to recognize the current needs at the scene as well as maintain reliable and continuous communication with the crisis center.

R. Moreno-Díaz et al. (Eds.): EUROCAST 2019, LNCS 12014, pp. 305–312, 2020.
https://doi.org/10.1007/978-3-030-45096-0_38

- **Executive Level** is the last, lower level, which consists in the cooperation of all emergency services at the scene of the incident, that is all physicians, paramedics, nurses, rescue and fire-fighting units.

The rescue operation site is organized in 3 zones:

- **Safe Zone** is the area where medical assistance is provided, medical tents are set up, secondary medical segregation (re-triage) is carried out and pick up spots are designated.
- **Transport Zone** occurs on the border of the safe zone and the danger zone. There are designated roads that are used to transport the injured from the place of danger. For people who can walk independently, separate escape routes are designated.
- **Immediate Danger Zone** is an area designated by the commander of state and volunteer fire brigades, who was the first to arrive at the site of the accident. Only fire brigade members who have the right rescue equipment can enter the zone of immediate danger.

Only firefighters can stay in the area of immediate danger. Here, triage of the victims is carried out. Firemen, after moving the injured people to the safe zone, hand them over to the first responder medical services.

All data collected by people carrying out triage are transferred to the coordinator - person coordinating medical rescue operations. Coordinator has the capability of of all the victims data collecting and their categorization of the urgency of evacuation to the safe zone, from where they will be transported to medical facilities for further assistance. Coordinator also has direct communication (usually via a radio or cellular network) with the dispatcher. This allows the flow of information on the number of victims, the possibilities of their admission to specific hospitals and allocation of the victims to specific medical facilities.

2.1 Triage Procedures for Wounded People

Triage possibilities differ depending on the zone in which the victims are located. The danger zone allows quick assessment of the victim in terms of the urgency of evacuation to the field medical point. In this zone, people without medical education (fire brigade rescuers) usually work in protective clothing which limit the possibility of a detailed examination of the victim.The safe zone with medical facilities allows the implementation of re-triage action based on the detailed assessment of the victim, followed by applying adequately advanced rescue procedures.

Due to the different competencies of rescuers performing triage of the victims and the environment in which triage is carried out, several proven procedures are currently used in on over the world:

Simple Triage And Rapid Treatment (START) is one of the oldest procedure of victims segregation [6], during mass casualty events. Its simplicity allows triage to be carried out even by staff without medical skills after a short training [6]. START allows granting one of four segregation priorities based on the assessment of the following physiological parameters [8]:

- ability to move in the designated direction (mobility and understanding of commands),
- the presence of breathing and respiratory rate,
- the presence of a radial pulse or capillary refill time,
- mental status.

Care Flight Triage (CFT) is a simple, three-step procedure that evaluates the patient's ability to walk, respond to commands, and the presence of breath and radial pulse. Due to its simplicity, the estimated time of triaging the victim is about 15 s. Despite its simplicity, the sensitivity of this algorithm is relatively high (82–99%) and the specificity level is about 96% [4,5].

Triage Sieve (TS) is based on the assessment whether the victim is walking, next examine respiratory rate and capillary refill time. This procedure does not require rescue action to be carried out by the triaging person (e.g. no airway opening is foreseen). It is based on observations and measurements, therefore it perfectly suits for the automation process using computer technology devices.

Sacco Triage Method (STM) involves assessing the victim's respiratory rate, radial pulse, motor response and their age. STM is the only method that in a score way determines the chances of survival of the victim during mass casualty event. It seems that this method is characterized by the highest specificity and sensitivity [7].

Sort, Assess, Lifesaving, Treatment/Transport - SALT is a slightly more complicated two-stage method. In the first step, this method recommends a general segregation of all people wounded in the incident. In this step the assessment of the general condition of the victim is performed as follows:

- if the victim is silent or in an evident state of life threat, then he will be triaged first,
- if victim moves, showing signs of life, then he will be triaged in the second order,
- if the victim walks and obeys commands, his individual categorization will take place after victims from previous two categories.

Then, in the order resulting from general segregation an individual triage of each victim is performed. It consists of all life-saving procedures (open airway, control hemorrhaging, make chest decompression) and then on breath assessment.

If victim is not breathing, then he is considered a person who can not be saved (black marker). The presence of breath allows to go on with further evaluation, and assessment of respiratory distress, the presence of a peripheral pulse and the ability to execute commands, and whether his hemorrhage was properly stopped. If all positive, then the scale of injuries is assessed and the yellow/delayed or green/minimal markers are assigned. If there is any negative, the chances of survival of the victim in this state are subjectively assessed as red/immediate or gray/expectant.

2.2   Techniques and Communication in Triage Realization

The above-mentioned triage systems are based on the classification of victims in the set of 3–4 categories. (i.e. red/immediate, yellow/delayed, green/minimal, gray/expectant and black/dead). Most (excluding STM) are based on the categorization of victim's' colors depending on their condition and urgency of evacuation. The SALT method introduces the gray/expectant category as intended to be resource-based [9].

In triage systems, the basis for categorization of the victims is the assessment of their consciousness state (e.g. according to the Alert, Verbal, Pain, Unresponsive scale), walking abilities, respiratory rate and the presence of heart rate pulses. The first two, START and CFT systems, are the most commonly used. Next two, TS and STM are the simplest for algorithmization and implementation using technical equipment. It is because, in the TS algorithm, there are no actions of a person performing triage (even such as opening the airway) and it does not use mental status assessment. Whereas the STM algorithm, based on the score scale, is directly dedicated to the implementation with the use of simple computing devices. The last of the presented techniques - SALT indicates that the triage process can be done in two stages. This is a important signal due to the fact that the second stage in this method can be repeated many times. It enables updating the situation view, adequate to the current state of the mass casualty incident victims

The process of medical categorization begins with the screening triage. The rescuer loudly asks all people on site, able to walk, to the green collection point. There, all people are examined by rescuers and initially marked with a green code. If the injured person worsens, they may be marked with a different color and redirected to the yellow or red zone. Remaining on the event venue victims are evaluated by a rescuer performing triage. By marking them with the right color, the notes are taken in order to have control over the number of examined people and their health condition. As of today, there are no specific procedures regarding the format of the notes being taken. After examining and marking all the injured, rescuers personally provide information to the coordinator of medical rescue operations, who fills in a collective data sheet. The coordinator of emergency medical services has a contact (via the radio or telephone) with the dispatcher assigned to service mass event. As a result, information on the number of injured people and the number of available hospital beds in individual emergency departments, intensive care and operating blocks can be communicated on an ongoing basis.

3   Smart Sensor Technologies for Triage Procedures

Modern technology offers a whole range of sensors that enable measurement and monitoring of selected physical quantities. The development of the wearable technology allowed to miniaturize the systems that monitor vital human activities using non-invasive methods.

3.1 Noninvasive Sensing of Human Vital Parameters

The triage procedures discussed above categorize the victims of the mass casualty. The measured values used as the basis for categorization are respiratory rate, peripheral pulse and capillary refill time (often substitute by heartbeats rate). Wearable and IoT technologies offer more in this area:

(a) **Respiration:** thoracic impedance respiratory effort belt. A wearable respirometer measures pulmonary ventilation and the carbon dioxide and oxygen levels of expired breath, and calculates whole body respiratory quotient (RQ) (i.e. the ratio of carbon dioxide produced to oxygen consumed in expired breath).

(b) **Pulse oximeter:** there are many available devices for noninvasive monitoring a victim's oxygen saturation (SO2) as well as their heart rate. Devices work on finger or ear.

(c) **Blood pressure:** device measures systolic and diastolic blood pressure, for accurate measurement a pressure cuff that is compressed and released, is necessary, which is inconvenient. New solution is cuff-free blood pressure estimation based on pulse transit time and heart rate. The measurements are made at wrist or elsewhere. Currently the lack of medically accepted accuracy is the main drawback.

(d) **Body temperature:** the best location for device settlement are forehead or axilla (under arm). Good contact with skin and reduction of heat flows are important.

(e) **Body position:** have the versatility to identify the primary lying positions: prone, supine, left, right and upright. Body position can be continuously monitored no matter how much the patient moves. They easily and comfortably attach to the thoracic respiratory effort belt.

An example of rather complex device is Universal Health-Sensor Platform proposed by Voler. It is pre-engineering prototyping system of selecting sensors and incorporating them into a device for measurement of vital, physiological human parameters.

3.2 Position Tracking and Sensing of the Environment Parameters

- **GPS locator:** For the needs of triage, we need to accurately detect the victim's medical status and location. It is also desirable (especially within immediate danger zone) to have the first responder's tracking systems. Both of them can assist coordinator to manage with large number of person in the disaster area. The mainstream in this area are GPS based system, which offers a set of GPRMC (rescuer movement tracking), GPGLL (victim location) frames.

- **Gas sensors:** the injured and rescuers are in the area where the mass accident occurred. It is desirable to monitor threats (especially if they are in an immediate danger zone) such as concentration of combustible fumes and explosive agents. Available microchip technologies propose miniaturized sensors for concentrations of such gases as carbon monoxide, methane or hydrogen sulfide

– **Ambient temperature and humidity** monitoring of victim environment is important because the victim is most often deprived of the possibility of independent relocation. In addition, this information can be used to correct the body temperature sensor indication of the victim.

Although the devices discussed above do not have a direct impact on the implementation of triage procedure, but they have the potential to increase it's efficiency and effectiveness. Some devices offer Bluetooth as interface providing a telecommunication links to remote locations.

4   IoT and LAN Communication Solutions

Wearable triage supporting device requires connectivity in order to transmit collected measurements to first responders and to the coordinator for analysis and storage.

The most frequent used Industry Scientific and Medical (ISM) band is 2.4 GHz used by such technologies as WiFi (IEEE 802.11), BLE (IEEE 802.2) and wireless personal area networks (IEEE 802.15.4). In this band transceivers can use wide frequency bands and are only restricted with maximum power radiated from antennas. This enables relatively high data throughput (several to dozens of Mbps) on short and medium communication ranges (usually up to 100 m).

In contrast to 2.4 GHz bands the sub-GHz frequencies have more restrictions regarding medium sharing between coexisting devices, but longer communication ranges.

4.1   Bluetooth Low Energy Communication Technology

Bluetooth Low Energy (BLE) is a mature radio communication technology that was designed with low-power operation in mind for short range applications. Recent, 5th version of BLE standard, introduces new interesting features while maintaining low power consumption, including; different communication throughput, extended communication range, larger payloads in advertisement messages, and high duty cycle advertisements.

While previous versions of BLE standard utilized only 1 Mbps throughput over 2 MHz width bandwidth, the 5th version also introduces faster communication 2 Mbps and two slower ones: 125 kbps and 500 kbps. Smaller throughput are achieved by modifying the coding scheme used. In 125 and 500 kbps modes packets are encoded using forward error correction (FEC) code with 8 and 2 symbols per bit respectively. This enables communication over less reliable communication channels and over larger distances.

New version of BLE standard also enables use of long payloads in advertisement messages (messages that are broadcasted in connection-less communication). Typically BLE allows for 31 bytes of data in advertisement payload while extended advertisements allow to transmit as much as 255 bytes of data.

New version of BLE also introduces low and high duty cycle advertisements. High duty cycle requires that advertisements are transmitted every 3.75 ms or less. Although high duty cycle advertisements cannot contain data they have potential benefits for the applications (e.g. shorter delays on connection or reconnection). High duty cycle also consumes radio bandwidth, therefore the device should use it not longer than 1.28 s.

4.2 Long Range Wide Area Network Communication

Long Range (LoRa) is one of the low-power and long-range wireless technologies dedicated to IoT applications where small amount of data are transmitted form large number of spatially distributed sensors to gateways and cloud servers. LoRa uses sub-GHz frequencies which have better propagation properties (smaller attenuation) and less interference compared to crowded 2.4 GHz spectrum.

Using long spreading sequences allows for long range transmissions (even up to 10–20 km in rural areas) with small throughput (250 bps). LoRa data packets can contain between 59 and 230 bytes of data depending on the spreading used.

LoRaWAN is one of the dedicated protocol stacks for LoRa networks, that inherently supports IoT applications using star of stars topology. In this approach LoRa enabled end-devices transmit messages over LoRa radio to gateways that route them to the Internet and LoRa Servers. Servers are responsible for routing messages, management of the network of gateways and ensuring security of communication.

4.3 Narrow Band IoT WAN Technology

Narrow Band IoT (NB-IoT) is a new cellular technology that is designed to operate in licensed frequency bands traditionally used by telecom operators. Technology is still under rollout and its deployments are limited in coverage. The advantage of NB-IoT is that it can coexist with other cellular technologies and thus can be introduced within existing operator's network and available frequency spectrum.

5 Conclusion

Contemporary, promising results in smart sensors and IoT technologies has pave their way to triage application, because they became relatively cheap and satisfactory reliable. It happened because of the rapid development of low-power, communication wearable and IoT technologies as well as miniaturization of senors and electronic devices in recent years.

Aforementioned properties of BLE and extensions introduced in 5th version of the standard have positive implication to support triage using smart sensors. The use of FEC enables longer communication distances and improves reliability thus enabling use of BLEv5 on accident site. Use of connection-less communication based on the advertisements improves coexistence of devices and enables information sharing between number of rescuers. Simultaneously high duty cycle advertisements can be used for establishment of connection in critical situation and exchange information, e.g. when victims condition drastically degrades.

Currently offered, dedicated wearable device can be used in triage procedures and will support first responders, medical doctors and hospitals in providing health care to casualties of mass-scale incidents. Utilization of low-power sensors, microcontrollers and communication technologies allow to provide health information of individual victim in real-time.

References

1. Albahri, O.S., et al.: Systematic review of real-time remote health monitoring system in triage and priority-based sensor technology: taxonomy, open challenges, motivation and recommendations. J. Med. Syst. **42**(5), 80 (2018). https://doi.org/10.1007/s10916-018-0943-4
2. Gao, T., et al.: The advanced health and disaster aid network: a light-weight wireless medical system for triage. IEEE Trans. Biomed. Circuits Syst. **1**(3), 203–216 (2007). https://doi.org/10.1109/TBCAS.2007.910901
3. Garner, A., Lee, A., Harrison, K., Schultz, C.H.: Comparative analysis of multiple-casualty incident triage algorithms. Ann. Emerg. Med. **2001**(38), 541–548 (2001)
4. Heller, A.R., Salvador, N., Frank, M., Schiffner, J., Kipke, R., Kleber, C.: Diagnostic precision of triage algorithms for mass casualty incidents. English version. Der Anaesthesist **68**(1), 15–24 (2017). https://doi.org/10.1007/s00101-017-0352-y
5. Jenkins, J.L., et al.: Mass-casualty triage: time for an evidence-based approach. Prehosp. Disaster Med. **23**(1), 3–8 (2008)
6. Kahn, C.A., Shultz, C.H., Miller, K.T.: Does START triage work? An outcomes assessment after a disaster. Ann. Emerg. Med. **54**, 424–430 (2009)
7. Lerner, E.B., Schwartz, R.B., Coule, P.L., Weinstein, E.W., et al.: Mass casualty triage: an evaluation of the data and development of a proposed national guideline. Disaster Med. Public Health Preparedness **2**(S1), S25–S34 (2013). https://doi.org/10.1097/DMP.0b013e318182194e
8. Navin, D.M., Sacco, W.J., Waddell, R.: Operational comparison of the Simple triage and Rapid treatment method and the Sacco triage method in mass casualty exercises. J. Trauma Acute Care Surg. **69**(1), 215–225 (2010)
9. Navin, D., Sacco, W.J.: Science and evidence-based considerations for fulfilling the SALT triage framework. Disaster Med. Public Health Preparedness **4**(1), 10–12 (2010)
10. Niswar, M., Wijaya, A.S., Ridwan, M., Adnan Ilham, A.A., Sadjad, R.S., Vogel, A.: The design of wearable medical device for triaging disaster casualties in developing countries. In: 2015 Fifth International Conference on Digital Information Processing and Communications (ICDIPC), pp. 207–212 (2015). https://doi.org/10.1109/ICDIPC.2015.7323030
11. Sakanushi, K., et al.: Electronic triage system for continuously monitoring casualties at disaster scenes. J. Ambient Intell. Humaniz. Comput. **4**(5), 547–558 (2012). https://doi.org/10.1007/s12652-012-0130-2

Motion Capture Analysis Supporting Lifting Technique Optimization for Occupational Safety Diagnosis

Ryszard Klempous[1](✉) , Jan Nikodem[1] , Konrad Kluwak[1] ,
Maciej Nikodem[1] , Anna Kołcz[3] , Paweł Gawłowski[4] , Jerzy Rozenblit[6],
Christopher Chiu[2] , and Marek Olesiak[5]

[1] Faculty of Electronics, Wrocław University of Science and Technology,
Wrocław, Poland
{ryszard.klempous,jan.nikodem,konrad.kluwak,maciej.nikodem}@pwr.edu.pl
[2] Faculty of Engineering and IT, University of Technology Sydney, Ultimo, Australia
christopher.chiu@uts.edu.au
[3] Department of Physiotherapy, Wrocław Medical University, Wrocław, Poland
anna.kolcz@umed.wroc.pl
[4] Department of Emergency Medical Services, Wrocław Medical University,
Wrocław, Poland
[5] Faculty of Engineering, University of Applied Sciences, Wałcz, Poland
[6] Faculty of Electrical and Computer Engineering, University of Arizona,
Tucson, USA

1 Introduction

Musculoskeletal function disorders are the most common health problem in the European Union. Improper strain on the musculoskeletal system, during the daily activities of work, constitutes an important source of concern because of the health effects of the employee, as well as the financial consequences for the employer. Additionally, time off work and social costs are also a notable concern. In some countries, musculoskeletal disorders represent 40% of employee compensation costs and up to 1.6% of the state's Gross Domestic Product [3].

The UK Health and Safety Executive performed human resource analysis determining that one out of four nurses are on sick leave as a result of back injury during their professional activities [4]. Moreover, over 5000 injuries occurring in this occupational group are a result of manual activity, and half during patient movement. Movement of patients is the main cause of work injury in the medical workplace, while support staff are often injured during heavy object handling. Another important element is the uncomfortable, static positions of the body during work activity that is a source of strain on the musculoskeletal system.

Diagnosing work safety to optimize the technique of lifting heavy objects, such as patient movement, should focus on the factors resulting from the occupation, which in the context of musculoskeletal system disorders include: lifting, supporting, stacking, pushing, pulling, and/or moving. The type of weights employees in the healthcare sector must deal with can be an inanimate object

© Springer Nature Switzerland AG 2020
R. Moreno-Díaz et al. (Eds.): EUROCAST 2019, LNCS 12014, pp. 313–320, 2020.
https://doi.org/10.1007/978-3-030-45096-0_39

such as a laundry container or a wheeled table, but mostly animated, i.e. lifting patients. The criteria for assessing the risks associated with manual load handling, in particular where spinal injury can occur, is defined in Annex I European Council Directive 90/269/EEC [3]:

- *Heavy:* Although no exact limit on safe weight is specified, for most people, an object with a weight of 20–25 kg is difficult to lift.
- *Large:* When it is not possible to apply the basic principles of lifting and moving, resulting in greater muscle fatigue.
- *Difficult to Handle:* With the risk of slipping from the hands, with the consequence of causing injury.
- *Unstable:* Due to uneven muscle load and rapid fatigue resulting from the object's center of gravity being away from the center of the worker's body.
- *Difficult to Reach:* By reaching with outstretched arms, in combination or with tilted and/or twisting of the trunk, as this requires conscious stabilization of the torso and increased muscle strength.
- *Shaped and/or Sized:* Being significant to limit the field of view of the employee, with the possibility of stumbling, lack of control, slipping or collision.

2   Spinal Column Mechanical Principles for Lifting

The structure of the spine consists of the following elements [6]:

- *Vertebrae:* The column made of bone elements between which there are intervertebral discs.
- *Discs:* The oval ring element built in the peripheral part of a strong, compacted fibro-collagenous tissue.
- *Nucleus:* The nucleus pulposus is the liquid-like element inside the fibrous ring.

The placement of the spinal bone structure is subject to constant pressure from the surrounding elements. Although it has elements of rigidity, it also has mobile structural characteristics, with mobility provided by the muscles and ligaments surrounding the spine. The spine in connection with the functions it performs is not completely straight, but has three physiological bends in the sagittal plane [6]:

- *Cervical Spine (C):* First part being forward bend, it is the cervical lordosis.
- *Thoracic Segment (Th):* Second part is bent slightly backward, it is the thorax kyphosis.
- *Lumbar Segment (L):* Lowest part of the spine, like the first part is also bent forward, it is called the lumbar lordosis.

Properly shaped bends of the spine cause the spine to achieve the so-called neutral setting. Although the spinal movements are physiological and healthy, the most effective in terms of functionality is when the spine has a neutral or safe position.

2.1 Reducing Undue Spinal Stress

In situations where the spine bends and twists too often, the intervertebral discs can break and constrict the surrounding structures. The most common problem is pressure on the nerve roots, which go from the spinal cord and run along the entire length of the spine, as they control the work of organs and receive pain stimuli. Nerve roots move with the body movement and receive information from the body. Nervous sensitivity becomes greater at the time of mechanical irritation. The ability to control defense mechanisms that arise from the load or irritation of periorbital structures is very strongly associated with muscle activity.

Employees in the health care sector make a number of mistakes related to everyday life and professional activities, including excessively bending the spine, instead of using the power generated during movement in the hip joints. When performing such activities, muscles stabilizing the torso should be active, stiffening or stabilizing the spine in this way. Repeated bending of the spine will eventually cause pain located in the lumbar region of the spine. Adopted body posture is closely related to the load on the joints. Compressive forces affect the joints perpendicular to them, with painful forces affecting the body when it is in certain positions under heavy loads. Limiting these forces allows for a proper body position, and prepare the muscles for strain beforehand.

3 Application of Motion Capture Analysis

Motion capture analysis (MCA) is the tracking and analysis of movements for a biological entity. In this work, lifting technique optimization for occupational safety diagnosis in conjunction with MCA is of interest as we need to study the movements of medical staff in their lifting practice in space, along with how they coordinate their muscles as they perform their maneuver in their regular, day-to-day activities. By making quantifiable studies of the gait of the subject over a period, specialist clinicians can make effective, interpretive analysis based on the age, health and personal history of the individual.

The technologies of MCA are well established, with an analysis of various methodologies considered for monitoring the lifting methodology of the subject. Gait analysis has transitioned from analogous methods in the late 1800's [7] into the digital age by the late 1980's, with the active industries being aerospace, biometric security, advanced medical science and commercial television broadcasting. As these industries have the resources to conduct MCA where financial constraints are not a priority, as such they have been focused on optimizing the precision and accuracy of gait analysis.

Hence, the technology of MCA is now far more applicable in broader-based applications – most notably for consumer and civilian commercial purposes. Along with the well-known applications of MCA in the personal entertainment and gaming fields; there is also a greater array of health science applications that are being explored in the medical domain, including home-based tele-health services and highly targeted, personalized medical patient care.

3.1   MCA for Lifting Practice Applications

In our research study, we will consider in-depth the chiropractic and osteopathic analysis that is applicable in our research into lifting technique optimization for occupational safety diagnosis, and how MCA can actively enhance the clinical diagnosis of correct lifting techniques. The principles of correct lifting practice is well reinforced in employment training along with follow-up analysis and study [9]. Using MCA enhances the training of good lifting techniques and reinforces positive, healthy practice as shown in Fig. 1.

Incorrect technique identification highlights to the candidate that they are compensating for muscular strain or other related difficulties and persisting with incorrect practice will lead to prolonged health issues over time. The key is to capture the main data points of the trainee during the initial preparation of bending over to the patient, undertaking the act of holding the patient and the stage of lifting the patient while load bearing. Monitoring staff techniques over time is essential to determine the effectiveness of the training platform [9].

3.2   Gait Capture Techniques

Marker-Less Gait Capture
Marker-less gait capture is a non-invasive approach to MCA. Marker-less gait capture has gained prominence in many fields including commercial gaming applications, most notably Microsoft Kinect, demonstrating its potential as it does not require additional equipment or tools besides the monitoring hardware. In addition, the removal of markers allows the greater exploration into gait analysis, as the preparatory time required to setup the equipment is simplified, while allowing for the subject to conduct their movements with their own uniform.

Marker Gait Capture
Active Marker Systems. It use 'active' markers as they require a power source. The markers listen to or observe the synchronization signals from the base monitor, by means of an incoming infra-red signal and respond by transmitting a corresponding signal. Time-of-Flight principles are used to triangulate the marker's location, as the time difference for each marker will vary slightly based on the marker's position for each joint on the human body.

Passive Marker Systems. It use "passive" markers, as the markers do not require a power source for operation. Typically, the use of reflective markers, shaped as spherical balls, are used. A multiple camera setup is used, employing five to twelve cameras, to record the movement measurements simultaneously. High-power infra-red strobes are utilized by the cameras to record the marker reflections placed across the human subject using Time-of-Flight concepts. To develop the lifting technique optimization for occupational safety diagnosis platform, a balance between flexibility and precision must be established. As we are developing an effective training resource for the working productivity of healthcare workers, the main importance is allowing the subject to conduct their movements with the least amount of intrusion while they perform the lifting maneuver [6].

1. Turn in bed toward lifter from back to left.   *6.* Move patient from sitting to supine position.

2. Reposition from lying in middle to bedside.   *7.* Transfer patient from sitting to wheelchair.

3. Turn in bed away from back to right side.   *8.* Reposition patient posterior on wheelchair.

4. Elevate from supine to the sitting position.   *9.* Reposition supine patient to the bed head.

5. Lift patient from edge of bed to the floor.   *10.* Standard Lift.

Fig. 1. Best practice technique for manual patient lifting

The summary of gait capture techniques to be considered in the study are considered in Table 1. Therefore, the use of a passive marker system is most suitable in this situation, as although precision is compromised compared to active marker systems, its lower cost and higher degree of flexibility means we can deploy the monitoring hardware with minimal supervision from a trained technician. As well, this helps to minimize the risk of error resulting from circumstances or situations that lead to incorrect movement analysis and final diagnosis, such as improper placement of markers on the monitored subject.

3.3   Current Motion Capture Technologies

Recognition of activities performed by a human is based on detecting and analyzing information, as obtained from a variety of sensor systems. The greater the array of sensors, the higher the accuracy of the data collected is enhanced,

Table 1. Identified gait capture technologies

	Marker system		Marker-less system
	Active marker	Passive marker	
Advantage	• Highest precision level as markers have unique identification	• Higher precision level over marker-less system • Lower cost over active marker system	• Non-invasive over to active marker systems • Lowest cost of implementation
Disadvantage	• Invasive marker usage • High cost of active markers	• Invasive marker usage • Higher cost over marker-less systems	• Higher post-process work required • Reduced accuracy over marker systems

while most importantly minimizing noise that affects the quality of the information gathers. Many modern commercial platforms integrate multiple sensor types into their hardware, so the task of sensor fusion is a feasible task with the supported libraries and development kits [9]. The data fusion operation typically takes place on the connected computing device, as the computational capability is greater and more capable than on the sensor equipment as shown in Table 2.

Table 2. Summary of various modalities for human motion capture

	R.G.B. video camera	Depth camera	Inertial sensor
Advantage	• Cost effective and wide availability • Easy operation • Provides rich scene texture information	• Low cost and available • Illumination insensitive • Works in darkness • Provides 3D structure • Easy operation • Color/texture insensitive environment	• Cost effective and readily available • High sample rate • Works in darkness • Works in unconfined
Disadvantage	• Requires subject in field of view • Sensitive to light • Sensitive to camera calibration • Intensive algorithms	• Requires subject in field of view • Different noise present • Depth data insensitive to variances in reflection • No color available	• Location sensitive • Sensor drift • Sensors need power • Multiple sensors for full body motion • Intrusive sensor gear

4 Proposed MCA Technologies for Lifting Technique Optimization

4.1 Motion Capture Systems Employed

At the Virtual Medical Technology Center of Wrocław University of Science and Technology, we employ the current experimental setup:

- *ToF Camera*: Microsoft Xbox Kinect, Softkinetic DepthSense 311 and 525.
- *OptiTrack System*: 8 OptiTrack Cameras with Motion Capture System.
- *Laboratory Setup*: 3 laboratories to carry out extensive measurement exams.

4.2   Background Research Utilized

Work-Related Musculoskeletal Disorders in Home-Care Nursing

The research case study of main risk factors by Carneiroa et al. [1] determines the factors that can lead to the absence or contribution to lumbar issues for health care workers, including nursing staff. The model of statistics that is proposed can rightly identify the discomfort associated with lumbar risk with a probability of 88.4%. The risk concerns include forearm and static posture, arm position, hand support and bed height.

Biomechanical Strain Based on Stabilizing Shoulder Joint

The work of Chowdhury et al. [2] examines musculoskeletal disorders (MSD), particularly concerning the joint of the shoulder, is measured with the Vicon motion capture platform and surface electromyography (SEMG). The recorded motion data was accomplished with Vicon MX system consisting of 8 cameras at 100 Hz sample rate. 20 markers were positioned at strategic landmarks of the participants. Arm muscle performance was assessed using SEMG to ascertain the shoulder strain for fatigue and muscle demand factors.

Systemic Framework for Ergonomic Evaluation of Patient Handling

Kumar and Ray [5] discuss how healthcare workers are routinely engaged in working with medical patients can suffer from various complexities as a result of uncomfortable positioning during transfers of patients in a manual way. Risk factors include inappropriate methods when dealing with medical patients, and the absence of formal training programs. As a result, ailments include back injuries, musculoskeletal disorders, arm, neck or knee injuries, carpal tunnel syndrome, high levels of significant physical stresses and anthropometric mismatch.

3D Bio-Mechanical Evaluation of Lower-Back Load

Skotte et al. [8] evaluate manual patient-handling work by using a 3D biomechanical model to determine the net torque at the junction of L4/L5 of the spine. The force plate was employed to measure the reactivity of the substrate and transducer of force is positioned in the patient bed for reaction taking place. EMG is adopted to record activity of the muscle by use of a video system (50-channels) using 5 cameras using the Peak Motus 4.3 development platform.

5   Conclusion

The optimum approach is focusing on the development of a motion capture system utilizing tag detection and analysis, whereby the candidate will be assessed in their current lifting approach and quantitatively assessed for their overall technique. Utilizing motion capture analysis algorithms and filtering excess signal noise, we then perform meta-tagging of key joint maneuvers to identify biomechanical points where the trainee can improve their lifting techniques.

The problem of determining the kinematic or locomotion activity of a subject matter is also of importance, specifically human subjects in a given space. The use of support vector machines, random forest or neural network approaches is required to analyze the human subject as they perform the maneuver and adjust their position accordingly.

Framing the problem within an appropriate structure is an essential task, such that the data can be prepared appropriately. These steps, once finessed and optimized effectively, are a semi-automated process and require minimal user intervention. Thus, we evaluate the main models for human activity recognition useful for patient lifting best practice and analyzing the lumbar sections.

In addition to assessing the quantitative analysis of the candidate trainees, the trainees are also requested to provide qualitative feedback on the system. This is to ensure the system must be beneficial in terms of human user interaction to the trainee and trainer to provide constructive feedback for further feature enhancement.

References

1. Carneiro, P., Braga, A.C., Barroso, M.: Work-related musculoskeletal disorders in home care nurses: study of the main risk factors. Int. J. Ind. Ergon. **61**, 22–28 (2017). https://doi.org/10.1016/j.ergon.2017.05.002
2. Chowdhury, S.K., Nimbarte, A.D., Hsiao, H., Gopalakrishnan, B., Jaridi, M.: A biomechanical shoulder strain index based on stabilizing demand of shoulder joint. Ergonomics **16**(12), 1657–1670 (2018). https://doi.org/10.1080/00140139.2018.1499967. http://www.tandfonline.com/action/journalInformation?journalCode=terg20
3. European Commission, Directorate-General for Employment, Social Affairs and Inclusion: Occupational health and safety risks in the healthcare sector, guide to prevention and good practice. Publications Office of the European Union (2013)
4. European Risk Observatory Report: Current and emerging occupational safety and health (OSH) issues in the healthcare sector, including home and community care. Publications Office of the European Union, Luxembourg (2014)
5. Ray, P.K., Maiti, J. (eds.): Healthcare Systems Management: Methodologies and Applications. MAC. Springer, Singapore (2018). https://doi.org/10.1007/978-981-10-5631-4
6. McGill, S.: Back Mechanic: The Step-by-Step McGill Method for Back Pain (2018). https://www.backfitpro.com/books/back-mechanic-the-mcgill-method-to-fix-back-pain/
7. Motion Capture Society: The History and Current State of motion capture (2019). http://www.motioncapturesociety.com/resources/industry-history
8. Skotte, J.H., Essendrop, M., Hansen, A.F., Schibye, B.: A dynamic 3D biomechanical evaluation of the load on the low back during different patient-handling tasks. J. Biomech. Sci. **35**, 1357–1366 (2002)
9. Skublewska-Paszkowska, M., et al.: Motion capture as a modern technology for analysing ergometer rowing. Adv. Sci. Technol. Res. J. **10**(29), 132–140 (2016). https://doi.org/10.12913/22998624/61941. http://www.astrj.com/motion-capture-as-a-modern-technology,61941,0,2.html

Advances in Biomedical Signal and Image Processing

ECG Morphological Changes Due to Age and Heart Rate Variability

Kyriaki Kostoglou$^{(\boxtimes)}$ (iD) and Carl Böck (iD)

Institute of Signal Processing, Johannes Kepler University, Linz, Austria
{kyriaki.kostoglou,carl.boeck}@jku.at

Abstract. The electrocardiogram (ECG) constitutes one of the most useful diagnostic tools for evaluating the overall health of the heart. ECG interpretation involves the assessment of various heartbeat interval features, as well as ECG wave morphological patterns and variations. However, electrocardiographic alterations are associated with a multitude of factors, which sometimes are difficult to differentiate. In this paper, we propose a system identification based methodology that quantifies the dynamic effects of heart rate variability (HRV) and age on the ECG morphology. Specifically, samples of the ECG waveform of healthy young and elderly subjects were modeled as linear and nonlinear autoregressive processes (AR). The effects of HRV were investigated by considering the HRV time-series as an exogenous input to the system. Age-related ECG wave alterations were also examined by statistically comparing the differences in the predictive performance of the AR models in the two groups.

Keywords: Heart rate variability · Ageing · ECG · Morphology · Radial basis functions · Autoregressive model · Exogenous input · Genetic algorithm

1 Introduction

Ageing is one of the multiple factors associated with electrocardiographic alterations. The normal ageing process induces changes in the cardiovascular and autonomic nervous system that are reflected in the electrocardiogram (ECG) [1]. Autonomic dysregulation in elderly and specifically prevalence of sympathetic tone over parasympathetic activity [2, 3] contributes to the increase of blood pressure and decrease of heart rate (HR) and heart rate variability (HRV) with age. In addition, increased vascular stiffness and aortic impedance observed in healthy elderly subjects has been linked with ECG QTc prolongations [4] i.e., increased duration of ventricular depolarization and repolarization. HRV (i.e., the capacity of the heart to respond and adapt to physiological challenges), which is known to be significantly influenced by age [5], has also by itself a profound effect on the ECG waveform characteristics. It has been shown, for example, that beat-to-beat QT interval variability can be partially explained by HRV [6–8]. Physiologically, this is described by the cardiac restitution mechanism whereby HR changes modulate the electrical excitation and repolarization of the heart [9]. Most of the aforementioned studies have focused on the effect of age and HRV on specific beat-to-beat ECG interval

© Springer Nature Switzerland AG 2020
R. Moreno-Díaz et al. (Eds.): EUROCAST 2019, LNCS 12014, pp. 323–330, 2020.
https://doi.org/10.1007/978-3-030-45096-0_40

variations (e.g. QT, PR). Such approaches, however, ignore the wealth of information contained in the remainder of the waveform shape. Herein, we investigated age and HRV related changes of the ECG waveform using system identification techniques. Specifically, we analyzed ECG signals from healthy young and elderly subjects. For both cohorts, the evolution of each sample of the extracted ECG waveform was modeled in time using both linear and nonlinear autoregressive (AR) models [10]. The effect of HRV on the ECG morphology was quantified as the improvement in the model predictive performance when considering HRV as an exogenous input.

2 Experimental Data

ECG signals were obtained from the Physionet/Fantasia database [11]. The database consists of ECG recorded from 20 young (21–34 years old) and 20 elderly (68–85 years old) healthy subjects in supine position, watching the Disney movie Fantasia. 60 Hz power line interference and harmonics were removed from the ECG signals by applying the PCA/SVD filtering method implemented in BioSig (remove5060hz.m). Baseline wander correction and high frequency noise (>100 Hz) removal was achieved using a Chebyshev type II filter. HRV was computed based on the timing of the R peaks (provided in the annotations). The non-uniformly sampled HRV time-series were interpolated in order to obtain uniformly spaced intervals and downsampled to 12 Hz. The ECG was sliced into single beats by considering 0.24 s and 0.44 s before and after the R peak, respectively (Fig. 1a – top panel). Each sample of the ECG waveform was then tracked in time, creating multiple time-series that describe the time evolution of each point of the waveform (Fig. 1a – bottom panel).

3 Methods

3.1 Linear Models - Autoregressive Model with Exogenous Input (ARX)

Autoregressive (AR) models have been widely used in time-series analysis to describe random processes that exhibit serial autocorrelation. An AR model predicts the future behavior of a time-series based on its past behavior. An extension of the AR is the *Autoregressive Model with Exogenous Input* (ARX). The ARX retains the structure of the AR model, but in addition it models the dynamic response of a system to an exogenous factor. In discrete time, an ARX model of order (p, q) is defined as [10],

$$y(n) = \sum_{i=1}^{p} a_i y(n-i) + \sum_{j=0}^{q} b_j x(n-j) + \varepsilon(n) = c^T \varphi(n) + \varepsilon(n) \quad (1)$$

where n represents the discrete time, $y \in R^{N \times 1}$ is the output or else the time-series under consideration, N is the total number of samples, $x \in R^{N \times 1}$ is the exogenous input, $\varepsilon \in R^{N \times 1}$ is assumed to be zero-mean white noise, $c^T = [a_1 \ldots a_p \, b_0 \ldots b_q]$ contains the model coefficients, whereas $\varphi^T(n) = [y(n-1) \ldots y(n-p) \, x(n) \ldots x(n-q)]$ is the regressor vector at time instant n. Based on Eq. (1), at each time point the output is expressed as the linear combination of its past values, as well as present and past values of the exogenous input. Note that if an exogenous input is not considered Eq. (1) reduces to a simple AR model. In matrix form Eq. (1) can be written as,

$$y = \Phi c + \varepsilon \tag{2}$$

where $\Phi \in R^{N \times d}$ is the regressor matrix, $c \in R^{d \times 1}$ is the coefficient vector and d is the total number of model coefficients (i.e., $d_{AR} = p$ for the AR case and $d_{ARX} = p+q+1$ for the ARX case). The unknown coefficients c can be estimated using the Least Squares (LS) solution,

$$\hat{c} = \left(\Phi^T \Phi \right)^{-1} \Phi^T y \tag{3}$$

The predicted output at each time point is given as,

$$\hat{y} = \Phi \hat{c} \tag{4}$$

3.2 Nonlinear Models - Radial Basis Function Based Autoregressive Model with Exogenous Input (RBF-ARX)

In AR/ARX models, the dependencies between present and past input/output lags are purely linear. One class of models that can actually describe complex nonlinear dynamics is the *state-dependent AR model with functional coefficients*, proposed by Vesin [12] as an extension of the exponential autoregressive (ExpAR) model. The state-dependent ARX model follows the same structure as the ARX, however its coefficients are nonlinear functions of a predefined state vector [12–14],

$$y(n) = \sum_{i=1}^{p} f_i\{\Upsilon(n)\} \cdot y(n-i) + \sum_{j=0}^{q} h_j\{\Upsilon(n)\} \cdot x(n-i) + \varepsilon(n) \tag{5}$$

where $f_i\{\Upsilon(n)\}$ is the i-th autoregressive functional coefficient and $h_j\{\Upsilon(n)\}$ the j-th exogenous term functional coefficient at time n. $\Upsilon(n) \in R^{l \times 1}$ is regarded as the state vector at time instant n and is usually defined as a subvector of $\varphi^T(n) = [y(n-1) \dots y(n-p) \, x(n) \dots x(n-q)]$. Each coefficient is expressed as a linear combination of a fixed number of radial basis functions (RBF),

$$f_i\{\Upsilon(n)\} = a_{i0} + \sum_{k=1}^{F} a_{ik} e^{\left(-\frac{\|\Upsilon(n) - z_{f_k}\|^2}{s_{f_k}} \right)} \tag{6}$$

$$h_j\{\Upsilon(n)\} = b_{j0} + \sum_{k=1}^{H} b_{jk} e^{\left(-\frac{\|\Upsilon(n) - z_{h_k}\|^2}{s_{h_k}} \right)} \tag{7}$$

where $Z_{f_k}, Z_{h_k} \in R^{l \times 1}$ are the centers of the k-th RBFs used for the autoregressive and the exogenous input terms, respectively, $s_f = [s_{f_1} \dots s_{f_F}]$ and $s_h = [s_{f_1} \dots s_{f_H}]$

contain the scaling parameters that control the RBF smoothness and $\boldsymbol{a}_i = [a_{i0} \cdots a_{iF}]$, $\boldsymbol{b}_j = [b_{j0} \cdots b_{jH}]$ are weight vectors. The idea behind Eqs. (6–7) is that the exponential term should become very small when $\boldsymbol{\Upsilon}(n)$ moves away from the center $\boldsymbol{Z}_k$. For simplicity, herein, we assumed that $F = H$, $\boldsymbol{Z}_{f_k} = \boldsymbol{Z}_{h_k}$ and $s_f = s_h$, i.e., both autoregressive and exogenous terms share the same RBFs. Based on the aforementioned assumptions, we reformulated Eq. (5) as,

$$y(n) = \boldsymbol{c}^T(n)\boldsymbol{\xi}(n) + \varepsilon(n) \tag{8}$$

where $\boldsymbol{c} \in \boldsymbol{R}^{d \times 1}$ is the coefficient vector, $\boldsymbol{\xi}(n) \in \boldsymbol{R}^{d \times 1}$ is the regressor and d is the total number of model coefficients ($d_{RBF-AR} = (F+1)p$, $d_{RBF-ARX} = (F+1)(p+q+1)$). For the RBF-ARX model, Eq. (8) can be written as,

$$y(n) = [\boldsymbol{a}_1 \cdots \boldsymbol{a}_p \ \boldsymbol{b}_0 \cdots \boldsymbol{b}_q]\{[\boldsymbol{\varphi}(n) \otimes 1]^{\circ} \boldsymbol{M}(n)\} + \varepsilon(n) \tag{9}$$

where $\otimes$ denotes the Kronecker product and $^{\circ}$ the Hadamard product. $\boldsymbol{c} = [\boldsymbol{a}_1 \cdots \boldsymbol{a}_p \ \boldsymbol{b}_0 \cdots \boldsymbol{b}_q]^T$ is the coefficient vector, $1 \in \boldsymbol{R}^{(F+1) \times 1}$ is a vector of ones, $\boldsymbol{\varphi}^T(n) = [y(n-1) \dots y(n-p) \ x(n) \dots x(n-q)]$ is the regressor vector used in the linear ARX models, $\boldsymbol{M}(n) = [\boldsymbol{m}(n) \cdots \boldsymbol{m}(n)]^T \in \boldsymbol{R}^{(F+1)(p+q+1) \times 1}$ and

$$\boldsymbol{m}(n) = \left[1 \ e^{\left(-\frac{\|\boldsymbol{\Upsilon}(n-1)-\boldsymbol{Z}_{f_1}\|^2}{s_{f_1}}\right)} \ \cdots \ e^{\left(-\frac{\|\boldsymbol{\Upsilon}(n-1)-\boldsymbol{Z}_{f_F}\|^2}{s_{f_F}}\right)}\right]^T \in \boldsymbol{R}^{(F+1) \times 1} \tag{10}$$

Equation (9) can be efficiently written in matrix form as follows,

$$\boldsymbol{y} = \boldsymbol{\Phi}\boldsymbol{c} + \boldsymbol{\varepsilon} \tag{11}$$

where $\boldsymbol{\Phi} \in \boldsymbol{R}^{N \times d}$ is the regressor matrix. The unknown coefficients $\boldsymbol{c}$ can be estimated using the Least Squares (LS) solution (Eq. (4)).

3.3 Model Order Selection and Hyperparameter Optimization

In the linear case, model order selection involves the appropriate choice of the orders p and q of the AR/ARX models. In the nonlinear case, model complexity is defined by two main components; the AR/ARX model structure (i.e., p and q), as well as the number of RBFs used to approximate the state-dependent coefficients. Hyperparameter optimization, on the other hand, involves the tuning of the RBF hyperparameters, i.e., the centers and the scaling parameters, which is a highly nonlinear optimization problem. Model order selection and hyperparameter optimization can be realized using for example exhaustive search. However, this can be a very time consuming or even sometimes impractical procedure. The present study proposes an heuristic approach based on a mixed integer Genetic Algorithm (GA) [15, 16], which is effective in searching complex multidimensional spaces without any prior information. The GA assesses different candidate solutions, i.e., combinations of hyperparameters and model structures, until it reaches a global minimum for a predefined fitness function. In the linear case, the candidate solutions for the AR/ARX models are of the form,

$$S_{AR} = p \tag{12}$$

$$S_{ARX} = \begin{bmatrix} p\, q \end{bmatrix} \tag{13}$$

where p and q are the orders of the autoregressive and exogenous terms, respectively. In the nonlinear case, the candidate solutions are of the form,

$$S_{RBF-AR} = \begin{bmatrix} p\ l\ F\ s_f\ \mathbf{Z}_{f_1}^T\ \ldots\ \mathbf{Z}_{f_F}^T \end{bmatrix} \tag{14}$$

$$S_{RBF-ARX} = \begin{bmatrix} p\ q\ l\ F\ s_f\ \mathbf{Z}_{f_1}^T\ \ldots\ \mathbf{Z}_{f_F}^T \end{bmatrix} \tag{15}$$

where l is the dimension of the state-dependent vector $\Upsilon(n)$, F is the total number of RBFs used to approximate the coefficients of the autoregressive and exogenous terms, $s_f \in R^{1 \times F}$ contain the RBF scaling parameters, and $\mathbf{Z}_{f_k} \in R^{l \times 1}$ define the centers of the RBFs. As fitness function we applied the commonly used Bayesian Information Criterion (BIC) [17],

$$BIC(S) = \frac{N}{2}\log\left(\frac{J}{N}\right) + \frac{d}{2}\log(N) \tag{16}$$

where N is the number of samples, d the total number of model coefficients ($d_{AR} = p$, $d_{ARX} = p + q$, $d_{RBF-AR} = (F+1)p$, $d_{RBF-ARX} = (F+1)(p+q+1)$) and $J = \sum_{n=1}^{N} e^2(n)$ is the sum of squares of the prediction error $e(n) = y(n) - \hat{y}(n)$.

3.4 Quantifying the Effect of HRV and Age on the ECG Waveform

The main goal of this work was to quantify the effect of HRV and age on the ECG waveform. To this end, we fitted AR/RBF-AR models to the extracted waveform time-series (Fig. 1a – bottom panel) of both young and elderly subjects and used them as reference models. Their predictive performance was then compared with that obtained when HRV was included as exogenous variable (ARX/RBF-ARX). The key assumption was that if HRV induced temporal dynamics on specific ECG waveform segments, including it as an exogenous input would increase prediction accuracy. As a measure of model performance, we used the normalized mean squared error (NMSE) between actual (y) and one-step ahead predicted ($\hat{y}$) time-series (Fig. 1b),

$$NMSE = \frac{\|y - \hat{y}\|_2^2}{\|y\|_2^2} \tag{17}$$

The NMSE essentially describes the predictability of each waveform sample from its past history (as well as the HRV past history in case of its inclusion as an exogenous input). Group differences were assessed using Kruskal-Wallis analysis of variance.

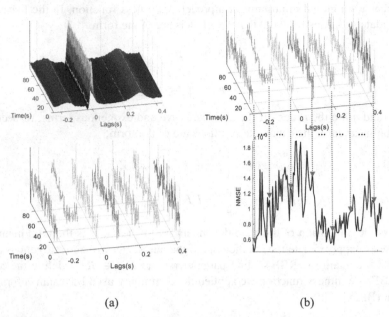

(a)   (b)

Fig. 1. (a) Time evolution of the beat to beat ECG waveform of a representative subject (top panel). All R peaks were placed at time lag 0. Segments of the waveform 0.24 s before and 0.44 s after the R peak were only considered. The colored lines represent the time evolution of representative samples of the waveform. The respective extracted standardized time-series can be found in the bottom panel. (b) Linear and nonlinear AR/ARX were fitted on the extracted time-series (in case of ARX models, HRV was also considered as an exogenous input). The predictive performance of the models was quantified by the NMSE between the actual output and the one-step ahead prediction. Each lag of the ECG waveform was therefore assigned with a unique NMSE value.

4   Results and Conclusions

The mean and standard deviation of the NMSE for both young and elderly subjects and for the different type of models is depicted in Fig. 2. Overall, RBF-ARX models exhibited higher predictive accuracy (i.e., smaller NMSE values). In the young group, the ECG segment around the R peak was less predictable compared to the elderly group, suggesting that R peak variations in the ECG of young subjects followed a more random pattern. Based on Fig. 3, using HRV as an exogenous input led to a NMSE improvement in both linear (i.e., ARX) and nonlinear (i.e., RBF-ARX) models and in both groups. The NMSE improvement was found to be greater for the young group compared to the elderly group, implying that HRV had a more pronounced effect on the ECG morphology of young subjects, which coincides with previous reports. In [18], a progressive decoupling between QT and HRV was observed with age due to increased sympathetic activity. The observed NMSE improvement was also significantly greater when using RBF-ARX models compared to ARX models indicating a HRV induced nonlinear modulation of the ECG waveform shape. Finally, we extracted ECG waveform segments were HRV had a significantly more pronounced effect in young than in elderly (Fig. 3) using both linear

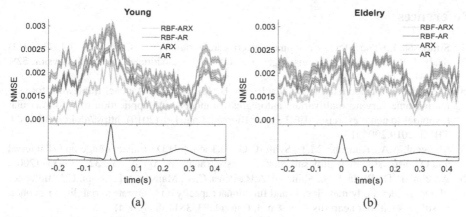

Fig. 2. NMSE ± std obtained by fitting AR, ARX, RBF-AR and RBF-ARX models to the time-series describing the time evolution of each sample of the ECG waveform in (a) young and (b) elderly subjects. The average waveform of each group is depicted in a subplot under each plot.

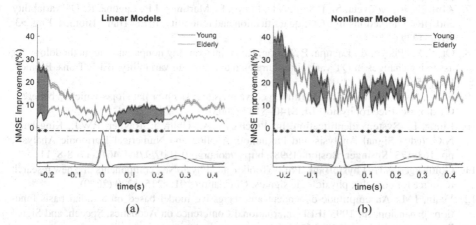

Fig. 3. Percentage improvement in NMSE (±std) by including HRV as an exogenous input in young and elderly subjects using (a) ARX (linear models) and (b) RBF-ARX (nonlinear models). The average ECG waveforms of each group are depicted under each plot. Horizontal bars reflect 4 sample periods from which average values were used to assess group differences in the NMSE improvement across time using Kruskal-Wallis analysis of variance (*p < 0.04). The grey shaded areas represent the segments where NMSE improvement was significantly greater in young compared to elderly subjects.

and nonlinear models. Nonlinear models were able to detect an extra segment that was missed out in the linear case (Fig. 3b). Physiological interpretation of the abovementioned results requires further investigation and will be examined in more detail in future work.

Acknowledgements. This work has been supported by the "LCM – K2 Center for Symbiotic Mechatronics" within the framework of the Austrian COMET-K2 program.

References

1. Simonson, E.: The effect of age on the electrocardiogram. Am. J. Cardiol. **29**, 64–73 (1972)
2. Seals, D.R., Esler, M.D.: Human ageing and the sympathoadrenal system. J. Physiol. **528**, 407–417 (2000)
3. Kostoglou, K., Robertson, A.D., MacIntosh, B., Mitsis, G.D.: A novel framework for estimating time-varying multivariate autoregressive models and application to cardiovascular responses to acute exercise. IEEE Trans. Biomed. Eng. 1–1 (2019). https://doi.org/10.1109/TBME.2019.2903012
4. Mangoni, A.A., Kinirons, M.T., Swift, C.G., Jackson, S.H.D.: Impact of age on QT interval and QT dispersion in healthy subjects: a regression analysis. Age Ageing **32**, 326–331 (2003)
5. Antelmi, I., De Paula, R.S., Shinzato, A.R., Peres, C.A., Mansur, A.J., Grupi, C.J.: Influence of age, gender, body mass index, and functional capacity on heart rate variability in a cohort of subjects without heart disease. Am. J. Cardiol. **93**, 381–385 (2004)
6. Valenza, G., et al.: Assessing real-time RR-QT frequency-domain measures of coupling and causality through inhomogeneous point-process bivariate models. In: 2014 36th Annual International Conference of the IEEE Engineering in Medicine and Biology Society, pp. 6475–6478 (2014)
7. Almeida, R., Gouveia, S., Rocha, A.P., Pueyo, E., Martinez, J.P., Laguna, P.: QT variability and HRV interactions in ECG: quantification and reliability. IEEE Trans. Biomed. Eng. **53**, 1317–1329 (2006)
8. Orini, M., Pueyo, E., Laguna, P., Bailón, R.: A time-varying nonparametric methodology for assessing changes in QT variability unrelated to heart rate variability. IEEE Trans. Biomed. Eng. **65**, 1443–1451 (2018)
9. Franz, M.R.: The electrical restitution curve revisited: steep or flat slope–which is better? J. Cardiovasc. Electrophysiol. **14**, S140–S147 (2003)
10. Ljung, L.: System identification. In: Procházka, A., Uhlíř, J., Rayner, P.W.J., Kingsbury, N.G. (eds.) Signal Analysis and Prediction. Applied and Numerical Harmonic Analysis, pp. 163–173. Springer, Boston (1998). https://doi.org/10.1007/978-1-4612-1768-8_11
11. Goldberger, A.L.: PhysioBank, PhysioToolkit, and PhysioNet: components of a new research resource for complex physiologic signals. Circulation **101**, e215–e220 (2000)
12. Vesin, J.M.: An amplitude-dependent autoregressive model based on a radial basis functions expansion. In: 1993 IEEE International Conference on Acoustics, Speech, and Signal Processing, vol. 3, pp. 129–132 (1993)
13. Shi, Z., Tamura, Y., Ozaki, T.: Nonlinear time series modelling with the radial basis function-based state-dependent autoregressive model. Int. J. Syst. Sci. **30**, 717–727 (1999)
14. Peng, H., Ozaki, T., Haggan-Ozaki, V., Toyoda, Y.: A parameter optimization method for radial basis function type models. IEEE Trans. Neural Networks **14**, 432–438 (2003)
15. Lawrence, D., et al.: Handbook of Genetic Algorithms. Van No Strand Reinhold, New York (1991)
16. Deep, K., Singh, K.P., Kansal, M.L., Mohan, C.: A real coded genetic algorithm for solving integer and mixed integer optimization problems. Appl. Math. Comput. **212**, 505–518 (2009)
17. Schwarz, G., et al.: Estimating the dimension of a model. Ann. Stat. **6**, 461–464 (1978)
18. Baumert, M., Czippelova, B., Porta, A., Javorka, M.: Decoupling of QT interval variability from heart rate variability with ageing. Physiol. Meas. **34**, 1435 (2013)

Overcomplete Multi-scale Dictionaries for Efficient Representation of ECG Signals

David Meltzer[1]ⓘ, David Luengo[1](✉)ⓘ, and Tom Trigano[2]ⓘ

[1] Universidad Politécnica de Madrid, 28031 Madrid, Spain
{david.meltzer,david.luengo}@upm.es
[2] Shamoon College of Engineering, 77245 Ashdod, Israel
thomast@sce.ac.il

Abstract. The electrocardiogram (ECG) was the first biomedical signal subject of extensive digital signal processing techniques. Essentially, the ECG consists of a cyclic sequence of relevant activations embedded into inactivity time sequences combined with interferences and noise. By its nature, it can be subject of representation as a sparse signal. This work describes an efficient method to create overcomplete multi-scale dictionaries that can be used for sparse ECG representation. Whereas most of the proposed methods to date use fixed waveforms that somehow resemble actual ECG shapes, the main innovation in our approach is selecting ECG waveforms recorded from actual patients. A relevant result of our method is the ability to process long lasting recordings from multiple patients. Simulations on patient actual records from Physionet's PTB Diagnostic ECG Database confirm the good performance of the proposed approach.

Keywords: Electrocardiogram (ECG) · LASSO · Overcomplete multi-scale signal representation · Dictionary construction · Sparse inference

1 Introduction

It is a well known fact that, since the viable introduction of the electrocardiogram (ECG) recording, its use has become so widespread that it is now commonly used in the health-care sector for obtaining indicators of patient health status. The use and interpretation of the ECG has been dramatically extended by means of the application of digital signal processing (DSP) techniques. Noise and interference removal, extraction of specific signals from the composite ECG, detection and characterization of waveforms are examples of solutions provided by DSP techniques [3].

The time representation of an ECG shows cyclic waveforms corresponding to QRS complexes, as well as P and T waveforms, embedded into non active time sequences corresponding to isoelectric intervals, all this together with noise

© Springer Nature Switzerland AG 2020
R. Moreno-Díaz et al. (Eds.): EUROCAST 2019, LNCS 12014, pp. 331–338, 2020.
https://doi.org/10.1007/978-3-030-45096-0_41

and interferences [12]. Therefore, the ECG can be considered a sparse signal. A number of sparse inference and representation techniques have been proposed for many types of signals (images, audio, recordings, biomedical waveforms, etc.) [4] since the introduction of the Least Absolute Shrinkage and Selection Operator (LASSO) regularizer [13].

Most of the works done regarding electrocardiographic signal processing and aiming for sparse representation of single-channel or multi-channel ECGs [1, 9, 11, 14] use fixed arbitrary waveforms that somehow resemble the characteristic shape of a QRS complex (e.g., a mexican hat wavelet). This type of approach leads to practical positive results that usually include a number of spurious activations which need a removal procedure before their potential use as physiologically interpretable signals. This is typically performed using a post-processing stage [9, 11] or by minimizing a complex non-convex cost function [10].

In this work, the authors propose a method to conform a multi-scale dictionary derived from a set of atoms that have their origin in ECG waveforms recorded from actual patients. The aforementioned dictionary is then used to obtain spare representations of ECGs using the LASSO regularizer. Numerical simulations show that the proposed approach leads to very sparse representations that both represent al QRS complexes without misses while lacking spurious activations, which eliminates the need for any post-processing.

The rest of this document is organized as follows. The next section states the problem of sparse representation of ECG signals, with special emphasis in the relevance of counting on an appropriate dictionary. Then, Sect. 3 describes the procedure followed to derive a multi-scale dictionary from one or more atoms that have their origin in ECG waveforms recorded from actual patients. Finally, the next section provides the results of experiments that validate the proposed approach using ECG records from the Physikalisch-Technische Bundesanstalt (PTB) [5] database from PhysioNet and the conclusions close the paper.

2   Sparse Representation Problem Formulation

Let us consider a single-lead discrete-time ECG, $y[n]$, obtained from a properly filtered and amplified continuous-time single-lead ECG, $y_c(t)$, using uniform sampling with a period $T_s = 1/f_s$, i.e., $y[n] = y_c(nT_s)$. Assuming that this signal is obtained as the superposition of a number of waveforms of interest (essentially QRS complexes, P and T waveforms) plus noise and interferences, then $y[n]$ can be expressed as:

$$y[n] = \sum_{k=-\infty}^{\infty} E_k \Phi_k(t_n - T_k) + \varepsilon[n], \quad n = 0, \ldots, N-1, \tag{1}$$

where T_k denotes the arrival time of the k-th electrical pulse; E_k its amplitude; Φ_k the associated, unknown pulse shape; and $\varepsilon[n]$ an additive, white Gaussian noise (AWGN) with variance σ^2. Equation (1) is known in the literature as the *shot-noise model*, and it is commonly used in the digital signal processing of biomedical signals. Note that, in real-world applications neither Φ_k, T_k nor E_k are known. Even so, if the most common shapes and durations of Φ_k are known, each one can be approximated using a time-shifted, multi-scale dictionary of waveforms from actual patients recordings with finite support $M \ll N$ and this approximation can then be used to infer the values of E_k and T_k. More precisely, let us define a set of P candidate waveforms, Γ_p for $p = 1, \ldots, P$, with a finite support of M_p samples such that $M_1 < M_2 < \cdots < M_P$ and $M = \max_{p=1,\ldots,P} M_p = M_P$. If properly chosen, these waveforms will provide a good approximation of the local behavior of the signal around each sampling point, thus allowing us to approximate (1) through the following model:

$$y[n] = \sum_{k=0}^{N-M-1} \sum_{p=1}^{P} \beta_{k,p} \Gamma_p[n - k] + \varepsilon[n], \quad n = 0, \ldots, N - 1, \qquad (2)$$

where the $\beta_{k,p}$ indicate the amplitude of the p-th waveform shifted to the k-th time instant, $t_k = kT_s$. It is possible to group all the candidate waveforms into a single matrix $\mathbf{A} = [\mathbf{A}_0 \ \mathbf{A}_1 \ \cdots \ \mathbf{A}_{N-M-1}]$, where the $N \times P$ matrices $\mathbf{A}_k$ (for $k = 0, \ldots, N - M - 1$) have column entries equal to $\Gamma_p[m - k]$ for $m = k, \ldots, k + M - 1$ and 0 otherwise. With this grouping, the model of (2) can be expressed in matrix form as follows:

$$\boldsymbol{y} = \mathbf{A}\boldsymbol{\beta} + \boldsymbol{\varepsilon}, \qquad (3)$$

where $\boldsymbol{y} = [y[0], \ldots, y[N-1]]^\top$ is an $N \times 1$ vector with all the ECG samples, $\boldsymbol{\beta} = [\beta_{0,1}, \ldots, \beta_{0,P}, \ldots, \beta_{N-M-1,1}, \ldots, \beta_{N-M-1,P}]^\top$ is an $(N - M)P \times 1$ coefficients vector, and $\boldsymbol{\varepsilon} = [\varepsilon[0], \ldots, \varepsilon[N - 1]]^\top$ is the $N \times 1$ noise vector. Note that matrix A can be seen as a global dictionary that contains $N - M$ replicas, $\mathbf{A}_k$ for $k = 0, 1, \ldots, N - M - 1$, of the candidate waveforms time shifted to $t_0 = 0$, $t_1 = T_s, \ldots, t_{N-M-1} = (N - M - 1)T_s$. Two measures can now be taken to cope with the uncertainty about the shape and duration of the pulses that can be found in $y[n]$: using several different waveforms with distinct timescales. The result is a time-shifted, multi-scale overcomplete (as $(N-M)P > N$) dictionary. It is important to remark that, once the dictionary signals are defined, the only remaining unknown term in (3) is $\boldsymbol{\beta}$. In this case, since the presence of relevant waveforms in $y[n]$ is typically sparse, the usual approach consists in enforcing sparsity in $\boldsymbol{\beta}$ by applying the so called LASSO, which minimizes a convex cost function composed of the L_2 norm of the reconstruction error and the L_1 norm of the coefficient vector,

$$\hat{\boldsymbol{\beta}} = \arg\min_{\boldsymbol{\beta}} \|\mathbf{y} - \mathbf{A}\boldsymbol{\beta}\|_2^2 + \lambda\|\boldsymbol{\beta}\|_1, \qquad (4)$$

where λ is a parameter defining the trade-off between the sparsity of $\boldsymbol{\beta}$ and the precision of the estimation.

3   Multi-scale Dictionary Derivation

As noted in the introduction, most previous works related to construction of sub-dictionaries $\boldsymbol{A}_k$ typically use a single waveform unrelated to actual ECG waveforms, like Gaussians [11] with different variances or the mexican hat wavelet

[9]. This work is an extension of [8], where a single waveform was used to construct the dictionary. This extension aims to populate a dictionary with multiple waveforms derived from actual ECG patients recordings, selected on the basis of a distance metric. Let $Q = 52$ be the recording sessions from different healthy control subjects in the database where, for simplicity reasons, a single channel is considered corresponding to the precordial V4 electrode. The following steps have been applied to each one of the sessions:

1. Identification of the fiducial points of every QRS complex in the session following the approach described in [6]. As a result, the characterization set of all the P-QRS-T waveforms is available in the session.
2. Discard of those records for which fiducial points cannot be reliably found. For the remaining records, all identified QRS complexes are extracted, centered with respect to R and resampled in such a way that they all end up being described with the same number of samples as the longest one, L_i samples.
3. Derivation of the average QRS waveform corresponding to a subject. The standard deviation is also computed as a safety measure: if it is too large, the resulting waveform is discarded.

At this point, a number of $Q' \leq Q$ average waveforms are made finally available from different patients. All of them can potentially be used to build sub-dictionaries. All Q' waveforms are highly correlated and thus using them all would result in a dictionary that would provide a poor performance and lead to high computation consumption. Therefore, in order to obtain a reduced dictionary composed of a few waveforms as differentiated as possible, we perform the following procedure:

1. Resample all the average QRS waveforms in such a way that they all have exactly the same number of samples as the longest one, $L = \max_{i=1,\ldots,Q'} L_i$ samples.
2. Normalize all the waveforms by removing their means and dividing by the square root of their ℓ_2 norms. Remove border effects following the technique described in [7].
3. Compute the correlation coefficient among each pair of waveforms,[1]

$$\rho_{ij} = \frac{C_{ij}}{\sqrt{C_{ii}C_{jj}}}, \qquad (5)$$

where C_{ij} denotes the cross-covariance between the i-th and j-th waveforms at lag 0 (i.e., without any time shift).
4. Select the waveform with the highest average correlation (in absolute value) with respect to the rest of candidate waveforms, i.e.,

$$\ell = \arg\max_{i=1,\ldots,Q'} \sum_{j=1}^{Q'} |\rho_{ij}|, \qquad (6)$$

---

[1] In practice, this only has to be done $Q'(Q'-1)/2$ times, since $\rho_{ii} = 1 \; \forall i$ thanks to the normalization and $\rho_{ij} = \rho_{ji}$.

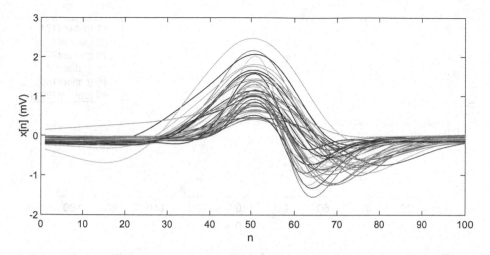

Fig. 1. $Q' = 44$ reliable average QRS complexes extracted from the $Q = 52$ healthy patients in the PTB database after resampling, normalization and removal of border effects.

which corresponds to the most representative waveform of all candidate waveforms.

5. If a number $K > 1$ of atoms is needed, additional waveforms can be sequentially selected from the remaining waveforms set:
    (a) Select the waveform with the highest average correlation (in absolute value) with respect to the remaining candidate waveforms (to obtain representative dictionary atoms).
    (b) Compute the correlation of the selected waveform w.r.t. the already accepted waveforms. If this correlation (in absolute value) is below a pre-established threshold γ (to avoid similar atoms), then accept it. Otherwise, discard it. In any case, remove the selected waveform from the pool of candidates.

Once K waveforms have been selected, all of them are resampled in order to obtain a multi-scale sub-dictionary composed of T different time scales. Note that the total number of available waveforms in the resulting dictionary is thus $P = KT$. Note also that the global dictionary is simply obtained by performing $N - M$ different time shifts on the resulting sub-dictionary [9].

4 Experimental Results

In this section we present the experimental results obtained both for building the dictionary and to perform sparse reconstruction of a number of actual ECG signals using it.

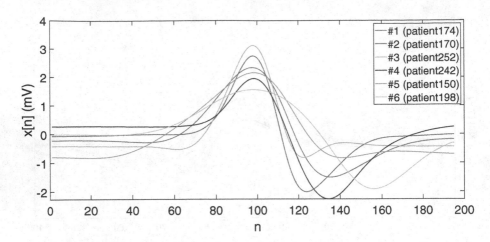

Fig. 2. Sub-dictionary composed of six R-centered average QRS waveforms.

4.1 Dictionary Construction

In order to construct the dictionary, we use the Physikalisch-Technische Bundesanstalt (PTB) database, compiled by the National Metrology Institute of Germany for research, algorithmic benchmarking and teaching purposes [2]. The ECGs were collected from healthy volunteers and patients with different heart diseases by Prof. Michael Oeff, at the Dep. of Cardiology of Univ. Clinic Benjamin Franklin in Berlin (Germany), and can be downloaded from Physionet [5]. The database contains 549 records from 290 subjects (aged 17 to 87 years), where each record includes 15 simultaneously measured signals: the 12 standard leads plus the 3 Frank lead ECGs [3,12]. Each signal is digitized using a sampling frequency $f_s = 1000\,\text{Hz}$ with a 16 bit resolution.

Out of the 268 subjects for which the clinical summary is available, we selected the $Q = 52$ healthy control patients in order to build the dictionary. From those patients, we were able to obtain reliable average QRS complexes in $Q' = 44$ patients. The average waveforms for these 44 patients, after resampling to $L = 100$ samples, normalization and removal of border effects, can be seen in Fig. 1. Note the large similarity among all waveforms when they are centered around the R peak. Given this set of average waveforms, the previously described selection process for atoms is performed. Figure 2 shows a sub-dictionary composed of the 6 atoms obtained by setting $\gamma = 0.9$. To finalize the construction of the dictionary, from each sub-dictionary atom a number of related waveforms are derived by resampling, so that each one has a duration that ranges from 60 ms to 160 ms in 10 ms steps. Hence, the resulting dictionary contains $P = 6 \times 11 = 66$ waveforms that can be easily time shifted in order to construct the sparse ECG representations performed in the following section.

4.2   Sparse ECG Representation

Now we test the constructed dictionary on 5 healthy patients from the PTB database. In order to solve (4), we use the CoSA (Convolutional Sparse Approximation) algorithm recently proposed in [15], which allows us to process the whole signals (approximately 115200 samples, nearly 2 min of recorded time each) at once (i.e., without having to partition them into several segments that have to be processed separately) in a reasonable amount of time. Since several signals showed a significant degree of baseline wander, before applying CoSA all signals were previously filtered using a third-order high-pass IIR (infinite impuse response) Butterworth filter designed using Matlab's filterDesigner: stop-band frequency $f_{stop} = 0.1\,\mathrm{Hz}$, pass-band frequency $f_{pass} = 1\,\mathrm{Hz}$, minimum stop-band attenuation $A_{stop} = 40\,\mathrm{dB}$, and maximun pass-band attenuation $A_{pass} = 1\,\mathrm{dB}$.

The results are displayed in Table 1, where each row is identified by the record patient number, the degree of sparsity (measured as the percentage of non-zero coefficients in β), and the relative error (measured as the percentage of the ℓ_2 norm of the residual error w.r.t. the ℓ_2 norm of the signal). Note the large degree of sparsity attained, which is slightly lower in all cases than the one achieved in [8]. The large relative error shown is due to the fact that the dictionary is optimized for the detection of the QRS complexes (which is usually the first step in ECG signal processing) and does not recover other existing waveforms in the signal (like P and T waves). This can be easily corrected by incorporating additional waveforms to the dictionary in the future. However, note also that this error is substantially lower than the one achieved in [8] using $K = 1$, thus confirming the interest of building dictionaries with multiple waveforms.

Table 1. Sparsity and relative error for 5 signals from the PTB database using the derived dictionary for $K = 1$ [8] and $K = 6$.

Signal	$K = 1$		$K = 6$	
	Sparsity	Rel. error	Sparsity	Rel. error
104	2.84%	30.14%	2.18%	9.89%
105	1.82%	57.74%	1.10%	30.93%
116	1.24%	49.69%	1.05%	14.10%
121	1.53%	24.39%	1.28%	4.94%
122	3.44%	36.23%	2.51%	13.58%

5   Conclusions

In this paper, we have presented a simple mechanism to build multi-scale dictionaries using several distinct QRS complexes directly extracted from real-world signals. The proposed approach has been used to model ECG signals from healthy patients, showing promising results in terms of the achieved sparsity and the reconstruction error. Future works will focus on the extension of this procedure to patients with cardiac diseases (where robust methods for fiducial point extraction will be essential) and the construction of dictionaries for the other relevant waveforms in the ECG (P and T waves).

References

1. Billah, M.S., Mahmud, T.B., Snigdha, F.S., Arafat, M.A.: A novel method to model ECG beats using Gaussian functions. In: 4th IEEE International Conference on Biomedical Engineering and Informatics (BMEI), vol. 2, pp. 612–616 (2011)
2. Bousseljot, R., Kreiseler, D., Schnabel, A.: Nutzung der EKG-signaldatenbank CARDIODAT der PTB über das internet. Biomedizinische Technik/Biomed. Eng. **40**(s1), 317–318 (1995)
3. Clifford, G.D., Azuaje, F., McSharry, P., et al.: Advanced Methods and Tools for ECG Data Analysis. Artech House, Boston (2006)
4. Elad, M.: Sparse and Redundant Representations: From Theory to Applications in Signal and Image Processing. Springer, New York (2010). https://doi.org/10. 1007/978-1-4419-7011-4
5. Goldberger, A.L., et al.: PhysioBank, PhysioToolkit, and PhysioNet: components of a new research resource for complex physiologic signals. Circulation **101**(23), e215–e220 (2000)
6. Israel, S.A., Irvine, J.M., Cheng, A., Wiederhold, M.D., Wiederhold, B.K.: ECG to identify individuals. Pattern Recogn. **38**(1), 133–142 (2005)
7. Luengo, D., Meltzer, D., Trigano, T.: An efficient method to learn overcomplete multi-scale dictionaries of ECG signals. Appl. Sci. **8**(12), 2569 (2018)
8. Luengo, D., Meltzer, D., Trigano, T.: Sparse ECG representation with a multi-scale dictionary derived from real-world signals. In: 41st IEEE International Conference on Telecommunications and Signal Processing (TSP), pp. 1–5 (2018)
9. Luengo, D., Monzón, S., Trigano, T., Vía, J., Artés-Rodríguez, A.: Blind analysis of atrial fibrillation electrograms: a sparsity-aware formulation. Integr. Comput.-Aided Eng. **22**(1), 71–85 (2015)
10. Luengo, D., Vía, J., Monzón, S., Trigano, T., Artés-Rodríguez, A.: Cross-products LASSO. In: IEEE International Conference on Acoustics, Speech and Signal Processing, pp. 6118–6122 (2013)
11. Monzón, S., Trigano, T., Luengo, D., Artes-Rodriguez, A.: Sparse spectral analysis of atrial fibrillation electrograms. In: IEEE International Workshop on Machine Learning for Signal Processing, pp. 1–6 (2012)
12. Sörnmo, L., Laguna, P.: Bioelectrical Signal Processing in Cardiac and Neurological Applications, vol. 8. Academic Press, Boston (2005)
13. Tibshirani, R.: Regression shrinkage and selection via the LASSO. J. Roy. Stat. Soc.: Ser. B (Methodol.) **58**(1), 267–288 (1996)
14. Trigano, T., Kolesnikov, V., Luengo, D., Artés-Rodríguez, A.: Grouped sparsity algorithm for multichannel intracardiac ECG synchronization. In: 22nd European Signal Processing Conference (EUSIPCO), pp. 1537–1541 (2014)
15. Trigano, T., Shevtsov, I., Luengo, D.: CoSA: an accelerated ISTA algorithm for dictionaries based on translated waveforms. Sig. Process. **139**, 131–135 (2017)

A Linear Parameter Varying ARX Model for Describing Biomedical Signal Couplings

Carl Böck[1,2](✉) [ID], Kyriaki Kostoglou[1] [ID], Péter Kovács[1] [ID], Mario Huemer[1] [ID], and Jens Meier[2]

[1] Institute of Signal Processing, Johannes Kepler University Linz, Linz, Austria
{carl.boeck,kyriaki.kostoglou,peter.kovacs,mario.huemer}@jku.at
[2] Department of Anesthesiology and Critical Care Medicine,
Kepler University Hospital, Linz, Austria

Abstract. Biomedical signal processing frequently deals with information extraction for clinical decision support. A major challenge in this field is to reveal diagnostic information by eliminating undesired interfering influences. In case of the electrocardiogram, e.g., a frequently arising interference is caused by respiration, which possibly superimposes diagnostic information. Respiratory sinus arrhythmia, i.e., the acceleration and deceleration of the heartrate (HR) during inhalation and exhalation, respectively, is a well-known phenomenon, which strongly influences the ECG. This influence becomes even more important, when investigating the so-called heart rate variability, a diagnostically powerful signal derived from the ECG. In this work, we propose a model for capturing the relationship between the HR and the respiration, thereby taking the time-variance of physiological systems into account. To this end, we show that so-called linear parameter varying autoregressive models with exogenous input are well suited for modeling the coupling between the two signals of interest.

Keywords: Heart rate variability · Biomedical signal couplings ·
System identification · Linear parameter varying ARX

1 Introduction

The electrocardiogram (ECG) has proven to be one of the most useful biomedical signals when it comes to cardiovascular disease detection. For this, clinically useful parameters are derived from the raw signal and evaluated by experts. One of these derived signals is the so-called heart rate variability (HRV), which is the reciprocal of the instantaneous heart rate (HR), i.e., the distance between two subsequent R-peaks (RR-interval), over time. The HRV has shown to be of great diagnostic value for several physical or mental disorders. This is based on the dependency of the HR on the autonomous nervous system (ANS), i.e., the ANS reacts on internal and external influences by constantly adapting the

© Springer Nature Switzerland AG 2020
R. Moreno-Díaz et al. (Eds.): EUROCAST 2019, LNCS 12014, pp. 339–346, 2020.
https://doi.org/10.1007/978-3-030-45096-0_42

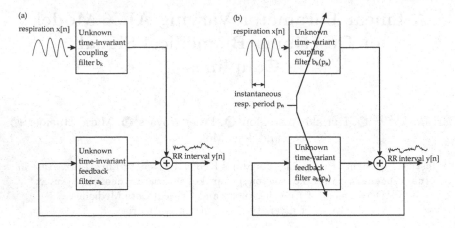

Fig. 1. (a) ARX system model vs. (b) LPV–ARX model.

HR. In general, increased HRV is indicative of better health [1]. Exploiting this information, HRV has been used as a biomarker in many clinical applications, e.g., for quantifying ANS imbalances [2], predicting subsequent cardiac events after myocardial infarction [3] or even assessing the mental workload during a cognitive task [4].

These studies, however, usually only evaluate the effects of the ANS onto the HR, thereby neglecting possible coupling with other sources which could significantly influence the HR. The so-called respiratory sinus arrhythmia is a well known phenomenon that describes the acceleration and deceleration of the HR during inhalation and exhalation, respectively. Ignoring such type of couplings could significantly impact the diagnostic process, leading to possible diagnostic errors. As a result, there have been attempts to model the underlying coupling, e.g., by determining the relationship between respiration and heart rate in the frequency domain [5]. However, in a recent study, Lenis et al. showed that the strength of the coupling depends on many factors, such as age or respiratory frequency [6]. In fact, the coupling is subject specific and, in some cases, even absent. Consequently, trying to eliminate non-existing effects of the respiration onto the HRV might lead to decreased signal quality in weakly coupled signals.

Lenis et al., were the first to investigate the relationship between HR and respiration using Wiener-Granger's causality. HR was modeled as an autoregressive (AR) process, whereas the amplitude of the respiration was considered as an exogenous input to the system (ARX), illustrated in Fig. 1(a). Significant improvements in the prediction error due to the inclusion of respiration suggested a respiratory influence on HR and therefore increased coupling.

One limitation of their work was the assumption of a time-invariant ARX model, which in general is not true for a changing respiratory frequency [7]. In our work, we tackle this limitation by allowing the model parameters to be time varying and specifically dependent upon the instantaneous respiratory period, leading to a linear parameter varying (LPV)–ARX model [8], which is depicted in Fig. 1(b) and will be introduced in Sect. 2. In order to evaluate our work, we recorded ECG and respiration signals from seven subjects performing paced breathing (Sect. 3). In Sect. 4 we compare our proposed model with the autoregressive (AR) and ARX models before concluding our work in Sect. 5.

2   LPV–ARX Model for HRV Estimation

The instantaneous RR-interval, i.e., the reciprocal of the instantaneous HR over time, can be modeled as single-input single-output (SISO) AR stochastic process,

$$y[n] = \sum_{k=1}^{N_a} a_k y[n-k] + \epsilon[n], \tag{1}$$

where $y[n]$ corresponds to a specific RR-interval at time instant n and $\epsilon[n]$ is assumed to be zero-mean white Gaussian noise. It is well-known that respiration significantly influences the length of an RR-interval, a phenomenon usually referred to as respiratory sinus arrhythmia [9]. As suggested in [6], this can be taken into account by defining the amplitude of the respiration as exogenous input $x[n]$, leading to the following SISO ARX model,

$$y[n] = \sum_{k=1}^{N_a} a_k y[n-k] + \sum_{k=0}^{N_b} b_k x[n-k] + \epsilon[n]. \tag{2}$$

Note that the output $y[n]$ in (2) is represented by a time-invariant linear combination of current and preceding input values (respiration amplitude) as well as preceding output values (instantaneous RR-interval). While time-invariance often is a valid assumption, in general this is not true for physiological systems, i.e., the coefficient vectors **a** and **b** vary over time. Specifically, it can be assumed that the dynamics of the system are externally modulated by certain time-varying (TV) parameters, known as scheduling variables (SV). Therefore, in our work, we assume that the coefficient vectors **a** and **b** have a static dependence on the respiratory period p_n, leading to the following LPV ARX model

$$y[n] = \sum_{k=1}^{N_a} a_k(p_n) y[n-k] + \sum_{k=0}^{N_b} b_k(p_n) x[n-k] + \epsilon[n], \tag{3}$$

where we use p_n instead of $p[n]$ for notational simplicity [8]. In order to identify the LPV–ARX model defined in (3) we recast the problem as linear regression, originally proposed in [10]. Hence, for describing the static dependence of the model parameters on p_n, **a** and **b** are expressed as linear combination of radial basis functions (RBFs) $\phi_{k_i}(p_n)$ and $\psi_{k_i}(p_n)$, i.e.,

$$a_k(p_n) = \boldsymbol{\alpha}_k^T \boldsymbol{\Phi}_k(p_n) = \alpha_{k_0} + \sum_{i=1}^{L_k} \alpha_{k_i} \phi_{k_i}(p_n), \qquad k = 1, \ldots, N_a, \tag{4}$$

$$b_k(p_n) = \boldsymbol{\beta}_k^T \boldsymbol{\Psi}_k(p_n) = \beta_{k_0} + \sum_{i=1}^{M_k} \beta_{k_i} \psi_{k_i}(p_n), \qquad k = 0, \ldots, N_b. \tag{5}$$

We further define a weight vector

$$
\mathbf{w} = \left[\alpha_{1_0}, \alpha_{1_1}, \ldots, \alpha_{1_{L_1}}, \alpha_{2_0}, \ldots, \alpha_{(N_a)_{L_{N_a}}}, \beta_{0_0}, \beta_{0_1}, \ldots, \beta_{0_{M_1}}, \beta_{1_0}, \ldots, \beta_{(N_b)_{M_{N_b}}} \right]^T
$$
$$
= \left[\boldsymbol{\alpha}_1^T, \ldots, \boldsymbol{\alpha}_{N_a}^T, \boldsymbol{\beta}_0^T, \ldots, \boldsymbol{\beta}_{N_b}^T \right]^T = [\mathbf{w}_1^T, \mathbf{w}_2^T, \ldots, \mathbf{w}_{\mathbf{N_c}}^T]^T \in \mathbb{R}^{d \times 1},
$$

where $N_c = N_a + N_b + 1$ and $d = \left[\sum_{i=1}^{N_a} (1 + L_i) \right] + \left[\sum_{i=1}^{N_b} (1 + M_i) \right]$, as well as an extended regressor

$$
\boldsymbol{\xi}[n] = \big[y[n-1], \Phi_{1_1}(p_n) y[n-1], \ldots, \Phi_{1_{L_1}}(p_n) y[n-1], y[n-2], \ldots,
$$
$$
\Phi_{(N_a)(L_{N_a})}(p_n) y[n - N_a], x[n], \ldots, \Phi_{0_{M_0}}(p_n) x[n], x[n-1], \ldots,
$$
$$
\Phi_{(N_b)(M_{N_b})}(p_n) x[n - N_b] \big]^T
$$
$$
= \big[\Phi_1^T(p_n) y[n-1], \ldots, \Phi_{N_a}^T(p_n) y[n - n_a], \Psi_0^T(p_n) x[n], \ldots,
$$
$$
\Psi_{N_b}^T(p_n) x[n - N_b] \big]^T
$$

If we now redefine $z_k[n] = y[n-k]$ and $\boldsymbol{\Theta}_k[n] = \boldsymbol{\Phi}_k[n]$ $(k = 1, \ldots, N_a)$ as well as $z_{N_a+1+k}[n] = x[n-k]$ and $\boldsymbol{\Theta}_{N_a+1+k}[n] = \boldsymbol{\Psi}_k[n]$ $(k = 1, \ldots, N_b)$, we obtain the extended regressor

$$
\boldsymbol{\xi}[n] = \big[\boldsymbol{\Theta}_1^T(p_n) z_1[n], \ldots, \boldsymbol{\Theta}_{N_a}^T(p_n) z_{N_a}[n], \boldsymbol{\Theta}_{N_a+1}^T(p_n) z_{N_a+1}[n], \ldots,
$$
$$
\boldsymbol{\Theta}_{N_a+1+N_b}^T(p_n) z_{N_a+1+N_b}[n] \big]^T . \tag{6}
$$

Consequently we can rewrite (3) as

$$
y[n] = \mathbf{w}^T \boldsymbol{\xi}[n] + \epsilon[n] = \sum_{k=1}^{N_{ab}} \mathbf{w}_k^T \boldsymbol{\Theta}_k(p_n) z_k[n] + \epsilon[n], \tag{7}
$$

and subsequently by using $\boldsymbol{y} = [y[1], \ldots, y[N]]^T$, $\boldsymbol{\Xi} = [\boldsymbol{\xi}[1], \ldots, \boldsymbol{\xi}[N]]$, and $\boldsymbol{\epsilon} = [\epsilon[1], \ldots, \epsilon[N]]^T$

$$
\mathbf{y} = \mathbf{w}^T \boldsymbol{\Xi} + \boldsymbol{\epsilon}, \tag{8}
$$

where N is considered to be the total number of samples. In order to obtain the unknown weighting coefficients $\mathbf{w}$ the least squares solution is used, i.e.,

$$
\hat{\mathbf{w}} = \left(\boldsymbol{\Xi}^T \boldsymbol{\Xi} \right)^{-1} \boldsymbol{\Xi}^T \mathbf{y}. \tag{9}
$$

At this point we need to define the two main components which characterize the LPV–ARX, i.e., the order of the ARX model itself and the number of RBFs together with their hyperparameters used for capturing the unknown dependence of coefficient vectors $\mathbf{a}, \mathbf{b}$ on the SV p_n. Since an exhaustive search for determining these parameters would not be feasible, we use a mixed integer genetic algorithm (GA) [11] with the Bayesian information criterion (BIC) [12]

$$\mathrm{BIC}(d) = \frac{N}{2} \log \left(\frac{J}{N} \right) + \frac{d}{2} \log (N) \tag{10}$$

as fitness function. In (10) N is again the number of samples, d corresponds to the total number of parameters, and $J = \sum_{k=0}^{N} (y[k] - \hat{y}[k])^2$, where $\hat{y}[k]$ is the predicted time series.

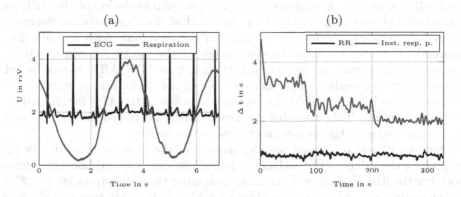

Fig. 2. (a) Exemplary raw ECG and respiration, (b) extracted instantaneous RR interval and respiratory period.

3   Experiments

In order to test the validity of the proposed model, ECG and respiration (Fig. 2(a)) were recorded for seven subjects (2 female, 5 male, 22–34 years old) performing controlled breathing at the frequencies 0.3 Hz, 0.4 Hz, and 0.5 Hz, respectively. Therefore, a predefined breathing pattern for every desired frequency was displayed for 125 s at a computer screen. The two signals were recorded at a sampling frequency of $f_s = 1200$ Hz and standard preprocessing for removing baseline wander and powerline interference was performed. Subsequently, the instantaneous RR interval and respiratory period were determined and resampled at 4 Hz to ensure equidistant sampling for both of the signals (Fig. 2(b)). Additionally, the SV, i.e., the instantaneous respiratory period, was normalized between 0 and 1.

For every recording three models (AR, ARX, LPV–ARX) were identified. The maximum model order evaluated by the GA was 12, following the suggestion of [6] to allow coupling between RR and respiration up to three seconds in the past [13]. For the LPV–ARX model, additionally the maximum number of basis functions for capturing the dependence of the coefficient vectors **a** and **b** on the instantaneous respiratory period was set to 10. The actual number of basis functions as well as the model order were optimally selected using the mixed integer GA scheme addressed in Sect. 2. In order to compare the performance of the models, we computed the absolute prediction error (APE), i.e., the absolute value of the difference between the measured and the predicted instantaneous HR ($|e_{p,AR}|$, $|e_{p,ARX}|$, $|e_{p,LPV}|$), as demonstrated in Sect. 4.

4   Results

Figure 3(a) shows the exemplary smoothed temporal evolution of the APE for a randomly chosen subject. One can observe that the absolute error decreases when incorporating respiratory information (i.e. using an ARX model). This approach, however, neglects the dependency of the model parameters on the instantaneous respiratory frequency. Introducing an LPV–ARX system model, as defined in (3), leads to a further decrease of the APE. The same trend can be observed in Fig. 3(b), which summarizes in boxplots the APE for all subjects and time instants. This validates the assumption, that the coefficient vectors **a** and **b** are driven by the instantaneous respiratory period.

Figure 3(c) and (d) depict this dependency of the coefficients on the SV p_n. In general, the values of the coefficients follow a subject-specific, non-linear function. For the first coefficient of the exogenous input this is illustrated in Fig. 3(c). For example, in subject 1 b_0 is small for a low SV (short respiratory period – high respiratory frequency), peaks at a specific respiratory frequency and decreases again with an increasing SV. This means, that the influence of that specific coefficient depends on the instantaneous respiratory period. This dependency is subject-specific, as illustrated in Fig. 3(c) for the 7 subjects. Similar observations can be made for the autoregressive coefficients **a**, which are depicted in Fig. 3(d) for a randomly chosen representative. For example, while a_1 decreases with an increasing respiratory period (lower respiratory frequency) a_3 increases. One possible interpretation would be, that for a higher respiratory frequency, the most recent value of the RR intervals has higher weight (due to physiological reasons), while for a lower respiratory frequency other coefficients become more important. These captured dependencies allow to improve the prediction of RR intervals.

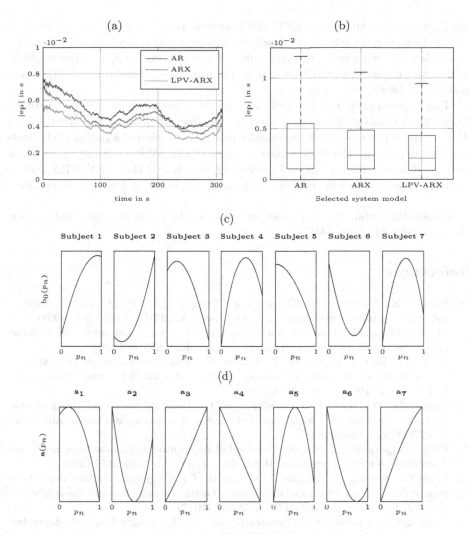

Fig. 3. (a) Smoothed temporal evolution of the APE for a randomly chosen subject, (b) boxplots of the APE for all subjects and time instants, (c) exogenous model parameters (first coefficient) for all subjects as a function of the SV, and (d) AR model parameters as a function of the SV for a randomly chosen subject.

5   Conclusion

Within this work we have implemented and evaluated an LPV–ARX model for capturing the influence of the respiration on the instantaneous HR. We assumed that the system dynamics depend on the respiratory period and consequently vary over time as a function of the breathing rate. The results suggest that at least for specific experimental setups, the respiratory frequency should not be neglected, as in the case of stress tests where the breathing frequency evolves significantly over time. The LPV–ARX approach allows to model the respiratory influence more accurately, leading to more reliable HRV–based diagnostic biomarkers. Furthermore, the dynamics of the system itself, i.e., the relationship between model coefficients and respiratory rate, (Fig. 3(c) and (d)) could potentially be of medical interest.

The experiments in this work were limited to paced breathing, therefore, future work involves the investigation of the effect of spontaneous breathing on HRV. Furthermore, we will investigate models, in which the model coefficients not only depend on the instantaneous values of the SV but also on its past values (i.e. dynamic dependency). Concluding, we showed that LPV–ARX system models are well suited for capturing the coupling between HR and respiration.

Acknowledgments. This work was supported by the Upper Austrian Medical Cognitive Computing Center (MC^3).

References

1. Stein, P.K., Bosner, M.S., Kleiger, R.E., Conger, B.M.: Heart rate variability: a measure of cardiac autonomic tone. Am. Heart J. **127**(5), 1376–1381 (1994)
2. Struhal, W., et al.: Heart rate spectra confirm the presence of autonomic dysfunction in dementia patients. J. Alzheimers Dis. **54**(2), 657–667 (2016)
3. Malik, M., Farrell, T., Cripps, T., Camm, A.: Heart rate variability in relation to prognosis after myocardial infarction: selection of optimal processing techniques. Eur. Heart J. **10**(12), 1060–1074 (1989)
4. Langewitz, W., Rüddel, H., Schächinger, H.: Reduced parasympathetic cardiac control in patients with hypertension at rest and under mental stress. Am. Heart J. **127**(1), 122–128 (1994)
5. Choi, J., Gutierrez-Osuna, R.: Removal of respiratory influences from heart rate variability in stress monitoring. IEEE Sens. J. **11**(11), 2649–2656 (2011)
6. Lenis, G., Kircher, M., Lázaro, J., Bailón, R., Gil, E.: Separating the effect of respiration on the heart rate variability using Granger's causality and linear filtering. Biomed. Sig. Process. Control **31**, 272–287 (2017)
7. Angelone, A., Coulter, N.A.: Respiratory sinus arrhythmia: a frequency dependent phenomenon. J. Appl. Physiol. **19**(3), 479–482 (1964)
8. Tóth, R.: Modeling and Identification of Linear Parameter-Varying Systems, vol. 403. Springer, Heidelberg (2010). https://doi.org/10.1007/978-3-642-13812-6
9. Hirsch, J.A., Bishop, B.: Respiratory sinus arrhythmia in humans: how breathing pattern modulates heart rate. Am. J. Physiol.-Heart Circ. Physiol. **241**(4), 620–629 (1981)
10. Bamieh, B., Giarre, L.: Identification of linear parameter varying models. Int. J. Robust Nonlinear Control **12**(9), 841–853 (2002)
11. Deep, K., Singh, K.P., Kansal, M.L., Mohan, C.: A real coded genetic algorithm for solving integer and mixed integer optimization problems. Appl. Math. Comput. **212**(2), 505–518 (2009)
12. Schwarz, G.: Estimating the dimension of a model. Ann. Stat. **6**(2), 461–464 (1978)
13. Pitzalis, M.V., et al.: Effect of respiratory rate on the relationships between RR interval and systolic blood pressure fluctuations: a frequency-dependent phenomenon. Cardiovasc. Res. **38**(2), 332–339 (1998)

ECG Segmentation by Adaptive Rational Transform

Gergő Bognár$^{(\boxtimes)}$ ⓘ and Sándor Fridli ⓘ

Department of Numerical Analysis, Faculty of Informatics,
ELTE Eötvös Loránd University, Budapest, Hungary
bognargergo@caesar.elte.hu, fridli@inf.elte.hu

Abstract. We propose a novel method to delineate and segment ECG heartbeats, i.e. to provide model curves for the P, QRS, and T waves, and to extract the fiducial points of them. The main idea of our method is to apply an adaptive transformation by means of rational functions to model the heartbeats and their waveforms. We suggest to represent the heartbeats with a linear combination of rational functions that are selected adaptively to the ECG signals through a non-linear optimization. This leads to a simple, yet morphologically accurate description of the heartbeats, and results a direct segmentation of them. Then, we derived the fiducial points based on the analytical model curves extracted from the rational representation. Multiple geometric concepts and their combination is discussed to this order. The evaluations were performed on the QT Database, and the results are compared to the previous ones, proving the efficiency of our method.

Keywords: ECG signals · Heartbeat segmentation · Fiducial point detection · Adaptive transformation · Rational function systems

1 Introduction

Computer-assisted electrocardiogram (ECG) analysis has been under intense research focus since decades and still today. Automated ECG processing techniques are important tools for medical doctors, which can effectively help to handle certain clinical situation (e.g. real-time and long-term monitoring). Besides the clinical practice, the spread of mobile and smart ECG devices demands reliable and efficient techniques. In this paper, we focus on the problem of ECG heartbeat delineation and segmentation. Normally, ECG heartbeats have similar morphology, and consist of certain waveforms, the so-called P wave, QRS complex, and T wave. The actual shape of this waveforms, their duration, and the

G. Bognár—Supported by the ÚNKP-18-3 New National Excellence Program of the Ministry of Human Capacities of Hungary.
S. Fridli—EFOP-3.6.3-VEKOP-16-2017-00001: Talent Management in Autonomous Vehicle Control Technologies - The Project is supported by the Hungarian Government and co-financed by the European Social Fund.

© Springer Nature Switzerland AG 2020
R. Moreno-Díaz et al. (Eds.): EUROCAST 2019, LNCS 12014, pp. 347–354, 2020.
https://doi.org/10.1007/978-3-030-45096-0_43

time interval between them carry medical information about the patient's cardiac condition. Also, cardiologists derive certain diagnostic descriptors based on the segmentation (e.g. QRS duration, QTc, VAT) that serve as objective metrics. To this order, the so-called fiducial points of these waveforms should be determined, that are the on- and offset, and peak points of the curves. The problem is ill-defined: the actually selected fiducial points may differ per cardiologist, although that does not interfere with their diagnosis. Also, the human-based evaluation is extremely time-consuming, even for a short measurement, which brings the computer-assisted techniques into the picture. The automatic ECG segmentation can help the diagnostic evaluation of the patient's current condition, track the changes in time, but it may also be utilized to detect abnormalities, as well.

We propose a novel method based on an adaptive rational transformation of the ECG heartbeats, and then the extraction and combination of geometric descriptors based on the model curves. Transformation methods have a long history in signal processing, and specifically in ECG signal processing. Here we only mention the trigonometric Fourier-transform, wavelets, and other orthogonal systems, like Hermite and Walsh. Although a transformation with a fixed system is in general efficient, adaptive methods, when the system itself has free system parameters that can be adapted to the signals, may perform better in certain cases. Namely, better approximation and representation properties may be achieved. Also, the transformation serves as a filtering and dimension-reduction of the original signal, resulting a model that captures only the relevant details of the waveforms. Here we propose to utilize an adaptive transformation based on rational function systems. These systems are well-known in signal processing and control theory, and previous studies show their possible applications in ECG signal processing [1–5,10]. The main idea behind using these specific systems to model ECG signals is their high flexibility, mathematical advantages, and the direct connection with the ECG waveforms. Namely, the adaptive rational system can be designed according to the shape of the heartbeats, thus the system parameters and the coefficients of the projection carry direct medical information. We acknowledge the RAIT Matlab Toolbox [13] that are involved for the calculations and simulations.

We also refer here to a few recent ECG segmentation results: a method based on low-pass-differentiation (LPD) [15], one based on wavelets [17], and one involving adaptive Hermite functions [12].

Our method is validated against the QT Database [14], available on PhysioNet [7]. This database is a common benchmark for heartbeat segmentation and QT evaluation methods, thus our results can be directly compared to the other methods. The database contains 105 records selected from other well-known database, where the original annotations were extended by fiducial points, determined by cardiologists. This results a total of 3623 annotated (normal) heartbeats, available on two leads (typically MLII and V1-6). Although this database is important for the objective evaluation and comparison of methods, it shows the difficulty and ill-defined nature of the problem: we can observe systematic and random differences between the annotations of two cardiologists.

2   Rational Function Systems

In this paper, an adaptive transformation by rational function systems is utilized to model ECG heartbeats. To this order, let us define the basic rational functions of the form:

$$r_{a,k}(z) := \frac{1}{(1 - \overline{a}z)^k} \qquad (z \in \mathbb{D}),$$

where $a \in \mathbb{D}$ is the so-called inverse pole, $k \in \mathbb{N}^+$ is the degree of $r_{a,k}$, and $\mathbb{D}$ denotes the (open) unit disk of complex numbers. We take the restriction of these functions to the unit circle $\mathbb{T}$, which fits the signal processing problem, considering the natural association between $\mathbb{T}$ and the interval $[-\pi, \pi)$. Given $n \in \mathbb{N}^+$ distinct inverse poles $\{a_k \in \mathbb{D} : k = 0, \ldots, n - 1\}$ associated with multiplicities $m_k \in \mathbb{N}^+$, our general signal model is as follows:

$$E(t) := \Re \left(\sum_{k=0}^{n-1} \sum_{\ell=1}^{m_k} c_{k\ell} \cdot r_{a_k,\ell}(e^{it}) \right) \qquad (t \in [-\pi, \pi)).$$

Here the coefficients $c_{k\ell} \in \mathbb{C}$ are determined as a least square approximation of the original signal, i.e. we take the orthogonal projection to the subspace spanned by the rational system (defined by the inverse poles and multiplicities). The problem can be discussed in the Hilbert-space $L^2(\mathbb{T})$ of square integrable function over $\mathbb{T}$, with the usual scalar product. The actual calculation of the coefficients, and the reconstruction of the model curve can performed efficiently, using only the basic mathematical operation. Here we remark that we have orthogonal (Malmquist–Takenaka) and biorthogonal [6] representations at hand, that can be expressed by the well-known Blaschke-functions. For more details on rational systems we refer to [9].

It the inverse poles and multiplicities, and so the rational system is given, then we have a Fourier-like transformation method with a rational basis, as defined above. The actual problem is the proper selection of these system parameters, adapted to the signals. The questions include the number, multiplicities, and values of the inverse poles. In general, pole identification is a non-linear optimization problem, where a certain, so-called *variable projection functional* [8, 11] needs to be minimized. The actual form of the functional, as well as the scope and strategy of the optimization, and the utilized method may differ per ECG processing problems. During the previous applications of the rational systems we have found that different problems require different parameter selection and representation methods [1, 11]. The one developed for ECG segmentation is discussed in Sect. 3.

3   Methodology

The proposed methods consists of the following steps: preprocessing and extraction of heartbeats, model identification and rational transformation, geometric feature extraction from the model curves, combination of the descriptors.

3.1 Preprocessing and Heartbeat Extraction

The goals of the first step are to reduce the noise, to approximately extract the heartbeat segments, and to precondition the signal for optimization step.

Before the rational transformation is applied, the ECG signal need to split into heartbeat segments. Here we utilize an adaptive fixed window scheme discussed in [2]. Each heartbeat segment is window around the R-peak, containing 100 samples before and 200 samples after that. Then, adaptively to the RR intervals, a few leading and trailing samples are cleared (faded to 0) in order to reduce the overlapping of the subsequent heartbeats in the window. This leads to a simple, yet rough estimation of the heartbeat segments that approximately contain the ECG waveforms. The R-peak locations are extracted from the QT Database annotations. We note that in a real application a heartbeat detector should be implemented as well.

ECG signals may suffer from several type of noise and artifacts, like electric noise, power line interference, and baseline wandering. Although the rational transformation itself acts as a filtering method, the pole identification is more stable if the signal is preprocessed using the usual techniques. On the other hand, it is important to locate the proper baseline for the geometric fiducial point extraction. Here we applied a low-pass filter with cutoff frequency of 35 Hz to reduce the high-frequency noise, and a two-pass filter to remove the baseline wandering. First, a wavelet-based method [18] is applied to the whole signal. Then, after the segmentation, the pre-R and post-R parts of the heartbeats are fitted and corrected with linear functions, in order to eliminate local oscillations and effects like ST depression.

Usually, the amplitudes of the ECG waveforms are not only different, but differently scaled. Namely, the R-peaks are usually much higher than the P and T-peaks. In order to compensate this effect, we produce preconditioned versions of the heartbeats for the optimization methods, where the amplitudes of the waveforms are estimated, and approximately normalized.

3.2 Adaptive Rational Transformation

As discussed in Sect. 2, the essential step of the adaptive rational transformation is the identification of the inverse poles. Previous studies show that it is reasonable to use three inverse poles, corresponding to the P, QRS, and T waves, and to choose higher multiplicity for the QRS complex, as it is usually the most complex part of the heartbeat. This way, after a proper pole selection, we can provide a morphologically accurate description of the heartbeats. Namely, the inverse poles approximately locate the waveforms, and describe their general behavior, and the linear coefficients reflect to the details of them. Moreover, the rational transformation provides a direct delineation of the waveforms. Previous studies work with per-patient and per-heartbeat combinations, i.e. when the same pole combination is utilized for every heartbeat of the records, or when each heartbeat is represented with an individual pole combination. Both concepts has its reasons and advantages. Namely, in the per-patient case, the pole combination

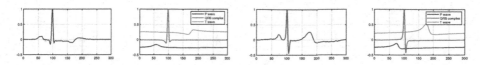

Fig. 1. Extracted model curves of the waveforms for two heartbeats from record sel100 (1–2) and sel16272 (3–4) of QT Database.

carry medical information about the average behavior of the patient's heart, and every heartbeat is represented with the same, patient-adapted basis. This makes the representations comparable, which is useful e.g. for classification [1,2]. In the per-heartbeat case, the pole combination reflects to the variations of the heartbeat, which leads to a better approximation, e.g. for compression [11].

Here, we suggest to use three inverse poles with a fixed $(1, 4, 1)$ multiplicities, respectively. This representation catches the basic behavior of the P and T waves, and the relevant details of the QRS complex, as well. Then the model for the heartbeats takes the form:

$$E(t) := \Re\left(c_0 + \underbrace{c_1 \cdot r_{a_1}(e^{it})}_{=:E_1^*(t)} + \underbrace{\sum_{j=1}^{4} c_{2j} \cdot r_{a_2,j}(e^{it})}_{=:E_2^*(t)} + \underbrace{c_3 \cdot r_{a_3}(e^{it})}_{=:E_3^*(t)} \right) \qquad (t \in [-\pi, \pi)),$$

where $c_* \in \mathbb{C}$ are the linear coefficients, $a_1, a_2, a_3 \in \mathbb{D}$ are the inverse poles, and E_1^*, E_2^*, E_3^* are the complex model curves corresponding to the P, QRS, and T waves, respectively. The segmented model curves for the waveforms are derived from the complex model curves above by the normalization:

$$E_k(t) := \Re\left(E_k^*(t) - \int_{-\pi}^{\pi} E_k^* \right) \qquad (t \in [-\pi, \pi), \; k = 1, 2, 3).$$

We propose to perform the pole optimization in two steps. First a global, patient-wise pole combination is determined for each record, then a pole combination for each heartbeat is selected based on the globally fitting poles. More precisely, the first optimization is performed including every annotated heartbeat of the record, the objective function is selected to be the sum of the mean squared approximation errors. This optimization if performed on the precon-ditioned heartbeats, because otherwise, the amplitude differences may mislead the optimization. Namely, the resulting pole combination may not fit our rep-resentation goals, i.e. that the inverse poles should distinctly correspond to the waveforms. The result of the first optimization is a globally fitting pole combi-nation, where the complex argument of the inverse poles correlate to the average location of the waveforms. The second optimization is performed for each heart-beat individually. Here, the objective function is the approximation error, and the search space is restricted to the neighborhood of the globally fitted poles. The result of the second optimization takes the variations of the locations and shapes of the waveforms into account, as well. In both cases, Hyperbolic Nelder–Mead

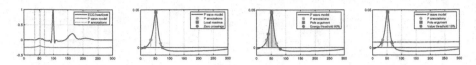

Fig. 2. Fiducial point extraction for a P wave: a heartbeat from record sel103 of QT Database (1), fiducial points extracted by geometric (2), model and energy (3), and modified geometric (4) approach.

[4, 16] optimization method is utilized. Validated on the QT Database, we have found that the proposed method leads to stable and morphologically accurate representation of the heartbeats and the waveforms. Figure 1 demonstrates the results of the delineation for two, differently shaped heartbeats.

3.3   Fiducial Point Extraction

The next goal is to extract the fiducial points of the P, QRS, and T waves, i.e. to find their on- and offset, and peak points.

The adaptive rational transformation discussed above results simple analytical model curves for the waveforms. Moreover, these curves act as filtered versions of the original waveforms that contains only the relevant morphological information about them. Our idea is to derive the fiducial points based on descriptors extracted from these analytical model curves. We also refer to [3], where the mathematical background of geometric interpretation is introduced, as well as evaluation for the QRS complexes. Here, the models are extended to the P and T waves, as well. In the following, we suggest multiple approaches to extract descriptors.

Geometric Approach. Based on a geometric point of view, the fiducial points can be associated with certain characteristic points (local extrema and zero crossing points) of the model curves. Here the proper location of the baseline is important, and the even and odd type of model curves need to be distinguished.

Model-Based Approach. The basic and elementary rational functions are localized in time corresponding to the complex argument of their inverse poles. Thus, the inverse poles carry information about the location of the waveforms, we can estimate the peaks based on them.

Modified Geometric Approach. The geometric approach above estimates the on- and offset points of an even model curves by the zeros crossing points. We have found that, in some cases, a better estimation can be given by a modified approach. Namely, we suggest to use the first point before and after the peak, where the absolute of the model curve reaches a threshold. Let $\alpha_k \in \mathbb{D}$ the peak location, and $g_k \in [0, 1]$ a given threshold ratio, then we are looking for the first or last time location $t^* \in (\alpha_k, \pi)$ or $[-\pi, \alpha_k)$ so that:

$$|E_k(t^*)| \leq g_k \cdot \max\{|E_k(t)| : t \in [-\pi, \pi]\} \qquad (k = 1, 2, 3).$$

Table 1. Performance evaluation and comparison to the reference works.

	Proposed		LPD [15]		Wavelet [17]		Hermite [12]	
	$\overline{\mu_e}$	$\overline{\sigma_e}$	$\overline{\mu_e}$	$\overline{\sigma_e}$	$\overline{\mu_e}$	$\overline{\sigma_e}$	$\overline{\mu_e}$	$\overline{\sigma_e}$
P_{on}	0.17	34.14	14.02	13.32	2.00	14.80	1.05	14.86
P_{peak}	**1.25**	**14.88**	4.78	10.56	3.60	13.20	11.10	14.58
P_{end}	0.09	35.54	−0.12	12.32	1.90	12.80	13.21	15.81
T_{peak}	−9.07	25.49	−7.19	14.28	0.20	13.90	−10.92	12.49
T_{end}	1.08	34.44	13.50	27.00	−1.60	18.10	5.19	16.83

$\overline{\mu_e}, \overline{\sigma_e}$: average bias and standard deviation of time differences (in ms).

Energy-Based Approach. Another suggestion, we found effective in some cases, is the first point before and after the peak, where the energy reaches a threshold. Again, let $\alpha_k \in \mathbb{D}$ the peak location, and $e_k \in [0, 1]$ a given threshold ratio, and we are looking for the first or last time location $t^* \in (\alpha_k, \pi)$ or $[-\pi, \alpha_k)$ so that:

$$\left| \int_{\alpha_k}^{t^*} |E_k(t)|^2 \, dt \right| \leq e_k \cdot \int_{-\pi}^{\pi} |E_k(t)|^2 \, dt \qquad (k = 1, 2, 3).$$

Figure 2 demonstrates the results of the different approaches for a P wave. As the final result, the peaks for the P wave are extracted by model-based, and for the T wave by geometric approach. The on- and offset points are estimated using a combination of the approaches, where we selected the thresholds by an empirical way. The adaptive selection of the thresholds may be part of a further research.

4   Results and Conclusion

We developed a segmentation and fiducial point extraction method for ECG heartbeats. The proposed method is based on a properly adjusted adaptive rational transformation that results a morphologically accurate delineation of the ECG waveforms, and a combination of multiple approaches to extract the fiducial points.

We validated our method on the QT Database using the common metrics. For every fiducial points, the time difference e between the database annotations and the predicted labels is evaluated. Then the average and the standard deviation of e is calculated, and averaged by the recordings. Table 1 presents the evaluated metrics, compared to the previous results. Here we discuss the results only for the P and T waves. We can conclude that the rational representation allows accurate localization of the P wave, and acceptable localization of the T wave.

References

1. Bognár, G., Fridli, S.: Heartbeat classification of ECG signals using rational function systems. In: Moreno-Díaz, R., Pichler, F., Quesada-Arencibia, A. (eds.) EUROCAST 2017. LNCS, vol. 10672, pp. 187–195. Springer, Cham (2018). https://doi.org/10.1007/978-3-319-74727-9_22

2. Bognár, G., Fridli, S.: ECG heartbeat classification by means of variable rational projection (to appear)
3. Bognár, G., Schipp, F.: Geometric interpretation of QRS complexes in ECG signals by rational functions. Ann. Univ. Sci. Bp. Sect. Comput. **47**, 155–166 (2018)
4. Fridli, S., Kovács, P., Lócsi, L., Schipp, F.: Rational modeling of multi-lead QRS complexes in ECG signals. Ann. Univ. Sci. Bp. Sect. Comput. **37**, 145–155 (2012)
5. Fridli, S., Lócsi, L., Schipp, F.: Rational function systems in ECG processing. In: Moreno-Díaz, R., Pichler, F., Quesada-Arencibia, A. (eds.) EUROCAST 2011. LNCS, vol. 6927, pp. 88–95. Springer, Heidelberg (2012). https://doi.org/10.1007/978-3-642-27549-4_12
6. Fridli, S., Schipp, F.: Biorthogonal systems to rational functions. Ann. Univ. Sci. Bp. Sect. Comput. **35**, 95–105 (2011)
7. Goldberger, A.L., et al.: PhysioBank, PhysioToolkit, and PhysioNet: components of a new research resource for complex physiologic signals. Circulation **101**(23), e215–e220 (2000)
8. Golub, G.H., Pereyra, V.: The differentiation of pseudo-inverses and nonlinear least squares problems whose variables separate. SIAM J. Numer. Anal. **10**(2), 413–432 (1973)
9. Heuberger, P.S.C., van den Hof, P.M.J., Wahlberg, B. (eds.): Modelling and Identification with Rational Orthogonal Basis Functions. Springer, London (2005). https://doi.org/10.1007/1-84628-178-4
10. Kovács, P.: Transformation methods in signal processing. Ph.D. thesis, ELTE Eötvös Loránd University, Budapest, Hungary, May 2016
11. Kovács, P.: Rational variable projection methods in ECG signal processing. In: Moreno-Díaz, R., Pichler, F., Quesada-Arencibia, A. (eds.) EUROCAST 2017. LNCS, vol. 10672, pp. 196–203. Springer, Cham (2018). https://doi.org/10.1007/978-3-319-74727-9_23
12. Kovács, P., Böck, C., Meier, J., Huemer, M.: ECG segmentation using adaptive Hermite functions. In: 2017 51st Asilomar Conference on Signals, Systems, and Computers, pp. 1476–1480, October 2017
13. Kovács, P., Lócsi, L.: RAIT: the rational approximation and interpolation toolbox for Matlab, with experiments on ECG signals. Int. J. Adv. Telecom. Elect. Sign. Syst. **1**(2–3), 67–752 (2012)
14. Laguna, P., Mark, R.G., Goldberg, A., Moody, G.B.: A database for evaluation of algorithms for measurement of QT and other waveform intervals in the ECG. In: IEEE Computers in Cardiology, pp. 673–676, September 1997
15. Laguna, P., Jané, R., Caminal, P.: Automatic detection of wave boundaries in multilead ECG signals: validation with the CSE database. Comput. Biomed. Res. **27**(1), 45–60 (1994)
16. Lócsi, L.: A hyperbolic variant of the Nelder–Mead simplex method in low dimensions. Acta Univ. Sapientiae Math. **5**(2), 169–183 (2013)
17. Martinez, J.P., Almeida, R., Olmos, S., Rocha, A.P., Laguna, P.: A wavelet-based ECG delineator: evaluation on standard databases. IEEE Trans. Biomed. Eng. **51**(4), 570–581 (2004)
18. Zhang, D.: Wavelet approach for ECG baseline wander correction and noise reduction. In: Proceedings of International Conference of the IEEE Engineering in Medicine and Biology Society, pp. 1212–1215 (2005)

Ensemble Learning for Heartbeat Classification Using Adaptive Orthogonal Transformations

Tamás Dózsa[1] , Gergő Bognár[1] , and Péter Kovács[1,2]( )

[1] Department of Numerical Analysis, Eötvös Loránd University, Budapest, Hungary
tamasdzs@gmail.com, bognargergo@caesar.elte.hu, kovika@inf.elte.hu
[2] Institute of Signal Processing, Johannes Kepler University, Linz, Austria

Abstract. In this work, we are focusing on the problem of heartbeat classification in electrocardiogram (ECG) signals. First we develop a patient-specific feature extraction scheme by using adaptive orthogonal transformations based on wavelets, B-splines, Hermite and rational functions. The so-called variable projection provides the general framework to find the optimal nonlinear parameters of these transformations. After extracting the features, we train a support vector machine (SVM) for each model whose outputs are combined via ensemble learning techniques. In the experiments, we achieved an accuracy of 94.2% on the PhysioNet MIT-BIH Arrhythmia Database that shows the potential of the proposed signal models in arrhythmia detection.

Keywords: ECG classification · Patient-specific feature extraction · Ensemble learning · Variable projection

1 Introduction

Recent advances in biomedical engineering make it possible to record physiological signals in various ways. For instance, ECG can be measured by portable devices, which highly increase the demand for computer-assisted interpretation and analysis of these signals, with an emphasis on arrhythmia detection. The problem of detecting cardiovascular illnesses can be presented as a classification task, where the ECG of patients has to be classified in a heartbeat to heartbeat manner. This means that after an initial segmentation and preprocessing of the measurements, we assign each heartbeat to one of the following classes: supraventricular (S), ventricular (V), fusion (F), unknown (Q), and normal (N). These classes were suggested in [1] and provide a basis for the comparison of our approach with other ECG classification algorithms. We use the PhysioNet MIT-BIH Arrhythmia Database [2] to evaluate the performance of the proposed method

EFOP-3.6.3-VEKOP-16-2017-00001: Talent Management in Autonomous Vehicle Control Technologies – The Project is supported by the Hungarian Government and co-financed by the European Social Fund.

© Springer Nature Switzerland AG 2020
R. Moreno-Díaz et al. (Eds.): EUROCAST 2019, LNCS 12014, pp. 355–363, 2020.
https://doi.org/10.1007/978-3-030-45096-0_44

and compare it to the state-of-the-art. This database includes a large number of annotated heartbeats and has been frequently used in automatic arrhythmia detection research [3].

Raw ECGs contain noise as well as diagnostically insignificant information. In order to obtain the best possible classification results, we expose the heartbeats to mathematical transformations, by which we extract the clinically relevant information from the signal. Then, for each heartbeat, we construct a feature vector that includes the parameters of the corresponding transformation. We consider a wavelet based linear model, and adaptive nonlinear models using three different function systems, i.e., B-splines with free knots [4,5], Hermite functions with free translation, dilation [6], and rational functions with free poles [7,8]. We note that the present approach builds on our previous ECG classification algorithm described in [9], however in that work ECG signals were assigned to 16 different classes, and the features were extracted using rational functions only.

After extracting the features, we train a support vector machine (SVM) for each model, i.e., wavelets, B-splines, Hermite and rational functions, using ten-fold cross-validation. Once the training is finished, we evaluate the classification accuracies on a test set that is independent of the training data. For each heartbeat, the result of the classification is a vector of posterior probabilities, which indicates the likelihood of the beat to belong to a certain class. Finally, we enhance the precision of the four individual classifications by applying ensemble learning strategies.

2   Feature Extraction

2.1   Adaptive Signal Models

The first step in the classification of a heartbeat signal is to extract a feature vector representation. In this work, we use linear and nonlinear mathematical transformations to construct the features for each heartbeat. Through this process we hope to obtain the information stored in the original noisy signal. Another advantage of using these transformations for feature extraction is the decrease in dimension. While the original heartbeat was given by $N \in \mathbb{N}$ samples, after the transformation it can be represented by $n \in \mathbb{N}$ $(n \ll N)$ parameters. This makes the subsequent classification task easier for the support vector machine.

Let us consider an ECG signal $f \in \mathcal{H}$ where $\mathcal{H}$ is a Hilbert-space. Furthermore let $\mathcal{S} \subset \mathcal{H}$ be a closed subspace and $\hat{f}$ be the orthogonal projection of f onto $\mathcal{S}$. The orthogonal projection can be expressed as the solution to

$$\mathrm{dist}(f, \mathcal{S}) := \min_{g \in \mathcal{S}} \|f - g\|_2 = \|f - \hat{f}\|_2 , \tag{1}$$

where $\|g\|_2 = \sqrt{\langle g, g \rangle}$ is induced by the corresponding dot product in $\mathcal{H}$.

If we now consider the orthonormal functions $\Phi_0, \Phi_1, \ldots, \Phi_{n-1}$ $(n \in \mathbb{N}_+)$ such that $\mathcal{S} = \mathrm{span}\{\Phi_0, \Phi_1, \ldots, \Phi_{n-1}\}$, the solution $\hat{f}$ to (1) can be expressed as:

$$\hat{f} = P_{\mathcal{S}} f := \sum_{k=0}^{n-1} c_k \Phi_k , \tag{2}$$

where $c_k = \langle f, \Phi_k \rangle$ denotes the coefficients. Given a suitable $\{\Phi_k \,|\, 0 \leq k < n\}$ function system, (2) seems to be a good method for extracting features. However, we note that ECG heartbeats show patient-to-patient variance in shape. Therefore, choosing a priori the set of functions that span $\mathcal{S}$ is inefficient, as the error of the approximation depends heavily on the signal.

One way to mitigate this problem is to replace the functions $\Phi_0, \Phi_1, \ldots, \Phi_{n-1}$ with an adaptive system $\{\Phi_k(\boldsymbol{\eta}; \cdot) \,|\, 0 \leq k < n\}$, which depends on the vector of nonlinear parameters $\boldsymbol{\eta} \in \mathbb{R}^m$. Adjusting the value of $\boldsymbol{\eta}$ changes the spanned subspace $\mathcal{S}(\boldsymbol{\eta})$, which lets us adapt the approach for each patient. We can express this adaptation in terms of minimizing the so-called variable projection (VP) functional [10]:

$$\min_{\boldsymbol{\eta} \in \mathbb{R}^m} r_2(\boldsymbol{\eta}) := \min_{\boldsymbol{\eta} \in \mathbb{R}^m} \|f - P_{\mathcal{S}(\boldsymbol{\eta})} f\|_2^2 = \min_{\boldsymbol{\eta} \in \mathbb{R}^m} \Big\| f - \sum_{k=0}^{n-1} c_k(\boldsymbol{\eta}) \cdot \Phi_k(\boldsymbol{\eta}; \cdot) \Big\|_2^2, \quad (3)$$

where $c_k(\boldsymbol{\eta})$'s denote the coefficients with respect to $\boldsymbol{\eta}$. In this work, we extracted the feature vectors from ECG heartbeats using four different models. Three of these can be expressed in terms of (3), while the wavelet based approach is a linear model that can be calculated via [11].

2.2   Rational Model

Here, we briefly describe the rational model used for feature extraction, which was introduced to model ECG signals in [7]. Let us consider the Malmquist–Takenaka (MT) system:

$$\Psi_k(\boldsymbol{b}; z) = \frac{\sqrt{1 - |b_k|^2}}{1 - \overline{b_k} z} \cdot \prod_{\ell=0}^{k-1} \frac{z - b_\ell}{1 - \overline{b_\ell} z} \qquad (z \in \mathbb{C}), \quad (4)$$

where the so-called inverse poles b_ℓ's lie in the unit disk $\mathbb{D}$. The MT system can be discretized by sampling these functions uniformly over the unit circle, i.e., $z_j = e^{i2\pi j/N}$ $(j = 0, \ldots, N-1)$, and we can define the matrix $\boldsymbol{\Phi}(\boldsymbol{b})_{jk} = \Phi_k(\boldsymbol{b}; z_j)$. According to (3), the best approximation of an ECG heartbeat $\mathbf{f} \in \mathbb{R}^N$ with $N \in \mathbb{N}$ samples can be reformulated as a VP problem:

$$\min_b r_2(\boldsymbol{b}) = \min_b \|\mathbf{f} - \boldsymbol{\Phi}(\boldsymbol{b}) \mathbf{c}(\boldsymbol{b})\|_2^2 = \min_b \|\mathbf{f} - \boldsymbol{\Phi}(\boldsymbol{b}) \boldsymbol{\Phi}^+(\boldsymbol{b}) \mathbf{f}\|_2^2, \quad (5)$$

where $\boldsymbol{\Phi}^+(\boldsymbol{b})$ denotes the Moore–Penrose inverse of $\boldsymbol{\Phi}(\boldsymbol{b})$. We extend this problem by optimizing $\boldsymbol{b}$ simultaneously for a sequence of $M \in \mathbb{N}$ heartbeats as follows:

$$\min_b \sum_{i=1}^{M} \|\mathbf{f}^{(i)} - \boldsymbol{\Phi}(\boldsymbol{b}) \boldsymbol{\Phi}^+(\boldsymbol{b}) \mathbf{f}^{(i)}\|_2^2. \quad (6)$$

Since the shape characteristics of ECG heartbeats remain similar in case of a single patient, we can construct an efficient algorithm for determining the optimal values of b. It is sufficient to solve (6) for the first few heartbeats of the recording, then use the resulting value of b for the rest of the heartbeats.

The feature vectors include the coefficients $c(b)$ and the error of the approximation. Additionally, we extended these features by the RR-interval information of the ECG, i.e., pre-RR, post-RR, local, and average RR-peak distances (see e.g., [11] and [12]). In the rational model, we used 3 different inverse poles ($a = (a_1, a_2, a_3)^T \in \mathbb{D}^3$) with the multiplicities of $(2, 4, 2)$, i.e., $b = (a_1, a_1, a_2, a_2, a_2, a_2, a_3, a_3)^T \in \mathbb{D}^8$. For each recording in the database, we took the first $M = 20$ heartbeats to calculate the optimal value of b in (6).

2.3   B-Spline Model

Let $[a, b] \subset \mathbb{R}$ be a real interval and $\ell \in \mathbb{N}$ ($\ell \ll N$) be the degree of splines, where N is the number of samples in the heartbeat. We now identify the function system in (3) as the set of B-splines $\{B_{\ell,k}(\tau; \cdot) \mid k = -\ell, \dots, n-1\}$, which is characterized by the knot vector $\tau = (t_{-\ell}, t_{-\ell+1}, \dots, t_{n+\ell})^T \in [a, b]^{n+2\ell+1}$. Then, the corresponding VP problem can be written in the form:

$$\min_{\tau} r_2(\tau) = \min_{\tau} \sum_{j=1}^{N} \left(f_j - \sum_{k=-\ell}^{n-1} c_k(\tau) \cdot B_{\ell,k}(\tau; x_j) \right)^2, \tag{7}$$

where $c_k(\tau)$'s denote the least-squares regression coefficients for the corresponding knot vector τ, and f_j represents the value of the signal sampled at $x_j \in [a, b]$. In order to solve (7) for cubic splines ($\ell = 3$), we applied an iterative knot-reduction algorithm [4]. Once the optimal knots have been identified, we can construct the feature vector that includes the coefficients $c_k(\tau)$'s, the error of the approximation as well as RR-interval information.

2.4   Hermite-Model

In addition to the B-spline and the rational models, we extracted features by using the system of adaptive Hermite-functions [6]. Let us consider the set of classical Hermite polynomials $\{h_k \mid k \in \mathbb{N}\}$, which are orthogonal with respect to the weighted dot product [13], i.e.,

$$\|h_k\|_2^2 \cdot \delta_{kj} = \langle h_k, h_j \rangle_w := \int_{\mathbb{R}} h_k(x) h_j(x) w(x) \mathrm{d}x \quad (j, k \in \mathbb{N}),$$

where $w(x) = e^{-x^2}$ is the corresponding weight function. Using these polynomials, the system of orthonormal Hermite functions can be defined as follows:

$$\Phi_k(x) = h_k(x) / \|h_k\|_2 \cdot \sqrt{w(x)} \quad (k \in \mathbb{N}). \tag{8}$$

To extend the model with nonlinear parameters, we transform the argument of the Hermite functions [6]. This yields the set of orthonormal functions

$$\Phi_k(\tau; \lambda; x) := \sqrt{\lambda} \cdot \Phi_k(\lambda(x - \tau)) \qquad (x, \tau \in \mathbb{R}, \lambda > 0), \tag{9}$$

where the dilatation parameter λ denotes the length of the unit, and the translation parameter τ determines the position of zero on the real line $\mathbb{R}$. The extension of the VP problem in (3) to affine Hermite functions is now straightforward. The resulting feature vector includes the nonlinear parameters λ, τ, the corresponding least-squares regression coefficients, the error of the approximation, and the RR-interval information.

3 Classification

3.1 Classifier

The heartbeats were classified using SVMs with radial basis kernel functions of the form: $K(\boldsymbol{x}_i, \boldsymbol{x}_j) \equiv \phi(\boldsymbol{x}_i)^T \phi(\boldsymbol{x}_j) = \exp(-\gamma \|\boldsymbol{x}_i - \boldsymbol{x}_j\|^2)$, $\gamma > 0$. In general, let $\{(\boldsymbol{x}_i, y_i) \mid \boldsymbol{x}_i \in \mathbb{R}^n, \ y_i \in \{1, -1\}^{\ell}, \ (i = 1, \dots, l)\}$ be the set of feature vector and class label pairs, where $l \in \mathbb{N}$ is the number of training samples. Then, SVM gives the solution to the following optimization problem [14]:

$$\underset{w,b,\xi}{\text{minimize}} \quad \frac{1}{2} \boldsymbol{w}^T \boldsymbol{w} + C \cdot \sum_{i=1}^{l} \xi_i$$

$$\text{subject to} \quad y_i(\boldsymbol{w}^T \phi(\boldsymbol{x}_i) + b) \geq 1 - \xi_i,$$

$$\xi_i \geq 0.$$

The method has two hyperparameters: $\gamma > 0$ parametrize the kernel, and $C > 0$ penalize the misclassification rate on the training set. The optimal values of these parameters are determined through cross-validation on the training set. Originally, SVM is a binary classifier that can be extended to multi-class problems in several ways. Here, we employed the one-by-one extension. The output of the classification for a given test sample is a vector of posterior probabilities $\mathbf{p} \in \mathbb{R}^n$, where $n \in \mathbb{N}$ is the number of classes, and p_i is the probability of the sample belonging to class i.

3.2 Classification Scheme

We performed the classification procedure in the following way:

1. For each of the heartbeats in the database, feature vectors were extracted using the models described in the previous sections. We refer to the feature vectors of a single model as a feature set.
2. Following the recommendation of [12] for a subject-oriented (inter-patient) classification, the heartbeats were divided into independent training (DS1) and test (DS2) set.

3. For each feature set, the optimal hyperparameters of SVM were determined using a tenfold cross-validation on the training set.
4. For each feature set, an SVM classifier was trained on the training set using the hyperparameters obtained from step 3.
5. For each feature set, the test set was classified using the SVM model trained in step 4, and then overall classification accuracy and confusion matrix was evaluated. In addition, the resulting posterior probabilities are also stored for each heartbeat.
6. Ensemble strategies were employed utilizing the classification outputs of the different feature sets.

3.3   Ensemble Learning

In order to enhance the classification, we combined the results derived from different feature extraction methods. To this order, we examined three possible ensemble strategies. In all cases, we utilized the predicted labels and the posterior probabilities of a given group of feature sets as the input of the ensemble. The idea is that the feature extraction methods have differences, they may highlight different information of the heartbeats. Thus, the combination of them, assuming their partial independence, may lead to a better final prediction.

The first ensemble strategy we employed is a simple vote. For each heartbeat, each feature set 'voted' by their predicted labels. The label that got most of the votes won, and was assigned as the final prediction of the heartbeat. In case of a tie, we chose randomly between the winners.

The second strategy is a weighted vote. This approach is similar to the first, but we weighted the votes by the posterior probabilities. This results a refined and better combination. The further advantage of this approach is that we could filter the reliability of the predictions by the final posterior probability.

The third strategy is ensemble learning. Here we gathered the posterior probability vectors yielded by each single model classification of the given heartbeat, and created a new feature vector from them (by summing the probabilities for each class from each result). Then, an another SVM classifier was trained and tested using these feature vectors, as introduced in (Sect. 3.2). We remark, that here class labels were predicted for the training data as well (using the same trained models), in order to produce training features for the ensemble learning.

4   Results

In our experiments, we tested the proposed classification methods on the Physionet MIT-BIH Arrhythmia Database [2] including at about 100000 heartbeats, with sufficient representation of each of the five classes (S, V, F, Q, N). In Table 1, the first horizontal section contains the results of the state-of-the-art ECG classification techniques. The middle part shows the individual classification results for each model in Sect. 2. The last block summarizes the classification accuracies we obtained by ensemble learning. The columns contain the name of the examined method, the way of extracting features, the classifier (linear discriminant (LD) or SVM), and the average accuracy across the entire test set. In Table 1, we used the following acronyms to abbreviate the name of features:

- LC : linear coefficients of the transformation method.
- RR: RR-interval features [11,12].
- PRD: percent root mean square difference, i.e., error of the approximation.
- NLP: nonlinear parameters of the adaptive models.

Table 1. Comparison of proposed methods with the state-of-the-art.

Method	Features	Classifier	Accuracy
de Chazal et al. 2004 [12]	Waveform (fiducial points) + RR	LD	86.1%
Llamedo et al. 2011 [15]	Waveform (VCG, wavelet) + RR	LD	93%
Ye et al. 2012 [11]	Wavelet + ICA (PCA) + RR	SVM	86%
B-spline model	LC + RR + PRD	SVM	90.7%
Rational model	LC + RR + PRD	SVM	82.1%
Wavelet model	LC + RR	SVM	92.5%
Hermite model	LC + RR + PRD	SVM	90.9%
Hermite model	LC + NLP + PRD + RR	SVM	**93.6%**
Simple vote	Predicted labels (all models)	–	92.0%
Simple vote	Predicted labels (Wavelet + B-spline)	–	92.4%
Vote based on probabilities	Posterior probabilities (all models)	–	93.4%
Vote based on probabilities	Posterior probabilities (Wavelet + B-spline)	–	**94.2%**
Ensemble learning	Posterior probabilities (all models)	SVM	89.4%
Ensemble learning	Posterior probabilities (Wavelet + B-spline)	SVM	93.8%

The results show that the way we construct the feature vectors highly influences the classification accuracy. For instance, let us consider the results of the Hermite model, which improved significantly once we extended the features by the nonlinear parameters of the model. Note that the ensemble techniques can also improve the average accuracy of the classification. Using ensemble strategies on all of the results however, is sometimes less efficient than applying them on a selection of individual classification outputs. This phenomenon is demonstrated through the last two rows of the ensemble block in Table 1. Only when the posterior probabilities of the B-spline and the wavelet based classifications were included did the ensemble learning yield better results.

5   Conclusion

In this work, we examined the potential of adaptive signal models to classify ECG signals. Namely, we used a wavelet based linear model, and three adaptive nonlinear models, i.e., B-splines, Hermite, and rational functions, to extract features for the classification. The feature extraction step is reformulated as a variable projection problem in order to adapt the shape of the basic functions to the patient's ECG signal.

We developed an SVM based heartbeat classification scheme, in which we trained the classifier on patient-specific feature sets. Then, the accuracy of the individual classifiers are improved via ensemble learning techniques. The experiments on the MIT-BIH Arrhythmia Database show that the proposed adaptive transform based approaches are able to extract the clinically relevant information from the heartbeat signals. As a consequence, the classification accuracies are reasonably high for the individual classifiers as well as for the ensembles learning. It turned out that the proposed algorithm outperforms other state-of-the-art techniques in terms of classification accuracy. However, the optimal selection of patient-specific features, the combination of individual classification outputs, and the analysis of other properties, such as sensitivity and specificity, requires further research.

References

1. Testing and Reporting Performance Results of Cardiac Rhythm and ST-Segment Measurement Algorithms. American National Standard, ANSI/AAMI/ISO EC57. 1998-(R) (2008)
2. Goldberger, A.L., et al.: PhysioBank, PhysioToolkit, and PhysioNet: components of a new research resource for complex physiologic signals. Circulation **101**, 215–220 (2000)
3. Moody, G.B., Mark, R.G.: The impact of the MIT-BIH arrhythmia database. IEEE Eng. Med. Biol. Mag. **20**, 45–50 (2001)
4. Gabbouj, M., Karczewicz, M.: ECG data compression by spline approximation. Signal Process. **59**, 43–59 (1997)
5. Kovács, P., Fekete, A.M.: Nonlinear least-squares spline fitting with variable knots. Appl. Math. Comput. **2019**(354), 490–501 (2019)
6. Dózsa, T., Kovács, P.: ECG signal compression using adaptive hermite functions. In: Loshkovska, S., Koceski, S. (eds.) ICT Innovations 2015. AISC, vol. 399, pp. 245–254. Springer, Cham (2016). https://doi.org/10.1007/978-3-319-25733-4_25
7. Fridli, S., Lócsi, L., Schipp, F.: Rational function systems in ECG processing. In: Moreno-Díaz, R., Pichler, F., Quesada-Arencibia, A. (eds.) EUROCAST 2011. LNCS, vol. 6927, pp. 88–95. Springer, Heidelberg (2012). https://doi.org/10.1007/978-3-642-27549-4_12
8. Fridli, S., Kovács, P., Lócsi, L., Schipp, F.: Rational modeling of multi-lead QRS complexes in ECG signals. Ann. Univ. Sci. Budapest Sect. Comp. **37**, 145–155 (2012)
9. Bognár, G., Fridli, S.: Heartbeat classification of ECG signals using rational function systems. In: Moreno-Díaz, R., Pichler, F., Quesada-Arencibia, A. (eds.) EUROCAST 2017. LNCS, vol. 10672, pp. 187–195. Springer, Cham (2018). https://doi.org/10.1007/978-3-319-74727-9_22
10. Golub, G.H., Pereyra, V.: The differentiation of pseudo-inverses and nonlinear least squares problems whose variables separate. SIAM J. Numer. Anal. **10**, 413–432 (1973)

11. Ye, C., Kumar, B.V.K.V., Coimbra, M.T.: Heartbeat classification using morphological and dynamic features of ECG signals. IEEE Trans. Biomed. Eng. **59**, 2930–2941 (2012)
12. de Chazal, P., O'Dwyer, M., Reilly, B.R.: Automatic classification of heartbeats using ECG morphology and heartbeat interval features. IEEE Trans. Biomed. Eng. **51**, 1196–1206 (2004)
13. Szegő, G.: Orthogonal Polynomials, 3rd edn. AMS Colloquium Publications, New York (1967)
14. Hsu, C.-W., Chang, C.-C., Lin, C.-J.: A Practical Guide to Support Vector Machine Classification. National Taiwan University, pp. 1–16 (2016)
15. Llamendo, M., Khawaja, A., Martínez, J.P.: Cross-database evaluation of a multi-lead heartbeat classifier. IEEE Trans. Inf. Technol. Biomed. **16**, 658–664 (2012)

Epileptic Seizure Detection Using Piecewise Linear Reduction

Yash Paul[iD] and Sándor Fridli[(✉)][iD]

Department of Numerical Analysis, Faculty of Informatics, Eötvös L. University,
Pázmány P. sétány 1/C, Budapest 1117, Hungary
yashpaul1234567@gmail.com, fridli@inf.elte.hu
http://numanal.inf.elte.hu

Abstract. In this paper we propose a hybrid approach to detect seizure segments in a given EEG signal. In our model the discrete EEG signal is naturally associated with a piecewise linear function. We apply two data reduction techniques within the model space, a new half-wave method in the time domain, and orthogonal projection with the Franklin system in frequency domain. The later one is a complete orthogonal system of piecewise continuous functions. As a result we obtain two reduced piecewise linear functions with low complexity that still preserve the main characteristics of the seizures in the signals. Then the components of the feature vector are generated from the parameters of the two reduced functions. Our choice for the model space, i.e. the space of piecewise continuous functions, is justified by its simplicity on the one hand, and flexibility on the other hand. Accordingly the proposed algorithm is computationally fast and efficient. The algorithm is tested on 23 different subjects having more than 100 hours long term EEG in the CHB-MIT database in several respects. It showed better performance compared to the state of the art methods for seizure detection tested on the given database.

Keywords: Epilepsy · Seizure detection · Signal modeling · Half-wave method · Franklin system

1 Introduction

Epilepsy is a neurological disorder which causes drastic effects to human brain. According to the latest study by different prominent medical institutions of the world related to epilepsy more than 2% of the population worldwide is suffering from epilepsy and 85% of those live in developing countries like India and China.

The first author was supported by EFOP-3.6.3-VEKOP-16-2017-00001: Talent Management in Autonomous Vehicle Control Technologies - The Project is supported by the Hungarian Government and co-financed by the European Social Fund.
This research of the second author was supported by the Hungarian Scientific Research Funds (OTKA) No K115804.

© Springer Nature Switzerland AG 2020
R. Moreno-Díaz et al. (Eds.): EUROCAST 2019, LNCS 12014, pp. 364–371, 2020.
https://doi.org/10.1007/978-3-030-45096-0_45

Every year more than 2.4 million new cases related to epilepsy are registered globally [1]. EEG signals are the most preferable among biomedical signals for the diagnosis of epilepsy and in most cases scalp EEG is used. There are a number of algorithms proposed to detect seizure and the majority of the algorithms is based on multichannels. The problem with the multichannel algorithms is that they require a huge amount of data to process in order to get good results. It slows down the speed of the method. Such algorithms are not accepted in small devices and in real time applications where response is expected in very short time with high accuracy. On the other hand state of the art single channel methods are fast but they are not as reliable and accurate as multichannel methods. We propose a single channel approach to detect seizures in a given EEG signal. Our method is a so called hybrid method, i.e. a combination of a time domain and a frequency domain method. The novelty in the proposed algorithm is that two piecewise linear models called half-wave decomposition and Franklin transformation are applied for the EEG signal. They reduce the complexity of the signal but preserve the important characteristics of seizures. Feature vector is constructed from both the half-wave and Franklin transformations and followed by classification.

2 Dataset and Channel Selection

2.1 Dataset

For our tests we used CHB-MIT Scalp EEG Database collected by Ali Shoeb [3] (Physionet, https://www.physionet.org/pn6/chbmit/) at the Children's Hospital Boston. It consists of EEG recordings from paediatrics subjects with intractable seizures. Recordings, grouped into 23 cases, were collected from 22 subjects (5 males, ages 3–22 yrs; and 17 females, ages 1.5–19 yrs). The start and end of each seizure is annotated. The signals were recorded with 23 common EEG channels at a sampling rate of 256 Hz.

2.2 Channel Selection

The channel selection is a challenging part in seizure detection and prediction algorithms. Taking many channels results in slow algorithms because of the higher computation demand. In the proposed method we use only one channel and show that it works well for seizure detection. For channel selection we follow the method proposed in [2]. Namely, we chose the one with least standard deviation (SD). The idea behind it is that unwanted artifacts, like eye blink or muscular movement, may produce sudden changes and so increase SD even in seizure free intervals in the signal. In our study we tested different channels, with different SD and found that channel having least SD gives the best result.

3 Methodologies Used

In our study we propose a novel EEG seizure detection hybrid method. In both domains, time and frequency, we use signal reduction processes. Then features are extracted from the reduced models. Our aim was to construct an effective but simple and fast method. Keeping these guiding principles in mind we came to the conclusion that the model of piecewise linear functions will be appropriate. The EEG devices provide a discrete signal, i.e. sequence of the sample values, that can be considered as a time series, or a piecewise constant function. A representation equivalent to them can be obtained by linear interpolation. This way we associate the discrete signal with a continuous piecewise linear function (pl-function), i.e. the signal is viewed as a piecewise continuous analog signal. Throughout the whole process we stay within this model space. This space is simple but it is rich enough for preserving the necessary properties of the signal. In addition, using a time window with 256 samples the point at which such functions are non-differentiable are all dyadic rationals. Such functions are easy to represent, because they are completely characterized by the endpoints of the linear segments. Moreover, all of the calculations reduce to simple arithmetic operations.

In the time domain we develop a new half-wave method for reducing the original function to a more simple one. The idea is to keep the relevant tendencies but eliminate the irrelevant ones in the signal. The nature of the seizure segments is that, usually they have high spikes rate and high amplitudes [4]. In the frequency domain we use orthogonal projection for reduction. We show that the Franklin system is the proper choice for that.

3.1   Signal Reduction in Time Domain: Half-Wave Method

The history of the so called half-wave method goes back to 40 years. Starting from the 70's of the 20th century to the first decade of this century this method was very popular to detect epileptic activities (seizures) form long EEG signals. It was used to identify spikes and sharp waves [4] as representatives of seizure and non seizure portions. Its main advantage is that normal and abnormal patterns of very long signals can be examined and identified easily. Different versions of half-wave methods have been proposed to this order. In them several criterions were applied for the definition and identification of half-wave formations within the signal. Also, various parameters like duration of the wave, frequencies, amplitude etc. and sophisticated methods based on them have been utilized for concluding whether epileptiform activity is found at that instance. Here we can not go into details. Instead we refer the readers to the following relevant publications [4–8].

Our motivation differs from those above. Namely, we do not want to identify individual spikes. Instead, we take a 1 s portion of the EEG signal which consists of 256 samples. Then we consider it as a pl-function, and we want to simplify it by eliminating irrelevant details. To this purpose we developed yet another half-wave method which is simple and fast.

Proposed Method of Half-Wave Generation. The idea behind the proposed half-wave method is to reduce the complexity of the signal and to retain prominent peaks in the signal. First we calculate the extremal points of the

original signal, drop the other values, and take the pl-function generated by the
extremal points. Since the minimum-maximum values alternate in the sequence
of extremal points, the graph of the resulting pl-function is a kind of wave form.
We find that in intervals when there is a tendency of increase the decrease in
the individual maxima→minima intervals are very small. They do not seem to
contribute much in seizure detection process. Therefore, their inclusion in the
half-wave is not necessary and can be dropped. Similar process is applied to
opposite direction, i.e. when the signal shows a decreasing tendency. In the proposed method we apply only one condition, which is very simple, in the reduction
process. After applying this condition the first time, the outcome is again a pl-
wave with less extremal points, and is called first level half-wave decomposition.
The process can be repeated. It is easy to see that after some steps it will not
make any further change, i.e. the next level decomposition coincides with the
previous one. Then it is called final or complete half-wave, and the previous
versions are called semi-half-wave decompositions. When we move from lower
to higher levels in half-wave decomposition we loose more and more details. It
is part of the reduction problem to decide which level is the best suitable for
seizure detection.

Now we provide the mathematical formalization of the proposed method. To
this order let $N \in \mathbb{N}$, and let $f : [0,1] \mapsto \mathbb{R}$ be a continuous function that is
linear on every subinterval of the form $[k/N, (k+1)/N]$ $(k = 0, \ldots, N-1)$. In
the first step we select the points of local extrema. Namely those for which the
following condition holds

$$f(k/N) > f((k-1)/N) \qquad \text{and} \qquad f(k/N) > f((k+1)/N),$$

or

$$f(k/N) < f((k-1)/N) \qquad \text{and} \qquad f(k/N) < f((k+1)/N).$$

Adding the two endpoints 0, and 1 to those satisfying the condition we obtain
an alternating sequence $0 = x_0 < x_1 < \cdots < x_{N_0} = 1$ of maximum-minimum
points ordered in increasing way. The points of this sequence along with the
values at them define the starting half-wave function f_0, which is the continuous
pl-function that is linear on the intervals $[x_k, x_{k+1}]$ $(k = 0, \ldots, N_0 - 2)$.

In the following steps we use criteria for the differences rather than for the
individual values of the corresponding function. Suppose that f_j is a continuous
pl-function with alternating extremal points $0 = x^{(j)} < x_1^{(j)} < \cdots < x_{N_j-1}^{(j)} = 1$.
Set $\Delta_k^{(j)} = x_{k+1}^{(j)} - x_k^{(j)}$ $(k = 0, \ldots, N_j - 1)$. Then for every pair $(x_k^{(j)}, x_{k+1}^{(j)})$
$(k = 1, \ldots, N_j - 2)$ we check wether the condition

$$|\Delta_k^{(j)}| > |\Delta_{k-1}^{(j)}| \qquad \text{or} \qquad |\Delta_k^{(j)}| > |\Delta_{k+1}^{(j)}|.$$

holds. If this condition holds for k then we consider that the segment connecting the values at $x_k^{(j)}$ and $x_{k+1}^{(j)}$ represents a significant change in the signal. Otherwise we consider that portion as an irrelevant detail and we will

erase the points $x_k^{(j)}$ and $x_{k+1}^{(j)}$ from the sequence of extremal points. It is easy to see that if the condition doesn't hold for a k then it does hold for $k+1$. Consequently, despite of taking overlapping pairs of consecutive points the erasure process goes pairwise. It means, that also the remaining sequence $0 = x^{(j+1)} < x_1^{(j+1)} < \cdots < x_{N_{j+1}-1}^{(j+1)} = 1$ is an alternating sequence of maximum-minimum points. This sequence again defines a continuous pl-function function f_{j+1}, a reduced half-wave function.

Then the starting pl-function is reduced from level to level. The process of course terminates at some level, when no points are dropped from the sequence of extrema. That is the final half wave-function generated by the original pl-function f.

3.2 Signal Reduction in Frequency Domain: Franklin Transform

The frequency domain part in our hybrid classification is an orthogonal projection using a proper orthogonal system. Recall that the our model space for the EEG signals is the family of continuous piecewise continuous functions. In order to perform an orthogonal projection, reduction in the frequency domain, that complies with our model we need an orthogonal system that consists of continuous piecewise continuous functions. This guarantees that the subspace spanned by the elements of the system is a subspace of our model space. Moreover, since we take 1 s long segments with 256 samples linearity must hold between any dyadic rationals of the form $k2^{-8}$ ($k = 0, \ldots, 256$). The combination of these requirements leads to the Franklin system as a natural choice.

The importance of the role of the Haar system in many applications, including signal processing problems, is hard to exaggerate. It is, among others, the simplest model for wavelets. Originally, in the construction of his system Alfred Haar was motivated by the problem of Schauder basis in the space of continuous functions $C([0,1])$. At that time no orthogonal system Ψ was known such that the Ψ-Fourier partial sums of every continuous function converge to the given function uniformly. The Haar system was the first example for such an orthogonal system. Ever since it turned out that the Haar system ($\mathcal{H}$) enjoys several nice and important properties in mathematics as well as in applications. There was, however, one imperfection in the construction from the point of the original motivation. Namely, the Haar functions themselves are not continuous, ie. do not belong to the space $C([0,1))$. In order to overcome this problem Faber [9] came to the idea to take the integral functions of the Haar functions. Then he of course received continuous functions, and hoped that the system Φ of these functions preserve the convergence property of $\mathcal{H}$. Indeed, the system Φ now called as Faber-Schauder system turned to be Schauder basis in $C([0,1])$. Recall that $h_n \in \mathcal{H}$ ($n \in \mathbb{N}$, $n = 2^m + k$, $0 \le k < 2^m$) is defined as

$$h_n = 2^{m/2}\chi_{[k/2^m,(2k+1)/2^{m+1})} - 2^{m/2}\chi_{[(2k+1)/2^{m+1}),(k+1)/2^m)},$$

where χ_A stands for the characteristic function of the set $A \subset [0,1]$. Hence we have that the nth Faber-Schauder function $\varphi_n(x) = \int_0^x h_n(t)\,dt$ is a roof shape function, continuous pl-function, on $[k/2^m, (k+1)/2^m]$. Finally, the Franklin system $\mathfrak{F} = \{\mathfrak{f}_n : n \in \mathbb{N}\}$ is generated from $\varPhi$ by Gram-Schmidt orthogonalization and normalization. Then $\mathfrak{F}$ is an orthonormal basis in $C[0,1)$. We note that it follows from the construction that $\mathfrak{f}_n$ $(n \in \mathbb{N}, n = 2^m + k, 0 \le k < 2^m)$ is a continuous pl-function, which is linear on every dyadic interval $[k/2^{m+1}, (k+1)/2^{m+1}]$. We conclude that $\mathfrak{F}$ satisfies all of the properties we formulated above with respect to the desired orthogonal system. We note that if f is a pl-function that corresponds to the EEG samples in a 1 s long record then the Franklin coefficients

$$\widehat{\mathfrak{f}_n} = \int_0^1 f \cdot \mathfrak{f}_n$$

can be accurately calculated by finite many arithmetic operations.

3.3 Feature Extraction

In the proposed method a hybrid feature vector is constructed from two piecewise linear models. Rectangular windows of size 1 s are applied with 256 samples in each window. This size turned to be appropriate and that agrees with the conclusion in [10]. In the time domain features are extracted from the half-wave reduction: total number of extremal points, slopes of linear segments, maximum of slopes, mean of extremal points, absolute minimum and maximum within the window. In the frequency domain we take the first 16 coefficients of the Franklin transform.

The final feature vector is constructed after performing tests using different combinations. We found that the above mentioned six features from time domain in the 4th level half-wave reduction and the first 16 Franklin coefficients form the best combination with KNN classifier for seizure classifications.

3.4 Classification

We have tested several classifiers commonly used for seizure detection, like k-nearest neighbor (KNN) algorithm, artificial neural network and support vector machines. We concluded that the KNN performs the best in our case.

We had to address the problem that the database is highly imbalanced. Namely, the CHB-MIT database has 10218 seizure seconds, which is only 1.6% of the total duration of the EEG signal (6400086 s). This makes the classifier biased to detect majority (non-seizure) class because of the unequal prior probabilities of the two classes. There are two popular methods to handle this problem:

(a) over-sampling (increasing the samples of minority class),
(b) under-sampling (reducing the samples of majority class).

Most of the pattern classification methods use over-sampling because there is no loss of information. In the proposed method, we applied the well known over sampling technique called Synthetic Minority Over-Sampling Technique (SMOTE) [17]. It neither exaggerates the Receiver Operating Characteristic curve of the extracted features, nor causes any over-fitting problem [18]. We used 3 iterations of SMOTE for each patient as recommended by Bhattacharya et al [2]. Each iteration increases the number of minority samples by 100%. The results of the comparison tests are presented in Table 1. It shows the effectiveness of our method.

Table 1. Comparsion with latest state of the art methods

Reference and year	Channel - patients considered	Training/test data	Classifier used	Average Sensitivity - Specificity -Accuracy (%)	False alarm rate
Bhattacharyya [2]	Multichannel-23	10 fold cross validation	RF	97.91–99.57–99.41	–
Sina [11]	Multiple-23	Leave-one-record-out	ADCD	96.00– –	0.12
Miaolin [12]	Multichannel-23	–		98.48– –	8.61
Chen [13]	Multichannel-23	Leave-one-subject-out cross validation	SVM	91.71– 92.89–92.30	–
Birjandtalab [14]	Multichannel-23	10 fold cross validation	RF-t-sne, KNN	– – 89.80	2.2
Tsiouris [15]	Multichannel-23	No training	Rule based	88– –	8.1
Samiee [10]	Multichannel-23	25% training	SVM, Log regg, RF	71.6–99.2	0.35
Khan [16]	Multichannel-5	80% training	LDA	100–83.6–91.8	–
Proposed work	Single channel-23	60% training	KNN	**99.92–98.38–99.3**	**0.027**

After applying the classifier, we analyzed the class labels. We experienced that in non-seizure time intervals some segments are mistakenly classified as seizure segments. The opposite situation occurs in seizure intervals. Therefore, we studied the result of the classification not only for the individual segment but for its 4 neighbors on each side. This way we could correct the status of most of the misclassified segments.

References

1. National Institute of Neurological Disorders and Stroke. http://www.ninds.nih. gov/. Accessed 15 Sept 2014
2. Bhattacharyya, A., Pachori, R.B.: A multivariate approach for patient specific EEG seizure detection using empirical wavelet transform. Journal **21**(6), 880–886 (2017)
3. Shoeb, A.H.: Application of machine learning to epileptic seizure onset detection and treatment. Ph.D. dissertation, Massachusetts Institute of Technology (2019)
4. Gotman, J., Gloor, P.: Automatic recognition and quantification of inter-ictal epileptic activity in the human scalp EEGArticle title. Electroencephalogr. Clin. Neurophysiol. **41**(5), 513–529 (1976)
5. Gevins, A.S.: Automated analysis of the electrical activity of the human brain (EEG): a progress report. Proc. IEEE **63**(10), 1382–1399 (1991)

6. Kooi, A.K.: Voltage-time characteristics of spikes and other rapid electroencephalographic transients: semantic and morphological considerations. Neurology **16**(1), 59–66 (1996)

7. Jasper, H., Kershman, J.: Electroencephalographic classification of the epilepsies. Arch. Neurol. Psych. **45**(6), 903–943 (1941)

8. Silva, L., Dijk, A., Smits, H.: Detection of nonstationarities in EEGs using the autoregressive model. an application to EEGs of epileptics. In: Dolce, G., Künkel, H. (eds.) CEAN Computerized EEG Analysis, pp. 180–199. Fischer, Stuttgart (1975)

9. Faber, G.: Über die Orthogonalfunktionen des Herrn Haar. Jahresber. Deutsch. Math. Verein. **19**, 104–112 (1910)

10. Samiee, K., Kovács, P., Gabbouj, M.: Epileptic seizure classification of EEG timeseries using rational discrete short time fourier transform. IEEE Trans. Biomed. Eng. **62**(2), 541–552 (2015)

11. Sina, K., Chou, C.: Adaptive seizure onset detection framework using a hybrid PCA-CSP approach. IEEE J. Biomed. Health Inf. **22**(1), 154–160 (2017)

12. Miaolin, F., Chou, C.: Detecting abnormal pattern of epileptic seizures via temporal synchronization of EEG signals. IEEE Trans. Biomed. Eng. **66**(3), 601–608 (2019)

13. Chen, D., Wan, S., Xiang, J., Bao, F.S.: A high-performance seizure detection algorithm based on Discrete Wavelet Transform (DWT) and EEG. PLoS ONE **12**(3), (2017)

14. Birjandtalab, J., Pouyan, M.B., Cogan, D., Nourani, M.: Automated seizure detection using limited-channel EEG and non-linear dimension reduction. Comput. Biol. Med. **82**, 49–58 (2017)

15. Tsiouris, K., Markoula, S., Konitsiotis, S., Koutsouris, D., Fotiadis, D.: A robust unsupervised epileptic seizure detection methodology to accelerate large EEG database evaluation. Biomed. Signal Process. Control **40**, 275–285 (2018)

16. Khan, Y.U., Rafiuddin, N., Farooq, O.: Automated seizure detection in scalp EEG using multiple wavelet scales. In: 2012 IEEE International Conference on Signal Processing, Computing and Control Proceedings, pp. 1–2. IEEE, Waknaghat Solan (2012) https://doi.org/10.1109/ISPCC.2012.6224361

17. Chawla, N.V., Bowyer, K., Hall, L.O., Kegelmeyer, W.P.: SMOTE: synthetic minority over-sampling technique. J. Artif. Intell. Res. **16**(1), 321–357 (2002)

18. López, V., Fernández, A., Morreno-Torres, H.G., Herrera, F.: Analysis of preprocessing vs. cost-sensitive learning for imbalanced classification. Open problems on intrinsic data characteristics. Exp. Syst. Appl. **39**(7), 6585–6608 (2012)

Improved Classification of Myoelectric Signals by Using Normalized Signal Trains

Philip Gaßner[(✉)] and Klaus Buchenrieder

Institut für Technische Informatik, Universität der Bundeswehr München,
85577 Neubiberg, Germany
{philip.gassner,klaus.buchenrieder}@unibw.de
https://www.unibw.de/technische-informatik

Keywords: EMG-Signals · Classification · Hand prosthesis

1 Introduction

Modern myoelectric hand prostheses, like the i-limb[TM] ultra from Touch Bionics and the Bebionic[TM] hand from RSLSteeper, are advanced multi-finger prostheses which can perform several hand movements and assume various gestures [5]. The control signals are obtained by preprocessing and classification of cutaneously derived myoelectric signals of residual muscles. Typically, three to five different motion states or hand positions can be distinguished with two sensors. As already explained in earlier studies [6], classification becomes increasingly difficult with a rising number of states or positions, since the decision spaces or feature clusters tend to overlap [4] and can hardly be separated statically. An improvement is suggested by Attenberger [1] and Hudgins et al. [4] showing that EMG-Signals are, to a certain degree, time-dependent.

In this contribution, we substantiate that a significant improvement of the classification can be attained by including the time-course of features obtained from the myosignal, resulting in significantly improved classification accuracy and classifier performance.

2 Method

The classical classification approach [2,3] is depicted in Fig. 1. As shown, the myoelectric signal is derived with cutaneous dual electrodes, amplified, filtered and features calculated. After calculation, these features create point clouds which form clusters. These tend to overlap even with only a few gesture classes. Figure 2a shows three overlapping clusters of feature points calculated from signals derived with two sensors. Figure 2b, presents eight overlapping clusters for which no meaningful classification can be made.

Obviously, clusters of gestures taken over several days are in fact more scattered and have more overlapping clusters. A separation of lapping clusters is

© Springer Nature Switzerland AG 2020
R. Moreno-Díaz et al. (Eds.): EUROCAST 2019, LNCS 12014, pp. 372–379, 2020.
https://doi.org/10.1007/978-3-030-45096-0_46

Fig. 1. Classical approach to record EMG-Signals and to control a hand prostheses.

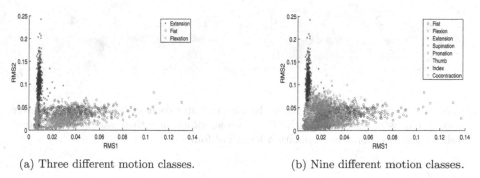

(a) Three different motion classes.   (b) Nine different motion classes.

Fig. 2. Point clusters with two sensors. On each is the RMS feature calculated. Three classes can already overlap, nine classes can not be distinguished.

practically impossible for statically generated points in the vector space, even when considering multiple projections of the point in the vector space. In contrast to the static approach, we use a dynamic approach in which the myogram for an entire movement of the upper extremity is considered. Furthermore, we use the insight that the corresponding time-courses always look almost identical, no matter if these were executed fast or slow. To be able to classify time-courses of different length, we normalize these, so that the feature trains have the same length, as illustrated in Fig. 3. The two subplots on the left and the two subplots on the right depict two different Signals for the same movement. The two upper subplots represent the classical approach, while the two lower frames depict the normalized approach. The classical approach uses a fixed window size. This means that each signal has a different number of resulting windows but in each window, the signal has the same number of data points. The upper left signal is divided into five windows, while the upper right one has only four. It can be discussed whether the last window belongs to the signal or not. It contains so few gesture data points, that it falls below a threshold value and is therefore often ignored. In order to see the similarities, between different movements of the same class and at the same time to distinguish them from other classes, a dynamic window size is used. This window size depends on the size to which the movement is to be normalized. Given a signal length l and a normalization size n, the resulting window size w corresponds to: $w = l/n$. Thus, each signal has the same normalization length which is independent from the original length. This is depicted in the lower two subplots. Noteworthy, each window contains a different amount of data points. Nevertheless, any features can now be calculated for each window and the signal remains normalized over time.

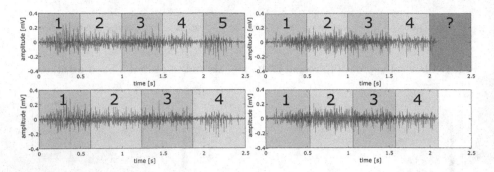

Fig. 3. The upper two subplots show the classical approach with a fixed window size on two signals with different length. The lower subplots show these signals divided into equalized windows for a normalization length of four.

If we look at the normalized signals within a three-dimensional space, it turns out that each movement follows a very similar pattern. We call these patterns feature-trains. Figure 4 presents feature-trains for movements of the two gestures Flexation and Extension. With only one feature for each sensor. If we look at feature-trains from above, we obtain a projection exhibiting two separable clusters. However, both clusters contain points that cannot be unambiguously assigned. This is particularly pronounced near the zero point of the X and Y axis. As the number of movement classes increases, it becomes increasingly difficult.

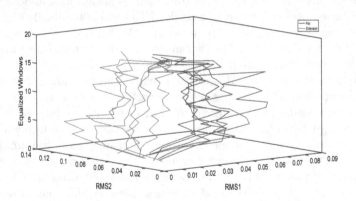

Fig. 4. Extension and fist as normalized signal trains.

For the classification w.r.t. this contribution, the following four features were used for classification:

1. Root mean Square (RMS)
2. Zero Crossing (ZC)
3. Approximate Entropy (ApEn)

4. Autoregressive coefficients with order four (AR)

For the study, we collected data from three probands, which performed nine different hand gestures with 15 movement repetitions on six different days, spread over more than three weeks. Thus, each movement was performed 90 times and a total of 810 repetitions were performed per person. The evaluation therefore spans across 2430 recorded movements. The nine hand gestures performed correspond to:

1. Cocontraction of the hand. (Con)
2. Extension of the wrist. (Ext)
3. Fist (Fist)
4. Flexation of the wrist. (Flex)
5. Extension of the index finger while flexing all other fingers. (Index)
6. Performing an "OK" sign, Extension of the three fingers pinky, ring

finger and middle finger while flexing the thumb and ring finger. (OK)
7. Thumb Up; Flexation of the four fingers, pinky, ring finger, middle finger and index finger while extending the thumb. (ThUp)
8. Pronation of the wrist. (Pron)
9. Supination of the wrist. (Sup)

3   Results

Based on 2430 recorded movements derived from three probands, Fig. 5 provides the results for 22 different classifiers and the achieved F1 score on average over all test probands for all days. Clearly all 22 classifiers rank better with the normalized method. In the worst case, the normalized procedure is 9% points (p.p.) better than the standard procedure. In the best case, it is 19 p.p. better and on average 14 p.p. better. A Fine Gaussian Support Vector Machine (SVMFineGaussian) achieved the least favorable classification results yielding only 20% with the standard method. With the normalized method, both a simple decision tree (SimpleTree) and a SVMFineGaussian achieved the most unpropitious results with 29%. In the worst case, the normalized method is on average therefore 9 p.p. better. The best results with the standard method were achieved with a Quadratic Support Vector Machine (SVMQuadratic) approach yielding 65%. This result is closely followed by a Cubic Support Vector Machine (SVMCubic) and a Bagged Decision Tree (BaggedTree) with 64% each. For the normalized method the SVMQuadratic scored best with 84% followed by the SVMCubic with 82% of the F1 score. Which is on average 19 p.p. better than the standard method.

Table 1 summarizes the average achieved F1 score for all probands achieved over the six days. If we look at the results of the individual movements in Table 1, we can see a very significant increase of more than 30 p.p. for the two movements Index and OK, and a significant increase of more than 20 p.p. for the two movements Cocontraction and Thumb Up.

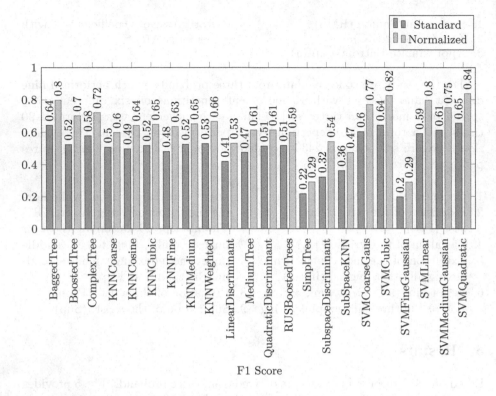

Fig. 5. Average F1 Score for 22 classifiers for each probands over six days.

Table 2 summarizes the average classification results individually. Note, that for proband 2 there is a negative delta for two gestures, the extension with −11.4 p.p. and the supination with −1 p.p., while all other gestures still have a positive delta. But even with the decrease of two classification rates for proband 2, the classification generally remains significantly better with the normalized procedure. The two gestures Index and OK have improved by 19 p.p.. For proband 2 three gestures evaluated above 90% (F1 Score) and four above 80%. With an increase of the F1 score from 31% to 92.4%, proband 1 shows the strongest improvements with the OK gesture. The gestures Cocontraction, Thumb Up and Index could also revealed a considerable improvement of 50 p.p. Thus, all nine gestures can be classified with an F1 score between 80.6% and 92.4%. This represents a significant improvement over the standard procedures. For proband 3 seven gestures increased around 10 p.p. resulting in seven gestures over 80% and the remaining two are over 70%, F1 Score.

Table 1. Comparison between the standard procedure and the normalized procedure on average for each gesture over all three probands with F1 Scores.

Gesture	Standard	Normalized	Δ
Con	54.0%	81.1%	27.1 p.p.
Ext	82.7%	96.7%	14.0 p.p.
Fist	66.6%	77.4%	10.8 p.p.
Flex	86.3%	89.6%	3.3 p.p.
Index	42.5%	77.3%	34.7 p.p.
OK	49.9%	83.1%	33.2 p.p.
Thumb Up	54.5%	80.9%	26.4 p.p.
Pron	72.9%	81.1%	8.2 p.p.
Sup	78.3%	86.4%	8.1 p.p.

Table 2. Average F1 Score for each probands over six days.

Gesture	Proband 1			Proband 2			Proband 3		
	Std.	Norm.	Δ	Std.	Norm.	Δ	Std.	Norm.	Δ
Con	38.6%	92.3%	53.7 p.p	56.3%	73.6%	17.3 p.p	67.3%	81.1%	13.9 p.p.
Ext	72.1%	88.8%	16.7 p.p	80.2%	68.7%	−11.4 p.p	95.7%	96.7%	1.0 p.p.
Fist	58.7%	80.6%	21.9 p.p	73.9%	83.2%	9.3 p.p	67.3%	77.4%	10.1 p.p.
Flex	79.0%	90.2%	11.1 p.p	93.9%	98.3%	4.4 p.p	86.0%	89.6%	3.6 p.p.
Index	29.4%	84.6%	55.3 p.p	31.1%	50.4%	19.3 p.p	67.1%	77.3%	10.1 p.p.
OK	31.0%	92.4%	61.4 p.p	47.3%	66.7%	19.4 p.p	71.5%	83.1%	11.6 p.p.
ThUp	30.6%	88.8%	58.2 p.p	61.6%	64.0%	2.4 p.p	71.4%	80.9%	9.5 p.p.
Pron	66.1%	83.2%	17.1 p.p	81.4%	93.8%	12.4 p.p	71.3%	81.1%	9.8 p.p.
Sup	67.9%	88.0%	20.1 p.p	93.4%	92.5%	−1.0 p.p	73.6%	86.4%	12.9 p.p

In Tables 3 and 4 it becomes apparent that not only the classification became better, also the gestures that could not be discerned before, can now be classified. The best result was archieved on day 3 with the gesture Thumb Up. It increased from an F1 Score of 0 to 0.987, while all other gestures improved as well. A similar extreme improvement was achieved on day 4 and 6 with the gesture OK. It improved by 98.1 p.p. and 87 p.p. each time from a F1 Score of 0. This results in an average improvement of 35.1 p.p. over all six days. The F1 Score is on average at 87.6%. For proband 2 the average is 76.8% and for proband 3 it is 83.7%.

Table 3. Average F1 Score of proband 1 for each the of days 1 to 3.

Gesture	Day 1			Day 2			Day 3		
	Std.	Norm.	Δ	Std.	Norm.	Δ	Std.	Norm.	Δ
Con	15.8%	98.70%	82.9 p.p	62.20%	89.4%	27.2 p.p	49.3%	91.4%	42.1 p.p
Ext	50.4%	94.5%	44.1 p.p	78.6%	86.7%	8.1 p.p	69.9%	85.1%	15.2 p.p.
Fist	58.9%	83.7%	24.8 p.p	55.6%	78.9%	23.3 p.p	48.7%	86.1%	37.4 p.p.
Flex	80.5%	89.2%	8.7 p.p	65.2%	80.0%	14.8 p.p	83.3%	89.3%	6.0 p.p.
Index	22.5%	87.3%	64.7 p.p	32.1%	85.7%	53.6 p.p	40.2%	87.0%	46.8 p.p.
OK	40.6%	98.0%	57.4 p.p	42.10%	90.9%	48.8 p.p	48.6%	98.1%	49.5 p.p.
ThUp	20.7%	96.3%	75.6 p.p	64.5%	75.3%	10.7 p.p	0.0%	98.7%	98.7 p.p.
Tin	65.5%	75.0%	9.5 p.p	71.8%	87.2%	15.4 p.p	74.9%	85.2%	10.3 p.p.
Tout	71.4%	97.4%	25.9 p.p	32.3%	82.0%	49.7 p.p	76.0%	92.3%	16.3 p.p

Table 4. Average F1 Score of proband 1 for each of the days 4 to 6.

Gesture	Day 4			Day 5			Day 6		
	Std.	Norm.	Δ	Std.	Norm.	Δ	Std.	Norm.	Δ
Con	25.8%	90.4%	64.6 p.p	44.6%	85.2%	40.6 p.p	33.8%	98.7%	65.0 p.p
Ext	69.1%	85.3%	16.2 p.p	90.5%	85.0%	−5.5 p.p	74.3%	96.1%	21.8 p.p.
Fist	49.7%	83.9%	34.3 p.p	66.3%	91.1%	24.9 p.p	72.9%	59.6%	−13.3 p.p.
Flex	78.8%	92.0%	13.2 p.p	83.9%	96.0%	12.1 p.p	82.4%	94.5%	12.1 p.p.
Index	31.1%	76.5%	45.4 p.p	22.5%	98.1%	75.6 p.p	27.8%	73.3%	45.5 p.p.
OK	0.0%	98.0%	98.1 p.p	54.5%	81.3%	26.7 p.p	0.0%	87.7%	87.7 p.p.
ThUp	56.0%	97.4%	41.5 p.p	20.3%	92.3%	72.0 p.p	22.2%	72.7%	50.5 p.p.
Tin	78.6%	70.6%	−8.1 p.p	59.1%	91.8%	32.7 p.p	46.5%	89.5%	43.0 p.p.
Tout	82.8%	88.9%	6.1 p.p	60.9%	77.4%	16.5 p.p	83.7%	90.0%	6.3 p.p

4   Conclusions

In this paper, we presented a method to normalize EMG data under consideration of time-dependence. Classification rates increase for all 22 classifiers, because
different gestures have unique time-dependencies or signal-trains. The results of
multi-classification for nine different, but similar movement types, substantiate
the outstanding properties of normalized signal-trains for myoelectric signals. In
the study brought forward here, the movements were performed over a period
of 6 days. An improvement was demonstrated for three probands. This contribution shows, that the classification of individual movements, using normalized
signal-trains, is favorable, even though classification can begin only after the
movement fully completes. However, current research suggests, that a positive
classification can already be made with a view to the future after the completion
of partial movement with very good results.

References

1. Attenberger, A.: Time analysis for improved upper limb movement classification. Doctoral thesis, Universität der Bundeswehr München, Neubiberg (2016)
2. Farina, D., et al.: The Extraction of neural information from the surface EMG for the control of upper-limb prostheses: emerging avenues and challenges. IEEE Trans. Neural Syst. Rehabil. Eng. **22**(4), 797–809 (2014)
3. Fougner, A., Stavdahl, Ø., Kyberd, P.J., Losier, Y.G., Parker, P.A.: Control of upper limb prostheses: terminology and proportional myoelectric control—a review. IEEE Trans. Neural Syst. Rehabil. Eng. **20**(5), 663–677 (2012)
4. Hudgins, B., Parker, P., Scott, R.N.: A new strategy for multifunction myoelectric control. IEEE Trans. Biomed. Eng. **40**(1), 82–94 (1993)
5. Riet, D.V.d., Stopforth, R., Bright, G., Diegel, O.: An overview and comparison of upper limb prosthetics. In: 2013 Africon, pp. 1–8 (2013)
6. Zardoshti-Kermani, M., Wheeler, B.C., Badie, K., Hashemi, R.M.: EMG feature evaluation for movement control of upper extremity prostheses. IEEE Trans. Rehabil. Eng. **3**(4), 324–333 (1995)

Hyperbolic Transformations of Zernike Functions and Coefficients

Zsolt Németh$^{(\boxtimes)}$, Ferenc Schipp, and Ferenc Weisz

Department of Numerical Analysis, Eötvös Loránd University,
Pázmány Péter stny. 1/C, Budapest 1117, Hungary
{nemeth,schipp,weisz}@numanal.inf.elte.hu

Abstract. Measurement and mathematical description of the corneal surface and the optical properties of the human eye is an active field in biomedical engineering and ophthalmology. One particular problem is to correct certain types of corneal shape measurement errors, e.g. ones that arise due to unintended eye-movements and spontaneous rotations of the eye-ball. In this paper we present the mathematical background of our recent approach, which is based on constructions of systems of orthonormal functions based on the well-known Zernike polynomials. For this, argument transformation by suitable Blaschke functions are used, as they correspond to the congruent transformations in the Poincaré disk model of the Bolyai–Lobachevsky hyperbolic geometry, making them a practical choice. The problem of discretization, and computation of the translated Zernike coefficients is also discussed.

Keywords: Zernike functions · Blaschke functions · Zernike coefficients · Hyperbolic Fourier series

1 Introduction

The cornea is the primary optical structure of the human eye, contributing the greatest part to the eye's total refractive power. During the past decades, plenty of measurement devices and experimental set-ups for corneal topography have been developed, in order to aid the understanding of the general and the individual optical characteristics of the corneal surfaces.

At the same time, similar statement can be made for the mathematical models used in descriptions of the corneal shape. The anterior surface of the cornea is normally close to spherical, but its shape - and as a consequence its optical - aberrations may result in decrease in the visual quality. For reviews of applied models, methods and devices, see e.g. [4,9].

The first author's research was supported by the Hungarian Government and co-financed by the European Social Fund under project EFOP-3.6.3-VEKOP-16-2017-00001: Talent Management in Autonomous Vehicle Control Technologies. The second and the third authors' research was supported by the Hungarian Scientific Research Funds (OTKA) No. K115804.

© Springer Nature Switzerland AG 2020
R. Moreno-Díaz et al. (Eds.): EUROCAST 2019, LNCS 12014, pp. 380–387, 2020.
https://doi.org/10.1007/978-3-030-45096-0_47

In the last few years, numerous experiments and related mathematical modeling and simulations were carried out by the second author of the present paper and affiliated coauthors, related to corneal measurement and shape description. These include development of an experimental multi-camera reflective cornea topographer [9] and the utilization of Zernike functions, and their discretization on the unit circle [5,7,8].

In Sect. 2, we discuss the motivations for our current research, and then in Sect. 3 we present the main mathematical tools of our method. In the closing section, some conclusions are drawn and further work is outlined.

2 Problem Description

Our motivation is based on some difficulties encountered during medical evaluations of corneal measurements. First, in [13] the authors draw attention to the inconsistencies of ocular reference axes and angles. These inconsistencies become an issue when different corneal measurement systems are used for patients, and their maps need to be compared, or aggregated. The need for a simplified management and correction of misalignments seems clear, and a pragmatic way to unify, standardize and align these measurements would be extremely helpful.

The review [10] serves as an excellent guide to ophthalmologists and biomedical engineers on the topics of elevation- based topography and pachymetry. It discusses and illustrates, among others, the importance of choosing the appropriate reference axis for the axial curvature calculations, and in creating such corneal maps. The authors underline the need for corneal map corrections, if for some reason or another, the choice of the reference axis were not perfect (Fig. 1).

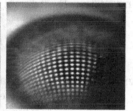

Fig. 1. A corneal measurement in progress.

Then, in a recent study [14], the repeatability of corneal measurements was evaluated for successive topography measurements taken in follow-up of LASIK refractive surgeries. Elevation maps taken with Scheimpflug topography were included in the study. For each patient, two maps were taken preoperatively, and then two at 1 month, and another two at 3 months after the operation. The maps were fitted to each other using an Iterative Closest Point algorithm, and were evaluated for repeatability within and amongst the operative stages. Also, the errors due particularly to rotational and translational misalignments were calculated. It is clear that the challenges posed by such longitudinal evaluations of successive topography measurements provide motivation for the development of new shape description, map alignment and correction methods.

3   Rational Zernike Functions and Coefficients

3.1   The Basic Zernike Functions and Their Discretization

The (basic) Zernike functions [1], introduced in 1934, are often used to express wavefront data on optical tests, since they are made up of terms that are of the same form as the types of aberrations often observed in optical tests [3]. Since then, they have become one of the most important and universally used mathematical tools in corneal topography. In practice, videokeratometers and Scheimpflug cameras permit accurate estimation of corneal surfaces. From height data it is possible to adjust analytical surfaces that will be later used for aberration calculation and ray trace solving. In this process, Zernike polynomials are often used as adjusting polynomials.

These functions form a complete orthogonal system on the unit disk $\mathbb{D} := \{z \in \mathbb{C} : |z| \leq 1\}$, and can be defined by separating the radial and angular factors, i.e. using $z = re^{i\phi}$ as the polar form of $z \in \mathbb{C}$, for $n \in \mathbb{N} := \{0, 1, \ldots\}$ let

$$Z_n^m(r, \phi) := R_n^m(r)e^{im\phi}, \quad (r \in [0,1], \phi \in [0, 2\pi), |m| \leq n),$$

where, with the Jacobi polynomials $P_n^{(\alpha, \beta)}$,

$$R_n^m(r) := (-1)^{\frac{n-m}{2}} r^m P_{\frac{n-m}{2}}^{(m,0)}(1 - 2r^2), \quad (2|n - m, m \in \mathbb{N}),$$

and $R_n^m := R_n^{-m}$ for $m < 0$. Now their orthogonality relation is given by

$$\int_0^1 \int_0^{2\pi} Z_n^m(r, \phi)\overline{Z_l^k(r, \phi)} r \, d\phi dr = \frac{\pi}{\sqrt{(n+1)(l+1)}} \delta_{n,l} \delta_{m,k},$$

with the double integral serving as the scalar product.

Now, since we have a complete orthogonal system, the Zernike series of a square integrable function $f \in L^2(\mathbb{D})$ defined on $\mathbb{D}$, is converging to f in this space, i.e.

$$f(z) = \sum_{n=0}^{\infty} \sum_{|m| \leq n} c_{n,m} Z_n^m(z), \quad (z = re^{i\phi} \in \mathbb{D}),$$

where the (Zernike-)coefficients $c_{n,m}$ are defined as the normalized scalar product of f and Z_n^m.

From a practical point of view, it is also important to note that an appropriate discretization on $\mathbb{D}$ has been introduced for Zernike functions [5], such that the scalar product needs to be evaluated only on the set of discrete points, and with proper weighting, interpolation is guaranteed and orthogonality is preserved. It turns out that the roots of the Legendre polynomials serve as a good discretization radially, while a uniform division may be used in azimuthally, i.e. with the choice of nodes

$$X_N = \left\{ z_{j,k} = \left(\sqrt{\frac{1 + \lambda_{k,N}}{2}}, \frac{2\pi j}{4N + 1} \right), \ k = 1, \ldots, N, \ j = 0, \ldots, 4N \right\},$$

where the numbers $\lambda_{k,N}$ notate the roots of the Legendre polynomial of degree N, and the (discrete) measure

$$\mu_N(z_{j,k}) = \frac{\mathcal{A}_{k,N}}{2(4N + 1)},$$

with the numbers $\mathcal{A}_{k,N}$ being the Cristoffel-numbers corresponding to the roots $\lambda_{k,N}$ (see e.g. [2]), we can define the discrete integral

$$\int_{X_N} f(z) \, d\mu_N = \sum_{k=1}^{N} \sum_{j=0}^{4N} f(z_{j,k}) \cdot \mu_N(z_{j,k}).$$

For this we have the discrete orthogonality of Zernike functions up to a certain degree:

Theorem 1 [5, Theorem 2.1]. *If $n + n' + |m| \leq 2N - 1$, $n + n' + |m'| \leq 2N - 1$, $n, n' \in \mathbb{N}$ and $m, m' \in \mathbb{Z}$, then*

$$\int_{X_N} \mathcal{Z}_n^m(z) \overline{\mathcal{Z}_{n'}^{m'}}(z) \, d\mu_N = \frac{\delta_{n,n'} \delta_{m,m'}}{\sqrt{(n+1)(n'+1)}}$$

Consequently, the limit of the discrete integrals of any function is the continuous integral with respect to the measure $dx dy / \pi$, as $N \to +\infty$. Several experiments and tests were carried out on corneal surface data with encouraging results, see e.g. [8].

3.2   Hyperbolic Translations of Zernike Functions

The proposed problem of transforming the Zernike coefficients (describing the aberrations), in order to express them in case of a scaled and/or rotated pupil, was recently discussed in the literature. I.e., several recent papers describe different approaches and propose possible solutions to this problem, see e.g. [6,11,16].

Our methods concerning rotations differ in approach from the previous ones: instead of Euclidean or polar geometry, we utilize the tools of the usual (Poincaré and Cayley–Klein) models of hyperbolic geometry. It is known that the Blaschke functions can be identified with the congruence transformations on the Poincaré disk model of the Bolyai–Lobachevsky hyperbolic geometry [12]. Consequently, we may describe translations on the hyperbolic plane by them, and these translations correspond to certain rotations of the cornea surface.

For an arbitrary pair $\mathfrak{a} = (a, \epsilon) \in \mathbb{B} := \mathbb{D} \times \mathbb{T}$, consisting of a complex rational pole a and a scaling parameter ϵ, let us define the Blaschke functions as

$$B_{\mathfrak{a}}(z) := \epsilon B_a(z), \ B_a(z) := \frac{z - a}{1 - \overline{a} z}, \quad (z \in \overline{\mathbb{D}}),$$

where $\mathbb{T} := \{z \in \mathbb{C} : |z| = 1\}$ notates the torus. These functions are bijections both on $\mathbb{D}$ and on $\mathbb{T}$, and analytic on $\mathbb{D} \cup \mathbb{T}$.

The set $\mathfrak{B} = \{B_{\mathfrak{a}|\mathbb{D}} : \mathfrak{a} \in \mathbb{B}\}$ with $\circ$ forms a group. The map $\mathfrak{a} \to B_{\mathfrak{a}}$ induces an isomorphic group on the set of parameters $\mathbb{B}$ with the corresponding operation $\circ$: $(\mathbb{B}, \circ)$. Let $\mathfrak{a}^-$ denote the *inverse* of $\mathfrak{a} \in \mathbb{B}$, for which $B_{\mathfrak{a}^-} = B_{\mathfrak{a}}^{-1}$. It is known, and easy to verify that $\mathfrak{a}^- = (-\epsilon a, \bar{\epsilon})$. We remark that in practice, it is often enough to consider a subgroup of these functions, e.g. those for which the point $z = 1$ is fixed under transformation (with $\epsilon = 1$).

Now let us introduce the hyperbolic translation operators

$$\left(T_{\mathfrak{a}^-}^{[s]} f\right)(z) := \left(\frac{\sqrt{\bar{\epsilon}(1 - |a|^2)}}{1 - \bar{a}z}\right)^s \cdot f(B_{\mathfrak{a}}(z)), \quad (s \in \mathbb{N}).$$

For these, it can be verified that the relation $T_{\mathfrak{a}_1}^{[s]}\left(T_{\mathfrak{a}_2}^{[s]} f\right) = T_{\mathfrak{a}_1 \circ \mathfrak{a}_2}^{[s]} f$ holds ($\mathfrak{a}_j \in \mathbb{B}, s \in \mathbb{N}$), and they form a representation of the Blaschke group. In our case, the choice $s = 1$, studied in detail in work [15], is particularly interesting, as the operator $T_{\mathfrak{a}} := T_{\mathfrak{a}}^{[1]}$ is unitary on the Hilbert space $L^2(\mathbb{D})$ w.r.t. the measure $dxdy/\pi$, i.e. it preserves the scalar product and consequently $\|T_{\mathfrak{a}}f\|_2 = \|f\|_2$.

The direct consequence of this is that the translated (or rational) Zernike functions (or Zernike–Blaschke functions) $T_{\mathfrak{a}} Z_n^m$ also form a complete and orthogonal system in $L^2(\mathbb{D})$, for any choice of $\mathfrak{a}$. When visualized, this new set of orthogonal functions resemble an adapted version of the original Zernike functions to eye-balls not looking straight in the desired direction, rather slightly rotated, but the usual invariances of the Zernike functions around the origin are preserved. Therefore they may be applied to correct corneal measurements subject to this kind of defects (Fig. 2).

Fig. 2. A Zernike function and its translated variants.

3.3 Discretization and Coefficient Transformation

Concerning the practical usage of the aforementioned model, we present two additional result in this subsection.

First, we have a discretization result for the translated systems of Zernike functions, based on the system of nodes X_N, making them directly applicable in practice. For this, consider an arbitrary $\mathfrak{a} \in \mathbb{B}$, and define the set of nodal points

$$X_N^{\mathfrak{a}} = \{B_{\mathfrak{a}}(z_{j,k}) \; : \; z_{j,k} \in X_N\},$$

with the discrete measure for $x_{j,k} \in X_N^{\mathfrak{a}}$ given by

$$\mu_N^{\mathfrak{a}}(x_{j,k}) = \frac{\mathcal{A}_{k,N}}{2(4N+1)} \cdot |B_{\mathfrak{a}}'(z_{j,k})|^2 = \mu_N(x_{j,k}) \cdot |B_{\mathfrak{a}}'(z_{j,k})|^2, \quad (z_{j,k} \in X_N).$$

For these, among others we have a result analogue to Theorem 1:

Theorem 2. *If* $n + n' + |m| \leq 2N - 1$, $n + n' + |m'| \leq 2N - 1$, $n, n' \in \mathbb{N}$ *and* $m, m' \in \mathbb{Z}$, *then*

$$\int_{X_N^{\mathfrak{a}}} (T_{\mathfrak{a}} Z_n^{m,\mathfrak{a}})(z) \overline{(T_{\mathfrak{a}} Z_{n'}^{m',\mathfrak{a}})}(z) \, d\mu_N^{\mathfrak{a}} = \frac{\delta_{n,n'} \delta_{m,m'}}{\sqrt{(n+1)(n'+1)}}.$$

Once again, the limit of the discrete integrals of a function is the value of the continuous integral with respect to the measure $dxdy/\pi$. The details and proofs, among some other results are covered in our work to appear [17].

Next, let us remind that in classical Fourier analysis, given the Fourier coefficients of a function, we can compute the Fourier coefficients with respect to a modulated system of complex exponentials, since the matrix of a translation operator in the time domain corresponds to the matrix of modulation by the same parameter in the frequency domain. Therefore, it is enough to construct the matrix (or, in practice, a sufficiently large finite submatrix) of the first to compute the latter shifted coefficients.

For our work, computing the Zernike–Blaschke coefficients from the Zernike coefficients $c_{n,m}$, given the underlying translation parameter $\mathfrak{a}$, could be practical e.g. when trying to compare the results of measurements taken at separate times and/or under different conditions, by normalizing the two sequences of aberration coefficients. In a theoretical point of view, the solution is analogue to the classical case.

Since the image of an orthonormal system under the translations $T_{\mathfrak{a}}$ is also orthonormal, we may use any such system to construct entries of the translation matrix, so now let us consider the functions

$$e_n(z) := \frac{z^n}{\sqrt{n+1}}, \quad (z \in \mathbb{D}, n \in \mathbb{N}).$$

With these, the $E(\mathfrak{a})$ matrix of the translation $T_{\mathfrak{a}^-}$ is given by

$$E(\mathfrak{a}) := \left[t_{m,n}(\mathfrak{a}^-)\right]_{m,n \in \mathbb{N}}, \quad t_{m,n}(\mathfrak{a}) = \langle T_{\mathfrak{a}^-} e_m, e_n \rangle.$$

Based on [7], for any $m \in \mathbb{N}$ and $a \in \mathbb{D}$ the generating function of Zernike functions can be expressed via Blaschke functions in the form

$$\frac{1}{1 - \overline{a}z} B_a^m(z) = \sum_{n=0}^{\infty} (-1)^n Z_{n+m}^{n-m}(a) z^n,$$

leading to many interesting connections between these classes. Namely, it can be used to directly verify the following addition formula, analogue to the functional equation of the exponential function

$$E(\mathfrak{a}_1 \circ \mathfrak{a}_2) = E(\mathfrak{a}_1)E(\mathfrak{a}_2), \quad (\mathfrak{a}_j \in \mathbb{B}),$$

and consequently enabling us to compute the coefficients with respect to the translated system.

Also, the same generator function formula should be used to express the matrix entries themselves: e.g., considering the previously mentioned practical case $\epsilon = 1$, for any $\mathfrak{a} = (a, 1)$, by the matrix representation we have that

$$T_{\mathfrak{a}} e_m = \sum_{n=0}^{\infty} t_{mn}(\mathfrak{a}) e_n,$$

where applying the formula gives

$$t_{mn}(\mathfrak{a}) = (-1)^n \sqrt{1 - |a|^2} \sqrt{\frac{n+1}{m+1}} Z_{n+m}^{n-m}(a),$$

so the matrix entries are expressed by values of suitable Zernike functions.

4   Concluding Remarks

In this paper we collected and summarized the most important mathematical concepts behind our recent work concerning corrections of corneal measurements where the eye-ball was in a slightly rotated position. This research lead us to many interesting theoretical results regarding Zernike and Blaschke functions, as well as to promising practical applications to this problem and to others as well. The cited works contain the exact formalizations and the proofs in more detail, and not only for the Bolyai–Lobachevsky model of hyperbolic geometry but also for the Cayley–Klein model, which could also turn out to be practically useful.

In the future, numerical simulation, as well as measurements on real corneal surfaces are to be carried out to verify the applicability of this model for the given purpose. We intend to explore its potentials, and hope to give more precise error bounds. Based on these we intend to formulate recommendations on its practical use.

References

1. Zernike, F.: Beugungstheorie des Schneidenverfahrens und seiner verbesserten Form, der phasenkontrastmethode. Physica **7**, 689–704 (1934)
2. Szegő, G.: Orthogonal Polynomials, vol. 23. American Mathematical Society Colloquium Publications, AMS, Cambridge (1967)

3. Wyant, J.C., Creath, K.: Basic Wavefront Aberration Theory for Optical Metrology. Applied Optics and Optical Engineering, vol. XI. Academic Press, Cambridge (1992)
4. Corbett, M., Rosen, E.S., O'Brart, D.P.S.: Corneal Topography: Principles and Practice. BMJ Publishing Group, London (1999)
5. Pap, M., Schipp, F.: Discrete orthogonality of Zernike functions. Math. Pann. **16**, 137–144 (2005)
6. Bará, S., Arines, J., Ares, J., Prado, P.: Direct transformation of Zernike eye aberration coefficients between scaled, rotated, and/or displaced pupils. J. Opt. Soc. Am. A. **23**, 2061–2066 (2006)
7. Pap, M., Schipp, F.: The voice transform on the Blaschke group II. Ann. Univ. Sci. Budapest Sect. Comp. **29**, 157–173 (2008)
8. Fazekas, Z., Soumelidis, A., Schipp, F.: Utilizing the discrete orthogonality of Zernike functions in corneal measurements. In: Proceedings of the World Congress on Engineering, London, UK (2009)
9. Soumelidis, A., Fazekas, Z., Bódis-Szomorú, A., Schipp, F., Németh, J.: Specular surface reconstruction method for multi-camera corneal topographer arrangements. In: Recent Advances in Biomedical Engineering, pp. 639–660 (2009)
10. Belin, M.W., Khachikian, S.S.: An introduction to understanding elevation-based topography: how elevation data are displayed - a review. Clin. Exp. Ophthalmol. **37**, 14–29 (2009)
11. Tatulli, E.: Transformation of Zernike coefficients: a Fourier-based method for scaled, translated, and rotated wavefront apertures. J. Opt. Soc. Am. A **30**, 726–732 (2013)
12. Schipp, F.: Hyperbolic wavelets. In: Rassias, T.M., Tóth, L. (eds.) Topics in Mathematical Analysis and Applications. SOIA, vol. 94, pp. 633–657. Springer, Cham (2014). https://doi.org/10.1007/978-3-319-06554-0_29
13. Chang, D.H., Waring, G.O.: The subject-fixated coaxially sighted corneal light reflex: a clinical marker for centration of refractive treatments and devices. Am. J. Ophthalmol. **158**, 863–874 (2014)
14. Zheng, X., et al.: Evaluating the repeatability of corneal elevation through calculating the misalignment between successive topography measurements during the follow up of LASIK. Sci. Rep. **7**, 1–7 (2017)
15. Lócsi, L., Schipp, F.: Rational Zernike functions. Ann. Univ. Sci. Budapest Sect. Comp. **46**, 177–190 (2017)
16. Li, L., Zhang, B., Xu, Y., Wang, D.: Analytical method for the transformation of Zernike polynomial coefficients for scaled, rotated, and translated pupils. Appl. Opt. **57**, F22–F30 (2018)
17. Németh, Z., Schipp, F.: Discrete orthogonality of Zernike-Blaschke functions. SIAM J. Numer. Anal. (2019, to appear)

Neural Personal Profile Identification Based on Environmental Performance Analysis of Intelligent Building

Andrzej Stachno[✉]

Department of Control Systems and Mechatronics,
Wroclaw University of Science and Technology, Wroclaw, Poland
andrzej.stachno@pwr.edu.pl

Abstract. For the needs of such identification of people staying in the building's premises, a profiling and personal identification algorithm was developed using artificial neural networks - the Neural Identification of the Organic Personal Profile - NIOPP. Neural identification, uses measurements of gas concentrations whose proportions and composition are an individual feature for every human being. The paper proposes a method of profiling and isolating people, based on measurements of CO_2 concentration, VOC, temperature and air humidity, and their analysis using algorithms using artificial neural networks. For each examined person, her personal profile was assigned, derived from a series of measurements of various environmental parameters of the room. The experiments carried out and their analysis showed that it is possible to identify individual people staying in the room. Each of the subjects was characterized by its individual profile, identifiable with very high accuracy, based on the analysis of basic parameters, which are identified by traditional gas sensors, temperature and humidity.

Keywords: Neural networks · Time series · Measurements of environmental parameters · Intelligent buildings

1 The Need for Analysis of Environmental Measures in the Intelligent Building

A lot of parameters are archived in an intelligent building. For example, these are measurements of temperature, humidity, wind speed, energy, gas concentration, etc. Some of these parameters can be influenced by existing building infrastructure, e.g. changing the temperature and humidity of rooms, but others can only be measured and analyzed. These parameters are independent of the impact of technical devices and carry a lot of interesting information about the building and people staying in it.

Appropriate separation and analysis of measurement information from sensors used in building automation enables the development of personal patterns, and on this basis, identification of people staying indoors. Because in real objects, measurement data come from many room users who occupy them sporadically or constantly, the mechanism of measurement information analysis must have autoadaptation capabilities. Such features

R. Moreno-Díaz et al. (Eds.): EUROCAST 2019, LNCS 12014, pp. 388–395, 2020.
https://doi.org/10.1007/978-3-030-45096-0_48

are characterized by algorithms using artificial neural networks. Subjecting the measurement results to neural analysis, allows for the current adaptation of the entire system to the current conditions that take place in the building.

2 Measurement Methods and Data Analysis

The measuring system was built based on distributed building automation - KNX. This system makes it possible to integrate over fifty six thousand sensory and executive devices that perform tasks of building automation. System topology from lines connected to areas (Fig. 1).

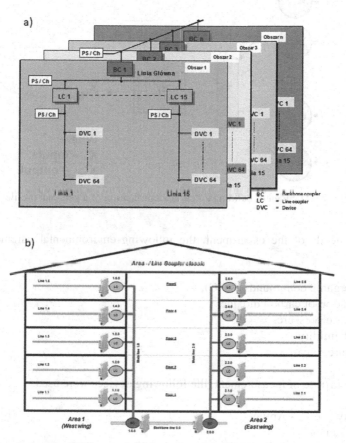

Fig. 1. (a) Topology of the KNX system, (b) Location of the KNX system topology in the building.

With this architecture, it is possible to link communications wiring devices, even in very large buildings. Devices included in the automation system can come from over 450 manufacturers from around the world and are compatible with each other at the communication level. This guarantees the verification of devices by a superior institution called the KNX Association. For the needs of the experiment, the system has been simplified to one line, in which there were measuring devices and an element of data archiving, which after proper processing were subjected to neural analysis. The idea of the analysis system is presented in Fig. 2.

Data input and output of Artificial Neural Networks for identification.

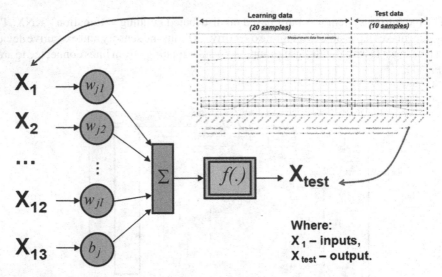

Fig. 2. The idea of building a neural identification of a personal profile.

For the needs of the experiment, the following environmental parameters were measured:

– Volatile organic compounds (VOC),
– Concentration of carbon dioxide,
– Atmospheric pressure,
– Relative humidity
– Temperature.

For the purpose of measurement, the following devices were used:

– Air quality sensor - Amun
– Presence sensor
– Air quality sensor - 2178 Jung
– PLC controller with data archiving module.

As a tool for neural analysis, an application written in the Matlab suite by MathWorks was used.

All measuring devices and data archiving communicated with each other using the KNX protocol.

3 Measurement Environment and the Course of the Experiment

Experiments of neuronal identification of people were made in a test room with an area of 36 [m²] and a volume of 100 [m³]. The room, test room with sensors, is depicted in Fig. 3.

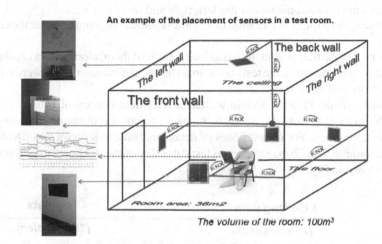

Fig. 3. Practical arrangement of measuring elements of internal environmental parameters of the building for the needs of the experiment.

Sensors are located on the walls and ceiling, connected by a communication bus to the data archiving server. Measurement data, reflecting the nine situations shown in Fig. 4.

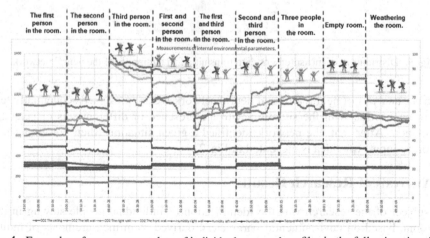

Fig. 4. Examples of measurement data of individual personal profiles in the following situations.

The measurements were made using multi-sensors operating in the KNX system, and the following parameters were analyzed:

- 4 measurements of CO_2 concentration (on the ceiling, on the left, right and front wall),
- 2 atmospheric pressure measurements (relative and absolute),
- 3 humidity measurements (on the left, right and front wall),
- 3 temperature measurements (on the left, right and front wall),
- 1 measurement of the concentration of volatile organic compounds (under the ceiling).

Three people participated in the experiment. Each of them, alone and in combination with other people, stayed in the test room. In addition, measurement data were collected from an empty and aired room.

Measurement data lasting 30 min with a measurement interval of 1 min were taken from each situation. In this way, for each situation a vector was obtained consisting of 13 measuring time series. For the purposes of neural analysis, this vector was divided into two parts: training data (20 samples) and test data (10 samples). The set of measurement vector is shown in Fig. 5.

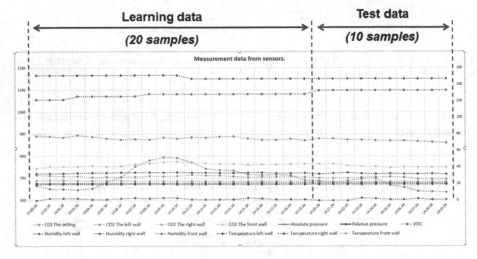

Fig. 5. Distribution of measurement data transmitted to the inputs of the neural network.

In the analysis of neural artificial neural network we are presented sequentially test data in connection with the situation with the presence of different sets of personal information. After that, the network identified a given situation when presenting test data on its inputs (the idea is presented in Fig. 2).

4   Analysis of Research Results

The subject of the research was the identification of individual people staying in the test room, based on environmental parameters, derived from measurements of multi-sensors used in building automation and their analysis with the use of artificial neural networks. The task of the proposed neural system was to learn the measurement pattern for all individuals individually and in groups, creating all possible combinations and additional situations: empty and ventilated rooms. Artificial neural network, based on previously presented patterns from measurements, identified the situation. In order to evaluate the results of the research, an algorithm was assigned assigning the value "one" to the situation of a correctly identified person and "zero" as a punishment for incorrect identification. For the situation of correct identification of all three people (or their absence), the maximum value is three. However, when all persons are incorrectly identified, the sum is zero (Fig. 6). The test was repeated ten times for each situation and the results were summed up.

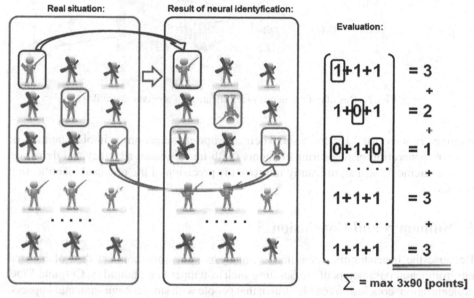

Fig. 6. The algorithm for calculating the weight for correct and incorrect identification of a personal profile.

Individual identification results are presented in Fig. 7. Out of all 90 test trials, 78 situations were identified (87%). The most identification errors were observed in the case of being alone in the second test room (5 out of 10 attempts) and the third (3 out of 10 attempts) of the person. Other errors, significantly affecting the result, concerned the identification of the second person staying at the same time and third in the room.

Since the analysis is based on the identification, data was measured internal environmental parameters of the building such as temperature, humidity, concentration of CO_2 and VOC can conclude that persons of a similar impact on the environment, for example. Exhaling a similar amount of CO_2 will be less recognizable by the neural system identification profile a passenger. Identification at the level of 50%, with the worst identified situation, however, gives the opportunity to improve the result by increasing the training data, or by modifying the internal parameters of the artificial neural network. It should also be remembered that standard sensors for measuring basic environmental

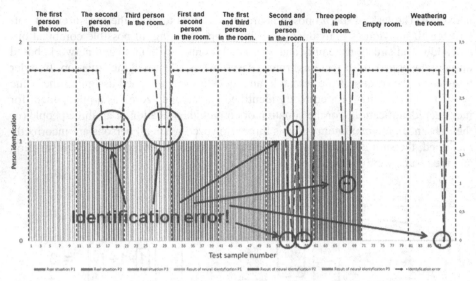

Fig. 7. Results of the neuron identification of a personal profile.

parameters were used for the tests. Their appropriate selection or implementation of a newer generation of measuring elements (with much greater accuracy and dynamics of measurement) will significantly improve the precision of the obtained identification results.

5   Summary and Conclusion

Because the basis for the identification analysis were measurement data of internal environmental parameters of the building such as temperature, humidity, CO_2 and VOC concentration, conclusions can be drawn that people with similar environmental impacts, e.g. exhaling a similar amount of CO_2, will be less well recognized by the neuronal personal profile identification system. Identification at the level of 50%, with the worst identified situation, however, gives the opportunity to improve the result by increasing the training data, or by modifying the internal parameters of the artificial neural network. It should also be remembered that standard sensors for measuring basic environmental parameters were used for the tests. Their appropriate selection or implementation of a newer generation of measuring elements (with much greater accuracy and dynamics of measurement) will significantly improve the precision of the obtained identification results.

References

1. Mantegna, R.N., Stanley, H.E.: An Introduction to Econophysics: Correlations and Complexity in Finance. PWN, Warsaw (2001)
2. Peitgen, H.O., Jurgens, H., Saupe, D.: Introduction to Fractals and Chaos. PWN, Warsaw (2002)

3. Technical Analysis of the Financial Markets, WIG Press (1999)
4. Jabłoński, A.: Intelligent buildings as distributed information systems. CASYS Int. J. Comput. Anticipatory Syst. **21**, 385–394 (2008)
5. Stachno, A., Jabłonski, A.: Hybrid method for forecasting next values of time series for intelligent building control. In: Moreno-Díaz, R., Pichler, F., Quesada-Arencibia, A. (eds.) EURO-CAST 2015. LNCS, vol. 9520, pp. 822–829. Springer, Cham (2015). https://doi.org/10.1007/978-3-319-27340-2_101

Systems Concepts and Methods in Touristic Flows

Re-aligning Business Ecosystem Data Sharing to Support City Hotel Operations Planning

Igor Perko[1](✉) ⓘ and Luka Smigoc[2]

[1] Faculty of Economics and Business, University of Maribor, Maribor, Slovenia
igor.perko@um.si
[2] Incon d.o.o. consulting group, Ljubljana, Slovenia

Abstract. The complexity of a successful tourist operations planning provides an everlasting challenge. It requires a vast array of data, managed and owned by multiple tourist business ecosystem players. Specifically, the rostering – planning staff and materials is especially hard to manage. In this paper, we elaborate information resources that have the potential to increase the planning accuracy in a well-developed tourist ecosystem with ever developing information systems. First, we identify the major tourist business ecosystem players, elaborate on their information related resources and needs, then we then examine their relations using system dynamics. Based on the developed model, a set of activities is proposed that would allow all the players to exploit the full potential of the data available, regarding the existing legal and ethical considerations.

The proposed model can be used for a scenario test, based on a case study of the tourist-oriented city, following a smart city path, located in Central Europe.

Invoking more detailed data, gathered from multiple sources and thereby increase in the rostering accuracy would significantly affect the optimisation of hospitality services.

Keywords: Hospitality · Predictive analytics · Smart city · System dynamics · Rostering · Tourist business ecosystem

1 Introduction

The complexity of tourist operations greatly exceeds the initial expectations by of many academic researchers [1]. It involves multiple players, which, only if coordinated perfectly, provide the desired tourist user experience. Planning these operations accurately is even harder [2], since the currently available data, gathered from multiple sources, combined with data on previous experiences is to be integrated in a meaningful manner to provide accurate predictions and smart suggestions. The premise is that the data storing and analysis is compliant with the GDPR regulation, adopted in the EU [3].

Multiple authors focused their research effort to the topic of managing the forthcoming use of the services offered to the tourists. Chen [4] discussed a decision system concepts, while Kulshrestha et al. [2] explored the non-linear autoregressive (NAR) neural networks and neuro-fuzzy systems in tourism demand forecasting. The involvement of behavior patterns, focused on of ecology factors was researched by Han et al. [5]. Not

© Springer Nature Switzerland AG 2020
R. Moreno-Díaz et al. (Eds.): EUROCAST 2019, LNCS 12014, pp. 399–406, 2020.
https://doi.org/10.1007/978-3-030-45096-0_49

enough effort though was put into addressing the issue of gathering and managing data, required to make such predictions.

An important segment of predictive decision processes is rostering. Ernst et al. [6] provide an overview of rostering applications, methods and models, while Smet [1], more recently, argues that academic rostering plans do not address the full complexity of multi-span dependent periods and thereby have limited application relevance. We can conclude that the currently proposed approaches do not have the capacity to address the complexity of the tourist operations planning and that the requisite information resources are to be identified to adequately resolve the problem.

One of the identified players is in the tourist data eco-system is a Smart city. Smart cities provide an organizational type, focused on providing a higher level of living experience for its inhabitants and visitors as already discussed in 1986 by Friedmann [7]. Batty et al. [8] identify six smart cities focus areas, ranging from the infrastructure to the creation of a space providing opportunities for urban populations.

The smart city integration and information sharing with its stakeholders is heavily researched and is found to be of great importance to support smart urban development. Caird [9], examined explicit reporting [10] and focused on knowledge sharing. The evidence of research in the field of information ownership, the issues of information asymmetry [11], management and sharing to/with the city stakeholders has not been thoroughly discussed yet.

Sigalatv et al. [12] claimed that to generate a real application of the smart concept in tourist cities, the collaboration of public and private actors, citizens and experts from different disciplines is essential. Smart tourism combines smart technologies to support all participants, providing tourist the best of experience in a location according to Gretzel [13].

The business relation, e-business as well as information sharing in tourism are reported as important [14]. Lalicic and Oender [15] combined the elements of a smart city and tourism planning and proposed co-participative approach in the planning process, whilst Nitti et al. added-on with the logistic optimization supported by the IoT [16].

Data, gathered by the tourist operators, enriched by the tourist feedbacks are an important resource for successful tourist operations planning [17]. The relations on data governance among the tourists, tour operators, and local tourist organizations are nevertheless largely unexplored.

System dynamics enables us to provide an oversight of complex systems where entities status and relations are determined by the outcome of repetitive behaviour loops as first discussed by Forrester [18] and was since then used to explain multiple complex relationships. Crnogaj et al. [19] for instance proposed a model for researching a sustainable entrepreneurship in the tourism sector, while Schianetz [20] proposed using system dynamics in strategic planning organisational learning and thereby creating a learning tourist destination.

In this paper, we address the of tourist operations planning complexity, identifying the important players in the system, the relations between them, built upon the feedback loops of their activities. Typically, the information resources consist of: the hotels internal resources, the smart city, the tour operators, the tourists etc. To provide a holistic manner perspective, a system dynamics model is designed, based the insights from the multiple existing research reports.

In the first part of the paper the backgrounds and the current state in the tourist business ecosystem is elaborated, related to the city hotel planning requirements. In the next part, using system dynamics a model is proposed, identifying current pathologies of relations among the ecosystem players and proposing mitigation activities.

The research, provided in this working paper should be continued by testing the proposed model on a real case. A mid-sized regional tourist focused city with the smart city initiative engaged is an appropriate candidate.

2 Hospitality Data Services Ecosystem

2.1 Identifying the Players

In the classic hospitality environment, the triangle of the players was simple: the Hospitality institutions, the travel agents and the tourists. The tourists make the reservation, through the tourist agents, or book the Hospitality resourced directly. The reservation data, combined with the experience on previous bookings enables the Hospitality institution to plan the resources with a certain degree of accuracy [21]. This process is performed for the short term planning, as well for the mid-term, seasonal planning (Table 1).

One of the main issues in hospitality planning is the lack of people, available in high seasons, combined with their re-allocation or potential unemployment during the off-season periods.

The main driving force in creating an active, data supported hospitality environment was the active marketing and opening new selling channels through web and mobile based portals, collecting feedforward and feedback by the users. The side-effect of this process was the creation of the data–rich environment, where multiple new data sources have emerged. Now the question is posted, weather and how this data should be used to increase the planning accuracy and adapt the planning to the tourist dynamics.

The standard hospitality player role in data storing changed considerably, with the new players adding in the data-rich ecosystem.

2.2 Data Storing Strategies

Players in hospitality data ecosystem differentiate in goal sets, data management capacities and authorizations. The model of traditional, new and potential data resources is presented in Fig. 1 and discussed later on.

The traditional relations are depicted in Blue, the new relations are depicted in green, and the potential relations with Smart cities are depicted in purple.

- **Hospitality institutions**: provide services to tourists directly or through the agents. They store data on booked and provided hospitality services, tourist properties and their feedbacks. They are particularly interested in booking tourist services, and optimizing the costs through effective planning [21]. Their capacities in storing and analysing data are usually rather limited and require decision-support ready data. The exception to the rule are global hospitality chains with high data storage and analytic capacities.

Table 1. Players in data ecosystem for hospitality planning

Player	Data stored	Implications for planning
Hospitality institutions	Data on the booked and used hospitality vacancies, the tourist properties and tourist feedbacks	Already used
Travel agents	Data on the tourist travel habits the tourist properties and tourist feedbacks	Reservations are already used, tourist feedbacks generally not
Tourists	They store and share their feedbacks data	Not used in planning
Tourist organisations	Provide statistical data on trends	Already used
Smart phone developers, and Mobile operators	Data from the mobile device sensors, as for instance location and movement style	Not used because of the lack in capacity and authority
Smart application developers	Store data, related to the smart application	Can be developed
Search engines developers	Store search history data and usually relate it to local data using the Geographical Information Systems (GIS) data	Not used because of the lack in capacity and authority
Social media developers	Store data on tourist experience and feedback by their community	Not used because of the lack in capacity and authority
Smart cities	Store data on traffic information, surveillance data, event planning and execution data, data on infrastructure, labour market	Share data and receive data aligned with their capacities and authorities

- **Travel agents:** act as an intermediary between the tourist and the Hospitality institution by answering the tourist expectations with a combination of hospitality services. Quite often they are organising travel services in form of regular or charter flights ship and bus connections. They store data on the tourist traveling habits, and feedbacks in the customer relationship management software. They are interested in fully addressing tourist expectations by providing the most convenient set of tourist destinations and hospitality services [22]. Their capacities in storing and analysing data vary considerably. Global travel agents possess high data storing and analytic capacities, while local agent capacities are rather limited and often rely on local expertise.
- **Tourists:** use their resources to explore tourist destinations. They store and share their feedbacks. Tourists are interested in using hospitality services that are aligned with

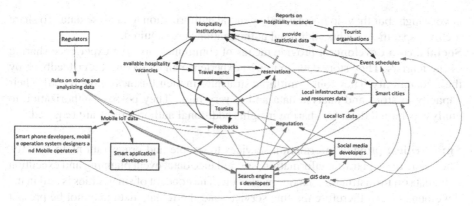

Fig. 1. Players and datasets

their particular interests and budget [23]. They are considered a main data source for the planning processes.

- **Tourist organisations:** provide statistical data on trends, predominantly based on data reported by Hospitality institutions and travel agents. They are interested in providing a general display of the activities and offers in the region/state. Their data management capacities are focused to summarize data.

The new, data focused players, in the tourist data-ecosystem are:

- **Smart phone developers, mobile operation system designers** and **Mobile operators**: provide basic services to mobile users, and connections between tourists and mobile application providers, they have the capacity to decode and store data from the mobile device sensors, as for instance location and movement style. They are focused in providing the high quality communication services and devices [24]. They store detailed data in raw form. Data storage is usually time limited, with relatively low capacity to analyse or aggregate data. Usually, the are not authorized to execute hospitality related analyses.

- **Smart app developers**: provide mobile apps, focused in addressing user information related needs, enhancing the real world experience. They store data, related to the application [25]. These can be specific or general. In specific apps, the capacity and authority to gather and analyse data is focused in a narrow segment of data with little of no value for the hospitality planning, with a clear exception of tourist focused smart apps.

Among the general classes of smart apps, we may identify:

- **Search engines developers**: provide active support in planning the tourist trips and provide on-site support for the tourists in exploring touristic destinations. They store search history data and relate it to local data using the Geographical Information Systems (GIS) data [26]. Their follow multiple business strategies, one of them is to promote search engine marketing [27]. Their capacity to store and analyse data and is very high, but they do possess only general authorization to analyse data. To share location specific insights additional authorizations are required.

- **Social media developers:** provide means of communication and experience sharing of the tourists. They store data on tourist experience and a second-order feedback by their community. They follow multiple strategies in their business models [28]. Their capacity to store and analyse data and is very high. They possess authorization to analyse personal data, for sharing insights additional authorizations are required.

- **Smart cities:** provide information services to people and organizations in the city. They store data on traffic information, surveillance data, event planning and execution data, data on infrastructure, labour market etc. The concept of smart cities is still in the development and therefore the line services and the related data may not be present [29]. Based on the smart city project state, the capacity to store and analyse tourist related data might vary considerably.

The Services, stored data and incentives are significantly more complex and overlapping. To cross-examine the data ecosystem, the data storing using strategies should be examined closely. We expect that the data storing and analysis processes are aligned with GDPR directive, with the regulator jet to play its role in closely examining the processes.

3 Summary

The proposed model is based on theory analysis, an overall examinations of the environment and feedbacks of field related experts. Therefore, it provides a place for further discussion, redesign and simulation on how the regulation and changes of the position of players would affect the development of the system.

The tourism data-ecosystem has gained new players. The traditional players: Tourists, Hosting institutions, Tourist agents, and Tourist organisations are now accompanied by Smart phone developers, Mobile operation system designers and Mobile operators, Smart application developers, Search engines developers, Social media developers.

Interestingly, the role of the new players is not in providing tourist services, it is focused in providing data services for exiting (and new players), which raises the complexity of relations among the players and provides potentials for further rearrangement. Arguably, the prospectus new player, not jet actively involved in the ecosystems are the Smart cities.

For further examination of the complex relations, data shared among the important players are to be examined closely.

At this stage, the proposed model shares light in relations of a newly formed digital ecosystem in the tourist environment and can therefore provide for the players in the ecosystem, the regulators and researchers.

References

1. Smet, P., Salassa, F., Berghe, G.V.: Local and global constraint consistency in personnel rostering. Int. Trans Oper. Res. **24**(5), 1099–1117 (2017)
2. Kulshrestha, A., Kulshrestha, A., Suman, S.: A hybrid intelligent model for tourism demand forecasting. Acta Turistica **29**(2), 157–179 (2017)
3. European_Commision: Regulation (EU) 2016/679 of the european parliament and of the council of 27 April 2016 on the protection of natural persons with regard to the processing of personal data and on the free movement of such data, and repealing Directive 95/46/EC (General Data Protection Regulation) (2016)
4. Chen, K.C.: Decision support system for tourism development: system dynamics approach. J. Comput. Inf. Syst. **45**(1), 104–112 (2004)
5. Han, H., Hsu, L.-T., Sheu, C.: Application of the theory of planned behaviour to green hotel choice: testing the effect of environmental friendly activities. Tourism Manage. **31**(3), 325–334 (2010)
6. Ernst, A.T., et al.: Staff scheduling and rostering: a review of applications, methods and models. Eur. J. Oper. Res. **153**(1), 3–27 (2004)
7. Friedmann, J.: The world city hypothesis. Dev. Change **17**(1), 69–83 (1986)
8. Batty, M., et al.: Smart cities of the future. Eur. Phys. J. Spec. Top. **214**(1), 481–518 (2012)
9. Caird, S.: City approaches to smart city evaluation and reporting: case studies in the United Kingdom. Urban Res. Pract. **11**(2), 159–179 (2018)
10. Caragliu, A., Del Bo, C., Nijkamp, P.: Smart cities in Europe. J. Urban Technol. **18**(2), 65–82 (2011)
11. Perko, I., Mlinaric, F.: Decreasing information asymmetry by sharing business data: a case of business non-payers sharing agency. Int. J. Risk Assess. Manage. **19**(1–2), 54 (2016)
12. Sigalat Signes, E., et al.: The need for a master plan for smart tourist cities. Methodological proposals based on participatory action. Pasos-Revista De Turismo Y Patrimonio Cultural **16**(2), 483–500 (2018)
13. Gretzel, U., et al.: Smart tourism: foundations and developments. Electron. Markets **25**(3), 179–188 (2015)
14. Fodor, O., Werthner, H.: Harmonise: a step toward an interoperable e-tourism marketplace. Int. J. Electron. Commer. **9**(2), 11–39 (2004)
15. Lalicic, L., Oender, I.: Residents' involvement in urban tourism planning: opportunities from a smart city perspective. Sustainability **10**(6), 1852 (2018)
16. Nitti, M., et al.: IoT Architecture for a Sustainable Tourism Application in a Smart City Environment. Mobile Information Systems (2017)
17. Sahin, I., Gulmez, M., Kitapci, O.: E-complaint tracking and online problem-solving strategies in hospitality management plumbing the depths of reviews and responses on TripAdvisor. J. Hospitality Tourism Technol. **8**(3), 372–394 (2017)
18. Forrester, J.W.: Industrial Dynamics, vol. 464. Pegasus Communications, Waltham (1961)
19. Crnogaj, K., et al.: Building a model of researching the sustainable entrepreneurship in the tourism sector. Kybernetes **43**(3–4), 377–393 (2014)
20. Schianetz, K., Kavanagh, L., Lockington, D.: The learning tourism destination: the potential of a learning organisation approach for improving the sustainability of tourism destinations. Tourism Manage. **28**(6), 1485–1496 (2007)
21. Altinay, L., Paraskevas, A.: Planning Research in Hospitality & Tourism. Routledge, London (2007)
22. Terblanche, N.S., Taljaard, A.: The perceived value and perceived benefits experienced by customers using travel agents. S. Afr. J. Bus. Manage. **49**(1), 1–13 (2018)

23. Markovic, S., Raspor, S., Komsic, J.: WHO ARE WELLNESS CUSTOMERS? AN EMPIR-ICAL STUDY IN THE CROATIAN HOTEL INDUSTRY/Kdo so velneski gosti? Empiricna studija v hrvaski hotelski industriji. Nase Gospodarstvo: NG **58**(1/2), 24–34 (2012)
24. Goadrich, M.H., Rogers, M.P.: Smart smartphone development: iOS versus Android. In: Cortina, T.J., et al. (ed.) Proceedings of the 42nd ACM Technical Symposium on Computer Science Education. SIGCSE 2011, pp. 607–612 (2011)
25. Kim, B.: The diffusion of mobile data services and applications: exploring the role of habit and its antecedents. Telecommun. Policy **36**(1), 69–81 (2012)
26. Vassio, L., et al.: You, the Web, and Your Device: Longitudinal Characterization of Browsing Habits. ACM Trans. Web **12**(4), 1–30 (2018)
27. Shih, B.-Y., Chen, C.-Y., Chen, Z.-S.: Retracted: an empirical study of an internet marketing strategy for search engine optimization. Hum. Factors Ergon. Manuf. Serv. Ind. **23**(6), 528–540 (2013)
28. Kaplan, A.M., Haenlein, M.: Users of the world, unite! The challenges and opportunities of social media. Bus. Horiz. **53**(1), 59–68 (2010)
29. Albino, V., Berardi, U., Dangelico, R.M.: Smart cities: definitions, dimensions, performance, and initiatives. J. Urban Technol. **22**(1), 3–21 (2015)

A Survey to Create Attractive Contents for Tourism -To Comprehend Other Cultures-

Yuko Hiramatsu[1(✉)], Atsushi Ito[2], Akira Sasaki[6], Kazutaka Ueda[3],
Rina Hayashi[4], Yasunari Harada[5], Hiroyuki Hatano[7], and Fumihiro Sato[1]

[1] Chuo University, 742-1 Higashinakano, Hachioji, Tokyo 192-039, Japan
{susana_y,fsato}@tamacc.chuo-u.ac.jp
[2] Utsunomiya University, 7-1-2 Yoto, Utsunomiya, Tochigi 321-8505, Japan
at.ito@is.utsunomiya-u.ac.jp
[3] University of Tokyo, 7-3-1 Hongo, Bunkyo-ku, Tokyo 113-8654, Japan
ueda@design-i.t.u-tokyo.ac.jp
[4] Okinawa Prefectural Government, 1-2-2 Izumizaki, Naha 900-8570, Japan
rina.h.1218@gmail.com
[5] Waseda University, 1-104, Totsuka-cho, Shinjyuku-ku, Tokyo 169-8050, Japan
harada@waseda.jp
[6] GClue Inc., 134-3 Ikkimachi Turuga, Aizu-wakamatsu-shi,
Fukushima 965-0006, Japan
akira@gclue.jp
[7] Mie University, 1577 Kurimamachiya-cho, Tsu city, Mie 514-8507, Japan
hatano@elec.mie-u.ac.jp

Abstract. Tourists use smartphone applications while traveling. Some applications are the same as their general use. Others are inclosing special contents for the area they are traveling. Smartphone applications make our travel convenient. However, if people feel something very convenience, they won't feel the trip great. We had researched the feeling of tourists and developed applications for tourists considering cognitive science.

Keywords: BLE beacon · Smartphone application · Tourism · Psychological effects

1 Introduction

UNWTO reported that international tourist arrivals grew 7.0% in 2017, the highest increase since the 2009 global economic crisis. A total of 1,326 million international tourist arrivals were recorded in destinations around the world, and some 86 million more than in 2016 [1]. 2,689,000 tourists visited Japan in January 2018. It went up by 7.5% from the year-earlier month by JNTO (Japan National Tourism Organization) [2]. Many tourists became to bring smartphones and use them on the trip to get some information about the area. Ministry of

© Springer Nature Switzerland AG 2020
R. Moreno-Díaz et al. (Eds.): EUROCAST 2019, LNCS 12014, pp. 407–415, 2020.
https://doi.org/10.1007/978-3-030-45096-0_50

Land, Infrastructure, Transport, and Tourism in Japan researched and found this tendency was remarkably increasing [3]. Now, mobile applications help users in planning travels. Also, they conveniently use the same tools during their trip; accommodation bookings, cab booking, route mapping, and information about the famous areas. However, is it enough to know much details conveniently for tourists? According to the psychology of tourism, the desire for novelty is essential for tourism. If tourists travel using an application which they use in their ordinary lives, they may not feel newness well. We have researched about tourists and developed an application for them in terms of psychology using Blue tooth Low energy (BLE) beacon. The rest of this paper is structured as follows. Section 2 examines related works. Section 3 describes the consideration of tourism at the viewpoints of psychology on the assumption of creating a smartphone application. Section 4 explains our two applications and results of experiments. Finally, in the conclusion section, we discuss how we can generate novelty for a tourist application.

2   Related Works

2.1   Application Using BLE Beacon

The global BLE beacon market is expected to grow at a compound annual growth rate of 307.2% from 2015–2020. About 80,000 units were shipped in 2015, and this number is expected to grow to 88.29 million units by 2020 quickly [4]. BLE beacons are mainly used for indoor location-based services to indicate locations and display information. For example, "Visualization Service for Congestion Degree Using BLE Beacons [5]" is one of those researches. This research aimed to alert the congestion risk to event operators by instantly grasping and visualizing the congestion degree at the event site. Casa Batllo in Spain is preparing the launch of the new visit with Virtual and Augmented Reality using beacons system by University Research Institute Robotics Information Communication Technologies [6]. For outdoor use, a new business called Beacon Bank uses beacons that having already been established and is based on a beacon sharing system [7].

2.2   Psychology of Tourism

The reason why people do travel is said that tourist motivation is a desire for novelty. Tae Hee Lee & Crompton, J. told "Novelty in the context of tourism, to conceptualize its role in the destination choice process, and to develop an instrument to measure novelty. The novelty construct was comprised of four interrelated but distinctive dimensions: thrill, change from routine, boredom alleviation, and surprise [8]".

3   Consideration About Tourism at the Viewpoints of Psychology to Create Our Smartphone Application

3.1   Psychology of Tourists

Tourists conveniently use same tools during their travel; accommodation bookings, cab booking, route mapping, and information about the famous areas. Nowadays we live in IoT Society. Many devices connect, and data is mining for each person. Such contents provide us safety and comfortable life. However, travel becomes some extension of ordinary lives using applications now. It seems that novelty is no longer a motivation for smartphone tourists. In ICT society, developers have sought to connect things or people by standardizing parts. Such connection brought us seam-less comfortable lives. They seldom bring us novelty to construct directly. On the other hand, it is not so easy to convey local traditional things, unique customs, or cultural originality by standardizing contents. Having a different viewpoint it means the subject of travel has changed. Tourists used to ask people in the area when they lost their way or want to know something in the area. Tourists were in a different culture from their own countries. They were strangers, and they used to accept new information or manners in the area from people living there. However, tourists become to play the leading parts on the trip as their ordinary lives using smartphone application now. They have fewer chances to say, "Excuse me", "Thank you" to people living in the area as newcomers. Tourists still want to contact with people in the area according to our research in 2015 [9] However, people in the region have little chances to talk to tourists who are looking at a smartphone screen. Such tendency makes one of the elements for tourism phobia. For tourism, one of the contents which tourists get novelty is another culture they have never had. Alison Malyn Shumate-Fowler wrote "The Psychological Aspects of Travel Abroad" [10]. They indicated a current issue that many people today are culturally sheltered, having no desire to open their minds beyond the boundaries of the nation. We have to create an attractive application to solve such a tendency.

3.2   Looking at the Display of Smartphone Application

We develop applications for a smartphone. The interface is a screen with light emission. According to the viewpoint of cognitive science and affordance theory, human behavior of reading objects is not so simple. Our eyes recognize and process different ways between looking at the screen with light emission and reading paper. The researches of Human Engineering explain differences in kinds of the medium we are looking [11]. However, there are not many pieces of research in this field. Dr. Onabe told the influences not only for short-term storage but also for long-term storage in his paper named "The Reason Why Scientific Documents have to be Read through Paper Media" [12]. Also, an experiment proved the superiority of paper to display by Dr. M Nakagawa et al. at the branch of neuroscience concerned with the brain (NIRS: Near-Infrared Spectroscopy) [12]. (See Fig. 1)

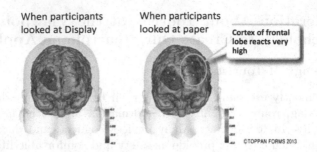

Fig. 1. The branch of neuroscience concerned with the brain (the news release by Toppanf), 23.7.2013 [13]

The results of the experiment showed that paper is superior to display for deeper understanding. When participants looked at papers, cortex of frontal lobe, which directs thinking and self-motivation, reacted very high. When tourists try to get some information about the roots or something they do not think about it deeply, the display is useful. However, if they try to understand some new or traditional culture in the area, the smartphone display will not make enough. We, creators, have to consider such a result of the experiment. If tourists feel something they have not known yet, we have to let them feel more active to think about the object. We try to create applications to make attractive contents for tourism, especially for specific points of the area to feel novelty.

4   Our Application

4.1   Aim and Methods

We planned to create a new application for tourists not only for convenience but also to perceive culture or custom politely. Tourists may be active in the place. Finally, we aim the application would help tourists and people in the area talk and respect each other. Tourists may have a chance to ask people living in the area about the local information with curiosity. To actualize this aim, we have two prerequisites. See Fig. 2. Human beings tend to pay attention to the open area. We apply such human tendency to our new applications. We concretely developed two applications as followings. Those are based on psychological effects. We developed two applications in Nikko [14,15], the world heritage site in Japan using BLE beacon: One is an orienteering application for students by Zeigarnik effect [16]. This effect explains that completed tasks are less recalled than uncompleted tasks. Schiffman & Greist Bousquet reported the evidence of the Zeigarnik effect in 1992 [17]. The other is an application for the National park at Oku-Nikko using Zeigarnik effect and Maslow's hierarchy of needs [18]. Figure 3 shows the contents of 2 applications. BLE beacons were set on the poles or the signboards by the roadside. We have our original function in colored points. Shop owners gave us not only information about their shop and but also about the areal and seasonal ones.

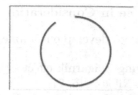

Fig. 2. How to make a remarkable point

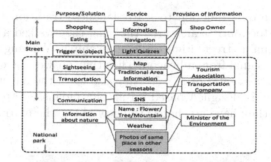

Fig. 3. Contents of 2 applications in Nikko

4.2 Our Beacon System and Screenshots of Our Application

We planned to use BLE beacons to create a new traditional road to the main shrine at Nikko for mains street (App No. 1). Also, we tried to show messages which were made by the people living in the area. Figure 4 explains the software components of our applications. BLE chip always scans the advertising message. When the operating system (OS) receives an advertising message, the OS forwards the message to the application. On the case of Core Location framework of iOS (7 or later), the message provides four properties of proximity, UUID, major, and minor. Using beacons, we send special local information.

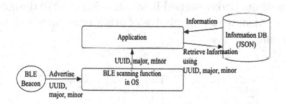

Fig. 4. The software components (both No. 1 and No. 2)

4.3 Contents and Interface in Consideration of Cognitive Science

We thought out those 2 points to develop our applications.

- Content: Quiz function using Zeigarnik effect (Main street at Nikko: No. 1 and National Park at Oku-Nikko: No. 2)
- Interface of App: considering Maslow's hierarchy of needs (National Park at Oku-Nikko: No. 2)

We created the quiz function to learn Japanese traditional cultural points for No. 1 App. After tourists answered the quiz, they walked a little and check the point at the main street. Figure 5 is an example. Walking along the road, tourists notice the signal from a beacon. Then they answer the quiz and find the Japanese lamp as the center of Fig. 5. They also learn the meaning of the mark of this lamp. That is designed based on an old Japanese letter. If they don't have such a quiz, they have no chance to know about the mark.

Fig. 5. Screens of quiz function No. 1 App

Setting BLE beacons in the national park of Oku-Nikko: No. 2 App, we had an experiment from February in 2018 (n = 20). We listed up to ten required elements of trips (See Fig. 6). Based on Maslow's hierarchy of needs, we added priority to the functions and designed it for Oku-Nikko. We designed an interface using these results. Also, we input photos of other seasons where tourists are now to feel some deficiency.

Elements of sightseeing (Oku-Nikko)	1	2	3	4	5	6	Function of App
Weather		O					Weather
New Information (Weather, Disaster, Bear, Event etc.)		O			O	O	Information
Transportation, Access		O					Bus (Timetable and route)
Restroom, Present location, Model cources	O	O			O		Map
High light, Gudance, Transportation, Food (Shops)	O	O			O		Pop-up
High light, Photos of seasons						O	Seasons Photo
Gidance, Origin, Photos of animals, floweres, mountains					O	O	Photo books
Event						O	Stamp rally
SNS, "Like"			O	O			SNS
Multi lingual		O					Setting

Fig. 6. Mapping among elements of information, Maslow's hierarchy of needs

4.4   Experiments

We asked tourists to install our application No. 1 at Tobu Nikko Station during 29th–30th August, 26th–27th September and 8th November 2015. N = 57: English (Foreigners) 15, Japanese 42. Users tended to rate our application as pleasant, interesting, and helpful. Figure 7 shows the evaluation of the operation. Foreign tourists evaluated higher than Japanese. They also evaluated our stamp function as "interesting," though the feature is not so useful. When the smartphone catches a beacon signal, the mascot character of Nikko is stamped with sound. Tourists enjoy it.

We also had an experiment of quiz function only in September 26–27, 2015(n = 28). After using this function, tourists evaluated "History/Culture" was higher than before. Also, the evaluation kept high about "History/Culture" after two months. For No. 2 application, we designed interface as Fig. 8. We will have experiments in 2019.

Fig. 7. A result of experiment (No. 1 App)

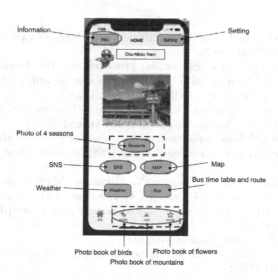

Fig. 8. Interface of the National Park Application at Oku-Nikko (No. 2 App)

5   Conclusion

We developed two applications with BLE beacons in Nikko considering psychological effects to make attractive points for tourists. The results of the experiment showed that tourists were interested in quiz function or stamps, which were not useful to their convenience or safety movement on the trip. They were interested in something they have not known yet and remember them after two months. The experiments are not finished, and we will continue to establish the validity of our applications using psychological effects. Also, we had a questionnaire to international students order to know how they evaluate signs in the main street in Nikko May in 2018 (n = 40, 15 countries.) in order to examine the linguistic gap among foreign tourists and people in the area. It is necessary to translate our traditional Japanese words into English. According to the results, Sentences of signboards with correct English is not always evaluated higher than wrong ones. On the other hand, some signboards evaluated high with spelling mistakes or grammatical errors: which shop owners tried to explain their Japanese sweets politely. Such sweets may be unknown things for foreigners. We also analyzed the results and found a correlation between "the satisfaction of the signboards" and "whether participants liked traveling or not" (r = 0.409). Novelty and curiosity bring tourists to attractive experiences. We will have experiments and consider how to update the contents of our application to communicate unique cultural objects.

Acknowledgments. This research is supported by JSPS KAKENHI Grant Number JP17H02249 and JP18K11849.

References

1. UNWTO: Tourism highlights 2018 Edition, p. 4. https://www.e-unwto.org/doi/pdf/10.18111/9789284419876
2. Japan National Tourism Organization, press release: The Number of foreigners Visiting Japan on January 2019 (estimated) (Japanese only). https://www.jnto.go.jp/jpn/news/press_releases/pdf/190220_monthly.pdf
3. Ministry of Land, Infrastructure, Transport and Tourism HP (Japanese only). http://www.mlit.go.jp/kankocho/news02_000190.html
4. Jesse, M.: Bluetooth beacons are teetering on the brink of ubiquity, with shipment volume expected to grow exponentially by 2020. Tecnavio Blog, 18 March 2016 (2016)
5. Sato, D., Mihara, Y., Sato, Y., Tanaka, Y., Miyamoto, M., Sakuma, S.: Information processing society of Japan. J. Consum. Device Syst. (CDS) **8**(1), 1–10 (2018)
6. Casa Batllo HP. https://www.casabatllo.es/ca/novetats/visita-con-realidad-aumentada-y-virtual/
7. Beacon Bank HP. https://beaconbank.jp/
8. Lee, T.-H., Crompton, J.: Measuring novelty seeking in tourism. J. Ann. Tour. Res. **19**, 732–751 (1992)
9. Hiramatsu, Y., Sato, F., Ito, A., et al.: Recovering the traditional street with BLE beacons base on classification of travelers. In: The 3rd WCCAIS. Dubai, UAE (2016)

10. Shumate-Fowler, A.M.: The psychological aspects of travel abroad. University of Tennessee - Knoxville, May 1995
11. Wright, P., Lickorish, A.: Proof-reading texts on screen and paper. Behav. Inform. Technol. **2**(3), 227–235 (2007)
12. Onabe, F.: The reason why scientific documents have to be read through paper media. SEN'I GAKKAISH **66**(5), 149 (2010)
13. IT media news: The experiment of neuroscience told people can understand higher paper than display (only in Japanese), 24 July 2013. https://www.toppan-f.co.jp/news/2013/0723.html
14. Hiramatsu, Y., et al.: A service model using bluetooth low energy beacons-to provide tourism information of traditional cultural sites. Serv. Comput. 14–19 (2016)
15. Ito, A., et al.: A study of psychological approach to design sightseeing support mobile application. In: Proceedings of INES 2018, June 2018
16. Zeigarnik, B.V.: On finished and unfinished tasks. In: Ellis, W.D. (ed.) A sourcebook of Gestalt psychology. Humanities Press, New York (1967)
17. Schiffman, N., Greist-Bousquet, S.: The effect of task interruption and closure on perceived duration. Bull. Psychonom. Soc. **30**(1), 9–11 (1992)
18. Maslow, A.H.: Motivation and Personality, 3rd edn. Pearson Education, Delhi (1987)

Experiments of LoRa to Develop Services for Tourists

Akira Sasaki[1], Munkhod Bayarsaikhan[1], Kingsam Law[1], Hiroyuki Hatano[3],
Atsushi Ito[1(✉)], Yuko Hiramatsu[2], and Fumihiro Sato[2]

[1] Utsunomiya University, 7-1-2 Yoto, Utsunomiya, Tochigi 321-8505, Japan
akira@gclue.jp, munju08@gmail.com, kingsamlawsan@gmail.com,
at.ito@is.utsunomiya-u.ac.jp
[2] Chuo University, 742-1Higashinakano, Hachioji, Tokyo 192-039, Japan
{susana_y,fsato}@tamacc.chuo-u.ac.jp
[3] Mie University, 1577 Kurimamachiya-cho, Tsu city, Mie 514-8507, Japan
hatano@elec.mie-u.ac.jp

Abstract. Low Power Wide Area (LPWA) is now becoming popular
for long-range license-free wireless communication technology. Bluetooth
and WiFi are commonly used for the license-free near field communication technique. However, they can cover 100 m or near. LPWA can
provide news services for long distance communication in the rural area.
We have been developing a sightseeing support application using BLE
beacon for six years near the World Heritage "Nikko" and now expanding
a service area to "Oku-Nikko" where is a mountain area with huge mush
and waterfalls, lakes, and mountains. A sightseeing support application
for Oku-Nikko requires to provide information about safety since there
is a mountain area. For that purpose, it is essential to observe hikers
in the broad field, and low cost, long distance telecommunication system is required. To design the tourist support network in Oku-Nikko,
we firstly understand the transmission model of LoRa. For that purpose, we performed some test to measure the transmission distance of
LoRa in different environments. In this paper, we would like to explain
an experiment of LoRa in Nikko National Park and around Utsunomiya
University. We discuss that results of the experiment show the one possibility to explain the transmission model of LoRa in Oku-Nikko and
Utsunomiya was Okumura-Hata model.

Keywords: LPWA · LoRA · Transmission model of LoRa

1 Introduction

Low Power Wide Area (LPWA) [1] is now becoming popular for long-range
license-free wireless communication technology. Bluetooth and WiFi are commonly used for the license-free near field communication technique. However,
they can cover 100 m or near. LPWA can provide news services for long-distance
communication (several 100 m - several km) in the rural area. LPWA is a name

© Springer Nature Switzerland AG 2020
R. Moreno-Díaz et al. (Eds.): EUROCAST 2019, LNCS 12014, pp. 416–424, 2020.
https://doi.org/10.1007/978-3-030-45096-0_51

of communication technologies that use sub-Giga Hz band. The sub-Giga Hz band has excellent penetration. It is expected that LPWA can provide several features for IoT applications such as low cost, low power consumption, long distance communication, a connection of a massive number of IoT devices, and small data transmission (100 bps–1 Mbps).

We have been developing a sightseeing support application using BLE beacon for six years near the World Heritage "Nikko" and now expanding a service area to "Oku-Nikko" where is a mountain area with huge mush and waterfalls, lakes, and mountains. A sightseeing support application in Oku-Nikko requires to provide information about safety since there is a mountain area. For that purpose, it is essential to observe hikers in the broad area, and low cost, long distance telecommunication system is required. To design the tourist support network in Oku-Nikko, we firstly understand the transmission model of LoRa. For that purpose, we performed some test to measure the transmission distance of LoRa in different environments.

In this paper, we would like to explain an experiment of LoRa in Nikko National Park and around Utsunomiya University. In this experiment, we used LoRa [2] that is an implementation of LPWA since it is easy to get devices.

In section two, we explain the outline of LPWA and tell about LoRa in section three. Then we mention the models to estimate the transmission distance. In section five, we describe the result of two experiments, one was performed in Oku-Nikko, and another was performed in Utsunomiya near our university. In section six, we discuss that the results show that the one possibility to explain the transmission model using the Okumura-Hata model may be useful. At last, in section seven, we mention the conclusion and further study.

2   Outline of LPWA

LPWA is strongly expected for communication technology for IoT systems. Ordinary communication technologies such as WiFi and Bluetooth since such technologies can connect only the adjacent area in 100 m since these technologies are designed for personal use.

LPWA can cover problems of existing technologies such as long distance and low power and become famous.

– LPWA has features as follows.
– Low cost
– low power (Except BLE, ordinary NFC technologies requires sufficient power supply)
– long distance (several 100 m - several km) (See Table 1)
– Connect many devices
– Small data (100 bps–1 Mbps)

The frequency band for LPWA is different in countries, and we should follow the law in each country. In Japan, 916.5–927.5 MHz is allowed to use for LPWA.

Also, it is required to follow the regulation of ARIB STD-T108 [6]. This regulation is defined for telemeter, tele-control, and data transmission equipment using the 920 MHz band. Frequency allocation of LPWAN in different countries is described in Table 2.

Table 1. Band and distance of LPWAN

Name	Band	Distance (m)
Bluetooth	2.4 GHz	Class1 100 m, Class2 10 m, Class3 1 m
WiFi	2.4 GHz, 5 GHz	10 m–100 m
LTE	2.4 GHz, 5 GHz	3 km–30 km
LoRa	920 MHz	Open space: 10 km, Town: 2 km
GIgfox	920 MHz	Open space: 30 km–50 km, Town: 3–5 km

Table 2. Frequency allocation of LPWAN

Country	Frequency (MHz)
Japan	916.5–927.5
U.S.A	902–928
Korea	917–923.5
EU	868–868.6
China	314–316, 430–434, 470–510, 779–787

3   Outline of LoRa

The most popular standard of LPWA is LoRa [2]. Especially, LoRa Alliance defines LoRaWAN [3]. The difference between LoRaWAN and LoRa is as follows. LoRa defines the modulation technology of the physical layer. On the other hand, the definition of LoRaWAN includes MAC layer. LoRaWAN specifies the interoperability of devices of LoRa. LoRa uses CSS (Chirp Spectrum Spread). By using spectrum spread with chirp signal, LoRa allows long distance communication. In the best case, LoRa allows communication of several tens of kilometers. When using LoRa, it is required to use two parameters: one is bandwidths (bw) and spreading factor (sf). Smaller bw allows to communicate in longer distance, and larger sf also allows to communicate in longer distance. However, if we would like to communicate longer distance, the transmission time becomes longer. The relation between bw and sf is described in Fig. 1.

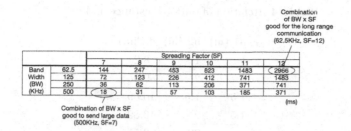

		Spreading Factor (SF)					
		7	8	9	10	11	12
Band	62.5	144	247	453	823	1483	2966
Width	125	72	123	226	412	741	1483
(BW)	250	36	62	113	206	371	741
(KHz)	500	18	31	57	103	185	371

Combination
of BW x SF
good for the long range
communication
(62.5KHz, SF=12)

(ms)

Combination of BW x SF
good to send large data
(500KHz, SF=7)

Fig. 1. The effect of SF and BW for the transmission time to send 10 bytes (ms)

The one of the largest benefit of LoRa is low power consumption. The comparison of power consumption of typical NFC technologies and LoRa is described in Table 3. Especially, the power consumption at the active case, it is 44% of BLE. So that, it is possible to send data from an IoT device for 10 years by using a small battery.

Table 3. Comparison of energy consumption of LPWAN

Name	Sleep (nA)	Active (mA)
Bluetooth LE	100	26
Zigbee	700	14.4
LoRa	100	10.5

In the next two sections, we explain the model of an electromagnetic wave in the broad area.

$$d = 3.57\sqrt{K}\left(\sqrt{h_1\,[\mathrm{m}]} + \sqrt{h_2\,[\mathrm{m}]}\right) \fallingdotseq 4.12\left(\sqrt{h_1\,[\mathrm{m}]} + \sqrt{h_2\,[\mathrm{m}]}\right)\,[\mathrm{km}]$$

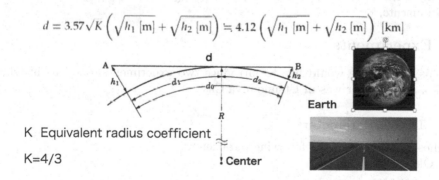

K Equivalent radius coefficient

K=4/3

Fig. 2. Outlook distance model

Table 4. Relation of outlook distance and height

h1 (m)	h2 (m)	d (km)
1	1	8.24
1	2	9.95
1.5	1.5	10.09
1.5	2	10.89
1	20	22.55

4   Model

4.1   Outlook Distance

Outlook Distance is the maximum distance that can be calculated by considering the curvature of the earth, as described in Fig. 2.

Table 4 shows some samples of the relation between the hight of a sender and a receiver, and an outlook distance. For example, if the sender and receiver are haled by users (about 1 m), the outlook distance is 8.24 km. And if the sender is 1 m and the receiver is 20 m, the outlook distance is 22.55 km.

4.2   Okumura-Hata-Model

The Okumura-Hata model is a radio propagation model for predicting the path loss of cellular transmissions in exterior environments, valid for microwave frequencies from 150 to 1500 MHz. It is an empirical formulation based on the data from the Okumura Model and is thus also commonly referred to as the Okumura-Hata model [4]. The model incorporates the graphical information from Okumura model and develops it further to realize the effects of diffraction, reflection, and scattering caused by city structures [2]. Additionally, the Okumura-Hata Model applies corrections for applications in suburban and rural environments.

5   Experiments

In this section, we would like to introduce two experiments, one was in Oku-Nikko, and another was in Utsunomiya City.

5.1   Device Parameters

In these trials, we set the following parameters.
   (Okuniko)

- bw: 125 MHz
- sf: 10
- Tx power: 13 dbm
- LoRa chip: RAK811
- gain of the antenna: 0 dbi

(Utsunomiya)

- bw: 62.5MHz
- sf: 12
- Tx power: 13dbm
- LoRa chip: ES920LR
- gain of the antenna: 0dbi

5.2 Experiment in Oku-Nikko

In Oku-Nikko, there is a big mash and forest called Senjyo-gahara. We set a transmitter in the parking lot of Senjyo-gahara and measured the reach of LoRa in Fig. 3a. Point 1, 400m West of the parking lot, we could receive the signal. At the Point 2, 2 km West from the parking lot, we received a signal every 5 min. Also, at the Point 3, 2.3 km West from the parking lot, we received a signal every 20 min. The result is shown in Fig. 3b.

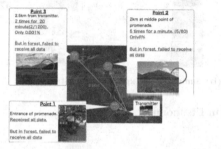 

(a) Experiment in Oku-Nikko   (b) Summary of Experiment in Oku-Nikko

Fig. 3. LoRa in Oku-Nikko

5.3 Experiment in Utsunomiya

In this experiment, we developed an application on Android to control LoRa (Fig. 4). We put the receiver on the roof of our building. The hight of our building is about 20 m. Then the transmitter moved to North. Figure 5a shows the result of the experiment in Utsunomiya. The signal of LoRa was received by the receiver when the transmitter was 4.5 km far from our building. Figure 5b shows the height of the transmitter.

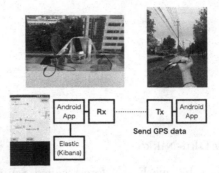

Fig. 4. Devices for experiment in Utsunomiya

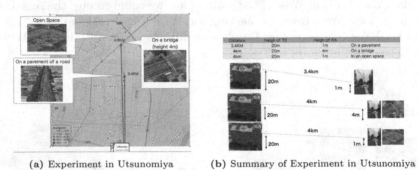

(a) Experiment in Utsunomiya   (b) Summary of Experiment in Utsunomiya

Fig. 5. LoRa in Utsunomiya

6   Discussion

Figures 6 and 7 show the Okumura-Hata-curve by using [5] in Oku-Nikko and Utsunomiya respectively.

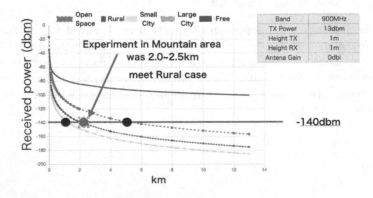

Fig. 6. Experiment in Oku-Nikko

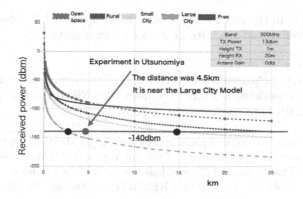

Fig. 7. Experiment in Utsunomiya

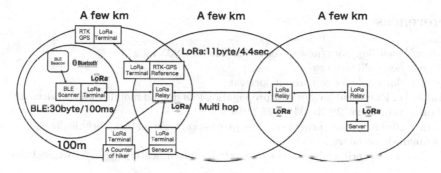

Fig. 8. Further study plan in Oku-Nikko

In Fig 6, our experiment shows the transmission distance was 2.0–2.5 km. This result fitted the rural area case of Okumura-Hata-curve when the band was 900 MHz, and both heights of Tx and Rx was 1 m. -140dbm is the threshold of signal strength of LoRa.

In Fig. 7, our experiment shows the transmission distance was 4.5 km. This result fitted the large city case of Okumura-Hata-curve when the band was 900MHz, and both heights of Tx was 1m, and Rx was 20 m.

So, we expect that the Okumura-Hata-model may give the proper estimation of the transmission distance of LoRa in Oku-Nikko and Utsunomiya.

7 Conclusion and Further Study

In this experiment, the reach of LoRa was 2 km in the forest and 700 m in the city area. There are some reports succeeded to transmit data using LoRa 5 to 10 km. We are planning to tune the transmitter and receiver and measure the transmission distance in both city area and forest and develop applications using features of LoRa such as counting the number of hikers and sending weather data in the mountains in Oku-Nikko area to provide safety information and navigate

424 A. Sasaki et al.

sightseeing people in the city area. We also thought that LPWA could be useful to observe children or older adults in the local community.

- Support more wide area.
- Continue to try measurement experiment at Utsunomiya University.
- Build target network using LoRa to connect Oku-Nikko and Univ.Utsunomiya (40 km) by multi-hops as described in Fig. 8.

Acknowledgement. Authors express special thanks to Mr.Wada and Mr.Suzuki of Nikko National Park Office of Ministry of the Environment, Ms.Wada, and Ms.Sato of Tochigi Prefectural Government Office and all members of the committee for increasing satisfaction of tourists in Nikko. JSPS KAKENHI Grant Number JP17H02249 supports this research.

References

1. http://www.3gpp.org/news-events/3gpp-news/1805-iot_r14
2. https://lora-alliance.org/
3. https://lora-alliance.org/about-lorawan
4. Hata, M.: Empirical formula for propagation loss in land mobile radio services. IEEE Trans. Veh. Tech. **29**(3), 317–325 (1980)
5. http://circuitdesign-jp.check-xserver.jp/wp-pre/technical/en/technicaltool/okumura-hata-curve/
6. https://hwww.arib.or.jp/english/std_tr/telecommunications/desc/std-t108.html

Evaluation of Sightseeing Support Application Using BLE Beacon in Oku-Nikko

Akira Sasaki[1], Rina Hayashi[2], Atsushi Ito[1(✉)], Yuko Hiramatsu[3],
Kazutaka Ueda[4], Yasunari Harada[5], Hiroyuki Hatano[1], and Fumihiro Sato[3]

[1] Utsunomiya University, 7-1-2 Yoto, Utsunomiya, Tochigi 321-8505, Japan
akira@gclue.jp, {at.ito,hatano}@is.utsunomiya-u.ac.jp
[2] Okinawa Prefectural Government, 1-2-2 Izumizaki, Naha 900-8570, Japan
rina.h.1218@gmail.com
[3] Chuo University, 742-1Higashinakano, Hachioji, Tokyo 192-039, Japan
{susana_y,fsato}@tamacc.chuo-u.ac.jp
[4] University of Tokyo, 7-3-1 Hongo, Bunkyo-ku, Tokyo 113-8654, Japan
ueda@design-i.t.u-tokyo.ac.jp
[5] Waseda University, 1-104, Totsuka-cho, Shinjyuku-ku, Tokyo 169-8050, Japan
harada@waseda.jp

Abstract. According to the spread of mobile devices such as a mobile phone, it is expected to use ICT (Information and Communication Technology) for sightseeing services. In Japan, the Tourism Authority of Japan has started to promote to use a smartphone application to support inbound traveler. In this situation, we are developing a sightseeing support application using BLE (Bluetooth Low Energy) beacon in the Nikko area. In the paper, we proposed a design method to design a sightseeing application applying two psychological effects, one is the Zeigarnik Effect, and another is Maslow's hierarchy of needs. Then we explain the trial and how the trial was failed. We also explain how to solve the problem that appeared during the trial.

Keywords: BLE beacon sightseeing support system · Smartphone · Solar battery

1 Introduction

According to the spread of mobile devices such as a mobile phone, it is expected to use ICT (Information and Communication Technology) for sightseeing services. In Japan, the Tourism Authority of Japan has started to promote to use a smartphone application to support inbound traveler [1]. In this situation, we are developing sightseeing support application [2] using BLE (Bluetooth Low Energy) beacon [3] in the Nikko area. In the paper [2], we proposed a design method to design a sightseeing application applying two psychological effects,

© Springer Nature Switzerland AG 2020
R. Moreno-Díaz et al. (Eds.): EUROCAST 2019, LNCS 12014, pp. 425–433, 2020.
https://doi.org/10.1007/978-3-030-45096-0_52

one is Zeigarnik Effect [4], and another is Maslow's hierarchy of needs [5]. Figure 1 shows the element of information for sightseeing in Oku-Nikko (mountain area) and their priority.

Elements of sightseeing (Oku-Nikko)	Levels of needs						Function of App
	1	2	3	4	5	6	
Weather	O						Weather
New Information (Weather, Disaster, Bear, Event etc.)	O			O	O		Information
Transportation, Access	O						Bus (Timetable and route)
Restroom, Present location, Model courses	O	O		O			Map
High light, Guidance, Transportation, Food (Shops)	O	O		O			Pop-up
High light, Photos of seasons					O		Seasons Photo
Guidance, Origin, Photos of animals, flowers, mountains				O	O		Photo books
Event					O		Stamp rally
SNS, "Like"			O	O			SNS
Multi lingual		O					Setting

Fig. 1. Information elements of sightseeing application for Oku-Nikko.

2   Design of Application for Oku-Nikko

Firstly, we listed up required elements of sightseeing and categorized into ten categories. Then we added priority to them based on Maslow's hierarchy of needs. At last, we added priority to functions of a mobile phone application based on the mapping of elements of sightseeing and Maslow's hierarchy of needs. Baes on this analysis, we designed our sightseeing application for Oku-Nikko. For example, all higher priority functions are accessible from the home screen, and some of them are in the tab bar to be accessible from all screens of the application. We added the photo book of seasons on the home screen to use Zeigarnik Effect to encourage visitors to revisit Oku-Nikko in the different seasons. Also, we expect that photo books of nature (mountain, flower, bird) may cause a similar effect. Figure 2 shows the UI of the application. When approaching to a beacon, a pop-up screen appears, and it informs explanation of that area and distance and walking time to nearest checkpoints such as a lake, waterfall, and bus stop as shown in Fig. 3.

3   Solar Beacon

In our previous application to navigate visitors from the Nikko-station to Toshogu-shrine, we used beacons with a small battery. That area is in the city area and easy to visit to repair beacons. However, Oku-Nikko is a mountain area. It is in high elevation and extensive field. So, it is difficult to visit there to perform the health check of beacons frequently. Beacons should be maintenance

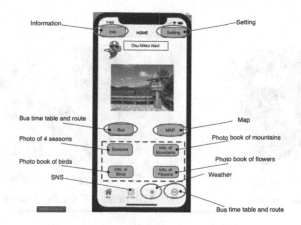

Fig. 2. UI of sightseeing application for Oku-Nikko.

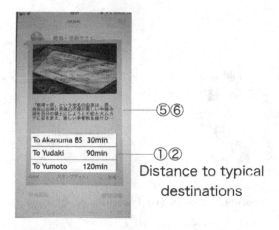

Fig. 3. Pop-up screen according to a beacon

free. We decided to use a beacon with a solar battery. Figure 4a shows the exterior of a solar beacon. The size is 7 cm × 8.5 cm × 3.5 cm. The diameter of the solar panel is 5 cm. Figure 4b shows the inside of a solar beacon. It consists of a solar panel, voltage converter, LiPo battery, and beacon (red round board). We designed this beacon works infinitely if 30% of a month is clear and shining sun.

4 Trial in Oku-Nikko

This summer, we set 31 BLE beacons with a solar panel in two areas of Oku-Nikko. Ten were installed around Chuzenji-Lake (Fig. 5a) and twenty-one were in Senjyo-gahara that is a big mash (Fig. 5b). Figure 5 shows an example of the beacons in Senjo-gahara area. Figure 6a shows a beacon on a panel in the mail walking road in the mush. Figure 6b shows a beacon on a signboard in the forest.

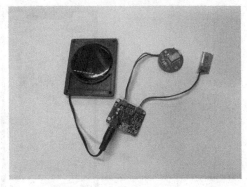

(a) Solar beacon   (b) Inside of a solar beacon

Fig. 4. Solar beacon

(a) Location of beacons around (b) Location of beacons in Senjyo-
Chuzenji-Lake   gahara

Fig. 5. Beacon map

5   Problems of the Trial

In 2018, during the trial, we had many problems on beacons that were installed in Oku-Nikko and could not perform the user trial. We want to explain the issues, such as water leaking of a solar beacon, shortage of solar energy, and describe how we tried to solve them.

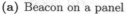

(a) Beacon on a panel   (b) Beacon on a signboard

Fig. 6. Beacons in Senjo-gahara

5.1 Water Leaking

The most severe issue was water leaking of the solar beacons. We set 31 beacons at the end of July 2018. However, more than half of them were broken immediately by water leaking after the heavy rain. Oku-Nikko is a mountain area so that it rains very hard. The broken solar beacon is shown in Fig. 7. The structure of a solar beacon is described in Fig. 8. The top is a transparent acrylic plate, and under the plate, there is a rubber plate. Under the rubber, there is a lid with a solar panel, as shown in Fig. 8. The bottom is a case to store the beacon and the battery. After the water leaking, as shown in Fig. 7a, there were a lot of water dots under the transparent acrylic plate. These waters prevent sunshine that should be used to generate electric power. Figure 7b shows the inside of a solar beacon with water.

So there are two possibilities of a route of water, one is between the transparent acrylic plate and rubber plate. Another possibility was an invisible crack of the bottom case.

To prevent the leaking water from the top, we decided to introduce polymer film. The polymer film has excellent material to protect water. After we changed the structure of a beacon, as shown in Fig. 8b. We think that the polymer film is useful to protect water from the screw holes.

The new beacon case works well. However, we still had a problem with water leaking.

We assume that there are some invisible cracks in the case since we made it be using a 3D printer. There are several ways to close cracks such as to paint waterproof material outside or melt the surface by dichloromethane. However, these techniques increase costs, so we would like to find a more straightforward but effective method.

(a) Outside   (b) Inseide

Fig. 7. Water leaking of beacon

Acrylic plate
Rubber
Lid w Solar Panel (printed, PLA)
Case (printed, PLA)

(a) Previous

Acrylic plate
Rubber
Lid w Solar Panel (printed, PLA)
Polymer film
Case (printed, PLA)

(b) New

Fig. 8. Structure of solar beacon case

5.2 Out of Battery

As explained in the previous section, some beacons were installed in the forest of Senjo-gahara as shown in Fig. 6b, and especially in the mid-summer, the forest was covered by leaves, and not enough sunshine was received by the solar panel of the beacon. In such a case, the solar beacons stopped because of the out of battery.

The solar beacon was designed if it gets solar light for 8 hours, it works at least one week.

So that, we redesign the solar beacon, and we decided to use Dye-Sensitized Solar Cell (DSC) [6]. This solar panel can generate enough power for BLE advertisement at low solar power. DSC can generate power under 200–10k lux. The sunshine is 10k–100k lux.

5.3   Other Issues

In Oku-Nikko, there are other severe conditions for a beacon. One is a low temperature in winter. In the mid-winter, it is lower than −20°. As shown in Fig. 9a, beacons are working in the snowfield. Also, even the water leaked inside, the frozen beacon worked properly, as shown in Fig. 9b. Also, in Oku-Nikko, there are some hot springs and around the hot springs "hydrogen sulfide" is generated. Hydrogen sulfide corrodes metals so that we worried that the BLE chip would be damaged by "hydrogen sulfide". However, for the two years test, the solar beacon is working around the hot spring.

(a) BLE beacon in Snow   (b) Frozen BLE beacon

Fig. 9. BLE beacon in winter

	Sender (Fixed)	Sender (move)
Receiver (move)	A #Navigation #Guide #Advertisement #Observation	B #Anti-theft #StreetPass Communication
Receiver (Fixed)	C #Sensor System #Message board	D #Mobility management #Observation #Entry Control

Fig. 10. Many applications of BLE beacons

6   Conclusion

In this paper, we explain the outline of sightseeing support system using BLE beacon and problems that happened during the trial. We want to restart trial before the summer vacation season.

According to the spread of mobile devices such as a mobile phone, it is expected to use ICT(Information and Communication Technology) for sightseeing services. In Japan, the Tourism Authority of Japan has started to promote to use a smartphone application to support inbound traveler. In this situation, we are developing a sightseeing support application using BLE (Bluetooth Low Energy) beacon in the Nikko area. In the paper, we proposed a design method to design a sightseeing application applying two psychological effects, one is Zeigarnik Effect, and another is Maslow's hierarchy of needs. Then we explain the trial and how the trial was failed. We also show how to solve the problem that appeared during the trial.

As described in Fig. 10, there are many possibilities to use BLE beacons. In this matrix, a sightseeing support system is in Type A. The sender is fixed as a beacon, and receivers move as a traveler. If both senders of information and receiver of it are fixed and embedded, they should be sensor networks as Type C. Type B is a particular use case since both sender and receiver are moving. This type is usually popular for a game application, however, this type of communication is useful when a large disaster happens. Type D is now becoming popular to control traffic. For example, we used a beacon to count the number of bicycles of a bike race in Japan. Each bike had a BLE beacon and at the start and goal, and each aid station, the receivers were installed. This test system found 99.3% of rides at the goal (3304 people in 3330 people). So, if we could design the receivers of BLE beacon, even for high-speed objects such as bike or car, it is possible to detect them.

Acknowledgement. Authors would like to express special thanks to Mr.Wada and Mr.Suzuki of Nikko National Park Office of Ministry of the Environment, Ms.Wada and Ms.Sato of Tochigi Prefectural Government Office and all members of the committee for increasing satisfaction of tourists in Nikko. They provided us information of Oku-Nikko and valuable advice. This research is supported by JSPS KAKENHI Grant Number JP17H02249. Also, the basis of this research was performed as a project of SCOPE (142303001).

References

1. http://www.mlit.go.jp/kankocho/shisaku/kokusai/ict.html. Accessed 20 May 2018
2. Ito, A., et al.: A study of psychological approach to design sightseeing support mobile application. In: Proceedings of INES 2018, June 2018

3. Bluetooth SIG: Specification of the Bluetooth System (2001). http://blog.bluetooth.com/bluetooth-sig-introduces-new-bluetooth-4-1-specification/. Accessed 20 May 2018
4. Zeigarnik, B.V.: On finished and unfinished tasks. In: Ellis, W.D. (ed.) A Sourcebook of Gestalt Psychology. Humanities Press, New York (1967)
5. Maslow, A.H.: Motivation and Personality, 3rd edn. Pearson Education, Delhi (1987)
6. https://en.wikipedia.org/wiki/Dye-sensitized_solar_cell

CAST Dynamic Modeling of Competitive Tourism Destinations: Gran Canaria and Its Nordic Markets

R. Moreno-Diaz Jr.$^{(\boxtimes)}$ and A. Rodríguez-Rodríguez

Instituto Universitario de Ciencias y Tecnologías Cibernéticas, ULPGC, Las Palmas, Spain
{roberto.morenodiaz,abraham.rodriguez}@ulpgc.es

Abstract. In this paper we consider tourism data as influenced by a number of economic and political factors expressed in a set of parameters within a classical, but retouched, CAST model: tourism is a complex reality that needs a not-so-simple approach. Starting on a general scheme consisting of two destinations that feed upon a market of total population P, we proceed by systematically studying its properties and various theoretical cases according to classical systems theory. At every step, real touristic correlates are explained and results compared with data from the evolving touristic situation of a specific destination, namely, Gran Canaria, and its tourism flow coming from its main northern Europe markets: Norway, Sweden, Finland and Denmark.

Keywords: Dynamic systems · Modelling · CAST · Tourism forecast · Tourism analysis · Competition · Gran Canaria

1 Background

Tourism is a key economic activity in today's world [1]. Some destinations depend greatly on it for its economic and social development, like Gran Canaria, almost 30% of its GDP and employment are directly related to touristic activity [2]. Tourism also generates an enormous amount of data concerning its own economic activity, people transportation, hotel or apartment stays, tourist expending [3] etc. Since the past 60s an increasing number or research studies have focused on the forecasting of tourism flux based on this ever growing data, today openly available from trusted web sites and monthly updated. These efforts have mainly used regression techniques to build forecasting systems of local tourism evolution, most of them complemented with and compared to the performance of neural networks techniques [4, 5]. In these models, tourism data (e.g. the monthly arrivals to a specific destination) is treated as a stochastic variable, and forecasting is made on a short term basis.

Figure 1 shows the general structure of the model. The touristic system is represented within the blue border box. It contains a block S, representing the share of people from population P (factor α) that wills to vacation on the specific product (e.g. sun-and-beach, cruise, cultural tourism, sports tourism etc.) of which two competing destinations $D1$ and $D2$ are offered. These two destinations compete both within the market (parameters

© Springer Nature Switzerland AG 2020
R. Moreno-Díaz et al. (Eds.): EUROCAST 2019, LNCS 12014, pp. 434–441, 2020.
https://doi.org/10.1007/978-3-030-45096-0_53

γ and δ) and between them (parameters μ_i), and all have an "exit" factor β, of tourists that decide not to vacationing again on the product or in those destinations.

The system theoretical part of the model is based on a generalization of an epidemiological type of differential equations [6] with reinforced terms for competition. The proposed dynamic model is used to explain touristic behaviour and relations between markets and competing destinations based on the possible values of all parameters involved. In these kind of models, behaviour description is quite more complex than in short-term time series data regression type, and characteristics of both the market (like economic situation or political relationship with the destination) and the destinations (like safety, quality of infrastructures, number of beds and airplane seats etc.) are embodied in the relating parameters used in the formal approach.

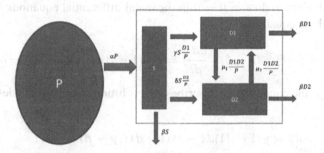

Fig. 1. The block structure of our proposal for a dynamic touristic system.

The system ruling equations are not difficult to derive from Fig. 1 and have the following expression, assuming that all exiting tourists (arrows with beta parameter) re-enter into P:

$$\frac{ds}{dt} = \alpha - \gamma s\,d1 - \delta s\,d2 - \beta s \tag{1}$$

$$\frac{dd1}{dt} = \gamma s\,d1 - \mu_1 d1\,d2 + \mu_2 d2\,d1 - \beta\,d1 \tag{2}$$

$$\frac{dd2}{dt} = \delta s\,d2 - \mu_2 d1\,d2 + \mu_1 d2\,d1 - \beta d2 \tag{3}$$

$$\beta(s + d1 + d2) = \alpha \tag{4}$$

2 Touristic Model for a Single Destination Without Competition

We graphically represent the scenario of a touristic system with only one destination (called $D1$) as shown in Fig. 2.

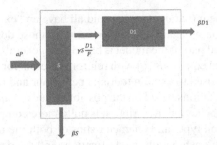

Fig. 2. Simplified scheme/model for a touristic system in a market with only one destination (no competition)

This is equivalent to do $\delta = \mu = 0$ in the initial differential equations system, thus leading to the three equations:

$$\frac{ds}{dt} = \alpha - \gamma s\, d1 - \beta s \quad \frac{dd1}{dt} = \gamma s\, d1 - \beta\, d1 \quad \beta(s + d1) = \alpha \tag{5}$$

Since $\alpha = \beta$, the equation that describes the evolution of travelers in destination *D1* is:

$$\dot{d}1 = \gamma(1 - d1)d1 - \beta d1 = d1((\gamma - \beta) - \gamma d1) \tag{6}$$

This is a first-order differential equation of the logistic type. The solution of this equation is the logistic curve of the following equation, where we have assumed the existence of an initial condition $d_1(0) = d_0$:

$$d_1(t) = \frac{(\gamma - \beta)d_0 e^{(\gamma - \beta)t}}{\gamma - \beta - \gamma d_0 + \gamma d_0 e^{(\gamma - \beta)t}} \tag{7}$$

The graphical representation of it with different arbitrary values for coefficients γ and β, is shown in Fig. 3. The choice of the coefficients' values depends on the critical points of the system and the stability of the solutions.

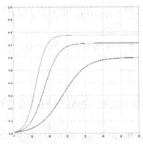

Fig. 3. Graphical representation of $d_1(t)$ with P = 1000, d0 = 0.01, different values of γ (0.25 blue, 0.35 red and 0.45, green) $\beta = 0.1$, $\gamma - \beta > 0$. Saturation is reached in $(\gamma - \beta)/\gamma$. X axis units arbitrary. (Color figure online)

The destination has capacity limitations (number of beds) or accessing limitations (limited number of flights) that have influence in the value of γ and it shows a maximum value in the number of visitors, which cannot become infinite. That would be the meaning of changing the γ parameter, as can be seen in Fig. 3. At some later point that flow must return home. Thus there is a change of sign in the exponent of the logistic equation, making the number of tourist to decrease as t increases enough. A graphical representation is shown in Fig. 4.

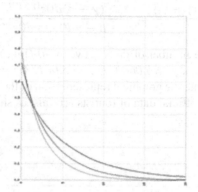

Fig. 4. The end of the touristic season, $\beta > \gamma$ or $\gamma - \beta < 0$, $(\gamma - \beta)$ changes the sign in every case and $\gamma = 0.1$, with $d_0 = 0.6$ (blue), $d_0 - 0.714$ (red), $d_0 - 0.777$ (green). X axis units, arbitrary. (Color figure online)

The destination's absorption of tourists is limited by the values of the coefficients of attraction and loss of visitors, and their meaning in terms of available lodging spaces and capacity of transport. The model provides the first approximation when the goal is to maximize the absorption by tuning the γ and β parameters. Assuming that the behaviour can be repeated in the future, this model represents a captive and seasonable market.

3   A Case Study of the Gran Canaria Touristic Destiny in the Nordic Markets

Data regarding touristic flow towards Gran Canaria have been recorded since the 90's and are publicly available both at the Canarian Institute of Statistics (ISTAC) [7] and in the website of AENA, the public manager for the Spanish airports. All these data are monthly updated and plotted as temporal series we get the graphs in Fig. 5a.

It can be observed the constant regularity and the season behavior in the flow of tourists. In Fig. 5b we compare the graphs seen in Figs. 3 and 4 with winter-summer waveform corresponding to the Norwegian market in 2006 and 2007.

As the characterization of a destiny without competition in a touristic market comes from the values of γ and β in the proposed model, we will carry out the calculus of these theoretical coefficients for the Norwegian market and destination Gran Canaria with the touristic and population data of year 2007. The population in Norway was $P = 4.737.171$. If we assume $D0$ as the official number of tourists registered in June 2017 we will have $D = 5313$, $d0 = D/P = 0.00128959$. The saturation value of the destination, is obtained as the greater of the monthly data, December, so that $(\gamma - \beta)/\gamma = 32655/P = 0.00695946$. In order to calculate the separated values of γ and β we take the value of November in the temporal series (31884, which is the value previous to the maximum, that represents in this case 97.63% of the value of December, which is the maximum value of saturation) and we substitute in the expression of the equation that is the solution of the differential Eq. (8).

$$\frac{0.9763(\gamma - \beta)}{\gamma} = \frac{(\gamma - \beta)d0e^{(\gamma - \beta)t}}{\gamma - \beta - \gamma d0 + \gamma d0e^{(\gamma - \beta)t}} \tag{8}$$

using $T = 152$, as it is the number of days between $d0$ (June) and the 97.63% of the saturation value (November), $\gamma = 5.066997$; $\beta = 5.081731$; $\gamma - \beta = 0.032266$. With all these data we can generate the graphical representation of the behavior, which is quite similar to generated using official data of tourists arrivals, as shown in Fig. 6.

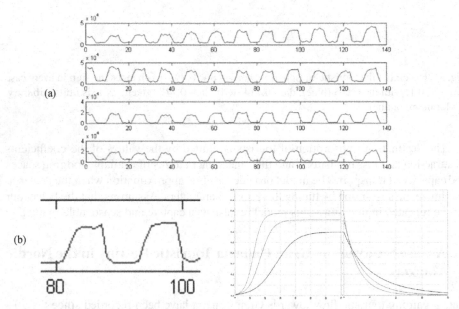

Fig. 5. (a) Temporal series of arrivals of Nordic tourists to Gran Canaria between January 200 and May 2011. From top to bottom: Norway, Sweden, Finland and Denmark. (b) Left, temporal series of Norway, two consecutive cycles summer-winter-summer years 2006–2007. Right, the result of the proposed dynamic model.

The same analysis can be repeated with the rest of the Nordic markets, obtaining their characteristic parameters with se same procedure. Following this methodology we can build a table with the different parameters for each touristic season in Gran Canaria, related to each Nordic market, as shown in Table 1, with data from 2007 to 2017.

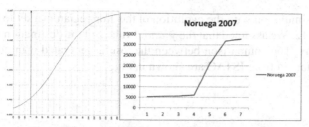

Fig. 6. Norway Summer-Winter 2007. Right, official arrivals data to Gran Canaria from June to December, time axe in months. Left, the logistic curve obtained with the dynamic model of destination without competition. The point where the axis crosses the curve is t = 0 in June. The x-axis of the model is time in days, and from t = −30 (May) up to t = 150 (December).

Table 1. Parameters that characterize the dynamic model of a touristic destination (Gran Canaria) without competition in the European Nordic markets.

	Year	P	D0	d0	gamma(g)	beta(b)	g-b	(g-b)/g
Noruega	2017	5341443	8516	0,00159433	3,39031603	3,35875526	0,03156077	0,00930909
Noruega	2016	5245041	8720	0,00166252	7,40408028	7,33545791	0,06862237	0,00926818
Noruega	2015	5179469	7785	0,00150305	4,54149833	4,50180875	0,03968957	0,00873931
Noruega	2014	5115710	8802	0,00172058	4,14845407	4,11036738	0,03808669	0,00918093
Noruega	2013	5050909	10887	0,00215545	3,02609938	2,99448922	0,03161016	0,01044584
Noruega	2012	5051275	9062	0,001794	5,26205193	5,20866756	0,05338437	0,01014516
Noruega	2011	4922598	8756	0,00177874	4,53991943	4,49882348	0,04109594	0,00905213
Noruega	2010	4860811	6927	0,00142507	6,16175273	6,11388416	0,04786858	0,00776866
Noruega	2009	4801002	5707	0,00118871	6,51893425	6,47427258	0,04466167	0,00685107
Noruega	2008	4744109	5796	0,00122173	5,70084588	5,65666534	0,04418054	0,00774982
Noruega	2007	4691845	5313	0,00113239	5,06699765	5,0317316	0,03526604	0,00695995
Suecia	2017	9903518	8539	0,00086222	13,4288536	13,3509099	0,07794375	0,0058042
Suecia	2016	9822013	7428	0,00075626	6,82152465	6,78292148	0,03860317	0,00565902
Suecia	2015	9741337	5833	0,00059879	9,79174772	9,74094015	0,05080757	0,00518882
Suecia	2014	9663747	5659	0,00058559	7,29831574	7,26010733	0,03820841	0,00523524
Suecia	2013	9583852	5776	0,00060268	6,61619078	6,57886782	0,02722206	0,00564116
Suecia	2012	9502905	4334	0,00045607	11,4151797	11,3614511	0,05372864	0,00470677
Suecia	2011	9422325	5224	0,00055443	5,52732283	5,50218089	0,02514194	0,00454867
Suecia	2010	9903518	8539	0,00086222	13,4288536	13,3509099	0,07794375	0,0058042
Suecia	2009	9264883	5039	0,00054388	13,3813117	13,3400999	0,04121178	0,0030798
Suecia	2008	9903518	8539	0,00086222	13,4288536	13,3509099	0,07794375	0,0058042
Suecia	2007	9120284	3677	0,00040317	21,7391284	21,6602979	0,07883049	0,0036262
Finlandia	2017	5546502	9861	0,00177788	13,0916146	13,0406196	0,05099508	0,00389525
Finlandia	2016	5518962	575	0,00010419	34,6923491	34,5529439	0,13940524	0,00401833
Finlandia	2015	5503297	378	6,8686E-05	33,5751765	33,4454344	0,12974217	0,00386423
Finlandia	2014	5471753	583	0,00010655	31,2595831	31,1285292	0,13105395	0,00419244
Finlandia	2013	5438853	171	3,144E-05	17,2882808	17,205448	0,08283278	0,00479127
Finlandia	2012	5546502	9861	0,00177788	13,0916146	13,0406196	0,05099508	0,00389525
Finlandia	2011	5381755	14592	0,00271138	14,6781478	14,6102057	0,06794203	0,00462879
Finlandia	2010	5354089	954	0,00017818	24,6179821	24,5295262	0,0884559	0,00359314
Finlandia	2009	5327328	881	0,00016537	20,4679195	20,4056474	0,06227213	0,00304243
Finlandia	2008	5301752	927	0,00017485	14,3614098	14,3059687	0,0554411	0,00386042
Finlandia	2007	5277967	889	0,00016844	37,2033254	37,0597767	0,14354878	0,00385849
Finlandia	2003	5219732	808	0,0001548	37,7119395	37,6027499	0,10918962	0,00289536
Dinamarca	2017	5705730	5945	0,00104194	11,8398198	11,782971	0,05684876	0,00480149
Dinamarca	2016	5681810	4706	0,00082826	11,5385463	11,484438	0,05410829	0,00468935
Dinamarca	2015	5657990	4450	0,0007865	9,53157027	9,49383138	0,03773889	0,00395936
Dinamarca	2014	5659715	4345	0,00076771	24,625124	24,5374698	0,08765419	0,00355954
Dinamarca	2013	5612633	4903	0,00087357	17,7921468	17,7173058	0,07484095	0,0042064
Dinamarca	2012	5588775	4583	0,00082004	13,1154199	13,0647772	0,05064272	0,00386131
Dinamarca	2011	5563768	2985	0,00053651	14,6571759	14,6011343	0,05604154	0,00382349
Dinamarca	2010	5537357	2970	0,00053636	16,2912497	16,2405138	0,05073587	0,0031143
Dinamarca	2009	5509528	2419	0,00043906	15,4431194	15,3973578	0,04576152	0,00296323
Dinamarca	2008	5481145	2253	0,00041105	19,2331131	19,1771206	0,05599246	0,00291125
Dinamarca	2007	5453842	2378	0,00043602	18,8582855	18,7876634	0,07062207	0,00374488
Dinamarca	2004	5411405	2232	0,00041246	11,7970984	11,7544001	0,04269833	0,00361939

We show a simulation with the evolution of the Norwegian market to Gran Canaria from 2009 to 2012. We assumed that the γ *and* β values of the destination were constant along these years. The comparison between the results generated using the model and the real data obtained from ISTAC are shown in Fig. 7.

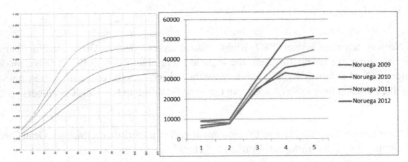

Fig. 7. Forecast of the proposed model (left, parameters set as explained in the text and increasing α: 6.4748 (blue), 6.4801 (red), 6.4884 (green) y 6.4954 (grey)) and real data of tourism flow from Norway to Gran Canaria (right) in winter seasons from 2009 to 2012. (Color figure online)

4   Conclusions

The generic dynamic model of Fig. 1 adapted for the specific case of a non-competitive touristic destination (Fig. 2) seems to fit with the touristic flow towards an insular destination, with a strong seasonal character in a set of markets where the crisis does not seem to have hit their holiday behaviour. The main parameters controlling the model behaviour (γ, β and its difference) can be used to adjust the dynamic system with the actual touristic evolution. This allows us to interpret in the opposite sense: if a destination wishes to raise the theoretical saturation limit $(\gamma - \beta)/\gamma$ it would be more efficient to widen the difference between γ and β and make γ larger. Thus, it is better to build customer loyalty so he does not leave the circuit (by keeping a small β) or, alternatively, making the duration of the trip longer so the latency of a small β should be larger. When γ grows, increasing the number of available lodging facilities or the number of flight seats, also affects the rate of tourist arrivals, reducing the time for saturation.

These parameters can be used to characterize a touristic destination based on the optimization of its load capacity for both cases (i.e. a mass tourism model). We could consider a year as a "good touristic year" when $\gamma - \beta$ is larger when compared to previous years, while keeping a large γ. For the Norwegian market depicted on top of Table 1, years 2010, 2016 and 2017 should be considered 'good years' when compared with the rest of the years. Using the same analysis for the Finish market, years 2007, 2014, 2015 and 2016 stand out.

Moreover, the market efficiency could also be classified for a medium and long term period, by calculating the average value of $\gamma - \beta$ for that period. So as stated in Table 1, the mean value for that difference in the case of the Norwegian market for the period from 2007 to 2017 is 0.0522; 0.0543 for the Swedish market; 0.0911 for the Finish; and

0.05827 for the Danish market. So, we could order the countries in descending order according to the efficiency of the touristic market as: Finland, Denmark, Sweden and Norway, which differs from the result we get when we order those countries by the number of tourists arriving from each market.

References

1. Travel and Tourism. Economic impact 2017. Report of the World Travel and Tourism Council, London, March 2017. www.wtcc.org
2. Summary Assessment of the Canary Islands, 2013. Report, ESIC, European Commission, Directorate General for Enterprise and Industry, November 2013
3. EUROSTAT Tourism Statistics. http://ec.europa.eu/eurostat/web/tourism/publications. Accessed 10 May 2019
4. Song, H., Liu, H.: Predicting tourist demand using big data. In: Xiang, Z., Fesenmaier, D.R. (eds.) Analytics in Smart Tourism Design. TV, pp. 13–29. Springer, Cham (2017). https://doi.org/10.1007/978-3-319-44263-1_2
5. Teixeira, F.: Tourism time series forecast with artificial neural networks. Rev. Appl. Manage. Stud. **12**, 26–36 (2014)
6. Luenberger, D.G.: Introduction to Dynamic Systems Theory. Models and Applications. Wiley, New York (1979)
7. Instituto Canario de Estadística. http://www.gobiernodecanarias.org/istac/. Accessed 10 May 2019

Towards a Simulation Model of Competition Between Touristic Destinations Using Dynamic Systems Tools

R. Moreno-Díaz Jr. and A. Rodríguez-Rodríguez[✉]

Instituto Universitario de Ciencias y Tecnologías Cibernéticas, ULPGC, Las Palmas, Spain
{roberto.morenodiaz,abraham.rodriguez}@ulpgc.es

Abstract. We describe a model based on dynamic systems theory to analyse the behaviour and flows of travellers between tourist markets and competing destinations, including a qualitative application, distinguishing several situations (destinations in mild competition and destinations in strong competition), to the case study of Gran Canaria and Tenerife, two competing island destinations. Our proposal is based on the mathematical theory of complex dynamic systems. Tourism figures are updated monthly and accessible through the website of the Regional Government Statistics Institute (ISTAC) [12] or the managing body of Spanish public airports (AENA) [13]. Being destinations accessible almost exclusively by air, tourist figures are much more reliable, include less dubious data than that of destinations accessible by road, train or boat which need to complement the official figures with other estimates [14], making the theoretical models we present to describe more accurately their actual evolution.

Keywords: Dynamic complex systems · Modelling · Tourism forecast · Market and destination analysis · Competition · Simulation · Gran Canaria

1 Models of Tourism Flows: From Stochastic to Analytical

Tourism is one of the most important economic activities in the world today in terms of turnover [1]. It is one of the pillars of the economy at all levels. There are regions, like the Canary Islands, whose industrial base has been tourism for decades [2] and specific destinations whose economy and society depend largely on tourism, such as Gran Canaria [3]. This sector generates an enormous amount of data that grows exponentially [4, 5], and is used to try to predict tourist flows and their evolution at local and regional levels. Many studies attempt to construct models of market behaviour and passenger flows [6–8]. Two forecasting techniques are recurrent: the analysis of time series and short-term prediction via linear regressions and the application of neural networks for prediction in the short and medium terms [9]. The models based on the theory of complex dynamic systems are rather scarce [10, 11]. We are motivated by this scarcity, as well as the need to include parameters that reflect the economic state of both, markets and destinations, and the relationships between them and between competing destinations, features that are not usually included in models based on linear regression and in many of those based

R. Moreno-Díaz et al. (Eds.): EUROCAST 2019, LNCS 12014, pp. 442–449, 2020.
https://doi.org/10.1007/978-3-030-45096-0_54

on neural networks. The monthly data on tourism received in a destination should not be considered isolated, stochastic or random: it actually shows aspects of the economic and social health of a specific market, of the acceptance of a destination, of its capacity to safely accommodate a certain number of visitors, of the viability of travel between the two and of the evolution of the political relations between destination and market. It is a complex reality that requires non-simple modelling allowing to forecast the evolution of the sector in situations of economic crisis (f.i. Great Recession) or political crisis (f.i. Brexit) and that facilitates decision-making in the affected business fields [15]. The model depends on a greater number of parameters, having to broaden the discussion on the relative and absolute values of them, which in turn generates a richer description of real situations with touristic significance that allow them to be formally modelled.

2 Fundamentals of the Dynamic Competition Model

Our formal model is based on a general dynamic system [16]. Parameters are introduced that take into account or reflect characteristics of both the market (economic situation, willingness to travel…) and the destination (safety, competitiveness, quality, and price) and of the relationship between the destinations (competition strategies, infrastructure improvement, emergence of problems in one of them, etc.). The structure of the model is shown in Fig. 1, where the coefficients α and β denote the proportion of tourists entering and leaving the system. They can express the improvement in economic conditions (e.g. with a higher α, which represents a higher proportion S of P inhabitants willing to travel to D1 or D2 competing destinations), or their worsening (e.g., β high is equivalent to a loss of tourists due to an increase in price, change of product, age etc.). The visitors who "leave" the system are recycled in the total population P, so that within the block of the system there is no direct loss of tourists.

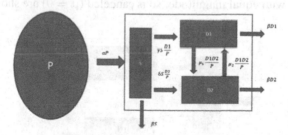

Fig. 1. Block structure of the dynamic model for touristic flows.

Coefficients γ and δ are parameters for destination choice, expressing the proportion of travelers who choose each of them. They mean the attraction of D1 and D2 (in terms of safety, cleanliness, quality…) and in the case of island destinations more markedly, the bottleneck due to the availability of airplane seats and accommodation.

The relationship between S and D1 (and D2) is expressed as proportional to the population S and the term D1/P and D2/P denoting the influence of the proportion of the population D1 and D2 that already know the destination (customer loyalty), the action of specialized travel agencies, direct marketing etc. Direct competition between destinations is denoted by $\mu 1$ and $\mu 2$, or competition coefficients, and we will assume that they are proportional to the travelers in each destination and to the ratio of "loyal customers" of D1 and D2 in relation to the total population P, constant. These coefficients express the transfer of tourists from one destination to another due to security problems, improvement of conditions of one destination (infrastructure, price, services…) without passengers leaving the system (coefficients β). From block diagram of Fig. 1, re-scaling by a 1/P factor, the four equations describing the system:

$$\frac{ds}{dt} = \alpha - \gamma s\, d1 - \delta s\, d2 - \beta s \qquad \frac{dd1}{dt} = \gamma s\, d1 - \mu_1 d1\, d2 + \mu_2 d2\, d1 - \beta\, d1 \quad (1)$$

$$\frac{dd2}{dt} = \delta s\, d2 - \mu_2 d1\, d2 + \mu_1 d2\, d1 - \beta d2 \qquad\qquad \beta(s + d1 + d2) = \alpha$$

Functions d1(t), d2(t) and s(t) take consistent values only in the range (0, 1). The model is non-linear and equivalent to an epidemiological type [16, 17] with reinforcement of competition and of "output" of the system, with factor β. We will consider the coefficients of entry and exit to be equal, $\alpha = \beta$, and we will add the expression $\mu = \mu_1 - \mu_2$ to denote the relative loss or gain of tourists due to the direct competition. Equations are:

$$\dot{d}1 = \gamma(1 - d1 - d2)d1 - \mu\, d1\, d2 - \beta d1 \qquad \dot{d}2 = \delta(1 - d1 - d2)d2 + \mu\, d1\, d2 - \beta d2 \quad (2)$$

3   Competition Without Predation Between Markets

Two competing destinations between which there is no competition exercised directly ($\mu_1 = \mu_2 = 0$) or with equal magnitude, so is canceled ($\mu = 0$) are shown in Fig. 2.

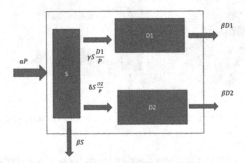

Fig. 2. Model for two competing destinations without mutual predation of tourists.

The new system of differential equations that rule the model is, then:

$$\dot{d}1 = ((\gamma - \beta) - \gamma(d2 + d1))d1 \qquad \dot{d}2 = ((\delta - \beta) - \delta(d2 + d1))d2 \quad (3)$$

The equilibrium points of the system, the algebraic values of d1 and d2 that solve:

$$0 = ((\gamma - \beta) - \gamma(d2 + d1))d1 \qquad 0 = ((\delta - \beta) - \delta(d2 + d1))d2 \qquad (4)$$

Among them the point $(d1^*, d2^*) = (0, 0)$, the extinction of both destinations. To solve the previous system of equations we initially assume that only one of the coordinates is positive for the corresponding equilibrium point. Suppose we do $d1^* = (\gamma - \beta)/\gamma$, and set $d2^* = 0$. The Jacobian matrix of the system yields the eigenvalues: $r_1 = \beta - \gamma$ and $r_2 = \delta - \beta - \delta(\gamma - \beta)/\gamma$.

For an asymptotically stable equilibrium point both eigenvalues must be negative which implies $\gamma > \beta$ (from r1) and $\gamma > \delta$ (from r2) so that d1 is greater than zero (and destination 1 survives) or $\delta > \gamma$ in the other case. One of the two destinations disappears from the market, as in Fig. 3, the final state being reached asymptotically.

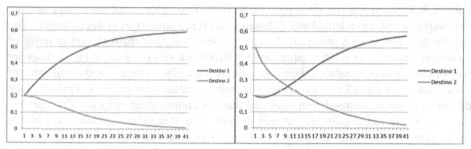

Fig. 3. The predicted evolution of two theoretical destinations competing on a market in uneven $(\gamma \neq \delta)$ conditions.

For the possibility of both destinations coexisting in equilibrium, we take the case that $\gamma = \delta$ in (4) so that the parts that include the nonlinearity of the model are equal and the equation is reduced to:

$$0 = (\gamma - \beta) - \gamma(d2 + d1) \qquad (5)$$

This implies the existence of infinite non-isolated equilibrium points $E(d1^*, d2^*)$ whose coordinates have to hold that, being greater than zero, their sum is in turn:

$$d_1^* + d_2^* = \frac{\gamma - \beta}{\gamma} \qquad (6)$$

Expression (6) is the equation of a line in the phase plane, where the infinite critical points are located. This yields two cases: the initial conditions fall above or below the line of infinite critical points. The evolution is described in Fig. 4. The coexistence of both markets is very unstable: the restriction $\gamma = \delta$ is very strong and any variation in one of the parameters causes the balance of survival to tilt and one of the markets disappears. Due to having a line of singularities in the phase plane towards which the evolution of both markets is attracted, the evolution of both markets will grow or decrease to equilibrium.

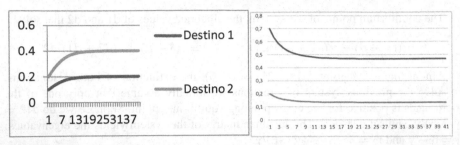

Fig. 4. Evolution of the tourists to two destinations competing evenly ($\gamma = \delta$) on the same market according to the proposed dynamic model, with the conditions of coexistence. Both markets "survive" mutual competition and grow (decrease) up to a level of equilibrium given by the (6).

Gran Canaria and Tenerife are destinations based on *sun and beach* model and known in Western Europe since the 1960s. Both destinations seek customers through marketing campaigns adapted and differentiated to each country as isolated markets. The two destinations have a preferential target in Germany, their main market in terms of customer volume. The relative situation of both destinations is shown in Fig. 5. They are well-known, solidly established destinations and candidates reach a theoretical value of their parameters γ and δ very similar as a measure of the knowledge and acceptance of the destination, the accommodation offer and their air communication factor. Comparative data of the "initial conditions" in this market show that Gran Canaria has a higher figure than Tenerife. The evolution of passenger arrivals is consistent with the theoretical competing destinations proposed model in their general characteristics: the curves do not cross each other and evolve almost in parallel.

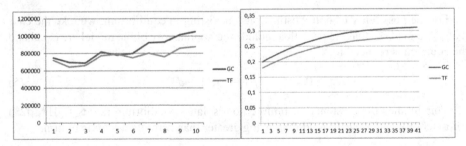

Fig. 5. Comparative evolution of absolute tourist arrivals from Germany to Gran Canaria (blue) and Tenerife (red) between 2008 and 2017. Annual data (left) and dynamic model (right). (Color figure online)

4   The Full Competition Model

For the most general case, we need to investigate the properties of the model when the parameters of entry and exit of tourists to the system are different, i.e. $\alpha \neq \beta$ and $\mu \neq 0$:

$$\dot{d}1 = \left(\left(\gamma\frac{\alpha}{\beta} - \beta\right) - (\gamma + \mu)d_2 - \gamma d_1\right)d_1 \qquad \dot{d}2 = \left(\left(\delta\frac{\alpha}{\beta} - \beta\right) - (\delta - \mu)d_1 - \delta d_2\right)d_2$$

$$(7)$$

The coordinates of the new acceptable equilibrium point must fulfill (again, with the two positive coordinates):

$$\gamma d_1 + (\gamma + \mu)d_2 = \gamma\frac{\alpha}{\beta} - \beta \qquad (\delta - \mu)d_1 + \delta d_2 = \delta\frac{\alpha}{\beta} - \beta \qquad (8)$$

The restrictions on the parameters must comply with in a necessary but not sufficient way:

$$\gamma > \delta > \mu; \gamma\alpha > \beta^2; \delta\alpha > \beta^2 \quad or\ equivalently: \quad \delta\left(\gamma\frac{\alpha}{\beta} - \beta\right) > (\gamma + \mu)\left(\delta\frac{\alpha}{\beta} - \beta\right)$$

$$(9)$$

In Sect. 3 the case of "mild" competition between two mature tourist destinations with a long history of common presence in European markets, Gran Canaria and Tenerife, was developed. In this section the situation becomes more complex, as it requires active competition between destinations and for this we have looked at the evolution over the last few years of the arrival of tourists to Gran Canaria and Tenerife from markets younger in their exploitation than the classic, and in which both Gran Canaria and Tenerife have been present with more aggressive tourism campaigns. The behavior of the flow of tourists from the Czech Republic, Iceland and Poland has been studied. These markets did not exist 15 years ago. Figures 6, 7 and 8 show the evolution of tourists to Gran Canaria and Tenerife from the Czech Republic.

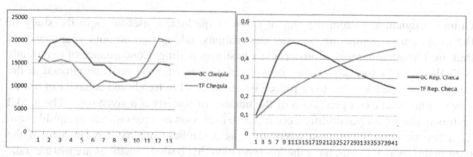

Fig. 6. Gran Canaria and Tenerife as competing destinations in the Czech Republic, 2005 onwards. Data evolution (left). Model (right, $\gamma = 0.041$; $\delta = 0.027$; $\beta = 0.016$; $\mu = 0.013$, $\alpha = \beta$).

In these examples the effect of direct competition between destinations in emerging markets is seen, and results consistent with ISTAC data. These markets have been subject to a strong economic crisis (Iceland) which can be interpreted as the "resetting" of the initial conditions and parameter values at a given moment used by one of the destinations to strengthen the values of its competition parameters. On the other hand, a recent market, with relatively stable economic situation from which both destinations start in equal conditions (Poland) shows that an adequate choice of the parameters at the initial moment makes it possible to explain the first evolution.

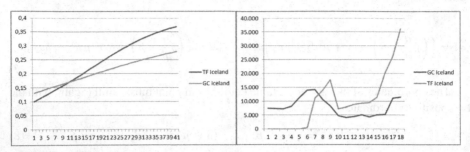

Fig. 7. Comparative evolution of the Icelandic market in GC and TF (right) with the proposed dynamic (left) model, $\alpha = 0 - 019$; $\beta = 0.016$. ISTAC data from 2000 to 2017.

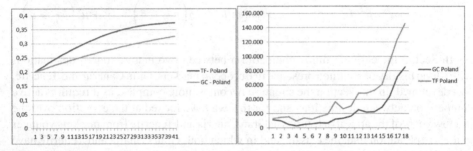

Fig. 8. Evolution of the dynamic model of full competition between GC and TF in Poland (left) with parameter values $\alpha = 0.019$; $\beta = 0.016$. On the right, ISTAC data from 2000 to 2017.

5   Conclusions

Complex dynamic system are shown to be of qualitative usefulness in the study of the evolution of competing touristic destinations, taking into account characteristics that are forgotten in more short-term stochastic modelling. Concordance of real trends with the model's forecasts shows it as a serious basis for the goals mentioned in the introduction: the focus has to be placed on the forecast of trends and behavior of tourist flows rather than exact prediction of the number of tourists at a given time. The model results in two major possibilities: competitive exclusion and coexistence in equilibrium. This second case is the most interesting, as it implies equality between two of the parameters, which in turn have the interpretation that both destinations are mature, take time to compete and have in fact achieved a mutual balance in a market that is important to both. This symbiotic relationship allows from specific initial conditions both destinations to evolve simultaneously and in the same way (increasing or decreasing) to the point of equilibrium. Any deviation in the value of the competition parameters (e.g. due to serious safety or quality problems at the destination leading to a decrease in the corresponding parameter) will cause one destination to disappear.

In the case of the model with full direct competition between them means that tourist arrivals will have a maximum and minimum in each destination depending on the moment in time being studied and on the initial conditions. This case, which involves a deeper study of the relationship between the values of the parameters of the system of equations, resembles the competition between Gran Canaria and Tenerife in markets much younger than those of the previous case, markets in which both destinations strive to make a niche in the holiday tourism system and therefore have large annual variations in the total number of tourists received, in some cases presenting annual maximums exchanged between the two destinations. The variability of situations suggests that in future developments of the model the time dependence of the system parameters must be considered, a dependency that in the case of destinations in mild competition we venture to affirm could be much smaller and possibly of a linear type closely linked to the variation of the general economic situation. Future work includes the characterization of markets and destinations based on the parameters using data mining tools; developing the bases of a system for forecasting tourism crises and a possible expert system of strategic economic, political advice in tourism for destinations with critical competition.

References

1. Travel and Tourism: Economic impact 2017. Report of the World Travel and Tourism Council, London, March 2017. www.wtcc.org
2. Moreno-Gil, S.: Tourism development in the Canary Islands. Ann. Tourism Res. **30**, 744–747 (2003). https://doi.org/10.1016/s0160-7383(03)00050-1
3. Summary Assessment of the Canary Islands, 2013: Report, ESIC, European Commission, Directorate General for Enterprise and Industry, November 2013
4. EUROSTAT. http://ec.europa.eu/eurostat/statistics-explained/index.php/Tourism_statistics. Accessed 10 May 2019
5. Song, H., Liu, H.: Predicting tourist demand using big data. In: Xiang, Z., Fesenmaier, D.R. (eds.) Analytics in Smart Tourism Design. TV, pp. 13–29. Springer, Cham (2017). https://doi.org/10.1007/978-3-319-44263-1_2
6. Teixeira, F.: Tourism time series forecast with artificial neural networks. Rev. Appl. Manag. Stud. **12**, 26–36 (2014)
7. Tularam, A., et al.: Modeling tourist arrivals using time series analysis: evidence from Australia. J. Math. Stat. **8**(3), 348–360 (2012)
8. Pai, P.F., Hung, K.C.: Tourism demand forecasting using novel hybrid system. Expert Syst. Appl. **41**, 3691–3702 (2014)
9. Yu, Y., et al.: Statistical modeling and prediction for tourism economy using dendritic neural network. Comput. Intell. Neurosci. (2017). https://doi.org/10.1155/2017/7436948
10. Song, L.: Tourism demand modelling and forecasting – a review of recent research. Tour. Manag. **29**, 203–220 (2008)
11. Garín-Muñoz, T.: Inbound international tourism to Canary Islands: a dynamic panel data model. Tour. Manag. **27**, 281–291 (2006)
12. Instituto Canario de Estadística. http://www.gobiernodecanarias.org/istac/. Accessed 10 May 2019
13. Aeropuertos Españoles y Navegación Aérea, AENA. http://www.aena.es/csee/Satellite?pagename=Estadisticas/Home. Accessed 10 May 2019
14. Claveria, O., Torra, S.: Forecasting tourism demand to Catalonia: neural networks vs. time series models. Econ. Model. **36**, 220–228 (2014)
15. What Brexit might mean for UK travel: Association of British Travel Agents, Deloitte. Report 2017 (2017). www.abta.com
16. Luenberger, D.G.: Introduction to Dynamic Systems. Theory, Models and Applications. Wiley, New York (1979)
17. Boyce, W.E., Di Prima, R.C.: Elementary Differential Equations and Boundary Problems, 10th edn. Wiley, New York (2012)

Systems in Industrial Robotics, Automation and IoT

IEC 61499 Runtime Environments: A State of the Art Comparison

Laurin Prenzel[1](✉), Alois Zoitl[2], and Julien Provost[1]

[1] Technical University Munich, Munich, Germany
{laurin.prenzel,julien.provost}@tum.de
[2] Johannes Kepler University, Linz, Austria
alois.zoitl@jku.at

Abstract. Networked automation devices, as needed for Industry 4.0 or Cyber Physical Production Systems, demand for new programming languages like the one defined in the IEC 61499 standard. IEC 61499 was originally released in 2005. Since then, different runtime environments—academic and commercial—surfaced: They partly differ in their execution semantics and behavior, and in the features they offer, e.g. Multitasking, Real-time performance, or Dynamic Reconfiguration. Users who want to apply this standard to their problem have to choose the right tool. This paper compares a selection of IEC 61499 runtime environments and outlines topics for further research.

Keywords: Archimedes · FBBeam · FBDK · 4diac FORTE · Fuber · ICARU_FB · ISaGRAF · nxtControl nxtIECRT · RTFM-RT

1 Introduction

We see a change in production automation towards more networked control devices demanding for new paradigms and languages allowing to more effectively and efficiently program them. The IEC 61499 defines a modeling language fulfilling these requirements [8]. Currently several runtime environments (RTEs) and IDEs provide implementations for IEC 61499.

Software tools for the IEC 61499 have been summarized before [5,20]. Some new developments in the area of IEC 61499 RTEs make it necessary to take a closer look at the available systems. More specifically, this paper takes a closer look at the execution semantics and the prominent features of currently available IEC 61499 RTEs. Whether one wants to try out the standard or implement a new RTE, it is important to recognize the differences of already existing implementations. While the differences of IDEs only affect the user experience during modeling, the RTE has to interpret the execution semantics of the standard.

This paper reviews the differences between a collection of existing RTEs and tries to find unclaimed research opportunities. After the basics of the IEC 61499 standard and its execution models are presented, the examined RTEs are introduced and compared. The findings are discussed in Sect. 4 and research opportunities are summarized in Sect. 5.

© Springer Nature Switzerland AG 2020
R. Moreno-Díaz et al. (Eds.): EUROCAST 2019, LNCS 12014, pp. 453–460, 2020.
https://doi.org/10.1007/978-3-030-45096-0_55

2   Background

The IEC 61499 standard has been the topic of many research papers. It was developed as an architecture for distributed, flexible systems that may be reconfigured dynamically [19].

The Function Block (FB) is the main component of the IEC 61499, encapsulating the functionality. It is used in FB networks to build applications. There are different types of Function Blocks, e.g. the *Basic FB* with a state machine and algorithms, or the *Composite FB* containing a network of other FBs.

Since the introduction of the IEC 61499 standard, there has been a discussion about its execution semantics and possible ambiguities [15]. Most notably, [7] classified different execution semantics on a theoretical level. Thus, for researchers and commercial users of the standard, it is important to know the available execution semantics and the most prevalent solutions. The different runtime environments (RTEs) may be compared on different levels.

There are *organizational characteristics*, such as the license of the project (open source or other), the status (commercial, research, or inactive), or the programming language employed. The *execution semantics* may be described by the trigger mechanism (cyclic or event-based) and the execution model of the RTE. Finally, runtime environments may be distinguished by the *features* they offer, such as real-time performance, multitasking, or dynamic reconfiguration.

2.1   Execution Models

The IEC 61499 does not strictly define the execution semantics of its models. This has led to a number of papers outlining these ambiguities [3,4,15]. Currently, there is no consistent framework to describe the execution semantics of an IEC 61499 implementation. Two different views are discussed here. Ferrarini and Veber [7] use the factors *Multitasking* and *Scan order* to describe 7 groups of possible implementation approaches (see Table 1). The first factor is whether the order in which FBs are scanned is fixed or not fixed. The second factor is whether multitasking is used, and if yes, how it is controlled. This leads to a total of 8 combinations, but Ferrarini and Veber exclude the case of a fixed scan order and not controlled multitasking.

Table 1. Possible implementation approaches according to Ferrarini and Veber [7]

		Multitasking implementation			
		Not used	Used, not controlled	Used, controlled, time slice	Used, controlled, FB slice
Scan order	Not fixed	A0	A1	A2	A3
	Fixed	A4	x	A5	A6

In addition to this classification, many publications have introduced their own names for the most common implementation. The earliest model is arguably NPMTR (*Non-Preemptive Multithreaded Resource*), which is employed in FBDK, and mentioned already in 2006 [16]. At a similar time, a sequential model was discussed in [21] and [4]. This model was later termed *Buffered Sequential Execution Model* (BSEM) [2]. Finally, [3] termed a third model, named *Cyclic Buffered Execution Model* (CBEM).

Table 2. Comparing key characteristics of IEC 61499 RTEs

Name	Organizational		Execution				Features		
	Open/ Closed src	Research/ Commercial	Language	Cyclic/ Event	Execution model	Ferrarini model	Real-time	Multi-tasking	Recon-figuration
Archimedes		R	Java C++	E	NPMTR	A1	Hard	Yes	Yes
FBBeam	O	R	Erlang	E	PMTR	A2	Soft	Yes	Yes
FBDK	C	R	Java	E	NPMTR	A1		Partly	Partly
4diac FORTE	O	R	C++	E	PMTR	A1	Hard	Yes	Yes
Fuber	O	R	Java	E	BSEM	A0		Yes	Yes
ICARU_FB	O	R	C	C	CBEM	A4	Hard	No	Yes
ISaGRAF	C	C	IEC 61131-3	C	CBEM	A4	Hard		
nxtIECRT	C	C	C++	E	PMTR	A1	Hard	Yes	Yes
RTFM-RT		R	C	E	PMTR	A1	Hard	Yes	

3 Methods

As introduced in the previous section, the IEC 61499 does not strictly define its execution semantics and thus different implementations are possible. This section presents a collection of runtime environments that have been implemented since the inception of the standard. An overview of the comparison is displayed in Table 2. A total of 9 different RTEs were compared based on information that was available from websites and publications.

In addition to the three execution models already introduced in the literature, an additional model (*PMTR*) was added. *NPMTR* describes non-preemptible multitasking resources. This explicitly excludes the preemptible multitasking resources, that nevertheless do not fall into the categories of buffered sequential or cyclic execution semantics. Thus, the *PMTR* name was chosen, to indicate the set of preemptible multitasking resources.

The assignment and collection was performed to the best of our knowledge. Where no reliable data was found, and the clues were inconclusive, the field was left blank. Following, the 9 RTEs are shortly presented.

3.1 Archimedes

There are three different runtime environments using similar execution semantics: *RTSJ-AXE* [17], *RTAI-AXE* [6], and *Luciol-AXE* [18]. They are implemented in Java and C++, and allow both reconfiguration and multitasking.

FBs may be implemented as independent tasks/threads, or combined in Function Block Containers.

3.2   FBBeam

In this Erlang-based IEC 61499 runtime environment, every FB is implemented as its own process, and scheduling is left to the Erlang Virtual Machine. Erlang processes do not share memory, and messages between processes are sent asynchronously. Because of the fair round-robin scheduling, only soft real-time performance can be guaranteed. Erlang includes sophisticated frameworks for distribution, dynamic reconfiguration, debugging and monitoring of distributed, highly concurrent systems [14]. Its execution model may be best described by *PMTR*, since FBs may be preempted.

3.3   FBDK FBRT

The *FBDK* (Function Block Development Kit) and the accompanying *FBRT* (Function Block Runtime Environment) allow the modeling and execution of IEC 61499 systems in a Java-based runtime environment [9]. Function Blocks are compiled to Java classes and scheduled in a depth-first manner. Instead of emitting events, the *FBRT* uses method calls to communicate between Function Blocks [20]. The execution model of the *FBRT* was referred to as Non-Preemptive Multithreaded Resource (NPMTR) [16].

3.4   4diac FORTE

4diac FORTE is the runtime environment provided by the Eclipse 4diac open source project [1, 22]. The implementation is based on C++ and uses the Event Chain concept described in [23] to achieve deterministic real-time performance by allowing the introduction of real-time constraints for Event Chains. Execution of an Event Chain may preempt execution of other event chains, thus the execution model *PMTR* seems the most appropriate.

3.5   Fuber

Fuber was build to investigate the different execution semantics of the IEC 61499 [4]. It executes in two threads: One for the execution of the ECC, and one for the scheduling of algorithms. Function Blocks and algorithms are assigned to FIFO queues and algorithms are interpreted on the fly instead of static compilation, thus allowing modification of the algorithm code during the execution. As the focus of this implementation is research about the execution semantics, real-time performance is not considered. *Fuber* employs the Buffered Sequential Execution Model (BSEM), where FBs are put in a FIFO ready queue [2].

3.6   ICARU_FB

ICARU_FB is a RTE for lightweight embedded systems, e.g. 8-bit Arduino boards. The IEC 61499 model is converted into C code. FBs are implemented as objects and events are passed directly to a variable in the destination FB object [13]. Since the execution is cyclic, and the FB are scanned in a fixed order, the most appropriate execution model for this RTE is CBEM and A4. Hard real-time performance may be achieved and dynamic reconfiguration is available.

3.7   ISaGRAF

ISaGRAF was the first commercial IEC 61499 implementation [5]. IEC 61499 Function Blocks are compiled to IEC 61131-3 code that may be executed on traditional IEC 61131-3 devices. Because of the IEC 61131-3 base, the execution is cyclic instead of event-triggered. Its execution model is referred to as Cyclic-Buffered Execution Model (CBEM) [3].

3.8   nxtControl nxtIECRT

According to [5], the solution provided by *nxtControl*, *nxtIECRT*, is based on the open source RTE *4diac FORTE*. Thus, the execution semantics should mostly be identical. The *nxtIECRT* RTE is a hybrid runtime system, that may execute both IEC 61131-3 and IEC 61499 systems [12]. Furthermore, *nxtIECRT* provides extensive features for changing control applications during system operation.

3.9   RTFM-RT

RTFM-RT is a RTE for the IEC 61499 built on the RTFM core language [10]. It is using the Event Chain concept and implements them as synchronous task chains [11]. The RTE is mostly build for real-time research. Threads of execution are preemptible and multitasking is possible, thus the model *PMTR* was assigned.

4   Discussion

Table 2 summarizes the findings of this paper. Up until now, the IEC 61499 has been implemented numerous times with various execution semantics. Most RTEs are open source and research projects, but there are at least 2 commercially available IEC 61499 RTEs. Both of them do not only implement the IEC 61499, but support also the languages of the IEC 61131-3. The implementation languages vary, but are mostly focused on Java and C/C++.

All RTEs except for two employ an event-triggered execution. Using the classification introduced by Ferrarini and Veber [7], most RTEs employ the semantics A0, A1, or A2, where no fixed scan order exists. *ISaGRAF* and *ICARU_FB* are the only implementations with a fixed scan order, falling into the category A4.

To the knowledge of the authors, the categories A3, A5, and A6 are currently not used, i.e. there are no RTEs with a fixed scan order and multitasking, or RTEs using FB slice multitasking. For categories A5 and A6 this may be because a fixed scan order with multitasking can be contradictory, since a multitasking implementation by itself may disturb a fixed scan order. If the next FB in the fixed scan order must wait for the previous FB to finish, multitasking is not possible. If it does not have to wait for the previous FB to finish, this would disturb the determinism of a fixed scan order implementation, since the previous FB might want to send events to the next FB in the scan order. For A2 and A3, only one implementation currently exists, that uses a fair scheduler with time slice preemption. Most other implementations do not prescribe the scan order, and either do not use multitasking, or do not control it.

Since the standard is aimed at industrial process measurement and control systems, most implementations claim to offer hard real-time performance. Multitasking is available in some RTEs but not all. Although Dynamic Reconfiguration has been the topic of multiple research papers, and many RTEs seem to support it, information about the usability or performance of the reconfiguration process is rare.

5   Conclusion

This paper summarizes some developments with respect to runtime environments of the IEC 61499 for users and researchers alike interested in working with IEC 61499 or wanting to implement their own RTE. Since the introduction of the standard, it has been implemented numerous times. Despite the ambiguities of the execution semantics, there exist both commercial and research runtime environments that may be used to control physical systems.

From a theoretic perspective, the existing and possible execution models call for a deeper investigation. The current classification frameworks help distinguish fundamental differences between the RTEs, but fail to describe the different execution models of the standard precisely. Given that the execution semantics of the standard have room for interpretation, it is even more important to differentiate between the implementations.

Given the availability of lightweight, multitasking embedded systems that require real-time performance, the IEC 61499 may offer suitable models for this application. In this regard, deterministic real-time scheduling of multitasking IEC 61499 systems may require further investigation.

Although the topic of Dynamic Reconfiguration has been addressed from a modeling perspective, and many runtime environments claim to allow Dynamic Reconfiguration, examples of Dynamic Reconfiguration with the IEC 61499 are rare. Most RTEs focus on the execution semantics, whereas the frameworks for deployment, distribution, configuration and reconfiguration are also key selling points of the IEC 61499.

References

1. 4diac: 4diac FORTE - the 4diac runtime environment (2019). https://www.eclipse.org/4diac/en_rte.php. Accessed 24 May 2019
2. Cengic, G., Akesson, K.: Definition of the execution model used in the Fuber IEC 61499 runtime environment. In: International Conference on Industrial Informatics. IEEE (2008)
3. Cengic, G., Akesson, K.: On formal analysis of IEC 61499 applications, Part B: execution semantics. IEEE Trans. Ind. Inform. **6**, 136–144 (2010)
4. Cengic, G., Ljungkrantz, O., Akesson, K.: Formal modeling of function block applications running in IEC 61499 execution runtime. In: Conference on Emerging Technologies and Factory Automation. IEEE (2006)
5. Christensen, J.H., et al.: The IEC 61499 function block standard: software tools and runtime platforms. ISA Automation Week (2012)
6. Doukas, G.S., Thramboulidis, K.C.: A real-time Linux execution environment for function-block based distributed control applications. In: International Conference on Industrial Informatics. IEEE (2005)
7. Ferrarini, L., Veber, C.: Implementation approaches for the execution model of IEC 61499 applications. In: International Conference on Industrial Informatics. IEEE (2004)
8. Harrison, R., Vera, D., Ahmad, B.: Engineering methods and tools for Cyber-Physical automation systems. Proc. IEEE **104**(5), 973–985 (2016)
9. Holobloc: FBDK 8.0 - the function block development kit. https://www.holobloc.com/fbdk8/index.htm. Accessed 24 May 2019
10. Lindgren, P., Lindner, M., Lindner, A., Pereira, D., Pinho, L.M.: RTFM-core: language and implementation. In: Conference on Industrial Electronics and Applications. IEEE (2015)
11. Lindgren, P., Lindner, M., Lindner, A., Vyatkin, V., Pereira, D., Pinho, L.M.: A real-time semantics for the IEC 61499 standard. In: Conference on Emerging Technologies Factory Automation. IEEE (2015)
12. nxtcontrol: nxtcontrol - nxtIECRT (2019). https://www.nxtcontrol.com/en/control/ Accessed 24 May 2019
13. Pinto, L.I., Vasconcellos, C.D., Rosso, R.S.U., Negri, G.H.: ICARU-FB: an IEC 61499 compliant multiplatform software infrastructure. IEEE Trans. Ind. Inform. **12**(3), 1074–1083 (2016)
14. Prenzel, L., Provost, J.: FBBeam: an erlang-based IEC 61499 implementation. In: International Conference on Industrial Informatics. IEEE (2019)
15. Strasser, T., Zoitl, A., Christensen, J.H., Sünder, C.: Design and execution issues in IEC 61499 distributed automation and control systems. IEEE Trans. Syst. Man Cybern. **41**(1), 41–51 (2011)
16. Sünder, C., et al.: Usability and interoperability of IEC 61499 based distributed automation systems. In: International Conference on Industrial Informatics. IEEE (2006)
17. Thramboulidis, K., Zoupas, A.: Real-time Java in control and automation: a model driven development approach. In: Conference on Emerging Technologies and Factory Automation, vol. 1. IEEE (2005)
18. Thramboulidis, K., Papakonstantinou, N.: An IEC 61499 execution environment for an aJile-based field device. In: Conference on Emerging Technologies and Factory Automation. IEEE (2006)

19. Vyatkin, V.: IEC 61499 as enabler of distributed and intelligent automation: state-of-the-art review. IEEE Trans. Ind. Inform. **7**(4), 768–781 (2011)
20. Vyatkin, V., Chouinard, J.: On comparisons of the ISaGRAF implementation of IEC 61499 with FBDK and other implementations. In: International Conference on Industrial Informatics. IEEE (2008)
21. Zoitl, A., Grabmair, G., Auinger, F., Sunder, C.: Executing real-time constrained control applications modelled in IEC 61499 with respect to dynamic reconfiguration. In: International Conference on Industrial Informatics. IEEE (2005)
22. Zoitl, A., Strasser, T., Valentini, A.: Open source initiatives as basis for the establishment of new technologies in industrial automation: 4DIAC a case study. In: International Symposium on Industrial Electronics. IEEE (2010)
23. Zoitl, A.: Real-time Execution for IEC 61499. Instrumentation Systems, and Automation Society, Pittsburgh (2009)

Skill-Based Motion Control with OPC UA and Deterministic Ethernet

Marius Beller[1]([⊠]), Ben Schneider[2]([⊠]), and Alois Zoitl[3]([⊠])

[1] ITQ GmbH, München, Germany
beller@itq.de
[2] fortiss GmbH, München, Germany
schneider@fortiss.org
[3] Johannes Kepler Universität, Linz, Austria
alois.zoitl@jku.at

Abstract. The paper contains the results of the concept and the experiments with an skill-based motion control approach, based on OPC UA. The set up is extended for basic experiments with deterministic Ethernet containing network performance with undisturbed and disturbing data traffic.

Keywords: Skill-based engineering · Motion control · Distributed industrial automation · IEC61499 · TSN · OPC UA

1 Introduction

Nowadays customer wishes increase and tighten the economic competition. This leads to a changing production strategy from mass production towards mass customization with the overall goal of fast and flexible reconfiguration of production systems [1]. Today's production technologies are based on the automation pyramid, whose horizontal automation levels have got own connectivity systems. This rigid management system needs to get more flexible to meet the challenging economic requirements. Vertical integration refers to the networks between hierarchical levels. The connection in vertical direction can enable the self-optimization of production resources, e.g. the on demand optimization of logistic operations in production. Therefore, a technology has to merge the requirements of communication standards from all automation pyramid levels. We show how to solve this connectivity problem by proposing a skill-based approach for motion control using OPC UA client-server and deterministic Ethernet.

2 Background

IEC 61499 is a standard for developing distributed industrial automation systems [2,3], based on models. The *Application Model* contains Function Blocks (FB) encapsulating system functionality (e.g., arithmetic operations, network

R. Moreno-Díaz et al. (Eds.): EUROCAST 2019, LNCS 12014, pp. 461–468, 2020.
https://doi.org/10.1007/978-3-030-45096-0_56

access, ...). FBs are triggered by events and a sequence of events (event chain) form an IEC 61499 compliant application. IEC 61499's *System Model* provides information about the physical setup of the target system, consisting of end devices (e.g., Programmable Logic Controllers (PLCs)) and network segments for connecting the different PLCs via network devices.

The *Distribution Model* maps certain parts of the modeled application to the end devices. Communication Service Interface Function Blocks (SIFB) are added manually to the distributed application in order to connect the different parts of the distributed application.

A modern way of real-time communication between different devices is the IEEE Time-sensitive Networking (TSN) standard. TSN is an extension of standard Ethernet (ISO OSI layer 2) and provides the network infrastructure for Ethernet-based protocols to be deterministic and real-time capable. These features are achieved by a subset of standards belonging to the IEEE 802.1 TSN family, which provide time synchronization (IEEE 802.1AS-Rev [4]), time-triggered scheduling (IEEE 802.1Qbv [5]), configuration (IEEE 802.1Qcc [6]) and many more.

3   Concept and Implementation

3.1   Concept

The increasing customisation of products requires a variable automation in production lines. This work shows an approach how smart factories could be realized using skill-based engineering according to [7] combined with deterministic and real-time capable Ethernet. Production processes can be realised by connecting separated skills. Skills are an abstract description of functions and interfaces and can be categorised in e.g. moving, linking, comparing, etc. Atomic skills are basic actions like a linear movement. Further, skills can be combined into composed skills. The aim of the composed skill is to offer an unified skill in the network to move an axis. First and foremost, a central skill client invokes the server methods offered in the network. To synchronise two axis, the central controller has to invoke the two axis clients at the same time.

3.2   Implementation

The chosen use case to synchronise two axes provides the possibility to experiment and examine basic requirements and behaviour of such a deterministic system, based on the Ethernet standard. The whole setup contains the demonstrator, a gantry robot, two step motor controller connected to a switch and a central control unit. The used motor controllers are BeagleBone Black (BBB) controller, open-hardware embedded computers running a Debian operating system with RT preempt patch. A BBB contains a Sitara AM3358BZCZ100 1 GHz processor and a SDRAM Memory with 512 MB. Additionally, there are 4 GB onboard flash and of course an Ethernet interface 10/100 RJ45. The used switch is a TTTech TSN switch called DESwitch Akro 6/0 TSN. The switch supports the

TSN standards IEEE 802.1Qbv, the VLAN priorities in standard IEEE 802.1Q as well as the IEEE 1588 standard, the Precision Time Protocol (PTP), to synchronise clocks (Fig. 1).

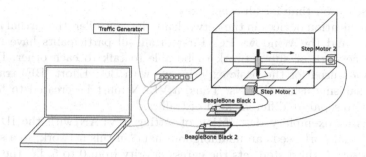

Fig. 1. Experimental hardware setup.

The PLCs contain the implementations, which are based on the IEC standard 61499. Applications are designed using the eclipse 4diac framework (Fig. 2).

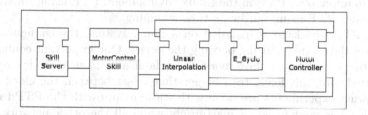

Fig. 2. Skill to move an axis.

The basic skill is realised with an independent function block that represents the Motor Controller function block. The Linear Interpolation, E_Cycle and Motor Controller function blocks define the skill itself. While the Motor Controller drives the stepper motor, the Linear Interpolation calculates the destination point in motor steps. This happens in 10 ms cycles, determined by the cycle function block. The MotorControl Skill offers a state machine. To be able to invoke the skill, the skill server provides the functionality in the network via OPC UA servers.

The task of the central orchestration is to activate methods, which are offered by servers in the network.

It is connected to the clients via an adapter socket, which allows to transfer event messages. The connection transfers events like start, cancel, etc. from the central controller to the clients. These are events, which invoke functions or transitions to change the state. When the control function block receives a starting event an entered target position for each axis is read in. Important point during the synchronisation of the movement of the two axes is, that the axes arrive at their destination at the same time. First of all, the central control unit must consider the physical constraints of the actuated skills. This is why a method is realised in this work, which detects the axis with the shortest path first. If the shortest distance is chosen, then it is multiplied with the slowest velocity offered by the Move Linear skills. The obtained target time is set as global destination time for all other axes.

Communication devices in the network are the controller, the virtual machine with Linux and the Windows PC. First of all, all participants have to be in the same network or sub-network to be able to talk to each other. Different addresses are used for the basic experiments with Best Effort (BE) traffic and TSN mechanisms using VLANs. Thus, a VLAN must be created to have the possibility to separate different kind of traffics.

This is an exemplary description of setting a VLAN with the ID 3. The created virtual port needs an unambiguous name in this network, so a static IP address is set. A third step sets the egress priority from 0 to 5, i.e. the priority of leaving Ethernet frames tagged with the priority 0 gets reset to the priority of 5. This additional priority shifting is needed, because messages leaving the runtime forte are set by default to priority 0.

A basic prerequisite of TSN is the synchronisation of the clocks from participating devices. Therefore the PTP protocol is used. There are two different methods to implement PTP in the Linux environment: PTP using software time stamping and PTP using hardware time stamping.

If the PTPd package is installed on a Linux system, the configuration file coordinates the settings during booting the device. One important configuration is the setting of master or slave mode. By default a dynamical mode assignment is supported, but this leads to a bigger time offset between the clock devices. The following experiments are done with static modes with the PTPd method. BeagleBone 1 is configured as masteronly while all the other network participants are declared as slaveonly. As a consequence the mode is set statically. An estimation about the accuracy is done by analysing the PTPd log-file. The offset fluctuates within a magnitude of microseconds.

This subsection comprises the main settings and features of the network set ups, running with TSN. The conducted experiments need three different messages streams: BE stream transmitting payload, Prioritized stream transmitting payload via TSN and Prioritized stream for network flooding. First, the priority system behind the IEEE 802.1Q defines, which tag corresponds with which priority. On this basis the TSN traffic is sent with a very high priority, e.g. tag no. 5, which matches priority 2 on VLAN 3. The disturbing traffic is set to another VLAN to ensure that the processing devices don't have to handle all of the frames, otherwise an internal queue overflow is risked. Thus, the flooding traffic is sent on VLAN 6 with a priority tag 3. Finally, the BE stream is sent on VLAN 5 with the lowest priority, the BE tag 0.

4   Experiments

The chosen way to demonstrate the function of two separately driven axes is to control a superimposed movement. The central control unit stays permanently in contact with the motor controller running on the two BeagleBone Blacks. Thus, the issue arises, what happens when disturbing network traffic tarnishes the communication. Therefore, two different experiment types are chosen to show the issue of non-deterministic communication in relation to a deterministic communication approach. On the one hand, the fundamental network experiment shows an impact of disturbing traffic to the performance of particular messages. On the other hand, the impact to the skill-based motion control setup is depicted.

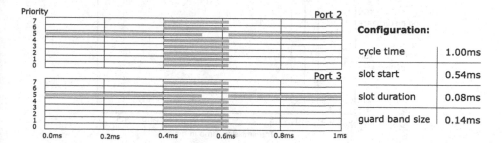

Fig. 3. TSN switch configuration.

The configuration of the switch ports 2 and 3 are depicted in Fig. 3. With the used TTTech kit it is possible to configure each port like depicted. The depicted ports two and three have a definite timeslot for sending only packages with priority 3. The grey bars stand for a blocked priority queue. If there is no bar, data can be sent. To ensure that the port is not busy with sending a message at starting point of a preferred message, guard bands are used. They protect the deadline by blocking other queues with a sufficient gap to the starting time of the preferred message and ensure that transmitting of the last frame is done when the preferred gate is opening. The magnitude of these configurations is within microseconds and considers only the TSN traffic on port 2 and 3. BE traffic can be used on all ports, like on a non-TSN switch.

The following Fig. 4 depicts the results of all network experiments. Like expected, the measurements with BE packages show a faster, but less reliable performance than TSN streams. It has been shown that the message transmission is influenced by the disturbing traffic like the requirements from the state of the art and related works confirm. The TSN experiments show the expected results as well. The mean of the TSN experiments is around 1071,8 µs and therefore higher than the mean of the executed BE measurements, confirmed by Hummen [8]. The difference occurs from the used IEEE 802.1Qbv Time-Aware Shaper [5]. If the sending node does not send messages at specific times, the packages are going to be queued in the switch. A cycle time of the used switch is 1 ms. Therefore, a latency greater than 1 ms occurs when the packet misses the slot of the current cycle and is therefore transmitted in the next cycle. Moreover, the lower the measured latency, the less valid is the result.

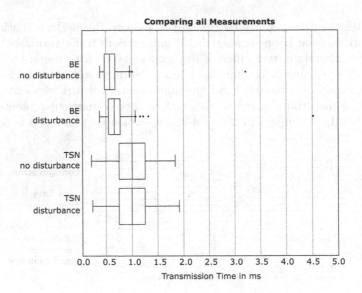

Fig. 4. Comparing measurements.

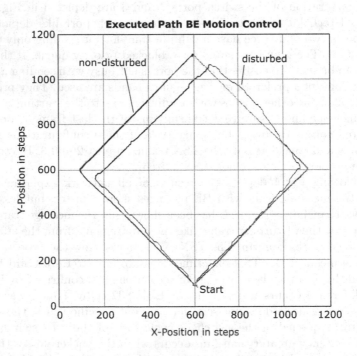

Fig. 5. Results of BE motion control without and with disturbing traffic.

The network experiments were conducted in a preferably stationary performance to guarantee repeatability at the best. Thus, one sample contains 60000 measurements. Measurements with Best Effort (BE) communication show a minimum latency of 325 µs and a maximum at 31974 µs. In contrast, measurements in a disturbed network shows a minimum latency of 318 µs and the maximum lies at 4525 µs. Comparing the results of the experiments, the experiment in a disturbed system shows more outliers than the one in an undisturbed environment (Fig. 5).

The difference is clearly visible between disturbed and non disturbed experiment. It was not achieved to run the whole motion control implementation with the TSN network. It is recognised, that the used hardware was not able to execute all needed configurations for the TSN network. The main issues were implementing a central control unit. The used set up reached its limit by running two different OPC UA clients, which are invoked in a period of 100 ms. Within the scope of this work, it was not achieved to do the central orchestration with the used PC. The approach recording incoming messages on a motor controller give an indication about the functionality of OPC UA over TSN.

5   Conclusion and Future Work

5.1   Conclusion

It was achieved, to realise a skill-based motion control approach, based on consumer Ethernet, to drive stepper motors. This leads to the required flexibility in automation [9]. With the realised motor controller, the demonstrator can be simple expanded by adding the third axis. The implementation provides a linear interpolation between the actual position and the target position. A more complex implementation would be a driven circular path. It requires a non linear interpolation and a higher resolution of the controlling. This and the attempt with more professional hardware could be an approach for further research. The measured performance is slower compared to tests by Kellermeier [10], who used existing proprietary systems. In spite of this difference, the TSN behaviour is comparable to related works. Optimising the TSN network performance needs a synchronised message exchange i.e. messages that can be send at a specific time point. Especially the use of the IEEE 802.1Qbv Time-Aware Shaper leads to a very rigid system. Referred to the time measurements, a benefit of TSN is shown. It was achieved to run the OPC UA communication with the TSN network in a reduced scope. The motion control of one axis is analysed within a TSN network. The measurements of incoming messages at the receiving node show similar characteristics with or without disturbing traffic. State of the art application in motion control with existing fieldbus systems operate within a reaction time of 1 ms. The implemented OPC UA application is able to operate in 100 ms, which is much higher than the actual state of the art. Nevertheless, TSN is a possibility to simplify the vertical integration by unify the communication mechanisms in horizontal and vertical levels. The combination with SOA, in form of skills, leads to very flexible software applications for industrial automation. Further TSN standards will improve the use and flexibility of an Ethernet-based real-time network.

5.2   Perspective

Different technologies were examined throughout this work. Since the time horizon for the project was limited, it focuses on explaining the foundations and elementary solutions for each technology. The first list below details some improvements and points for further research. The closing comments aim for carrying on research in the real-time capable Ethernet domain.

– The used hardware is a key aspect when implementing the motor controller. Other than in this thesis, a hardware encoder should be used to be certain of the executed steps of a motor. Based on such an encoder, a real controlling circuit could be set up.
– For better performance in motion control, the operating times of the motor control cape must be faster. Therefore, motor drives with response times in 1 ms magnitude are needed.
– By activating the hardware time stamping for PTP, a more precise time synchronisation between the network participants can be achieved.
– The performance of the network could be accelerated by using OPC UA with publish and subscribe. Thus, the cyclical transmission of data, especially in case of motion control, could be improved.

References

1. Weyer, S., Schmitt, M., Ohmer, M., Gorecky, D.: Towards Industry 4.0 - standardization as the crucial challange for highly modular, multi-vendor production system. IFAC-PapersOnLine **48**(3), 579–584 (2015)
2. IEC 61499 Part 1: Architecture. IEC
3. Zoitl, A., Lewis, R.: Modelling Control Systems Using IEC 61499. The Institution of Engineering and Technology, London (2014)
4. IEEE 802.1ASRev - Timing and synchronization for time-sensitive applications. IEEE
5. IEEE 802.1Qbv - Enhancements for scheduled traffic. IEEE
6. IEEE 802.1Qcc - Stream reservation protocol (SRP) enhancements and performance improvements. IEEE
7. Dorofeev, K., Zoitl, A.: Skill-based engineering approach using OPC UA programs. In: 2018 IEEE 16th International Conference on Industrial Informatics (INDIN), Porto 2018, pp. 1098–1103 (2018). https://doi.org/10.1109/INDIN.2018.8471978
8. Hummen, R., Kehrer, S., Kleinberger, O.: TSN - time sensitive networking (2016)
9. Koren, Y.: The Global Manufacturing Revolution: Product-Process-Business Integration and Reconfigurable Systems. Wiley (2010). https://doi.org/10.1002/9780470618813
10. Kellermeier, K., Pieper, C., Flatt, H., Wisniewski, L., Biendarra, A.: Performance evaluierung von PROFINET RT Geräten in einem TSN-basierten backplane. In: Jasperneite, J., Lohweg, V. (eds.) Kommunikation und Bildverarbeitung in der Automation. TA, pp. 40–53. Springer, Heidelberg (2018). https://doi.org/10.1007/978-3-662-55232-2_4

Enhancing Industrial Maintenance Through Intelligent Data Analysis

Patrick Praher[1], Bernhard Freudenthaler[1]($\boxtimes$), Werner Schröder[2],
and Florian Sobieczky[1]

[1] Software Competence Center Hagenberg, Softwarepark 21, 4232 Hagenberg, Austria
{patrick.praher,bernhard.freudenthaler,
florian.sobieczky}@scch.at
[2] BMW Motors, Hinterbergerstraße 2, 4400 Steyr, Austria
werner.schroeder@bmw.com

Abstract. For years, the amount of data generated in many industrial production plants has been said to have great potential for improving maintenance processes. In order to leverage this potential in practice, however, it is necessary to overcome a number of hurdles from automated data exchange, linking separate data sources, evaluating the actual data quality to the automated evaluation of existing data. In the project "Smart Maintenance" together with our industrial partners BMW Motors Steyr and BRP Rotax, we have developed a practical procedure to analyze the operating-, error- and sensor-data in a user-friendly web interface. This enables us to make the data utilizable for improving maintenance processes. The core functionality consists of various filter and aggregation mechanisms. Based on these different forms of visualization allow the intuitive interpretation of events in order to integrate new contexts into the daily routine of maintenance planning.

Keywords: Predictive maintenance · Industrial log visualization · Heatmaps

1 Introduction and Motivation

In large manufacturing industries, maintenance is usually based on carrying out service tasks at known intervals or on special monitoring techniques such as the measurement of temperatures or vibrations. In the first case either the manufacturer specifies the intervals or the system operator determines them over the years which requires a lot of know-how by the plant personnel. In the second case data is collected for specific problem scenarios, using mostly expensive sensor technology, and subsequently analyzed (condition monitoring). In either case, the data produced by plant control systems, some of which are already being stored, often remains unnoticed.

In the project "Smart Maintenance" we tried to overcome these classic approaches and used these additional data sources. Established manufacturers of engines such as our partners from BMW Motors Steyr and BRP Rotax already have systems that store all messages available from the plant control system centrally and persistently. Over the last few years, large amounts of data have been recorded, but most of them are nearly unused.

© Springer Nature Switzerland AG 2020
R. Moreno-Díaz et al. (Eds.): EUROCAST 2019, LNCS 12014, pp. 469–476, 2020.
https://doi.org/10.1007/978-3-030-45096-0_57

These range from operating to error and sensor-data. Thereby, the main problems are the lack of structure as these log files where mostly not intended to be further analyzed, and the data volume from hundreds of systems.

To overcome these challenges, we identified the following requirements for an application in close cooperation with our industrial partners:

Identification of Critical Installations. Due to the large number of production lines and unstructured messages, it is currently difficult to identify problematic machines and components. This process is particularly important for the selection of assembly lines that are subject to a detailed manual risk assessment.

Diagnosis/Analysis of Known Problems. In many cases, it is important for the technicians to analyze the cause during or after a shutdown in order to prevent future problems. For this purpose, it is essential to be able to search the historical data of the plant control systems in a fast and intuitive way.

Optimization of Procurement Orders in the Course of Maintenance. In the current maintenance processes, parts are replaced either in regular intervals or when faults occur. New evaluations that allow an overview of all similar systems in the entire plant could enable a further optimization of spare parts procurement.

Early Detection of Problems/Irregularities. The three requirements described above relate to the consideration of historical data. In order to get closer to the goal of predictive maintenance with the limited possibilities of the existing data, the application should enable the visualization of trends in alarm messages. The identification of problematic components within the large and complex system is of great importance.

Based on these requirements a prototypical application was developed to support maintenance activities. The specially adapted filter and aggregation methods allow the use of a large number of alarm messages from plant control systems on a cross-divisional level. The provided visualizations enable an intuitive handling of the data.

The rest of the paper is structured in the following way: In Sect. 2 we will present related work in the field of log file analysis and visualization. Section 3 gives a description of the system architecture and visualization techniques developed and applied for the described scenario. The prototypical application is demonstrated in Sect. 4. Finally, we provide our concluding remarks and hints for future work in Sect. 5.

2   Related Work

The main challenge in the project is to identify problems in large, unstructured amounts of data. For this purpose, visual methods were chosen, since maintenance technicians with little knowledge about data analysis should use the application.

In the last years tools like Kibana[1] und Datadog[2] were developed to visualize data sets. Those tools support many different visualization options from simple line plots over

---

[1] https://www.elastic.co/products/kibana.
[2] https://www.datadoghq.com/.

histograms to heatmaps. The main reason for not using these tools is the complexity of data (pre)processing required in order to use these visualization options.

The basic structure of the message data from programmable logical controllers (PLCs) is very similar to classic log files from server software, operating systems or firewalls. In this area methods for visualization often use clustering or graphs [1, 2]. Basic variants of heatmaps are used in order to detect anomalous user activity [3], fraud [4], usage patterns [5] or analyze the development of infectious diseases [6].

In contrast to these applications, we count each type of message in time slots and use these counts as a basis for the heatmap. We inspect the data at different levels of granularity regarding the timeslots and the grouping of messages (e.g., by keywords or machine assemblies), which greatly help to identify and diagnose equipment problems. The most similar approach from a visual point of view is called HMAP [7].

We chose to develop the application in R[3] Shiny[4]. This allowed us to reuse the existing data analysis methods developed in the course of the project. In contrast to more heavy weight desktop user interface (UI) frameworks like Microsoft WPF[5] or Java Swing[6], Shiny allows a fast implementation of the software prototype. Therefore, we can get fast feedback about the usability and functionality from our project partners. R[7] or Python[8] Notebooks would have been another alternatives for rapid prototyping but this would have come at the expense of usability.

3 Visualization of Alarm Data

In this chapter we first describe the structure of the application. Then we will discuss the characteristics of the visualization and the applicability of trend recognition.

3.1 System Architecture

The data flow from the industrial plants to the finished analyses is shown Fig. 1. The imported data can be pre-selected using extensive filter functions (I). These enable the selection of predefined categories (e.g., programmable logic controller), restrict the observation period and filter by message text. It is possible to search through all messages texts to easily find the messages related to specific components or machines. The result from the search can be manually edited to exclude or include single messages. It is possible to save this selection as a so-called message group.

The message groups are the basis for the next analysis step but also allows to quickly reload a filter combination with new or changed data in the future. In the next step the data can be aggregated in several ways (II) to give users new perspectives of the facilities. One such perspective is the overview of all groups for the entire plant. Regardless of aggregation, grouping or filtering, several visualization options are available which will be described in the following.

---

[3] https://www.r-project.org/.

[4] https://shiny.rstudio.com/.

[5] https://docs.microsoft.com/en-us/dotnet/framework/wpf/.

[6] https://docs.oracle.com/javase/tutorial/uiswing/.

[7] https://rmarkdown.rstudio.com/r_notebooks.html.

[8] https://ipython.org/notebook.html.

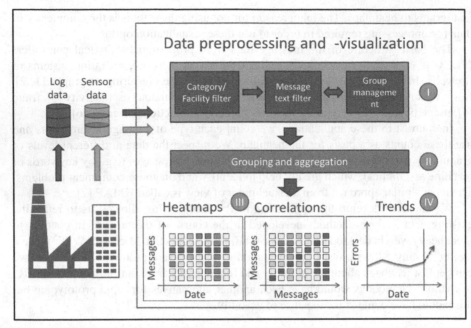

Fig. 1. Illustrates the process of data collection, preprocessing, and visualization in typical industrial scenarios.

3.2 Visualization

Two different visualization options (III) are available:

1. The most commonly used method is used to visualize the frequency of messages over time. The representation is a variant of a heatmap shown Fig. 2: the darker the color in a field, the higher the number of messages in this time frame. The X-axis represents the time line and the Y-axis the selected messages. This plot allows the representation of frequencies of many messages or aggregated groups at once (up to 250) in an easily readable format. Since the quality of the status and alarm messages is often neglected, sometimes the same message is issued many times in a very short period of time. In order to make a clear representation possible, however, there is the option to scale the number of messages exponentially. In order to be able to quickly extract exact information in large plots (many messages over a long period of time, e.g., >1 year), a click in the plot area displays the number of messages, the date and the message name in the information area. All plots can be easily exported for documentation purposes.

2. The second variant for visualization is the calculation of the correlations between the selected message counts, which are displayed as a matrix. The color of the intersections shows the strength of the correlation. In order to easily identify groups of messages that occur frequently together, it is possible to apply cluster algorithms. By default, the Pearson correlation coefficient is used. Depending on the underlying data and the granularity of the timeslots the application of robust methods (e.g. Spearman rank correlation coefficient) is better suited.

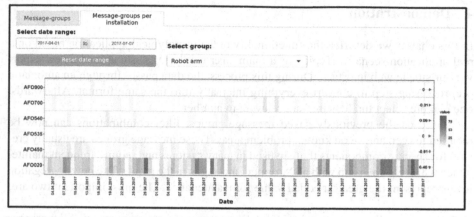

Fig. 2. Shows a visualization of message counts per timeslot from industrial production machines at BMW Motors Steyr. The messages are filter for the keywords "Robot arm" which describes a specific component that occurs at many different places in the whole plant. These messages are grouped per "AFO" which corresponds to specific organizational units. The intensity of the color shows the count per timeslot per group. The last column indicates whether the count per timeslot shows an increasing, decreasing or no trend.

3.3 Trends

To provide additional support for maintenance personnel, trends for the message frequency are calculated. At the moment we use linear models for the calculation in most cases. Depending on the application it is necessary to vary the observation period. The relevant duration varies from a few days to months, depending on the application. These trends can be visualized within the heatmaps as an arrow at the end of each row (last point in time). Color-coding of the arrows improves the readability. To get a better estimate of the trend, a numeric value (the slope of the linear model) gives information about the trend's strength. Additionally, a tab panel shows the trends as a list sorted by their slope. This makes it possible to quickly and easily identify problematic components based on the forecast. As with the visualization techniques, trend analysis can be applied to unprocessed, grouped and aggregated data.

3.4 Technologies

In many data analysis projects R Notebooks[9] are used since they provide a fast and reproducible first look on the data. In the first project phase algorithms specifically for reading and preprocessing data are developed. The possibility to reuse these software components makes R Shiny an adequate option to develop prototypical software applications for industrial partners. The use of web technologies in combination with a large library of statistical methods and extensive visualization options is the ideal combination for prototyping such an application.

---

[9] https://rmarkdown.rstudio.com/r_notebooks.

4 Demonstration

In this chapter we describe the functionality of the prototypical application based on a real application scenario. Typically, a maintainer would regularly upload a new export via our simple web interface. During this process, the data passes through an automatic preprocessing step to convert everything internally into the same format. Afterwards, one can pre-select the files that are relevant to him/her.

Based on the previously saved message groups, filter combinations can now be recalled to keep an eye on known problem areas. These message groups are usually created for specific components that are used in many systems and require frequent maintenance work (e.g., a group with all "gripper" messages in the plant). The new aggregation levels represent the greatest added value for maintenance. The most important two are:

- *Overview of all message groups*: Each line represents a message group. All messages in this group are summed up. This allows fast identification of problematic components across the plant.
- *Message groups details per installation*: Here the messages are visualized within a group and are summed up for each system. Based on the message group overview, it is possible to quickly link the problem to individual systems. Figure 2 shows a screenshot of this perspective. At the top left it is possible to restrict the date range. On the top right you can select the relevant message group. In the example it can be seen that with the latest data, alarm messages occur in the group "Robot Arm" especially at the system AFO020.

As new problems occur, the maintenance personnel can use the filter functionality for analyzing root causes. Due to the easy structure, new filter parameters can be saved as groups and can be monitored with the described views henceforth.

The colored arrows in the last column help to quickly identify trends in the message counts. This feature can be especially useful if the counts between the machines/groups (displayed as rows) differ a lot. For example, a rise of warnings from 2 to 10 per timeslot could be indicative of a new problem, but due to a high number of messages (e.g., 50 per timeslot) on other machines within the same group, the difference is barely visible.

As a result, our application supports the maintenance personnel to fulfill the scenarios described at the beginning of this paper in the following ways:

- *Identification of critical installations*: The clear visualizations of the frequency of alarm messages, the extensive filter options and additional aggregation levels make it easier and faster to identify problematic installations. This function is particularly useful for further detailed analyses, as facilities can be identified more quickly.
- *Diagnosis/analysis of known problems*: The flexible filter mechanisms for the message text and the message time open up new possibilities for identifying the causes of faults. This root cause analysis is also the basis for a better understanding of the fault relationships and thus for a better early identification of emerging problems.
- *Tuning/optimization of procurement orders in the course of maintenance*: The new aggregation options allow better planning of the procurement of spare parts, since

defects which occur on several systems with the same or similar components can easily be identified.

- *Early detection of problems/irregularities*: By calculating trends for individual alerts as well as for groups and systems, an increase in faults can be detected more quickly. Often, such an increase (sometimes over several days to weeks) indicates a fault before it can be detected by the machine operator or serious damage to the machine happens.

5   Conclusion and Future Work

The presented application allows a good usage of the available data with regard to maintenance requirements: (i) The new perspectives resulting from the aggregation and filter functions provide new starting points for fault diagnosis and maintenance planning. (ii) The application allows to extract additional information from the fault messages of the plant control systems, which could only be stored but could not be evaluated until now. Based on the available data, no long-term forecasts can be made, but short-term trends can be derived. (iii) The possibility to analyze similar components (e.g. "proximity switches") across all systems opens up new perspectives for maintenance planning. The clearly arranged representations enable a quick identification of problematic components.

Future Work: Integration into existing systems via API (Application Programming Interface) is very important for the usability of the application. Only the automatic data exchange allows the practical application of trend analysis and can lead to a stronger integration into the process of maintenance planning. The functions shown here represent a first step towards the digitalization of maintenance processes in industrial plants. In order to gain a deeper insight into the conditions and processes of industrial plants, it is necessary to extract data with higher information content from the plant control systems. This ranges from standardized and finer graduated status messages to exact sensor data of the individual components. This data contains the potential for accurate and long-term predictions of the conditions within the plant.

The second major topic for future work concerns the possibility of predicting specific events over a longer period of time. From our point of view, we are still at the beginning of this development, mainly due to the limited quality of available data from real-world industrial environments. Nevertheless, with a complete concept from data generation and recording to analysis, we are getting a big step closer to this vision. With our simple trend analysis, we have taken a first step in this direction, but there is still a lot of potential for improved algorithms in this area.

Since data from the industrial environment always present challenges with regard to quality (e.g., outliers), robust learning methods were researched in the "Smart Maintenance" project [8, 9]. In the future, analyses based on these methods could be integrated into the application.

Acknowledgments. The research reported in this paper has been partly done in the project "Smart Maintenance", funded by FFG (project no. 843650), the project "AutoDetect", funded by "Innovative Upper Austria, call Digitalization" (FFG project no. 862019) and by the Austrian Ministry for Transport, Innovation and Technology, the Federal Ministry for Digital and Economic Affairs, and the Province of Upper Austria in the frame of the COMET center SCCH.

References

1. Takada, T., Koike, H.: Tudumi: information visualization system for monitoring and auditing computer logs. In: Proceedings International Conference Information Visualisation, January 2002, pp, 570–576 (2002). https://doi.org/10.1109/IV.2002.1028831
2. Longtong, Y., Narupiyakul, L.: Suspect tracking based on call logs analysis and visualization. In: 20th International Computer Science and Engineering Conference: Smart Ubiquitous Computing and Knowledge, ICSEC 2016 (2017). https://doi.org/10.1109/ICSEC.2016.7859900
3. Hanniel, J.J., Widagdo, T.E., Asnar, Y.D.W.: Information system log visualization to monitor anomalous user activity based on time. In: Proceedings 2014 International Conference on Data and Software Engineering, ICODSE 2014 (2014). https://doi.org/10.1109/ICODSE.2014.7062673
4. Chang, R., et al.: Scalable and interactive visual analysis of financial wire transactions for fraud detection. Inf. Vis. **7**, 63–76 (2008). https://doi.org/10.1057/palgrave.ivs.9500172
5. Guo, H., Gomez, S.R., Ziemkiewicz, C., Laidlaw, D.H.: A case study using visualization interaction logs and insight metrics to understand how analysts arrive at insights. IEEE Trans. Vis. Comput. Graph. **22**, 51–60 (2016). https://doi.org/10.1109/TVCG.2015.2467613
6. DeBold, T., Friedman, D.: Battling Infectious Diseases in the 20th Century: The Impact of Vaccines. http://graphics.wsj.com/infectious-diseases-and-vaccines/
7. Frei, A., Rennhard, M.: Histogram Matrix: Log file visualization for anomaly detection. In: 3rd International Conference on Availability, Reliability and Security Proceedings, ARES 2008, pp. 610–617 (2008). https://doi.org/10.1109/ARES.2008.148
8. Kogler, A., Traxler, P.: Efficient and Robust Median-of-Means Algorithms for Location and Regression, pp. 0–7 (2016). https://doi.org/10.1109/SYNASC.2016.35
9. Kogler, A., Traxler, P.: Parallel and robust empirical risk minimization via the median trick. In: Blömer, J., Kotsireas, I.S., Kutsia, T., Simos, D.E. (eds.) MACIS 2017. LNCS, vol. 10693, pp. 378–391. Springer, Cham (2017). https://doi.org/10.1007/978-3-319-72453-9_31

Simulator for Planning Collision-Free Trajectories in Manipulation of Objects Applications

J. S. Martinez-Caldas, C. H. Rodriguez-Garavito, Carolina Peña-Ortega, Alvaro A. Patiño-Forero[⊠], and Guillermo A. Camacho

Universidad de La Salle, Cra 2 No 10-70, Bogota, Colombia
{juansmartinez21,cerodriguez,caropena,alapatino,
gacamacho}@unisalle.edu.co

Abstract. This article presents the functional description of a simulator that plans trajectories in an automatic fashion in order for a Motoman HP20D industrial robot to move box-like objects from an initial to a final position avoiding obstacles in its workspace. The simulator sets up robot positioning based on the data entered by the user as well as the position of obstacles (boxes) by using an offline workspace reconstruction based on a computer vision tool, the main component of which is an RGB-D camera. The vision system estimates the position, orientation and size of a set of boxes to create a virtual representation in the simulator. In addition to that, a collision detection module, cost-efficient in computational terms, is described as the structural block of the trajectory planning process. Finally, the work space road map is obtained through a lazy PRM algorithm, as a global planner, and a type-A* search algorithm, as a local planner. This way, a collision-free trajectory is obtained and animated in the simulator as the final result of the general planning process.

Keywords: Path planning · Motoman HP20D · Lazy PRM · Box detection · Kinect

1 Introduction

One of the main issues in manipulator robotics is finding the best path that allows manipulator movement from an initial to a final configuration contemporarily complying with workspace restriction requirements [7,11]. For this reason, a particular interest has arisen with respect to modern path planning simulation strategies due to the difficulty of elaborating optimal paths applied to robots with different levels of freedom as well as to workspaces containing different objects [4]. In fact, the motivation for developing these strategies arises because robots are becoming increasingly useful in industrial applications where they have to carry out tasks, such as optimum palletizing of continuous loads,

Universidad De La Salle.

R. Moreno-Díaz et al. (Eds.): EUROCAST 2019, LNCS 12014, pp. 477–484, 2020.
https://doi.org/10.1007/978-3-030-45096-0_58

in workspaces containing a considerable number of obstacles. This is a highly interesting topic in logistic operations. Solutions may be classified into two categories according to their scope: (1) Optimum pattern planning, (2) Automatic stacking machines. The former are in charge of modeling stacking characteristics and calculating a packing pattern that maximizes the available volume and meets load and container restrictions [1–3,5,6,15]. The latter instead design mechanical systems capable of manipulating loads and implementing the optimum calculated solution [8,14,16,17]. Research is currently focused on applications that solve both problems at a time so as to develop integral solutions that take into account packing pattern effects on stacking strategies. To this end, the relevance of an artificial vision system enabling to characterize stacking machine's workspace has surged for the purpose of solving load characteristics identification and collision-free trajectory planning issues. This article presents a simulator that reconstructs the workspace of a stacking cell and carries out the collision-free trajectory planning between a predefined pair of positions. The purpose of this simulator is serving as a path validation platform in real stacking applications. The article is divided into the following sections: Sect. 2 presents the path simulator description, Sect. 3 shows and analyzes the final simulator implementation results and conclusions are summarized in Sect. 4.

2   Trajectory Planning Simulator

The interaction between box stacking path simulator's functional blocks is shown in Fig. 1. Each process carried out by the simulator is described hereunder.

2.1   Virtual Environment

Blocks 1 and 2 represent the work environment of the trajectory planning simulator. Those consist of a 1:1 reconstruction of Universidad de La Salle's Robotics Lab, where a Motoman HP20D robot is located. The LAB-Robot CAD model is then integrated in a Unity platform environment. The CAD simulation environment result can be observed in Fig. 2 in comparison with the real lab.

Additionally, a mathematical model is required to describe the movement of the Motoman Robot HP20D. This definition is presented in two equations: the first one is named direct kinematic model, its process begins with an articular position of the robot so as to obtain the end effector framework of reference. $T_e^b = T_0^b T_1^0(q_1) T_2^1(q_2) \ldots T_6^5(q_6) T_e^6$ [13]. The second is the inverse kinematic model, in which the process begins with the spatial description of robot's end effector so as to obtain the arch coordinates of its kinematic chain. $\theta = [\theta_i]$, $i = 0 \ldots n$ [10].

2.2   3D Object Recognition

The object recognition pose for stacking applications consists of finding position, orientation and size descriptors with respect to a set of boxes in an RGB-D image. The Fig. 3 summarizes a processing sequence to carry out this task [12].

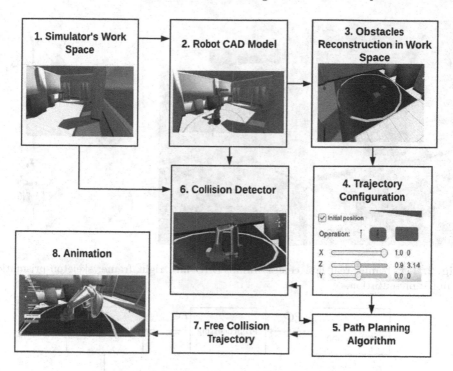

Fig. 1. Flow chart simulator process.

The image acquisition phase captures a point cloud describing the packing scenario, i.e. the set of boxes, floor and elements surrounding the stacking cell. The preprocessing phase aligns the point cloud with the gravity vector and eliminates the points representing the floor plane. The clustering phase groups points using each image voxel's position and the number of groups is determined by the same Clustering algorithm: MeanShift. The elimination of clusters not describing box-like objects is further developed in the filtering phase. Said task is carried out using a thresholding process based on cluster size, inclination and height. Properties are calculated during the features extraction phase: size (length, height and width), the position referred to the geometrical center of the upper side of the box and its orientation. In this instance, position and orientation results are calculated with respect to the RGB-D camera reference system. It is necessary to carry out a transformation to the base reference system so as to ease up the subsequent path calculation step. This is the very task carried out by the last block of the processing chain. In the Fig. 4 the final processing is presented. We can identify the base reference system with a sub-index k as well as the reference system of each box in the scenario. These systems contain intended orientation and position data.

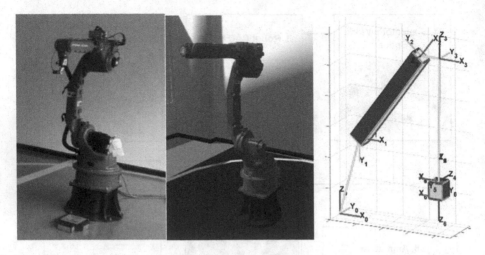

Fig. 2. Left frame: real lab. center frame: CAD lab. right frame: skeleton-prismatic robot representation.

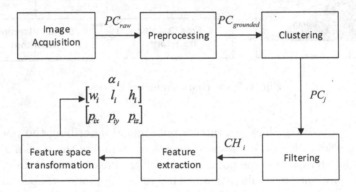

Fig. 3. Processing line

2.3 Collision Detector Algorithm

The method proposed for collision detection is a computationally efficient algorithm as it simplifies the issue of detecting interferences between the HP20D robot links and, on its turn, between said links and the objects located in the workspace (virtually reconstructed boxes to be stacked). It also simplifies the detection of intersections between bounding boxes, four face prisms covering each object to be analyzed (see Fig. 2, right frame).

This way, the bounding-boxes intersection becomes the progressive detection of intersections among the plans that shape each bounding box' face, which is equivalent to detecting the intersection of rectangles in space. The detailed description of the implemented collision detection algorithm is presented in [13].

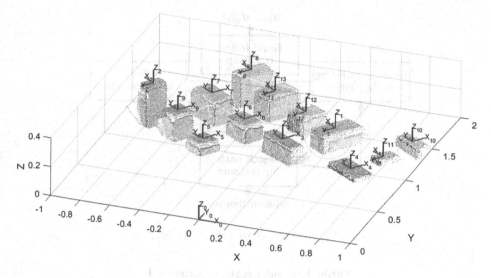

Fig. 4. Objects process

2.4 Lazy PRM Path Planning Algorithm

The method implemented herein is a variation of the original PRM proposed by Kavraky, the difference with respect to the PRM one [9], is that all configurations are assumed to be collision-free in the resulting road map a q_{start}, q_{end}, and a number of uniformly distributed nodes are set so as to create a roadmap that links pairs of close nodes by creating paths. The shorter path from q_{start} y q_{end} in the road map is found via a local search algorithm, then a verification is carried out as to whether the selected path is collision-free. Should collision be detected, the nodes and paths that compose this trajectory will be removed from the Roadmap. The process may end in two ways: if a feasible trajectory is found from the initial to the final configuration, the algorithm will then return the trajectory, to the contrary, should a feasible trajectory not be found, the algorithm adds nodes to the Roadmap and begins searching again. The steps composing this algorithm as well as their sequence can be observed in Fig. 5.

3   Results

The results of the Lazy PRM algorithm tests applied to the real robot with 6 degrees of freedom in a Lab environment are presented in this section, the planner was developed in C# using the Unity videogame engine for result simulation purposes. Experiments have been conducted with a computer equipped with an Intel Core I7 5th generation, 1.8 to 2.4 GHz, RAM 8 GB and a 64 bits processor. In the test environment an initial number of nodes $N_{init} = 60$, a neighboring radium $M_{neigh} = 60$, a collision detection interpolation step $M_{coll} = 200$, and a number of added nodes $N_{enh} = 10$ were set up.

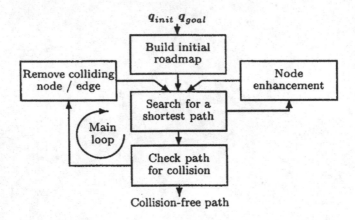

Fig. 5. Flow chart lazy PRM [9].

Table 1. Results of the experiment 1.

Experiment 1							
Position (m)	X/S	Z/L	Y/U	RX/R/W	RY/B/L	RZ/T/H	R
Initial Position (m)	1	0.3	−0.4	0	3.14	0	-
Goal Position (m)	1	0.3	0.4	0	3.14	0	-
Initial Position (rad)	−0,38056	1,06463	−0,34970	−0,00383	1,41580	1,95515	-
Goal Position (rad)	0,38056	1,06463	−0,34970	0,00383	1,41580	1,18645	-
Second Position (rad)	−0,29882	0,98118	−0,25044	0,53768	1,06660	1,70249	-
Third Position (rad)	0,20100	0,82875	−0,38809	1,38193	−1,42471	0,51027	-
Box 1	0,4	0	−0,6	0,2	0,7	0,8	0
Box 2	0,4	0	0,4	0,4	0,4	0,6	0
Time (s)	10						

Three different experiments were developed, see Table 1, 2, and 3, in each one of them the end effector's initial and final positions are set up as well as obstacle size and position characterized by an increasing degree of difficulty after consecutive experiments so as to assess trajectory generation.

Table 2. Results of the experiment 2.

Experiment 2							
Position (m)	X/S	Z/L	Y/U	RX/R/W	RY/B/L	RZ/T/H	R
Initial Position (m)	1	0.7	1	0,6	3.14	0	-
Goal Position (m)	1	0.7	−0.9	0	1	0	-
Initial Position (rad)	0,75485	0,88161	0,04464	−0,99767	1,05930	1,65381	-
Goal Position (rad)	−0,73281	0,83738	−0,01083	0	0,84822	2,30361	-
Second Position (rad)	−0,02186	1,00807	0,50100	1,48815	1,779990	−0,10779	-
Box 1	0,5	0	−0,7	0,6	0,7	0,8	0,4
Box 2	0,4	0	0,5	0,4	0,4	0,9	−0,3
Time (s)	420						

Table 3. Results of the experiment 3.

Experiment 3							
Position (m)	X/S	Z/L	Y/U	RX/R/W	RY/B/L	RZ/T/H	R
Initial Position (m)	1	1.6	0.8	0.6	3.14	0	-
Goal Position (m)	1	0.5	0.2	0	3,14	0	-
Initial Position (rad)	0,67474	0,49090	0,61165	0	-0,12075	0,89605	-
Goal Position (rad)	0,19739	0,78127	-0,53640	0	1,31768	1,37340	-
Second Position (rad)	-1	0,156613	-0,0634754	0,708756	1	0,2835549	-
Box 1	0,6	0	-0,7	0,4	0,6	1,3	0,6
Box 2	0,4	0	0,5	0,4	0,4	1,4	0
Time (s)	32						

4   Conclusions

The result of the trajectory planning algorithm shows an average response time of 150 s. In all cases, a feasible and collision-free trajectory is obtained, thus demonstrating that the planner autonomously generates a set of paths. Due to random nature of Roadmap creation, trajectory points are always different. The time the simulator takes to solve a problem depends directly upon the resolution of the initial Roadmap, the number of points added in the context of the Lazy PRM algorithm improvement process, obstacle size and initial and final end effector's position.

The simulator developed in this study allows interconnectivity with the real HP20D robot with which it is expected to conduct stacking test in a real environment.

The main contributions of this work are two: the first one consists of the real-time implementation of the Lazy PRM algorithm as a result of the effective implementation of the collision detector. The second relevant contribution is the integration of simulator modules in the Unity environment by leaving open user interaction via virtual reality.

References

1. Alonso, M.T., Alvarez-Valdes, R., Parreño, F., Tamarit, J.M.: Algorithms for pallet building and truck loading in an interdepot transportation problem. Math. Probl. Eng. **2016** (2016). https://doi.org/10.1155/2016/3264214
2. Alvarez-Valdes, R., Parreño, F., Tamarit, J.M.: A GRASP/path relinking algorithm for two- and three-dimensional multiple bin-size bin packing problems. Comput. Oper. Res. **40**, 3081–3090 (2013). https://doi.org/10.1016/j.cor.2012.03.016
3. Camacho-Muñoz, G.A., Alvarez-Martinez, D., Cuellar, D.: An approach for the pallet building and loading problem. In: Universitat Pompeu Fabra (ed.) Proceeding of the MIC and MAEB 2017 Conferences Proceeding of the MIC and MAEB 2017 Conferences, pp. 38–43. Universitat Pompeu Fabra, Barcelona (2017). ISBN 978-84-697-4275-1

4. Cheng, X., Zhao, M.: Analysis on the trajectory planning and simulation of six degrees of freedom manipulator. In: 2018 3rd International Conference on Mechanical, Control and Computer Engineering (ICMCCE), pp. 385–387. IEEE (2018)
5. Easy Cargo: Easy Cargo (2016). http://www.easycargo3d.com/es/
6. Esko: Cape Pack (2016). https://www.esko.com/en/products/overview/cape-pack/overview/
7. Han, X., Wang, T., Liu, B.: Path planning for robotic manipulator in narrow space with search algorithm. In: 2017 2nd International Conference on Advanced Robotics and Mechatronics (ICARM), pp. 339–344. IEEE (2017)
8. Institut für Technische Logistik: Parcel Robot (2013). http://donar.messe.de/exhibitor/cemat/2014/S731673/parcel-robot-pr-information-sheet-eng-315227.pdf
9. Kavraki, L., Bohlin, R.: Path planning using lazy PRM. In: International Conference on Robotics and Automation, pp. 521–528. IEEE (2000)
10. Leonardo, M.L.D.: Interfaz natural para la programación de un robot manipulador a través de un Kinect (2014). http://repository.lasalle.edu.co/bitstream/handle/10185/3969/45101413-2014.pdf?sequence=3&isAllowed=y
11. Mu, Y., Zhang, L., Chen, X., Gao, X.: Optimal trajectory planning for robotic manipulators using chicken swarm optimization. In: 2016 8th International Conference on Intelligent Human-Machine Systems and Cybernetics (IHMSC), vol. 2, pp. 369–373. IEEE (2016)
12. Rodriguez-Garavito, C.H., Camacho-Munoz, G., Álvarez-Martínez, D., Cardenas, K.V., Rojas, D.M., Grimaldos, A.: 3D object pose estimation for robotic packing applications. In: Figueroa-García, J.C., Villegas, J.G., Orozco-Arroyave, J.R., Maya Duque, P.A. (eds.) WEA 2018. CCIS, vol. 916, pp. 453–463. Springer, Cham (2018). https://doi.org/10.1007/978-3-030-00353-1_40
13. Rodriguez-Garavito, C.H., Patiño-Forero, A.A., Camacho-Munoz, G.A.: Collision detector for industrial robot manipulators. In: Graña, M., et al. (eds.) SOCO'18-CISIS'18-ICEUTE'18 2018. AISC, vol. 771, pp. 187–196. Springer, Cham (2019). https://doi.org/10.1007/978-3-319-94120-2_18
14. TEUN: TEUN takes a load off your hands (2012). http://www.teun.com/en/
15. TOPS Software Corporation. Total optimization packaging software: MaxLoad Pro (2016)
16. Univeyor: Empticon - efficient and ergonomically designed emptying of containers (2014)
17. Vaculex: Vaculex working with ease (2015). http://www.vaculex.com/references/case-studies/case-study-posten-logistics-orebro/

Real-Time IoT-Based Production Planning and Control of Industrial Robots in an Automated Cyber-Physical Production System Under Dynamic Conditions: Lessons Learned from a Make-to-Order Usage Case

Joachim Berlak[1], Julia Berg[2], Michael Stangl[3], and Luciano Baumgart[4(✉)]

[1] Institute for Automatization and Industrial Management (IAIM), FOM University, Campus Munich, Arnulfstr. 30, 80335 Munich, Germany
joachim.berlak@fom.com

[2] Fraunhofer-Einrichtung fuer Gießerei-, Composite- und Verarbeitungstechnik, Provinostr. 52, 86153 Augsburg, Germany
julia.berg@igcv.fraunhofer.de

[3] software4production GmbH, Anton-Boeck-Str. 34, 81249 Munich, Germany
michael.stangl@softwareproduction.com

[4] Lorenscheit Automatisierungstechnik GmbH, Marienauer Weg 7, 21368 Dahlenburg, Germany
l.baumgart@moving-production.com

Abstract. Industry 4.0, IoT, and cyber-physical production systems (CPPSs) are regarded as a key factor for manufacturing companies to become more efficient, flexible, and responsive to market changes. However, all but real-time bidirectional communication between shop floor cyber-physical systems (CPSs) and IoT-based production planning and control (PPC) in a cloud environment become especially challenging regarding the de facto state of technology, as we indicate. Many CPS/CPPS projects fail in industrial practice. We describe the design and implementation of a highly automated CPPS in a real-time make-to-order usage case for the production of prescription lenses based on an environment that requires real-time communication if it is to work. We use the project experiences to explain the lessons learned and derive a holistic approach to IoT-PPC CPS and CPPS design and implementation.

Keywords: Industry 4.0 · IoT · Automation · Robotics · Production planning and control · OPC UA · CPS · CPPS

1 Introduction

While the focus today in Western industry is on swift, flexible manufacturing of high-end customer-specific products instead of low-cost and medium-cost off-the-shelf goods [1], this strategy is affected by global pressure on prices, costs, and delivery times by

© Springer Nature Switzerland AG 2020
R. Moreno-Díaz et al. (Eds.): EUROCAST 2019, LNCS 12014, pp. 485–492, 2020.
https://doi.org/10.1007/978-3-030-45096-0_59

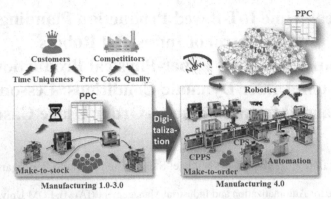

Fig. 1. Transformation of manufacturing owing to digitalization

global markets, combined with unpredictable dynamics in all business areas [2]. Figure 1 indicates these forces on the left.

To compete under these conditions, manufacturing companies must become more efficient, flexible, and responsive to market changes [3]. However, today's production planning and control (PPC) cannot fulfill these market challenges as intended [4]. Thus, IT has been used and regarded in the past decade as a tool to decrease costs and improve performance and efficiency [5–10]. Since 2010, in Germany, this evolutionary process of digitalization has been labeled Industry 4.0 [11]. By automating business and manufacturing processes using virtual or physical robotics, there is a shift to make-to-order production systems [12]. The Internet of things (IoT) is now regarded as the main driver of Industry 4.0 [13]. Thus, smart devices or cyber-physical systems (CPSs) are primary enablers of flexibility and productivity [14]. CPSs consist of embedded systems with the ability to communicate [15]. Since a CPS can interact with other CPSs, all elements of a CPS must be designed and must be able to cross-link in order to build a cyber-physical production system (CPPS) at the plant level [16]. Owing to these market changes, the bidirectional vertical and horizontal communication and information exchange must occur in close to real time [16]; however, for the real-time cooperation between robotics, IoT, and PPC within a CPS/CPPS, this is a major challenge, as we indicate. We research the state-of-the-art of robotics, IoT, and PPC regarding real-time communication. We will then present a Greenfield design and implementation of a highly automated CPPS using robotics and real-time IoT-PPC. We will describe the lessons learned as implications for robotics, IoT, and PPC. Finally, we will propose a holistic approach to CPS/CPPS design with robotics and IoT-PPC. This is needed to transform today's manufacturing via digitalization.

2 Design and Implementation of a Highly Automated CPPS in a Real-Time Make-to-Order Usage Case

We will now describe the design and implementation of a highly automated CPPS in a real-time make-to-order use case for the production of prescription lenses.

2.1 Initial Situation and Requirements

After a consumer has selected frames at an optician, the prescription lenses are ordered and produced by a so-called lab [17]. All lenses are one-of-a-kind and are made to order. Thus, the question how to address challenges in future lens production (see Fig. 2) is shaping all activities in this industry. Within the scope of this 2017 Greenfield project, the principles of digitalization, robotics, and IoT were applied. The requirements were to build a plant that manufactures 5,000 lenses per day with 30% so-called speed orders produced within a 4.5-h production time and next-day delivery. A maximum of 10 human operators were to be employed per shift in 24/7 operations. Thus, an >85% automation level of all processes had to be achieved and controlled in real time. To implement this new concept as a role model for future lens production, we defined a cloud-based IoT approach as a must for scalability. We will now focus our research on an industrial robot-based CPS within the overall CPPS.

2.2 Sectoring Robot CPS Design and Implementation Usage Case

To set research boundaries, we focus on the robot cell depicted in Fig. 2.

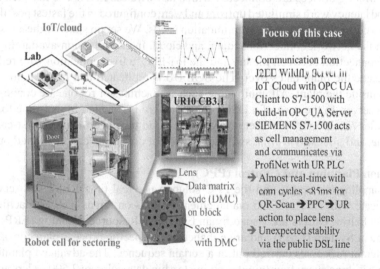

Fig. 2. The robot cell as CPS controlled by the IoT PPC

Sectors are handled manually by operators at 10 doors initiated and visualized by the IoT-PPC on an LCD screen. We will describe the IoT and the PPC foci later; we start with the robotics focus.

Robotics

We designed this robot cell with a Universal Robot UR10 CB 3.1. A robot-based CPS is usually equipped with an own PLC. Here, the control is transferred from the PLC level to the PPC-IoT level, with the operator performing only basic material handling operations. As interface between the PLC and the IoT-PPC, the OPC-UA protocol and a SIEMENS S7-1500 with integrated OPC UA server is used to act as cell control for this CPS. The robot is programmed to safely move every needed combination of waypoints, and knows the coordinates of every position, indicated by a door number and a position number. The appropriate movement path is started by the PLC that also inhabits the background CPS logic. To decide the right operation, 2-D DMC barcode scanners of lenses and doors are used, and the PPC-IoT remains informed about the lenses reaching and leaving the robot cell.

Internet of Things (IoT)

To get scalability and security, a lab-internal hosting of all necessary software we discard in favor of a private cloud-based approach. The main goal in that case is to achieve 24/7 operations by 99.7% availability of the entire IT infrastructure, because of the potential costs and lost turnover due to downtime. However, the crucial part is the public DSL line between the plant and the private cloud hosting the application servers as well as the SQL database server. We realized the plant-cloud connection by a duplicated 1 Gigabit VPN-secured public DSL line. The PPC is installed on the application server and communicates with for instance the machines and robots via a local 1 Gigabit cable-based network. Mobile devices are connected with a fast wireless LAN. The network speeds, traffic, and latency were simulated upfront and were configured in the fastest possible way in order to cover the real-time communication needs. We set up state-of-the-art security to protect the network connections, data, and cloud. In case of a non-availability of the network connection between the lab and the IoT-PPC, a live replication with redundant servers inside the plant takes over. The SQL DB is replicated live from cloud with the SQL DB inside the plant. All equipment, such as machines or robots, are connected via a domain server. In the case of a DSL problem, there is a switch in real-time to the lab server. After resolution, cloud server sync and cloud take over again. Worst-case tests were done, and almost real-time switchover without downtime can be carried out.

Production Planning and Control (PPC)

The IoT application server and the PPC solution use real-time REST webservices to communicate with ERP and lab management systems on top as well as machines and equipment below. Orders are issued by an Enterprise Resource Planning (ERP) or Lab Management System (LMS) and are enhanced by a specific process plan consisting up to 20 different processes carried out in a certain sequence. The advanced planning and scheduling is done every four minutes owing to a big data volume: 2,500 orders are 5,000 lenses, which means a total of up to 100,000 processes to be scheduled backlog-free with finite capacities, and batching according to the recipe of the lens is carried out. As a result, two to four minutes' calculation duration for scheduling can be achieved under these conditions. Thus, we implemented a cascaded approach for real-time production control. The main idea is to achieve and establish sustainable communication that can handle communication losses.

3   Lessons Learned

The IoT-based PPC of Industrial Robots via OPC UA has been running stable in this 24/7 operations production environment. That's an interesting fact because we expected the DSL line having latency and further issues resulting from OPC UA being actually not real-time-able. In the following section, we describe the lessons learned.

3.1   Implications for Robotics

Today, robot programming's focus is on solving a given task and surrounding conditions such as productivity by deriving an appropriate robot program in an iterative, trial-and-error approach with only a robotics focus. In the IoT-PPC use case, the local smartness and communication sustainability concerning the PPC had to be discussed, designed, and implemented. The robotics programming is then done within this tolerance area, in part because the IoT-PPC could be unavailable owing to for instance network connectivity issues. If this occurs and the robot would wait for a certain command from the PPC, there would be a deadlock, downtime, and productivity loss. Thus, holistic solutions had to be implemented (see Fig. 3).

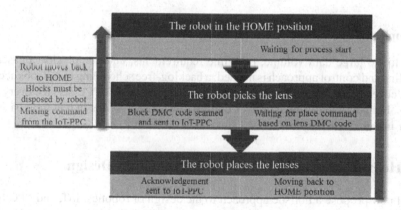

Fig. 3. Procedures in the case of communication loss between the robotics and the IoT-PPC

The cascaded approach always starts with the robot starting in and from a to-be-defined position (HOME) for the robotics and the IoT-PPC. The communication is push-oriented, and always starts from the IoT-PPC acting as the server and the robot as the client, and every communication step is implemented as a stable handshake procedure. Without IoT-PPC information, a process cannot be completed properly, because the robot lacks important information; thus, an automated terminate procedure had to be implemented in the robot system to reset the process by itself after a specific time-out period when either the robot's command did not arrive at the IoT-PPC, or vice versa. After communication loss, the robot may clear the gripper and may prepare for the next process to start, as soon as the connection to the server is re-established, but the IoT-PPC cannot initiate these steps. Thus, follow-up strategies had to be implemented on the robot so as to prevent a process getting stuck after a communication loss. If proper communication between the IoT-PPC and the robots is ensured, most errors can be handled by strategies implemented in the IoT-PPC outside robotics, which is a major lesson learned. However, some errors to be resolved by a human operator. Thus, the training, guiding, assisting, and alerting of operators are critical in this environment.

3.2   Implications for the Internet of Things

The main goal for IT or IoT specialists is to design and implement an infrastructure that allows 24/7 operations by securing the desired availability of 99.7% as agreed service level. Thus, we focused on the SQL database (DB) as the backbone for data and the public DSL line availability. The IoT design concept followed the idea of having a redundant server in the lab and the SQL DB being replicated live from the cloud with the server in the lab. We connected the equipment via a domain server. In case of a DSL public line connectivity problem, there is a real-time switch to the lab server. When the public line is available again and the problem is resolved, the cloud server syncs the SQL DB back and the cloud takes over again. We proved this mechanism in several swap tests. However, owing to costs, the server hardware in the lab is less powerful than the cloud. Thus, production carries on, but at a lower speed, which is sufficient for this 0.3% scenario.

3.3   Implications for Production Planning and Control

Owing to the large data volume, real-time requirements, and complexity, a cascaded scheduling and control approach is needed: a backlog-free scheduling for all jobs according to delivery date and recipe is running as an automatic IoT-PPC service every four minutes. Further, a real-time conveyor control service routes jobs in real time based on e.g., for instance machine states.

4   A Holistic Approach to IoT-PPC CPS/CPPS Design

We will now propose a holistic approach to the design of robotics, IoT, and PPC based on the lessons learned in this case. In Fig. 4, the three disciplines are symbolized by three gear wheels of the same size. It is only when these three work together seamlessly that the entire CPPS works as intended. Three main strategies should be considered for the three disciplines: design cooperative and communicative robotics, design a sustainable IT/IoT infrastructure, and design a real-time service-based PPC. First, all the disciplines must be involved from the outset and the interdependencies must be understood, in order to solve the given CPPS/CPS conceptual formulation. The CPPS's logistical performance and productivity relates to a cooperative and holistic approach, which must be carried out structurally. This case also proved that the involvement of a very limited number of highly skilled and experienced persons from the three domains is a key success factor [18].

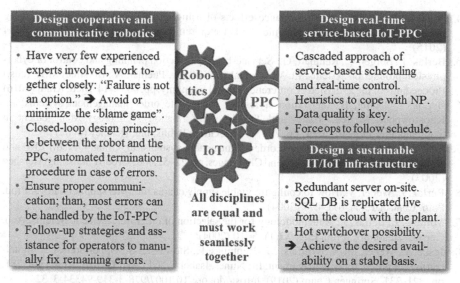

Fig. 4. A holistic approach to CPS/CPPS design with robotics and IoT-PPC

5 Summary and Outlook

We have derived a holistic approach to CPS/CPPS design with robotics, IoT, and PPC. The main strategies to be considered for the three disciplines are, the design of cooperative and communicative robotics, the design of a sustainable IT/IoT infrastructure, and the design of a real-time service-based PPC. All disciplines must be involved from the outset, and their interdependencies must be understood. This is needed as a basis to transform today's manufacturing via digitalization.

As future research directions, we propose on one hand to use the Technology Acceptance Model (TAM) [19] to evaluate the propositions derived in this holistic approach to CPS/CPPS design. While our key findings are not rocket science, many CPS/CPPS projects fail in practice. Thus, it can be assumed that some technology acceptance problem type could be the reason. On the other hand, we propose aligning this holistic approach to the different process and procedure models in robotics, IoT, and PPC. The evaluation of these three derived key principles should also be verified by quantitative and/or qualitative research in different usage cases.

References

1. Brecher, C.: Integrative Production Technology for High-Wage Countries. Springer, Berlin (2012). https://doi.org/10.1007/978-3-642-21067-9
2. Jeschke, S.: Automation, Communication and Cybernetics in Science and Engineering. Springer, Berlin (2014). https://doi.org/10.1007/978-3-319-08816-7
3. Abele, E., Reinhart, G.: Zukunft der Produktion: Herausforderungen, Forschungsfelder, Chancen, pp. 121–147. Carl Hanser, Munich (2011)

4. Tenhiälä, A., Helkiö, P.: Performance effects of using an ERP system for manufacturing planning and control under dynamic market requirements. J. Oper. Manag. **36**, 147–164 (2015)
5. Berlak, J., Berger, C., Reinhart, G.: Service-based production planning and control of cyber-physical production systems. In: Versendaal, J., Kittl, C., Pucihar, A., Borstnar, M.K. (eds.) Proceedings of the 29th Bled eConference Digital Economy, pp. 403–414. Bled, Kranj (2016)
6. Berlak, J., Deifel, B.: Activation styles for changeable order management systems. In: Khosrowpour, M. (ed.) Issues and Trends of Information Technology Management in Contemporary Organizations, pp. 70–77. Idea Group Publishing, Hershey (2002)
7. Berlak, J., Deifel, B.: Changeable order management systems. In: Grant, G. (ed.) ERP and Data Warehousing: Current Issues and Challenges, pp. 22–52. Idea Group Publishing, Hershey (2003)
8. Berlak, J., Weber, V.: How to configure viable supply chains for SME suppliers. Int. J. Prod. Plan. Control **15**(7), 671–677 (2004)
9. Milberg, J., Berlak, J.: A methodology for the selection of order management systems. Ann. German Acad. Soc. Prod. Eng. **XI**(1), 5–10 (2004)
10. Jeske, T., Weber, M.-A., Würfels, M., Lennings, F., Stowasser, S.: Opportunities of digitalization for productivity management. In: Nunes, Isabel L. (ed.) AHFE 2018. AISC, vol. 781, pp. 321–331. Springer, Cham (2019). https://doi.org/10.1007/978-3-319-94334-3_32
11. Lasi, H., Fettke, P., Kemper, H.-G., Feld, T., Hoffmann, M.: Industry 4.0. J. Bus. Inf. Syst. Eng. **6**(4), 239–242 (2014)
12. Lacity, M., Willcocks, L.P.: A new approach to automating services. MIT Sloan Manag. Rev. **58**, 40–49 (2017)
13. Shancang, L., Da, X.L., Shanshan, Z.: The internet of things: a survey. Inf. Syst. Front. **17**(2), 243–259 (2015)
14. Bauernhansl, T.: Industrie 4.0 in Produktion, Automatisierung und Logistik: Anwendung, Technologien und Migration, pp. 38–120. Springer, Wiesbaden (2014). https://doi.org/10.1007/978-3-658-04682-8
15. El Kadiri, S., Grabot, B., Thoben, K., et al.: Current trends on ICT technologies for enterprise information systems. Comput. Ind. **6**(79), 14–33 (2016)
16. Kolberg, D., Berger, C., Pirvu, B.-C., Franke, M., Michniewicz, J.: Cy-ProF – Insights from a framework for designing cyber-physical systems in production environments. Procedia CIRP **57**, 32–37 (2016)
17. Berlak, J.: INDUSTRY 4.0/ AMP 2.0: what is it all about and how labs can profit. Mafo **1**(13), 10–18 (2017)
18. Brooks, F.P.: The mythical Man Month: Essays on Software Engineering. Addison-Wesley/Longman, Boston (1995)
19. Davis, F.D.: Perceived usefulness, perceived ease of use, and user acceptance of information technology. MIS Q. **13**(3), 319–340 (1989)

A Smart and Flexible Study Course for Industry 4.0 – Systems Engineering

Dirk Jacob(✉) [iD]

University of Applied Sciences Kempten, Bahnhofstr. 61, 87435 Kempten, Germany
dirk.jacob@hs-kempten.de

Abstract. The demands of the interlinked production processes of industry 4.0 to engineers are versatile. Engineers shall know the tools to realize production processes automatically, understand different production processes to implement sensor technologies where needed, integrate network technologies to interconnect all components and develop software tools to run the production and to analyze the collected data. Therefore, the qualification of engineers must be adapted to integrate new competences in the engineering education.

Keywords: Digitalization of production · Industry 4.0 · Teaching

1 Content of the Course

Digitization in production confronts companies with new problems [1–3]. Software and agile development methods influence both, product development and production [4]. At present, there are far too few skilled workers available for these challenges who can consider the engineering aspects as well as the possibilities of information technologies into account in developing systems and who are able to create added value [5, 6].

Until a few years ago, automation technology was predominantly limited to controlling sensors and actuators on the field level via PLC and exchanging minimal information with the superordinate level. The result was the classic automation pyramid with a rigid hierarchical structure [7]. Using new communication structures, this model can be broken up, so that the information from the production can be accessed at any time in the entire company network [8]. Based on these changes new opportunities in the production environment arise. Current curricula of degree programs in the field of production and automation technologies don't or only partially cover these opportunities. The considerably increased proportion of information technology in future production systems is often given as little attention in the current degree programs as the integrated crosslinking of the fields of automation technology, starting with mechanics, via actuators and sensors for electrical engineering and electronics, to information technology and artificial intelligence.

To build these competences, a new study course Systems Engineering was set up. The three universities in Augsburg, Kempten and Neu-Ulm have therefore joined forces to the Digital and Regional project, which is funded by the Bavarian Ministry of Science and Culture as part of the Bavarian regionalization offensive. The current shortcomings

R. Moreno-Díaz et al. (Eds.): EUROCAST 2019, LNCS 12014, pp. 493–499, 2020.
https://doi.org/10.1007/978-3-030-45096-0_60

and needs of the industry were identified in joint workshops with companies in the field of production technology and possible contents of the new degree program discussed. About half of the contents of the Systems Engineering degree program include engineering modules such as mechanics, design, electrical engineering, control engineering and automation technology. The other half of the modules are related to information technology, such as programming, networks and data communication, safe industrial systems, distributed systems and the fundamentals of Industry 4.0. The students are therefore trained for application-oriented technical programming with a simultaneous understanding of the system for the three areas of electrics/electronics, mechanics and computer science and thus for networked technical systems.

2 Study Model

A dual study is considered a very attractive variant of a practical oriented study course. The current models of Hochschule Dual Bayern, the study program with in-depth practice as well as the collaborative study, have been established for several years. However, when studying with in-depth practice, in which students complete a course of study and work as interns in the company during the lecture-free period, the feedback from the companies is that the proportion of time students spend in the practical phase is too small. In the case of combined study, in which an apprenticeship is completed in the company parallel to the studies, the time that the student spends in the company from the second year of training is also severely restricted. Here, too, only the lecture-free periods are available for the training content. Another disadvantage is the low connection of the training content in the company and the teaching content at the university.

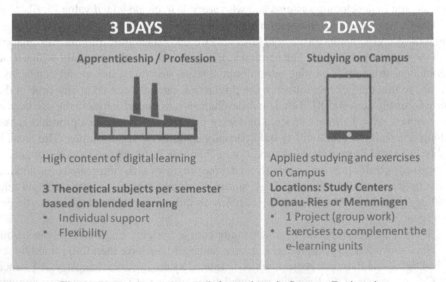

Fig. 1. Time schedule per week for students in Systems Engineering

For the Systems Engineering degree program, a part-time study model has been developed that offers new opportunities for combining study and work in the company. The basis for this is a part-time study program with 20 CP (ECTS) instead of 30 CP (ECTS) per semester in combination with the integration of digital teaching. Digital teaching methods are used for the flexibilization of the time allocation of students, so that only two days a week attendance at the university is necessary (see Fig. 1).

On the other days, the student can work in the company and work on the digital content during his free time. Another focus of this model is the general structure of each semester with three subject-specific modules of 5 CPs each and a coupled project module of 5 CPs. The subject matter of the 3 theory modules is bundled in a project that the students work on in teams. As a result, the theoretically developed content can be linked directly with a practical implementation. The tasks for this project module can also originate from cooperating companies to handle realistic tasks. Through the projects the students are intensively coached for teamwork. This also provides mutual support by students with different educational backgrounds.

For the realization of the study three different models are possible:

1. Parallel to their studies, the students complete an apprenticeship as a skilled worker (e.g. computer scientist, industrial mechanic, electronics technician, mechatronics engineer). The contents of the vocational training are coordinated with the IHK Schwaben, as well as the attendance days in the vocational school. After 2.5 years, the students complete the exam to become a skilled worker. Thereafter, he continues to be involved in the business three days a week and thus gains further practical knowledge.
2. The students are also involved as interns in a company at the beginning of their studies. Thus, they can continuously be integrated in a trainee program in the company and be permanently active in projects through the permanent presence in the company. Due to the considerably more intensive involvement in the companies compared to traditional study models of the study with in-depth practice, the student gains a lot of practical know-how parallel to the studies.
3. The student has already completed an apprenticeship as a technician or master and uses the combination of part-time study in conjunction with high digital teaching content as an opportunity for further education, with moderately reduced working hours.

Due to the practical knowledge of the students developed parallel to the studies, the practical semester can be credited, so that a reduction of the nominal 11 semester standard period of study to 9 semesters is possible (see Fig. 2).

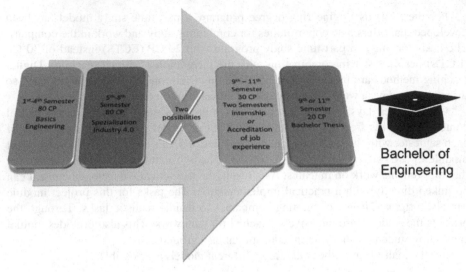

Fig. 2. Timetable of the part-time degree program Systems Engineering

3 Study Content and Didactic Methods

The method of the Flipped Classroom is predominantly used to convey the theoretical content. The students receive this content in the form of educational videos supplemented with quizzes and exercises in digital form (see Fig. 3). In addition, a general exchange of information between the students, both with each other and with the lecturers outside the attendance phases is guaranteed. The material provided on a weekly basis is to be processed in preparation for the days of attendance at the learning center, so that the

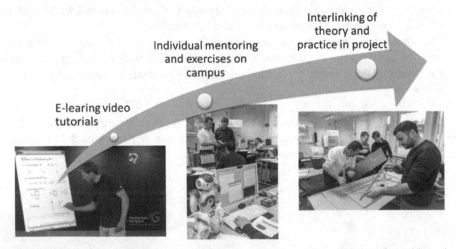

Fig. 3. Teaching and learning forms of the degree program Systems Engineering with project integration

questions of content that are relevant to the lecturer can then be answered individually and further exercises can be processed.

The digital part of the study program facilitates the integration of the study into the everyday life of the students as well as the individualized scheduling and implementation for the lecturers. This opens the opportunity for students to study at the same time as their professional and family life, without causing too much stress. In addition to the lectures offered by the lecturers, the students will be supervised by lecturers on the attendance days before and after the actual event, so that questions regarding the content of the lectures can be clarified.

4 Study Centers and Used Technologies

The concept of the degree program considered that companies that are not located in metropolitan areas frequently lose workers who continue to qualify through studies at companies that are located near the study location and thus in a metropolitan area. For this reason, the two study centers Memmingen and Nördlingen were set up, where the attendance phases of the students are carried out.

The attendance days are carried out in parallel at both study centers. By transferring the lectures to the other study center, both groups of students can work simultaneously. In the process, one view of the lecturers and the students is transferred to the other study location, presentations and table addresses are displayed on a large touchscreen, which, coupled with a media server, can also be used to share student monitor contents. These contents are also transmitted to the other study center. For simple communication, a conference microphone is available at each table for the students, so that contributions from all participants are possible.

A pure implementation of teaching at the e-learning level was deliberately avoided, as the on-site attendance phases on the one hand create a group bond and dynamics that should reduce the drop-out rate, which is extremely high in the case of pure e-learning services. In addition, the individual contact between students and lecturers is important in order to realize a support of the individual students, which is also required due to the heterogeneous learning biographies of the students. Here is the combination of digital teaching, where the individual content can be selectively retrieved repeatedly, and personal feedback as ideal.

To form a co-operative group of students from both study centers, a 2-day team-building event will be held right at the beginning of the first semester. As a result, the students get to know each other personally, which promotes cooperation both through the digital media and through the two learning centers. In addition to this, at least once per semester, subject-oriented excursions are carried out jointly by both study centers in order to promote the cohesion of the group both in content and in person.

As learning platforms Moodle and JupyterHub are in service. Here, the video clips produced in the video lab, the quiz, tasks and program code are deposited and released one to two weeks in advance for students for editing. The students can thus work out the contents chronologically by sifting through the individual instructional videos with content-related topics and using the accompanying quiz and short questions to immediately test whether they have understood the contents. Editing the corresponding exercises will apply the learned content. For content-related questions outside the time of atten-dance, chat groups are available on telegram, in which the lecturers are also involved. The lecturers can support, if questions cannot be solved within the student groups.

The examination concept puts competence-oriented testing in the foreground. There-fore, the cognitive competences in the theory module and the application-oriented com-petences in the respective project of the semester are checked. In the programming events, therefore, the exams are also conducted online using the tools used in the events.

5   Cooperation with Companies

In addition to the discussion of the study content in the course design, events are held regularly with the companies that cooperate with the degree program. At these round tables, current topics that concern the degree program are discussed and suggestions for improvement made by the companies are included. Likewise, the discussion of current technical topics with experts from industry and university is promoted. The events ensure a quick and fast feedback loop to clarify possible ambiguities and problems in a timely manner.

Another option for companies to cooperate with the degree program is to participate in project work. Through tasks from the companies, which are processed by students in the context of the semester projects, the students get the opportunity to solve practical topics in discussion with the companies involved. Through teamwork, students can strengthen the methodological and personal skills that are essential when working on projects in teams.

6   Summary

The part-time degree program Systems Engineering offers new approaches in terms of content as well as concepts for studying automation technology, considering the increasing digitization of production and the resulting new challenges. Through the integration of digital teaching methods and a part-time study model, it is possible to make the study more flexible and more individualized so that it is possible to study even with heterogeneous learning biographies. An important goal in the design was a close interaction of theory and practice. This is possible through the combination of part-time study, digital learning concepts and intensive on-site learning units in learning groups. This offers the possibility of realizing different study concepts adapted to the needs of the economy. A corresponding combination of teaching and practical work is currently not offered in any other model of dual university concepts that has become established in Germany. Even in an international environment, a correspondingly close integration of teaching and practical work in the company is not known and can serve as a model for further study courses. The VDMA has honored the new and application-oriented concept of the study program with the special prize "Best Machinery House 2017", the Bavarian Ministry of Science and Culture awarded the degree program for its innovative didactic approach with the Prize for outstanding teaching in the spring of 2018.

References

1. Roth, A. (ed.): Einführung und Umsetzung von Industrie 4.0, p. 3. Springer, Heidelberg (2016). https://doi.org/10.1007/978-3-662-48505-7
2. Schmidt, R.F., Jacob, D., Thalhofer, U.: Systems engineering - Dual Studieren im Teilzeitmodell mit digitaler Unterstützung. In: BWP Berufsbildung in Wissenschaft und Praxis, vol. 47, no. 2, pp. 32–35 (2018)
3. Huber, W.: Industrie 4.0 in der Automobilproduktion. Ein Praxisbuch, p. 21. Springer Fachmedien, Wiesbaden (2016). https://doi.org/10.1007/978-3-658-12732-9
4. Gilchrist, A.: Industry 4.0. The Industrial Internet of Things, p. 42. Apress, New York (2016)
5. Bauernhansl, T., ten Hompel, M., Vogel-Heuser, B. (eds.): Industrie 4.0 in Produktion, Automatisierung und Logistik. Anwendung, Technologien, Migration, p. 13. Springer Vieweg, Wiesbaden (2014)
6. Stetter, R.: Bildung 4.0 für Unternehmen. In: IndustryArena, no. 3, pp. 28–29. Langenfeld (2016)
7. Heinrich, B., Linke, P., Glöckler, M.: Grundlagen Automatisierung, p. 4. Springer Vieweg, Wiesbaden (2017)
8. Kleinemeier, M.: Von der Automatisierungspyramide zu Unternehmenssteuerungs-Netzwerken. In: Handbuch Industrie 4.0, Teil 1, pp. 219–226. Springer, Berlin (2017)

Simulation-Based Design and Evaluation of a Smart Energy Manager

Tobias Rodemann[1]([✉])[iD] and Kai Kitamura[2][iD]

[1] Honda Research Institute Europe, Offenbach, Germany
tobias.rodemann@honda-ri.de
[2] Department of Systems and Control Engineering, Tokyo Institute of Technology,
Tokyo, Japan
kitamura.k.ad@m.titech.ac.jp
http://www.honda-ri.de

Abstract. In this work we describe an advanced development environment for energy management systems using a combination of a Modelica-based simulation tool for multi-physics systems and a controller implemented in the Python scripting language, exchanging information via the FMI (Functional Mockup Interface) standard. As an example, we present the development of a simple but robust Electric Vehicle (EV) charging controller for a smart home with a Photo Voltaic system. The performance of the controller is evaluated using conventional criteria like annual energy costs and peak load plus two newly developed customer satisfaction indicator (CSI) functions.

Keywords: Digital twin · Energy management optimization · Customer satisfaction indicators · Smart home

1 Introduction

The dramatic changes in energy systems towards more and cheaper renewable energies, open up new possibilities for more efficient operation of energy systems. An example we look at in this work is the integration of electric mobility into homes with a Photo Voltaic (PV) system. It is a common problem, that excess PV energy has to be fed back to the grid, reducing the profitability of the system and potentially destabilizing the electricity grid. With a proper control strategy, Electric Vehicle (EV) batteries could be used to store electric energy from the PV system. An energy manager (EM) is used to control the flow of energy between house (PV system) and EV.

Several articles (for example [3,5]) have already outlined how problems of this type can be solved in an optimal way, however, they require a prediction of future energy demands and production plus substantial computing power. The relatively modest saving potential often does not suffice to compensate for the investment in stronger CPUs and/or cloud computing access. Therefore in practice, often simple rule-based systems are employed, where computing

© Springer Nature Switzerland AG 2020
R. Moreno-Díaz et al. (Eds.): EUROCAST 2019, LNCS 12014, pp. 500–507, 2020.
https://doi.org/10.1007/978-3-030-45096-0_61

requirements are low, and the rules are easy to understand. Here, we are looking at the development of such a rule-based EM for a small building with a PV system and single EV plus charging station. The EM should be operating to minimize energy costs by maximizing self-consumption of PV power, to minimize charging peaks and to maximize customer satisfaction, leading to three separate and conflicting optimization targets. In order to facilitate the development of such a controller, several key components are required that will be outlined in the following:

1. A multi-physics simulation environment that can be used to model a variety of scenarios at a high simulation speed (much faster than real time) while at the same time incorporating all relevant physical effects of the system.
2. A development environment for the energy manager software that is easy to use and capable of supporting advanced tools in the field of AI. We have opted for Python (www.python.org) as a platform to develop and test our controller due to the availability of a large number of open-source libraries in the field of machine learning and data mining.
3. A coupling between the simulator and the EM, so that two different software frameworks, both optimized for the task, can be used. The ultimate target is a Software-in-the-loop (SiL) testing framework, where the EM can be connected seamlessly to the real system after it was tested on the simulation system.
4. A definition of the objective functions to be considered. Here it is important to consider the various requirements of the customer. Specifically we need to consider the customer perspective that evaluates the quality of a charging process.

2   Simulation Model

While developing a controller that handles a single objective well is relatively straightforward, finding a good balance for all objectives in many different scenarios is rather challenging. Quite obviously, the development and validation of such a controller can not be done with a real system due to the disturbances to the inhabitants and the limited control over external factors like weather and user behavior. We have therefore decided to employ a simulation system that models relevant physical effects for building and car. Our simulator [1] uses the Modelica language [2] which is well-suited for the modeling of multi-physics systems. In Fig. 1 a view of the model in the simulation tool is shown.

2.1   Simulation-Controller Interface

In order to link a controller written in Python with a detailed physical building simulation we are using the Functional Mockup Interface (FMI) [4]. Originally developed for connecting different simulation tools, FMI is used to link two different programs (Modelica physical simulation and the Python EM logics) via a connecting interface. A view of the different components is shown in Fig. 1.

A controller interface block based on Functional Mockup Units (FMUs) is embedded in the simulation model. This serves as an interface to the EM software implemented in Python via a coupling software called SIMBUS.

3   Controller Approaches

In this work we compare four different rule-based EMs of increasing complexity that control the charging of the EV, depending on the following external inputs: current SoC (EV battery state of charge), time to planned departure t_{Remain}, PV surplus power $P_{Surplus}$ (the current power produced by the PV system minus the current energy consumption of the building, excluding the charging system).

3.1   Basic EM: PMax

The most basic control logic (often referred to as 'dumb charging') is to charge the car with maximum power ($P_{Max} = 7.36\,\mathrm{kW}$) as soon as the EV is connected and until it is full. This strategy provides the maximum customer satisfaction but also generates strong peaks and often uses less PV surplus power than other approaches.

3.2   Surplus Charging

This approach only charges the car using PV surplus power, therefore maximizing the self-consumption of PV power. However this comes at the cost of occasional low CSI values, especially, when weather conditions are bad and not enough surplus power is available.

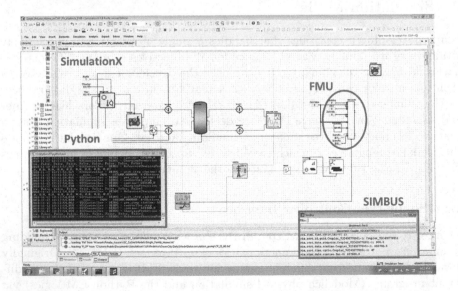

Fig. 1. Schematic view of the simulation environment including FMU coupling.

3.3   Emergency Charging: Last2H

This control approach is a surplus charging strategy, but if the car is not fully charged two hours before planned departure, the EM charges the car with maximum power until it is full. This approach provides a better compromise than the first two methods. However, it still responds poorly under some specific conditions. One example is a customer that arrives in the late afternoon (no more PV surplus) and wants to leave in the morning. The Last2H approach would wait all night (for PV surplus) and then charge with full power in the morning. This would generate substantial peaks in the grid and leave the car at a low SoC level for all of the night.

3.4   New Controller

In order to deal with the issues of the Last2H controller, we add a simple predictive component. Based on historical data (the last 7 days) we predict the amount of PV surplus we can expect in the time till departure ($\overline{P_{Sur}}$). The remaining energy that is probably not going to be provided by the PV system is taken from the grid, but distributed equally over the charging time (P_{Distri}). We also add an emergency charge component that provides the remaining energy evenly distributed in the last 2 h. This approach combines the merits of the three other approaches and only requires a simple addition to the control structure and hardware (a memory to store PV surplus of the last days). The flowchart of our new approach is shown in Fig. 2.

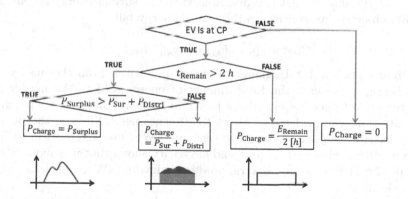

Fig. 2. The flowchart of our new energy management controller logic. The EM first verifies if the EV is at the charging point (CP), then checks if the emergency charging has to be engaged. If the current power surplus is much larger than predicted only surplus power is used, otherwise the controller provides the estimated surplus power plus power from the grid.

In Fig. 3 the differences in charging patterns for the four different control strategies are visualized for one example day.

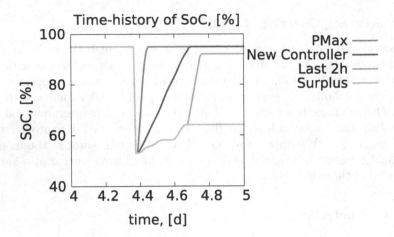

Fig. 3. Typical charging process for each controller during one typical day.

4 Objective Functions

To investigate the performance of a controller one needs to compute a number of performance indicators. The necessary data was generated by the simulation model for a complete simulated year. The simulation covers typical weather patterns and was also tested with different EV usage. The results shown here correspond to a charging scenario where the EV is connected to the charging station during the day, so that it is available when PV surplus energy is generated. The first objective we consider is the annual energy bill:

$$Cost = c_{\text{Buy}} \cdot E_{\text{Grid}} - c_{\text{Sell}} \cdot E_{\text{FeedIn}}. \tag{1}$$

E_{Grid} represents the total amount of energy purchased from the master grid, while E_{FeedIn} represents the total amount of energy sold to the master grid. With reference to general electricity price in Germany, the price for purchased electricity from the grid (c_{Buy}) is set to 30 cents per kWh, and the price for selling electricity (c_{FeedIn}) is set to 10 cents per kWh. The difference in the price between purchased electricity and sold electricity shows that it is more efficient in terms of cost to consume electric power obtained by PV as much as possible within the home.

The second objective is the peak power which represents the maximum purchased power from the master grid in one year. Peak Power is often used as an indicator to be minimized when developing smart home systems and energy management controllers. The larger Peak Power, the higher the load on the grid which might lead to blackouts. Especially in the case when designing systems which include hundreds of EVs, Peak Power must be properly considered. We note that for many customers, peak power also influences the annual electricity bill, but this was not considered in this work.

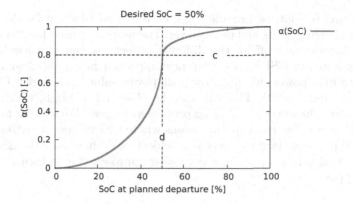

Fig. 4. CSI_α with $SoC_{desired} = 0.5$ and $c = 0.8$.

4.1 Customer Satisfaction Indicator

In order to properly represent the customers' mobility demand, we introduce two new objectives via customer satisfaction indicators (CSI) that compare the user's (modeled) requirements with the result of the charging process. The CSIs consider two different aspects of the charging process:

Final State of Charge: CSI_α. We assume that before the charging commences the customer provides the intended departure time and desired SoC ($SOC_{desired}$). At the time of departure, we compare the desired SoC with the achieved value (SoC) according to the following equation (see also Fig. 4):

$$CSI_\alpha = \begin{cases} c\left\{1 - \sqrt{1 - \left(\frac{SoC}{SoC_{desired}}\right)^2}\right\} & (SoC < SoC_{desired}) \\ c + (1-c)\sqrt{1 - \left(\frac{SoC-100}{SoC_{desired}-100}\right)^2} & (SoC \geq SoC_{desired}) \end{cases} \tag{2}$$

The parameter c represents the customer satisfaction achieved when the car is charged to the intended level. As one can see, providing more energy than requested will lead to relatively small gains in CSI. On the other hand failing to reach the requested value quickly deteriorates the CSI level.

Intermediate State of Charge: CSI_β. The second part of the charging CSI considers the SoC level during the charging process. The rationale behind this is that the customer might have to leave earlier than expected and would prefer to have a fully charged car as soon as possible. We therefore compute CSI_β by computing the mean level of SoC during the charging process minus the SoC at arrival.

5 Results

We simulated the operation of our four controllers for one complete year each and compute the performance objectives. In Fig. 5 we see that the surplus controller has the lowest costs and peak power, but also the worst CSI values. The max power charging in contrast provides high customer satisfaction for the charging process but also high costs and peak power. The more advanced Last2H approach provides a better trade-off for the different objectives, but still has high peak load values and low CSI scores. Our new approach has reduced annual costs compared to max power charging, low peak power values, and higher CSI values than Surplus and Last2H. This can also be observed in Fig. 6, which shows a boxplot of CSI values over all charging processes of a year. We see that for Surplus and Last2H strategies, there are occasions where CSI values are extremely low, which would probably lead to a very low subjective evaluation of the EM system. In contrast, CSI values for our new controller approach stay in higher ranges for both CSI types.

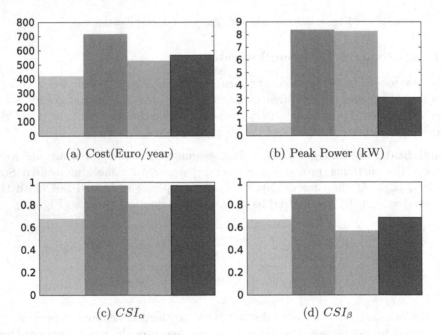

Fig. 5. Comparison of objective functions with four controllers (*from left to right: Surplus, PMax, Last2H, our approach*). CSI are mean values over a year.

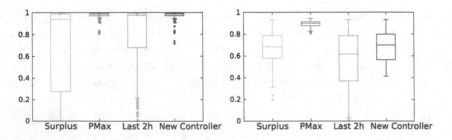

Fig. 6. Boxplot of CSI values (*left: CSI_α, right: CSI_β*) for one year.

6   Summary and Conclusion

In this work we have introduced a simulation-based development and test environment for a smart home energy management system. A new controller approach was presented and evaluated for different scenarios. In order to better include the customer's view, we defined two new objective functions, so called customer satisfaction indicators, that evaluate the success of the charging process from a user perspective. We have shown that our new approach exhibits very competitive performance compared to three other controllers, with only a limited amount of extra complexity. Using the simulation approach we could complete the model set-up, controller development, CSI definition, and system tests within a 6 student months project, which is much faster than any development based on real-world pilot studies.

References

1. ESI-ITI: SimulationX 3.8. https://www.simulationx.com/
2. Fritzson, P., Bunus, P.: Modelica - a general object-oriented language for continuous and discrete-event system modeling. In: Proceedings of the 35th Annual Simulation Symposium, pp. 14–18 (2002)
3. Lu, X., Liu, N., Chen, Q., Zhang, J.: Multi-objective optimal scheduling of a DC micro-grid consisted of PV system and EV charging station. In: 2014 IEEE Innovative Smart Grid Technologies - Asia (ISGT ASIA), pp. 487–491, May 2014. https://doi.org/10.1109/ISGT-Asia.2014.6873840
4. Rodemann, T., Unger, R.: Smart company digital twin - supporting controller development and testing using FMI. In: Proceedings of the Japanese Society of Automotive Engineers Spring Meeting (2018)
5. van der Meer, D., Chandra Mouli, G.R., Morales-Espa Mouli, G., Elizondo, L.R., Bauer, P.: Energy management system with PV power forecast to optimally charge EVs at the workplace. IEEE Trans. Ind. Inform. **14**(1), 311–320 (2018). https://doi.org/10.1109/TII.2016.2634624

Authentication of Internet Connected White Goods Using Gestures or Key Sequences

Thomas Schlechter[1(✉)] and Johannes Fischer[2]

[1] University of Applied Sciences Upper Austria, 4600 Wels, Austria
thomas.schlechter@ieee.org
[2] Bosch Connected Devices and Solutions GmbH, 72760 Reutlingen, Germany
johannes.fischer@bosch-connectivity.com
https://www.fh-ooe.at/
https://www.bosch-connectivity.com/

Abstract. In the context of IoT, more and more white goods (e.g., water boiler, micro wave, washing machine) are connected to the internet for various purposes from the manufacturers side. In many countries, the consumer has the right to access the data generated and transmitted by his own devices. To be compliant with this right, the manufacturer has to guarantee the access of the data to the consumer without violating his privacy. This means, it has to be guaranteed, that the user is able to access his own data only, while no one else is able to access his data. Many methodologies to implement this might be thought of, while in this proposal we introduce an approach of a straight forward implementation covering easy and good user experience and also enabling securing privacy issues.

Keywords: IoT · Privacy · Security · Authentication · White goods · Confidentiality · Availability · Integrity · User experience · Connectivity · Smart devices

1 Introduction

Intelligent or smart devices are getting populated in our every day's life continuously. An ever increasing portion of those devices possess connectivity to the internet, building the class of IoT devices. While many of those are kind of seamless to the user, like smart meters for logging and transmitting resource consumption for, e.g., water or electricity, many more devices occur more present in the people's households. Those include connected coffee and washing machines as well as fridges or hoovers - which are all white goods. The deeper sense of this new connectivity offers many advantages for both the user and the consumer, as will be described later in this paper. The problem to be solved is, that an owner of a white good connected to the internet deserves to access the data published by his own device, while the access to this data needs to be exclusive to him.

© Springer Nature Switzerland AG 2020
R. Moreno-Díaz et al. (Eds.): EUROCAST 2019, LNCS 12014, pp. 508–512, 2020.
https://doi.org/10.1007/978-3-030-45096-0_62

In this paper we propose an intuitive solution to this problem. The paper is structured as follows. After providing some more insight in the topic in Sect. 2, Sect. 3 states the main problem(s) and focuses on the underlying legal base line. The proposed solution is given in Sect. 4 while Sect. 5 closes the paper.

2 Advantages Using Connected Devices and Information Sharing

The advantages for sharing information while white goods are in operation are manifold and both on the manufacturer's and consumer's side. On the manufacturer's side, examples include

- Enabling predictive maintenance compared to regular maintenance (this is especially valuable if the devices are not owned by the consumer, but leased).
- Collecting device data to monitor the white goods performance. This allows improvements on the fly for the next device generation lowering the internal testing and research amount and budget.
- Collecting information about the user behavior. In this context, both extra services may be offered to steer and foster a certain desired user behavior, while also features for new developments may be derived from the gathered user data.
- Offering additional services is connecting the user closer to the company.

Concerning the consumer, the following advantages may be listed:

- Gamification: the device can be observed and controlled remotely, e.g., via a smart phone application.
- Automated reordering of expendable goods, like coffee pads or water softening agent accessories.
- Potentially, based on the user profile additional useful services or device features may be offered by the company.
- Special offers for expendable goods based on the individual automatically detected user profile.

For sure, the lists above may only be seen as exemplary and by far not complete. However, also some disadvantages arise. Some core issues focus purely on the gathered and generated flood of data and related security and privacy issues. This fact will be explained in the following section.

3 Problem Statement and Legal Baseline

In many countries, the consumer has the right to access the data generated and transmitted by his own devices. To be compliant with this right, the manufacturer has to guarantee the access of the data to the consumer without violating his privacy. This means, it has to be guaranteed, that the user is able to access his own data only, while no one else is able to access his data.

This fact raises the liability of the white goods' manufacturers to implement security measures to prevent hacking the device and/or stealing data by any means of hacking attack (e.g., backdoor attack, eavesdropping, phishing) and also to guarantee the availability and integrity of the user data (e.g, by preventing denial of service attacks and spoofing). In Europe, this liability is prescribed in the European Union in the General Data Protection Regulation (GDPR), which has been established in April 2016 and mandatorily entered into force from May 2018.

The right for information is based on Art.15 GDPR [1]. On the other hand side, both policies of Privacy by Design and Privacy by Default need to be followed, described in more detail in Art.25 GDPR [1]. Punishment fees up to 20M€ or up to 4% of the previous year's worldwide profit may have to be paid in case of breaking those rules (besides others not relevant for this topic). The punishment details are described in Art.83 Abs.5 GDPR [1].

According to Art.20 GDPR [1], the information has to be provided in a certain structured format. Therefore, a good approach for any operator collecting person related data is to automatically integrate the possibility for reporting in their devices aside with a secure procedure guaranteeing privacy for the user as well.

As has been shown, the secure handling of the mentioned data contents is on the one hand side in the companies' own interest to built and remain trust among the customers, and is on the other side mandatory by law. Therefore, up to date security measures may be installed. Best in class security measures do not only fulfill the technical core requirements, but are also intuitive, easy to use and operation error proof to guarantee an excellent user experience without bothering the user with technical details or multiple passwords.

4   Proposed Solution

The proposed implementation includes an intuitive method for the owner of an internet connected white good to access his personal data sent by his white good, while preserving data privacy both for peregrine data from a third parties point of view and his own data from his personal point of view.

The proposed method is quite straight forward. The basis is, that the white good under interest is connected to the internet. To get access to the relevant data, the user connects to the data base of the manufacturer. This can, e.g., be done using an app or a web page. The critical issue is how to authorize yourself to this backend. The proposed implementation involves a feedback of the user which guarantees his physical presence at the device of interest, while he potentially still needs to know some specific fixed authorization data. The idea is, that apart from any well known fixed authorization procedure, a physical authorization procedure shall be implemented, which together with standard authorization methods uniquely identifies the interrogator as the valid user and owner of the device. Within this proposal, a user always sends a request to access his own data to the manufacturers data base. Doing this, the user implicitly addresses a unique white good connected to the internet, more precisely connected to the manufacturers data base. This device may have a unique ID, however, this ID may be faked. To ensure, that the requesting user is the user authorized to access the data, the manufacturer is initiating, the following procedure, which is also illustrated in Fig. 1.

- The requesting user contacts the manufacturer to get access to his/her device related data.
- The first authorization stage is approved, containing fixed authorization entities, like TAN, MobileTan, PhotoTAN, Password, etc.
- A physical authorization instance is shared with the user. Basically, a defined interaction with the device of interest is negotiated. The specific sequence may be shared via app, via e-mail, via web pages, etc. The only important thing is, that it will be shared with the initiating user on a real time base.
- The user follows the desired interaction. This can be, e.g., a defined key sequence on a coffee machine, a specific choice on a rotary switch on a washing machine, or even more generally a forced gesture on a touch screen.

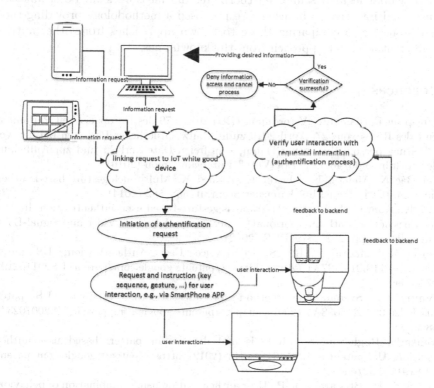

Fig. 1. Schematic of the proposed authentication process.

Related to this proposal the choice of the individual physical feedback loop is not limited to the aforementioned approaches. Any physical pro-active interaction triggered by the users provider is valid.

Several researchers and developers dealt with similar problems in the past, e.g., proposing gesture recognition authentication procedures [2,3], two-step auxiliary device based authentication of consumer requests [4,5], or geometric and biometric pattern approaches for authentication [6,7]. However, none of them are as easy to implement and simple as the described implementation, while still the main security and privacy features remain valid, or do not fulfill the desired functionality.

5   Conclusion

In this paper we pointed out the (dis-)advantages of data sharing connected white goods along with necessary measures for secure and reliable private data exchange. This includes data confidentiality, integrity, and availability from a technical security measure perspective, and also mandatory follow the specific local or global legal baseline. Furthermore, the measure shall be seamless to the user and intuitive to be used. We proposed a methodology providing those corner stones, also comparing those to known approaches from other authors and differentiated our approach from the known ones.

References

1. European Parliament: "Verordnung (EU) 2016/679 des Europaeischen Parlaments und des Rates vom 27. April 2016 zum Schutz natuerlicher Personen bei der Verarbeitung personenbezogener Daten, zum freien Datenverkehr und zur Aufhebung der Richtlinie 95/46/EG (DSGVO)." European Union (2016)
2. Sae-Bae, N., Memon, N., Isbister, K., Ahmed, K.: Multitouch gesture-based authentication. IEEE Trans. Inf. Forensics Secur. 9, 568–582 (2014)
3. Lai, K., Konrad, J., Ishwar, P.: Towards gesture-based user authentication. In: Proceedings of the Ninth International Conference on Advanced Video and Signal-Based Surveillance, pp. 282–287. IEEE (2012)
4. Hito, G., Madrid, T.R.: Smart Device User Authentication, US patentus US20,110,219,427A1 (2011). https://patents.google.com/patent/US20110219427A1/en
5. White, C.: System and method for authenticating products, US patentus US20,070,234,058A1 (2007). https://patents.google.com/patent/US20070234058A1/en
6. Venkatha Raghavan, S.: Methods and devices for pattern-based user authentication, US patentus US8,191,126B2 (2012) https://patents.google.com/patent/US8191126B2/en
7. Saevanee, H., Bhatarakosol, P.: User authentication using combination of behavioral biometrics over the touchpad acting like touch screen of mobile device. In: Proceedings of the International Conference on Computer and Electrical Engineering, pp. 82–86. IEEE (2008)

Author Index

514   Author Index

Printed in the United States
By Bookmasters